9th Edition

The Manager's Legal Handbook

Lisa Guerin, J.D.
Sachi Barreiro, J.D.

NINTH EDITION	JANUARY 2018
Cover Design	SUSAN PUTNEY
Production	SUSAN PUTNEY
Proofreading	SUSAN CARLSON GREENE
Index	VICTORIA BAKER
Printing	BANG PRINTING

ISSN: 2167-5724 (print)

ISSN: 2332-2357 (online)

ISBN: 978-1-4133-2464-8 (pbk)

ISBN: 978-1-4133-2465-5 (epub ebook)

This book covers only United States law, unless it specifically states otherwise.

Please note

We believe accurate, plain-English legal information should help you solve many of your own legal problems. But this text is not a substitute for personalized advice from a knowledgeable lawyer. If you want the help of a trained professional—and we'll always point out situations in which we think that's a good idea—consult an attorney licensed to practice in your state.

Acknowledgments

The authors would like to thank:

On the first edition, our wonderful editor, Shannon Miehe, whose sense of humor, organizational skills, lightning-fast speed, and careful editing made working on this book a pleasure.

On subsequent editions, our editor and friend, Stephanie Bornstein, who helped transform the book into a must-have legal guide for managers.

Mary Randolph, Jake Warner, and Janet Portman, all of whom helped us figure out how to organize this material—and how to avoid the dreaded "scope creep."

Ella Hirst, Alayna Schroeder, Drew Wheaton, and Stephen Stine for meticulously researching and compiling the state charts.

Stan Jacobsen, for his research help and ever-positive attitude.

John M. True, III, formerly of Leonard Carder, LLP, in Oakland, California, for writing some of the privacy material and helping out with the information on unions.

Philip Monrad, also of Leonard Carder, for his generous help with the unions chapter.

About the Authors

Lisa Guerin worked for Nolo as a research and editorial assistant during her years as a law student at Boalt Hall School of Law. After a stint as a staff attorney at the U.S. Court of Appeals for the Ninth Circuit, Lisa worked primarily in the field of employment law, in both government and private practice. Lisa has litigated on behalf of her clients in all levels of state and federal courts and in agency proceedings. Lisa returned to Nolo as an editor, where she specialized in employment law and civil litigation.

Sachi Barreiro is a legal editor at Nolo specializing in employment law and workers' compensation law. Before joining Nolo, Sachi was in private practice as an employment lawyer, advising businesses on their legal obligations and litigating a variety of employment matters. Prior to that, she gained valuable litigation experience representing plaintiffs in personal injury lawsuits. Sachi received her law degree with high honors from the University of San Francisco School of Law.

Table of Contents

Navigating the Maze of Employment Law

Some managers learn the hard way that good intentions aren't enough. In these days of burgeoning employment laws, regulations, and lawsuits, successfully and safely managing workers (employees and independent contractors alike) requires a whole lot more than just following your instincts. Lawmakers and courts have created a complicated web of dos and don'ts that covers the entire spectrum of workplace issues, from hiring to firing and everything in between. If you are a supervisor, manager, or human resources specialist, you'll need to learn how to navigate this legal maze or risk serious trouble for your company and yourself.

Fortunately, learning how to manage workers on a daily basis doesn't have to be time-consuming, difficult, or even unpleasant. This book takes these complicated issues and boils them down to your basic obligations, so you can feel confident that you're managing your employees effectively and within the confines of the law.

How to Use This Book

This book gives you the information you need to deal with many common workplace concerns and issues. Each chapter focuses on a specific employment law topic—such as hiring, compensation and hours, privacy in the workplace, and so on—and breaks that subject down into the issues managers are most likely to face.

Of course, every company is different, and every manager has varying areas of responsibility and expertise. And, not every manager will have the authority to make ultimate decisions on matters of policy or serious personnel matters, such as firing and layoffs. The information in this book provides some legal background that will help you understand your role in the process, however your company defines it.

Each chapter includes:

- **Frequently Asked Questions (FAQs).** We introduce you to the chapter topic through succinct answers to questions that managers and employers commonly face.

- **Topic Headings.** We break down the chapter's topic into a series of separate sections, so that you can get right to the information you need. That way, you can focus only on the rules that apply to the situation at hand without having to wade through an entire chapter looking for your answer.

- **Lessons From the Real World.** Learn from the failures and victories of companies that have been taken to court by their employees.

- **Legal Dos and Don'ts.** We provide a handful of strategies to follow—and traps to avoid—as you implement the information in each chapter.

- **Test Your Knowledge.** Find out how well you understand each topic by taking our end-of-chapter quiz and checking your answers.
- **50-State Charts.** At the end of the chapter, we provide you with a summary of information on your state's legal requirements, in addition to the federal law covered in the chapter.

You can read through the entire book at once, you can pick and choose among chapters of special interest to your company, or you can use the book as a desk reference by consulting particular sections as issues come up. No matter how you use the book, the basic information we provide will help answer your most common employment questions.

This book covers rules for private employers only. It does not apply to government employees, who are typically subject to other laws.

The federal laws we discuss are the minimum requirements that employers in all states must follow. However, many states have additional laws that may be more restrictive. As you read through this book, keep in mind that when both a federal and state law apply, your company must follow whichever rule is more beneficial to the employee.

Additional Resources

Although most managers can find everything they need in this book, you might occasionally have a problem that requires you to seek additional help. We will alert you to those potential trouble spots and point you toward resources that can give you the extra information you need.

The appendix (at the end of the book) contains a list of resources you can consult for more information. These resources include:

- contact information for the federal agencies that enforce federal workplace laws, including the Equal Employment Opportunity Commission (EEOC), the Occupational Safety and Health Administration (OSHA), the Department of Labor (DOL), and the Federal Trade Commission (FTC).
- contact information for the state agencies that enforce state workplace laws, including state departments of labor and state fair employment offices.

Get Updates and More Online

When there are important changes to the information in this book, we'll post updates online, on a page dedicated to this book: **www.nolo.com/back-of-book/ELBA.html** You'll find other useful information there, too, including legal updates and blog posts.

Hiring

Hiring can be a tough task for managers. It's challenging enough to find the right person for the job, someone with the skills, attitude, personality, and other important qualities to be a success at your company. When you add legal concerns into the mix, hiring can seem like a truly daunting responsibility.

But you can't just ignore your legal obligations when interviewing applicants and hiring new employees. Federal and state employment laws reach beyond current employees; many also protect those who apply for jobs. For example, such laws might prohibit discriminatory job postings, put limits on the information you can gather in a background check, or outlaw certain kinds of applicant screening tests. What's more, the things you say and do during the hiring process could come back to haunt you and your company, particularly if an employee claims that you offered a job contract or promised job security.

The good news is that following sensible and careful hiring practices will keep your company out of immediate legal trouble, will help you find the most qualified employees, and—by screening out problem employees from the get-go—will help prevent management headaches and possible lawsuits down the road.

This chapter explains the legal ins and outs of hiring and provides practical advice on how to find, interview, and seal the deal with your lucky new hire.

Job Postings

Your legal obligations start at the very beginning: advertising for an open position. Although a job posting might seem innocuous, the words you use can get your company in trouble. In particular, it's important to watch out for language that could be interpreted as discriminating against applicants based on a characteristic protected by federal or state law, such as race or gender. (To learn which characteristics are protected by federal and state law, see Chapter 3.)

Some off-limits topics are obvious: Most managers know that a job ad can't state "Only white males need apply." But companies can also get into trouble by posting an ad that discriminates on a more subtle level, even if that wasn't their intention.

For example, let's say you want to hire a technician for your company's information systems department. Almost all of the technician's day would be spent at a computer. On occasion, however, technicians at your company have to install new equipment, which might require them to carry computers, monitors, printers, and so on. Should you write a job posting saying that applicants must be able to lift at least 50 pounds? Well, that kind of requirement would screen out applicants with certain disabilities, as well as disproportionate numbers of women. Because the lifting is only occasional and could be accomplished by other means—using machinery, for example—including such a requirement in your ad could be found to be discriminatory.

Frequently Asked Questions About Hiring

Do I have to advertise open positions?

No. Although federal, state, and local governments are typically required to post openings, private companies are not. Nonetheless, there are some very good reasons to advertise:

- You can choose from a larger pool of applicants, which increases your odds of finding the best person for the job.
- You avoid unintentional discrimination. For example, if you rely solely on word of mouth when looking for applicants, and you only know people of your own race or ethnicity, then your hiring process might be biased.
- You can avoid the appearance of nepotism or favoritism. If you hire your friends, family members, or neighbors to come work for you, the employees who currently report to you might think you'll play favorites. By posting open positions and choosing your hires from a broad range of applicants, you can show your employees that you hire—and manage—based on merit alone. (For advice on effective and legal job advertisements, see "Job Postings," above.)

Are there questions I can't ask during a job interview?

Yes. Several topics are off limits. For example, you may not ask whether an applicant has a disability, what country an applicant comes from—and, in some states—whether an applicant has ever been arrested. (To learn what questions you can and cannot ask an applicant during an interview, see "Interviews," below.)

Are there things I shouldn't say when I'm trying to convince a really strong applicant to take a job?

Absolutely. Although you might be tempted to sell your company during a job interview with a hot prospect, don't overdo it. If you exaggerate—or flat out lie—about the position, the company's future, or other important facts, and the applicant takes the job based on your statements, he or she can sue the company if your statements turn out to be false. Likewise, avoid any statements that promise job security or continued employment if the applicant takes the position. (For more information on statements to avoid when hiring, see "Making Promises," below.)

Can I ask whether an applicant has a disability?

No. The Americans with Disabilities Act (ADA) prohibits you from asking whether an applicant has a disability. Instead, you should focus your interview questions on the applicant's abilities. For example, you may ask whether and how an applicant would perform each essential function of the job. If you know that an applicant has a disability (because it is obvious or the applicant has told you about it), you may ask whether the applicant will need an accommodation to perform the job. (For more on avoiding disability discrimination when hiring, see "Applicants With Disabilities," below.)

Can I ask every applicant to take a lie detector test?

No. The Employee Polygraph Protection Act (EPPA) prohibits lie detector tests by all but a few types of employers, such as those that provide certain types of security services or those that manufacture pharmaceuticals. (For more information on what tests you can ask applicants to take, see "Testing Applicants," below.)

Frequently Asked Questions About Hiring (continued)

Can I run background checks on applicants?
It depends on the information you plan to collect and who collects it. In general, you can check information that is relevant to the job for which you are hiring. However, state and federal laws restrict you from gathering or using certain types of records (such as medical records or criminal records). And, if you plan on having a third party run a background check, you must get the applicant's written consent in advance. (See "Background Checks," below, for more information.)

Can I hire teenagers to do clerical work?
Generally, yes. Teenagers who are at least 16 years old may work unlimited hours in any profession that the government has not deemed hazardous. You can also hire younger teens, although the law restricts how many hours they may work and the types of jobs they may do. (For more information, see "Young Workers," below.)

If I want to offer someone a job, do I have to do it in writing?
There is no law that governs how you offer someone a job. You can do it in person, over the phone, or with a formal letter. However, you should probably send written offer letters to make sure potential hires understand exactly what you are offering. Offer letters aren't without their pitfalls, however, so be careful what you write. (To learn more, see "Offer Letters," below.)

When I hire someone, should I use a written contract?
It depends on the circumstances. In most cases, you probably won't want to use a contract because it will give up your right to fire at will. However, there might be times when a written contract is a good idea, such as when you want the employee to make a long-term commitment to the company. (To learn about when you should use an employment contract, see "Written Employment Contracts," below.)

What forms or paperwork do new employees have to complete?
In addition to paperwork your company requires—such as an acknowledgment form for the employee handbook, a confidentiality agreement, or an emergency contact form—you should also ask employees to complete the following documents:

- IRS Form W-4, *Withholding Allowance Certificate*. Employees use this form to tell you how many allowances they are claiming for tax purposes and, therefore, how much you should withhold from their paychecks.
- USCIS Form I-9, *Employee Eligibility Verification*. You and the employee must each complete a portion of this form to verify that the employee is eligible to work in the United States.
- New Hire Reporting Form. The new hire reporting program requires employers to report basic identifying information on all new employees to a state agency, to be used to locate parents who owe child support.

(For more on these requirements, see "Checklist: First-Day Paperwork," below.)

Similarly, avoid words or descriptions that imply you have a discriminatory preference. For example, let's say you are looking for a sales representative. If you use the term, "salesman" in your ad, it implies that you are only looking for men (and therefore that you would discriminate against female applicants). The same precaution applies to terms like "handyman" or "waiter."

So what can you say? If you follow two basic rules, you should steer clear of trouble:

- **Focus on the essential functions of the job.** In other words, advertise only for the skills or characteristics that the job absolutely requires. For example, if you are looking for someone to proofread magazine articles, you probably don't need someone with a B.A. in science unless your magazine is a professional scientific journal. If there is an up-to-date job description for the position, you can use it to focus the ad appropriately.

- **Pay attention to the literal meaning of the words you use.** This is particularly important with the suffix "-man"—as in "salesman," "repairman," and so on (try "salesperson" and "general repair person" instead)—or gendered positions such as "waiter" (use "server" or "wait staff" instead). It is also important to be cautious when using words that refer to age. For example, targeting your job ads to "recent college grads" would likely discourage older workers from applying for the position, which could lead to an age discrimination lawsuit.

Ban-the-Box Laws Restrict Inquiries About Criminal History

In the last several years, an increasing number of states and cities have passed laws prohibiting employers from asking an applicant about criminal history early on in the hiring process. Called "ban-the-box" laws, these laws were originally aimed at removing a common question on job applications that required applicants to check a box if they had a criminal record. Nearly ten states, and many cities, have adopted ban-the-box laws. While these laws vary in the particulars, employers are generally not allowed to ask about criminal history—on a job application or otherwise—until the applicant comes in for an interview or receives a conditional offer of employment. Some of these laws also require employers to give the applicant an opportunity to explain any criminal history or require employers to consider certain criteria in evaluating criminal history. To learn if your state has such a law, see "State Laws on Employee Arrest and Conviction Records," at the end of this chapter.

Interviews

The spontaneous and unpredictable nature of the job interview makes it rife with traps, even for managers with the best of intentions. Well-meaning, innocent comments could be construed by an applicant as prejudicial or used as the basis of a discrimination lawsuit.

For example, let's say an applicant speaks with an accent you've never heard before.

You might be curious about where the applicant is from. However, if you ask about the applicant's national origin, and the applicant doesn't get the job, your question could make the applicant wonder whether ethnicity played a role in your decision.

On the other hand, you don't want to get so hung up on every word you say that you defeat the purpose of the interview: to learn about the applicant's skills and experience so you can choose the best-qualified candidate for the position.

Here are some tips that will help you stay out of legal trouble while also getting the information you need to make the right choice:

- **Don't ask about any characteristic that the law prohibits you from considering in making your decision.** (To learn about these protected characteristics, see Chapter 3.) For example, you can't base your hiring decisions on an applicant's religious beliefs or race, so you shouldn't be asking about those things in your interviews. For ideas on how to get information while staying within the bounds of federal law, see the "Preemployment Inquiries" chart at the end of this chapter.

- **Respect the applicant's privacy.** Although federal law does not require you to do so, many state laws and rules of etiquette do. For example, asking applicants in California about their sexual fantasies (yes, that actually happened in a real-life case) violates their state-protected right to privacy. (For more information on privacy in the workplace, see Chapter 6.)

- **If an applicant raises a delicate subject, it's usually best to skirt the issue.** Unless the topic is directly related to the position—for example, the applicant reveals that he or she has a disability and will need an accommodation to perform the job—politely steer the conversation in another direction. Although it might seem a bit awkward, you'll be better off in the long run if you don't take the applicant's comments as an invitation to pry into his or her relationship troubles or political beliefs.

- **Ask open-ended questions to get the candidate talking.** There's a big difference between a closed question (such as "How many supervisory positions have you held?") and an open one (such as "Tell me about your most recent experience supervising others"). The more open your questions, the more you invite the candidate to talk. This will not only give you the factual information you need to make a decision, but will also let you see how well applicants express themselves and think on their feet.

- **Ask behavioral questions, if possible.** It can be tough to find out whether applicants possess important, yet somewhat intangible qualifications, such as problem-solving skills or the ability to work well as part of a team. If you just come out and ask, all but the most dim-witted applicants are going to know the correct answer. ("Are you good at solving problems?" "You bet!") On the other hand, if you ask the applicant to describe specific instances in which he or she had to use those skills, you're more likely to get a helpful response. To find out about a candidate's problem-solving skills, for example, you could say, "Tell me about a problem you recently faced in your current position and how you handled it."

- **Focus on what the job really requires.** If you have a job description for the position, use it to script some interview questions that will help you find out whether the applicant has the necessary skills and experience. If you don't have a job description, create a list of the essential tasks for that position, then craft questions that will help you figure out whether the applicant can meet these requirements. Remember, the law absolutely allows you to ask questions that directly relate to the requirements of the job you are trying to fill.

- **Cover similar ground with each applicant.** You can't ask exactly the same questions of each applicant, nor should you. After all, you don't want to miss the opportunity to ask spontaneous follow-up questions or delve more deeply into particular topics. On the other hand, you should try to cover the same basic topics and general questions with each applicant. This will help you compare candidates when it's time to choose your hire; it will also help you avoid claims of discrimination by applicants who don't get the job.

Asking for Social Media Account Passwords

Many companies look online for publicly available information on job or promotion applicants, including on Facebook and other social networking sites. But the Maryland Department of Corrections took this common practice a step further when it asked employee Robert Collins to hand over his Facebook password during a job recertification interview.

The situation was publicized when the American Civil Liberties Union filed a lawsuit on Collins's behalf in 2011. Soon after, Maryland passed a law banning this practice, and several states have followed suit.

Over two dozen states now have laws that prohibit or place restrictions on this practice. In most of these states, it is illegal for an employer to make an applicant hand over the password to his or her private social media account or pull up the account in the employer's presence. (Check out the website of the National Conference of State Legislatures, www.ncls.org, for current information on state laws in this area.)

Facebook has weighed in on the issue, making it a violation of the site's code of conduct to "share or solicit a Facebook password." In response to the publicity surrounding the Maryland case, Facebook's Chief Privacy Officer warned employers that they could expose themselves to "unanticipated legal liability" by demanding user passwords.

Making Promises

A common mistake managers make during the hiring process is to exaggerate the prospects of the business ("We're expanding like wildfire; those stock options will be worth millions in no time!") or play up the security of the job ("As long as you do good work, you won't lose your job"). Lots of companies and managers embellish when they're trying to sell an especially desirable applicant on a job. No harm in that, right?

Wrong. If you tell a prospective employee something about a job, you'd better be able to back it up. If the employee takes the job in part because of what you said, then that employee may be allowed to sue if your promises or statements later prove false. Courts sometimes decide that a promise or statement you make to a prospective employee turns into a contract if the employee accepts the job offer because of what you said. If the position doesn't live up to your statements, your company has broken the contract and might have to pay damages to the employee.

It's easy to avoid making inflated promises if you follow one simple rule: Tell the truth. After all, job applicants are trying to figure out whether the job will fit with their career goals, skills, and lives outside the workplace. They deserve to know the truth so they can make the right decision.

This strategy will not only keep you out of legal trouble, but will also increase your chances of finding an employee who is right for the job and for your business. No one wants a disgruntled employee on the payroll. If you've told the applicant the truth and he or she still wants the job, then you've probably found a good fit.

 Lessons From the Real World

A California company paid the price for aggressively recruiting an employee with promises it couldn't keep. Rykoff-Sexton, Inc., promised Andrew Lazar job security, significant pay increases, an eventual executive position, and a bright future with a company that was financially strong. Lazar took the bait and left a lucrative job in New York City, his home of 40 years.

Although Lazar excelled in his new job, the pay increases and bonuses never came. Eventually, Rykoff fired Lazar because of a "reorganization."

Lazar sued and won. He argued to the California Supreme Court that Rykoff should have to keep the promises it used to recruit him, and the court agreed. The court decided that Rykoff's broken promises amounted to fraud because it knew the promises were untrue when it made them.

Lazar v. Rykoff-Sexton, Inc., 12 Cal.4th 631 (1996).

Here are a few rules that will help you avoid common promise pitfalls:

- **Don't make predictions about your company's financial future.** Even if you honestly believe that your company is headed for the Fortune 500, keep your optimism to yourself. If the applicant asks about the company's prospects, stick to the facts. If you make any statements about what the future might bring, clearly identify them as hopes, not predictions. For example, you might say, "Our business has continued to grow despite the economic downturn, and we're hoping that trend will continue," but you shouldn't say, "We'll be the industry leader by this time next year."

- **Don't estimate the future value of stock options.** Let's face it: You simply can't know what your company's stock options will be worth in the future. It's fine to explain the stock option program to applicants and to tell them that you hope the options will be valuable, but don't say things like, "When these options vest, we'll all be millionaires!"

- **Don't say anything that might limit your right to make personnel decisions in the future.** If you tell an applicant that your company fires workers only for poor performance, this will limit your ability to terminate that person for any other reason—such as personality conflicts or economic downturns—if he or she accepts the job.

Similarly, if you promise pay increases at regular intervals, the employee could hold you to that promise, even if the flagging economy or the employee's performance don't justify a raise.

- **If layoffs are likely, say so.** If your company is considering staff reductions and there is even a remote chance that the applicant you are interviewing might lose that new job as a result, disclose this before the applicant accepts the job. Otherwise, you may find your company slapped with a lawsuit, especially if the employee left a secure job elsewhere to come work for your company. Of course, this strategy might make it difficult to find new employees, but it really isn't fair (or legal) to hire people on false pretenses.

- **Be accurate in describing the position.** Don't exaggerate to land an applicant, and don't play bait and switch by offering an applicant one job, then placing him or her in another. It might not matter much to you who does what, but it will matter a lot to the employee. An employee who accepts the position based on statements that turn out to be false might have grounds for a lawsuit.

Applicants With Disabilities

Of all the antidiscrimination laws, perhaps none confuses managers more than the Americans with Disabilities Act (ADA), especially when it comes to hiring. Managers want to find out if the person they hire can actually perform the job but often aren't sure how to explore this issue without running afoul of the law. (For information on how the ADA applies to employees, see Chapter 3.)

If you remember one simple rule, you'll be in good shape: You can ask candidates about their abilities, but not about their disabilities. This means that you can ask how an applicant would perform each function of the job, but you can't ask whether the applicant has any disabilities that will prevent him or her from performing each function of the job.

One way to ensure that you stay within the rules is to attach a detailed job description to the application or describe the job duties to applicants during the job interview. Then ask how the applicant plans to perform the job. This approach gives applicants an opportunity to talk about their qualifications and strengths. It also gives them a chance to let you know if they need reasonable accommodations to do the job.

If you choose to ask applicants how they would perform the job duties, you should ask these questions of all applicants. It's illegal to single out those whom you suspect might have a disability. If an applicant has a "known" disability—a disability that the applicant has disclosed or that is obvious (for example, if the applicant uses a wheelchair)—and it reasonably appears that the applicant might

not be able to perform the job's functions, you may ask how the applicant would perform those functions or whether the applicant would need an accommodation to do so.

Generally, you may not ask an applicant questions—on an application or during a job interview—that are likely to require the applicant to reveal a disability. The Equal Employment Opportunity Commission (EEOC), the federal agency that interprets and enforces the ADA, gives the following examples of questions you should not ask:

- Do you have a disability that would interfere with your ability to do the job?
- How many days were you sick last year?
- Have you ever filed for workers' compensation? Have you ever been injured on the job?
- Have you ever been treated for mental health problems?
- What prescription drugs are you currently taking?

You may, however, ask questions like these:

- Can you perform all of the functions of this job?
- How would you perform each of the job functions?
- What certifications and licenses do you hold?
- Tell me about your education and work history.
- Can you meet the attendance requirements of this job?

If you have no reason to believe that the applicant has a disability, you may not ask whether the applicant will need an accommodation to perform the job. If, however, you know that the applicant has a disability—because it is obvious, for example, or because the applicant has told you about it—you may ask about accommodations.

Testing Applicants

Many companies like to use preemployment tests as a way to screen out applicants who are not suitable for a job. These tests include skills tests, aptitude tests, psychological tests, personality tests, honesty tests, medical tests, and drug tests.

Although you are allowed to do some testing of applicants, both state and federal law impose numerous restrictions on what you can do. Because these restrictions are often vague and open to conflicting interpretations, you should use only the tests that are absolutely necessary. You should also consult with a lawyer before administering the test to make sure that it will pass legal muster in your state.

Avoiding Disability Discrimination

For all tests—including those described below—you must take care to avoid discriminating against applicants who are protected by the Americans with Disabilities Act (ADA). (For information on the ADA,

see Chapter 3.) To ensure that a test does not unfairly screen out people with disabilities, it must accurately measure people's skills, not their disabilities. For example:

- Avoid testing mental, sensory, manual, or speaking skills unless they are job-related. For example, even though a typing test is a manual test that will screen out people who have particular impairments, it is acceptable if you are filling a job for a typist. However, requiring a typing test for a janitorial position probably won't fly.
- Accommodate people with disabilities by giving them a test that is "disability neutral" whenever possible. For example, if you are giving a written test to applicants for a sales position to test their knowledge of sales techniques, you can administer the test orally to a blind applicant. This is a reasonable accommodation because sight is not required for the job, but it is required to take the test.

Skills Tests

Skills tests range from something as simple as a typing test to something as complicated as an architectural drafting test. Generally speaking, these tests are legal as long as they genuinely test a skill necessary to perform the job, do not violate the ADA (see above), and do not unfairly exclude anyone based on a protected characteristic.

Aptitude, Psychological, and Personality Tests

Some companies use written tests—often in a multiple choice format—to learn about an applicant's general abilities, personality, and work style. However, using these tests leaves you vulnerable to various types of lawsuits. For example:

- A multiple-choice aptitude test might discriminate against minority applicants or female applicants because it really reflects test-taking ability rather than actual job skills. (Studies have shown that some aptitude tests are biased against women and minority test takers.)

- A personality test can be even riskier. Such a test might invade a person's privacy by inquiring into topics that are personal in nature, such as sexual preferences or religious beliefs. (Many states specifically protect a person's right to privacy, even from inquiries by employers.) In addition, these tests can lead to discrimination lawsuits. For example, if you decide not to hire someone based on his or her answers to questions dealing with religious issues, the applicant could argue that you illegally discriminated based on his or her religion. (For more about discrimination, see Chapter 3.)

- Psychological and personality tests are treated like medical tests (see below) when they ask for answers that would indicate whether the applicant has a mental disorder or impairment. If

they do, they will be governed by the Americans with Disabilities Act (ADA) and all of its restrictions. (For more on hiring and the ADA, see "Applicants With Disabilities," above.)

If you decide to use one of these types of tests, proceed with extreme caution. Make sure that the test has been screened scientifically for validity and that it genuinely correlates to necessary job skills. Review the test carefully for any questions that might intrude into an applicant's privacy. And, depending on the complexity and purpose of the test you use, your company might need to hire an expert to interpret the results.

Lie Detector and Honesty Tests

The federal Employee Polygraph Protection Act (EPPA) generally prohibits employers from requiring applicants to take a lie detector test or from asking applicants about the results of previous lie detector tests. The law contains a few narrowly defined exceptions for certain types of employers, including those that provide armored car, alarm, or guard services, and those that manufacture, distribute, or dispense pharmaceuticals.

Even though no federal law specifically outlaws written honesty tests, these tests sometimes violate federal and state antidiscrimination or privacy laws. Plus, the tests can be unreliable.

Some states have adopted their own rules about polygraph tests, some of which are stricter than the federal law. To find out what your state requires, see "Employee Polygraph Examination Laws," at the end of this chapter.

Lessons From the Real World

Rent-A-Center, Inc., a company that offers furniture and other household goods on a rent-to-own basis, required applicants for certain management positions to take the Minnesota Multiphasic Personality Inventory test (MMPI), answering questions such as:

- I see things or animals or people around me that others do not see.
- My soul sometimes leaves my body.
- At times I have fits of laughing and crying that I cannot control.
- I have a habit of counting things that are not important such as bulbs on electric signs, and so forth.

Applicants who were required to take the test sued, arguing (among other things) that the test violated the ADA because it was a medical examination designed to reveal mental impairments. Although the trial court rejected this argument, the federal Court of Appeals agreed with the applicants. Rent-A-Center stopped using the MMPI and was ordered to destroy all test results in its possession; it also had to pay the plaintiff class's attorneys' fees.

Karraker v. Rent-A-Center, 492 F.3d 896 (7th Cir. 2007); *Karraker v. Rent-A-Center,* 411 F.3d 831 (7th Cir. 2005).

Medical Tests

Medical testing is tricky. To avoid violating the Americans with Disabilities Act, you shouldn't ask for an applicant's medical history or conduct any medical exam before you make a job offer.

However, once you decide to offer the applicant a job, you can make the offer conditional on the applicant's passing a medical exam. However, you must require the exam for all entering employees doing the same job. If you only require people whom you believe or know to have disabilities to take the exam, you will be violating the Americans with Disabilities Act. If the exam would screen out disproportionately large numbers of applicants with disabilities, you may administer it only if it is job related and correlates to necessary job skills.

The Genetic Information Nondiscrimination Act (GINA) prohibits employers from asking or requiring applicants to provide genetic information, including through genetic tests. Even though the ADA allows employers to require a post-offer medical exam, as described above, that exam may not include genetic testing, nor may it include the collection of family medical history. Employers must instruct their health care providers not to collect genetic information as part of any employment-related medical exam. If an employer discovers that a health care provider is nonetheless requesting this information, it must take reasonable steps to put a stop to it by, for example, no longer using that provider.

Drug and Alcohol Tests

The laws on drug testing vary widely from state to state. In general, employers have much more leeway to test job applicants than current employees. However, several states have imposed certain procedural requirements that employers must follow. For example, you might be required to give notice to applicants that the job is a drug-tested position, to test only after making a conditional offer of employment, or to provide applicants with a copy of positive test results. And, a minority of states restrict the occupations for which you may drug test, such as safety-sensitive positions. Consult "State Drug and Alcohol Testing Laws," at the end of this chapter, for information on your state's rules.

Background Checks

When you are making hiring decisions, you might need a bit more information than applicants provide. After all, some folks—surveys estimate between 30% and 40% of applicants—give false or incomplete information in employment applications. And workers probably don't want you to know certain facts about their past that might disqualify them from getting a job. Generally, it's good policy to do a little checking before making a job offer.

However, you do not have an unfettered right to dig into applicants' personal affairs. Workers have a right to privacy in certain personal matters, a right they can enforce by suing your company if you pry too deeply. How can you avoid crossing this line? Here are a few tips to keep in mind when gathering information on an applicant:

- **Make sure your inquiries are related to the job.** If you decide to do a background check, stick to information that is relevant to the job for which you are considering the worker. For example, if you are hiring a security guard who will carry a weapon and be responsible for large amounts of cash, you might reasonably check for past criminal convictions. (However, see "Criminal records," below, for some restrictions.)

- **Ask for consent.** You are on safest legal ground if you ask the applicant, in writing, to consent to a background check. Explain clearly what you plan to check and how you will gather information. This gives applicants a chance to take themselves out of the running if there are things they don't want you to know. It also prevents applicants from later claiming that you invaded their privacy. If an applicant refuses to consent to a reasonable request for information, you may legally decide not to consider that applicant for the position.

- **Be reasonable.** Managers can get their employers into legal trouble if they engage in background check overkill. You will not need to perform an extensive background check on every applicant. Even if you decide to check, you probably won't need to get into excessive detail for every position. If you find yourself questioning neighbors, ordering credit checks, and performing exhaustive searches of public records every time you hire a clerk or counterperson, you need to scale your efforts back.

In addition to these general considerations, specific rules apply to certain types of information:

- **School records.** Under federal law and the laws of some states, educational records—including transcripts, recommendations, and financial information—are confidential. Because

of these laws, most schools will not release records without the consent of the student. And some schools will only release records directly to the student.

- **Consumer and credit reports.** If you hire an outside party—such as a consumer reporting agency or private investigator—to conduct a background check or credit check on an applicant, you will need to follow special rules. Among other things, you'll need to get the applicant's written

Lessons From the Real World

After a handful of interviews and long-distance communications, including half a dozen phone calls and 20 email exchanges, Microsoft's Associate General Counsel, Michele Gammer, offered Mitchell Schley a job as a senior attorney. The offer letter, which Schley signed and returned, said that the job was at will, and that his employment was contingent on the successful completion of a background and reference check, among other things.

At the time, Schley was living and working in New Jersey. Gammer encouraged Schley to give notice to his current employer, recommended a real estate agent, and helped facilitate his purchase of a home in Washington from someone she knew. After Schley put down a deposit of $30,000 on the new home, put his New Jersey home on the market, and began to relocate, Gammer told him that his start date would have to be delayed while the company investigated a felony charge that came up in his

background check. Schley told Gammer that the charge was frivolous and that the person who made the complaint had dropped it; he also sent Gammer documents supporting his claims. A few days later, Gammer contacted Schley to tell him that Microsoft was revoking the job offer. Schley had to immediately resell the home he purchased in Washington and was out of work for two years afterwards. He sued Microsoft.

The court threw out Schley's claim that Microsoft broke an employment contract, because the job was to be at will. Because Microsoft had reserved the right to fire him at any time, the company had the legal right to revoke the offer. However, the court allowed Schley to bring his claim of promissory estoppel: Because he was promised the job and was encouraged to quit his job and buy a new home based on that promise, Microsoft could be legally held liable for the damages he suffered as a result.

Schley v. Microsoft, Civ. No. 08-3589 (D. New Jersey, 2008).

consent and inform the applicant if you decide not to hire him or her based on something you found in the report. (See "Ordering Consumer Reports," below, for more information.)

- **Criminal records.** The law varies from state to state on whether, and to what extent, a private employer may consider an applicant's criminal history in making hiring decisions. Some states don't allow you to ask about arrests that did not lead to convictions, convictions that occurred well in the past, juvenile crimes, or sealed records. Some states allow you to consider convictions only if the crimes are relevant to the job or only for certain positions (such as nurses, child care workers, private detectives, and other jobs requiring licenses). And, some states allow you to consider criminal history only at certain times in the hiring process (see "Ban-the-Box Laws Restrict Inquiries About Criminal History," above). To learn more about your state's laws, see "State Laws on Employee Arrest and Conviction Records," at the end of this chapter.

- **Workers' compensation records.** You may only consider information contained in the public record from a workers' compensation appeal in making a job decision if the applicant's injury might interfere with his or her ability to perform required duties.

- **Medical records.** Under the Americans with Disabilities Act, you may inquire about an applicant's ability to perform specific job duties, but you may not request medical records. Companies cannot make job decisions (on hiring or promotion, for example) based on an applicant's disability, as long as the employee can do the job, with or without a reasonable accommodation. Employers also can't discriminate on the basis of genetic information, nor may they request or require that applicants provide such information. Some states also have laws protecting the confidentiality of medical records.

- **Social media profiles.** Many employers consider public posts on Facebook or other social media websites when making hiring decisions. While employers are generally free to view posts that applicants have made available to the public, there is the potential for an employer to come across information that it is not allowed to consider in making job decisions— such as the applicant's religion, ethnic background, or disability. An applicant who is turned down for a job might argue that the decision was based on improper criteria. To avoid this dilemma, you might want to have someone other than the decision maker view social media pages and weed out any information pertaining to a protected class. (Different rules apply to applicants' private social media profiles; see "Asking for Social Media Account Passwords," above, for more information.)

- **Records of military service.** Members and former members of the armed forces have a right to privacy in their service records. These records may be released only under limited circumstances, and consent is generally required. However, the military may disclose name, rank, salary, duty assignments, awards, and duty status without the member's consent.
- **Driving records.** You should check the driving record of any employee whose job will require large amounts of driving (delivery persons or bus drivers, for example). These records are available, sometimes for a small fee, from the state's motor vehicles department.

Ordering Consumer Reports

Employers that use an outside agency to gather background information on an applicant must follow the guidelines set forth in the Fair Credit Reporting Act (FCRA). Contrary to its title, the FCRA applies to a lot more than just credit checks. The FCRA applies to all "consumer reports," which is defined broadly to include any information about an applicant's credit, character, reputation, or mode of living.

Many employers hire consumer reporting agencies to gather information about an applicant's credit history, job history, criminal record, driving record, or other information. Before ordering this type of report, though, you need to follow certain procedural steps required by the FCRA. The same is true if you plan to hire a private investigator, or any other party, to look into an applicant's background.

The FCRA, which is enforced by the Federal Trade Commission (FTC), requires that you do all of the following:

- Get the applicant's written consent in advance.
- Warn the applicant if you plan to reject him or her based on the report (called a "pre-adverse-action notice).
- Give the applicant a final notice (called an "adverse action notice") if you ultimately decide to reject him or her based on the report.

The purpose of these rules is to ensure accuracy in the reporting of a consumer's credit history and other personal information by letting consumers know when these reports are checked, whether the reports include disqualifying information, and how consumers can challenge incorrect entries. Given how often credit and consumer reports are consulted by employers, lenders, and landlords—it makes sense that the law builds in a few consumer protections.

Get Written Consent

Before you order a background check, you must notify the applicant that you plan to do so and get the applicant's written authorization. This notice and authorization must be set forth in a separate document that doesn't include other information. In other words, it can't be a section of your employment application.

Send a Pre-Adverse Action Notice

If you plan to reject the applicant based on something in the report, you must send the applicant a notice stating your intention to do so. This notice, called a "pre-adverse action notice," must also include two documents: (1) a copy of the consumer report, and (2) a copy of a notice from the Federal Trade Commission entitled "A Summary of Your Rights Under the Fair Credit Reporting Act," which tells the applicant how to challenge any incorrect information in the report, among other things.

(The consumer reporting agency that sent you the report should also give you a copy of the FTC's Summary of Rights; if it doesn't, you can find a copy at the FTC's website, www.ftc.gov.)

Send an Adverse Action Notice

Once you have made a final decision not to hire the applicant based on information contained in the report, you must send the applicant another document called an "adverse action notice." This notice explains that you are not hiring the applicant and provides additional information on the applicant's rights, including the right to dispute the accuracy of the report and the right to obtain an additional copy.

State Law Restrictions on Credit Reports

Other than the FCRA, federal law does not place restrictions on an employer's use of credit reports in making hiring decisions. As long as employers follow the notice and consent requirements, they are free to check credit reports and use them as the basis for denying employment.

However, several states have passed laws prohibiting employers from pulling credit reports or limiting the use of credit reports in making employment decisions. In addition to the District of Columbia, the following states have such laws: California, Colorado, Connecticut, Delaware, Hawaii, Illinois, Maryland, Nevada, Oregon, Vermont, and Washington. Although the rules vary from state to state, many of these laws limit credit checks to managerial or other sensitive positions where the applicant will have significant financial responsibilities or access to large sums of money.

Young Workers

Many jobs around an office and in a business are perfect for younger workers. For example, if you need someone to photocopy documents for an hour or two a day, a high school student who comes in after school might be just what you're looking for. The student gets experience and extra pocket money, and your company gets someone who is willing to work just a few hours a week on the cheap.

The history of child labor in this country isn't quite so benign, however. Children once worked long hours in hazardous jobs—such as manufacturing and mining—for very little money. They didn't attend school, and they often suffered serious—even fatal—health problems.

To protect child workers, the federal and state governments passed laws regulating the type of work children can do, the number of hours they can work, and the types of businesses that can employ them.

Before you hire any worker younger than 18, you should check both federal and state law. We describe the federal law here. To find out about your state child labor law, contact your state department of labor. (See Appendix A for contact information).

The Fair Labor Standards Act (FLSA) is the federal law that governs child labor. Virtually all employees and businesses must follow the FLSA, except for a handful of businesses, including small farms. To learn out about exceptions to FLSA requirements, check out the website of the U.S. Department of Labor—the federal agency that enforces the FLSA—at www.dol.gov.

Hazardous Jobs

According to the U.S. Department of Labor, workers younger than 18 may never perform the following types of hazardous jobs (some exceptions are made for apprentices and students):

- manufacturing or storing explosives
- being an outside helper on a motor vehicle
- coal or other mining
- logging and sawmilling
- anything involving power-driven, wood-working machines
- anything involving exposure to radioactive substances and ionizing radiations
- anything involving power-driven hoisting equipment
- anything involving power-driven metal-forming, punching, and shearing machines
- meat packing or processing (including anything involving power-driven meat slicing machines)
- anything involving power-driven bakery machines
- anything involving power-driven paper products machines
- manufacturing brick, tile, and related products
- anything involving power-driven circular saws, band saws, and guillotine shears
- wrecking, demolition, and shipbreaking operations

- roofing and work performed on or near roofs, including installing or working on antennas and rooftop appliances, and
- excavation operations.

Jobs That Involve Driving

Special rules apply to jobs that involve driving. As noted above, employees younger than 18 may not work as outside helpers on a vehicle. Employees who are 16 and younger also may not drive on public roads as part of their jobs. An employee who is at least 17 may drive on public roads as part of a job only if all of the following are true:

- The driving takes place during daylight hours only.
- The minor has a valid state driver's license for the type of driving involved.
- The minor has completed a driver's education course and has no moving violations.
- The vehicle weighs no more than 6,000 pounds.
- The vehicle is equipped with seat belts, and the employer has told employees to use them when driving.
- The driving is only occasional and incidental to the job, defined as taking up no more than a third of the workday and 20% of the minor's total weekly hours.

Even if all of the above conditions are met, a 17-year-old is legally prohibited from driving:

- a towing vehicle
- any vehicle other than a car or truck

- route deliveries or sales
- to transport property, goods, or passengers for hire
- to make urgent, time-sensitive deliveries (including pizza)
- with more than three passengers, even if they are also employees
- beyond a 30-mile radius from the workplace, or
- more than two trips per day to deliver goods to customers or to transport passengers (other than other employees).

Agricultural Jobs

If you own or operate a farm or another type of agricultural business, the following child labor rules apply to you:

- You may hire a worker who is 16 or older for any work, whether hazardous or not, for unlimited hours.
- You may hire a worker who is 14 or 15 for any nonhazardous work outside of school hours.
- You may hire a worker who is 12 or 13 for any nonhazardous work outside of school hours if the child's parents work on the same farm or if you have their written consent.
- You may hire a worker who is ten or 11 if you've been granted a waiver by the U.S. Department of Labor to employ the youngster as a hand-harvest laborer for no more than eight weeks in any calendar year.

- You can hire your own children to do any kind of work on the farm, regardless of their ages.

Nonagricultural Jobs

If you seek to hire a youngster for work that is nonagricultural, the following rules apply:

- You may hire a worker who is 18 or older for any job, hazardous or not, for unlimited hours.
- You may hire a worker who is 16 or 17 years old for any nonhazardous job, for unlimited hours.
- You may hire a worker who is 14 or 15 years old outside school hours in various nonmanufacturing, nonmining, and nonhazardous jobs, but some restrictions apply. The teen cannot work more than three hours on a school day, more than eight hours on a nonschool day, more than 18 hours in a school week, or more than 40 hours in a nonschool week. Also, the work cannot begin before 7 a.m. or end after 7 p.m., except from June 1 through Labor Day, when evening hours are extended to 9 p.m.

Offer Letters

Offer letters are typically used with at-will employees to state the basic terms of employment, such as job title and rate of pay. When done right, an offer letter does not restrict an employer's ability to change the terms of employment or terminate the employee for any reason, at any time.

When it comes to offer letters, keep them short and sweet. The same rules that apply to job interviews apply to offer letters: Stick to the facts and don't make promises you can't keep. Applicants might some day try to turn an offer letter into a contract that sets the terms and conditions of the job or limits your company's right to fire or discipline them.

Avoid using language that makes promises or assurances about the employment relationship. For example, if you tell the applicant "We look forward to a long and happy relationship with you" or "We think you have a bright future at this company," the applicant might assume that you're offering more than the normal "at-will" employment and that you won't end the employment relationship without good cause. If you want to fire the employee in the future, these words might come back to haunt you.

Similarly, don't specify job duties, benefits, pay schedules, vacation/sick leave, or any other benefit you might want to change in the future. The employee might argue that your letter created a contract and try to hold the company to it.

So what can you say? You might want to:

- congratulate the applicant
- confirm the job title
- name the applicant's supervisor
- state the starting salary or hourly rate, and
- establish a start date.

In addition, if you haven't or won't offer the applicant a written contract for employment (the vast majority of employees don't have written employment contracts), confirm in writing that employment is at will, meaning that there is no employment contract and you can fire the employee at any time for any reason that isn't illegal. It's also a good idea to have the employee sign an acknowledgment at the end of the letter, to show that he or she read and understood its contents. (For more about at-will employment, see "At-Will Employment" in Chapter 4.)

Written Employment Contracts

A written employment contract is a document that an employer and an employee sign, setting forth the detailed terms of their relationship with each other. In addition to clearly describing what the employee is going to do for the employer (the job) and what the employer is going to do for the employee (the salary), the contract can address many other issues, including:

- the duration of the job (for example, one year, two years, or until a certain project is complete)
- the specifics of the employee's responsibilities
- the employee's benefits (for example, health insurance, vacation leave, or disability leave)
- grounds for termination

- limitations on the employee's ability to compete with your company once the employee leaves
- protection of company trade secrets and client lists
- who will own the employee's work product (for example, if the employee writes books or invents gadgets for your company), and
- a method for resolving any disputes between the employee and the company.

The distinguishing feature of an employment contract is that it binds the company to hire the employee for a set period of time. You should carefully consider the advantages and disadvantages of this type of arrangement before committing your company.

Advantages

Employment contracts can make sense if you want or need to control the employee's ability to quit. For example, if the employee is a high-level manager or executive, or if the employee is especially valuable to the company (such as the administrator who is the organizational backbone of the office), then a contract can protect the company against the sudden, unexpected loss of the employee. It can lock the employee into a specific term (for example, two years), or it can require the employee to provide enough notice to allow your company to find and train a suitable replacement.

Employment contracts can also protect your company if the employee will have access to confidential and sensitive business information. You can insert confidentiality clauses into the contract that prevent the employee from disclosing this information or using it for personal gain. (For more on this topic, see "Nondisclosure Agreements" in Chapter 10.)

Similarly, a contract can prevent employees from competing against your company after they move on to other pursuits, at least in some states. (For more on this topic, see "Noncompete Agreements" in Chapter 10.)

Sometimes, you can also use an employment contract as a way to entice a highly skilled individual to accept a job offer. Job security and beneficial terms often sweeten the deal enough to convince a highly desirable applicant who is on the fence to join your team.

Finally, an employment contract can give the company greater control over the employee. If you specify the standards for the employee's performance and grounds for termination, you might have an easier time terminating an employee who doesn't live up to those standards.

Disadvantages

An employment contract is a two-way street: Just as the contract requires the worker to stay for a certain period of time, it limits your company's right to fire the worker during the same period (except for the reasons stated in the contract). Your company also won't have the ability to alter the terms of the employment as its business needs change. To alter the terms, you'll have to renegotiate the contract and offer the employee some new benefit in exchange for the alteration to make the new agreement binding. And, no matter what you offer, the employee is free to reject any proposed new terms. These factors can make the renegotiation process time-consuming and complicated.

For example, let's say you sign a two-year contract with a new employee. If, six months later, you decide you don't need the employee after all, you can't terminate the relationship. If you do, you will set your company up for a breach of contract lawsuit. Similarly, if you promised benefits in the contract, the company can't stop paying for them before the term is up without breaching the contract and risking a lawsuit.

Another disadvantage of employment contracts is that they always contain an unwritten obligation, imposed by law, to deal fairly with the employee. In legal terms, this is called the "covenant of good faith and fair dealing." If you treat an employee with whom you have signed a contract in a way that seems unfair, your company could end up in court.

Finally, there are ways to protect the company's sensitive information and business interests without using an employment contract for a specific period of time. For example, you can have an at-will employee sign a standalone confidentiality agreement to prevent disclosure of the company's trade secrets. (For more information, see Chapter 10.)

Checklist: First-Day Paperwork

When your new hire shows up on the first day of work, there will be lots to do, including plenty of forms to be completed. Use this checklist to make sure you don't forget any important paperwork. (Of course, your company might not use every form on this list—or might have come up with additional paperwork of its own—so make sure you modify this checklist if necessary.)

Required Government Paperwork

☐ USCIS Form I-9, *Employment Eligibility Verification*. The federal government requires employers to complete this form verifying that new hires are eligible to work in the United States. Get more information at www.uscis.gov.

☐ IRS Form W-4, *Withholding Allowance Certificate*. New employees use this form to tell your company how much income tax to withhold from their paychecks. Go to www.irs.gov for information.

☐ New hire reporting information. Employers must provide information on new employees to a state agency, which uses it to find parents who owe child support. For information on your state's requirements, go to www.acf.hhs.gov/ccs and select the "Employers" tab.

Company Forms

☐ Signed offer letter or employment contract

☐ Employee handbook acknowledgment form (see Chapter 4)

☐ Acknowledgment of company email policy (see Chapter 6)

☐ Benefits paperwork, such as enrollment forms

☐ Emergency contact information

☐ Acknowledgment of receiving company property, such as a cell phone, car, or laptop computer to be used off-site

☐ Other agreements, such as confidentiality agreement or arbitration agreement

Legal Dos and Don'ts: Hiring

Do:

- **Focus on the essential elements of the job.** You can avoid problems with antidiscrimination and privacy laws by remembering your hiring goal: to find an applicant who can do the job well. Keeping your eyes on the prize will stop you from delving into an applicant's personal affairs, religious beliefs, medical conditions, or other forbidden topics.

- **Use written contracts sparingly.** A written contract is a great way to seal the deal with a stellar applicant whom you want to retain. It's also a fast track to the courthouse if used with an employee whom you might have to fire or lay off.

- **Put your offer in writing.** No law requires you to use written offer letters, but they're an easy and effective way to make sure the applicant knows exactly what the job entails. If you are offering an at-will job, spelling that out will help you document your intentions.

Don't:

- **Shade the truth.** Always be honest when dealing with job applicants. Someone who accepts a job based on your false statements about the job can ask a court to hold the company to your promises or to pay for your misrepresentations.

- **Get too personal.** Privacy laws differ from state to state, but you'll always be on shaky legal ground if you delve into an applicant's personal life.

- **Test unless you really need to (and you've cleared the test with a lawyer).** The law of testing is changing all the time, which makes it a ripe source of lawsuits for invasion of privacy, disability discrimination, and more. The good news is that the vast majority of companies can make sound hiring decisions without resorting to testing.

Test Your Knowledge

Questions

1. You should ask every applicant exactly the same questions when interviewing for a position. ☐ True ☐ False

2. You may ask applicants with disabilities whether and how they could perform the essential functions of the position. ☐ True ☐ False

3. It's best to ask only about verifiable facts during an interview, such as where an applicant works or what positions he or she has held. ☐ True ☐ False

4. You can make promises to an applicant during the hiring process, as long as employees at your company have to sign an at-will agreement. ☐ True ☐ False

5. If an applicant brings up his or her religion, it's okay to ask questions and state your opinions about it. ☐ True ☐ False

6. A company can require all applicants to take a personality test. ☐ True ☐ False

7. You always have the right to look at an applicant's credit report when making hiring decisions. ☐ True ☐ False

8. It's a good idea to send an offer letter to successful applicants. ☐ True ☐ False

9. A company should never offer applicants a written employment contract. ☐ True ☐ False

10. Antidiscrimination laws and other workplace restrictions apply only to employees, not to job applicants. ☐ True ☐ False

Test Your Knowledge (continued)

Answers

1. False. Although you should cover the same basic ground with every applicant, you shouldn't script the entire interview. Otherwise, you'll miss opportunities to follow up on issues applicants raise and delve more deeply into areas of interest or concern.

2. True. While you can't ask applicants about their disabilities, you can ask about their abilities. Just be sure to ask all applicants this question, not just those whom you suspect of having a disability.

3. False. You should certainly find out what positions an applicant has held, but the most informative answers come from open-ended queries that invite the applicant to talk about his or her experience and skills.

4. False. An at-will agreement is not a silver bullet, especially if an applicant left a good position to come to work for your company based on your false statements. If you entice someone with promises that won't come true, you could have a lawsuit on your hands.

5. False. Even if an employee brings up a delicate topic, it's best to simply move on. If you get into a discussion and say something that the employee finds distasteful or biased, the fact that the employee raised the issue in the first place won't save you from a discrimination claim.

6. False. It depends on the test, how it's administered, what it measures, and what you use it for. Courts have found that some personality tests are discriminatory or violate the applicant's right to privacy.

7. False. It depends; some states prohibit employers from using an applicant's credit report in making hiring decisions. In states that allow it, federal law requires employers to get the applicant's consent, in writing, before running a credit check.

8. True. You can use the offer letter to set forth the basic terms of the job and let future employees know that they will be working at will, if that's your company's policy.

9. False. Written employment contracts should be the exception rather than the rule, but there are circumstances when it makes sense to use one.

10. False. Antidiscrimination laws apply to every stage of the employment relationship, including job postings, applications, interviews, and actually selecting your new hire.

Preemployment Inquiries

Note: This chart provides guidance on how to avoid questions that could run afoul of federal antidiscrimination laws. While not all of the subjects listed below are expressly protected by federal law, the EEOC has stated that certain subjects are closely tied to discrimination based on a protected characteristic (for example, questions about marital status or number of children are commonly used to discriminate against women). Many states have laws that protect additional characteristics; to learn more, see the "State Laws Prohibiting Discrimination in Employment" chart at the end of Chapter 3.

Subject	Lawful Preemployment Inquiries	Unlawful or Risky Preemployment Inquiries
Name	Applicant's full name Have you ever worked for this company under a different name? Is any additional information relative to a different name necessary to check work record? If yes, explain.	Original name of an applicant whose name has been changed by court order or otherwise Applicant's maiden name
Address or duration of residence	How long have you been a resident of this state or city?	Do you rent or own?
Birthplace	None	Birthplace of applicant Birthplace of applicant's parents, spouse, or other close relatives Requirement that applicant submit birth certificate, naturalization, or baptismal record
Age	Are you 18 years old or older? This question may be asked only for the purpose of determining whether applicants are of legal age for employment.	How old are you? What is your date of birth? What year did you graduate from high school?
Religion or creed	None	Inquiry into an applicant's religious denomination, religious affiliations, church, parish, pastor, or religious holidays observed
Race or color	None	Complexion or color of skin Inquiry regarding applicant's race
Photograph	None	Any requirement for a photograph prior to hire
Height	None	Inquiry regarding applicant's height (unless you have a legitimate business reason)
Weight	None	Inquiry regarding applicant's weight (unless you have a legitimate business reason)
Marital or familial status	Is your spouse employed by this employer?	Are you single or married? Do you have any children? Is your spouse employed? What is your spouse's name?

Preemployment Inquiries (continued)		
Subject	**Lawful Preemployment Inquiries**	**Unlawful or Risky Preemployment Inquiries**
Gender	None	Mr., Miss, Mrs., Ms., or any inquiry regarding gender Inquiry as to ability or plans to reproduce or advocacy of any form of birth control
Disability	These [provide applicant with list] are the essential functions of the job. How would you perform them?	Inquiries regarding an individual's physical or mental condition that are not directly related to the requirements of a specific job
Citizenship	Are you legally authorized to work in the United States on a full-time basis?	Questions about the subjects below are unlawful, but the applicant might be required to reveal some of this information as part of the federal I-9 process: • Country of citizenship • Whether an applicant is naturalized or a native-born citizen; the date when the applicant acquired citizenship • Requirement that an applicant produce naturalization papers or first papers • Whether applicant's parents or spouse are naturalized or native-born citizens of the United States, and, if so, the date when such parent or spouse acquired citizenship
National origin	Inquiry into language applicant speaks and writes fluently	Inquiry into applicant's lineage, ancestry, national origin, descent, parentage, or nationality, unless part of the federal I-9 process in determining employment eligibility Nationality of applicant's parents or spouse Inquiry into applicant's native language or how applicant acquired ability to read, write, or speak a foreign language
Education	Inquiry into the academic, vocational, or professional education of an applicant and public and private schools attended	
Experience	Inquiry into work experience Inquiry into countries applicant has visited	
Arrests	Have you ever been convicted of a crime? Are there any felony charges pending against you?	Inquiry regarding arrests that did not result in conviction (except for law enforcement agencies)
Relatives	Names of applicant's relatives already employed by this company	Address of any relative of applicant, other than address (within the United States) of applicant's father and mother, husband or wife, and minor dependent children

Preemployment Inquiries (continued)		
Subject	Lawful Preemployment Inquiries	Unlawful or Risky Preemployment Inquiries
Notice in case of emergency	Name and address of person to be notified in case of accident or emergency	Name and address of nearest relative to be notified in case of accident or emergency
Organizations	Inquiry into the organizations of which an applicant is a member, except for organizations which by name or character of indicate the race, color, religion, national origin, or ancestry of its members	List all clubs, societies, and lodges to which the applicant belongs
Personal finance	None	Inquiries about financial problems, such as garnishment or bankruptcy

Employee Polygraph Examination Laws

Alaska

Alaska Stat. § 23.10.037

Employers covered: All

What's prohibited: Employer may not suggest, request, or require that employee or applicant take a lie detector test.

California

Cal. Lab. Code § 432.2

Employers covered: All

What's prohibited: Employer may not demand or require that employee or applicant take a lie detector test.

What's allowed: Employer may request a test, if applicant is advised in writing of legal right to refuse to take it.

Connecticut

Conn. Gen. Stat. Ann. § 31-51g

Employers covered: All, including employment agencies

What's prohibited: Employer may not request or require that employee or applicant take a lie detector test.

Delaware

Del. Code Ann. tit. 19, § 704

Employers covered: All

What's prohibited: Employer may not suggest, request, or require that employee or applicant take a lie detector test in order to obtain or continue employment.

District of Columbia

D.C. Code Ann. §§ 32-901 to 32-903

Employers covered: All

What's prohibited: Employer may not administer, have administered, use, or accept the results of any polygraph examination.

Hawaii

Haw. Rev. Stat. § 378-26.5

Employers covered: All

What's prohibited: Employer may not require employee or applicant to take lie detector test.

What's allowed: Employer may request test if current or prospective employee is told, orally and in writing, that refusing to take test will not result in being fired or hurt chances of getting job.

Idaho

Idaho Code § 44-903

Employers covered: All

What's prohibited: Employer may not require an employee or applicant to take a lie detector test.

Illinois

225 Ill. Comp. Stat. § 430/14.1

Employers covered: All

What's prohibited: Unless directly related to employment, examination may not include questions about:

- political, religious, or labor-related beliefs, affiliations, or activities (that are lawful)
- beliefs or opinions on racial matters, or
- sexual preferences or activity.

Iowa

Iowa Code § 730.4

Employers covered: All

What's prohibited: Employer may not request, require, administer, or attempt or threaten to administer a lie detector test; may not request or require that employee or applicant sign waiver of any action prohibited by this law.

Maine

Me. Rev. Stat. Ann. tit. 32, § 7364

Employers covered: All

Employee Polygraph Examination Laws (continued)

What's prohibited: Employer may not request, require, suggest, or administer a polygraph test.

What's allowed: Employee may voluntarily request a test if all these conditions are met:

- Results cannot be used against employee.
- Employer must give employee a copy of the law when employee requests test.
- Test must be recorded or employee's witness must be present during the test, or both (upon employee's request).

Maryland

Md. Code Ann. [Lab. & Empl.] § 3-702

Employers covered: All

What's prohibited: Employer may not require or demand that employee or applicant take a lie detector test.

What's required: All employment applications must include specified notice that no person can be required to take a lie detector test as a condition of obtaining or continuing employment and must include space for applicant to sign and acknowledge notice.

Massachusetts

Mass. Gen. Laws ch. 149, § 19B

Employers covered: All

What's prohibited: Employer may not request, require, or administer a lie detector test.

What's required: All employment applications must include specified notice that it is unlawful to require a lie detector test as a condition of obtaining or continuing employment.

Michigan

Mich. Comp. Laws §§ 37.203, 338.1719

Employers covered: All

What's prohibited: Employer may not request, require, administer, or attempt or threaten to

administer a lie detector test; may not request or require that employee or applicant sign waiver of any action prohibited by this law.

What's allowed: Employee may voluntarily request a test if all of these conditions are met:

- The employee is given a copy of the law before taking the test.
- The employee is given copies of the test results and reports.
- No questions are asked about sexual practices; marital relationship; or political, religious, or labor or union affiliations, unless the questions are relevant to areas under examination.
- The examiner informs employee:
  - of all questions that will be asked
  - of the right to accept, refuse, or stop the test at any time
  - that the employee is not required to answer questions or give information, and
  - that any information volunteered could be used against the employee or made available to the employer, unless otherwise agreed to in writing.

Minnesota

Minn. Stat. Ann. §§ 181.75, 181.76

Employers covered: All

What's prohibited: Employer may not directly or indirectly solicit or require an applicant or employee to take a lie detector test.

What's allowed: Employee may request a test, but only if employer informs employee that test is voluntary. Results of voluntary test may be given only to those authorized by employee.

Montana

Mont. Code Ann. § 39-2-304

What's prohibited: Employer may not require an employee or applicant to take a lie detector test.

Employee Polygraph Examination Laws (continued)

Nebraska

Neb. Rev. Stat. § 81-1932

Employers covered: All

What's prohibited: Employer may not require an employee or applicant to take a lie detector test.

What's allowed: Employer may request that test be taken, but only if all of these conditions are met:

- No questions are asked about sexual practices; marital relationship; or political, religious, or labor or union affiliations.
- An examinee is given written and oral notice that the test is voluntary and may be discontinued at any time.
- An examinee signs a form stating that the test is being taken voluntarily.
- Prospective employees are asked only job-related questions and are not singled out for testing in a discriminatory manner.
- An employee is requested to take the test only in connection with a specific investigation.
- The results of a test are not the sole reason for terminating employment.
- All questions and responses are kept on file by the employer for at least one year.

Nevada

Nev. Rev. Stat. Ann. §§ 613.480 to 613.510

Employers covered: All

Exceptions: Manufacturers or distributors of controlled substances; providers or designers of security systems and other security personnel; ongoing investigation

What's prohibited: Employer may not directly or indirectly require, request, suggest, or cause a lie detector test to be taken; may not use, accept, refer to, or ask about the results of any test. May not take adverse employment action solely on the basis of test results or a refusal to take test.

What's allowed: Nevada law allows testing in the same limited circumstances as the federal EPPA, with similar rules and restrictions on when and how the test is given.

New Jersey

N.J. Stat. Ann. § 2C:40A-1

Employers covered: All

Exceptions: Employers that deal with controlled, dangerous substances

What's prohibited: Employer may not influence, request, or require applicant or employee to take a lie detector test.

What's allowed: Employers who are allowed to test must observe all of these rules:

- The job must require direct access to the controlled substance.
- The test is limited to the preceding 5 years.
- Questions must be work-related or pertain to improper handling, use, or illegal sale of legally distributed controlled dangerous substances.
- The test taker has the right to legal counsel.
- The written copy of test results must be given to the test taker upon request.
- Test information may not be released to any other employer or person.
- The employee or prospective employee must be informed of the right to present results of a second independently administered test prior to any personnel decision being made.

New York

N.Y. Lab. Law §§ 733 to 739

Employers covered: All

What's prohibited: Employer may not require, request, suggest, permit, or use results of a lie detector test.

Employee Polygraph Examination Laws (continued)

Oregon

Ore. Rev. Stat. Ann. §§ 659.840, 659A.300

Employers covered: All

What's prohibited: Employer may not require an employee or applicant to take a lie detector test.

Pennsylvania

18 Pa. Cons. Stat. Ann. § 7321

Employers covered: All

Exceptions: Employers with positions that have access to narcotics or dangerous drugs

What's prohibited: Employer may not require an employee or applicant to take a lie detector test.

Rhode Island

R.I. Gen. Laws §§ 28-6.1-1 to 28-6.1-4

Employers covered: All

What's prohibited: Employer may not request, require, subject, nor directly or indirectly cause an employee or applicant to take a lie detector test.

Tennessee

Tenn. Code Ann. §§ 62-27-123, 62-27-128

Employers covered: All

What's prohibited: Employer may not take any personnel action based solely upon the results of a polygraph examination. No questions may be asked about:

- religious, political, or labor-related beliefs, affiliations, or activities (that are lawful)
- beliefs or opinions about racial matters
- sexual preferences or activities
- disabilities covered by the Americans with Disabilities Act, or
- activities that occurred more than five years before the examination, except for felony convictions and violations of the state drug control act.

(There is an exception where the examination is part of an investigation of illegal activity in one of the above subject areas.)

What's required: Prospective examinee must be told if examiner is a law enforcement or court official and informed that any illegal activity disclosed may be used against examinee. Must receive and sign a written notice of rights including:

- right to refuse to take the test or to answer any question
- right to terminate examination at any time
- right to request an audio recording of examination and pretest interview, and
- right to request examination results within 30 days of taking it.

Vermont

Vt. Stat. Ann. tit. 21, §§ 494 to 494e

Employers covered: All

Exceptions: Employers whose primary business is sale of precious metals, gems, or jewelry; whose business includes manufacture or sale of regulated drugs and applicant's position requires contact with drugs; employers authorized by federal law to require a test

What's prohibited: Employer may not request, require, administer, or attempt or threaten to administer a lie detector test. May not request or require that employee or applicant sign waiver of any action prohibited by state law. May not discriminate against employee who files a complaint of violation of laws.

When testing is allowed, no questions may be asked about:

- political, religious, or labor union affiliations
- sexual practices, social habits, or marital relationship (unless clearly related to job performance), or
- any matters unrelated to job performance.

Employee Polygraph Examination Laws (continued)

What's required: Prior to taking test examinee must receive a copy of state laws and a copy of all questions to be asked. Must be told that any information disclosed could be used against examinee or made available to employer, unless there is a signed written agreement to the contrary. Examinee must be informed of rights including:

- right to accept or refuse to take examination
- right to refuse to answer any questions or give any information
- right to stop examination at any time, and
- right to a copy of examination results and of any reports given to employer.

Virginia

Va. Code Ann. § 40.1-51.4:3

Employers covered: All

What's prohibited: Employer may not require an applicant to answer questions about sexual activities in a polygraph test, unless the sexual activity resulted in a conviction for violation of state law.

What's required: Any record of examination results must be destroyed or maintained on a confidential basis, open to inspection only upon agreement of the employee.

Washington

Wash. Rev. Code Ann. § 49.44.120

Employers covered: All

Exceptions: Applicant or employee who manufactures, distributes, or dispenses controlled substances, or who works in a sensitive position directly involving national security

What's prohibited: Employer may not require, directly or indirectly, that an employee or applicant take a lie detector test.

West Virginia

W.Va. Code §§ 21-5-5a to 21-5-5d

Employers covered: All

Exceptions: Employees or applicants with direct access to controlled substances

What's prohibited: Employer may not require or request, directly or indirectly, that an employee or applicant take a lie detector test; may not knowingly use the results of a lie detector test.

Wisconsin

Wis. Stat. Ann. § 111.37

Employers covered: All

Exceptions: Manufacturers or distributors of controlled substances; providers or designers of security systems and other security personnel; ongoing investigation

What's prohibited: Employer may not directly or indirectly require, request, suggest, or cause an applicant or employee to take a lie detector test; may not use, accept, refer to, or inquire about the results of a test. May not take adverse employment action solely on the basis of test results or a refusal to take test. May not discriminate or retaliate against employee who files a complaint of violation of laws.

What's allowed: Wisconsin law allows testing in the same limited circumstances as the federal EPPA, with similar rules and restrictions on when and how the test is given.

State Drug and Alcohol Testing Laws

Note: Some states have drug or alcohol testing laws that apply to all employers of a certain size in the state. Other states' laws apply only to employers that choose to establish a drug-free workplace in order to qualify for a workers' compensation discount. These programs may not only allow employers to test, but actually require employers to test in certain circumstances. Finally, some states are not included in this chart because they do not have a general drug and alcohol testing statute governing private employers. However, other statutes or case law (from court decisions) may also apply. Check with an employment lawyer or your state department of labor for more information.

Alabama

Ala. Code §§ 25-5-330 to 25-5-340

Employers affected: Employers who establish a drug-free workplace program to qualify for a workers' compensation rate discount.

Testing applicants: Employer must test applicants upon conditional offer of employment. May test only those applying for certain positions, if based on reasonable job classifications. Job ads must include notice that drug and alcohol testing required.

Testing employees: Random testing permitted. Must test:

- after an accident that results in lost work time
- upon reasonable suspicion (reasons for suspicion must be documented and made available to employee upon request)
- as required by employer's routinely scheduled fitness for duty exams, and
- as follow-up to a required rehabilitation program.

Employee rights: Employees have 5 days to contest or explain a positive test result. Employer must have an employee assistance program or maintain a resource file of outside programs.

Notice and policy requirements: All employees must have written notice of drug policy. Must give 60 days' advance notice before implementing testing program. Policy must include consequences of refusing to take test or testing positive.

Alaska

Alaska Stat. §§ 23.10.600 to 23.10.699

Employers affected: Employers with one or more full-time employees.

Testing applicants: Employer may test applicants for any job-related purpose consistent with business necessity and the terms of the employer's policy.

Testing employees: Employers are not required to test. Random testing permitted. Employer may test:

- for any job-related purpose consistent with business necessity
- to maintain productivity or safety
- as part of an accident investigation or investigation of possible employee impairment, or
- upon reasonable suspicion.

Employee rights: Employer must provide written test results within 5 working days. Employee has 10 working days to request opportunity to explain positive test results; employer must grant request within 72 hours or before taking any adverse employment action.

Notice and policy requirements: Before implementing a testing program employer must distribute a written drug policy to all employees and must give 30 days' advance notice. Policy must include consequences of a positive test or refusal to submit to testing.

Arizona

Ariz. Rev. Stat. §§ 23-493 to 23-493.11

Employers affected: Employers with one or more full-time employees.

State Drug and Alcohol Testing Laws (continued)

Testing applicants: Employer must inform prospective hires that they will undergo drug testing as a condition of employment.

Testing employees: Statute does not encourage, discourage, restrict, prohibit, or require testing. Random testing permitted. Employees may be tested:
- for any job-related purpose
- to maintain productivity or safety
- as part of an accident investigation or investigation of individual employee impairment, or
- upon reasonable suspicion.

If employer tests, all compensated employees must be included in the program, including officers, directors, and supervisors.

Employee rights: Policy must inform employees of their right to explain positive results.

Notice and policy requirements: Before conducting tests employer must give employees a copy of the written policy. Policy must include the consequences of a positive test or refusal to submit to testing.

Arkansas
Ark. Code Ann. §§ 11-3-203, 11-14-101 to 11-14-112

Testing applicants: Employers who establish a drug-free workplace program to qualify for a workers' compensation rate discount: must test for drug use upon conditional offer of employment. May test only those applying for certain positions, if based on reasonable job classifications. Employer may test for alcohol. Job ads must include notice that testing is required.

All employers: may not test applicant unless employer pays for the cost of the test, and upon written request, provides a free copy of the report to the employee or applicant.

Testing employees: Employers who establish a drug-free workplace program to qualify for a workers' compensation rate discount must test any employee:

- upon reasonable suspicion
- as part of a routine fitness-for-duty medical exam
- after an accident that results in injury, and
- as follow-up to a required rehabilitation program.

Employer may test for any other lawful reason.

All employers: may not test employee unless employer pays for the cost of the test, and upon written request, provides a free copy of the report to the employee or applicant.

Employee rights: Employer may not refuse to hire applicant or take adverse personnel action against an employee on the basis of a single positive test that has not been verified by a confirmation test and a medical review officer. An applicant or employee has 5 days after receiving test results to contest or explain them.

Notice and policy requirements: Employer must give all employees a written statement of drug policy, including the consequences of a positive test or refusal to submit to testing. Employer must give 60 days' advance notice before implementing program.

Connecticut
Conn. Gen. Stat. Ann. §§ 31-51t to 31-51bb

Employers affected: All employers.

Testing applicants: Employer must inform job applicants in writing if drug testing is required as a condition of employment. Employer must provide copy of positive test result.

Testing employees: Employer may test when there is reasonable suspicion that employee is under the influence of drugs or alcohol and job performance is or could be impaired.

Random testing is allowed only:
- when authorized by federal law
- when employee's position is dangerous or safety sensitive

State Drug and Alcohol Testing Laws (continued)

- when employee drives a school bus or student transportation vehicle, or
- as part of a voluntary employee-assistance program.

Employee rights: Employer may not take any adverse personnel action on the basis of a single positive test that has not been verified by a confirmation test.

Florida

Fla. Stat. Ann. §§ 440.101 to 440.102

Employers affected: Employers who establish a drug-free workplace program to qualify for a workers' compensation rate discount.

Testing applicants: Employers must test job applicants upon conditional employment offer. May test only those applying for certain positions, if based on reasonable job classifications. Job ads must include notice that testing is required.

Testing employees: Must test employee:
- upon reasonable suspicion
- as part of a routine fitness-for-duty medical exam, and
- as part of a required rehabilitation program.

Random testing and testing for any other reason is neither required nor precluded by the law.

Employee rights: Employees who voluntarily seek treatment for substance abuse cannot be fired, disciplined, or discriminated against, unless they have tested positive or have been in treatment in the past. All employees have the right to explain positive results within 5 days. Employer may not take any adverse personnel action on the basis of an initial positive result that has not been verified by a confirmation test and a medical review officer.

Notice and policy requirements: Prior to implementing testing, employer must give 60 days' advance notice and must give employees written copy of drug policy. Policy must include consequences of a positive test result or refusal to submit to testing.

Georgia

Ga. Code Ann. §§ 34-9-410 to 34-9-421

Employers affected: Employers who establish a drug-free workplace program to qualify for a workers' compensation rate discount.

Testing applicants: Employer must test on conditional offer of employment. May test only those applying for certain positions, if based on reasonable job classifications. Job ads must include notice that testing is required.

Testing employees: Must test any employee:
- upon reasonable suspicion
- as part of a routine fitness-for-duty medical exam
- after an accident that results in an injury, and
- as part of a required rehabilitation program.

Random testing and testing for any other lawful reason is neither required nor prohibited.

Employee rights: Employees have 5 days to explain or contest a positive result. Employer must have an employee assistance program or maintain a resource file of outside programs. Initial positive result must be confirmed.

Notice and policy requirements: Employer must give applicants and employees notice of testing and must give 60 days' notice before implementing program. All employees must receive a written policy statement; policy must state the consequences of refusing to submit to a drug test or of testing positive.

Hawaii

Haw. Rev. Stat. §§ 329B-1 to 329B-5

Employers affected: All.

Testing applicants: Same conditions as current employees.

Testing employees: Employer may test employees only if these conditions are met:

State Drug and Alcohol Testing Laws (continued)

- employer pays all costs including confirming test
- tests are performed by a licensed laboratory
- employee receives a list of the substances being tested for (and medications that could cause a positive result)
- there is a form for disclosing medicines and legal drugs, and
- the results are kept confidential.

Notice and policy requirements: If employer uses an on-site screening test, it must follow the instructions on the package. If an employee or applicant tests positive in an on-site test, the employer must direct the employee or applicant to go to a licensed laboratory, within four hours, for a follow-up test. If the employee or applicant doesn't go to the lab, the employer can fire, refuse to hire, or take other adverse action against the employee or applicant only if the employer provided written notice of both of the following:

- The employer followed the required procedures for the on-site test.
- The employee or applicant could refuse to take the test.

If the employee or applicant refused or failed to take the test, the employer can take adverse action.

Idaho
Idaho Code §§ 72-1701 to 72-1716

Employers affected: Employers who establish a drug-free workplace program to qualify for a workers' compensation rate discount and/or prohibit employees fired for drug or alcohol use from qualifying for unemployment compensation.

Testing applicants: Employer may test as a condition of hiring.

Testing employees: May test for variety of reasons, including:

- following a workplace accident
- based on reasonable suspicion

- as part of a return-to-duty exam
- at random, or
- as a condition of continued employment.

An employer who follows drug-free workplace guidelines may fire employees who refuse to submit to testing or who test positive for drugs or alcohol. Employees will be fired for misconduct and denied unemployment benefits.

Employee rights: An employee or applicant who receives notice of a positive test may request a retest within 7 working days. Employee must have opportunity to explain positive result. If the retest results are negative, the employer must pay for the cost; if they are positive, the employee must pay. Employer may not take any adverse employment action on the basis of an initial positive result that has not been verified by a confirmation test.

Notice and policy requirements: Employer must have a written policy that includes a statement that violation of the policy may result in termination due to misconduct, as well as what types of testing employees may be subject to.

Illinois
775 Ill. Comp. Stat. § 5/2-104(C)(2)

Employers affected: Employers with 15 or more employees.

Testing employees: Statute does not "encourage, prohibit, or authorize" drug testing, but employers may test employees who have been in rehabilitation.

Indiana
Ind. Code Ann. §§ 22-9-5-6(b), 22-9-5-24

Employers affected: Employers with 15 or more employees.

Testing employees: Statute does not "encourage, prohibit, or authorize" testing, but employers may test employees who have been in rehabilitation.

State Drug and Alcohol Testing Laws (continued)

Iowa

Iowa Code § 730.5

Employers affected: Employers with one or more full-time employees.

Testing applicants: Employer may test as a condition of hiring.

Testing employees: Statute does not encourage, discourage, restrict, limit, prohibit, or require testing. Employer may conduct unannounced, random testing of employees selected from the entire workforce at one site, all full-time employees at one site, or all employees in safety-sensitive positions. Employers may also test:
- upon reasonable suspicion
- during and after rehabilitation, or
- following an accident that caused a reportable injury or more than $1,000 property damage.

Employee rights: Employee has 7 days to request a retest. Employers with 50 or more employees must provide rehabilitation for any employee testing positive for alcohol use who has worked for at least 12 of the last 18 months and has not previously violated the substance abuse policy. Employer must have an employee assistance program or maintain a resource file of outside programs.

Notice and policy requirements: Must have written drug test policy that includes consequences of positive result and refusal to take test. Employer may take action only on confirmed positive result.

Kentucky

Ky. Rev. Stat. 304.13-167; 803 Ky. Admin. Code 25:280

Employers affected: Employers who establish a drug-free workplace to qualify for a workers' compensation premium discount.

Testing applicants: Must test for drugs and alcohol after conditional offer of employment.

Testing employees: Must test for drugs:
- upon reasonable suspicion
- following a workplace accident that requires medical care
- as a follow-up to an Employee Assistance Program (EAP) or rehabilitation program for drug use, and
- upon being selected using a statistically valid, random, unannounced selection procedure.

Must test for alcohol:
- upon reasonable suspicion
- following a workplace accident that required medical care, and
- as a follow-up to an EAP or rehabilitation program for alcohol use.

Employee rights: Employee must have an opportunity to report use of prescription or over-the-counter medicines after receiving a positive test result.

Notice and policy requirements: Employer must have a written drug-free workplace policy. Employer must distribute and post notice of how it will determine whether employees have violated the policy and the consequences of violating the policy.

Louisiana

La. Rev. Stat. Ann. §§ 49:1001 to 49:1012

Employers affected: Employers with one or more full-time employees. (Does not apply to oil drilling, exploration, or production.)

Testing applicants: Employer may require all applicants to submit to drug and alcohol test. An employer must use certified laboratories and specified procedures for testing if it will base its hiring decisions on the results of the test.

Testing employees: Employer may require employees to submit to drug and alcohol test. An employer that will take negative action against an employee

State Drug and Alcohol Testing Laws (continued)

based on a positive test result must use certified laboratories and specified procedures for testing.

Employee rights: Employees with confirmed positive results have 7 working days to request access to all records relating to the drug test. Employer may allow employee to undergo rehabilitation without termination of employment.

Maine

Me. Rev. Stat. Ann. tit. 26, §§ 681 to 690

Employers affected: Employers with one or more full-time employees.

Testing applicants: Employer may require applicant to take a drug test only if offered employment or placed on an eligibility list.

Testing employees: Statute does not require or encourage testing. Employer may test based upon probable cause but may not base belief on a single accident, an anonymous informant, or off-duty possession or use (unless it occurs on the employer's premises or nearby, during or right before work hours); must document the facts and give employee a copy. May test randomly when there could be an unreasonable threat to the health and safety of coworkers or the public. Testing is also allowed when an employee returns to work following a positive test.

Employee rights: Employee who tests positive has 3 days to explain or contest results. Employee must be given an opportunity to participate in a rehabilitation program for up to 6 months; an employer with more than 20 full-time employees must pay for half of any out-of-pocket costs. After successfully completing the program, employee is entitled to return to previous job with full pay and benefits.

Notice and policy requirements: All employers must have a written policy, which includes the consequences of a positive result or refusing to submit to testing. Policy must be approved by the state department of labor. Policy must be distributed to each employee at least 30 days before it takes effect. Any changes to policy require 60 days' advance notice. An employer with more than 20 full-time employees must have an employee assistance program certified by the state office of substance abuse before implementing a testing program.

Maryland

Md. Code Ann., [Health-Gen.] § 17-214

Employers affected: Law applies to all employers.

Testing applicants: May use preliminary screening to test applicant. If initial result is positive, may make job offer conditional on confirmation of test results.

Testing employees: Employer may require substance abuse testing for legitimate business purposes only.

Employee rights: The sample must be tested by a certified laboratory; at the time of testing employee may request laboratory's name and address. An employee who tests positive must be given:

- a copy of the test results
- a copy of the employer's written drug and alcohol policy
- a written notice of any adverse action employer intends to take, and
- a statement of employee's right to an independent confirmation test at own expense.

Minnesota

Minn. Stat. Ann. §§ 181.950 to 181.957

Employers affected: Employers with one or more employees.

Testing applicants: Employers may require applicants to submit to a drug or alcohol test only after they have been given a job offer and have seen a written notice of testing policy. May test only if required of all applicants for same position.

Testing employees: Employers are not required to test. Employers may require drug or alcohol testing

State Drug and Alcohol Testing Laws (continued)

only according to a written testing policy. Testing may be done if there is a reasonable suspicion that employee:

- is under the influence of drugs or alcohol
- has violated drug and alcohol policy
- has been involved in a work-related accident, or
- has sustained or caused another employee to sustain a personal injury.

Random tests permitted only for employees in safety-sensitive positions. With 2 weeks' notice, employers may also test as part of an annual routine physical exam. Employer may test, without notice, an employee referred by the employer for chemical dependency treatment or evaluation or participating in a chemical dependency treatment program under an employee benefit plan. Testing is allowed during and for two years following treatment.

Employee rights: If test is positive, employee has 3 days to explain the results; employee must notify employer within 5 days of intention to obtain a retest. Employer may not discharge employee for a first-time positive test without offering counseling or rehabilitation; employee who refuses or does not complete program successfully may be discharged.

Notice and policy requirements: Employees must be given a written notice of testing policy which includes consequences of refusing to take test or having a positive test result. Two weeks' notice required before testing as part of an annual routine physical exam.

Mississippi

Miss. Code Ann. §§ 71-7-1 to 71-7-33, 71-3-121, 71-3-205 to 71-3-225

Employers affected: Employers with one or more full-time employees. Employers who establish a drug-free workplace program to qualify for a workers' compensation rate discount must implement testing procedures.

Testing applicants: May test all applicants as part of employment application process. Employer may request a signed statement that applicant has read and understands the drug and alcohol testing policy or notice.

Testing employees: May require drug and alcohol testing of all employees:

- upon reasonable suspicion
- as part of a routinely scheduled fitness-for-duty medical examination
- as a follow-up to a rehabilitation program, or
- if they have tested positive within the previous 12 months.

May also require drug and alcohol testing following an employee's work-related injury, for purposes of determining workers' compensation coverage. Testing is also allowed on a neutral selection basis.

Employee rights: Employer must inform an employee in writing within 5 working days of receipt of a positive confirmed test result; employee may request and receive a copy of the test result report. Employee has 10 working days after receiving notice to explain the positive test results. Employer may not discharge or take any adverse personnel action on the basis of an initial positive test result that has not been verified by a confirmation test. Private employer who elects to establish a drug-free workplace program must have an employee assistance program or maintain a resource file of outside programs.

Notice and policy requirements: 30 days before implementing testing program employer must give employees written notice of drug and alcohol policy which includes consequences:

- of a positive confirmed result
- of refusing to take test, and
- of other violations of the policy.

State Drug and Alcohol Testing Laws (continued)

Montana

Mont. Code Ann. §§ 39-2-205 to 39-2-211

Employers affected: Employers with one or more employees.

Testing applicants: May test as a condition of hire, but only for applicants who will work in:

- a hazardous work environment
- a security position
- a position that affects public safety or health
- a position with a fiduciary relationship to the employer, or
- a position that requires driving.

Testing employees: Same job restrictions apply to employees as to applicants. Employees in these positions may be tested:

- upon reasonable suspicion
- after involvement in an accident that causes personal injury or more than $1,500 property damage
- as a follow-up to a previous positive test, or
- as a follow-up to treatment or a rehabilitation program.

Employer may conduct random tests as long as there is an established date, all personnel are subject to testing, the employer has signed statements from each employee confirming receipt of a written description of the random selection process, and the random selection process is conducted by a scientifically valid method. Employer may require an employee who tests positive to undergo treatment as a condition of continued employment.

Employee rights: After a positive result, employee may request additional confirmation by an independent laboratory; if the results are negative, employer must pay the test costs. Employer may not take action or conduct follow-up testing if the employee presents a reasonable explanation or medical opinion that the original results were not caused by illegal drug use; employer must also remove results from employee's record.

Notice and policy requirements: Written policy must be available for review 60 days before testing. Policy must include consequences of a positive test result.

Nebraska

Neb. Rev. Stat. §§ 48-1901 to 48-1910

Employers affected: Employers with 6 or more full-time and part-time employees.

Testing employees: Employers are not required to test. Employer may require employees to submit to drug or alcohol testing and may discipline or discharge any employee who refuses, tests positive, or tampers with the test sample.

Employee rights: Employer may not take adverse action on the basis of an initial positive result unless it is confirmed according to state and federal guidelines.

North Carolina

N.C. Gen. Stat. §§ 95-230 to 95-235

Employers affected: Law applies to all employers.

Testing applicants: May test as a condition of hire. Applicant has right to retest a confirmed positive sample at own expense. If first screening test produces a positive result, applicant may waive a second examination that is intended to confirm the results.

Testing employees: Employers may, but are not required to, test. Testing must be performed under reasonable, sanitary conditions, and must respect individual dignity to the extent possible. Employer must preserve samples for at least 90 days after confirmed test results are released.

Employee rights: Employee has right to retest a confirmed positive sample at own expense.

State Drug and Alcohol Testing Laws (continued)

North Dakota

N.D. Cent. Code §§ 34-01-15, 65-01-11

Employers affected: All employers

Testing applicants: May test as a condition of hire.

Testing employees: Employer may test following an accident or injury that will result in a workers' compensation claim, if employer has a mandatory policy of testing under these circumstances, or if employer or physician has reasonable grounds to suspect injury was caused by impairment due to alcohol or drug use.

Employee rights: Employer who requires drug testing of any applicant or employee must pay for the test.

Ohio

Ohio Admin. Code § 4123-17-58

Employers affected: Employers who establish a drug-free safety program may qualify for a workers' compensation rate bonus.

Testing applicants: Must test all applicants and new hires.

Testing employees: Must test employees:
- upon reasonable suspicion
- following a return to work after a positive test, and
- after an accident which results in an injury requiring off-site medical attention or property damage.

Employers must test at random to meet requirements for greater discounts.

Employee rights: Employer must have an employee assistance plan. Employers who test at random to qualify for greater discount must not terminate employee who tests positive for the first time, comes forward voluntarily, or is referred by a supervisor. For these employees, employer must pay costs of substance abuse assessment.

Notice and policy requirements: Policy must state consequences for refusing to submit to testing or for violating guidelines. Policy must include a commitment to rehabilitation.

Oklahoma

Okla. Stat. Ann. tit. 40, §§ 551 to 565

Employers affected: Employers with one or more employees.

Testing applicants: May test applicants.

Testing employees: Statute does not require or encourage testing. Before requiring testing, employer must provide an employee assistance program. Random testing is allowed. May test employees:
- upon reasonable suspicion
- after an accident resulting in injury or property damage
- on a random selection basis
- as part of a routine fitness-for-duty examination, or
- as follow-up to a rehabilitation program.

Employee rights: Employee has right to retest a positive result at own expense; if the confirmation test is negative, employer must reimburse costs.

Notice and policy requirements: Before requiring testing employer must: adopt a written policy; give a copy to each employee and to any applicant offered a job; and allow 10 days' notice. Policy must state consequences of a positive test result or refusing to submit to testing.

Oregon

Ore. Rev. Stat. §§ 659.840, 659A.300, 438.435

Employers affected: Law applies to all employers.

Testing applicants: Unless there is reasonable suspicion that an applicant is under the influence of alcohol, no employer may require a breathalyzer test as a condition of employment. Employer is not prohibited from conducting a test if applicant consents.

State Drug and Alcohol Testing Laws (continued)

Testing employees: Unless there is reasonable suspicion that an employee is under the influence of alcohol, no employer may require a breathalyzer or blood alcohol test as a condition of continuing employment. Employer is not prohibited from conducting a test if employee consents.

Employee rights: No action may be taken based on the results of an on-site drug test without a confirming test performed according to state health division regulations. Upon written request, test results will be reported to the employee.

Rhode Island

R.I. Gen. Laws §§ 28-6.5-1 to 28-6.5-2

Employers affected: Law applies to all employers.

Testing applicants: May test as a condition of hire.

Testing employees: May require employee to submit to a drug test only if there are reasonable grounds, based on specific, documented observations, to believe employee may be under the influence of a controlled substance that is impairing job performance.

Employee rights: Employee must be allowed to provide sample in private, outside the presence of any person. Employee who tests positive may have the sample retested at employer's expense and must be given opportunity to explain or refute results. Employee may not be terminated on the basis of a positive result but must be referred to a licensed substance abuse professional. After referral, employer may require additional testing and may terminate employee if test results are positive.

South Carolina

S.C. Code Ann. §§ 41-1-15, 38-73-500

Employers affected: Employers who establish a drug-free workplace program to qualify for a workers' compensation rate discount.

Testing applicants: Employer is not required to test applicants to qualify for discount.

Testing employees: Must conduct random testing among all employees.

Employee rights: Employee must receive positive test results in writing within 24 hours.

Notice and policy requirements: Employer must notify all employees of the drug-free workplace program at the time it is established or at the time of hiring, whichever is earlier. Program must include a policy statement that balances respect for individuals with the need to maintain a safe, drug-free environment.

Tennessee

Tenn. Code Ann. §§ 50-9-101 to 50-9-114

Employers affected: Employers who establish a drug-free workplace program to qualify for a workers' compensation rate discount.

Testing applicants: Must test applicants for drugs upon conditional offer of employment. May test only those applying for certain positions, if based on reasonable job classifications. May test for alcohol after conditional offer of employment. Job ads must include notice that drug and alcohol testing is required.

Testing employees: Employer must test upon reasonable suspicion; must document behavior on which the suspicion is based within 24 hours or before test results are released, whichever is earlier; and must give a copy to the employee upon request. Employer must test employees:

- if required by employer policy as part of a routine fitness-for-duty medical exam
- after an accident that results in injury, or
- as a follow-up to a required rehabilitation program.

May test employees who are not in safety-sensitive positions for alcohol only if based on reasonable suspicion.

State Drug and Alcohol Testing Laws (continued)

Employee rights: Employee has the right to explain or contest a positive result within 5 days. Employee may not be fired, disciplined, or discriminated against for voluntarily seeking treatment unless employee has previously tested positive or been in a rehabilitation program.

Notice and policy requirements: Before implementing testing program, employer must provide 60 days' notice and must give all employees a written drug and alcohol policy statement. Policy must include consequences of a positive test or refusing to submit to testing.

Utah

Utah Code Ann. §§ 34-38-1 to 34-38-15

Employers affected: Employers with one or more employees.

Testing applicants: Employer may test any applicant for drugs or alcohol as long as management and employer also submits to periodic testing.

Testing employees: Employer may test employee for drugs or alcohol as long as management also submits to periodic testing. Employer may require testing to:

- investigate possible individual employee impairment
- investigate an accident or theft
- maintain employee or public safety, or
- ensure productivity, quality, or security.

Employer may suspend, discipline, discharge, or require treatment on the basis of a failed test (confirmed positive result, adulterated sample, or substituted sample) or a refusal to take test.

Notice and policy requirements: Testing must be conducted according to a written policy that has been distributed to employees and is available for review by prospective employees.

Vermont

Vt. Stat. Ann. tit. 21, §§ 511 to 520

Employers affected: Employers with one or more employees.

Testing applicants: Employer may not test applicants for drugs or alcohol unless there is a job offer conditional on a negative test result and applicant is given written notice of the testing procedure and a list of the drugs to be tested for.

Testing employees: Random testing not permitted unless required by federal law. Employer may not require testing unless:

- there is probable cause to believe an employee is using or is under the influence
- employer has an employee assistance program which provides rehabilitation, and
- employee who tests positive and agrees to enter employee assistance program is not terminated.

Employee rights: Employer must contract with a medical review officer who will review all test results and keep them confidential. Medical review officer is to contact employee or applicant to explain a positive test result. Employee or applicant has right to an independent retest at own expense. Employee who successfully completes employee assistance program may not be terminated, although employee may be suspended for up to 3 months to complete program. Employee who tests positive after completing treatment may be fired.

Notice and policy requirements: Must provide written policy that states consequences of a positive test.

State Drug and Alcohol Testing Laws (continued)

Virginia

Va. Code Ann. § 65.2-813.2

Employers affected: Employers who establish drug-free workplace programs to qualify for workers' compensation insurance discount.

Testing applicants: State law gives insurers the authority to establish guidelines and criteria for testing.

Testing employees: State law gives insurers the authority to establish guidelines and criteria for testing.

West Virginia

W.Va. Code §§ 21–3E–1 to 21–3E–16

Employers affected: Employers with one or more full-time employees.

Testing applicants: Same conditions as current employees.

Testing employees: Employers may test for a wide variety of reasons, including:

- following a workplace accident
- to deter or detect substance abuse
- to investigate employee theft or misconduct
- to protect the safety of employees, customers, or the general public
- to maintain productivity or quality of services
- or to protect company property or information. Testing must be paid for by the employer and conducted by an approved laboratory.

Employee rights: Employees and applicants must be given the opportunity to provide information relevant to the test, such as current prescription drug use or medical information. They also have the right to challenge the result and order retesting of the sample at their own cost.

Notice and policy requirements: Employers must have a written testing policy in place and distribute it to employees and applicants.

Wyoming

Wyo. Stat. Ann. 27-14-201; Wyo. Rules & Regulations, WSD WCD Ch. 2, § 8

Employers affected: Employers that establish a drug and alcohol testing program approved by the state Department of Workforce Services may receive a workers' compensation discount of up to 10% of the base rate for the employer's classification.

Testing applicants: Must test applicants for drugs; may test applicants for alcohol. Job announcements must state that testing is required.

Testing employees: Must test employees:

- upon reasonable suspicion
- following a workplace accident, and
- at random.

Must follow testing protocols prescribed in regulations (including "strong recommendation" that post accident testing be done by blood sample).

Employee rights: Employee has 5 days to contest or explain a positive result.

Notice and policy requirements: Employer must have written policy including consequence of positive result or refusing to submit to test. Must give notice 60 days prior to testing.

State Laws on Employee Arrest and Conviction Records

The following chart summarizes state laws and regulations on whether an employer can ask about or access an employee's or prospective employee's past arrests or convictions. It includes citations to statutes and agency websites, as available.

Many states allow or require private sector employers to run background checks on workers, particularly in fields like child care, elder care, home health care, private schools, private security, and the investment industry. Criminal background checks usually consist of sending the applicant's name (and sometimes fingerprints) to the state police or to the FBI. State law may forbid hiring people with certain kinds of prior convictions, depending on the kind of job or license involved.

Federal law allows the states to establish procedures for requesting a nationwide criminal background check to find out if a person has been "convicted of a crime that bears upon the [person's] fitness to have responsibility for the safety and well-being of children, the elderly, or individuals with disabilities." (42 U.S.C.A. § 5119a(a)(1).)

If your state isn't listed in this chart, then it doesn't have a *general statute* on whether private sector employers can find out about arrests or convictions. There might be a statute about your particular industry, though. Additionally, your state might have applicable case law (from court decisions) that apply to your particular situation.

It's always a good idea to consult your state's nondiscrimination enforcement agency or labor department to see what kinds of questions you can ask. The agency guidelines are designed to help employers comply with state and federal law. For further information, contact your state's agency.

Alabama
Ala. Code §§ 15-27-1, 15-27-6

Rights of employees and applicants: Need not disclose expunged records on employment application.

Arizona
Ariz. Rev. Stat. § 13-904(E)

Rights of employees and applicants: Unless the offense has a reasonable relationship to the occupation, an occupational license may not be denied solely on the basis of a felony or misdemeanor conviction.

Agency guidelines for preemployment inquiries: Office of the Attorney General, Guide to Premployment Inquiries, at www.azag.gov/sites/default/files/documents/files/PRE-EMPLOYMENT_INQUIRIES.pdf.

California
Cal. Lab. Code §§ 432.7, 432.8 (also, see 2 CCR § 11017.1)

Rules for employers:

May not ask about, seek, or use records pertaining to:
- arrests that did not lead to conviction
- participation in or referral to pretrial or post-trial diversion program
- convictions that have been judicially sealed, dismissed, or expunged
- non-felony convictions for marijuana possession that are more than two years old
- juvenile criminal history, including arrests, detentions, processings, adjudications, and court dispositions that occurred while applicant was subject to the juvenile court system.

May ask about, seek, or use records pertaining to:
- arrest if applicant is awaiting trial
- convictions other than those mentioned above (even if no sentence is imposed).

Agency guidelines for preemployment inquiries: Department of Fair Employment and Housing, "Employment Inquiries," DFEH-161 at www.dfeh.ca.gov/wp-content/uploads/sites/32/2017/06/DFEH-161.pdf

State Laws on Employee Arrest and Conviction Records (continued)

Colorado

Colo. Rev. Stat. §§ 24-72-702(1)(f)(I), 8-3-108(m)

Rules for employers: May not ask an applicant to disclose records of civil or military disobedience, unless the incident resulted in a guilty plea or conviction. May not ask about information contained in sealed criminal records. May not ask about expunged records where employee was arrested due to mistaken identity.

Rights of employees and applicants: Need not disclose any information in a sealed criminal record; may answer questions about sealed arrests or convictions as though they never occurred. Need not disclose information in an expunged record relating to arrest due to mistaken identity.

Agency guidelines for preemployment inquiries: Colorado Civil Rights Division, "Pre-Employment Inquiries" at https://drive.google.com/file/d/0B2Rq MM3zUzjtNTdZdklGV2tDS3c/view.

Connecticut

Conn. Gen. Stat. Ann. §§ 46a-79, 46a-80, 31-51i

Rules for employers: Employer may not ask about criminal records in an initial employment application, unless required to by law or the position requires a security or fidelity bond. If exception applies and employment application form contains question concerning criminal history, it must include a notice in clear and conspicuous language that (1) the applicant is not required to disclose the existence of any arrest, criminal charge, or conviction, the records of which have been erased; (2) define what criminal records are subject to erasure; and (3) any person whose criminal records have been erased will be treated as if never arrested or convicted and may swear so under oath. Employers may not discriminate against applicants or employees on the basis of arrests or convictions that have been erased

or for which an employee or applicant has received a provisional pardon or certificate of rehabilitation. Employer may not disclose information about a job applicant's criminal history except to members of the personnel department or, if there is no personnel department, person(s) in charge of hiring or conducting the interview.

Rights of employees and applicants: Employee may file a complaint with the Labor Commissioner if employer asks about criminal records on employment application. May not be asked to disclose information about a criminal record that has been erased; may answer any question as though arrest or conviction never took place.

Special situations: Applicants may not be denied a license, permit, registration, or other authorization to engage in a particular trade solely on the basis of a criminal conviction, unless the agency determines that the applicant isn't suitable based on: the nature of the crime and its relationship to the job; any rehabilitation the person has completed; and how long it has been since the conviction. A consumer reporting agency that issues a consumer report that is used or is expected to be used for employment purposes and that includes in such report criminal matters of public record concerning the consumer shall provide the consumer who is the subject of the consumer report (1) notice that the consumer reporting agency is reporting criminal matters of public record, and (2) the name and address of the person to whom such consumer report is being issued.

Delaware

Del. Code Ann. tit. 11, § 4376

Rights of employees and applicants: Do not have to disclose an arrest or conviction record that has been expunged.

State Laws on Employee Arrest and Conviction Records (continued)

District of Columbia

DC Code 32-1342

Rules for employers: Employers with 11 or more employees:

- May not ask about or require an applicant to disclose any arrest or criminal accusation that is not pending or that did not lead to a conviction.
- May not ask about or require an applicant to disclose a conviction until after a conditional offer of employment is made.
- Employer may only withdraw conditional offer based on a legitimate business reason.
- Employers need not comply for certain positions, including those working with minors and vulnerable adults.

Rights of employees and applicants: If employer withdraws conditional offer based on criminal history, applicant has the right to request within 30 days: all records collected by the employer, including criminal records, and a notice of the applicant's right to file an administrative complaint with the Office of Human Rights.

Florida

Fla. Stat. Ann. §§ 112.011, 768.096, 943.0585, 943.059

Rules for employers: Employers need not conduct criminal background checks. However, employers are legally presumed not to have been negligent in hiring if they conduct a background investigation before hiring employees, including a criminal records check. If the employer conducted such a check and did not discover any information reasonably demonstrating that the employee was unfit for the job (or for employment in general), the employer is entitled to a presumption that it did not act negligently.

Rights of employees and applicants: May not be disqualified to practice or pursue any occupation or profession that requires a license, permit, or certificate because of a prior conviction, unless it was for a felony or first-degree misdemeanor and is directly related to the regulatory standards for that line of work. Employee whose criminal record is expunged or sealed may deny the existence of the arrest, except when seeking employment in certain occupations or obtaining certain licenses.

Georgia

Ga. Code Ann. §§ 35-3-34, 35-3-34.1, 35-3-37, 42-8-62, 42-8-63, 42-8-63.1

Rules for employers: In order to obtain a criminal record from the state Crime Information Center, employer must supply the individual's fingerprints or signed consent. Employer will not be provided with records of arrests, charges, and sentences for first-time offenders where the individual was exonerated. Where, pursuant to Georgia's First Offender Statute, the charges were dismissed without an adjudication of guilt, the discharge may not be used to disqualify candidates except for specific occupations. If an adverse employment decision is made on the basis of the records provided, employer must disclose all information in the record to the employee or applicant and tell how it affected the decision.

Rights of employees and applicants: Probation for a first offense is not a conviction and may not be disqualified for employment once probation is completed, except for certain occupations.

Hawaii

Haw. Rev. Stat. §§ 378-2, 378-2.5, 831-3.2

Rules for employers: Arrest records: It is a violation of law for any employer to refuse to hire, to discharge, or to discriminate in terms of compensation, conditions, or privileges of employment because of a person's arrest or court record.

Convictions: May inquire into a conviction only after making a conditional offer of employment, may

State Laws on Employee Arrest and Conviction Records (continued)

withdraw offer if conviction has a rational relation to job. May not examine any convictions over 10 years old.

Rights of employees and applicants: If an arrest or conviction has been expunged, may state that no record exists and may respond to questions as a person with no record would respond.

Agency guidelines for preemployment inquiries: Hawaii Civil Rights Commission, "Pre-Employment Inquiries (Application Forms and Job Interviews)" at http://labor.hawaii.gov/hcrc/publications.

Idaho

Agency guidelines for preemployment inquiries: Idaho Department of Labor, "A Guide to Lawful Applications and Interviews" at https://labor.idaho.gov/publications/GuidetoLawful.pdf and Idaho Commission on Human Rights, "Pre-Employment Inquiries - Discrimination Pitfalls" at http://human rights.idaho.gov/discrimination/pre_employment.html

Illinois

775 Ill. Comp. Stat. § 5/2-103, 20 Ill. Comp. Stat. Ann. 2630/12, 820 Ill. Comp. Stat. Ann. 75/15

Rules for employers: All employers: It is a civil rights violation to ask an applicant about arrests or criminal records that have been expunged or sealed, or to use the fact of an arrest or an expunged or sealed record as a basis for refusing to hire or renew employment. Law does not prohibit employer from using other means to find out if person actually engaged in conduct leading to arrest. Job applications must clearly state that the applicant is not required to provide information about sealed or expunged records of convictions or arrest.

Employers with 15 or more employees: Except in limited situations, employer may not ask about criminal history or criminal records until the applicant is selected for an interview, or if there is none, until a conditional offer of employment has been made.

Indiana

Ind. Code § 35-38-9-10

Rules for employers: Employer may ask about criminal record only in terms that exclude expunged convictions or arrests. It is unlawful discrimination to refuse to employ someone based on a sealed or expunged arrest or conviction record. Information about expunged convictions is not admissible evidence in negligent hiring lawsuit against employer who relied on expungement order in deciding to hire the employee.

Rights of employees and applicants: May answer any question as though expunged arrest or conviction never occurred. May not be discriminated against on the basis of a conviction or arrest that has been expunged or sealed.

Special situations: Sealed or expunged arrest or conviction record may not be used to refuse to grant or renew a license, permit, or certificate necessary to engage in any activity, occupation, or profession.

Iowa

Agency guidelines for preemployment inquiries: Iowa Workforce Development, Successful Interview Guide, Summary Guide to Application and Pre-Employment Questions, at www.iowawork forcedevelopment.gov/sites/search.iowaworkforce development.gov/files/Successful%20Interviewing %20Guide_70-0006.pdf.

Kansas

Kan. Stat. Ann. §§ 12-4516; 22-4710

Rules for employers: Cannot require an employee to inspect or challenge a criminal record in order to obtain a copy of the record to qualify for employment, but may require an applicant to sign a release to allow employer to obtain record to determine fitness for employment. Employers

State Laws on Employee Arrest and Conviction Records (continued)

can require access to criminal records for specific businesses. Employer is not liable for making hiring or contracting decision based on applicant's criminal record, as long as it reasonably bears on applicant's trustworthiness or the safety or well-being of customers or other employees.

Rights of employees and applicants: Need not disclose expunged records on employment application except for sensitive positions enumerated in Kan. Stat. Ann. §12-4516(2) (A)-(K).

Agency guidelines for preemployment inquiries: Kansas Human Rights Commission, "Guidelines on Equal Employment Practices: Preventing Discrimination in Hiring," at www.khrc.net/hiring.html.

Kentucky
Ky. Rev. Stat. Ann. §§ 431.073, 431.076

Rights of employees and applicants: Need not disclose expunged records on employment application.

Louisiana
La. Rev. Stat. Ann. § 37:2950

Rights of employees and applicants: Prior conviction cannot be used as a sole basis to deny an occupational or professional license, unless conviction directly relates to the license being sought and the reasons for denial are stated explicitly, in writing.

Special situations: Protection does not apply to medical, engineering and architecture, or funeral and embalming licenses, among others listed in the statute.

Maine
Me. Rev. Stat. Ann. tit. 5, § 5301

Rights of employees and applicants: A conviction is not an automatic bar to obtaining an occupational or professional license. Only convictions that directly relate to the profession

or occupation, that include dishonesty or false statements, that are subject to imprisonment for more than 1 year, or that involve sexual misconduct on the part of a licensee may be considered.

Agency guidelines for preemployment inquiries: The Maine Human Rights Commission, "Pre-Employment Inquiry Guide," at www.maine.gov/mhrc/guidance /pre-employment_inquiry_guide.htm, suggests that asking about arrests is an improper race-based question, but that it is okay to ask about a conviction if related to the job.

Maryland
Md. Code Ann. [Crim. Proc.], §§ 10-109, 10-301, 10-306; Md. Regs. Code § 09.01.10.02

Rules for employers: May not inquire about criminal charges that have been expunged or criminal records that have been shielded under the Maryland Second Chance Act. May not use a refusal to disclose information as sole basis for not hiring an applicant.

Rights of employees and applicants: Need not refer to or give any information about an expunged charge or shielded record. A professional or occupational license may not be refused or revoked simply because of a conviction; agency must consider:

- the nature of the crime and its relation to the occupation or profession
- the conviction's relevance to the applicant's fitness and qualifications
- when conviction occurred and other convictions, if any, and
- the applicant's behavior before and after conviction.

Agency guidelines for preemployment inquiries: DLLR's Office of Fair Practices, "Guidelines for Pre-Employment Inquiries Technical Assistance Guide," at www.dllr.maryland.gov/oeope/preemp.shtml.

State Laws on Employee Arrest and Conviction Records (continued)

Massachusetts

Mass. Gen. Laws ch. 6, § 171A; ch. 151B, § 4; ch. 276, § 100A; Mass. Regs. Code tit. 804, § 3.02

Rules for employers: Unless federal or state law disqualifies applicants with certain convictions from holding position, may not ask about criminal record information of any kind on initial written application. If job application has a question about prior arrests or convictions, it must include a formulated statement (that appears in the statute) that states that an applicant with a sealed record is entitled to answer, "No record." May not ask about arrests that did not result in conviction. May not ask about first-time convictions for drunkenness, simple assault, speeding, minor traffic violations, affray, or disturbing the peace; may not ask about misdemeanor convictions 5 or more years old unless applicant has another conviction within the last 5 years.

Rights of employees and applicants: If criminal record is sealed, may answer, "No record" to any inquiry about past arrests or convictions.

Special situations: Employer must give applicant a copy of criminal record before asking about it. Employer must give applicant a copy of record after making adverse job decision (if it didn't already provide the record). Additional rules apply to employers that conduct 5 or more criminal background checks per year.

Agency guidelines for preemployment inquiries: Massachusetts Commission Against Discrimination, "Employment Discrimination on the Basis of Criminal Record," at www.mass.gov/mcad/resources/employers-businesses/emp-fact-sheet-discrim-criminal-record-gen.html

Michigan

Mich. Comp. Laws § 37.2205a

Rules for employers: May not request information on any misdemeanor arrests or charges that did not result in conviction. May ask about felony arrests and misdemeanor or felony convictions.

Rights of employees and applicants: Employees or applicants are not making a false statement if they fail to disclose information they have a civil right to withhold.

Agency guidelines for preemployment inquiries: Michigan Department of Civil Rights, "Pre-Employment Inquiry Guide," at www.michigan.gov/documents/mdcr/Preemploymentguide62012_388403_7.pdf.

Minnesota

Minn. Stat. Ann. §§ 364.01 to 364.03; 181.981

Rules for employers: Employers may not ask, consider, or require applicants to disclose criminal record or history until selected for an interview or, if there is no interview, until a conditional offer of employment is made. However, employer may notify applicants that particular criminal records will disqualify applicants from holding particular jobs.

Rights of employees and applicants: No one can be disqualified from pursuing or practicing an occupation that requires a license, unless the crime directly relates to the occupation. Agency may consider the nature and seriousness of the crime and its relation to the applicant's fitness for the occupation. Even if the crime does relate to the occupation, a person who provides evidence of rehabilitation and present fitness cannot be disqualified.

Agency guidelines for preemployment inquiries: Employee's criminal record is not admissible in any civil lawsuit against the employer based on the employee's actions if: the lawsuit is based on the employer's compliance with the state's "ban the box" law; the employee's record was sealed or pardoned prior to the actions; the employee's record consists only of arrests or charges that did not lead to conviction; or the employee's job duties did not create any greater risk of harm than being employed in general or interacting with the public outside of work.

State Laws on Employee Arrest and Conviction Records (continued)

Agency guidelines for preemployment inquiries: Minnesota Department of Human Rights, "Criminal Background" at http://mn.gov/mdhr/employers/criminal-background/

Mississippi

Miss. Code Ann. § 99-19-71

Rules for employers: Employer may ask applicant if expunction order has been issued regarding the applicant.

Rights of employees and applicants: Applicant need not disclose expunged arrest or conviction when responding to inquiries.

Missouri

Mo. Rev. Stat. § 314.200

Rights of employees and applicants: No one may be denied a license for a profession or occupation primarily on the basis that a prior conviction negates the person's good moral character, if the applicant has been released from incarceration by pardon, parole, or otherwise, or the applicant is on probation with no evidence of violations. The conviction may be considered, but the licensing board must also consider the crime's relation to the license, the date of conviction, the applicant's conduct since the conviction, and other evidence of the applicant's character.

Montana

Mont. Admin. Rule 24.9.1406

Rules for employers: Employer should not ask questions about arrests at any point in the hiring process. Employers may ask about convictions, however.

Nebraska

Neb. Rev. Stat. § 29-3523

Rules for employers: May not obtain access to information regarding arrests after one year if no charges are filed by prosecutor decision; after two years if no charges are filed as a result of completed diversion; or after three years if charges were filed but were dismissed by the court. May not ask about sealed records in an employment application.

Rights of employees and applicants: As to sealed records, employee may respond as if the offense never occurred.

Nevada

Nev. Rev. Stat. Ann. §§ 176A.850, 179A.100(3), 179A.190, 179.285, 179.301

Rules for employers: Unless applicant consents, employer may obtain only records of convictions or incidents for which the applicant or employee is currently within the criminal justice system, including parole or probation. Employer does not, however, need written consent to access all information contained in a criminal record of a sex offender or someone who is convicted of a crime against a child.

Rights of employees and applicants: Employees not be required to disclose sealed convictions, or convictions for which they were honorably discharged from probation (except to a gaming establishment or state employer).

Agency guidelines for preemployment inquiries: Nevada Equal Rights Commission, "Guide to Pre-Employment," at http://detr.state.nv.us/Nerc_pages/premployment_guide.htm.

New Hampshire

N.H. Rev. Stat. Ann. § 651:5 (X)

Rules for employers: May ask about a previous criminal record only if question substantially follows this wording, "Have you ever been arrested for or convicted of a crime that has not been annulled by a court?"

New Jersey

N.J. Stat. Ann. §§ 5:5-34.1, 5:12-89, 5:12-91, 32:23-86, 34:6B-11 to 34:6B-19; N.J.A.C. 13:59-1.2, N.J.A.C. 13:59-1.6

State Laws on Employee Arrest and Conviction Records (continued)

Rules for employers: May not publish a job advertisement that states that applicants who have been arrested or convicted will not be considered for the position. May not ask applicants about criminal records during the initial employment application process, unless the applicant voluntarily offers such information. Employer may ask about criminal records after an initial interview. Employer may not refuse to hire an applicant based on a criminal record that has been expunged or pardoned.

Rights of employees and applicants: Applicant who is disqualified for employment based on criminal record must be given adequate notice and reasonable time to confirm or deny accuracy of information.

Special situations: There are specific rules for casino employees, longshoremen and related occupations, horse racing, and other gaming industry jobs.

New Mexico

Criminal Offender Employment Act, N.M. Stat. Ann. §§ 28-2-3, 28-2-4

Special situations: For a license, permit, or other authority to engage in any regulated trade, business, or profession, a regulating agency may consider felony and convictions for misdemeanors involving moral turpitude. Such convictions cannot be an automatic bar to authority to practice in the regulated field, but may be disqualifying if they relate directly to the profession, the agency determines after investigation that the applicant isn't sufficiently rehabilitated to warrant the public's trust, or the field is teaching or child care (for certain offenses).

New York

N.Y. Correct. Law §§ 750 to 754; N.Y. Exec. Law § 296 (15), (16)

Rules for employers: It is unlawful discrimination to ask about any arrests or charges that did not result in conviction, unless they are currently pending. Employers also may not ask about sealed convictions

or youthful offender adjudications. Employers with 10 or more employees may not deny employment based on a conviction unless it relates directly to the job or would be an "unreasonable" risk to property or to public or individual safety. Employer must consider 8 factors listed in statute. If employer considers these factors and makes a reasonable, good-faith decision to hire or retain employee, there's a rebuttable presumption that evidence of the employee's criminal history should be excluded in any subsequent lawsuit for negligent hiring or retention.

Rights of employees and applicants: Upon request, applicant must be given, within 30 days, a written statement of the reasons why employment was denied.

Agency guidelines for preemployment inquiries: New York State Division of Human Rights, www.dhr. ny.gov/sites/default/files/pdf/arrest_conviction.pdf.

North Carolina

N.C. Gen. Stat. § 15A-146

Rights of employees and applicants: May not ask applicants about expunged arrests, charges, or convictions.

Rights of employees and applicants: Person whose arrest or charge was expunged may omit expunged entries in response to questions.

Special situations: Licensing board may not automatically deny professional or occupational license to applicant based on criminal history. If board is authorized to deny license based on crime of fraud or moral turpitude, must consider:

- level and seriousness of crime
- when crime occurred
- age of applicant when crime occurred
- circumstances of crime
- relationship between crime and profession or occupation

State Laws on Employee Arrest and Conviction Records (continued)

- prison, parole, rehabilitation, and employment records since crime was committed
- any subsequent criminal activity, and
- affidavits and other documents, including character references.

North Dakota
N.D. Cent. Code § 12-60-16.6

Rules for employers: May obtain records of arrests (adults only) occurring in the past three years or of convictions, provided the information has not been purged or sealed.

Agency guidelines for preemployment inquiries: North Dakota Department of Labor, "Employment Applications and Interviews," www.nd.gov/labor/publications/docs/employment.pdf.

Ohio
Ohio Rev. Code Ann. §§ 2151.357, 2953.33, 2953.55

Rules for employers: May inquire only into convictions or bail forfeitures that have not been sealed, unless question has a direct and substantial relationship to job.

Rights of employees and applicants: May not be asked about arrest records that are sealed; may respond to inquiry as though arrest did not occur.

Oklahoma
Okla. Stat. Ann. tit. 22, § 19(F)

Rules for employers: May not inquire into any criminal record that has been expunged.

Rights of employees and applicants: If record is expunged, may state that no criminal action ever occurred. May not be denied employment for refusing to disclose sealed criminal record information.

Oregon
Or. Rev. Stat. §§ 181A.230, 181A.240, and 181A.245, 659A.030

Rules for employers: Employer may not ask about criminal convictions on an employment application. Employer may ask about criminal convictions only after an initial interview or after a conditional offer of employment has been made.

Employer may request information from state police department about convictions and arrests in the past year that have not resulted in dismissal or acquittal. Before making request, employer must notify employee or applicant; when submitting request, must tell department when and how person was notified. May not discriminate against an applicant or current employee on the basis of an expunged juvenile record unless there is a "bona fide occupational qualification."

Rights of employees and applicants: Before state police department releases any criminal record information, it must notify employee or applicant and provide a copy of all information that will be sent to employer. Notice must include protections under federal civil rights law and the procedure for challenging information in the record. Record may not be released until 14 days after notice is sent.

Pennsylvania
18 Pa. Cons. Stat. Ann. § 9125

Rules for employers: May consider felony and misdemeanor convictions only if they relate to person's suitability for the job.

Rights of employees and applicants: Must be informed in writing if refusal to hire is based on criminal record information.

Rhode Island
R.I. Gen. Laws §§ 12-1.3-4, 13-8.2-1 through 8, 28-5-7(7)

Rules for employers: It is unlawful to include on an application form or to ask as part of an interview if the applicant has ever been arrested or charged with any

State Laws on Employee Arrest and Conviction Records (continued)

crime. Application form may not include questions about arrests, charges, or convictions, except questions about convictions for specific offenses which would legally disqualify the applicant for the position under federal or state law, or would preclude bonding (if bonding is required for the position). May ask about convictions during the first interview or later.

Rights of employees and applicants: Do not have to disclose any conviction that has been expunged. As to sealed records for arrests due to mistaken identity, employee may respond as if the offense never occurred.

Special situations: Those convicted of crimes may apply to the parole board for a Certificate of Recovery and Re-Entry, stating that the holder has achieved certain rehabilitation goals. Parole board will consider applications for a certificate one year or more after conviction of a misdemeanor, or three years or more after conviction of a nonviolent felony. Although the purpose of this certificate is to assist the holder in reentering society, employers are not liable for denying employment based on prior conviction(s), even if the applicant holds a certificate.

Agency guidelines for preemployment inquiries: Rhode Island Commission for Human Rights, Pre-Employment Inquiries Guidelines, at www.richr. state.ri.us/pei.pdf.

South Carolina

S.C. Code Ann. § 40-1-140

Rights of employees and applicants: Person may not be denied authorization to practice, pursue, or engage in regulated profession or occupation based on prior conviction, unless it relates directly to the profession or occupation or the applicant is found unfit or unsuitable based on all available information, including the prior conviction.

South Dakota

Agency guidelines for preemployment inquiries: South Dakota Division of Human Rights, "Pre-Employment Inquiry Guide," at www.sdra.org/dwnld/ preemplo.htm suggests that an employer shouldn't ask or check into arrests or convictions if they are not substantially related to the job.

Texas

Tex. Crim. Proc. Code Ann. § 55.03; Tex. Fam. Code Ann. § 58.003

Rights of employees and applicants: Employee may deny the occurrence of any arrest that has been expunged. An employee whose juvenile records have been sealed is not required to disclose in a job application that the employee was the subject of a juvenile court proceeding.

Vermont

13 Vt. Stat. Ann. §§ 7606 to 7607; 21 Vt. Stat. Ann. § 495j

Rules for employers: May not ask about criminal history on an employment application, except for specific offenses that would disqualify the applicant for the position under state or federal law. Employer may ask about criminal history during an interview or once the applicant has been deemed qualified for the position.

Rights of employees and applicants: Need not disclose arrests or convictions that have been expunged or sealed.

Virginia

Va. Code Ann. § 19.2-392.4

Rules for employers: May not require an applicant to disclose information about any arrest or criminal charge that has been expunged.

Rights of employees and applicants: Need not refer to any expunged charges if asked about criminal record.

State Laws on Employee Arrest and Conviction Records (continued)

Washington

Wash. Rev. Code Ann. §§ 43.43.815, 9.94A.640(3), 9.96.060(3), 9.96A.020; Wash. Admin. Code § 162-12-140

Rules for employers:

Arrest records: Employer who asks about arrests must ask whether the charges are still pending, have been dismissed, or led to conviction that would adversely affect job performance and the arrest occurred within the last 10 years.

Convictions: Employer who obtains a conviction record must notify employee within 30 days of receiving it and must allow the employee to examine it. May make an employment decision based on a conviction only if conviction or release from prison occurred less than 10 years before and the crime reasonably relates to the job duties.

Rights of employees and applicants: If a conviction record is cleared or vacated, may answer questions as though the conviction never occurred. A person convicted of a felony cannot be refused an occupational license unless the conviction is less than 10 years old and the felony relates specifically to the occupation or business.

Special situations: Employers are entitled to obtain complete criminal record information for positions that require bonding, or that have access to information affecting national security, trade secrets, confidential or proprietary business information, money, or items of value. Employers may also obtain record to assist an investigation of suspected employee misconduct that may also be a penal offense under federal or state law.

Agency guidelines for preemployment inquiries: Washington Human Rights Commission, "Preemployment inquiry guide," at http://apps.leg.wa.gov/WAC/default.aspx?cite=162-12.

West Virginia

W.Va. Code § 49-4-723

Rules for employers: Employers may not discriminate on the basis of juvenile criminal records that have been expunged.

Agency guidelines for preemployment inquiries: West Virginia Bureau of Employment Programs, "Pre-employment Inquiries Technical Assistance Guide," at www.wvcommerce.org/App_Media/assets/pdf/workforce/WFWV_Afirmative_Action_Pre-employment_Inquiries.pdf. The state's website says that employers can only make inquiries about convictions directly related to the job.

Wisconsin

Wis. Stat. Ann. §§ 111.31 and 111.335

Rules for employers: It is a violation of state civil rights law to discriminate against an employee on the basis of a prior arrest or conviction record.

Arrest records: May not ask about arrests unless there are pending charges. May not reject applicant unless pending charges are substantially related to the job or would preclude required bonding.

Convictions: May not ask about convictions unless charges substantially relate to job or would preclude required bonding.

Special situations: Employers are entitled to obtain complete criminal record information for positions that require bonding and for burglar alarm installers.

Agency guidelines for preemployment inquiries: Wisconsin Department of Workforce Development, Equal Rights Division, Civil Rights Bureau, "Fair Hiring & Avoiding Loaded Interview Questions," at dwd.wisconsin.gov/er/civil_rights/discrimination/avoiding_discriminatory_interview_questions.htm

Wyoming

Wyo. Stat. § 7-13-1401

Rights of employees and applicants: If an arrest or charge has been expunged, may respond to questions as if arrest or charge never occurred.

Compensation and Hours

No matter how much you encourage creativity, camaraderie, and good cheer in your team or department, you know that employees don't show up every day for the sheer fun of it: They want to get paid (as, probably, do you). Pay is, perhaps, the most basic part of the employment relationship: Employees are paid in return for their labor. Despite the simplicity of this exchange, however, the legal rules governing pay and work can get pretty complicated. And managers—who often have to participate in setting pay levels, deciding whether employees should receive overtime, and figuring out how to pay employees who travel for business, among other things—can easily get caught in the middle.

This chapter covers some compensation basics, including:

- setting pay levels
- minimum wage
- overtime
- paying for on-call and travel time
- flexible work schedules
- deductions and wage garnishments
- equal pay for men and women, and
- record-keeping requirements.

While not every manager will need to know the information in this chapter, it's important to read if any of the following is true: You work in human resources or payroll or otherwise have to deal with compensation issues, you have some input into the pay levels of those who report to you, or you assign or approve employee schedules. (This chapter might also answer some of your questions about your own paycheck.)

The Fair Labor Standards Act

The Fair Labor Standards Act (FLSA), 29 U.S.C. §§ 201 and following, is the primary federal law governing wages and hours. The FLSA sets the federal minimum wage; establishes rules for overtime pay, child labor, and paycheck deductions; and requires businesses to keep certain records showing the pay and hours of their workers.

Although not every company is subject to the FLSA, most are. Generally, a business is covered if it has $500,000 or more in annual sales. However, smaller companies will still be covered if their employees work in what Congress calls "interstate commerce." Engaging in interstate commerce has historically been defined broadly, to include making phone calls to or from another state, sending mail out of state, or handling goods that have come from or will go to another state. As a result, most employees are covered. The wage and hour rules also apply to employees who work from their homes.

Certain types of workers are not entitled to the minimum wage or overtime pay. These include:

- independent contractors (only employees are covered by the FLSA; for more information about independent contractors, see Chapter 9)

- outside salespeople (a salesperson who works a route, for example)
- employees of seasonal amusement or recreational businesses (such as ski resorts or county fairs)
- employees of certain small newspapers and newspaper deliverers
- workers engaged in fishing operations
- employees who work on small farms, and
- certain switchboard operators.

Many states also have their own wage and hour laws, some of which provide workers with more protections than the FLSA (and place more obligations on companies). To make things a bit trickier, a business must follow whichever rule (state or federal) that gives its workers more protection. This means you might have to abide by a patchwork of laws, applying a minimum federal standard in some locations and a more protective state standard in others. For example, if

---

Frequently Asked Questions About Compensation and Hours

How should I decide what to pay people?

Here are five steps to help you set the pay rate for any given position: (1) Clearly define the job and the level of talent necessary to do it well; (2) examine your company's budget to determine what you can afford to pay; (3) look internally at what others in your company are being paid for similar jobs; (4) gather external information on what other companies pay for similar jobs; and (5) find out the job candidate's pay requirements. (For an explanation of these five steps, see "Deciding What to Pay People," below.)

Do we have to pay the minimum wage to employees who receive tips?

It depends. Under federal law, as long as an employee regularly earns at least $30 per month in tips, the employee can be paid as little as $2.13 an hour (called a "tip credit"). However, that amount plus the tips the employee actually earns must add up to at least the federal minimum wage ($7.25 per hour).

If the employee's total earnings fall short of the minimum wage, the employer must make up the difference. Some states, however, don't allow employers to take such a generous tip credit or allow a tip credit at all. (For more information on minimum wage laws, see "The Minimum Wage," below.)

Are managers entitled to overtime pay?

It depends. Under federal law, employees are entitled to overtime pay unless they fall within an exemption. Managers will generally qualify as exempt under the "executive" exemption if they earn at least $455 per week, spend most of their time managing two or more employees, and have authority on hiring and firing decisions. (For more, see "Overtime," below.)

If an employee goes on an overnight business trip, do we have to pay for every hour the employee spends away from home, even hours spent sleeping or eating?

No. You must pay for the hours the employee actually spends working, of course. You also have

Frequently Asked Questions About Compensation and Hours (continued)

to pay for travel time, but only if the employee travels during his or her regular working hours. (These are the rules for overnight trips; the rules for one-day trips are different. For the full story, see "Travel Time," below.)

Are employees entitled to be paid for on-call time, even if they don't have to stay at work?
Employees are entitled to be paid for every on-call hour spent at the worksite. If employees aren't required to remain at the workplace, they are entitled to be paid for on-call time only if their activities are significantly restricted during those hours. (For more on paying for on-call time, see "On-Call Time," below.)

If I allow one or a few workers to work on a flexible schedule, do I have to allow everyone to do so?
No. Certain positions are better suited for flexible schedules than others. As long as your decision about who can work a flexible schedule isn't based on an illegal reason, such as race, gender, or age (and you stay within the bounds of overtime laws), you can allow only some workers to work flextime. (For more information, see "Flexible Work Schedules," below.)

Can I put an exempt employee on unpaid suspension while I investigate a claim that he or she sexually harassed a coworker?
If you dock an exempt employee's pay, you risk making that employee nonexempt—and, therefore, entitled to earn overtime—unless an exception applies. One of these exceptions allows employers to put exempt employees on unpaid

suspension for violating workplace conduct rules, but only if the employer has a written policy regarding such suspensions that applies to all employees. (For more information, see "Pay Docking and Unpaid Suspensions," below.)

Can we deduct money from a worker's paycheck to repay a cash advance?
The answer is yes under the federal law, even if it would bring the employee's earnings below minimum wage, as long as you get the employee's consent. But some states don't allow employers to make these kinds of deductions. (For more on withholding pay, see "Garnishments," below.)

Are female employees entitled to be paid as much as male employees, even if their jobs are different?
No. Under the Equal Pay Act, men and women are entitled to equal pay for doing substantially the same work. But if men and women's job duties differ significantly, equal pay is not required. (For more on the Equal Pay Act, see "Equal Pay," below.)

Can I get rid of employees' payroll records once they leave the company?
No. Federal law requires employers to keep certain records—including records on wages, hours, deductions, overtime, and pay dates—for each of its workers. You have to keep these records for three years, even if the worker leaves your company. (For more information on these rules, see "Record-Keeping Requirements," below.)

your company does business in a state that requires a higher minimum wage but sets lower standards for child labor, it will have to follow the state minimum wage law while applying the stricter federal child labor rules.

To find out more about your state's law —and how it compares to federal law— contact your state labor department. (See the appendix for contact information.)

Deciding What to Pay People

While the bulk of this chapter covers the rules of wage and hour law, we begin with the most basic compensation question first: How do you figure out what to pay for which jobs? And what if the jobs are similar but require different levels of experience or skill? The following sections provide you with the tools you need to craft compensation packages that pay fairly for the work done and, hopefully, attract employees who will do the job well.

Steps to Determine What to Pay

While there are many shifting variables to consider when determining pay, the process can be summed up in five steps:

Step 1: Clearly define the job and the level of talent necessary to do it well.

Step 2: Examine your company budget to determine what you can afford to pay.

Step 3: Look internally at what others in your company are being paid for similar jobs (to achieve "internal equity").

Step 4: Gather external information on what other companies pay for similar jobs (called "external market data"). To do this, you might wish to gather both quantitative data (for example, surveys) and qualitative or anecdotal data (for example, asking those in your professional network what they pay or finding out what your job applicants have been earning).

Step 5: Find out the job candidate's pay requirements.

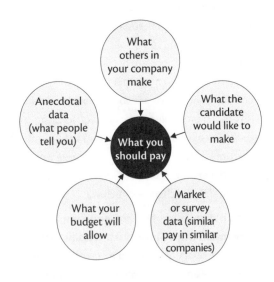

While doing this work might take a little time, it will be time well spent: You will be able to attract better candidates and justify your pay requests to management.

And, the pay you determine will be fair and appropriate.

Define the Job

Until you understand precisely what you are paying for, you cannot begin to know how much you should pay. Each type of job could conceivably have many different levels or requirements that you compensate differently. Your best bet is to capture the job exactly as you know it to be currently and then begin your pay determination there.

Start with a good job description. (For help writing one, see *The Job Description Handbook*, by Margie Mader-Clark (Nolo).) If you do not have a job description, spend a few minutes answering the following questions:

- What are the primary functions of this job? What must a person in this position absolutely do to perform the job successfully?
- What other responsibilities does the job have? Might you add any responsibilities in the near future?
- What skills and abilities are necessary to do this job? Are there any special requirements needed, such as licenses, certificates, or certain educational requirements?
- Are there any special characteristics of this job to consider, such as unusual work hours, significant travel, being on call, or dangerous or undesirable job duties?

Examine Your Budget

Of course, one of the biggest determinants of what you will pay an employee is how much your business can afford. After clarifying the job description, this is the first thing to consider when hiring or promoting someone. How much you can afford to pay will differ depending on the type of company you work for:

- **Small businesses.** Small business owners typically know exactly what their constraints are when setting pay. Often, while they would like to hire more senior or managerial-level candidates, their budgets only allow for hiring entry-level employees.
- **Private companies.** Privately held companies vary in their level of sophistication about compensation structures. Get familiar with your company's approach and make sure that you are on the same page as your company's finance and human resources departments when getting ready to set a pay package.
- **Public companies.** Publicly owned companies are more likely to have formal compensation structures and even people to help you determine pay. Nevertheless, be prepared with a clear definition of the job, an understanding of whether the position has been budgeted for, and what that budget includes (for example, whether it covers just the salary, or fringe benefits or bonuses as well).

With your budget number in hand, you now have the "top line" of what you can pay someone: an amount of compensation that you cannot exceed (although your company may have a process to do so if it's absolutely necessary). You can now move on to figure out where, from the top line down, you should set your pay.

Consider What Others in Your Company Make

Paying fairly across like positions within a company—known as "internal equity"—can be a loaded issue for many workplaces. How many times have you heard complaints about a new hire making more than someone who has been with the company for years? It's a good idea to generate a report that shows the title, level, and compensation of similarly situated employees (you don't need their names for this exercise). Then, consider the following:

- **Current pay levels.** What are people in similar positions within your company making? Keep in mind that positions need not be exactly the same or even in the same job family to be considered in an internal equity study. For instance, if you are hiring a director of marketing, it's helpful to understand compensation of not only other marketing directors at your company, but directors in other corporate functions as well. It is also a good idea to consider the pay of those directly below or above the position.

Compression (pay that is too close to the level above or below) can lead to problems when it comes time to give someone a raise.

- **Starting pay levels.** What did people in these similar positions make when they first started (and how long ago was that)?

- **Education or experience levels.** The newcomer might have much more experience than your other employees, which could warrant more pay. If so, be prepared to justify the higher pay, because employees might very well learn what their coworkers are making.

- **Requirements of the job.** You might have added responsibilities to the position, making it different from an existing position. For example, if you are hiring an international sales manager to open a new sales branch for India, his or her position might be very different from the other six sales managers on your staff. While their titles are the same, the other six all came to work for existing businesses and were not responsible for opening their own sales branches. This is a significant difference in the requirements of the job (as well as the experience necessary to do that job successfully) that could warrant higher pay.

Studying internal equity can be complex; don't let it become anything more than a guideline to help you set pay for a particular job. You might ultimately decide to hire at a compensation level well above or below what others are currently making. As long as you can clearly explain the differences in the job requirements or tasks, you should be able to justify your decision.

Gather External Market Data

Next, find out what other companies pay employees in the same or similar positions. There are two main sources for this data: surveys and anecdotal information. Both have advantages and disadvantages. Surveys provide concrete quantitative data across a broad spectrum, but unfortunately tend to become stale so quickly that, by the time they are published, they are already outdated (although the Internet is helping to alleviate this problem). Qualitative anecdotal data suffers from not being very scientific and tapping into a smaller pool of information, but can be even more relevant because of its freshness; it can tell you what people earn right now.

Surveys. A quick Internet search can often provide fairly decent external market data on a whole variety of positions. Try visiting www. salaryexpert.com, glassdoor.com, or other job websites like Indeed.com. When looking at survey information on these websites, you will see that most of the information is broken up into a few different pieces:

- **Geographical information.** Pay will always vary based on location due to factors

such as cost of living and supply and demand. Auto mechanics might be more prevalent in Detroit than in Anchorage, for example, and their pay may vary accordingly.

- **Level of the job.** This is where your job definition will come in handy. Typically there are about three levels listed for any job: entry, mid, and high. Titles used to define these three levels vary. For example, you might be hiring for an "associate," "junior," or "senior" position (as in "associate clerk") or hiring for the position plus a "1," "2," or "3" (as in "clerk 2"), and so on. Be sure to look for data that matches the level of the job for which you are setting pay.

- **Industry.** The industry or type of industry also helps to determine pay for any given position. Fast-growing industries, such as high tech or biotech, typically pay more than well-established industries, such as shipping and manufacturing. Pay is often a function of supply and demand: In newer industries, you might need to pay more for new skill sets, whereas in more established industries, there are usually more people with the proper training to choose from.

Take any survey information you find with a grain of salt. As mentioned above, it could be outdated, and it might not be a direct match with your position. But like internal equity, it can provide another guideline to help you set pay.

Anecdotal information. While surveys might seem scientific and important, often the freshest data will come from professional organizations, colleagues in your field, and even the candidates themselves. Anecdotal information you glean from speaking to people can also be more relevant than survey data because it is usually more targeted to the position you are filling.

You can gather anecdotal information from a number of different sources. At meetings of professional organizations to which you belong, check in with your peers to find out what they are currently paying people. Also, read organizational newsletters and websites, especially if they list classifieds for open positions.

You can also get such information from applicants who come in to interview for the position. It's a fair question to ask them not only their salary requirements, but also their current salaries.

CAUTION

Some locations ban salary history questions. In an effort to stop the cycle of wage discrimination, Massachusetts became the first state to pass a law—which takes effect on July 1, 2018—prohibiting employers from asking applicants about their current or previous pay. The rationale is that, when employers base salary on an applicant's prior salary, pay inequality ends up following women from job to job. Some cities have already banned this practice, and several other states are considering similar legislation. You can find regular updates on these laws at the online companion page for this book. (See the introductory chapter for the link.)

Understand the Candidate's Requirements

By looking at your budget, you determined the top line of what you can pay for a given position. Internal equity and external market data gave you some parameters for what you should pay to be competitive and fair. The last piece of the puzzle is finding out what the job candidate will accept. This is the bottom line of what you can pay.

Once you narrow the pool of applicants down to one or two real candidates for the position, you will need to ask the candidates both what they made in their last position (which you might have already done in gathering anecdotal information from all of the applicants in the previous step) and what they would accept from you for the new position (don't phrase it this way, of course!). To make such a question sound better and not seem like you are trying to lowball the candidate, ask a question such as, "What pay would seem reasonable to you if you were to join us?" With a stroke of good luck, this number will be below your top line number and within your other guidelines. Often, however, you will need to massage the numbers and use some creative techniques (as described below) to come up with a compensation package that is acceptable to both the candidate and your company.

Putting It All Together

After going through all five steps, how do you turn all of this information into a pay package? In a perfect world, your top line is the same as or higher than what the candidate is willing to accept. If this is not the case, consider the following creative techniques for making the numbers work:

- Establish base pay that reasonably falls within your parameters, but allows for pay increases in the future.
- Offer bonuses or variable pay based on performance on top of the base pay. Bonuses can be short-term (at signing or after 90 days), midterm (after six months or at annual performance appraisals), or long-term (designed to retain an employee). Make sure you communicate the entire compensation package to the candidate, not just the base pay.
- Offer stock or stock options to the candidate.
- You can often make up differences in what a candidate would like to make and what you can afford by offering noncash compensation, such as enhanced vacation benefits, paid parental leave, or educational assistance.

All of these elements can be part of a compensation package. Most of them will require different levels of company approval, so check your policies before offering them. If you are creative with the different tools your company has to offer and can tailor the compensation package to the individual, you should be able to hire your chosen candidate.

The Minimum Wage

Many managers will never have to worry about the minimum wage. However, if you supervise low-wage or tipped employees, if you participate in determining compensation, or if you implement your company's pay program (for example, you work in human resources or payroll), you need to know the basic rules.

Federal law requires employers to pay employees a minimum wage (currently $7.25 an hour). States may impose a higher minimum wage requirement, and many do. The federal law is always the minimum. That is, a company must pay the higher amount, whether it's state or federal. For information on your state's minimum wage requirements, see "State Minimum Wage Laws for Tipped and Regular Employees," at the end of this chapter.

How It's Paid

Although the minimum wage is an hourly standard, employees don't have to be paid by the hour for the minimum wage requirement to kick in. Employees entitled to the minimum wage may receive a salary, commission, wages plus tips, or piece rate, as long as the total amount paid divided by the total number of hours worked by the employee equals at least the minimum wage.

Living Wage Laws

Some cities and counties have passed "living wage" ordinances, requiring certain businesses to pay their workers more than the federal or state minimum wage. The living wage rate is usually calculated by figuring out how much a full-time worker would have to make to support a family of four at or above the poverty line in that geographic area. Some living wage laws also require employers to provide certain benefits or allow employers to pay a lower wage if they already provide benefits.

City and county governments often impose these requirements in areas where the cost of living has skyrocketed beyond that of the rest of the country (such as San Francisco and New York). If your company does business in an area with a high cost of living, there is likely to be a living wage law.

Many of these laws cover only companies that have contracts with, or receive subsidies from, the state or county, but some apply more broadly to all private employers in the area. Check with your city or county government (or consult a local attorney) for information about local living wage laws.

Minimum Wage for Younger Workers

Under federal law, younger workers—those under the age of 20—may be paid a lower minimum wage for the first few months of a job. These workers are entitled to at least $4.25 an hour during their first 90 days of employment. (Note that these are calendar days—including weekends and holidays— not days that the employee actually works.)

Workers who reach their 20th birthdays are entitled to the standard minimum wage, even if they have not yet put in 90 days at your company.

Some states don't allow a youth minimum wage. In these states, younger workers are entitled to the same minimum wage as anyone else.

Employees Who Receive Other Types of Compensation

Under federal law and the laws of some states, companies might be allowed to pay less than the minimum wage to employees who receive other types of compensation. For example, if your company provides room and board to employees, the company can deduct money from their paychecks as reimbursement— even if they'll end up with less than the minimum wage for that pay period—as long as the employee agrees to this arrangement in writing. See "Garnishments," below, for more information.

Tips

Special rules apply to employees who receive tips as part of their compensation. For example, employers in most states can take a tip credit: They can pay employees who receive tips a lower minimum wage. Tipped employees may also be required to pool their tips with other employees.

Tip Basics

The basic rule of tips is that they belong to employees, not the employer. Employees can't be required to give any of their tips to the company, except as part of a valid tip pooling arrangement (see "Tip Pooling," below)—and even then, the tip pool must be divided only among certain employees. The employer can't be part of the pool.

It's not as easy as you might think to figure out exactly how much of what a customer pays is a "tip." Take, for example, bills paid by credit card: If the employer has to pay the credit card company a processing fee, some states allow the employer to subtract a proportionate amount of the designated tip to cover its expenses (for example, if the processing fee is 3%, the employer could deduct 3% of the tip). Other states—most notably, California—require employers to give the employee the full tip indicated by the customer and pay the fee themselves.

Mandatory Service Charges

What about those mandatory service charges that are often tacked on to bills for large tables, private parties, and catered events? Under federal law and in most states, this isn't considered a tip. Even if the customer thinks that money is going to the server and doesn't leave anything extra on the table, the employer can keep any money designated as a "service charge." The law generally considers this part of the contract between the patron and the establishment, not a voluntary acknowledgment of good service by an employee. Many employers give at least part of these service charges to employees, but that's the employer's choice—employees have no legal right to that money.

A couple of states have different rules, however, intended to make sure customers know what they're paying for. For example, New York's highest court recently held that companies must give all mandatory service charges to their employees unless they make it clear to customers that the company is keeping the money. And, the state of Washington requires companies to tell customers—on menus and receipts—what portion of a mandatory service charge goes to the employee who served the customer.

Tip Credits

Under federal law and the laws of most states, employers may pay tipped employees less than the minimum wage, as long as employees receive enough in tips to make up the difference. This is called a "tip credit." The credit itself is the amount the employer doesn't have to pay. The applicable minimum wage (federal or state) minus the tip credit is the least the employer can pay tipped employees per hour. For example, the current tip credit allowed under federal law is $5.12. After subtracting the tip credit from the current federal minimum wage ($7.25 − $5.12), the amount left over ($2.13) is the minimum that an employer must pay a tipped employee per hour. If the employee doesn't earn enough in tips during a given shift to bring the employee's total compensation up to at least the minimum rate wage, the employer has to pay the difference.

Employees are entitled to notice if the employer plans on taking a tip credit. This notice must include:

- the hourly cash wage the employer will pay the employee
- the amount that the employer will take as a tip credit (that is, the amount the employer will count toward the employee's wages)
- that the employee is entitled to retain all tips received except any amount the employee is required to contribute to a valid tip pooling arrangement, and
- that the tip credit won't apply to any employee who has not been informed of these requirements.

This notice doesn't have to be in writing; employers may inform employees orally, if they wish. As a practical matter, however, employers that plan to take a tip credit should provide written notice, so they can later prove that they properly notified employees, if necessary.

Most states allow employers to take a tip credit, although the amount varies from state to state. However, some states don't allow a tip credit at all, including California, Minnesota, and Oregon (among others). To find out what's allowed in your state, see "State Minimum Wage Laws for Tipped and Regular Employees" at the end of this chapter.

Tip Pooling

Many states allow employers to set up a mandatory tip pool. In a tip pool, employees are required to chip in all or a portion of their tips, which are then divided among a group of employees. A valid tip pool must follow certain guidelines, though. An employee can't be required to pay more into the pool than is customary and reasonable, and the employee must be able to keep at least the full minimum wage (that is, the employee can't be required to contribute any part of the tips the employer is counting toward the minimum wage).

Only employees who regularly receive tips can be part of the pool. Employees can't be required to share their tips with employees who don't usually receive their own tips, like dishwashers or cooks. And no employers are allowed in the pool: Tips from a tip pool can't go to the company or, in some states, managers or supervisors.

Overtime

Federal and state laws require most employers to pay overtime. The overtime premium is 50% of the employee's regular hourly rate. This means an employee who works overtime must be paid time and a half—the employee's usual hourly wage plus the 50% overtime premium—for every overtime hour worked.

Employees are entitled to overtime unless they fall within a specific exception set out in the law. Employees who are eligible for overtime are called "nonexempt" employees, and those who are not eligible for overtime are called "exempt" employees. Exempt employees must meet certain requirements by law; it is not enough to pay someone a salary and call them exempt. Misclassifying employees can be a very costly mistake if your company faces a lawsuit or a government audit. Because this is an area where a lot of managers get in trouble, it's worth taking some time to learn the rules.

Weekly Versus Daily Standard

Federal law and the laws of most states impose a weekly overtime standard, which means that nonexempt employees are entitled to overtime when they work more than 40 hours in a week, regardless of how many hours they work in a day. For example, Alex is a nonexempt employee who works 12 hours on Monday and six hours on Tuesday (and doesn't work any more hours in the week). He is not entitled to receive overtime under the weekly overtime standard, even though he worked more than eight hours on Monday.

California and a handful of other states have a daily overtime standard, which means that nonexempt employees are also entitled to overtime when they work more than eight hours in a day. Let's take Alex from the paragraph above. In a daily overtime state, he would be entitled to overtime pay for the four extra hours he worked on Monday, even though he didn't even come close to working 40 hours in the week.

How to Calculate the Overtime Rate

For employees who are paid by the hour, it's fairly simple to calculate the overtime rate. The overtime rate is 1.5 times the employee's hourly wage. For example, if an employee is paid $10 per hour, the overtime rate is $15 per hour.

For salaried employees who are not exempt from the overtime laws, you'll need to do some calculations to figure out the employee's hourly rate. First, take the employee's salary and divide that amount by 52 weeks. For example, if an employee is paid $30,000 per year, he or she makes $576.92 per week. Next, take that amount and divide it by the number of hours the employee works each week. For example, if an employee works 40 hours a week, he or she earns $14.42 per hour. Now you have the employee's hourly rate of pay, which you multiply by one-and-a-half. The employee's overtime rate is $21.63.

If an employee receives other forms of compensation, such as commissions or non-discretionary bonuses, those will need to be factored into the employee's overtime rate. These amounts should be added to the employee's total compensation for the week when determining the hourly rate. Certain types of payments need not be included in the overtime rate, including business and travel expenses, gratuities, and discretionary bonuses (bonuses that are paid at the employer's option, rather than due to meeting certain standards or criteria, such as a holiday bonus).

Classification Rules for White-Collar Employees

Administrative Employee

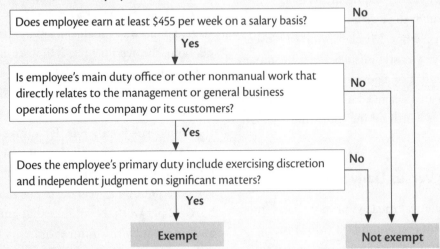

Does employee earn at least $455 per week on a salary basis? — No

Yes ↓

Is employee's main duty office or other nonmanual work that directly relates to the management or general business operations of the company or its customers? — No

Yes ↓

Does the employee's primary duty include exercising discretion and independent judgment on significant matters? — No

Yes ↓

Exempt / **Not exempt**

Executive Employee

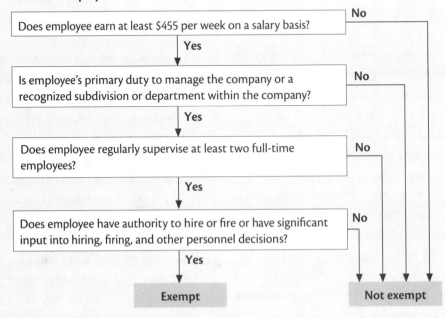

Does employee earn at least $455 per week on a salary basis? — No

Yes ↓

Is employee's primary duty to manage the company or a recognized subdivision or department within the company? — No

Yes ↓

Does employee regularly supervise at least two full-time employees? — No

Yes ↓

Does employee have authority to hire or fire or have significant input into hiring, firing, and other personnel decisions? — No

Yes ↓

Exempt / **Not exempt**

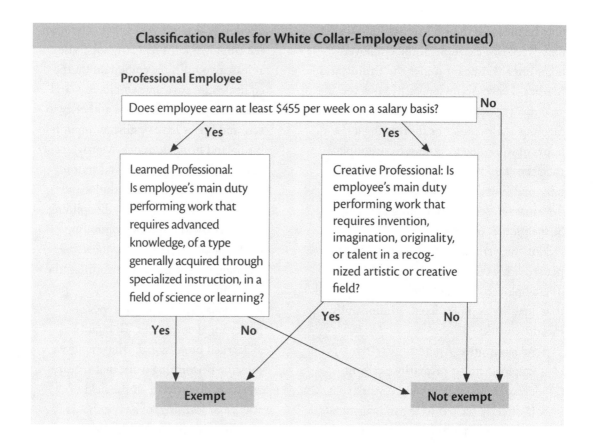

Classification Rules for White Collar-Employees (continued)

Professional Employee

Does employee earn at least $455 per week on a salary basis?

Learned Professional: Is employee's main duty performing work that requires advanced knowledge, of a type generally acquired through specialized instruction, in a field of science or learning?

Creative Professional: Is employee's main duty performing work that requires invention, imagination, originality, or talent in a recognized artistic or creative field?

Exempt

Not exempt

Which Employees Are Entitled to Overtime

If a business is covered by either the FLSA or a state overtime law, then all of its employees are entitled to overtime unless they are exempt (that is, unless they fit into an exception to the overtime rules).

Probably the most common—and confusing —exceptions to the overtime laws are for so-called "white-collar" workers. Employees whom the law defines as "administrative, executive, or professional"

need not be paid overtime. To be considered such, employees must:

- be paid on a salary basis, and
- spend most of their time performing job duties that fall under an exemption category.

An employee who is paid on a salary basis must earn at least $455 per week and must receive the same salary every week, regardless of how many hours the employee works or the quantity or quality of the work performed. There are only a few circumstances in which a salaried worker may be paid less than his or her full salary for a week (for example, if the employee takes unpaid time off under the Family and Medical Leave Act). Generally, however, if an employer docks an employee's pay (for not meeting a sales target or for missing a few hours of work due to illness, for example), then the employee is not paid on a salary basis and is entitled to overtime. (For more information, see "Pay Docking and Unpaid Suspensions," below.)

Not every employee who earns $455 or more per week is exempt from overtime, though. The employee must also be performing work that qualifies as professional, administrative, or executive work:

- **Administrative.** An administrative employee must primarily perform office or other nonmanual work that is directly related to the management or business operations of the employer or its customers and must exercise discretion and independent judgment regarding significant issues. (The last requirement generally means that the employee makes decisions after weighing different courses of action, rather than following established guidelines or procedures.) For example, an insurance adjuster or executive assistant to a CEO might qualify under this category, depending on their duties and authority to make decisions.
- **Executive.** An executive employee's primary duty must be managing the employer's enterprise or a recognized

division or department of that enterprise; the employee must regularly supervise at least two full-time employees (or the equivalent in part-time employees); and the employee must have the authority to hire and fire or have significant input into hiring and firing decisions. Management duties include supervising and training employees, assigning work duties and schedules, setting pay rates, disciplining employees, planning and controlling the budgeting, selecting the tools and techniques to be used in performing the work, and more.

- **Professional.** There are two types of professional employees. To qualify as a "learned professional," the employee must be performing work that requires advanced knowledge in the field of science or learning, of a type that is usually attained through an advanced course of study. Examples include doctors, lawyers, scientists, professors, engineers, certified public accountants, and registered nurses. To qualify as a "creative professional," the employee must be performing work that requires invention, imagination, originality, or talent in a recognized creative or artistic field. Examples include actors, musicians, sculptors, painters, and novelists.

The FLSA has a number of other exemptions, many of which are specific to certain industries. For example, there are exemptions for certain farmworkers, salespeople, drivers, mechanics, and computer professionals.

Some states also have their own exemptions or set more strict criteria for the white-collar exemptions. Whether an employee meets the requirements of an exemption is usually decided on a case-by-case basis. Because misclassifying employees can lead to large overtime and other wage claims, you should consult with a lawyer if you have any questions.

Minimum Salary Requirement Expected to Increase

In 2015, the Department of Labor (DOL) passed a final rule to increase the minimum weekly salary from $455 per week to $970 per week for the white-collar exemptions. However, the new rule was put on hold before it could take effect. After a change in leadership at the DOL, the agency announced plans to revise the rule to establish a weekly threshold that is lower than $970 per week. You can find legal updates on the online companion page for this book; see the introductory chapter for the link.

Compensatory Time Is Not Allowed

Some companies adopt a policy of giving their employees compensatory, or "comp," time—an hour off at some later date for every extra hour worked—instead of paying them overtime. But, as many managers are surprised to learn, these policies are generally illegal under federal law, at least for private employers (state and local governments can offer comp time in certain circumstances). The reason? They preclude employees from collecting an overtime premium: the extra pay to which they are entitled for working more than a set number of hours (for example, time and a half for working more than 40 hours under federal law).

This means that if you wish to give your employees time off instead of money for extra hours worked, you cannot simply establish an hour-for-hour policy (that is, telling the employee to take an hour off for every hour of overtime worked). You can, however, reduce the employee's hours in the same pay period in order to keep the employee's paycheck constant. To make the math come out right, the employee must take an hour and a half off for every extra hour worked.

For example, take an employee who works 40 hours a week, at a rate of $20 an hour, and earns $1,600 per two-week pay period (or $800 per week). If the employee works ten extra hours during the first week, he or she would be entitled to an overtime rate of $30 for ten hours, which is $300. To keep the paycheck consistent, the employee would need to take 15 hours off in the second week of the pay period. In other words, the employee would work only 25 hours at his or her regular rate and receive $500, instead of $800, for that week. The employee's paycheck for the pay period would still be $1,600 ($1,100 for the first week and $500 for the second week).

Unauthorized Overtime

The FLSA requires that employees be paid whenever they are "suffered or permitted" to work. This means that you must pay employees when they work overtime, even if they do it voluntarily or without getting permission. This doesn't, however, mean that you have to let employees work unlimited overtime. Instead, you can communicate a clear policy to your employees requiring that all overtime be authorized in advance. When an employee works unauthorized overtime, you can discipline them for violating company policy (while still paying them for the overtime). Employees will quickly get the message that they need to get permission to work overtime if they want to keep their jobs.

Meal and Rest Breaks

The FLSA doesn't require employers to give employees time off for meals or other breaks during their work days. Federal law does, however, provide some rules on what counts as a true break, for which employees don't have to be paid, and what should be compensable work time. These rules are explained below.

Some state laws require employers to provide meal or rest breaks, and some states require employers to pay for this time. In recent years, there have been a number of class action lawsuits against employers that don't provide the time off mandated by these laws. The dollar amounts in these cases add up fast: Multiply what the company owes a single employee for a half-hour's work by the number of employees in the company, and multiply that by the number of days for which employees can recover (often two or even three years). Once you tack on penalties, court costs, and attorneys' fees (for the company and for the employee's lawyers, if they win), companies are looking at a multimillion-dollar exposure. And it all could have been avoided if only they didn't make employees work through lunch.

What Counts as a Break?

Under the FLSA, employers are not required to provide meal or rest breaks. However, if they choose to do so, they must pay for any breaks that are 20 minutes or less.

If the break is for more than 20 minutes—for example, the employee takes a half-hour lunch break—the employer doesn't have to pay for any of that time. This is true only if the employee is completely relieved of all work duties during the break. If an employee has any responsibilities during the break, that time must be paid. For example, an employee who has to cover the phones or wait for a delivery while eating lunch must be paid for that time.

State Laws

As noted above, some states require employers to provide meal breaks. Typically, these laws require employers to provide employees with at least a half-hour for lunch when they are scheduled to work five or more hours. And, a handful of states also require employers to provide brief paid rest breaks during the day (typically ten minutes for each four-hour shift). For a summary of these laws, see "State Meal and Rest Break Laws," at the end of this chapter.

Lactation Breaks

Many new mothers return to work while they are still breast-feeding, which often means that they will need one or more breaks during the day to pump breast milk. For employers, providing these breaks makes good sense. It allows women to return to work more quickly after having a baby, enhances employee loyalty, and provides mothers and babies with the proven health benefits of breast-feeding.

The federal Patient Protection and Affordable Care Act—better known as the health care reform law—requires employers to provide breaks to nursing mothers. Many states also have laws that require employers to provide a certain amount of time off and a designated location for expressing breast milk at work.

What the Health Care Reform Law Requires

Under federal law, employers must provide reasonable break time for nursing mothers to pump breast milk for up to one year after the child's birth. Employers are not required to pay for this break time, unless the employee uses her normal paid breaks for such purposes.

Lessons From the Real World

In December 2006, a Pennsylvania jury ordered Wal-Mart to pay more than $78 million in damages to a class of 170,000 current and former employees. The employees claimed that they were required to work through their breaks and work "off the clock"—that is, after they had punched out for the day. They argued that Wal-Mart's failure to pay them for this time violated the company's own policies and the state's laws on payment of wages and overtime.

Pennsylvania law doesn't require employers to pay for employee breaks. However, the employees claimed that they didn't really get to take breaks. Instead, they had to work through these periods, even though they weren't paid. Wal-Mart argued, among other things, that employees were encouraged to take their breaks and that it shouldn't be held responsible if some employees chose to work instead. Apparently, the jury didn't find this argument very persuasive.

On top of the jury's award, the judge ordered Wal-Mart to pay more than $62 million in penalties and almost $50 million to the employees' attorneys, for a whopping total of more than $187 million. Wal-Mart appealed to the Pennsylvania Supreme Court, which upheld the jury award. The case is now on appeal to the United States Supreme Court. (You can find links to decisions and articles on the case at www.walmartpaclassaction.com, a site maintained by the employees' attorneys.)

The employer must also provide private space, other than a bathroom, for this purpose. Your company doesn't have to dedicate a room solely for pumping, although it can. If an employee's office is reasonably private, she can pump there; your company might have to provide some alterations (such as a window shade) for this purpose. For employees who don't have private workspace, the company can allow them to pump in a vacant office or conference room, for example, as long as the space is adequate and private.

Although the federal law applies to all employers, it includes an exception for employers with fewer than 50 employees. These employers need not allow lactation breaks if doing so would impose an "undue hardship," defined as significant expense or difficulty, considering the employer's size, structure, and resources.

State Laws

Some state lactation break laws require only that employers allow employees to use their regular breaks to express breast milk. Other states go further and require employers to provide additional breaks or allow breaks after the child's first year. Like the federal law, some states also require employers to provide an appropriate space for pumping.

Even if your company doesn't have to comply with the federal law (because providing breaks would pose an undue hardship, as defined above), it might still have to allow breaks under applicable state law. To find out whether your state has a law on this issue, see "State Meal and Rest Break Laws," at the end of this chapter.

Travel Time

Employees who are entitled to overtime pay also have the right to be paid for some hours they spend traveling for work. If your employees routinely travel as part of their jobs or go on business trips that take them out of the area, you'll need to be able to figure out whether (and how much) they are entitled to be paid for this time.

Although employees are not entitled to be paid for time spent commuting to and from work, they must be paid for travel time that is part of the job. If, for example, employees are required to go out on service calls, the time spent traveling to and from the customers' homes must be paid. Also, if employees are required to take employer-provided transportation from a central location to the worksite, they may have to be paid for this time.

Even though commuting time is not normally compensated, an employee who is required to come to the workplace at odd hours to deal with emergency situations might be entitled to pay. For example, if a mechanic works a regular 9-to-5 schedule but is sometimes called in during the night shift to repair equipment that has broken down, the mechanic is entitled to be paid for the extra trip to work.

Special rules apply to employees who occasionally travel to another location for business. The rules depend on whether the trip includes an overnight stay.

Day Trips

If you send an employee on a day trip, the employee is entitled to pay for hours spent in transit. For example, if an employee has to drive two hours each way to get to an out-of-town business meeting, the company must pay for the four hours of total travel time. If the employee goes straight from home to the meeting and back, the company can deduct the time it would otherwise have taken the employee to commute to work.

Pay for Travel Time: One-Day Trip

Time spent traveling	_____
Minus usual commute time	− _____
Equals compensable travel time	= _____

> **EXAMPLE:** It usually takes Polly about 30 minutes each way to commute to the office. You send her to a business meeting in a city that's two hours away. Polly doesn't come into the office at all that day and instead drives from her home straight to the meeting and straight home again afterwards. She is entitled to three hours of paid travel time in addition to the time she spends working:
>
>   4 hours travel time
> − 1 hour usual commute time
> = 3 hours compensable travel time

Overnight Trips

When an employee spends the night out of town, the rules are different. Of course, the employee must be paid for all of the time he or she spends actually working. However, whether the employee is entitled to pay for time spent in transit depends on when the travel takes place. Employees are entitled to pay for time spent traveling during the weekday, if it falls within their regular work hours. However, they are also entitled to be paid for weekend travel that takes place during these same hours, even if they ordinarily work only Monday through Friday.

Pay for Travel Time: Overnight Trip

Time spent traveling	_____
Minus travel time outside usual work hours	− _____
Equals compensable travel time	= _____

> **EXAMPLE:** You send Polly to attend a three-day business conference out of town. Her usual schedule is 9 a.m. to 5 p.m., Monday through Friday. She leaves her home to head for the airport at 5 a.m. Wednesday morning and arrives at the conference in time for the 9 a.m. orientation. Because the conference ends late on Friday, she returns home Saturday morning, catching an 8 a.m. flight and pulling into her driveway at home by noon. Of course, Polly is entitled to pay for all of the hours she actually spends at

the conference, even if it goes beyond her regularly scheduled hours. In addition, she is entitled to three hours of travel time. She must be compensated for the time she spent traveling on Saturday from 9 a.m. to noon because it fell within her normal work hours. The rest of her travel was before her regular starting time of 9 a.m., so it does not need to be compensated.

Rate for Travel Pay

When travel time is compensable, employers must pay employees at least the applicable minimum wage. This means employers can pay employees a lower rate for travel time than their normal rate (unless the employee also works during travel time, for example, on a train or during a flight). However, this approach has some practical downsides. For example, you'll need to carefully track the employee's hours, adjust the rates, and deal with more complicated overtime calculations. In many cases, it's not worth the administrative headache.

On-Call Time

Under federal law, employees are entitled to be paid for time that their employer controls and that benefits their employer. Generally, this includes time that the employee cannot spend as he or she wishes, even if that time is not spent working. For example, an employee who has to cover the phones while eating lunch is entitled to be paid for that time, even if the phones aren't ringing.

If employees are required to stay on company premises or at a customer's location while waiting for a work assignment, they are entitled to be paid even if they do not spend that time actually working. For example, a mechanic who knits a sweater while waiting for a customer to arrive or an assistant who does a crossword puzzle while waiting for an assignment is entitled to be paid for that time.

If employees must be on call elsewhere—for example, at home—they are entitled to be paid for those hours during which they have little or no control and which they cannot use for their own enjoyment or benefit. In short, if you place significant restrictions on an employee who is on call, that employee should be paid. There are few hard-and-fast rules in this area. Generally, the more constraints on an employee, the more likely he or she should be paid.

Here are some factors a court or agency might consider when deciding this issue:

- **How many calls an employee gets while on call.** The more calls an employee has to respond to, the more likely he or she is entitled to pay, particularly if any of the calls require the employee to report to work or give immediate advice or guidance over the phone.
- **How long an employee has to respond after a call.** If employees are required to report to work immediately after being paged, for example, they have a better

argument that they should be paid for their time.

- **Where an employee can go while on call.** Employees who must stay within a limited distance from work are more likely to be entitled to compensation.

- **What employees can do while on call.** The more rules imposed on on-call workers, such as a ban on alcohol or a requirement that they respond quickly and in person to calls (which can be difficult if the employee is out running or taking the kids to school), the more likely it is that they are entitled to pay for this time.

As with nonworking travel time, employers can set different hourly rates for on-call time, as long as employees receive at least minimum wage. See "Rate for Travel Pay," above, for more information.

Flexible Work Schedules

As we all know, it can sometimes seem impossible to work full time during business hours and simultaneously meet our family and other personal obligations, whether they include caring for a child, helping an elderly parent, or taking care of our own health needs. More and more companies are starting to respond to their workers' needs for flexibility by allowing employees to work flexible schedules or what is often referred to as "flextime."

Lessons From the Real World

Shelly Reimer was a nurse at Dakota Heartland Health Systems. She and her coworkers were required to spend some time "on call." They did not have to be at the workplace during this time, but they had to be reachable by cell phone, beeper, or regular phone; they had to be able to report to the hospital within 20 minutes of getting called; and they had to refrain from drinking alcohol or using "mind-altering" drugs or medications while on call. Dakota Heartland paid the nurses less than the minimum wage for time spent on call.

Reimer and her coworkers sued, arguing that they were entitled to at least the minimum wage for the time they spent on call. But the court disagreed. Finding that the restrictions placed on nurses were minimal, the court noted that they "could play sports, work at home, go shopping, or visit friends and neighbors" while on call. The court also found that nurses typically were not called in more than once per shift and that once a nurse was called in to work, she was paid at her regular rate. Because nurses were free to engage in a variety of activities, and because they were called in relatively rarely, the court found that their time did not have to be compensated at minimum wage.

Reimer v. Champion Healthcare Corp., 258 F.3d 720 (8th Cir. 2001).

Helping employees meet their family or personal needs can pay off for the company as well. Allowing employees to work flexible schedules can reduce distractions on the job and increase worker productivity, loyalty, and job satisfaction, which in turn reduces turnover and related costs. This section describes flextime and its legality; for more on other types of personnel policies that can help employees balance work and family, see "Family-Friendly Workplace Policies" in Chapter 4.

Flextime Defined

Generally speaking, an employee who works on a flexible schedule still works full time but simply does his or her work during what might not be considered normal business hours. This means that instead of working 9:00 a.m. to 5:00 p.m., an employee might, for example, work 7:00 a.m. to 3:00 p.m. to be home to provide care for his or her children after school, work 11:00 a.m. to 7:00 p.m. in order to take an elderly parent to morning physical therapy, or work 8:00 a.m. to 6:00 p.m. four days a week to have a full day off to care for his or her infant. (Other types of work arrangements such as working part time or job sharing are discussed in "Family-Friendly Workplace Policies" in Chapter 4.)

Flextime is not the same thing as compensatory or "comp" time: In comp time, an employee works overtime—beyond his or her regular work hours—in order to earn additional time off. This practice is generally not permitted. (See "Compensatory Time Is Not Allowed," above.) Flextime, on the other hand, is a policy whereby your company allows its workers to work a regular eight-hour day or 40-hour week, but doesn't require the work to be done during normal business hours.

Is Flextime Legal?

On the whole, flextime is perfectly legal, with two caveats. First, if any employee wants to work more than eight hours in one day, your company must be careful to follow any state overtime laws that apply. Under federal law, an employee who works no more than 40 hours in a week, regardless of how many hours he or she works per day, has not worked overtime and is not entitled to overtime pay. So, for example, an employee who works four ten-hour days and then has three days off need not be paid overtime. However, a handful of states have laws that provide a daily overtime standard. In these states, workers are entitled to overtime if they work more than a set number of hours in a day, even if they ultimately work fewer than 40 hours in a week.

So, if you allow a worker to work more than the set number of hours per day, you might have to pay overtime unless the law explicitly allows you and your employees to agree on an alternative workweek. California and Colorado are among the states that have a daily overtime standard. To find out the rules in your state, including whether you and your employees can arrange an alternative workweek schedule, contact your state labor department. (See the appendix for contact information.)

Second, as with any employment benefit your company establishes, you cannot discriminate unlawfully based on race, gender, religion, age, disability, or any other protected characteristic in providing the benefit. This doesn't mean that you have to let everyone work a flexible schedule; it just means that you cannot decide who has access to the benefit based on an impermissible characteristic. For example, if you give flexible schedules to all of the men in a particular position, you must also give flexible schedules to the women in that position.

Obviously, certain jobs are more suited to a flexible schedule. For example, jobs that do not need to be done during business hours or that do not require the worker to be present when other employees are present—such as editing books or accounting—might allow a flexible schedule, whereas jobs that must be done while the business is open—such as reception or computer support for employees—might not. If appropriate, flextime may also be used as a reasonable accommodation for an employee with a disability. (See "Disability," in Chapter 3, for more on reasonable accommodations.)

If your company chooses to institute flexible work schedules, you could hear some grumbling from those not allowed to work flexible hours. To reduce the chances of this happening, you should establish clear, consistent policies that can be administered fairly. For more on establishing personnel policies in general, see Chapter 4. For more information on instituting flexible work schedules, contact any of the number of organizations that work on such issues, including research organizations like the Families and Work Institute (www. familiesandwork.org), and consulting groups such as Catalyst (www.catalyst.org).

Are Employers Required to Provide Flexible Schedules?

In most cases, employers are not required to grant—or even consider—an employee's request for a flexible work schedule. However, there are a few exceptions to this rule. First, under federal and state disability laws, you might need to consider a flexible schedule as a reasonable accommodation for an employee with a disability. Second, some states similarly require employers to provide reasonable accommodations to pregnant employees, which could include flexible scheduling. Third, a few places have flextime laws that impose requirements on employers. For example, in Vermont, employers are required to consider flextime requests from employees at least twice a year and engage in a dialogue with the employee about possible arrangements. Some cities, such as San Francisco, have similar laws. Contact your state labor department or local government for more information.

Pay Docking and Unpaid Suspensions

Some managers discipline employees by docking their pay or putting them on unpaid suspensions for violating workplace rules. However, this type of policy can create big problems if applied to an exempt employee: that is, an employee who is not entitled to overtime pay because he or she is paid on a salary basis and meets the job duties of the executive, professional, or administrative exemptions.

What's Wrong With Docking Pay?

To qualify as exempt, employees have to be paid a set amount each pay period, without any reductions based on the quantity or quality of work they do. If you dock their pay, you might inadvertently make them nonexempt employees and thereby entitle them to overtime. As you might guess, the money saved by docking the employee's salary could be far exceeded by the money the company could have to pay out in overtime.

Under federal law, exempt employees—those who are not entitled to overtime—must earn at least $455 per week (or $23,660 per year) and be paid on a salary basis. (For more information, see "Which Employees Are Entitled to Overtime," above.) This means that all or some of the employee's salary is a fixed amount that doesn't depend on how many hours they work, how much work they accomplish, or the quality of their work. As long as these employees do some work during the week, they are entitled to their full weekly pay, unless the time they take off falls into one of the exceptions described below.

Permissible Salary Deductions

Employers may make salary deductions without jeopardizing the employee's exempt status for the following reasons:

- to take one or more full days off for personal reasons
- to go on unpaid leave under the Family and Medical Leave Act (see Chapter 5 for information on the FMLA)
- for one or more full days of disability or illness, if the employer has a plan that compensates employees for this time off (for example, a sick leave policy)
- to offset any amounts the employee receives as jury fees, witness fees, or military pay (however, employers may not deduct for the time spent away from work during the week)
- during the employee's first or last week of work, if the employee does not work a full week
- as a penalty imposed in good faith for infractions of safety rules of major significance (rules that prevent serious danger in the workplace), or
- to serve an unpaid disciplinary suspension of one or more full days imposed in good faith for infractions of workplace conduct rules, but only if the employer has a written policy regarding such suspensions that applies to all employees.

As you can see, many of the deductions discussed above are permitted only when the employee takes one or more full days off work. In other words, deductions for partial-day absences are generally not allowed. For example, if an employee takes a few hours off to run an errand or to attend a doctor's appointment, you cannot deduct his or her pay. However, deductions for partial-day absences are allowed during the employee's first or last week of work and for intermittent leave taken under the FMLA.

Actual Practice of Improper Deductions

A company will be penalized if it has an "actual practice" of making improper deductions from an exempt employee's salary. Among the factors a court or government agency will consider when making this determination are:

- the number of improper deductions
- the time period during which the deductions were made

 Lessons From the Real World

Life Time Fitness paid its senior managers a set amount of base salary twice a month, along with a monthly bonus payment based on the manager's year-to-date performance. In 2004, the compensation program reserved the company's right to take back previous bonus payments, by reducing a manager's base salary payments, if his or her performance dropped below a certain level. After 2004, the program was tweaked, but still allowed the company to reduce a manager's base pay for performance that didn't meet certain standards. In 2005, a number of managers had their base pay reduced under the program in three separate pay periods.

The managers sued, claiming that Life Time's program amounted to illegal pay docking and that all of them were entitled to overtime pay as a result. The court had a complicated job in this case because the Department of Labor changed the rules relating to pay docking in August of 2004. Under the old rules, an employer could be held liable for improper pay docking if it had an employment policy creating a "significant likelihood" of such reductions even if no deductions were actually made. Although no managers actually received reduced pay before the rules changed, the court found that Life Time's written policies clearly communicated that deductions were likely and therefore found in favor of the managers for this time period.

However, Life Time fared better for the time period after the rules changed. Under the new rules, employers were liable only if they had an "actual practice" of making deductions. The court found that the managers were entitled to overtime compensation only during the three pay periods when illegal deductions were actually made.

Baden-Winterwood et al. v. Life Time Fitness, Inc., 566 F.3d 618 (6th Cir., 2009).

- how many employees were subjected to improper salary deductions and where those employees worked
- how many managers were responsible for taking improper deductions and where those managers worked, and
- whether the company has a clearly communicated policy that either permits or prohibits improper deductions.

Deductions that are isolated or inadvertent will not be considered an actual practice of unlawful deductions, as long as the employer reimburses the employee for the money improperly withheld.

A company that has an actual practice of making improper deductions will lose the overtime exemption for all employees who work in the same job classification(s) and who work for the same managers responsible for making the deductions. In other words, if you make improper deductions, your company will have to pay overtime to everyone who reports to you and holds the same position as the employee whose pay you docked.

However, there is a "safe harbor" provision, which allows employers to avoid overtime liability if certain requirements are met. A company can take advantage of the safe harbor if all of the following are true:

- The company has a clearly communicated policy prohibiting improper deductions (including a complaint procedure).

- The company reimburses the employee for the money improperly withheld.
- The company makes a good-faith effort to comply with the law in the future.

An employer will not be protected by the safe harbor if it continues to make unlawful deductions after receiving employee complaints, however.

Garnishments

A company might be legally obligated to deduct money from a worker's paycheck to satisfy certain debts, such as child support or tax debts. In addition, you might be allowed to deduct money to satisfy the worker's debt to the company (for a cash advance, for example). However, except in very limited circumstances, an employer is not allowed to withhold money if it would make the worker's pay fall below minimum wage.

Wage Garnishment, Child Support Orders, and Tax Debts

If you receive a court order or notice from a government agency requiring you to withhold money from a worker's paycheck, simply follow the instructions in the documents. Generally, an employer might be required to deduct money from a worker's paycheck in three situations:

- **Wage garnishments.** A court might order your company to withhold money to satisfy certain debts, including student loan debts, alimony or spousal support, or money owed to someone who won a lawsuit against the worker. This type of order is called a wage "attachment" or "garnishment." The paperwork you receive from the court will generally tell you how much to deduct and where to send the money, although you might first have to tell the court how much the worker earns.

- **Child support orders.** When a judge orders a parent to pay child support, the judge will automatically issue a wage withholding order. This order requires the employer to deduct the amount owed each month from the worker's paycheck, and then send that money to the parent who has custody of the child.

- **Wage levy notices.** The Internal Revenue Service (IRS) has the right to take some portion of a worker's wages to satisfy his or her unpaid tax debt. In these situations, the employer will receive a wage levy notice from the IRS indicating the amount to be deducted (and sent to the government). Generally, state tax agencies have the same right.

Federal law prohibits employers from firing workers because their wages have been garnished to pay any one debt, no matter how many separate orders or lawsuits have been filed to collect that debt. However, a worker whose wages are garnished to pay off more than one debt can be terminated,

under federal law. Some states don't allow termination of workers because their wages have been garnished for more than one debt, however. Some states protect employees from being fired for having certain wage garnishment orders, such as an order for child support or spousal support. Other states prohibit employers from firing employees unless they have a certain number of wage garnishment orders (for example, more than two or three in a year).

Federal law limits how much can be deducted from a worker's paycheck for wage garnishments and child support orders. For most debts, an employer may deduct either 25% of the worker's actual earnings per pay period (after tax and required state and federal deductions) or the amount by which the worker's actual earnings exceed 30 times the minimum hourly wage, whichever is less. For child support or alimony orders, up to 50% of the worker's actual earnings may be taken if the worker is currently supporting a spouse or dependent child (other than the person for whom the money is being taken) and up to 60% if the worker is not. More may be taken from workers who are well behind in their support payments.

Wage garnishments can be tricky. If you have any questions about a wage garnishment or other withholding order, contact the authority that sent the order (for example, the IRS or a particular court). You might also consider asking a lawyer for advice.

Deductions to Pay a Debt to the Employer

If an employee owes the company money—for a salary advance, for example—the company is entitled under federal law to withhold money from the employee's paycheck to pay itself back. You can deduct the principal of the amount owed, even if the deduction would bring the employee's earnings below minimum wage. However, deductions for interest or administrative charges cannot bring the employee's earnings below minimum wage. And, you must get the employee's consent first. If you plan on making this type of deduction, it's best to document the loan or advance and get the employee's consent to the deductions in writing.

However, some states prohibit employers from deducting money from their workers' paychecks or limit the circumstances under which they can do so. For more information on your state's law, contact your state labor department (see the appendix for contact information).

Deductions for Food and Lodging

Employers are allowed to deduct the reasonable cost of meals and housing provided to workers, even if this would result in the worker's pay falling below minimum wage. However, these deductions are allowed only if *all* of the following are true:

- The company regularly provides room and board for workers.

- The items were provided for the benefit of the employee.
- The employee was told, before the arrangement began, that the company planned to take the deductions.
- The employee voluntarily agreed, in writing, to accept less than the minimum wage in exchange for the food and lodging provided.

Some states place additional limits on deductions for food and lodging. For example, some allow employers to deduct only a specified amount for each meal provided. To learn more about your state's law, contact your state labor department.

Other Deductions

Generally, an employer may not deduct money from a worker's paycheck to reimburse itself for other business expenses if doing so would cause the worker's pay to fall below the minimum wage. Examples of expenses subject to this rule include:

- uniforms (including dry cleaning costs)
- tools used in the employee's work
- financial losses incurred in the ordinary course of business (for example, a shortfall in a cash register or a customer's failure to pay a bill)
- employer-mandated medical examinations, and
- damage to or theft of company property.

Some states prohibit employers from charging their workers for these types of business expenses at all. Check with your state department of labor to find out what expenses (if any) can be charged back to workers.

Equal Pay

The Equal Pay Act (EPA), 29 U.S.C. § 206(d), prohibits employers from paying employees of one sex at a lower rate than employees of the opposite sex for doing equal work. The law was intended to combat what the Supreme Court called the "ancient but outmoded belief that a man, because of his role in society, should be paid more than a woman." *Corning Glass Works v. Brennan*, 417 U.S. 188, 195 (1974). Despite this gender-specific intent, however, the EPA protects both men and women from wage discrimination based on sex. (This section covers equal pay only. For more on gender discrimination, see "Gender, Pregnancy, and Sexual Harassment" in Chapter 3.)

What Is Equal Work?

Male and female employees are entitled to equal pay even if their jobs are not absolutely identical. The law requires only that their jobs be "substantially" equal for the equal pay requirement to kick in. That is, the jobs must require equal skill, effort, and responsibility, and they must be performed under similar working conditions.

Job titles do not determine whether two jobs are substantially equal. For example,

you may not pay a male "administrative assistant" more than a female "secretary" if both do essentially the same tasks. Similarly, jobs that have the same official name might require different degrees of responsibility or effort, allowing men and women holding those jobs to be paid at different rates. For example, a college might be able to pay the coach of its men's basketball team more than the coach of its women's basketball team, if the men's coach brings in more revenue and both coaches were given equal support and resources.

What Is Equal Pay?

The EPA doesn't just apply to wages. It also applies to benefits—such as insurance coverage, pensions, and use of a company car—and other forms of compensation, like vacation time, profit sharing, and bonuses. In other words, you must also provide equal fringe benefits to workers of both sexes who are performing substantially equal work.

Managers can get into trouble here: If you make certain benefits or perks available to only some of your reports, you must make sure that those benefits are not being doled out along gender lines. If men and women doing the same work don't receive the same benefits, that could be an EPA violation. And, even if they aren't doing equal work, providing benefits based on an employee's gender would constitute illegal sex discrimination (see Chapter 3).

EEOC to Collect Pay Data on Employees

In 2016, the Equal Employment Opportunity Commission (EEOC) announced a new rule to add pay data to the EEO-1 report, a form it uses to gather information about the race, ethnicity, and gender of a company's employees in each job category. By requiring employers to provide information on their employees' wages and work hours, the EEOC hopes to detect and correct wage inequality based on protected characteristics. Only employers with 100 or more employees are required to submit the annual EEO-1 form. The new form is scheduled to be issued for the March 2018 reporting period. However, the current administration has expressed its plans to minimize government regulations, which could lead to reconsideration of the rule in the near future. For updates, check out this book's online companion page (see the introductory chapter for the link).

However, this doesn't mean that men and women must receive identical paychecks. The EPA requires workers to be paid at the same rate, not the same amount. If workers are paid on commission or by the piece, for example, they must be paid according to the same formula (for example, 10% of the company's gross profit on each sale or $1 per piece). But it's okay if one worker earns more than another because he or she was more productive (for instance, because the worker made more sales or turned out more work in a given pay period than other workers doing the same job).

Financial incentives for good performance work the same way. You can't offer only salesmen the opportunity to earn a bonus for high sales volume while denying the same opportunity to saleswomen.

Exceptions to the EPA

There are four exceptions to the EPA. Workers of one sex may be paid more for doing equal work if the difference is based on one of the four following factors:

- **Seniority.** Workers who have been with the company for a long time may be paid more than workers with shorter tenure, even if this results in workers of one sex making more than workers of the other.
- **Merit.** For example, if you give performance-based raises, you may give a higher raise to workers whose performance is better, regardless of gender.
- **Quantity or quality of production.** An employer may pay by the piece, for example, or pay higher rates for better quality work, as long as both men and women have the opportunity to earn this higher rate.
- **Any factor other than sex.** This "catchall" exception is intended to encompass the myriad reasons why one worker might be paid more than another—as long as they are unrelated to the worker's gender. For example, if you must pay a shift premium to entice workers to cover the night shift, that would not violate

the EPA. Nor would offering a worker a higher starting rate based on his or her salary at a previous job.

For a discussion of gender discrimination, see "Gender, Pregnancy, and Sexual Harassment" in Chapter 3.

Record-Keeping Requirements

Under the Fair Labor Standards Act, employers must keep records on wages, hours, deductions, and pay dates for all of their employees. These records must be kept for three years, even after a worker leaves the company.

Although employers must create administrative systems that properly preserve these records, the good news is that you are not required to keep them in any particular form. For example, you don't necessarily have to use a time clock, as long as you have some other method of reliably recording employees' work hours.

What Records Must Be Kept?

Generally, an employer must keep records showing all of the following for each employee:

- name, address, occupation, sex
- birth date, if the worker is under the age of 19
- Social Security number
- hour and day when the workweek begins
- total hours worked in each workday and workweek
- basis for calculating wages (for example by the hour or by piece rate)

- total daily or weekly regular earnings
- the worker's regular hourly pay rate in any week when the worker works overtime
- total overtime pay for each workweek
- any deductions from or additions to pay for each pay period
- total wages paid for each pay period, and
- date of the payment and the pay period covered for each payment.

Employers might be required to keep additional information for certain workers, including those who work at home, those who receive tips, those who live at the worksite, or those who earn the youth minimum wage.

State law might require employers to keep additional records or keep records for a longer period of time. To find out, contact your state labor department. (Contact information is available in the appendix.)

Penalties for Failure to Keep Records

If an employer doesn't keep records as required, an individual employee or the U.S. Department of Labor could sue the company for inadequate record keeping alone. However, these claims usually come up only in the context of a larger lawsuit (for failing to pay overtime or taking improper deductions from workers' paychecks, for example).

The real danger of failing to keep adequate records is that your company will be unable to prove that it complied with wage and hour laws if the government or an employee challenges its practices. For example, if the Department of Labor decides to audit your company, you won't have any proof that you are complying with the law. This might encourage the government to dig deeper into your company's employment practices, something you probably want to avoid.

In addition, if your company is unlucky enough to wind up on the wrong end of an employee lawsuit, it won't have records to prove the employee was paid properly. And once workers offer some evidence that they worked any hours for which they were not paid, the burden shifts to the company to prove its workers wrong. A company that hasn't kept records won't be able to meet this burden.

Legal Dos and Don'ts: Compensation and Hours

Do:

- **Require approval for overtime.** If your reports work overtime—even without your knowledge or permission—the company will have to pay them for it. Cut down on surprises by requiring employees to get your approval in advance. And discipline employees who continue to work unauthorized overtime (but still pay them the overtime).

- **Conduct an annual job classification audit.** Once a year, review the job titles, classifications, and actual responsibilities of the employees reporting to you. Make sure employees who are classified as exempt from wage and hour laws meet the legal requirements.

- **Keep proper records.** Companies must keep certain payroll records for three years. Failing to keep required records is not only against the law; it will also hinder your company's ability to defend itself if employees sue for unpaid wages.

Don't:

- **Give comp time.** It's illegal for private employers to use comp time, but some managers have an informal practice of allowing it anyway. Even if your employees would rather take comp time than be paid overtime, don't fall into this habit.

- **Pay more attention to job titles than job duties.** When it comes to eligibility for overtime and compliance with equal pay and other wage discrimination laws, job titles don't matter. It's what employees actually do on the job that determines your company's obligations.

- **Dock an exempt employee's pay.** Find another way to discipline exempt employees for poor performance or minor misconduct. If you reduce an exempt employee's salary for these reasons, you risk making that employee—and all other employees who work for you in the same job classification—eligible for overtime.

Test Your Knowledge

Questions

1. When setting pay for a position, you should build a spreadsheet to calculate the value of the job based on the average pay internally (at your company) and at similar jobs externally (at other companies). ☐ True ☐ False

2. You don't have to pay tipped employees a regular wage as long as they earn at least the minimum wage in tips. ☐ True ☐ False

3. Only employees who are paid by the hour are entitled to earn overtime. ☐ True ☐ False

4. Nonexempt employees must be paid for every hour spent traveling for business. ☐ True ☐ False

5. Employees who must stay at the worksite while waiting to be called for work are entitled to be paid for that time. ☐ True ☐ False

6. If my company allows one employee to work a flexible schedule, it must allow all employees to do so. ☐ True ☐ False

7. You can never pay an exempt employee less than his or her full salary. ☐ True ☐ False

8. You do not have to honor a wage garnishment order unless the employee gives you permission to withhold the money from his or her paycheck. ☐ True ☐ False

9. All men and women who hold the same position must receive the same pay. ☐ True ☐ False

10. Once an employee quits or is fired, you can recycle or destroy that employee's pay records. ☐ True ☐ False

Test Your Knowledge (continued)

Answers

1. False. To set pay, you should go through a multistep process that takes into account your company's budget, internal equity (what others in your company make), external market data (what other companies pay for similar positions), and the employee's bottom line. While averages will give you guidelines for setting pay, do not use them as absolutes.

2. False. Tipped employees must be paid at least $2.13 an hour under federal law, or more, if their tips combined with this wage don't add up to at least the minimum hourly wage. State laws often require employers to pay more, and some don't allow a tip credit at all.

3. False. The right to earn overtime is not determined by how the employee is paid, but by the employee's job duties. Salaried employees can be either exempt or nonexempt.

4. It depends on the length of the trip and when the travel takes place. An employee who takes a one-day trip is entitled to be paid for all hours spent traveling, less the employee's usual commute. An employee on an overnight trip is entitled to be paid only for travel that falls during the employee's regular daily work hours (including those hours on weekends).

5. True. Employees who must be on call at the worksite are entitled to be paid for that time.

6. False. You can allow only certain employees to work flexible schedules as long as you do not make your decision for an illegal reason, such as discrimination. Seniority, whether the job is suited to a flexible schedule, and accommodating a worker with a disability, for example, are all legally valid reasons why you might allow one employee but not another to work a flexible schedule.

7. False. There are limited circumstances in which you can dock an exempt employee's salary (if the employee takes family and medical leave or violates an important safety rule, for example).

8. False. You must honor valid wage garnishment orders, no matter how the employee feels about it.

9. False. Men and women who hold the same position can receive different compensation if the differential treatment is based on seniority, quantity or quality of work, merit, or any factor other than sex.

10. False. You must keep payroll records for three years after an employee leaves.

State Minimum Wage Laws for Tipped and Regular Employees

The chart below gives the basic state minimum wage laws. Depending on the occupation, the size of the employer's business, or the conditions of employment, the minimum wage may vary from the one listed here. Minimum wage rates in a number of states change from year to year; to be sure of your state's current minimum, contact your state department of labor or check its website, where most states have posted the minimum wage requirements. (See the appendix for contact information.) Also, some local governments have enacted ordinances that set an even higher minimum wage—contact your city or county government for more information.

"Maximum Tip Credit" is the highest amount of tips that an employer can subtract from the employee's hourly wage. An employer cannot take the full tip credit if the employee doesn't earn enough in tips to make the applicable minimum wage. If an employee's tips exceed the maximum tip credit, the employee gets to keep the extra amount.

"Minimum Cash Wage" is the lowest hourly wage that an employer can pay a tipped employee (assuming the employee makes enough in tips to make the applicable minimum wage).

State and Statute	Notes	Basic Minimum Hourly Rate (*=tied to federal rate)	Maximum Tip Credit	Minimum Cash Wage for Tipped Employee	Minimum Tips to Qualify as a Tipped Employee (monthly unless noted otherwise)
United States 29 U.S.C. § 206; 29 U.S.C. § 203	This is the current federal minimum wage	$7.25	$5.12	$2.13	More than $30
Alabama	No minimum wage law				
Alaska Alaska Stat. § 23.10.065	Adjusts annually for inflation, posted at http://labor.alaska.gov/lss/whact.htm	$9.80	No tip credit	$9.80	N/A
Arizona Ariz. Rev. Stat. § 23-363	Adjusts annually for inflation, posted at www.azica.gov/labor-minimum-wage-main-page; does not apply to small businesses (those with gross revenue of less than $500,000 that are exempt from federal minimum wage laws)	$10 ($10.50 on January 1, 2018; $11 on January 1, 2019)	$3.00	$7 ($7.50 on January 1, 2018; $8 on January 1, 2019)	
Arkansas Ark. Code Ann. §§ 11-4-210 and 11-4-212	Applies to employers with 4 or more employees	$8.50	$5.87 (increases as minimum wage increases)	$2.63	Not specified

State Minimum Wage Laws for Tipped and Regular Employees (continued)

State and Statute	Notes	Basic Minimum Hourly Rate (*=tied to federal rate)	Maximum Tip Credit	Minimum Cash Wage for Tipped Employee	Minimum Tips to Qualify as a Tipped Employee (monthly unless noted otherwise)
California *Cal. Lab. Code § 1182.12*		Employers with 25 or fewer employees: $10.50 (in 2018), and $11 (in 2019). Employers with 26 or more employees: $11 (in 2018) and $12 (in 2019).	No tip credit	Same as for non-tipped employees	N/A
Colorado *Colo. Const. Art. 18, § 15; 7 Colo. Code Regs. § 1103-1:3*	Adjusted annually for inflation, posted at www.coworkforce.com	$10.20 (in 2018) and $11.10 (in 2019)	$3.02	$7.18 (in 2018) and $8.08 (in 2019)	More than $30
Connecticut *Conn. Gen. Stat. Ann. §§ 31-58(j), 31-60; Conn. Admin. Code § 31-61-E2*		$10.10	36.8% for wait staff in hotel and restaurant industries; 18.5% for bartenders.	$6.38 for wait staff in hotel and restaurant industries; $8.23 for bartenders (increases as minimum wage increases)	$10 per week (full-time employees); $2 per day (part-time employees)
Delaware *Del. Code Ann. tit. 19, § 902(a)*		$8.25	$6.02	$2.23	More than $30
District of Columbia *D.C. Code Ann. § 32-1003*		$12.50 ($13.25 on July 1, 2018; $14.00 on July 1, 2019)	$9.17 (increases as minimum wage increases)	$3.33 ($3.89 on July 1, 2018; $4.45 on July 1, 2019)	Not specified

State Minimum Wage Laws for Tipped and Regular Employees (continued)

State and Statute	Notes	Basic Minimum Hourly Rate (*=tied to federal rate)	Maximum Tip Credit	Minimum Cash Wage for Tipped Employee	Minimum Tips to Qualify as a Tipped Employee (monthly unless noted otherwise)
Florida Fla. Const., Art. X § 24; Fla. Stat. Ann. § 448.110	Adjusted annually for inflation, posted at www.floridajobs.org	$8.10	$3.02	$5.08	More than $30
Georgia Ga. Code Ann. § 34-4-3	Applies to employers with 6 or more employees and more than $40,000 per year in sales	$5.15	Minimum wage does not apply to tipped employees	N/A	N/A
Hawaii Haw. Rev. Stat. §§ 387-1 to 387-2		$10.10	75¢, but only if the employee makes at least $7 more than minimum wage with tips	$9.35	More than $20
Idaho Idaho Code §§ 44-1502; 44-1503		$7.25	$3.90	$3.35	More than $30
Illinois 820 Ill. Comp. Stat. § 105/4; Ill. Admin. Code tit. 56, § 210.110	Applies to employers with 4 or more employees (and all employers with respect to domestic workers)	$8.25	40%	$4.95	At least $20
Indiana Ind. Code Ann. § 22-2-2-4	Applies to employers with 2 or more employees	$7.25*	$5.12	$2.13	Not specified
Iowa Iowa Code § 91D.1	In first 90 calendar days of employment, minimum wage is $6.35	$7.25	40%	$4.35	At least $30
Kansas Kan. Stat. Ann. § 44-1203	Applies to employers not covered by the FLSA	$7.25	$5.12	$2.13	Not specified

State Minimum Wage Laws for Tipped and Regular Employees (continued)

State and Statute	Notes	Basic Minimum Hourly Rate (*=tied to federal rate)	Maximum Tip Credit	Minimum Cash Wage for Tipped Employee	Minimum Tips to Qualify as a Tipped Employee (monthly unless noted otherwise)
Kentucky Ky. Rev. Stat. Ann. § 337.275		$7.25*	$5.12	$2.13	More than $30
Louisiana	No minimum wage law				
Maine Me. Rev. Stat. Ann. tit. 26, §§ 663(8), 664		$10.00; $11.00 on January 1, 2019	50%	$6.00; $7.00 on January 1, 2019	More than $30
Maryland Md. Code Ann., [Lab. & Empl.] §§ 3-413, 3-419		$9.25 ($10.10 on July 1, 2018)	$5.62 (increases as minimum wage increases)	$3.63	More than $30
Massachusetts Mass. Gen. Laws ch. 151, § 1; Mass. Regs. Code tit. 454, § 27.03		$11	$7.25	$3.75	More than $20
Michigan Mich. Comp. Laws §§ 408.412 to 408.424	Applies to employers with 2 or more employees. Beginning in 2019, the minimum wage will be adjusted annually according to the consumer price index.	$9.25	$5.52 (increases as minimum wage increases)	38% of the minimum wage, which is $3.38	Not specified
Minnesota Minn. Stat. Ann. § 177.24	Beginning in 2018, the minimum wage will be increased annually for inflation.	$9.50 for large employers; $7.75 for small employers (businesses with annual gross volume of sales of less than $500,000)	No tip credit	Same as for non-tipped employees	N/A
Mississippi	No minimum wage law				

State Minimum Wage Laws for Tipped and Regular Employees (continued)

State and Statute	Notes	Basic Minimum Hourly Rate (*=tied to federal rate)	Maximum Tip Credit	Minimum Cash Wage for Tipped Employee	Minimum Tips to Qualify as a Tipped Employee (monthly unless noted otherwise)
Missouri *Mo. Rev. Stat. §§ 290.502, 290.512*	Doesn't apply to retail or service business with gross annual sales of less than $500,000. Adjusted annually based on cost of living; posted at https://labor.mo.gov/DLS/MinimumWage.	$7.70	50%	$3.85	Not specified
Montana *Mont. Code Ann. §§ 39-3-404, 39-3-409; Mont. Admin. R. 24.16.1508 & following*	Federal minimum wage for businesses with gross annual sales of more than $110,000. $4.00 for others. Adjusted annually; posted at http://erd.dli.mt.gov/labor-standards/wage-and-hour-payment-act/minimum-wage-history	$8.15	No tip credit	$8.15	N/A
Nebraska *Neb. Rev. Stat. § 48-1203*	Applies to employers with 4 or more employees	$9	$6.87	$2.13	Not specified
Nevada *Nev. Rev. Stat. Ann. §§ 608.100, 608.160, 608.250; Nev. Admin. Code 608.100; Nev. Const. Art. 15 § 16*	Adjusted annually, posted at labor.nv.gov	$7.25 if employer provides health benefits; $8.25 if no health benefits provided	No tip credit	$7.25 if employer provides health benefits; $8.25 if no health benefits provided	N/A
New Hampshire *N.H. Rev. Stat. Ann. § 279:21*		$7.25*	55%	45%	More than $30
New Jersey *N.J. Stat. Ann. § 34:11-56a4*	Adjusted annually based on consumer price index; posted at http://lwd.dol.state.nj.us/labor	$8.44*	$6.31	$2.13 (suggested, not required)	Not specified

State Minimum Wage Laws for Tipped and Regular Employees (continued)					
State and Statute	Notes	Basic Minimum Hourly Rate (*=tied to federal rate)	Maximum Tip Credit	Minimum Cash Wage for Tipped Employee	Minimum Tips to Qualify as a Tipped Employee (monthly unless noted otherwise)
New Mexico *N.M. Stat. Ann. § 50-4-22*		$7.50	$5.37	$2.13	More than $30
New York *N.Y. Lab. Law § 652*		$10.40; $11.10 on December 31, 2018	Depends on occupation	Depends on occupation	Depends on occupation
North Carolina *N.C. Gen. Stat. §§ 95-25.2(14), 95-25.3*		$7.25	$5.12	$2.13	More than $20
North Dakota *N.D. Cent. Code § 34-06-22; N.D. Admin. Code R. 46-02-07-01 to -03*		$7.25	33% of minimum wage	$4.86	More than $30
Ohio *Ohio Rev. Code Ann. § 4111.02; Ohio Const. art. II § 34a*	Same as federal minimum wage for employers with gross income under $299,000; adjusted annually, posted at www.com.ohio.gov/dico	$8.15	50%	$4.08	More than $30
Oklahoma *Okla. Stat. Ann. tit. 40, §§ 197.2, 197.4, 197.16*	Applies to employers with 10 or more full-time employees OR gross annual sales over $100,000 not otherwise subject to FLSA	$7.25	50% of minimum wage for tips, food, and lodging combined	$3.63	Not specified
Oregon *Ore. Rev. Stat. §§ 653.025, 653.035(3)*	Adjusted annually; posted at www.boli.state.or.us	$10.25 ($10.75 on July 1, 2018; $11.25 on July 1, 2019)	No tip credit	$10.25 ($10.75 on July 1, 2018; $11.25 on July 1, 2019)	N/A

State Minimum Wage Laws for Tipped and Regular Employees (continued)					
State and Statute	Notes	Basic Minimum Hourly Rate (*=tied to federal rate)	Maximum Tip Credit	Minimum Cash Wage for Tipped Employee	Minimum Tips to Qualify as a Tipped Employee (monthly unless noted otherwise)
Pennsylvania *43 Pa. Cons. Stat. Ann. §§ 333.103 and 333.104; 34 Pa. Code §§ 231.1 and 231.101*		$7.25*	$4.42	$2.83	More than $30
Rhode Island *R.I. Gen. Laws §§ 28-12-3 & 28-12-5*		$9.60	$5.71	$3.89	Not specified
South Carolina	No minimum wage law				
South Dakota *S.D. Codified Laws Ann. §§ 60-11-3 to -3.1*	Adjusted annually based on cost of living; posted at http://dlr.sd.gov/employment_laws/minimum_wage.aspx	$8.65	50%	$4.33	More than $35
Tennessee	No minimum wage law				
Texas *Tex. Lab. Code Ann. §§ 62.051 & 62.052*		$7.25	$5.12	$2.13	More than $20
Utah *Utah Code Ann. § 34-40-102; Utah Admin. R. 610-1*		$7.25	$5.12	$2.13	More than $30
Vermont *Vt. Stat. Ann. tit. 21, § 384(a); Vt. Code R. 24 090 003*	Applies to employers with 2 or more employees; adjusted annually, posted at www.vtlmi.info	$10.50	50% for employees of hotels, motels, restaurants, and tourist places	$5.00 (increases as minimum wage increases)	More than $120
Virginia *Va. Code Ann. §§ 40.1-28.9 and 28.10*	Applies to employees not covered by FLSA	$7.25	Tips actually received	Minimum wage less tips actually received	Not specified

State Minimum Wage Laws for Tipped and Regular Employees (continued)					
State and Statute	**Notes**	**Basic Minimum Hourly Rate (*=tied to federal rate)**	**Maximum Tip Credit**	**Minimum Cash Wage for Tipped Employee**	**Minimum Tips to Qualify as a Tipped Employee (monthly unless noted otherwise)**
Washington *Wash. Rev. Code Ann. § 49.46.020; Wash. Admin. Code § 296-126-022*	Adjusted annually; posted at www.lni.wa.gov	$11.50; $12.00 on January 1, 2019	No tip credit	$11.50; $12.00 on January 1, 2019	N/A
West Virginia *W.Va. Code §§ 21-5C-1, 21-5C-2, 21-5C-4*	Applies to employers with 6 or more employees at one location who are not covered by the FLSA	$8.75	70% of minimum wage	$2.62 (increases as minimum wage increases)	Not specified
Wisconsin *Wis. Admin. Code DWD § 272.03*		$7.25	$4.92	$2.33	Not specified
Wyoming *Wyo. Stat. § 27-4-202*		$5.15	$3.02	$2.13	More than $30

State Overtime Rules

This chart covers private-sector employment only. The overtime rules summarized are not applicable to all employers or all employees. Occupations that generally are not subject to overtime laws include health care and attendant care, emergency medical personnel, seasonal workers, agricultural workers, camp counselors, nonprofits exempt under the FLSA, salespeople working on a commission, transit drivers, babysitters and other household workers, and many others. For more information, contact your state's department of labor and be sure to check its website, where most states have posted their overtime rules. (See appendix for contact details.)

Alabama

No state overtime rules that differ from FLSA.

Alaska

Alaska Stat. §§ 23.10.060 and following

Time and a half after x hours per DAY: 8

Time and a half after x hours per WEEK: 40

Employment overtime laws apply to: Employers of 4 or more employees; commerce or manufacturing businesses.

Notes: Voluntary flexible work hour plan of 10-hour day, 40-hour week, with premium pay after 10 hours is permitted.

Arizona

No state overtime rules that differ from FLSA.

Arkansas

Ark. Code Ann. §§ 11-4-211, 11-4-203

Time and a half after x hours per WEEK: 40

Employment overtime laws apply to: Employers of 4 or more employees.

Notes: Employees in retail and service establishments who spend up to 40% of their time on nonexempt work must be paid at least twice the state's minimum wage ($572 per week).

California

Cal. Lab. Code §§ 500 to 511; Cal. Lab. Code § 513; Cal. Code Regs. tit. 8, §§ 11010 and following

Time and a half after x hours per DAY: Eight; after 12 hours, double time. Agricultural employees only: after 10 hours per day (From 2019 to 2022, this will gradually decrease to eight hours per day.)

Time and a half after x hours per WEEK: 40. On 7th day: time and a half for the first 8 hours; after 8 hours, double time. Agricultural employees only: after 60 hours per week (From 2019 to 2022, this will gradually decrease to 40 hours per week.)

Notes: Employee may make written request to work make-up time for hours taken off for personal obligations. As long as total hours don't exceed 11 in a day or 40 in a week, employer won't owe daily overtime. Employer may not encourage or solicit employees to request make-up time. Employees may, by majority vote in a secret ballot election, opt for an alternative workweek of four 10-hour workdays, in which case the employer will not owe overtime.

Colorado

7 Colo. Code Regs. § 1103-1:4

Time and a half after x hours per DAY: 12 hours in one workday or 12 consecutive hours

Time and a half after x hours per WEEK: 40

Employment overtime laws apply to: Employees in retail and service, commercial support service, food and beverage, health & medical industries.

Connecticut

Conn. Gen. Stat. Ann. §§ 31-76b and 31-76c; Conn. Admin. Code § 31-62-E1

Time and a half after x hours per WEEK: 40. On 7th consecutive workday, time and a half for all hours worked.

State Overtime Rules (continued)

Notes: In restaurants and hotels, time-and-a-half pay required for the 7th consecutive day of work or for hours that exceed 40 per week.

Delaware

No state overtime rules that differ from FLSA.

District of Columbia

D.C. Code Ann. § 32-1003(c); D.C. Mun. Regs. tit. 7, § 906

Time and a half after x hours per WEEK: 40

Notes: Employees must be paid one hour minimum wage for each day a split shift is worked, but not if the employee lives on the premises.

Florida

No state overtime rules that differ from FLSA.

Georgia

No state overtime rules that differ from FLSA.

Hawaii

Haw. Rev. Stat. §§ 387-1; 387-3

Time and a half after x hours per WEEK: 40. Dairy, sugarcane, and seasonal agricultural work: 48 hours per week.

Notes: No employer shall employ any employee in split shifts unless all of the shifts within a period of twenty-four hours fall within a period of fourteen consecutive hours, except in case of extraordinary emergency.

Idaho

No state overtime rules that differ from FLSA.

Illinois

820 Ill. Comp. Stat. §§ 105/3(d), 105/4a

Time and a half after x hours per WEEK: 40

Employment overtime laws apply to: Employers with 4 or more employees (and all employers with respect to domestic workers)

Notes: Collective bargaining agreement ratified by Illinois Labor Relations Board may provide for different overtime provisions.

Indiana

Ind. Code Ann. § 22-2-2-4(k)

Time and a half after x hours per WEEK: 40

Notes: Collective bargaining agreements ratified by the NLRB may have different overtime provisions. Domestic service work is not excluded from overtime laws.

Iowa

No state overtime rules that differ from FLSA.

Kansas

Kan. Stat. Ann. § 44-1204

Time and a half after x hours per WEEK: 46

Kentucky

Ky. Rev. Stat. Ann. §§ 337.050, 337.285; 803 Ky. Admin. Regs. § 1:060

Time and a half after x hours per WEEK: 40

Louisiana

No state overtime rules that differ from FLSA.

Maine

Me. Rev. Stat. Ann. tit. 26, § 664(3)

Time and a half after x hours per WEEK: 40

Maryland

Md. Code Ann., [Lab. & Empl.] § 3-420

Time and a half after x hours per WEEK: 40; 48 hours for bowling alleys and residential employees caring for the sick, aged, intellectually disabled, or mentally ill in institutions other than hospitals; 60 hours for agricultural work that is exempt from the overtime provisions of the federal act.

State Overtime Rules (continued)

Massachusetts
Mass. Gen. Laws ch. 151, § 1A

Time and a half after x hours per WEEK: 40. Time and a half for work on Sunday and certain holidays (for retail employees).

Employment overtime laws apply to: All employers for 40 hours a week; employers with more than 7 employees for Sunday and holiday overtime.

Michigan
Mich. Comp. Laws §§ 408.412 and 408.414a

Time and a half after x hours per WEEK: 40

Employment overtime laws apply to: Employers of 2 or more employees.

Minnesota
Minn. Stat. Ann. § 177.25

Time and a half after x hours per WEEK: 48

Mississippi
No state overtime rules that differ from FLSA.

Missouri
Mo. Rev. Stat. §§ 290.500 and 290.505

Time and a half after x hours per WEEK: 40; 52 hours for seasonal amusement or recreation businesses.

Montana
Mont. Code Ann. §§ 39-3-405 and 39-3-406

Time and a half after x hours per WEEK: 40; 48 hours for students working seasonal jobs at amusement or recreational areas.

Nebraska
No state overtime rules that differ from FLSA.

Nevada
Nev. Rev. Stat. Ann. § 608.018

Time and a half after x hours per DAY: Eight, if (1) employee receives health benefits from employer and employee's regular rate of pay is less than 1½ times the minimum wage, or (2) employee does not receive health benefits from employer and employee's rate of pay is less than $12.375 per hour.

Time and a half after x hours per WEEK: 40

Notes: Employer and employee may agree to flextime schedule of four 10-hour days.

New Hampshire
N.H. Rev. Stat. Ann. § 279:21(VIII)

Time and a half after x hours per WEEK: 40

New Jersey
N.J. Stat. Ann. §§ 34.11-56a4 and 34.11-56a4.1

Time and a half after x hours per WEEK: 40

New Mexico
N.M. Stat. Ann. § 50-4-22(d)

Time and a half after x hours per WEEK: 40

New York
N.Y. Lab. Law §§ 160(3), 161; N.Y. Comp. Codes R. & Regs. tit. 12, § 142-2.2

Time and a half after x hours per WEEK: 40 for nonresidential workers; 44 for residential workers.

Notes: In some industries, employees must be given 24 consecutive hours off per week. See N.Y. Lab. Law § 161.

North Carolina
N.C. Gen. Stat. §§ 95-25.14, 95-25.4

Time and a half after x hours per WEEK: 40; 45 hours a week in seasonal amusement or recreational establishments.

North Dakota
N.D. Admin. Code § 46-02-07-02(4)

Time and a half after x hours per WEEK: 40; 50 hours per week, cabdrivers.

State Overtime Rules (continued)

Ohio

Ohio Rev. Code Ann. § 4111.03

Time and a half after x hours per WEEK: 40

Employment overtime laws apply to: Employers who gross more than $150,000 a year.

Oklahoma

No state overtime rules that differ from FLSA.

Oregon

Ore. Rev. Stat. §§ 652.020, 653.261, 653.265

Time and a half after x hours per WEEK: 40

Notes: Time and a half required after 10 hours a day in canneries, driers, packing plants, mills, factories, and manufacturing facilities.

Live-in domestic workers must receive time and a half for hours in excess of 44 per workweek.

Pennsylvania

43 Pa. Cons. Stat. Ann. § 333.104(c); 34 Pa. Code § 231.41

Time and a half after x hours per WEEK: 40

Rhode Island

R.I. Gen. Laws §§ 28-12-4.1 and following, 5-23-2(d)

Time and a half after x hours per WEEK: 40

Notes: Time and a half for Sunday and holiday work is required for most retail businesses (these hours are not included in calculating weekly overtime).

South Carolina

No state overtime rules that differ from FLSA.

South Dakota

No state overtime rules that differ from FLSA.

Tennessee

No state overtime rules that differ from FLSA.

Texas

No state overtime rules that differ from FLSA.

Utah

No state overtime rules that differ from FLSA.

Vermont

Vt. Stat. Ann. tit. 21, §§ 382, 384(b); Vt. Code R. § 24 090 003

Time and a half after x hours per WEEK: 40

Employment overtime laws apply to: Employers of 2 or more employees; doesn't apply to retail or service establishments, hotels, motels, or restaurants (among other industries).

Virginia

No state overtime rules that differ from FLSA.

Washington

Wash. Rev. Code Ann. § 49.46.130

Time and a half after x hours per WEEK: 40

West Virginia

W.Va. Code §§ 21-5c-1(e), 21-5c-3

Time and a half after x hours per WEEK: 40

Employment overtime laws apply to: Employers of 6 or more employees at one location.

Wisconsin

Wis. Stat. Ann. §§ 103.01, 103.02, 103.03; Wis. Admin. Code DWD §§ 274.01, 274.03, 274.04

Time and a half after x hours per WEEK: 40

Employment overtime laws apply to: Manufacturing, mechanical, or retail businesses; beauty parlors, laundries, restaurants, hotels; telephone, express, shipping, and transportation companies.

Wyoming

No state overtime rules that differ from FLSA.

State Meal and Rest Break Laws

Note: In many states, employees who qualify as professional, executive, or administrative workers are exempt from these meal and rest break requirements. Also, some states are not listed in this chart because they do not have general meal or rest break laws for employees in the private sector. However, some states have special break rules for specific occupations or industries, which are beyond the scope of this chart. For more information, contact your state labor department. (See the appendix for details.)

Alabama

Breast-feeding: No employment-specific laws. However, breast-feeding is allowed in any public or private location where the mother's presence is authorized.

Arkansas

Ark. Stat. Ann. § 11-5-116

Applies to: All employers.

Breast-feeding: Reasonable unpaid breaks to express breast milk; if possible, break time to run concurrently with other breaks.

California

Cal. Lab. Code §§ 512, 1030; Cal. Code Regs. tit. 8, §§ 11010–11170

Applies to: Employers in most industries.

Exceptions: Motion picture and other occupations. See wage orders, *Cal. Code Regs. tit. 8, §§ 11010 – 11160,* for additional exceptions.

Meal Break: 30 minutes, unpaid, after 5 hours, except employer and employee can agree to waive meal period if employee works 6 hours or less. Second 30-minute unpaid meal period when employee works more than 10 hours a day, except employer and employee can agree to waive the second meal period if the employee works 12 hours or less and

took the first meal period. On-duty paid meal period permitted when nature of work prevents relief from all duties and parties agree in writing.

Rest Break: Paid 10-minute rest period for each 4 hours worked or major fraction thereof; as practicable, in the middle of the work period; not required for employees whose total daily work time is less than 3½ hours.

Breast-feeding: Reasonable unpaid breaks to express breast milk; if possible, break time to run concurrently with other breaks.

Colorado

Colo. Code Regs. tit. 7 § 1103-1:7 and 1:8

Applies to: Retail and service, food and beverage, commercial support service, and health and medical industries.

Exceptions: Numerous exceptions are listed in the regulation.

Meal Break: 30 minutes, unpaid, after 5 hours of work; on-duty paid meal period permitted when nature of work prevents break from all duties.

Rest Break: Paid 10-minute rest period for each 4 hours or major fraction worked; if practical, in the middle of the work period.

Breast-feeding: Reasonable unpaid time to express breast milk for up to two years after child's birth.

Connecticut

Conn. Gen. Stat. Ann. §§ 31-51ii, 31-40w

Applies to: All employers, except as noted.

Exceptions: Employers who pay for rest breaks as described below, those with a written agreement providing other break rules, and those granted an exemption for reasons listed in statute.

Meal Break: 30 minutes, unpaid, after first 2 hours of work and before last 2 hours for employees who work 7½ or more consecutive hours.

State Meal and Rest Break Laws (continued)

Rest Break: As alternative to meal break, a total of 30 minutes paid in each 7½-hour work period.

Breast-feeding: Employee may use meal or rest breaks for breast-feeding or expressing breast milk.

Delaware

Del. Code Ann. tit. 19, § 707

Applies to: All employers, except as noted.

Exceptions: Employers with alternative written agreement and those granted exemptions specified in statute. Law does not apply to teachers.

Meal Break: 30 minutes, unpaid, after first 2 hours and before the last 2 hours, for employees who work 7½ consecutive hours or more.

Breast-feeding: Reasonable accommodations for limitations of a person related to pregnancy, childbirth, or a related condition may include break time and appropriate facilities for expressing breast milk.

District of Columbia

D.C. Code Ann. §§ 2-1402.82, 32–1231.01-32–1231.03

Applies to: All employers

Breast-feeding: Reasonable unpaid time to express breast milk; runs concurrently with other paid or unpaid breaks provided by employer. Employer must make reasonable efforts to provide a private, sanitary location (other than a toilet stall) for expressing breast milk. Employer must provide reasonable accommodations to nursing mothers, unless it would cause an undue hardship.

Florida

Breast-feeding: No employment-specific laws. However, breast-feeding is allowed in any public or private location where the mother's presence is authorized.

Georgia

Ga. Code Ann. § 34-1-6

Applies to: All employers.

Breast-feeding: At employer's discretion, reasonable unpaid break time to express breast milk. Breast-feeding is allowed in any public or private location where the mother's presence is authorized.

Hawaii

Haw. Rev. Stat. §§ 378-2, 378-91 to 93

Applies to: All employers.

Breast-feeding: Reasonable unpaid break time to express breast milk for one year after child's birth.

Illinois

820 Ill. Comp. Stat. §§ 140/3, 260/10

Applies to: All employers.

Exceptions: Employees whose meal periods are established by collective bargaining agreement.

Employees who monitor individuals with developmental disabilities or mental illness, or both, and who are required to be on call during an entire 8-hour work period; these employees must be allowed to eat a meal while working.

Meal Break: 20 minutes, no later than 5 hours after the beginning of the shift, for employees who work 7½ or more continuous hours. Hotel room attendants are entitled to a 30-minute meal break if they work at least 7 hours.

Rest Break: In addition to meal break, hotel room attendants must receive two paid 15-minute rest breaks, if they work at least 7 hours.

Breast-feeding: Reasonable unpaid break time to express breast milk.

Indiana

Ind. Code § 22-2-14

Applies to: Employers with 25 or more employees.

Breast-feeding: Employer must make reasonable efforts to provide a private space, other than a restroom, for an employee to express breast milk during nonworking hours.

State Meal and Rest Break Laws (continued)

Kansas

Kan. Admin. Reg. 49-30-3

Applies to: Employees not covered under FLSA.

Meal Break: Not required, but if less than 30 minutes is given, break must be paid.

Breast-feeding: No employment-specific laws. However, breast-feeding is allowed in any public or private location where the mother's presence is authorized.

Kentucky

Ky. Rev. Stat. Ann. §§ 337.355, 337.365; 803 KAR 1:065

Applies to: All employers, except as noted.

Exceptions: Written agreement providing different meal period; employers subject to Federal Railway Labor Act.

Meal Break: Reasonable off-duty period close to the middle of the shift; cannot be required to take it before the third or after the fifth hour of work. Coffee breaks and snack time do not count toward the meal break.

Rest Break: Paid 10-minute rest period for each 4-hour work period; rest period must be in addition to regularly scheduled meal period.

Breast-feeding: No employment-specific laws. However, breast-feeding is allowed in any public or private location where the mother's presence is authorized.

Maine

Me. Rev. Stat. Ann. tit. 26, § 601

Applies to: All employers, except those with fewer than 3 employees on duty who are able to take frequent breaks during the workday.

Exceptions: Collective bargaining or other written agreement between employer and employee may provide for different breaks.

Meal Break: 30 minutes after 6 consecutive hours of work, except in cases of emergency. Time may be unpaid if employee is completely relieved of duty.

Breast-feeding: Adequate unpaid time to express breast milk, or employee may use rest or meal time, for up to 3 years following childbirth.

Maryland

Md. Code Ann., Lab. & Empl. § 3-710

Applies to: Retail establishments with 50 or more retail employees.

Exceptions: Employees who work in an office or who work at a single location with 5 or fewer employees are not covered.

Meal Break: 30 minutes, unpaid, after 6 consecutive hours of work.

Rest Break: 15 minutes, unpaid, when working 4 to 6 consecutive hours. (This may be waived if the employee works less than 6 hours). Employees working 8 or more consecutive hours must receive a 15-minute unpaid break for every additional 4 consecutive hours after a meal break.

Breast-feeding: No employment-specific laws. However, breast-feeding is allowed in any public or private location where the mother's presence is authorized.

Massachusetts

Mass. Gen. Laws ch. 149, §§ 100, 101

Applies to: All employers, except as noted.

Exceptions: Excludes iron works, glass works, paper mills, letterpresses, print works, and bleaching or dyeing works. Attorney general may exempt businesses that require continuous operation if it won't affect worker safety. Collective bargaining agreement may also provide for different breaks.

Meal Break: 30 minutes, if work is for more than 6 hours.

Minnesota

Minn. Stat. Ann. §§ 177.253, 177.254, 181.939

Applies to: All employers.

Exceptions: Excludes certain agricultural and seasonal

State Meal and Rest Break Laws (continued)

employees. A collective bargaining agreement may provide for different rest and meal breaks.

Meal Break: Sufficient unpaid time for employees who work 8 consecutive hours or more.

Rest Break: Paid adequate rest period within each 4 consecutive hours of work to utilize nearest convenient restroom.

Breast-feeding: Reasonable unpaid break time to express milk.

Mississippi

Miss. Ann. Code § 71-1-55

Breast-feeding: Employee may use meal or rest break for expressing breast milk.

Missouri

Breast-feeding: No employment-specific laws. However, breast-feeding is allowed in any public or private location where the mother's presence is authorized.

Montana

Breast-feeding: No employment-specific laws. However, breast-feeding is allowed in any public or private location where the mother's presence is authorized.

Nebraska

Neb. Rev. Stat. §§ 48-212, 48–1102

Applies to: Meal break provisions: assembly plant, workshop, or mechanical establishment.

Breast-feeding provisions: employers with 15 or more employees.

Exceptions: Other written agreement between employer and employees.

Meal Break: 30 minutes off premises for each 8-hour shift.

Breast-feeding: Employers with 15 or more employees must provide reasonable accommodation

to nursing mothers, unless it would cause an undue hardship. Accommodation may include breaks and an appropriate location for expressing breast milk.

Nevada

Nev. Rev. Stat. Ann. § 608.019, AB 113, § 5

Applies to: Employers with two or more employees.

Exceptions: Employees covered by collective bargaining agreement; exemptions for business necessity.

Meal Break: 30 minutes for 8 continuous hours of work.

Rest Break: Paid 10-minute rest period for each 4 hours or major fraction worked; as practicable, in middle of the work period; not required for employees whose total daily work time is less than 3½ hours.

Breast-feeding: Reasonable unpaid breaks to allow an employee to express breastmilk for a child under one year of age. (Applies to: All employers. Exceptions: Employers with fewer than 50 employees, if complying would cause an undue hardship.)

New Hampshire

N.H. Rev. Stat. Ann. § 275:30-a

Applies to: All employers.

Meal Break: 30 minutes after 5 consecutive hours, unless the employer allows the employee to eat while working and it is feasible for the employee to do so.

New Mexico

N.M. Stat. Ann. § 28-20-2

Breast-feeding: Flexible unpaid breaks to use breast pump in the workplace.

New York

N.Y. Lab. Law §§ 162, 206-c

Applies to: Factories, workshops, manufacturing facilities, mercantile (retail and wholesale) establishments.

State Meal and Rest Break Laws (continued)

Meal Break: Factory employees, 60 minutes between 11 a.m. and 2 p.m.; mercantile employees, 30 minutes between 11 a.m. and 2 p.m. If a shift starts before 11 a.m. and ends after 7 p.m., every employee gets an additional 20 minutes between 5 p.m. and 7 p.m. If a shift starts between 1 p.m. and 6 a.m., a factory employee gets 60 minutes, and a mercantile employee gets 45 minutes, in the middle of the shift. Labor commissioner may permit a shorter meal break; the permit must be in writing and posted conspicuously in the main entrance of the workplace.

Breast-feeding: Reasonable unpaid break time to express breast milk for up to three years after child's birth.

North Carolina

Breast-feeding: No employment-specific laws. However, breast-feeding is allowed in any public or private location where the mother's presence is authorized.

North Dakota

N.D. Admin. Code § 46-02-07-02

Applies to: Applicable when two or more employees are on duty.

Exceptions: Waiver by employee or other provision in collective bargaining agreement.

Meal Break: 30 minutes for each shift over 5 hours; unpaid if employee is completely relieved of duties.

Breast-feeding: No employment-specific laws. However, breast-feeding is allowed in any public or private location where the mother's presence is authorized.

Oklahoma

Okla. Stat. Ann. tit. 40, § 435

Breast-feeding: Reasonable unpaid breaks to breast-feed or express breast milk.

Oregon

Ore. Rev. Stat. 653.077; Ore. Admin. R. §§ 839-020-0050, 839-020-0051

Applies to: All employers except as noted.

Exceptions: Agricultural workers and employees covered by a collective bargaining agreement.

Meal Break: 30 minutes for employees who work at least six hours, unpaid if relieved of all duties; paid time to eat if employee cannot be relieved of duty; a shorter paid break (but no less than 20 minutes), if employer can show that it is industry practice or custom. If shift of 7 hours or less, meal break must occur between hours 2 and 5; if shift longer than 7 hours, meal break must be between hours 3 and 6.

Rest Break: Paid 10-minute rest period for each 4 hours or major fraction worked; if practical, in the middle of the work period. Rest period must be in addition to usual meal break and taken separately; can't be added to meal period or deducted from beginning or end of shift to reduce length of total work period. Rest period is not required for certain solo adult employees serving the public, although they must be allowed to use restroom.

Breast-feeding: Employers with 25 or more employees must provide a 30-minute unpaid break for every 4 hours worked to express breast milk, for up to 18 months after child's birth.

Pennsylvania

43 P.S. § 1301.207

Applies to: Employers of seasonal farmworkers.

Meal Break: Seasonal farm workers are entitled to a 30-minute meal or rest break if they work at least 5 hours.

Breast-feeding: No employment-specific laws. However, breast-feeding is allowed in any public or private location where the mother's presence is authorized.

State Meal and Rest Break Laws (continued)

Rhode Island

R.I. Gen. Laws §§ 28-3-8, 28-3-14, 23-13.2-1, 28–5–7.4

Applies to: Meal break provisions: employers with 5 or more employees. Breast-feeding provisions: employers with 4 or more employees.

Exceptions: Employers of health care facility or employers with fewer than 3 employees on any shift.

Meal Break: 20 minutes, unpaid, within a 6-hour shift or 30 minutes, unpaid, within an 8-hour shift.

Breast-feeding: Reasonable unpaid break time to breast-feed infant or express breast milk. Employers with 4 or more employees must provide reasonable accommodations to nursing mothers, which may include break time and private space for expressing breast milk, other than a restroom.

South Carolina

Breast-feeding: No employment-specific laws. However, breast-feeding is allowed in any public or private location where the mother's presence is authorized.

South Dakota

Breast-feeding: No employment-specific laws. However, breast-feeding is allowed in any public or private location where the mother's presence is authorized if the mother is in compliance with all other laws.

Tennessee

Tenn. Code Ann. §§ 50-2-103(h), 50-1-305

Applies to: Employers with 5 or more employees.

Meal Break: 30 minutes unpaid for employees scheduled to work 6 consecutive hours or more, unless workplace environment provides ample opportunity for appropriate meal break. Tipped employees who work in food or beverage service may waive right to meal break if employee requests waiver, knowingly and voluntarily, in writing, and employer consents. Employer may not coerce employee into waiving right to meal break. Employer must post waiver policy that includes a form stating the employee's right to a break, how long the waiver will last, and how the employee or employer may rescind the waiver.

Breast-feeding: Reasonable unpaid break time to express breast milk.

Texas

Breast-feeding: No employment-specific laws. However, breast-feeding is allowed in any public or private location where the mother's presence is authorized.

Vermont

Vt. Stat. Ann. tit. 21, § 304

Applies to: All employers.

Meal Break: Employees must be given reasonable opportunities to eat and use toilet facilities during work periods.

Rest Break: Employees must be given reasonable opportunities to eat and use toilet facilities during work periods.

Breast-feeding: Reasonable time to express breast milk for up to three years after the child's birth. Breaks can be paid or unpaid. Employer not required to provide breaks if it would substantially disrupt its operations.

Virginia

Breast-feeding: No employment-specific laws. However, breast-feeding is allowed in any public or private location where the mother's presence is authorized.

Washington

Wash. Admin. Code §§ 296-126-092, 296-131-020

Applies to: All employers except as noted.

State Meal and Rest Break Laws (continued)

Exceptions: Newspaper vendor or carrier, domestic or casual labor around private residence, sheltered workshop; separate provisions for agricultural labor.

Meal Break: 30-minute break, if work period is more than 5 consecutive hours, not less than 2 hours nor more than 5 hours from beginning of shift. This time is paid if employee is on duty or is required to be at a site for employer's benefit. Employees who work 3 or more hours longer than regular workday are entitled to an additional half hour, before or during overtime.

Agricultural employees: 30 minutes if working more than 5 hours; additional 30 minutes if working 11 or more hours in a day.

Rest Break: Paid 10-minute rest break for each 4-hour work period, scheduled as near as possible to midpoint of each work period. Employee cannot be required to work more than 3 hours without a rest break. Scheduled rest breaks not required where nature of work allows employee to take intermittent rest breaks equivalent to required standard.

West Virginia

W.Va. Code § 21-3-10a

Applies to: All employers.

Meal Break: At least 20-minute break for each 6 consecutive hours worked, unless employees are allowed to take breaks as needed or to eat lunch while working.

Rest Break: Rest breaks of 20 minutes or less must be counted as paid work time.

Wisconsin

Wis. Admin. Code § DWD 274.02; Wis. Stat. Ann. § 103.935.

Applies to: *Wis. Admin. Code § DWD 274.02* (all employers); *Wis. Stat. Ann. § 103.935* (migrant workers)

Meal Break: For most workers, 30-minute meal period is recommended but not required. Meal period should be close to usual meal time or near middle of shift. Shifts of more than 6 hours without a meal break should be avoided. If employee is not free to leave the workplace or relieved of all duties for at least 30 minutes, meal period is considered paid time. For migrant workers employed exclusively in agricultural labor, 30-minute meal period required after 6 continuous hours of work, unless the shift can be completed in an additional hour.

Rest Break: For migrant workers not employed exclusively in agricultural labor, rest period of at least 10 minutes within each 5 hours of continuous employment.

Breast-feeding: No employment-specific laws. However, breast-feeding is allowed in any public or private location where the mother's presence is authorized.

Discrimination

Discrimination is a negative force in any setting in American culture, but it's particularly destructive when it occurs in the workplace, where an individual's livelihood is at stake. Discrimination undermines employee loyalty, destroys employee morale, and reduces productivity and work quality. It can also lead to costly and painful lawsuits and cause irreparable harm to a company's reputation.

In addition to the obvious moral and ethical reasons to prevent discrimination, it makes good business sense for employers to keep discrimination out of the workplace. The burdens of preventing and remedying discrimination fall heavily on managers; after all, you are the ones who represent the company to its employees, have an opportunity to see what's really going on in the workplace, and are responsible for important personnel decisions that could form the basis for a discrimination lawsuit.

This chapter provides an overview of the kinds of employment discrimination that federal and state laws prohibit, tips on how you can prevent discrimination and harassment in your workplace, and what to do if an employee complains of discrimination.

Antidiscrimination Laws

Discrimination becomes a legal issue only when a state or federal law or local ordinance declares that a characteristic is "protected."

Once that happens, an employer subject to the law cannot base employment decisions on that characteristic.

To know what forms of discrimination are prohibited, you must know a little about your federal, state, and local laws. Some of these laws apply only to businesses of a particular size (for example, five or more employees). In addition, each state's law is slightly different. For example, some states prohibit discrimination on the basis of sexual orientation, while others do not. To learn which characteristics are protected by your state antidiscrimination laws, see "State Laws Prohibiting Discrimination in Employment," at the end of this chapter.

Employer Duties Under Antidiscrimination Laws

In addition to not discriminating against its own employees, an employer must take steps to prevent discrimination at the workplace. And when discrimination does occur, the company must act quickly to stop it.

This means employers must:

- have policies that prohibit discrimination and tell employees what to do if they experience discrimination
- make sure its managers and supervisors don't discriminate
- make sure its policies and procedures don't have an unfair impact on a protected group of people (discussed in more detail below)

Frequently Asked Questions About Discrimination

What types of discrimination are illegal in the workplace?

If a characteristic is specifically listed in a federal or state antidiscrimination law, or even in a local ordinance, then it is illegal to discriminate against someone on the basis of that characteristic. Under federal law, employers may not discriminate on the basis of race, color, national origin, religion, sex, disability, age (40 and older only), genetic information, or citizenship status. State and local laws might prohibit discrimination on the basis of additional characteristics, such as marital status or sexual orientation. (See "Antidiscrimination Laws," above, for more information.)

Can we require employees to speak only English when customers are present?

An English-only rule is allowed only if it is necessary for business reasons and is not too restrictive. For example, a rule that requires employees to speak English to English-speaking customers is probably fine. However, a rule that prohibits employees from speaking another language to each other or with customers who speak that language is probably not. (See "Race and National Origin," below, for more information.)

Is it age discrimination to hire a younger applicant who knows a broad range of cutting-edge computer programs over an older applicant who barely understands word processing?

No. You are not discriminating when you choose the most qualified candidate for a position. As long as the job requires the type of computer skills the younger applicant has, you're on safe ground. Age discrimination problems arise when you make assumptions based on age. For example, if you simply assumed that the older applicant didn't have up-to-date computer skills but he or she was actually a technology whiz, you could get into trouble. (For more information, see "Age," below.)

Can I choose to reassign a pregnant employee to a job that requires less physical work or travel?

Generally, no. Unless the employee requests an accommodation or reassignment, you cannot force one upon her. As long as a pregnant employee can perform her job duties, treating her differently based solely on her pregnancy is a form of sex discrimination. (For more information, see "Gender, Pregnancy, and Sexual Harassment," below.)

Is it illegal to receive genetic information about an employee if we didn't request it?

Generally, no. Although the Genetic Information Nondiscrimination Act (GINA) makes it illegal for employers to acquire genetic information about employees and their family members, there's an exception for information you receive inadvertently. For example, if an employee tells you that he has a genetic condition or you overhear a conversation about it, that doesn't violate the law. This exception also applies if you receive genetic information from a health-care provider in response to a lawful request for medical information (for example, as part of an FMLA certification), as long as you tell the provider not to give you genetic information. GINA supplies suggested language you can use to tell providers not to include genetic information. (For more on these rules, see "Genetic Information," below.)

Frequently Asked Questions About Discrimination (continued)

Our company has a largely gay clientele; can we give an edge in hiring to gay and lesbian applicants?

As a legal matter, it depends on the laws of your city and state. More than 20 states, the District of Columbia, and many cities and counties prohibit discrimination in private workplaces on the basis of sexual orientation. These laws apply equally to heterosexuals and homosexuals. Even if this type of discrimination isn't prohibited where you do business, however, discrimination is never a good idea. It can lead to other types of lawsuits, bad publicity, and more. And really, what should be important to your company is that employees understand the needs of its primarily gay customers, not whether the employees are gay themselves. (See "Sexual Orientation," below, for more information.)

Do we have to let a religious employee take his or her Sabbath day off?

It depends on how that would affect your company. Employers are required to reasonably accommodate their employees' religious practices, unless it would cause undue hardship. If it's relatively easy to switch employee schedules around, you are probably legally obligated to give this employee the day off. On the other hand, if no other employees are willing to work that day and employee schedules depend on seniority, this employee might not have the right to an accommodation. (See "Religion," below, for more information.)

If an employee with a disability asks for a specific reasonable accommodation, do we have to provide it?

Not necessarily. Once an employee asks for an accommodation, the employer must brainstorm with the employee to figure out what kinds of accommodations might work. However, you don't have to provide the exact accommodation the worker requests, nor do you have to provide an accommodation if it would cause your company undue hardship. (For information on accommodating disabilities, see "Disability," below.)

- investigate complaints of discrimination (see "Investigating Complaints" in Chapter 11), and
- take effective action against those who discriminate.

All of this might sound complicated, but it really isn't. If you and the company's other managers base all of your employment decisions on criteria related to the job, that's half the battle. If someone does complain about discrimination, or if prejudicial behavior otherwise comes to your attention, follow your company's reporting policies. And don't retaliate or allow retaliation against the victim.

Federal Antidiscrimination Laws

The main federal laws that managers should be aware of are:

- Title VII of the Civil Rights Act ("Title VII")
- the Age Discrimination in Employment Act (ADEA)
- the Equal Pay Act (EPA)
- the Immigration Reform and Control Act (IRCA)
- the Americans with Disabilities Act (ADA), and
- the Genetic Information Nondiscrimination Act (GINA).

We describe each of these laws below. Some laws apply to all employers, while others apply only to employers of a certain size. However, even if your company is so small that some of these federal laws don't apply, that's not a license to discriminate. Not only is it bad business, but it also might violate a state law that covers smaller employers.

Although they each protect different characteristics, federal antidiscrimination laws have a lot in common:

- **They prohibit retaliation.** All of the federal laws (and most state laws) prohibit employers from retaliating against applicants or employees who assert their rights under the law. For example, an employer cannot fire someone for complaining about race discrimination. This is an area where managers can really get into trouble, because they are often the ones deciding whether to separate, move, discipline, or otherwise take action that affects the employees involved. To learn more about this issue, see "Retaliation" in Chapter 11.
- **They cover the entire employment relationship.** The federal laws prohibit discrimination in all terms, conditions, and privileges of employment, including hiring, firing, compensation, benefits, job assignments, shift assignments, promotions, discipline, and more.
- **They prohibit neutral practices that harm a protected group.** Each law prohibits employer practices that seem neutral but have a disproportionate or unfair impact on a protected group of people. A neutral practice that has an unfair impact on a certain group is legal only if the employer has a valid business reason for using it. For example, a strength requirement for a job might be legal—even though it could exclude a disproportionately high number of women from that job—if an employer is filling a position for which lifting a certain amount is a requirement, such as a job in the logging industry. A strength requirement would not, however, be valid for a desk job.
- **Harassment is always a no-no.** In addition to prohibiting discrimination on the basis of the listed characteristics, all of the laws prohibit harassment based on those characteristics as well.

Title VII of the Civil Rights Act of 1964

Title VII of the Civil Rights Act of 1964 (Title VII) prohibits employers from discriminating on the basis of:

- race
- color
- religion
- sex (including pregnancy and childbirth), or
- national origin (including membership in a Native American tribe).

A very narrow exception to Title VII allows an employer to discriminate on the basis of religion, sex, or national origin (but not race or color) if a characteristic is intrinsic to the job, called a "bona fide occupational qualification" or BFOQ in legal lingo. For example, if you need to hire an actor to play the role of Hamlet's mother or you need to hire attendants for a women's restroom, you can discriminate against men in filling these positions. However, to rely on this exception, an employer must be able to show that no member of the group it discriminated against could meet the requirements of the job, which is a very tough standard to meet.

Title VII applies to:

- private employers with 15 or more employees
- state governments and their political subdivisions and agencies

- the federal government
- employment agencies
- labor organizations, and
- joint labor-management committees and other training programs.

The Age Discrimination in Employment Act

The Age Discrimination in Employment Act (ADEA) prohibits discrimination against employees who are age 40 or older. It does not protect people who are younger than 40 from being discriminated against on the basis of age. (Some state laws do, however.)

The ADEA applies to:

- private employers with 20 or more employees
- the federal government and its agencies
- interstate agencies
- employment agencies, and
- labor unions.

Although state government workers are protected by the ADEA, they do not have the right to sue their employers (the state for which they work) in court to enforce their rights. Only the Equal Employment Opportunity Commission (EEOC), the federal agency that interprets and enforces the ADEA, may sue a state to protect state employees from age discrimination. (To learn more about age discrimination, see "Age," below.)

The Equal Pay Act

The Equal Pay Act (EPA) requires that employers provide men and women with equal pay for substantially equal work. It applies to all employers, regardless of size. For more about this law, see "Equal Pay" in Chapter 2.

The Immigration Reform and Control Act of 1986

The Immigration Reform and Control Act of 1986 (IRCA) prohibits employers from discriminating against applicants or employees on the basis of citizenship or national origin. On the flip side, however, the IRCA also makes it illegal for employers to knowingly hire or employ people who are not legally authorized to work in the United States. Employers must keep records verifying that their employees are authorized to work in the United States (using Form I-9).

The IRCA applies to employers with four or more employees. For more information, see "Race and National Origin," below.

The Americans with Disabilities Act

The Americans with Disabilities Act (ADA), prohibits employers from discriminating against a person with a disability in any aspect of employment.

The ADA applies to:
- private employers with 15 or more employees
- local governments and their agencies
- employment agencies, and
- labor unions.

Employees of the federal government are protected from disability discrimination by a different law (the Rehabilitation Act). Like the ADEA, the ADA protects state employees, but those employees do not have the right to sue their state in court. Only the EEOC may sue a state to protect its employees from disability discrimination.

Genetic Information Nondiscrimination Act

The most recent addition to the civil rights laws is named GINA: the Genetic Information Nondiscrimination Act. GINA prohibits health insurers from using genetic information to deny insurance coverage or determine premiums. It also prohibits covered employers from making employment decisions based on an applicant's or employee's genetic information, and it requires employers to keep employee genetic information confidential.

GINA applies to:
- private employers with 15 or more employees
- the federal government
- state governments
- private and public employment agencies
- labor organizations, and
- joint labor-management committees.

Race and National Origin

Employment discrimination on the basis of race or national origin still happens more often than anyone wants to believe. It exacts a very high price, both from its victims and from the companies where it occurs. Recent lawsuits prove the point: Large companies have paid millions of dollars to compensate victims of race and national origin discrimination and to pay for their own complicity in encouraging or allowing a discriminatory atmosphere to flourish in the workplace.

Race Discrimination

An employer commits race discrimination when it makes job decisions on the basis of race or when it adopts seemingly neutral job policies that disproportionately affect members of a particular race.

Federal and state laws forbid race discrimination in every aspect of the employment relationship, including hiring, firing, promotions, compensation, job training, or any other term or condition of employment. For example, an employer discriminates when it refuses to hire Latinos, promotes only white employees to supervisory positions, requires only African American job applicants to take drug tests, or refuses to allow Asian American employees to deal with customers.

Which Federal Antidiscrimination Laws Apply to Your Company?

Not every antidiscrimination law applies to every employer. Federal antidiscrimination laws apply only to private employers with more than a minimum number of employees, and the minimum number is different for each law.

Name of Law:	Discrimination Prohibited on the Basis of:	Applies to:
Title VII	Race, color, religion, sex, or national origin	Employers with 15 or more employees
Age Discrimination in Employment Act	Age (age 40 or older)	Employers with 20 or more employees
Americans with Disabilities Act	Physical or mental disability	Employers with 15 or more employees
Equal Pay Act	Sex (wage discrimination only)	All employers
Immigration Reform and Control Act	Citizenship status, national origin	Employers with 4 or more employees
Genetic Information Nondiscrimination Act	Genetic information	Employers with 15 or more employees

An employer that discriminates on the basis of physical characteristics associated with a particular race—such as hair texture or color, skin color, or facial features—also commits race discrimination.

Even employment policies or criteria that seem to be neutral are discriminatory if they have a disproportionate impact on members of a particular race. For example, a height requirement might screen out disproportionate numbers of Asian American and Latino job applicants. Or an employment policy requiring men to be clean-shaven might discriminate against African American men, who are more likely to suffer from pseudofolliculitis barbae (a painful skin condition caused and exacerbated by shaving).

Rules or policies that have a disproportionate impact on people of a certain race will pass legal muster only if the employer can show that there is a legitimate and important work reason for the policy. For example, a height requirement might be legitimate if the company can show that an employee must be at least a certain height to operate a particular type of machinery.

National Origin Discrimination

An employer discriminates on the basis of national origin when it makes employment decisions based on a person's ancestry, birthplace, or culture, or on linguistic characteristics or surnames associated with a particular ethnic group. For example, an employer that refuses to hire anyone with a Hispanic-sounding last name is discriminating, as is an employer who won't allow anyone with an accent to work with the public.

Language Rules

An employer may prohibit on-duty employees from speaking any language other than English, but only if it can show that the rule is necessary for business reasons. If your company has an English-only rule, you must tell employees when they have to speak English (for example, whenever customers are present) and the consequences of breaking the rule. And, if an employee challenges the English-only rule, the company will have to defend the rule's scope. A rule that forbids workers from ever speaking another language, even during breaks or when a customer who speaks that language is present, is probably too broad.

Accent Rules

Because an employee's accent is often associated with his or her national origin, employers must tread carefully when making employment decisions based on accent. An employer may decide not to hire or promote an employee to a position that requires oral communication in English only if the employee's accent substantially affects his or her ability to communicate clearly. However, if the employee's accent does not impair his or her ability to be understood, you may not make job decisions on that basis. For example, a company cannot adopt a blanket rule that employees who speak accented English may not work in customer service positions.

Lessons From the Real World

A federal judge in Dallas ordered a Texas company to pay its Spanish-speaking workers $700,000 in damages for requiring them to speak only English on company premises. The judge found that the policy discriminated against the workers based on their national origin.

The company's policy prohibited workers from speaking Spanish during lunch, on breaks, when making personal telephone calls, and before and after work if they were in the building. The rule even prevented a Spanish-speaking husband and wife from speaking Spanish to each other when they ate lunch together. In fact, the only time employees were allowed to speak Spanish was when serving the company's Spanish-speaking customers.

The company disciplined and terminated employees who violated the policy. Even employees who tried to follow the policy but occasionally slipped up and allowed a Spanish word or phrase to enter into the conversation were disciplined.

Because the company could not provide a legitimate reason for such a broad rule, the court held that it was discriminating on the basis of national origin.

Equal Employment Opportunity Commission v. Premier Operator Services, Inc., 113 F.Supp.2d 1066 (N.D. Texas 2000).

Companies Pay the Price for Discrimination

Companies have been hit with huge verdicts—or have agreed to pay massive settlements—to employees who have been discriminated against or harassed on the basis of race or national origin. For example:

- Consolidated Freightways Corporation of Delaware agreed to pay $2.75 million to settle a racial harassment lawsuit filed by the EEOC. Twelve African American employees alleged that they were subjected to racial intimidation, threats, assault, racist graffiti, and property damage, among other things.

- The Equal Employment Opportunity Commission (EEOC) announced a $50 million settlement of a race and sex discrimination lawsuit against the clothing retail company Abercrombie & Fitch. Among the allegations was a claim that the clothier refused to hire female and nonwhite applicants because they did not fit the image or "look" the company was trying to project in the marketplace.

- Coca-Cola settled a class action race discrimination lawsuit for $192.5 million. African American employees said that Coke imposed a racial "glass ceiling" by discriminating against them in pay and promotions. Of the total settlement, $36 million was earmarked for monitoring the company's employment practices to make sure that the discrimination stopped.

Lessons From the Real World

In 2006, a California jury awarded two Federal Express drivers more than $61 million in damages, one of the largest verdicts in the nation that year. The drivers, who were Lebanese American, claimed that they were harassed and discriminated against based on their national origin. They said that their manager called them offensive names, such as "terrorists," "camel jockeys," and "Hezbollah," and that the company did nothing to stop the harassment, despite repeated complaints.

The jury awarded the drivers even more than they requested, ordering FedEx to pay them $5 million each in compensatory damages and $25 million each in punitive damages. The jury also ordered the manager who harassed them to pay more than $500,000 to each driver.

Although a judge later reduced the jury award, finding it excessive, the drivers still received a substantial sum in damages. FedEx was ordered to pay around $12.4 million in damages, while the manager was ordered to pay $400,000 to the drivers.

"Top Ten Jury Verdicts of 2006: Lebanese-American FedEx Drivers Win Workplace Harassment Suit," by Dick Dahl (*Lawyers USA*).

Harassment Based on Race or National Origin

Harassment on the basis of race and national origin is also prohibited. Harassment is unwelcome conduct based on a person's race or national origin that is severe or frequent enough to create an intimidating, hostile, or offensive work environment or that must be endured as a condition of continued employment. Harassing conduct might include racial slurs, jokes about a particular ethnic group, comments or questions about a person's cultural habits, or physical acts of particular significance to a certain racial or ethnic group, such as posting an offensive picture or hanging an offensive object near an employee's workspace, like a swastika or noose.

Age

There's a saying: "Hire a young doctor and an old lawyer." A young doctor, the theory holds, will have cutting-edge skills and knowledge of all the latest research and techniques; the old lawyer will have the experience and gravitas needed to convince a jury. If the adage resonates with you, you are not alone: Stereotypes based on age fill our culture, from the irresponsible, beer-loving college student to the stale and slow, 60-something middle manager.

While the stereotypes may abound, it is illegal for your company to act on such age-based preconceptions when making employment decisions. A number of state and federal laws prohibit discrimination and harassment against employees and applicants because of age.

The Age Discrimination in Employment Act

The Age Discrimination in Employment Act (ADEA) is the major federal law that addresses age discrimination. This law prohibits employers from discriminating against employees and applicants who are 40 years of age or older. It does not, however, prohibit discrimination against people who are younger than 40. (Some state laws do; see the discussion below.) If you are a private employer with 20 or more employees, you must follow the ADEA.

The ADEA prohibits discrimination in all phases of the employment relationship, except benefits and early retirement, which are addressed by a different law. (See "Discrimination in Benefits," below.) Not only does the ADEA prohibit you from discriminating against older workers in favor of those who are younger than 40, it also prohibits you from discriminating among older workers who are protected by the act. For example, you can't hire a 43-year-old instead of a 53-year-old simply because of age.

The ADEA also prohibits seemingly neutral employment practices that have a disparate impact on older workers, although the rules for these cases are slightly different than for other types of discrimination claims. In a disparate impact age discrimination case, the employee must point to a specific employment practice (such as a policy, screening test, or job requirement) that led to the disparate impact. And, the employer can escape liability if it can prove that its practice was based on a reasonable factor other than age.

To prove that it relied on a reasonable factor other than age (RFOA), the employer must show both that the factor was reasonably designed to achieve a legitimate business purpose, and that the employer applied the factor in a way that reasonably achieves that purpose. The EEOC has stated that the following items should be considered when deciding whether an employer's practice or policy counts as an RFOA:

- the extent to which the factor is related to the employer's stated business purpose
- the extent to which the employer defined the factor accurately and applied it fairly, including whether managers and supervisors received training as to how to apply the factor in making decisions in order to avoid discrimination
- the extent to which the employer limited supervisors' discretion to evaluate employees subjectively, particularly if the factor is known to be subject to negative stereotypes based on age
- the extent to which the employer assessed the adverse impact of its practice on older employees, and
- how much the practice harmed older workers (in severity and number) and whether the employer took steps to reduce that harm, given the burden involved in taking such steps.

The ADEA also prohibits workplace harassment on the basis of age.

State Laws

Many state laws also prohibit discrimination on the basis of age. Although some of these laws mirror the federal law and only protect people 40 and older, other laws are broader and protect workers of all ages.

State laws tend to cover employers with fewer than 20 employees, so you might have to comply with your state law even if your company isn't covered by the federal law. To find out more about the age discrimination law in your state, see "State Laws Prohibiting Discrimination in Employment," at the end of this chapter.

Discrimination in Benefits

The federal Older Workers Benefit Protection Act (OWBPA) makes it illegal to use an employee's age as a basis for discrimination in benefits. Like the ADEA, this act only protects people who are at least 40 years old. Also like the ADEA, this act applies to private employers with 20 or more employees, government employers, and unions.

The OWBPA prohibits age discrimination in the provision of fringe benefits, such as life insurance, health insurance, disability benefits, pensions, and retirement benefits. Typically, this means that employers must provide equal benefits to older and younger workers. For some types of benefits, however, employers can meet this nondiscrimination requirement by spending the same amount on the benefit provided to each group, even if older workers receive lesser benefits. In some circumstances, employers are also allowed to provide lesser benefits to older workers if those workers receive additional benefits— from the government or the employer—to make up the difference. Because these rules can get complicated, you'll need to talk to a lawyer to make sure you're in compliance.

Waivers

The ADEA also imposes special rules on waivers of the right to sue for age discrimination. A waiver (sometimes called a release or an agreement not to sue) of ADEA rights is valid only if it is knowing and voluntary. To meet this standard, the waiver must:

- be part of a written agreement between the employer and employee
- be written in language understandable to the employee
- specifically refer to the employee's rights or claims under the ADEA
- not require the employee to waive any rights or claims that may arise after the agreement is signed, and
- give the employee something of value (for example, a severance package) in exchange for the waiver, beyond anything to which the employee is already entitled.

Employers must advise employees, in writing, to consult with an attorney before signing a waiver. They must also give employees 21 days to consider the agreement (or 45 days, if the waiver is part of an exit incentive program offered to a group of employees) and seven days to revoke the agreement after signing. Additional rules apply to exit incentive programs or other termination programs offered to a group of employees.

Gender, Pregnancy, and Sexual Harassment

As with race or national origin discrimination, employment discrimination on the basis of sex still takes place with surprising regularity today. Despite federal and state laws prohibiting discrimination on the basis of sex—which the law defines to include pregnancy and related conditions—employers still make the mistake of making decisions along gender lines or treating pregnant employees differently just because they are pregnant. Such mistakes can cost a company dearly in lawsuit judgments and settlements.

Gender and Pregnancy Discrimination

An employer commits sex discrimination when it makes job decisions on the basis of sex or pregnancy or when it adopts seemingly neutral job policies that disproportionately affect members of one gender.

Federal and state laws forbid sex discrimination in every aspect of the employment relationship, including hiring, firing, promotions, compensation, job training, or any other term or condition of employment. For example, an employer discriminates based on gender when it promotes only men to supervisory positions, hires only women to work in tipped service positions, denies only women the chance to participate in training opportunities, or reassigns pregnant employees to "dead-end" positions based on the assumption that they won't return to work after giving birth.

Even employment policies or criteria that seem to be neutral are discriminatory if they have a disproportionate impact on members of a particular gender. For example, a height or strength requirement might screen out disproportionate numbers of female job applicants. Such rules or policies will pass legal muster only if the employer can show that there is a legitimate and important work reason for the policy. For example, a strength requirement might be legitimate if the employee needs to be able to lift a certain amount of weight in order to load and transport heavy goods on a regular basis.

When it comes to pregnancy, you can avoid sex discrimination by following two basic rules: (1) Do not make any decisions about the employee based solely on the fact that she is pregnant; and (2) treat pregnant employees the same way you would treat any other temporarily disabled employees, such as a worker who had surgery. If your pregnant employee is able to perform her job duties, you may not reassign her or change any of her job duties or any other term or condition of her job simply because she is pregnant.

If she is having trouble performing her job duties due to pregnancy-related conditions (for example, extreme nausea or medically required bed rest), under basic federal anti-discrimination law you must treat her as you would any nonpregnant, temporarily disabled worker. For instance, if you offer light duty or paid time off to workers who are injured on the job, you typically must offer your pregnant employee the same type of accommodation on the same terms.

Beyond Title VII, however, your pregnant employee might have additional rights under the federal and/or state family and medical leave laws or under additional state laws that protect pregnant workers or require transfer or reasonable accommodation if the worker requests it. For more information, see "Family and Medical Leave" and "Pregnancy and Parental Leave" in Chapter 5, and contact your state labor and fair employment agencies. (Contact information is included in the appendix.)

Supreme Court Addresses Accommodation for Pregnant Employees

Peggy Young was working for United Parcel Service (UPS) as a driver when she became pregnant with her first child. On the advice of her doctor, Young told UPS that she could not lift more than 20 pounds and asked to be accommodated. UPS refused, telling Young that heavy lifting was an essential part of her job. After she was placed on unpaid leave and lost her medical benefits, Young sued UPS.

Under federal law, employers must treat pregnant employees the same as other employees who are "similar in their ability or inability to work." Young produced evidence that UPS provided light duty to other employees, including those who were injured on the job and those who had lost their driving certifications by the Department of Transportation. Because UPS accommodated these employees, Young argued that she was entitled to accommodation. UPS, however, argued that it provided accommodations only to a specific subset of employees who were limited in their ability to work. UPS did not accommodate a number of other employees, including those who had suffered off-the-job injuries. Because it wasn't singling out pregnant employees for worse treatment, UPS argued that it was not required to accommodate Young.

The Supreme Court held that employers don't necessarily need to accommodate pregnant employees any time they accommodate a group of nonpregnant workers. However, they must have a legitimate, nondiscriminatory reason for doing so. The fact that it might be more expensive or inconvenient to accommodate pregnant employees is not a legitimate reason for different treatment. In light of these guidelines, the Supreme Court remanded the case to the lower court to decide whether UPS had a sufficiently strong reason for accommodating some employees, but not pregnant employees. *Young v. UPS*, 135 S.Ct. 1338 (2015).

Sexual Harassment

Sexual harassment is a form of sex discrimination. As with sex discrimination, Title VII is the main federal law that prohibits sexual harassment. (See "Antidiscrimination Laws," above.) In addition, each state has its own law prohibiting sexual harassment.

Sexual harassment is any unwelcome sexual advance or conduct on the job that must be endured as a condition of continued employment or that is severe or frequent enough to create an intimidating, hostile, or offensive working environment. Any conduct of a sexual nature that makes an employee uncomfortable has the potential to be sexual harassment. Sexual harassment can also include harassment that is not sexual in nature, but is based on one's gender. This type of harassment often takes place when women enter workplaces that have been traditionally male dominated and are belittled and treated poorly because they are women.

Given such a broad definition, it is not surprising that sexual harassment comes in many forms. The following are all examples of sexual harassment:

- A supervisor implies to an employee that the employee must go on a date with him or her to receive a promotion. (In legal lingo, this is sometimes called "quid pro quo" harassment.)
- Employees regularly tell sexually explicit jokes within earshot of the office manager, who finds the jokes offensive.
- A cashier at a store pinches and fondles a coworker against the coworker's will.
- Several employees post sexually explicit jokes on an office intranet bulletin board.
- An employee sends emails to coworkers that contain sexually explicit language and jokes.
- A male sales clerk makes demeaning comments about female customers to his coworkers.
- A secretary's coworkers belittle her and refer to her by sexist or demeaning terms.
- The only woman on an otherwise all-male construction crew routinely has her work tools taken or damaged by her male coworkers.

The harasser can be the victim's supervisor, manager, or coworker. The harasser can even be a nonemployee, such as a customer or a vendor.

Anyone Can Be Sexually Harassed

Although it might sound counterintuitive, sexual harassment knows no gender: Men can sexually harass women, and women can sexually harass men. Men can also sexually harass men, and women can sexually harass women. This is sometimes referred to as "same-sex harassment."

Same-sex harassment does not need to be motivated by sexual desire. For example, courts have held that sexual harassment occurs when a male employee is subjected to sex-related comments or actions by male coworkers in an attempt to humiliate him. The rules on same-sex harassment can get complicated, though, especially when it appears that the victim was targeted due to his or her sexual orientation—which is not a protected class under Title VII. In other words, a male employee who is harassed for being gay is not protected, but a male employee who is harassed because of his gender (or for not living up to gender stereotypes) is protected. Sound confusing? That's because the courts are still trying to figure out how to handle same-sex harassment. (For more information, see "Sexual Orientation," below.)

The bottom line is that you should try to prevent harassment in any form, regardless of where it falls on the legal spectrum. For information on how you can—and should—prevent sexual harassment in the workplace, see "Preventing Sexual Harassment" in Chapter 4.

Genetic Information

Although more than half of the states ban genetic discrimination, federal law didn't prohibit genetic discrimination by private employers until relatively recently. The Genetic Information Nondiscrimination Act (GINA), passed in 2008, makes it illegal for employers to gather or use genetic information, and it requires employers to maintain the confidentiality of any genetic information they obtain through legal means.

The nondiscrimination provision is fairly straightforward: Employers may not make employment decisions based on an employee's or applicant's genetic information, or the

Navigating GINA's Safe Harbor for Discrimination

If your company requests medical information about employees (for example, to support an employee's request for a reasonable accommodation under the ADA or request for medical leave under the FMLA), it might receive genetic information in response. This will be considered inadvertent—and fall within the first exception to GINA—as long as your company tells the information provider, up front, not to give you genetic information. The final regulations interpreting GINA suggest using the following language to make sure you gain the protection of this safe harbor:

"The Genetic Information Nondiscrimination Act of 2008 (GINA) prohibits employers and other entities covered by GINA Title II from requesting or requiring genetic information of an individual or family member of the individual, except as specifically allowed by this law. To comply with this law, we are asking that you not provide any genetic information when responding to this request for medical information. 'Genetic information' as defined by GINA, includes an individual's family medical history, the results of an individual's or family member's genetic tests, the fact that an individual or an individual's family member sought or received genetic services, and genetic information of a fetus carried by an individual or an individual's family member or an embryo lawfully held by an individual or family member receiving assistive reproductive services."

genetic information of an employee's or applicant's family member. Genetic information includes the results of genetic tests or the manifestation of a particular disease or disorder in the employee's family. For example, an employer may not refuse to hire an applicant because she carries BRCA1 or BRCA2 (the genes thought responsible for most inherited breast cancers) or fire an employee because he carries the trait for sickle cell anemia. Whether the employer is motivated by stereotypes or stigma associated with the disease or by a desire to reduce health care costs, decisions like these are illegal.

Acquiring Genetic Information

With a few exceptions, GINA prohibits employers from requiring or asking employees to provide genetic information (for example, by requiring genetic testing as a condition of employment). Employers also may not purchase genetic information about employees or their family members.

As explained below, there are a handful of exceptions to the general prohibition on acquiring genetic information from employees. Even if one of these exceptions applies, however, employers may not use the genetic information as a basis for employment decisions. Employers must also keep the information confidential as explained in "Confidentiality of Genetic Information," below.

Here are some of the exceptions that are most likely to apply, although there are others as well:

1. The employer acquires genetic information "inadvertently." This exception is intended to cover casual conversations among coworkers, overheard comments, information volunteered by employees, or unsolicited emails (for example, a request that coworkers sponsor an employee on a walkathon to support research into a particular genetic disease).

2. The employer acquires the information through health or genetic services it offers (as part of a wellness program, for example), but only if all of the following are true:
   - The health or genetic services are reasonably designed to promote health or prevent disease.
   - Providing information is voluntary, meaning that employees are not required to provide it or penalized for choosing not to provide it. Employers cannot offer financial inducements to employees in exchange for their genetic information. (There is a limited exception to this rule for the employee's spouse, but not the employee's children.)
   - The employee gives prior, knowing, voluntary, and written authorization for the services.
   - Only the employee or family member receiving services, along with the genetic counselor or health care professional

involved in providing the services, receives individually identifiable information about the results.

- Any individually identifiable information resulting from the services is available only for the purpose of those services and is not disclosed to the employer except in aggregate terms that don't reveal individual identities.

3. The employer requires family medical history from the employee to comply with the certification requirements of the Family and Medical Leave Act (see Chapter 5) or a similar requirement under a state family and medical leave law, or an employer policy.

4. The employer gets the information from documents that are commercially and publicly available. This exception applies to newspapers, magazines, and books, for example, but not to medical databases or court records. This exception doesn't apply if the employer accesses these sources with the intent to gather employee genetic information or was likely to acquire genetic information from viewing them.

Confidentiality of Genetic Information

Employers that have genetic information about an employee must keep it on separate forms and in separate files, and treat it as a confidential medical record. This means the employer must treat this information as it treats medical information under the ADA:

The information must be kept separately from regular personnel files and revealed only in limited circumstances to certain people (for example, to government officials investigating the company's compliance with the law).

Lessons From the Real World

Although GINA has been on the books for nearly a decade, the first case to go trial is believed to be in 2015. A few years prior, Atlas Logistics Group Retail Services—a company that stores groceries for retail stores—was facing an unpleasant workplace issue: It appeared that someone was repeatedly defecating in one of its warehouses. As part of its investigation to catch the so-called "devious defecator," Atlas collected saliva samples from several of its employees in hopes of matching the DNA to the fecal matter. Two of the employees, who were ultimately exonerated by the DNA results, sued their employer for illegally collecting their genetic information in violation of GINA. A jury found in favor of the two employees, slapping Atlas with a verdict of over $2.2 million. The majority of the award was for punitive damages, intended to punish the employer for what appeared to be a blatant violation of the law. (The award was later reduced by a judge to $300,000 for each employee, the maximum allowed under the law.)

Lowe v. Atlas Logistics Group Retail Services (Atlanta), LLC, 102 F.Supp.3d 1360 (N.D. Ga. 2015); Lauren Walker, "False Poop Tests Lead to $2.2 Million Lawsuit," *Newsweek* (June 25, 2015).

Genetic information may be disclosed only in the following circumstances:

- to the employee or family member to whom the information pertains, on written request
- to an occupational or health researcher for research conducted in compliance with Part 46 of Title 45 of the Code of Federal Regulations (these are the Department of Health and Human Services' rules for the protection of human research subjects)
- in response to a court order, but the employer may disclose only the genetic information expressly authorized by that order. If the court order was obtained without the employee's or family member's knowledge, the employer must notify the employee or family member of the order and of any genetic information that was disclosed as a result.
- to government officials investigating compliance with GINA, if the information is relevant to the investigation
- in connection with the employee's compliance with the certification requirements of the Family and Medical Leave act or a similar state law
- to a government health agency, but only information about the manifestation of a disease or disorder in an employee's family member that concerns a contagious disease that presents an imminent hazard of death or life-threatening illness. The employer must inform the employee of the disclosure.

Sexual Orientation and Gender Identity

Traditionally, LGBT employees have had little protection from discrimination and harassment in the workplace. Times are changing, however, and protections for gay, lesbian, and transgender employees have grown in recent years.

Under federal antidiscrimination laws, sexual orientation and gender identity are not protected classes. However, there are some situations in which courts have allowed LGBT employees to sue for employment discrimination under federal law. In these cases, an LGBT employee alleges that he or she was discriminated against for not conforming to gender stereotypes. For example, a gay employee who was harassed by male coworkers for being too "effeminate" was allowed to sue for sex discrimination. In another case, a transgender employee was allowed to sue for sex discrimination when she was fired by her employer after revealing her plans to transition from a male to female and beginning to dress more femininely.

Based on what it saw as a growing trend by the courts, the EEOC has taken the position in recent years that all discrimination based on sexual orientation or gender identity necessarily violates Title VII's prohibition against sex discrimination. Consistent with this position, the EEOC has pursued cases against employers for discrimination on these grounds. In 2015 alone, the EEOC received over 1,400 charges of discrimination based on sexual orientation and gender identity.

So far, two federal appeals courts have weighed in on this issue, at least with regard to sexual orientation. The U.S. Court of Appeals for the Eleventh Circuit recently ruled that Title VII does not prohibit discrimination based on sexual orientation. (*Evans v. Georgia Reg'l Hosp.*, 850 F.3d 1248 (11th Cir. 2017).) Only weeks later, the U.S. Court of Appeals for the Seventh Circuit ruled the opposite. (*Hively v. Ivy Tech Cmty. Coll. of Indiana*, 853 F.3d 339 (7th Cir. 2017).) The U.S. Department of Justice recently filed papers in a case before the Second Circuit, advocating the court to hold that Title VII does not prohibit sexual orientation discrimination. This area of law is still in flux. Legal updates will be posted on this book's online companion page. (For the link, see the introductory chapter.)

Supreme Court Rulings on Same-Sex Marriage

In 2013, the Supreme Court struck down part of the Defense of Marriage Act (DOMA), which defined marriage, for federal purposes, as a union between one man and one woman. (*United States v. Windsor*, 133 S.Ct. 2675 (2013).) Although the case was about whether a same-sex spouse could take advantage of the spousal exclusion for purposes of the federal estate tax, the Court's decision to remove the "one man and one woman" restriction applied much more broadly.

In the employment field, the DOMA decision meant that same-sex spouses could not be excluded from federal laws that provide benefits to married couples. For example, under the federal Family and Medical Leave Act, an eligible employee may take time off work to care for a spouse with a serious health condition. As a result of the DOMA decision, employers cannot prevent an employee from taking FMLA leave to care for a same-sex spouse.

However, the DOMA decision applied only to federal benefits. It did not prohibit states from outlawing same-sex marriage. In these states, employers could still discriminate against same-sex spouses in providing benefits under state laws.

In 2015, the Supreme Court took same-sex marriage rights one step further by legalizing same-sex marriages in all 50 states. (*Obergefell v. Hodges*, 135 S.Ct. 2584 (2015).) As a result, same-sex spouses can no longer be excluded from benefits provided to married couples under state laws.

It's important to note that the Supreme Court rulings do not make sexual orientation a protected class under federal antidiscrimination laws. In other words, they do not give gay and lesbian employees any additional rights to sue their employers for discrimination. However, the decisions will likely lead to further challenges under Title VII, asking courts to declare once and for all that discrimination on the basis of "sex" includes sexual orientation discrimination. It remains to be seen whether these challenges will be successful.

State and Local Laws

A number of state and local laws expressly prohibit private employers from discriminating on the basis of sexual orientation and gender identity. Almost half the states prohibit sexual orientation discrimination in private employment, along with the District of Columbia, and numerous cities and counties also prohibit sexual orientation discrimination in the workplace.

To find out whether your state, county, or city has this type of law, see "State Laws Prohibiting Discrimination in Employment," below.

Religion

The federal law against religious discrimination has two components: The law prohibits employers from discriminating based on someone's religion (for example, that an employee is Jewish, Catholic, Muslim, or Baptist), and it requires employers to accommodate a person's religious practices and beliefs (for example, if an employee needs time after lunch to pray or if an employee needs Saturdays off to observe the Sabbath).

The first part is fairly simple. You can't refuse to hire someone, decide to promote someone, or make any other employment decisions because of the person's religion.

The second part is more complicated. You must work with employees to make it possible for them to practice their religious beliefs, within reason. This might mean not scheduling an employee to work on a Sabbath day or relaxing a company dress code so that an employee can wear religious garments. The only time an employer does not have to accommodate an employee is when it would pose an undue hardship for the business. For instance, if changing an employee's schedule to accommodate a religious belief would wreak havoc on your company's seniority-based scheduling system and cause serious morale problems among other employees, you might not have to accommodate the worker.

As with many legal terms, it can be tough to figure out exactly what "accommodation" and "hardship" mean in the practical context of your workplace. The following sections look at the meaning of these terms.

Accommodation

If an employee has a sincere religious belief that conflicts with an employment rule or requirement, the law requires you to accommodate the employee's beliefs, working with the employee to find a way around the conflict. This does not mean that you have to accept any accommodation that the employee suggests. If you don't like the employee's idea, you can suggest one of your own. In this way, the two of you should engage in a negotiation process that balances the employee's religious rights with your need for the job to get done.

Examples of reasonable accommodations include:

- flexible scheduling
- changes to a grooming or dress code
- splitting shifts, and
- transferring an employee to a different position.

Undue Hardship

You do not have to make an accommodation for an employee's religious beliefs that will cause your company an undue hardship. This means that you can deny an accommodation that would:

- cost too much money (anything more than a minor cost is too much when it comes to religious accommodations)
- substantially harm the morale of other employees (in other words, more than mere grumbling), or
- substantially disrupt work routines.

Expression of Religious Beliefs

Some employees wish to—or believe that their religion requires them to—express their religious beliefs in the workplace by, for example, posting religious messages in their workspaces, using religious language (such as "God bless you" or "Praise the Lord") when communicating with others, or attempting to proselytize coworkers. In these situations, it can be difficult to balance the rights of the religious employee with the rights of others who do not share that employee's beliefs.

Employers Must Offer Accommodation When a Religious Need Is Suspected

Do applicants and employees need to explicitly request a religious accommodation? Or is it enough that the employer suspects the need for accommodation? The U.S. Supreme Court answered these questions in a recent case involving a young Muslim woman who was denied employment with Abercrombie & Fitch.

The famed retailer declined to hire Samantha Elauf because she wore a hijab—a religious headscarf—to her interview. According to Abercrombie, the headscarf violated its "look policy," which did not allow head wear of any kind. However, instead of discussing the look policy with Elauf and considering accommodations, Abercrombie simply refused to hire her. Elauf sued, alleging that Abercrombie discriminated against her due to her religion.

In its defense, Abercrombie argued that it didn't have actual knowledge that Elauf needed a religious accommodation because she never requested one. However, the Supreme Court rejected this argument, holding that actual knowledge is not a requirement. It was enough that Abercrombie suspected that Elauf needed a religious accommodation and refused to hire her on that basis.

Equal Employment Opportunity Commission v. Abercrombie & Fitch Stores, Inc., 135 S.Ct. 2028 (2015).

Lessons From the Real World

As part of a workplace diversity program, Hewlett Packard hung posters of employees, including one featuring an employee who was labeled as gay. In response, employee Richard Peterson posted passages from the Bible condemning homosexuality. Peterson claimed that he had a duty to expose evil and that he intended the messages to be hurtful to his gay and lesbian coworkers whom he hoped would read the messages, repent, and be saved.

After Peterson was fired for refusing to take down the passages, he sued for discrimination on the basis of religion. A federal Court of Appeals rejected his claim. The court found that Peterson's desire to express his religious beliefs could not be accommodated without requiring his employer to allow other employees to be demeaned.

Peterson v. Hewlett-Packard, 358 F.3d 599 (9th Cir. 2004).

According to the EEOC, employers must allow employees to engage in religious expression as long as it doesn't create an undue hardship. And, employers may not restrict religious expression more heavily than other forms of expression that have a similar impact on workplace efficiency.

What do these rules mean in practice? Unfortunately, it's not entirely clear. Some courts have held that an employer has no duty to accommodate an employee's religious expression when it could constitute harassment against other employees or it contravenes the employer's diversity or nondiscrimination policies. On the other hand, some courts have found in the employee's favor when his or her behavior was merely "annoying" or created mild discomfort for others. In light of this confusion, the best practice is to consult with a lawyer if an employee's religious expression is causing others to feel uncomfortable.

Disability

The federal Americans with Disabilities Act (ADA) and similar state laws prohibit discrimination against employees and applicants with disabilities and require employers to accommodate them unless it would cause an undue hardship.

Who Is Covered

The ADA and most state laws protect "qualified workers with disabilities." A qualified worker is someone who can perform the essential duties of the job, with or without some form of reasonable accommodation from the employer.

A worker who falls into one of the following three categories is considered disabled under the ADA:

- The worker has a physical or mental impairment that substantially limits a major life activity (such as the ability to walk, talk, see, hear, breathe, reason, work, or take care of oneself) or a major bodily function (such as the proper functioning of the immune system, brain, or respiratory system). Impairments that are episodic or in remission qualify as disabilities if they substantially limit a major life activity when active.

- The worker has a record or history of impairment. In other words, you may not make employment decisions based on an employee's past disability.
- The employer regards the worker—even incorrectly—as having a disability. In other words, you can't treat workers less favorably because you believe that they have disabilities, even if you are wrong.

In addition, for an impairment to be a disability under the ADA, it must be long-term. Temporary impairments, such as pregnancy or broken bones, are not covered by the ADA (but they might be covered by other laws; for example, see "Gender and Pregnancy Discrimination," above).

Measures an employee takes or uses to mitigate the effects of a disability may not be considered in determining whether the employee's impairment limits major life activities or major bodily functions. For example, an employee might have a serious condition that is largely controlled by medication. When considering whether that employee has a disability, the employer must look at the employee's condition as it would be if the employee were not using medication to control it. The only exception to this rule is for the corrective power of ordinary prescription glasses and contact lenses,

which may be considered when determining whether an employee has a disability.

Reasonable Accommodation

Accommodating a worker means providing assistance or making changes to the job or workplace that will enable the worker to do the job. For example, an employer might change the height of a desktop to accommodate a worker in a wheelchair, provide TTY telephone equipment for a worker whose hearing is impaired, or provide a quiet, distraction-free workspace for a worker with attention deficit disorder.

It is the employee's responsibility to inform you of his or her disability and request a reasonable accommodation; managers are not legally required to guess at what might help the employee do the job. However, once an employee reveals a disability, you must engage in what the law calls a "flexible interactive process," which is essentially a brainstorming dialog with the worker to figure out what kinds of accommodations might be effective and practical. Your company does not have to provide the precise accommodation the worker requests, but you must work together to come up with a reasonable solution.

However, you don't have to provide an accommodation if it would cause your company "undue hardship": significant difficulty or expense given the circumstances. (Note that this is a higher standard to meet than the standard for religious accommodation, as described above.) For instance, if the cost of an accommodation would eat up an entire year's profits (building a new wing on an office building, for example), it isn't required. Whether implementing an accommodation qualifies as undue hardship depends on a number of factors, including:

- the cost of the accommodation
- the size and financial resources of the business
- the structure of the business, and
- the effect the accommodation would have on the business.

Your company and the employee might have different opinions about what constitutes a reasonable accommodation and what would be an undue hardship. If you're unsure whether a disabled employee is entitled to a specific accommodation, you might want to get some legal help from a lawyer.

Alcohol and Drugs

Alcohol and drug use pose special problems under the ADA. Employees who use (or have used) alcohol or drugs might have disabilities under the law. However, an employer can require these employees to meet the same work standards—including not drinking or using drugs on the job—as everyone else.

Here are some guidelines to follow when dealing with these tricky issues:

- **Alcoholism.** Alcoholism is a disability covered by the ADA. This means that an employer cannot fire or discipline a worker simply because he or she is an alcoholic. However, an employer can fire or discipline an alcoholic worker for failing to meet work-related performance and behavior standards imposed on all employees, even if the worker fails to meet these standards because of drinking.
- **Illegal drug use.** The ADA does not protect employees who currently use or are addicted to illegal drugs. These workers do not have disabilities within the meaning of the law and therefore don't have the right to be free from discrimination or to receive a reasonable accommodation. However, the ADA does cover workers who are no longer using illegal drugs and have successfully completed (or are currently participating in) a supervised drug rehabilitation program.
- **Use of legal drugs.** If an employee is taking prescription medication or over-the-counter drugs to treat a disability, you must reasonably accommodate that employee's use of drugs and the side effects that the drugs have on the employee.

For more information, see "Drugs and Alcohol" in Chapter 7.

Legal Dos and Don'ts: Discrimination

Do:

- **Use only job-related criteria when making decisions.** If you always have sound business reasons for your actions, employees are less likely to complain of discrimination, and much less likely to win any discrimination claims they might make.
- **Keep an open door.** The more comfortable employees are talking to you about problems and concerns, the more likely they are to come to you for help rather than running to a lawyer. Communication is the best way to nip problems in the bud.
- **Act out of enlightened self-interest.** Most managers want to keep their companies out of trouble. But if you need a little more incentive to refrain from engaging in harassing or discriminatory behavior, remember this: In some states, managers can be held personally liable for harassment or discrimination they commit themselves.

Don't:

- **Hurt by helping.** Although it might seem like a good idea to move a victim out of a discriminatory or harassing environment, even well-intentioned actions taken against a victim might constitute retaliation. Solve these types of problems by moving the accused, not the accuser.
- **Drag your feet.** When you don't take immediate action to stop discrimination or harassment, you cost the company money. Allowing misconduct to continue causes morale and productivity to drop, and it could set your company up to lose a million-dollar lawsuit.
- **Jump to conclusions.** Always report claims of discrimination and harassment. Managers get in trouble when they assume that they know what happened, that their employees wouldn't lie to them, or that "it could never happen here," for instance.

Test Your Knowledge

Questions

1. Only large companies need to worry about complying with antidiscrimination laws. ☐ True ☐ False

2. Once a manager learns about discrimination, he or she should report it immediately, even if the employee is reluctant to come forward. ☐ True ☐ False

3. It is illegal to consider an employee's accent when filling a position, even if the job requires extensive customer communication. ☐ True ☐ False

4. It is discriminatory to hire or promote an employee based on age, even if all of the applicants are over the age of 40. ☐ True ☐ False

5. If an employee voluntarily reveals that he or she has a particular genetic disease, you may take that information into account when making decisions about promotions and other employment matters. ☐ True ☐ False

6. You may require an employee to accept a light-duty position if she is pregnant. ☐ True ☐ False

7. Because no federal law prohibits discrimination based on sexual orientation, employers are free to discriminate against gay and lesbian applicants or employees. ☐ True ☐ False

8. You are never allowed to take an employee's religion into account when making employment decisions. ☐ True ☐ False

9. As a manager, you are responsible for asking your reports whether they have disabilities and whether they need accommodations to do their jobs. ☐ True ☐ False

10. An employee can sue your company for disability discrimination even if he or she does not have a disability. ☐ True ☐ False

Test Your Knowledge (continued)

Answers

1. False. Some federal antidiscrimination laws apply to very small companies. And every state has an antidiscrimination law; some of these laws apply to every employer in the state, regardless of size.

2. True. Once you know about discrimination, the company is legally obligated to take steps to stop it, even if the employee who tells you about it doesn't want to come forward.

3. False. If an employee's accent is so pronounced that it seriously impairs the employee's ability to be understood, you may refuse to place that employee in a position that requires strong communication skills.

4. True. If you hire a 45-year-old applicant rather than a 65-year-old applicant because of age, that's discriminatory.

5. False. Even if the employee provides the information voluntarily, you may not make employment decisions based on genetic information.

6. False. As long as the employee is able to work her usual job, you may not move her simply because she is pregnant.

7. False. Some federal courts have interpreted Title VII's prohibition against sex discrimination to include discrimination based on sexual orientation. A number of states, the District of Columbia, and many cities and counties also expressly prohibit discrimination on the basis of sexual orientation. And, even if it's not prohibited in your region, making decisions based on an employee's sexual orientation—or any other factor unrelated to work—can lead to other kinds of trouble.

8. False. If a worker needs a reasonable accommodation to practice his or her religious beliefs, you are legally required to take the worker's needs into account in deciding whether you can offer an accommodation.

9. False. Employees are responsible for telling you that they have disabilities and need accommodations. Once an employee does so, you are legally obligated to work with the employee to try to come up with an accommodation that will work for the employee and the company.

10. True. If you make decisions based on your erroneous belief that an employee has a disability, or based on an employee's history of disability, that's disability discrimination.

State Laws Prohibiting Discrimination in Employment

Note: Federal law makes it illegal to discriminate on the basis of race, color, national origin, sex (including pregnancy, childbirth, and related medical conditions), age (40 and over), disability (including AIDS/HIV), religion, and genetic information. The following states have their own laws protecting certain classes from discrimination.

Alabama

Ala. Code §§ 25-1-20, 25-1-21

Law applies to employers with: 20 or more employees

Private employers may not make employment decisions based on:
- Age (40 and older)

Alaska

Alaska Stat. §§ 18.80.220, 18.80.300, 47.30.865

Law applies to employers with: One or more employees

Private employers may not make employment decisions based on:
- Age
- Ancestry or national origin
- Physical or mental disability
- Gender
- Marital status, including changes in status
- Pregnancy, childbirth, and related medical conditions, including parenthood
- Race or color
- Religion or creed
- Mental illness

Arizona

Ariz. Rev. Stat. §§ 41-1461, 41-1463, 41-1465

Law applies to employers with: 15 or more employees

Private employers may not make employment decisions based on:
- Age (40 and older)
- Ancestry or national origin

- Physical or mental disability
- AIDS/HIV
- Gender
- Race or color
- Religion or creed
- Genetic testing information

Arkansas

Ark. Code Ann. §§ 11-4-601, 11-5-403, 16-123-102, 16-123-107

Law applies to employers with: Nine or more employees

Private employers may not make employment decisions based on:
- Ancestry or national origin
- Physical, mental, or sensory disability
- Gender
- Pregnancy, childbirth, and related medical conditions
- Race or color
- Religion or creed
- Genetic testing information

California

Cal. Gov't. Code §§ 12920, 12926.1, 12940, 12941, 12945; Cal. Lab. Code § 1101

Law applies to employers with: Five or more employees

Private employers may not make employment decisions based on:
- Age (40 and older)
- Ancestry or national origin
- Physical or mental disability
- AIDS/HIV
- Gender
- Marital status
- Pregnancy, childbirth, and related medical conditions
- Breastfeeding
- Race or color

State Laws Prohibiting Discrimination in Employment (continued)

- Religion or creed
- Sexual orientation
- Genetic testing information
- Gender identity, gender expression
- Medical condition
- Political activities or affiliations
- Status as victim of domestic violence, sexual assault, or stalking
- Military and veteran status

Colorado

Colo. Rev. Stat. §§ 24-34-301, 24-34-401, 24-34-402, 24-34-402.5, 27-65-115; Colo. Code Regs. 708-1:60.1, 708-1:80.8

Law applies to employers with: One or more employees; 25 or more employees (marital status only)

Private employers may not make employment decisions based on:

- Age (40 and older)
- Ancestry or national origin
- Physical, mental, or learning disability
- AIDS/HIV
- Gender
- Marital status (only applies to marriage to a coworker or plans to marry a coworker)
- Pregnancy, childbirth, and related medical conditions
- Race or color
- Religion or creed
- Sexual orientation, including perceived sexual orientation
- Lawful conduct outside of work
- Mental illness
- Transgender status

Connecticut

Conn. Gen. Stat. Ann. §§ 25-4-1401, 46a-51, 46a-60, 46a-81a, 46a-81c

Law applies to employers with: Three or more employees

Private employers may not make employment decisions based on:

- Age
- Ancestry or national origin
- Present or past physical, mental, learning, or intellectual disability
- Gender
- Marital status, including civil unions
- Pregnancy, childbirth, and related medical conditions
- Race or color
- Religion or creed
- Sexual orientation (includes having a history of such a preference or being identified with such a preference)
- Genetic testing information
- Gender identity or expression
- Arrests or convictions that have been erased, pardoned, or rehabilitated

Delaware

Del. Code Ann. tit. 19, §§ 710, 711, 724

Law applies to employers with: Four or more employees

Private employers may not make employment decisions based on:

- Age (40 and older)
- Ancestry or national origin
- Physical or mental disability
- AIDS/HIV
- Gender
- Marital status
- Pregnancy, childbirth, and related medical conditions
- Race or color
- Religion or creed
- Sexual orientation
- Genetic testing information
- Gender identity

State Laws Prohibiting Discrimination in Employment (continued)

- Status as victim of domestic violence, sexual offense, or stalking
- Family responsibilities
- "Reproductive health decisions"

District of Columbia

D.C. Code Ann. §§ 2-1401.01, 2-1401.02, 2-1401.05, 2-1402.82, 7-1703.03, 32-131.08

Law applies to employers with: One or more employees

Private employers may not make employment decisions based on:

- Age (18 and older)
- Ancestry or national origin
- Physical or mental disability
- Gender, including reproductive health decisions
- Marital status, including domestic partnership
- Pregnancy, childbirth, and related medical conditions, including parenthood and breastfeeding
- Race or color
- Religion or creed
- Sexual orientation
- Genetic testing information
- Enrollment in vocational, professional, or college education
- Family duties
- Source of income
- Place of residence or business
- Personal appearance
- Political affiliation
- Victim of intrafamily offense
- Gender identity or expression
- Status as unemployed
- Tobacco use

- Reproductive health decisions
- Any reason other than individual merit

Florida

Fla. Stat. Ann. §§ 448.075, 760.01, 760.02, 760.10, 760.50

Law applies to employers with: 15 or more employees

Private employers may not make employment decisions based on:

- Age
- Ancestry or national origin
- "Handicap"
- AIDS/HIV
- Gender
- Marital status
- Pregnancy, childbirth, and related medical conditions
- Race or color
- Religion or creed
- Sickle cell trait

Georgia

Ga. Code Ann. §§ 34-1-2, 34-5-1, 34-5-2, 34-6A-1 and following

Law applies to employers with:

- 15 or more employees (disability)
- 10 or more employees (gender) (domestic and agricultural employees not protected)
- One or more employee (age)

Private employers may not make employment decisions based on:

- Age (40 to 70)
- Physical, mental, or learning disability
- Gender (wage discrimination only)

Hawaii

Haw. Rev. Stat. §§ 378-1, 378-2, 378-2.5; Hawaii Admin. Rules § 12-46-182

Law applies to employers with: One or more employees

State Laws Prohibiting Discrimination in Employment (continued)

Private employers may not make employment decisions based on:
- Age
- Ancestry or national origin
- Physical or mental disability
- AIDS/HIV
- Gender
- Marital status
- Pregnancy, childbirth, and related medical conditions, including breastfeeding
- Race or color
- Religion or creed
- Sexual orientation
- Genetic testing information
- Arrest and court record (unless there is a conviction directly related to job)
- Credit history or credit report, unless the information in the individual's credit history or credit report directly relates to a bona fide occupational qualification
- Gender identity and gender expression
- Status as a victim of domestic or sexual violence (if employer has knowledge or is notified of this status)

Idaho

Idaho Code §§ 39-8303, 67-5902, 67-5909, 67-5910

Law applies to employers with: Five or more employees

Private employers may not make employment decisions based on:
- Age (40 and older)
- Ancestry or national origin
- Physical or mental disability
- Gender
- Pregnancy, childbirth, and related medical conditions
- Race or color
- Religion or creed
- Genetic testing information

Illinois

410 Ill. Comp. Stat. § 513/25; 775 Ill. Comp. Stat. §§ 5/1-102, 5/1-103, 5/1-105, 5/2-101, 5/2-102, 5/2-103; 820 Ill. Comp. Stat. §§ 105/4, 180/30; Ill. Admin. Code tit. 56, § 5210.110

Law applies to employers with: 15 or more employees; one or more employees (disability only)

Private employers may not make employment decisions based on:
- Age (40 and older)
- Ancestry or national origin
- Physical or mental disability
- Gender
- Marital status
- Pregnancy, childbirth, and related medical conditions
- Race or color
- Religion or creed
- Sexual orientation
- Genetic testing information
- Citizenship status
- Military status
- Unfavorable military discharge
- Gender identity
- Arrest record
- Victims of domestic violence
- Order of protection status
- Lack of permanent mailing address or having a mailing address of a shelter or social service provider

Indiana

Ind. Code Ann. §§ 22-9-1-2, 22-9-2-1, 22-9-2-2, 22-9-5-1 and following

Law applies to employers with: Six or more employees; one or more employees (age only); 15 or more employees (disability only)

State Laws Prohibiting Discrimination in Employment (continued)

Private employers may not make employment decisions based on:

- Age (40 to 75)
- Ancestry or national origin
- Physical or mental disability
- Gender
- Race or color
- Religion or creed
- Off-duty tobacco use
- Status as a veteran
- Sealed or expunged arrest or conviction record

Iowa

Iowa Code §§ 216.2, 216.6, 216.6A, 729.6

Law applies to employers with: Four or more employees

Private employers may not make employment decisions based on:

- Age (18 or older)
- Ancestry or national origin
- Physical or mental disability
- AIDS/HIV
- Gender
- Pregnancy, childbirth, and related medical conditions
- Race or color
- Religion or creed
- Sexual orientation
- Genetic testing information
- Gender identity
- Wage discrimination

Kansas

Kan. Stat. Ann. §§ 44-1002, 44-1009, 44-1112, 44-1113, 44-1125, 44-1126, 65-6002(e)

Law applies to employers with: Four or more employees

Private employers may not make employment decisions based on:

- Age (40 or older)
- Ancestry or national origin
- Physical or mental disability
- AIDS/HIV
- Gender
- Race or color
- Religion or creed
- Genetic testing information
- Military service or status

Kentucky

Ky. Rev. Stat. Ann. §§ 207.130, 207.135, 207.150, 342.197, 344.010, 344.030, 344.040

Law applies to employers with: Eight or more employees

Private employers may not make employment decisions based on:

- Age (40 or older)
- Ancestry or national origin
- Physical or mental disability
- AIDS/HIV
- Gender
- Pregnancy, childbirth, and related medical conditions
- Race or color
- Religion or creed
- Occupational pneumoconiosis with no respiratory impairment resulting from exposure to coal dust
- Off-duty tobacco use

Louisiana

La. Rev. Stat. Ann. §§ 23:301 to 23:368

Law applies to employers with: 20 or more employees; 25 or more employees (pregnancy, childbirth, and related medical condition only)

State Laws Prohibiting Discrimination in Employment (continued)

Private employers may not make employment decisions based on:
- Age (40 or older)
- Ancestry or national origin
- Physical or mental disability
- Gender
- Pregnancy, childbirth, and related medical conditions
- Race or color
- Religion or creed
- Genetic testing information
- Sickle cell trait
- Being a smoker or nonsmoker

Maine
Me. Rev. Stat. Ann. tit. 5, §§ 19302, 4552, 4553, 4571 to 4576; tit. 26, § 833; tit. 39-A, § 353

Law applies to employers with: One or more employees

Private employers may not make employment decisions based on:
- Age
- Ancestry or national origin
- Physical or mental disability
- AIDS/HIV
- Gender
- Pregnancy, childbirth, and related medical conditions
- Race or color
- Religion or creed
- Sexual orientation, including perceived sexual orientation
- Genetic testing information
- Gender identity or expression
- Past workers' compensation claim
- Past whistleblowing
- Medical support notice for child

Maryland
Md. Code, [State Government], §§ 20-101, 20-601 to 20-608; Md. Code Regs. 14.03.02.02

Law applies to employers with: 15 or more employees

Private employers may not make employment decisions based on:
- Age
- Ancestry or national origin
- Physical or mental disability
- AIDS/HIV
- Gender
- Marital status
- Pregnancy, childbirth, and related medical conditions
- Race or color
- Religion or creed
- Sexual orientation
- Genetic testing information
- Civil Air Patrol membership
- Gender identity

Massachusetts
Mass. Gen. Laws ch. 149, § 24A, ch. 151B, §§ 1, 4; Code of Massachusetts Regulations 804 CMR 3.01

Law applies to employers with: Six or more employees

Private employers may not make employment decisions based on:
- Age (40 or older)
- Ancestry or national origin
- Physical or mental disability
- Gender
- Marital status
- Race or color
- Religion or creed
- Sexual orientation
- Genetic testing information
- Military service

State Laws Prohibiting Discrimination in Employment (continued)

- Arrest record
- Gender identity
- Status as a veteran

Michigan

Mich. Comp. Laws §§ 37.1103, 37.1201, 37.1202, 37.2201, 37.2202, 37.2205a, 750.556

Law applies to employers with: One or more employees

Private employers may not make employment decisions based on:

- Age
- Ancestry or national origin
- Physical or mental disability
- AIDS/HIV
- Gender
- Marital status
- Pregnancy, childbirth, and related medical conditions
- Race or color
- Religion or creed
- Genetic testing information
- Height or weight
- Misdemeanor arrest record
- Civil Air Patrol membership

Minnesota

Minn. Stat. Ann. §§ 144.417, 181.81, 181.974, 363A.03, 363A.08

Law applies to employers with: One or more employees

Private employers may not make employment decisions based on:

- Age (18 to 70)
- Ancestry or national origin
- Physical, sensory, or mental disability
- Gender
- Marital status

- Pregnancy, childbirth, and related medical conditions
- Race or color
- Religion or creed
- Sexual orientation, including perceived sexual orientation
- Genetic testing information
- Gender identity
- Member of local commission
- Receiving public assistance
- Familial status (protects parents or guardians living with a minor child)

Mississippi

Miss. Code Ann. § 33-1-15

Law applies to employers with: One or more employees

Private employers may not make employment decisions based on:

- Military status
- No other protected categories unless employer receives public funding

Missouri

Mo. Rev. Stat. §§ 191.665, 213.010, 213.055, 375.1306

Law applies to employers with: Six or more employees

Private employers may not make employment decisions based on:

- Age (40 to 70)
- Ancestry or national origin
- Physical or mental disability
- AIDS/HIV
- Gender
- Race or color
- Religion or creed
- Genetic testing information
- Off-duty use of alcohol or tobacco

State Laws Prohibiting Discrimination in Employment (continued)

Montana

Mont. Code Ann. §§ 49-2-101, 49-2-303, 49-2-310

Law applies to employers with: One or more employees

Private employers may not make employment decisions based on:

- Age
- Ancestry or national origin
- Physical or mental disability
- Gender
- Marital status
- Pregnancy, childbirth, and related medical conditions
- Race or color
- Religion or creed

Nebraska

Neb. Rev. Stat. §§ 20-168, 48-236, 48-1001 to 48-1010, 48-1102, 48-1104

Law applies to employers with: 15 or more employees; 20 or more employees (age only)

Private employers may not make employment decisions based on:

- Age (40 or older)
- Ancestry or national origin
- Physical or mental disability
- AIDS/HIV
- Gender
- Marital status
- Pregnancy, childbirth, and related medical conditions
- Race or color
- Religion or creed
- Genetic testing information (applies to all employers)

Nevada

Nev. Rev. Stat. Ann. §§ 613.310 and following; 2017 Nevada Laws Ch. 271 (A.B. 113), 2017 Nevada Laws Ch. 496 (S.B. 361)

Law applies to employers with: 15 or more employees

Private employers may not make employment decisions based on:

- Age (40 or older)
- Ancestry or national origin
- Physical or mental disability
- AIDS/HIV
- Gender
- Pregnancy, childbirth, and related medical conditions, including breastfeeding
- Race or color
- Religion or creed
- Sexual orientation, including perceived sexual orientation
- Genetic testing information
- Use of service animal
- Gender identity or expression
- Opposing unlawful employment practices
- Credit report or credit information (with some exceptions)
- requesting leave or reasonable accommodation due to status as victim of domestic violence (applies to all employers).

New Hampshire

N.H. Rev. Stat. Ann. §§ 141-H:3, 354-A:2, 354-A:6, 354-A:7

Law applies to employers with: Six or more employees

Private employers may not make employment decisions based on:

- Age
- Ancestry or national origin
- Physical or mental disability
- Gender

State Laws Prohibiting Discrimination in Employment (continued)

- Marital status
- Pregnancy, childbirth, and related medical conditions
- Race or color
- Religion or creed
- Sexual orientation
- Genetic testing information
- Victims of domestic violence, harassment, sexual assault, or stalking
- Off-duty use of tobacco products

New Jersey

N.J. Stat. Ann. §§ 10:5-1, 10:5-4.1, 10:5-5, 10:5-12, 10:5-29.1, 34:6B-1, 43:21-49

Law applies to employers with: One or more employees

Private employers may not make employment decisions based on:

- Age (18 to 70)
- Ancestry or national origin
- Past or present physical or mental disability
- AIDS/HIV
- Gender
- Marital status, including civil union or domestic partnership status
- Pregnancy, childbirth, and related medical conditions
- Race or color
- Religion or creed
- Sexual orientation, including affectional orientation and perceived sexual orientation
- Genetic testing information
- Atypical heredity cellular or blood trait
- Accompanied by service or guide dog
- Military service
- Gender identity
- Unemployed status

New Mexico

N.M. Stat. Ann. §§ 24-21-4, 28-1-2, 28-1-7, 50-4A-4; N.M. Admin. Code 9.1.1

Law applies to employers with:

- Four or more employees
- 50 or more employees (marital status only)
- 15 or more employees (sexual orientation and gender identity only)

Private employers may not make employment decisions based on:

- Age (40 or older)
- Ancestry or national origin
- Physical or mental disability
- Gender
- Marital status
- Pregnancy, childbirth, and related medical conditions
- Race or color
- Religion or creed
- Sexual orientation (including perceived sexual orientation)
- Genetic testing information
- Gender identity
- Serious medical condition
- Domestic abuse leave

New York

N.Y. Exec. Law §§ 292, 296; N.Y. Lab. Law § 201-d

Law applies to employers with: Four or more employees; all employers (sexual harassment only)

Private employers may not make employment decisions based on:

- Age (18 and over)
- Ancestry or national origin
- Physical or mental disability
- Gender
- Marital status
- Pregnancy, childbirth, and related medical conditions

State Laws Prohibiting Discrimination in Employment (continued)

- Race or color
- Religion or creed
- Sexual orientation, including perceived sexual orientation
- Genetic testing information
- Lawful recreational activities when not at work
- Military status or service
- Observance of Sabbath
- Political activities
- Use of service dog
- Arrest or criminal accusation
- Domestic violence victim status
- Familial status
- Gender identity and transgender status

North Carolina

N.C. Gen. Stat. §§ 95-28.1, 95-28.1A, 127B-11, 130A-148, 143-422.2, 168A-5

Law applies to employers with: 15 or more employees

Private employers may not make employment decisions based on:

- Age
- Ancestry or national origin
- Physical or mental disability
- AIDS/HIV
- Gender
- Race or color
- Religion or creed
- Genetic testing information
- Military status or service
- Sickle cell or hemoglobin C trait
- Use of lawful products off site and off duty

North Dakota

N.D. Cent. Code §§ 14-02.4-02, 14-02.4-03, 34-01-17

Law applies to employers with: One or more employees

Private employers may not make employment decisions based on:

- Age (40 or older)
- Ancestry or national origin
- Physical or mental disability
- Gender
- Marital status
- Pregnancy, childbirth, and related medical conditions
- Race or color
- Religion or creed
- Lawful conduct outside of work
- Receiving public assistance
- Keeping and bearing arms (as long as firearm is never exhibited on company property except for lawful defensive purposes)
- Status as a volunteer emergency responder

Ohio

Ohio Rev. Code Ann. §§ 4111.17, 4112.01, 4112.02

Law applies to employers with: Four or more employees

Private employers may not make employment decisions based on:

- Age (40 or older)
- Ancestry or national origin
- Physical, mental, or learning disability
- AIDS/HIV
- Gender
- Pregnancy, childbirth, and related medical conditions
- Race or color
- Religion or creed
- Military status
- Caring for a sibling, child, parent, or spouse injured while in the armed services

State Laws Prohibiting Discrimination in Employment (continued)

Oklahoma

Okla. Stat. Ann. tit. 25, §§ 1301, 1302; tit. 36, § 3614.2; tit. 40, § 500; tit. 44, § 208

Law applies to employers with: 1 or more employees

Private employers may not make employment decisions based on:

- Age (40 or older)
- Ancestry or national origin
- Physical or mental disability
- Gender
- Pregnancy, childbirth, and related medical conditions (except abortions where the woman is not in "imminent danger of death")
- Race or color
- Religion or creed
- Genetic testing information
- Military service
- Being a smoker or nonsmoker or using tobacco off duty

Oregon

Ore. Rev. Stat. §§ 25-337, 659A.030, 659A.122 and following, 659A.303

Law applies to employers with: One or more employees; 6 or more employees (disability only)

Private employers may not make employment decisions based on:

- Age (18 or older)
- Ancestry or national origin
- Physical or mental disability
- Gender
- Marital status
- Pregnancy, childbirth, and related medical conditions
- Race or color
- Religion or creed
- Sexual orientation
- Genetic testing information

- Parent who has medical support order imposed by court
- Domestic violence victim status
- Refusal to attend an employer-sponsored meeting with the primary purpose of communicating the employer's opinion on religious or political matters
- Credit history
- Whistleblowers
- Off-duty use of tobacco products

Pennsylvania

43 Pa. Cons. Stat. Ann. tit. 43 §§ 954–955

Law applies to employers with: Four or more employees

Private employers may not make employment decisions based on:

- Age (40 to 70)
- Ancestry or national origin
- Physical or mental disability
- Gender
- Pregnancy, childbirth, and related medical conditions
- Race or color
- Religion or creed
- Relationship or association with a person with a disability
- GED rather than high school diploma
- Use of service animal

Rhode Island

R.I. Gen. Laws §§ 12-28-10, 23-6.3-11, 28-5-6, 28-5-7, 28-6-18, 28-6.7-1

Law applies to employers with: Four or more employees; one or more employees (gender-based wage discrimination only)

Private employers may not make employment decisions based on:

- Age (40 or older)

State Laws Prohibiting Discrimination in Employment (continued)

- Ancestry or national origin
- Physical or mental disability
- AIDS/HIV
- Gender
- Pregnancy, childbirth, and related medical conditions
- Race or color
- Religion or creed
- Sexual orientation, including perceived sexual orientation
- Genetic testing information
- Domestic abuse victim
- Gender identity or expression
- Homelessness

South Carolina

S.C. Code §§ 1-13-30, 1-13-80

Law applies to employers with: 15 or more employees

Private employers may not make employment decisions based on:
- Age (40 or older)
- Ancestry or national origin
- Physical or mental disability
- AIDS/HIV
- Gender
- Pregnancy, childbirth, and related medical conditions
- Race or color
- Religion or creed

South Dakota

S.D. Codified Laws Ann. §§ 20-13-1, 20-13-10, 60-2-20, 60-12-15, 62-1-17

Law applies to employers with: One or more employees

Private employers may not make employment decisions based on:
- Ancestry or national origin
- Physical or mental disability

- Gender
- Race or color
- Religion or creed
- Genetic testing information
- Preexisting injury
- Off-duty use of tobacco products

Tennessee

Tenn. Code Ann. §§ 4-21-102, 4-21-401 and following, 8-50-103, 50-2-201, 50-2-202

Law applies to employers with: Eight or more employees; one or more employees (gender-based wage discrimination only)

Private employers may not make employment decisions based on:
- Age (40 or older)
- Ancestry or national origin
- Physical, mental, or visual disability
- Gender
- Race or color
- Religion or creed
- Use of guide dog
- Volunteer rescue squad worker responding to an emergency

Texas

Tex. Lab. Code Ann. §§ 21.002, 21.051, 21.082, 21.101, 21.106, 21.402

Law applies to employers with: 15 or more employees

Private employers may not make employment decisions based on:
- Age (40 or older)
- Ancestry or national origin
- Physical or mental disability
- Gender
- Pregnancy, childbirth, and related medical conditions
- Race or color

State Laws Prohibiting Discrimination in Employment (continued)

- Religion or creed
- Genetic testing information

Utah

Utah Code Ann. §§ 26-45-103, 34A-5-102, 34A-5-106

Law applies to employers with: 15 or more employees

Private employers may not make employment decisions based on:

- Age (40 or older)
- Ancestry or national origin
- Physical or mental disability
- AIDS/HIV
- Gender
- Pregnancy, childbirth, and related medical conditions, includes breastfeeding
- Race or color
- Religion or creed
- Sexual orientation
- Genetic testing information
- Gender identity

Vermont

Vt. Stat. Ann. tit. 21, §§ 495, 495d; tit. 18, § 9333

Law applies to employers with: One or more employees

Private employers may not make employment decisions based on:

- Age (18 or older)
- Ancestry or national origin
- Physical, mental, or emotional disability
- AIDS/HIV
- Gender
- Race or color
- Religion or creed
- Sexual orientation
- Genetic testing information
- Gender identity

- Place of birth
- Credit report or credit history

Virginia

Va. Code Ann. §§ 2.2-3900, 2.2-3901, 40.1-28.6, 40.1-28.7:1, 51.5-41

Law applies to employers with: One or more employees

Private employers may not make employment decisions based on:

- Age
- Ancestry or national origin
- Physical or mental disability
- AIDS/HIV
- Gender
- Marital status
- Pregnancy, childbirth, and related medical conditions
- Race or color
- Religion or creed
- Genetic testing information

Washington

Wash. Rev. Code Ann. §§ 38.40.110, 49.12.175, 49.44.090, 49.44.180, 49.60.030, 49.60.040, 49.60.172, 49.60.180, 49.76.120; Wash. Admin. Code § 162-30-020

Law applies to employers with: Eight or more employees; one or more employees (gender-based wage discrimination only)

Private employers may not make employment decisions based on:

- Age (40 or older)
- Ancestry or national origin
- Physical, mental, or sensory disability
- AIDS/HIV
- Gender
- Marital status
- Pregnancy, childbirth, and related medical conditions, including breastfeeding

State Laws Prohibiting Discrimination in Employment (continued)

- Race or color
- Religion or creed
- Sexual orientation
- Genetic testing information
- Hepatitis C infection
- Member of state militia
- Use of service animal
- Gender identity
- Domestic violence victim

West Virginia

W. Va. Code §§ 5-11-3, 5-11-9, 15–1K–4, 16-3C-3, 21-5B-1, 21-5B-3

Law applies to employers with: 12 or more employees; one or more employees (gender-based wage discrimination only)

Private employers may not make employment decisions based on:

- Age (40 or older)
- Ancestry or national origin
- Physical or mental disability, or blindness
- AIDS/HIV
- Gender
- Race or color
- Religion or creed
- Off-duty use of tobacco products
- Membership in the Civil Air Patrol (for employers with 16 or more employees).

Wisconsin

Wis. Stat. Ann. §§ 111.32 and following

Law applies to employers with: One or more employees

Private employers may not make employment decisions based on:

- Age (40 or older)
- Ancestry or national origin
- Physical or mental disability
- Gender
- Marital status
- Pregnancy, childbirth, and related medical conditions
- Race or color
- Religion or creed
- Sexual orientation, including having a history of or being identified with a preference
- Genetic testing information
- Arrest or conviction record
- Military service
- Declining to attend a meeting or to participate in any communication about religious matters or political matters
- Use or nonuse of lawful products off duty and off site

Wyoming

Wyo. Stat. §§ 27-9-102, 27-9-105, 19-11-104

Law applies to employers with: Two or more employees

Private employers may not make employment decisions based on:

- Age (40 or older)
- Ancestry or national origin
- Disability
- Gender
- Pregnancy, childbirth, and related medical conditions
- Race or color
- Religion or creed
- Military service or status

Personnel Basics

Effective management starts with good personnel policies. Fair and sensible policies can help improve performance and productivity while discouraging misconduct. They can also help prevent lawsuits by employees or investigations by government agencies, or at least lay the groundwork for a solid defense. Here, you'll find information on:

- at-will employment
- employee handbooks
- antiharassment policies
- communication skills
- performance evaluations
- personnel files, and
- policies to help employees balance work and family obligations.

Even if your job duties don't include creating policies, you should to be familiar with the information in this chapter. It will help you understand the legal framework within which you carry out your day-to-day supervisory responsibilities. And it will help you with basic management tasks, such as evaluating performance, communicating with employees, keeping personnel records, and more.

Personnel Policies and the Law

When it comes to personnel policies, there are surprisingly few legal requirements. For example, no law dictates that a company must have an employee handbook, let alone what should go in it. (Although there are a few types of policies you might have to put in writing—such as a notice about family and medical leave or, in some states, a smoking policy—you don't have to put them in an employee handbook.) You also aren't legally obligated to evaluate your employees, let alone use a particular form or follow a specified timetable. And although federal and state laws prohibit harassment, employers don't have to adopt a certain type of antiharassment policy.

So why take the time and trouble to develop sound personnel policies? Because

---

Frequently Asked Questions About Personnel Policies

What is at-will employment?
Employees who work at will can be fired at any time, for any reason that is not illegal, and they have the right to quit at any time. In every state but Montana, employees are presumed to work at will unless they have an employment contract limiting the employers' right to fire. (For more on

at-will employment, including steps you can take to avoid changing an at-will employee's status inadvertently, see "At-Will Employment," below.)

Does every company need an employee handbook?
No law requires employers to have an employee handbook, but it's a good idea. A handbook tells employees about workplace rules in an efficient,

Frequently Asked Questions About Personnel Policies (continued)

uniform way. Employees will know what is expected of them and what they can expect of the company. And your company will be able to prove that all employees were aware of the rules if a worker later decides to sue. (For suggestions on what to include in an employee handbook, see "Employee Handbooks," below.)

Do we need a sexual harassment policy?
Absolutely. The Supreme Court has held that an effective antiharassment policy, which includes a procedure for making complaints, can provide a defense to certain types of sexual harassment lawsuits. And a good policy can prevent sexual harassment from happening in the first place, by letting workers know what kinds of behavior cross the line, and what action the company will take against a harasser. (To learn more, see "Preventing Workplace Harassment," below.)

How can I improve my communication with my coworkers and employees?
Here are a few principles you can follow to improve your communication at work: Understand your audience; tailor your message appropriately (for your goals and your audience); deliver your message using the right medium (email is appropriate only for certain things); and speak and write clearly and concisely. (For an explanation of these principles, see "Communicating With Employees Effectively," below.)

How do I avoid legal problems when giving performance evaluations?
First, decide on the job requirements and performance goals you want each employee to meet. Create specific criteria that are directly related to the employee's success on the job. Write down the criteria you choose and let your employees know the basis for their evaluations in advance; or, better yet, ask your employees to help you come up with appropriate performance goals. (For more on evaluating your workers, see "Performance Appraisal," below.)

What documents should I keep in an employee's personnel file?
Your company should have a personnel file for each employee. Keep every important job-related document in the file, including job applications, offer letters, employment contracts, benefits and salary information, government forms, performance evaluations, and memos about disciplinary actions. Do not keep medical records or I-9 forms in personnel files. (For more on personnel files, see "Creating and Maintaining Personnel Files," below.)

What are some of the things I can do to make our workplace more family-friendly without costing the company a lot of money?
There are many policies you can institute in the workplace to help your employees balance the competing demands of work and family without significant cost to your company, including: flexible work schedules; telecommuting; job sharing or part-time work schedules; flexible spending accounts; and employee assistance programs that help employees find child care, after-school care, or elder care. (For more on such policies, see "Family-Friendly Workplace Policies," below.)

they keep the workplace running smoothly and keep your company out of legal trouble. Written policies tell workers what the company expects of them and what they can expect in return. A fair evaluation process helps managers keep track of workers' performance, notice and reward those who are doing well, and warn and assist those who are getting off track. A good sexual harassment policy will help prevent misconduct in the first place, as well as encourage workers to bring problems to the company's attention so they can be resolved before they get out of control. And policies that help employees balance work and family obligations will decrease distractions and absenteeism, while increasing worker productivity and loyalty.

We can't emphasize the legal benefits of solid personnel policies enough. If your company is unfortunate enough to be sued by a former worker, good personnel policies will be crucial to its defense. Performance evaluations can be used to show that a worker was fired for poor performance and was given notice and an opportunity to improve before being shown the door. Written policies can help show that a worker was fired for misconduct and knew the rules and the consequences of violating them. And if your company maintains complete personnel files, it will have all the documents necessary to prove that, for example, a worker generated customer complaints, signed a noncompete agreement, or received written warnings.

State Law

Some states have laws that apply to various personnel issues. For example, many states give workers the right to see their personnel files (or, at least, certain documents in those files). (See "State Laws on Access to Personnel Records," at the end of this chapter, for information on your state's law.) In addition, many states have codified the principle of employment at will. This age-old legal doctrine is not written down in any federal statute, but virtually every state (except Montana) recognizes it, and many have incorporated it into their own statutes. Your state labor department should be able to tell you whether your state has any other laws that relate to your personnel policies.

At-Will Employment

Private employers in the United States start off with the law on their side when dealing with employees. Although workers have specified rights in some situations, employers generally have plenty of latitude to make the employment decisions they feel are right for their businesses. This latitude is protected by the legal doctrine of "employment at will." At-will employees are free to quit at any time, for any reason, and employers are free to fire them at any time, for any reason, unless that reason is illegal. An illegal reason is one that is discriminatory (see Chapter 3) or retaliatory (see "Retaliation" in Chapter 11), violates a statute or public policy, or is in bad faith (see "Illegal Reasons for Firing Employees" in Chapter 12).

Companies that avoid these no-nos may fire an at-will employee for even the most whimsical or idiosyncratic reasons: having annoying mannerisms, poor fashion sense, or lousy eating habits, for example. Employers are also free to change the terms of employment—job duties, compensation, or hours, for example—for any reason that isn't illegal. Workers can agree to these changes and continue working or reject the changes and quit. In other words, the employment relationship is voluntary. An employer cannot force its employees to stay forever, and employees cannot force their employers to keep them on indefinitely.

Montana is the only state that does not recognize the doctrine of employment at will. Employers in the Big Sky state must have "good cause" to fire an employee who has completed the company's probationary period, or if there is no probationary period, worked for the company for at least six months. (For more on what constitutes good cause, see Chapter 12.)

Legal Limitations on At-Will Employment

The doctrine of at-will employment gives employers protection from wrongful termination claims. But this protection is limited in two important ways:

- **Employment contracts.** The doctrine doesn't apply to employees who have an employment contract, whether written, oral, or implied, that puts some limits on the company's right to fire them. For these employees, the language or nature of the contract usually spells out the terms of employment, including when and for what reasons the employees can be fired. (See "Firing Employees With Employment Contracts" in Chapter 12 for more information.)
- **State or federal laws.** Congress, state legislatures, and judges have carved out several exceptions to the doctrine of employment at will. Generally, as stated above, these exceptions prevent employers from taking any negative action against an employee (including disciplining, demoting, or firing) that is illegal: in bad faith, in violation of public policy, or for a discriminatory or retaliatory reason. (See "Illegal Reasons for Firing Employees" in Chapter 12 for more information.)

Practical Limitations on At-Will Employment

Although the law gives employers the right to fire or change the job of an at-will employee for any reason, no matter how frivolous, employers who lack a sensible basis for employment decisions take legal and practical risks. These risks include:

- **Productivity and morale problems.** If you fire or discipline a worker without a good reason, the rest of the workforce will be confused and uneasy. Employees who believe they might be fired or demoted even if they are doing a good job have less incentive to follow performance standards and other rules of the workplace.

- **Recruiting and hiring difficulties.** Once word gets out that an employer fires or disciplines employees without good reason, new employees will be harder to find. After all, why should an employee take a job where he or she could get fired at any time if another employer offers a little job security or at least a fair shake?

- **Lawsuits.** An employee who has been treated unfairly is more motivated to sue. And despite the doctrine of employment at will, most jurors have been or are employees and will empathize with the fired worker. Juries find ways to punish employers they perceive to be unfair, arbitrary, or callous (for example, by finding that an irrational or arbitrary reason for firing was really a pretext for illegal discrimination). And even if an employee ultimately loses a lawsuit, the employer will spend precious time and money fighting it in court.

Because of this, most employers fire or demote workers only for legitimate business reasons, which other workers (and a judge or jury, if it comes to that) will understand. However, smart employers also hang on

to their at-will rights, just in case. Even if your company generally fires only for cause, maintaining the right to fire at will can provide a valuable legal defense if your company ends up in court.

Preserving Your At-Will Rights

If you want to keep your company's right to fire and discipline employees on its own terms, don't make promises or adopt policies that restrict that right. For example, don't tell employees that they will only be fired for certain reasons or that they will have jobs as long as they do good work. Despite your good intentions, a disgruntled former employee can use these statements as evidence of an employment contract that eliminates employment at will.

Here are some steps you can take to protect your company's right to fire and discipline employees at will:

- **State that employment is at will.** In written employment policies, including the employee handbook or personnel manual, state clearly that employment at your company is at will and explain what this means.

- **Ask employees to sign an at-will acknowledgment.** Consider asking employees to sign a simple form or offer letter acknowledging that their employment is at will. A worker who has signed such a form will have a difficult time refuting it later.

- **Don't promise continued employment.** If you tell employees that their jobs are secure, that they will not be fired without good cause, or even that the company has never had to fire a worker, you risk creating an expectation (and a contract) that they will not be fired. Avoid these types of comments; they are particularly common when interviewing potential employees and giving performance reviews.
- **Train managers.** With few exceptions, the actions and statements of company managers will be legally attributable to your company. If your job includes training other managers, make sure they understand company policies and procedures, especially regarding discipline, performance reviews, and employment at will. If managers make any statements or take any actions contrary to these policies—like promising that workers won't be fired—the company might lose its at-will rights.
- **Keep disciplinary options open.** If your company has a progressive discipline policy, make sure it includes clear language preserving the right to fire employees at will. If the policy lists

Lessons From the Real World

Annunzio Ferraro worked as a security guard at the Hyatt hotel in Milwaukee. His job application form, which he signed, said that his employment could be terminated at any time. However, Hyatt's employment manual stated that employees would only be fired for just cause and outlined a progressive discipline policy under which employees would generally receive at least two prior warnings for similar offenses before getting fired. The manual allowed the company to fire an employee immediately for a "severe rule violation."

Ferraro was fired for physically assaulting a hotel guest. Amazingly, he then sued for wrongful termination, claiming that the hotel breached an implied employment contract by firing him without the two prior warnings promised in its disciplinary policy.

The Wisconsin Supreme Court agreed with Ferraro on one important issue: The court found that Hyatt's disciplinary policy created an implied contract promising that Ferraro would be fired only for just cause.

However, the court found that Ferraro's assault on a hotel guest constituted a "severe rule violation" and gave the hotel ample cause for termination, particularly since it was not Ferraro's first offense. Ferraro had previously hit an intoxicated guest, raised his voice in argument with a guest, and been accused of harassing the hotel's female employees, all in the space of less than a year. Faced with this less-than-stellar record, the court threw out a jury's verdict in Ferraro's favor, finding that no jury could reasonably believe Hyatt had breached Ferraro's implied employment contract.

Ferraro v. Koelsch et al., 368 N.W.2d 666 (Wis. 1985).

offenses for which firing is appropriate, it should state that the list is not exhaustive and that the company reserves the right to fire for any reason.

- **Don't refer to employees as "permanent."** Many employers have an initial probationary or temporary period for new employees, during which the company is free to fire the worker. Workers who survive this period are sometimes called "permanent" employees, who are entitled to benefits and so forth. To some courts, this language implies that an employee who becomes permanent can be fired only for good cause. If your company uses a probationary period and you are responsible for writing company policies, don't use the word "permanent" and make it clear that the company retains the right to fire at will once the probationary period is over.

Employee Handbooks

Many companies—especially smaller businesses—get along fine without an employee handbook. (They might still need certain stand-alone policies, though, such as an antiharassment policy.) But at some point, particularly as your company grows, it makes good business sense to create one. Although compiling the policies will take some effort, your company will save time, headaches, and possibly legal fees in the long run.

The benefits of having an employee handbook are many. Every employee will receive the same, consistent information about workplace rules, benefits, company procedures, and other important issues. Employees will know what is expected of them and what they can expect from your company, particularly in the areas of performance, attendance, and discipline. The handbook can tell workers a bit about the history of the business and the company's structure and values. And the handbook will provide a measure of legal protection if an employee or former employee decides to sue.

What to Include in an Employee Handbook

Effective employee handbooks vary widely in size, style, and content. Some large corporations produce handbooks that come in multiple volumes and cover every possible aspect of the business. Smaller companies might have a more limited handbook that covers only the basics and could probably fit into a pamphlet.

No matter which approach your company chooses, its handbook should incorporate the company's style and values. A handbook doesn't have to be written in legalese to be effective. In fact, the best policies are written in plain English. A handbook should communicate policies to workers in language they will understand.

Here are some topics to consider covering in a handbook. If you are assigned the responsibility of creating, updating, or troubleshooting your company's handbook, you can use this list as a starting point:

- **Information about the company.** If your company has an organizational chart, mission statement, or written history, you can include it here.
- **At-will statement.** If your company is an at-will employer, you should include a statement to that effect in the handbook. (See "At-Will Employment," above, for more information.)
- **Hiring rules.** Explain any rules or policies the company follows when hiring workers, including job postings, antidiscrimination policies, referral bonuses, and any testing required of new workers or applicants.
- **Pay.** Set out the rules on overtime, on-call time, wage garnishments, and so on. If the company has policies on expense reimbursements and pay advances, include them as well. And let workers know when they will be paid and according to what formula (for example, by commission or piece rate).
- **Hours.** Set the rules on rest breaks and meal breaks, attendance policies, schedules, flextime or other flexible scheduling arrangements, and time cards, if applicable. (For more information on compensation and hours, see Chapter 2.)
- **Leave.** If your company offers sick leave, vacation, parental leave, pregnancy or disability leave, leave for civic duties, sabbaticals, bereavement leave, or other time off, explain those policies here. (You

can find information on leave policies in Chapter 5.)
- **Performance.** If your company gives performance evaluations, explain the process here. (See "Performance Appraisal," below, for more information.)
- **Benefits.** Explain the benefits available to employees, including health insurance, dental and vision coverage, life insurance, disability insurance, pensions or other retirement plans, profit sharing, and the like.
- **Discrimination and harassment.** Include a statement that discrimination and harassment violate company policies and will not be tolerated. State that immediate action will be taken against wrongdoers. (For more on discrimination and sexual harassment, see "Preventing Workplace Harassment," below, and Chapter 3.)
- **Complaints and investigations.** Describe how employees can report harassment or other misconduct. Tell employees how to make complaints, describe what steps the company will take to investigate, and state that retaliation will not be allowed against a worker who complains in good faith. Encourage employees to report any concerns immediately. (For more on investigations, see "Investigating Complaints" in Chapter 11.)
- **Health and safety.** Detail any safety-related workplace rules (for example, that hard hats must be worn in certain areas) and

any special health and safety issues that apply to your company. And encourage workers to bring health and safety concerns to management right away. (For more on health and safety issues, see Chapter 7.)

- **Violence.** State clearly that violence and threats of violence will be taken seriously. Explain how employees can report threats and violent incidents, and lay out your company's safety plan in case of violence. (For more on violence, see "Workplace Violence" in Chapter 11.)

- **Privacy.** If your company monitors workers' phone calls, voicemail, email, or Internet use—or if it conducts any workplace searches or surveillance—let workers know. (For more about privacy issues in the workplace, see Chapter 6.)

- **Use of company property.** Be clear about employee use of computer equipment, email, company cars, communications equipment (phones and cell phones, for example), copiers, and so on.

- **Workplace conduct.** Include not only company standards of conduct (for example, no fighting or no conflicts of interest) but also policies on grooming, uniforms, and having visitors at work.

- **Social media.** While you can't prohibit employees from talking about the company on social media, you can create a social media policy that limits the disclosure of confidential information, that states that discriminatory or harassing comments are not acceptable, and that directs employees to explain that their opinions do not reflect the views of the company. (For more information, see "Protected Concerted Activity" in Chapter 8.).

- **Confidentiality.** Clearly define what company information is confidential and not to be disclosed, such as the company's financial data, customer and vendor lists, formulas, processes, marketing strategies, and the like. (See Chapter 10 for more information on protecting the company's proprietary information.)

- **Discipline.** If your company has a progressive discipline policy, describe it here. You can also describe what infractions constitute grounds for termination, but be sure to keep management's options open. (Disciplinary policies are covered in Chapter 11.)

- **Firing.** Detail any layoff and termination policies, including provisions regarding severance, return of company property, and references. (Firing and layoffs are covered in Chapters 12 and 13.)

For more detailed information and sample policies that you can modify, cut, and paste for use in your company, see *Create Your Own Employee Handbook,* by Lisa Guerin and Amy DelPo (Nolo).

Don't Create Obligations That Will Haunt Your Company Later

Some courts interpret the language in employee handbooks as contracts that create binding obligations on employers. If you include any unconditional promises in your company's employee handbook, there's a very real possibility that employees or former employees might try to enforce those promises in court. Here are some of the most common trouble spots:

- **Promises of continued employment.** Don't put language in the handbook that promises employees a job as long as they follow company rules. A court might interpret this as a contract of employment, guaranteeing that employees will not be fired without good cause. Instead, state in the handbook that your company reserves the right to terminate employees for reasons not stated in the handbook or for no reason at all. Even though the company may never have to rely on this language to defend against a wrongful termination claim, at least employees will know where they stand. (See "At-Will Employment," above, for more details.)

- **Conduct not covered by the handbook.** Of course, no handbook can cover every possible workplace situation. It's best to make this clear to employees by saying so in the handbook. Otherwise, employees might argue that any action the company takes that goes beyond what's explicitly set forth in the handbook is unfair.

- **Progressive discipline.** Many employers follow some form of "progressive discipline" for performance problems or less serious forms of misconduct (attendance problems, difficulties getting along with coworkers, or missing deadlines, for example). Often, discipline starts with informal coaching, then a verbal warning, followed by a written warning, then termination. Whatever system your company uses, don't obligate managers to follow a particular disciplinary pattern in every circumstance. It's better to leave the company's options open, to make sure it can fire workers, if necessary, without facing a legal challenge. (See "Disciplining Workers" in Chapter 11 for more information.)

- **Right to change the handbook.** You cannot be sure that the employment policies you come up with today will stand the test of time. Your company might later decide to change or eliminate a policy or to branch out into other endeavors that make additional policies necessary. Either way, the handbook should state that the company reserves the right to change the policies at any time, for any reason (provided you give notice to employees). This will give your company the necessary leeway to keep its policies in tune with its business.

Once you've created a comprehensive employee handbook, set aside time to review and update it regularly as company policies and procedures change. An outdated handbook doesn't do the company or its employees any good; it might even create confusion or unwanted legal obligations. A periodic handbook review will also help you identify changes you want—or need—to make to company policies.

Preventing Workplace Harassment

As explained in Chapter 2, most private employers have a responsibility to provide a workplace free of discrimination and harassment. While sexual harassment is perhaps the most well-known form of harassment, harassment based on any other protected characteristic—such as race or religion—is also illegal. In fact, in 2016, the Equal Employment Opportunity Commission (EEOC) received 23,528 complaints of workplace harassment other than sexual harassment.

As a manager, you are on the front lines when it comes to avoiding, preventing, and reporting harassment. The company is liable for your actions, which means that your failure to act appropriately can get the company in a lot of trouble. If you harass employees yourself, your company will be legally responsible. And if employees report harassment to you or you otherwise become

aware that harassment is taking place, your company will be on the hook, even if you choose to look the other way. That's why it's so important to learn what harassment is and what you should do if it takes place.

Harassment Defined

Harassment is unwelcome conduct based on a protected characteristic and:

- which the employee must endure as a condition of continued employment, or
- which is severe or frequent enough to create a work environment that the average person would find intimidating, hostile, or abusive (referred to as a "hostile work environment" claim).

Unwelcome conduct covers a wide variety of comments and actions, including derogatory name-calling, displaying offensive cartoons or pictures, physical assaults or threats, insults, offensive jokes or stories, inappropriate gestures, imitations, and more. For example, making fun of someone's religious attire or practices, imitating someone with a limp or speech impediment, or criticizing an ethnic hairstyle, can all qualify as harassing behavior.

Sexual harassment includes any unwelcome conduct of a sexual nature, including groping, repeated requests for dates, comments on a person's appearance or attractiveness, telling sexual jokes or stories, inquiries about the employee's sex life, massages or other touching, displaying sexual images or drawings, and more. Even compliments, gifts, and other attention can qualify as sexual harassment if it is unwanted and unwelcome.

Sex-based harassment does not need to be sexual in nature. Negative comments or actions about gender also qualify as illegal harassment, such as telling sexist jokes or repeating gender stereotypes. This often happens when women enter workplaces that have been traditionally male dominated. For example, a woman who joins an all-male construction crew might find sexist graffiti on her locker, her car defaced, or that her male coworkers won't back her up on dangerous work tasks. (See "Gender, Pregnancy, and Sexual Harassment," in Chapter 3.)

Employer Liability for Harassment

Your company's liability for workplace harassment depends, in part, on who is doing the harassing. Employers are always responsible for harassment committed by a supervisor that results in a tangible employment action, such as a promotion, termination, change in pay, transfer, or change in hours or work assignments. For example, if one of your managers only gives promotions to women who agree to go on dates with him or her, your company will be liable—even if no one else at the company knew what was going on.

If harassment by a supervisor doesn't result in a tangible employment action, your company will still be liable unless it can prove both of the following:

- The company made reasonable efforts to prevent and correct the harassing behavior.

- The employee failed to take advantage of the company's established complaint procedure (or other corrective measures offered by the employer).

For example, suppose an employee complains that her manager constantly comments on her appearance, asks about her sex life, and inappropriately touches her. Your company might have a viable defense to a sexual harassment lawsuit if you had a strong antiharassment policy in place, you regularly provided harassment training to supervisors, and you promptly investigated the employee's harassment complaint and took corrective action (such as firing the manager, providing additional harassment training, and reiterating the company's anti-harassment policy and complaint procedure to employees).

When it comes to harassment by an employee's coworkers or nonemployees (such as a client or vendor), your company will be liable if it knew, or should have known, about the harassment and failed to take timely action to correct the situation. For example, if a manager overhears an employee using racial epithets and making racist jokes, your company has an obligation to investigate and take action to prevent further harassment—even if no one makes a formal complaint.

Strategies for Prevention

There are a number of steps that a company can take to reduce the risk of workplace harassment:

- **Adopt a clear antiharassment policy.** In its employee handbook, your company should include a clear policy prohibiting harassment. The policy should define harassment (including sexual harassment); state in clear terms that harassment will not be tolerated; warn that the company will discipline or fire any wrongdoers; set out a clear procedure for employees to make harassment complaints; state that complaints will be investigated fully; and assert that the company will not tolerate retaliation against anyone who complains about harassment.

- **Train employees.** Once a year, your company should require employees to attend antiharassment training. These sessions should teach employees what harassment is, explain that employees have a right to a workplace free of harassment, review the company's complaint procedure, and encourage employees to come forward with concerns.

- **Train supervisors and managers.** At least once a year, your company should train supervisors and managers in a separate antiharassment training session. (A few states, including California, now require such trainings, at least for certain employers.) The sessions should educate managers and supervisors about harassment and explain how to deal with complaints they receive or problems they observe.

Lessons From the Real World

A male employee successfully sued his employer for sexual harassment because his coworkers made fun of him for not being "manly" enough.

Antonio Sanchez endured a lot of abuse for his less-than-macho ways. Coworkers referred to him as "she" and "her," told him that he walked and carried his tray "like a woman," made derisive comments because he did not have sex with a female friend, and taunted him for behaving like a woman.

Understandably, this barrage of verbal abuse upset and angered Sanchez. He complained to the general manager, an assistant manager, and the human resources director, but got no relief.

Eventually he sued, arguing that the abuse amounted to illegal sexual harassment. The court agreed. It said that Sanchez's coworkers abused him because he did not conform to their gender-based stereotypes. This was sexual harassment, plain and simple, and the employer had a legal obligation to stop the harassment once it knew about it.

Nichols v. Azteca Restaurant Enterprises, Inc., 256 F.3d 864 (9th Cir. 2001).

- **Monitor your workplace.** You and other managers should walk the floor periodically. Talk to employees about the work environment. Ask for their input. Look around the workplace itself. Do you see any offensive posters or notes? Keep the lines of communication open.

- **Take all complaints seriously.** If someone complains about harassment, immediately follow your company's reporting procedure. Prompt and thorough investigation can help your company defend against harassment lawsuits. If the complaint turns out to be valid, the company's response should be swift and effective. (For more information, see "Investigating Complaints" in Chapter 11.)

Communicating With Employees Effectively

More than any other aspect of successful management and leadership, good communication skills can have an enormously positive impact on your workforce. On the flip side, few things are as damaging to a workplace as poor communication. There are countless advantages to mastering good communication skills. Effective communication enhances your ability to:

- solve problems (and perhaps even anticipate them)
- supervise others successfully
- develop solid work relationships
- create a clear and compelling vision for your team (and your company)
- manage workflow between individuals and groups
- make well-informed decisions
- foster good performance, and
- eliminate poor performance.

Most of us believe that we know what we mean before we say something. Why,

then, do so many people consistently misunderstand us and get what we say wrong? Good communication is multifaceted. To communicate effectively, you need to get your point across in a way that whomever you're talking to can truly understand. Here are a few guiding principles to help you make yourself heard:

- Listen first.
- Understand your audience.
- Tailor your message appropriately (for your goals and your audience).
- Deliver your message using the right medium.
- Speak and write well.

Listen

Listening to others is probably the most overlooked aspect of good communication in the workplace. In their haste to make their own points, direct others, provide input, or just get things done, many managers issue declarative statements and pay little attention to the effect they have on those who hear them. Your ability to really listen, to understand what someone else is saying, and to incorporate that information into whatever you are doing, directly improves your skills and abilities as a manager.

The easiest way to build your listening skills is in a one-on-one environment. As you go about communicating something to an employee or coworker, stop and ask if he or she is clear on what you are saying. As the employee answers, listen closely and then repeat the answer back to the speaker, paraphrasing. Then ask, "Am I understanding you correctly?" Too often, managers ask questions and, as those questions are being answered, are already preparing their responses. By knowing that you will have to paraphrase the answer you hear back to the speaker, you can train yourself to really listen to what is being said.

Depending on your responsibilities as a manager, you might have to communicate with small and large groups in addition to individuals. Yet the importance of listening to your audience remains. How many times have you been sitting in a meeting, listening to a presentation, and noticed that your mind has wandered, perhaps sinking you into such boredom that you might even shut your eyes? If the speaker was paying close attention and listening to the cues of the audience, he or she would have known to either shorten the presentation or punch it up somehow to recapture the audience. When you are the speaker in such a situation, always stay alert to how your information is being received. Check in with your audience frequently for questions (you're really testing to see if they are still listening!) and shorten or modify your material if you see that you are losing people.

Understand Your Audience

Another common mistake in workplace communication is failing to consider whom you are speaking to and how that listener best receives information. Do not assume that everyone absorbs information like you do. Although it might be more comfortable for you to fall back on what works best for you, chances are that what works for you won't work for everyone.

In one-on-one communication, especially with employees whom you manage, simply ask the listener how he or she would like to communicate. Some employees might prefer to receive a written email rather than a phone call or voicemail if you are providing directives or instructions. Others might prefer to have a back-and-forth conversation. Some employees might require time to process or think about issues before they discuss them. For such folks, you'll want to set up meetings thoughtfully and provide an agenda in advance so that they know what you are expecting of them.

When it comes to providing criticism or negative feedback, you should be particularly sensitive to the needs of individual employees. For instance, it is never appropriate to criticize someone's work in a group setting. Some people need to be taken aside, have the issue pointed out to them, and then participate in deciding how to correct the issue. Others might want to be told what is wrong and how they could do it better, directly and forthrightly. By spending time with your team and learning how each of them hears things best, you will be much more effective in the long run.

In larger audiences, know whom you are talking to and how well they understand the material being presented. You might have heard the old adage that newspaper articles are written at the sixth-grade level, so that they are understood by all. While this guideline might work for the public as a whole, if you present a sixth-grade level presentation to the board of directors of your company, you'll probably be searching for a new job soon. Your audience will greatly appreciate being engaged at the appropriate level of their knowledge and interests.

Tailor Your Message Appropriately

Once you know your audience, put that information to work. There are many ways to tailor a message; knowing what you want to accomplish is key to getting the message across effectively. You should consider not only your audience, but also the goal of your communication.

If you need to deliver the same information to a variety of different people, you might need to tailor your message differently depending on your goal for communicating with each group. For example, imagine that you are a manager in a small company that is about to be sold to a larger company. You manage a very diverse group of individuals, from warehouse personnel to freelance writers. You know that the information will affect your reports differently, so you should prepare the appropriate communication for

each group you will face. When delivering the news to the freelance writers, you might, for example, focus more on the future plans of the new company and how the work they are currently doing will be folded into those plans. For the warehouse staff, however, you might focus on their employment status in particular, letting them know what will likely happen to their positions.

Deliver Your Message Using the Right Medium

Another key to effective communications at work is to deliver your message using the right medium of communication, whether in a conversation, an email, a meeting, or a written memo.

While the advent of email has been a huge boon to efficiency and consistency, email can be very dangerous when used to avoid difficult conversations or to vent frustrations. Email is appropriate for getting your simple questions answered quickly, making large group announcements, or documenting a conversation after the fact. But, unfortunately, email is often misused, allowing people who are uncomfortable with direct confrontation to raise difficult subjects while avoiding the reactions they provoke. This can be terribly destructive to effective communication at work because it can feel inappropriate or even cruel to the recipient. Also, when you send an email, you have no way of knowing how the recipient is interpreting your communication, which can cause needless and sometimes harmful misunderstandings.

Given the obvious limitations of email, even if it is your preferred method of communicating with employees, you must consider all of the possible ways you can deliver information at work and choose the most appropriate and effective medium. Consider the following:

- **Email.** As mentioned above, email is a great tool to update people, pass along materials, make brief announcements, provide status reports, ask and answer simple questions, and the like. It is not appropriate for many other kinds of communication.

- **Voicemail.** A bit more personal than email, voicemail allows you to convey meaning with your tone of voice. It is appropriate for leaving a short instruction or requesting an in-person conversation or meeting.

- **One-on-one conversations.** These are in-person meetings (or telephone conversations if the person you are speaking to is at another location). Conversation is a terrific medium for reviewing any performance issues, getting updated on work in progress, setting goals, and discussing how your employee is doing overall. It also provides direct and immediate feedback, the key to strong two-way communication.

- **Small group meetings.** This medium is best for making group decisions, gathering input from multiple sources, educating or training people, brain-storming ideas, and so on. A small group meeting should still involve two-way communication, allowing discussions, questions, and feedback.

- **Large group meetings.** This medium is best for bringing a larger number of people up to speed on specific issues in the same way at the same time. The larger the group, the more difficult it will be to engage in two-way communication, collect feedback, or make decisions.

- **Informal gatherings or hallway conversations.** Take advantage of these opportunities to get to know your team better outside the work environment. Be careful not to hand out or take on any action items during such communication, though, as assignments can be quickly forgotten.

The key point here is to match your medium or vehicle for communication with the message. Don't use a large group meeting to be critical of an employee, but do use it to celebrate someone's accomplishments. Don't use email to blow off steam if you're angry, but do use it to appropriately share information on a specific issue. And, most importantly, don't hide behind passive communication vehicles like email or voice-mail when you really need to have a direct, courageous conversation with someone.

Speak and Write Well

Finally, put some time and care into your written and spoken communication. Be clear and concise. Use words correctly. Check for typos and misspellings, even in internal emails, and especially in external presentations, memos, or correspondence. Such carelessness in a business setting is distracting and looks unprofessional.

Beyond these negatives, there are many more positive reasons why you should put care and thought into all your communications in the workplace:

- You appear more professional and knowledgeable.

- You garner credibility and respect.
- You will convey your point without distraction.
- You can be much more compelling when making an argument.
- You can effectively model good communication practices for employees and coworkers.

Improving your communication skills not only helps you in your current workplace, but it is also an investment in your own professional development. There are countless books and training courses available on how to write more clearly, improve your presentation skills, and the like. For more information, check out the

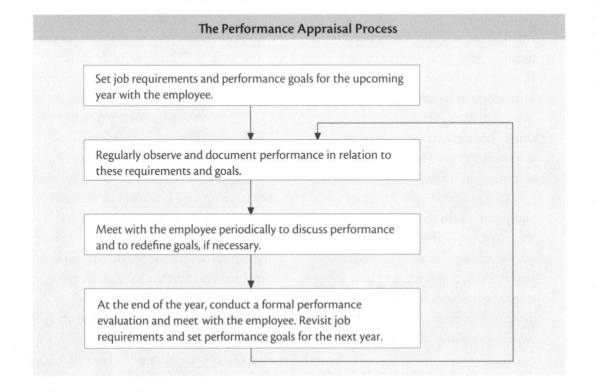

The Performance Appraisal Process

Set job requirements and performance goals for the upcoming year with the employee.

Regularly observe and document performance in relation to these requirements and goals.

Meet with the employee periodically to discuss performance and to redefine goals, if necessary.

At the end of the year, conduct a formal performance evaluation and meet with the employee. Revisit job requirements and set performance goals for the next year.

American Management Association, online at www.amanet.org, which provides training and seminars on communication skills; and the book *Harvard Business Review on Communicating Effectively* (2011).

Performance Appraisal

Managers who routinely review employee performance and conduct regular employee evaluations reap tremendous benefits. The evaluation process nips a lot of employment problems in the bud. Your reports will know what you expect of them; will receive feedback, praise, and criticism of their work; and will have notice of any shortfalls in their performance or conduct. You can recognize and reward good employees and identify and coach workers who are having trouble. And the communication involved in any good evaluation process ensures that you will stay in tune with the needs and concerns of the workers you supervise

Performance evaluations can also keep your company out of legal trouble. They help you track and document employee problems. If you ever need to fire or discipline a worker, you will have written proof that you gave the employee notice and a chance to correct the problem, which will go a long way toward convincing a jury or judge that you acted fairly. This section provides an overview of the performance appraisal process; for more detailed information and forms you can use in your workplace, see *The Performance Appraisal Handbook,* by Amy DelPo (Nolo).

Create Job Requirements and Performance Goals

Before you can accurately evaluate an employee's performance, you need some way to measure that performance. For each employee in a particular position, you will need to come up with job requirements and performance goals.

Job requirements describe what you want a worker in a particular job to accomplish and how you want the job done. These requirements apply across the board, to every worker who holds the same position. For example, a job requirement for a salesperson might be to make $40,000 in sales per quarter; for a customer service representative, to answer each call cheerfully; for a delivery driver, to have a missed delivery rate of 5% or less. Make sure requirements are achievable and directly related to the employee's job. If other managers supervise some employees who hold the same position, work together to come up with requirements all of you will use.

Performance goals, on the other hand, should be tailored to each employee; they will depend on the individual worker's strengths and weaknesses. For example, a goal for a graphic artist might be learning a new software design program; for an accounting professional, a goal might be to take the exam to become a Certified Public Accountant. Your workers can help you decide on reasonable goals.

Once you have defined the requirements and goals for each position and worker, write them down separately and hand them out to your reports. This will let employees know what you expect and what they will have to achieve during the year to receive a positive evaluation.

Keep Track of Employee Performance

Throughout the year, track the performance of each employee. Keep a performance log for each worker, either on your computer or on paper. Note memorable incidents or projects involving that worker, whether good or bad. For example, you might note that a worker was absent without calling in, worked overtime to complete an important project, or participated in a community outreach program on behalf of the company.

If an employee does an especially wonderful job on a project or really fouls something up, consider giving immediate feedback. Orally or in writing, let the employee know that you noticed and appreciate the extra effort, or that you are concerned about the employee's performance. If you choose to give this kind of feedback orally, make a written note of the conversation for the employee's personnel file.

Conduct Performance Evaluations

At least once a year, formally evaluate the worker by writing a performance evaluation and meeting with the worker to discuss it. First, gather and review all of the documents and records relating to the employee's performance, productivity, and behavior. Review your performance log for the employee and the employee's personnel file. You might also want to take a look at other company records relating to the worker, including sales records, call reports, productivity records, time cards, budget reports, and the like.

Once you have reviewed these records and gathered your thoughts about the employee's work, write the evaluation (or, if you will solicit input from other managers, ask each of them to complete an evaluation and compile them). Although a performance evaluation can take many forms, it should include:

- each requirement or goal you set for that worker and that job
- your conclusion as to whether the employee met the requirement or goal, and
- the reasons that support your conclusion.

Many companies use some kind of numerical scale or grading system to indicate how well the employee did on each goal or requirement. If yours is one of them, you should include these ratings in your evaluation. You should also leave space on the form for the employee's comments and your notes on your meeting with the employee.

When you have finished writing the evaluation, set up a meeting to discuss it with the employee. Remember, this is likely to be one of the most important meetings you have with that worker all year, so be sure to schedule enough time to discuss each issue thoroughly. At the meeting, let the worker know what you think he or she did well and what he or she needs to improve. Using your evaluation as a guide, explain your conclusions about each requirement and goal. Listen carefully to the worker's comments, and ask the worker to write them down on the evaluation form. Take notes on the meeting and include those notes on the form.

Tips for Performance Appraisal

Giving evaluations can be difficult. A worker who is criticized might react defensively. And, sometimes, no one understands what merits a positive evaluation. If workers feel that you take it easy on some of them while coming down hard on others, resentment will build. Avoid problems by following these rules:

- **Be specific.** When you set requirements and goals for your workers, spell out exactly what they will have to do to achieve them. For example, don't say "work harder" or "improve quality." Instead, say "increase sales by 20 percent over last year" or "make three or fewer errors per day in data input." Similarly, when you evaluate a worker, give specific examples of what the employee did well or needs to improve.
- **Give deadlines.** If you want to see improvement, give the worker a timeline for turning things around. If you expect

something to be done by a certain date, say so.
- **Be realistic.** If you set unrealistic or impossible requirements and goals, everyone will be disheartened. They will have little incentive to do their best if they know they will still fall short. Don't make your requirements too easy to achieve, but do take into account the realities of your workplace.
- **Be honest.** If you avoid telling a worker about performance problems, the worker won't know which areas need improvement. Be sure to give the bad news, even if it is uncomfortable.
- **Be complete.** Write your evaluation so that an outsider reading it would be able to understand exactly what happened and why. Remember, the evaluation could potentially become evidence in a lawsuit, should the employee ever sue. If it does become evidence, you will want the judge and jury to see why you rated the employee as you did.
- **Evaluate performance, not personality.** Focus on how well (or poorly) the worker did the job, not on the worker's personal characteristics or traits. Don't say, "You are angry and emotional." Instead, focus on the workplace conduct that is the problem. For example, you might write "You have been insubordinate to your supervisor twice in the past six months. This behavior is unacceptable and must stop."

- **Listen to your employees.** The evaluation process will seem fairer to workers if they have an opportunity to express their concerns, too. Ask employees what they enjoy about their jobs and working at the company. Also ask about any concerns or problems each employee has or whether the employee needs additional resources. You'll gain valuable information, and the employee will feel like a real participant in the process. In rare cases, you might even learn something that could change your evaluation.

Creating and Maintaining Personnel Files

Paperwork can be a bore, but setting up and maintaining personnel files will pay off in the long run. You will have all the important documents that relate to each employee in one place, easily accessible when it's time to make decisions on promotions or layoffs, file tax returns, or comply with government audits. And if you have to fire a problem employee, careful documentation can protect your company from legal trouble.

What Goes in a Personnel File

Begin a personnel file for each of your employees on the date of hire. (If you are a manager or supervisor, talk to your human resources department about who should set up the personnel file and whether you should keep your own files on your reports or submit all documents to the employee's main file.)

All important job-related documents should go in the file, including:

- the employee's job application and/or résumé
- letters of reference provided by or for the employee or notes from your conversations with references
- the offer letter
- IRS Form W-4: *Employee's Withholding Allowance Certificate*
- forms relating to the employee's benefits
- emergency contact forms
- a signed acknowledgment that the employee received and read the employee handbook
- performance evaluations
- other documents relating to the employee's performance (such as written warnings, memos on disciplinary actions, recognition for good performance, and complaints or compliments from customers)
- records of attendance at, or completion of, training programs
- records of promotions, pay raises, and transfers
- any contract, written agreement, receipt, or other acknowledgment between the employee and the employer (such as a noncompete agreement, an employment contract, or an agreement relating to a company-provided car), and

- documents relating to the worker's departure from the company (such as reasons why the worker was fired or let go, unemployment documents, COBRA forms, and other benefit documents).

Although an employee's personnel file should contain every important job-related document, don't go overboard. In many states, employees have the right to view their personnel files (or at least certain items, such as contracts or other documents they have signed). In the worst-case scenario, that file could turn into evidence in a lawsuit brought by a disgruntled former employee. Indiscreet entries that do not directly relate to an employee's job performance and qualifications—like references to an employee's private life or political beliefs; unsubstantiated criticisms; or comments about an employee's race, sex, or religion—will come back to haunt your company. A good rule of thumb: Don't put anything in a personnel file that you would not want a jury to see.

What Does Not Go in a Personnel File

Although most employment-related documents should be kept in a worker's personnel file, there are a couple of exceptions to this rule. First, medical records should not go in a worker's personnel file. If a worker has a disability, the employer is legally required to keep all of the worker's medical records in a separate file and limit access only to a very few people. A similar rule applies to records of genetic information (under the Genetic Information Nondiscrimination Act, as explained in Chapter 3) and family and medical leave records (under the Family and Medical Leave Act, covered in Chapter 5). The best practice is to segregate all medical information into a separate file for each worker, whether or not it fits squarely within the definition provided by one of these laws.

Second, Form I-9, the form you must complete for each employee verifying eligibility to work in this country, should be kept in a separate file. The U.S. Citizenship and Immigration Service (USCIS), the agency that replaced the INS, is entitled to inspect these forms. If you keep these forms in a worker's personnel file, the USCIS will be looking at all those other documents as well. Not only does this compromise workers' privacy, but it also might open your company up to additional questions and investigation.

How to Maintain a Personnel File

Establish a time to periodically review each employee's personnel file, perhaps when you conduct the employee's evaluation. During this review, consider whether the documents in the file are accurate, up to date, and complete. Some questions to consider:

- Does the file reflect all of the employee's raises, promotions, and commendations?
- Does the file contain every written evaluation of the employee?

- Does the file show every warning or other disciplinary action taken against the employee?
- If company policy provides that written warnings or other records of discipline will be removed from an employee's file after a certain period, have they been removed?
- If the employee was on a performance improvement plan, a probationary or training period, or other temporary status, has it ended? Has the file been updated to reflect the employee's current status?
- If the employee handbook has been updated since the employee started work, does the file contain a receipt or acknowledgment for the most recent version?
- Does the file contain current versions of every contract or other agreement between the company and the employee?

Once you get a regular filing system in place (for example, to make sure every new document a worker signs goes in the personnel file), these annual reviews should only take a few minutes.

Who May See Personnel Files

Generally, personnel files should be treated as private records belonging to the company and its employees. Obviously, not everyone in the company should be allowed to rummage through the performance evaluations, salaries, and job applications of other employees. But, some employees might have a legitimate need to view the information in a personnel file. For example, you or another manager might need to review performance evaluations to decide whether to promote an employee, or the human resources manager might need to review an employee's salary information to decide what to pay a new hire in the same position.

Treat personnel files like any other private company records: Keep them confidential and store them in a locked cabinet (or a password-protected database). Allow only those with legitimate business reasons to have access to the files. For example, a reasonable policy might give only the human resources manager, the individual employee's manager, and the employee the right to see the employee's file. This will protect employees' privacy and limit opportunities for inappropriate documents to find their way into the files.

Employees' Rights to See Their Own Personnel Files

Most states give employees some right to view the contents of their own personnel files. This right may be limited, however. In some states, employers must provide workers with copies of certain documents in their files. In others, the employee may only review the file in person, sometimes in the presence of a company representative. And in some states, the company can withhold certain documents that might compromise another person's privacy, such as letters of reference or investigation reports that include witness statements. To find out your state's rules, see "State Laws on Access to Personnel Records," at the end of this chapter.

Even if your state does not expressly allow employees to inspect their personnel files, however, it's a sensible policy to allow them to do so, or at least to inform them about documents that are in their files. If you are planning to take action against an employee based on material in the personnel file—a customer complaint or documented performance problems, for example—let the employee know. That way, the employee will have a chance to explain or discuss the problem and an opportunity to improve. An employee who finds negative information in a file only after being fired is likely to believe, rightly or wrongly, that those documents were created after the fact.

Family-Friendly Workplace Policies

In addition to the personnel policies that you must adopt, an increasing number of companies today are choosing to adopt policies that help their employees to meet the competing demands of work and family.

Family-Friendly Policies Defined

For a variety of reasons, a growing number of companies today are adopting personnel policies that help their employees balance work and family obligations. Such policies are often referred to as "family-friendly policies," and they benefit more than just employees with young children. In fact, employees with elderly parents or other relatives for whom they must care, or employees who have their own health or personal needs that interfere with work, can benefit from such policies as well.

Adopting family-friendly policies can be an inexpensive yet effective way to attract workers to your company these days, when the costs of employee benefits can be astronomical. You might not think of allowing workers more flexibility with their schedules or providing workers help to locate child or elder care services, for example, as traditional employment benefits. Yet such policies can be valuable and inexpensive tools to attract the best workers, especially if your company isn't able to pay for the most comprehensive health insurance plan or make large matching contributions to their 401(k)s.

In addition, your company can reap cost savings by adopting policies that let employees deal with family or other matters that would otherwise be distracting or interrupt their work. Family-friendly policies can increase loyalty, job satisfaction, and productivity, while reducing absenteeism, turnover, and the associated costs of finding and training new workers. Global consulting company Deloitte estimated that offering flexible work arrangements to 30,000 employees in the United States helped save $41.5 million in turnover and affiliated costs in 2003, while pharmaceutical company Merck & Co. estimated that it cost $38,000 to give an average employee a six-month parental leave with partial pay and benefits, as compared to $50,000 to replace the employee. (Elyane Robertson Demby, "Do Your Family-Friendly Programs Make Cents?" *HR Magazine*, January 2004.)

Below are some of the types of family-friendly policies that companies around the nation are implementing. (Note that these are just a handful of potential policies: The possibilities are limited only by the imaginations of your company's policymakers.)

- **Flexible work schedules.** This means allowing employees to work full time, yet outside of normal business hours, whether it be 7:00 a.m. to 3:00 p.m., ten hours for four days a week, or a varying schedule each day. It can also mean the flexibility to leave work when necessary to take an elderly parent to a doctor's appointment or pick up a sick child early from school. (For more on flextime, see "Flexible Work Schedules" in Chapter 2.)

- **Telecommuting.** This refers to allowing employees to work off site—for example, from home—for some or all of their workweek.

- **Job sharing.** This means allowing two employees to share one full-time job, alternating days or shifts (one working mornings and the other afternoons, for example).

- **Flexible spending accounts.** These are tax-saving vehicles that allow employees to set aside pretax money from their income (like a 401(k)) which they can then use to reimburse their dependent care costs and medical expenses.

- **Employee assistance programs (EAPs) or work/life programs.** These are general terms for a host of supportive services that companies provide to their employees, such as resource lists or other help finding child care, after-school care, or elder care providers.

- **Caregiving services.** Some companies go as far as providing financial assistance for child care nearby, providing on-site child care, or providing emergency caregiver services to be used when planned child or elder care falls through.

- **Allowing employees to donate sick or vacation time to each other.** Should one employee have an emergency situation, this allows others to help that employee out (while not requiring the company to provide any additional sick or vacation leave). (For more on sick and vacation time, see "Vacation and Sick Leave" in Chapter 5.)

- **Providing additional family and medical leave.** This means either providing more unpaid leave than is legally required or providing partial or total pay during an employee's otherwise unpaid leave. (For more on family and medical leave, see Chapter 5.)

Are Family-Friendly Policies Legal?

As with all employment benefits your company provides, any family-friendly policies your company decides to adopt will be legally sound as long as the company offers and administers such policies fairly, consistently, and free from illegal discrimination. Again, this does not mean that you have to provide every worker with the same family-friendly benefits; it just means that you cannot decide who gets such benefits based on an impermissible reason, such as race, gender, national origin, religion, age, or disability. Your company may, for example, decide to provide paid family and medical leave only for top executives as part of an executive compensation package. Or you may decide who gets to work a flexible schedule based on seniority with the company. In addition, where appropriate, some of these policies may be used as reasonable accommodations for employees with disabilities (for example, allowing a worker to work flextime, share a job, or telecommute). (See "Disability" in Chapter 3 for more on reasonable accommodations.)

Once you make such a policy, however, you cannot discriminate in offering it by, for example, allowing only mothers access to such benefits, but not fathers. One note of caution here: Some state and local laws prohibit discrimination based on sexual orientation and/or marital status, so be sure to follow any such laws that apply to your company when administering family-friendly policies. For more information on impermissible discrimination, see Chapter 3 and contact your state fair employment practices agency. (Contact information is in the appendix.)

While some might complain that family-friendly policies favor workers who have children over those who don't or favor women over men, this is not necessarily true, as long as you make such policies available equally to all workers who might need them. For example, if you offer paid maternity leave, offer paid paternity leave, too. If you offer flexible work schedules to care for children after school, offer this benefit equally to mothers and fathers. If you allow job sharing or part-time work for parents of young children, allow the same for workers who need to care for an elderly parent or sick spouse. In short, be sure to make all of your family-friendly policies clear and consistent and to administer them fairly, without regard to race, gender, national origin, religion, age, disability, or any other characteristics protected by your state and local laws.

For more information on family-friendly workplace policies, consult one of the many organizations that focus on helping employees balance work and family, including the following:

- The Families and Work Institute (www.familiesandwork.org)
- The National Partnership for Women and Families (www.nationalpartnership.org)
- Catalyst (www.catalyst.org), and
- *Working Mother Magazine* (www.workingmother.com), which publishes an annual list of the best 100 companies to work for based on their family-friendly policies.

Legal Dos and Don'ts: Personnel Basics

Do:

- **Keep your door open.** All good management practices and policies are based on communication between workers and managers. Keep your ear to the ground by having an open door policy that encourages your reports to come to you with concerns or ideas, and by listening to what they have to say. You might be surprised at what you hear.

- **Blaze a paper trail.** Any time you evaluate, discipline, take a complaint from, or investigate an employee, write it down. Keeping a written record of an employee's performance and conduct is the best way to keep your company out of court. If you later have to fire that employee, your documents will make it much harder for him or her to find a lawyer willing to take the case.

- **Get help from your reports.** Your policies and practices will be most effective if workers believe they are reasonable and fair, which is more likely if they had a hand in their development. Encourage employees to help you develop performance requirements and goals, come up with training programs, or suggest ways you can help them do their jobs more effectively.

Don't:

- **Sugarcoat the truth.** Most of us dislike giving bad news or disappointing others. But when you are giving evaluations or administering discipline, you have to be honest. Employees will improve only if you tell them exactly what you expect and where they have fallen short.

- **Treat some workers better than others.** Discrimination claims start with inconsistency: treating some workers better (or worse) than others. By knowing your company's policies and applying them evenhandedly, you will avoid playing favorites or picking on scapegoats, practices sure to land your company in legal trouble.

- **Procrastinate.** Putting off important tasks is a bad habit for a variety of reasons, but managers who procrastinate can create lots of unnecessary problems. If you are always timely with your performance evaluations and personnel documents, you will be able to avoid claims that you created evidence after the fact to justify termination or other discipline.

Test Your Knowledge

Questions

1. All employees work at will unless they have a written employment contract stating otherwise. ☐ True ☐ False

2. Managers should always have a good reason for firing an employee, even if the employee works at will. ☐ True ☐ False

3. As long as company policies are written down in an employee handbook, managers are free to supervise employees and make decisions as they see fit. ☐ True ☐ False

4. You have no obligation to report or take action to stop sexual harassment unless the victim is willing to make a complaint in writing. ☐ True ☐ False

5. Antiharassment training is not just a good idea; it might also be legally required. ☐ True ☐ False

6. Because it is so efficient, you should always communicate with employees you supervise via email. ☐ True ☐ False

7. You should give employees feedback throughout the year, not just at formal, year-end reviews. ☐ True ☐ False

8. I-9 forms should not be kept in employees' regular personnel files. ☐ True ☐ False

9. Employees are not entitled to see what's in their personnel files. ☐ True ☐ False

10. Family-friendly policies are discriminatory because they only benefit workers who have children. ☐ True ☐ False

Test Your Knowledge (continued)

Answers

1. False. If you make promises about continued employment to an employee, orally or in writing (for example, in an employee handbook), you risk creating an oral or implied contract that the employee will be fired only for good cause or other specified reasons.

2. True. Even if you have the legal right to fire at will, you don't gain anything by using it. Firing employees without a good reason leads to morale problems and employee lawsuits.

3. False. Written policies in an employee handbook are meaningless if managers don't follow those policies consistently.

4. False. Once a manager learns of harassment—whether through a complaint, personal observation, or any other means—the company is legally obligated to take action to stop it. Employees need not make a written complaint to put the company on notice.

5. True. Some states require companies to provide antiharassment training to managers.

6. False. Email is a great tool for certain types of communication, such as to document a conversation after it occurs or to make brief announcements. It is not, however, appropriate for many kinds of communication, such as providing feedback on an employee's performance or delivering bad news. Never use email as a way to avoid conversations that make you uncomfortable.

7. True. Ongoing feedback, both positive and negative, is an important part of a successful performance evaluation system.

8. True. I-9 forms should be kept in a separate file, so government auditors will be able to review them without rummaging through other employee personnel documents.

9. False. Most states give employees and former employees a right to see at least some of the documents in their personnel files.

10. False. Instituting policies that help workers balance the demands of work and family can benefit all workers, regardless of whether they have children or not. Flexible work schedules, job sharing, and flexible spending accounts can all help workers to care for elderly parents or sick spouses or partners or to meet their own health or other needs. As long as such policies are written and applied consistently, fairly, and without regard to such protected characteristics as gender, race, national origin, age, and the like, they are legally sound.

State Laws on Access to Personnel Records

This chart deals with only those states that authorize access to personnel files. Generally, an employee is allowed to see evaluations, performance reviews, and other documents that determine a promotion, bonus, or raise; access usually does not include letters of reference, test results, or records of a criminal or workplace-violation investigation. Under other state laws, employees might have the right to access their medical records, payroll records, and records of exposure to hazardous substances; these laws are not included in this chart.

Alaska

Alaska Stat. § 23.10.430

Employers affected: All

Employee access to records: Employee or former employee may view and copy personnel files.

Conditions for viewing records: Employee may view records during regular business hours under reasonable rules.

Copying records: Employee pays (if employer requests).

California

Cal. Lab. Code §§ 1198.5; 432

Employers affected: All employers subject to wage and hour laws

Employee access to records: Employee or former employee has right to inspect personnel records relating to performance or to a grievance proceeding, within 30 days of making a written request for records. Employer may redact the names of any nonmanagerial employees. Employer need not comply with more than one request per year from a former employee. If employee files a lawsuit against employer that relates to a personnel matter, the right to review personnel records ceases while the suit is pending.

Written request required: Yes. If employee makes an oral request, the employer must supply a form to make a written request.

Conditions for viewing records: Employee may view personnel file at reasonable times, during break or nonwork hours. If records are kept offsite or employer does not make them available at the workplace, then employee must be allowed to view them at the storage location without loss of pay. If former employee was terminated for reasons relating to harassment or workplace violence, employer may provide copy of records or make them available offsite.

Copying records: Employee or former employee also has a right to a copy of personnel records, at the employee's cost, within 30 days of making a written request.

Connecticut

Conn. Gen. Stat. Ann. §§ 31-128a to 31-128h

Employers affected: All

Employee access to records: Employee has right to inspect personnel files within 7 business days after making a request, but not more than twice a year. Former employee has right to inspect personnel files within 10 business days after making a request.

Written request required: Yes.

Conditions for viewing records: Employee may view records during regular business hours in a location at or near worksite. Employer may require that files be viewed in the presence of designated official.

Copying records: Employer must provide copies within 7 days (current employee) or 10 days (former employee) after receiving employee's written request; request must identify the materials employee wants copied. Employer may charge a fee that is based on the cost of supplying documents.

State Laws on Access to Personnel Records (continued)

Employee is entitled to a copy of any disciplinary action against the employee within 1 business day after it is imposed; employer must immediately provide terminated employee with a copy of the termination notice.

Employee's right to insert rebuttal: If employee disagrees with information in personnel file and cannot reach an agreement with employer to remove or correct it, employee may submit an explanatory written statement (a "rebuttal"). Rebuttal must be maintained as part of the file. Employer must inform employee of the right to submit a rebuttal in evaluation, discipline, or termination paperwork.

Delaware

Del. Code Ann. tit. 19, §§ 730 to 735

Employers affected: All

Employee access to records: Current employee, employee who is laid off with reemployment rights, or employee on leave of absence may inspect personnel record; employee's agent is not entitled to have access to records. Unless there is reasonable cause, employer may limit access to once a year.

Written request required: At employer's discretion. Employer may require employee to file a form and indicate either the purpose of the review or what parts of the record employee wants to inspect.

Conditions for viewing records: Records may be viewed during employer's regular business hours. Employer may require that employees view files on their own time and may also require that files be viewed on the premises and in the presence of a designated official.

Copying records: Employer is not required to permit employee to copy records. Employee may take notes.

Employee's right to insert rebuttal: If employee disagrees with information in personnel file and cannot reach an agreement with employer to remove or correct it, employee may submit an explanatory written statement (a "rebuttal"). Rebuttal must be maintained as part of the personnel file.

Illinois

820 Ill. Comp. Stat. §§ 40/1 to 40/12

Employers affected: Employers with 5 or more employees

Employee access to records: Current employee, or former employee terminated within the past year, is permitted to inspect records twice a year at reasonable intervals, unless a collective bargaining agreement provides otherwise. An employee involved in a current grievance may designate a representative of the union or collective bargaining unit, or other agent, to inspect personnel records that may be relevant to resolving the grievance. Employer must make records available within 7 working days after employee makes request (if employer cannot meet deadline, may be allowed an additional 7 days).

Written request required: At employer's discretion. Employer may require use of a form.

Conditions for viewing records: Records may be viewed during normal business hours at or near worksite or, at employer's discretion, during nonworking hours at a different location if more convenient for employee.

Copying records: After reviewing records, employee may get a copy. Employer may charge only actual cost of duplication. If employee is unable to view files at worksite, employer, upon receipt of a written request, must mail employee a copy.

State Laws on Access to Personnel Records (continued)

Employee's right to insert rebuttal: If employee disagrees with any information in the personnel file and cannot reach an agreement with employer to remove or correct it, employee may submit an explanatory written statement (a "rebuttal"). Rebuttal must remain in file with no additional comment by employer.

Iowa
Iowa Code §§ 91B.1, 91A.2

Employers affected: All employers with salaried employees or commissioned salespeople

Employee access to records: Employee may have access to personnel file at time agreed upon by employer and employee.

Conditions for viewing records: Employer's representative may be present.

Copying records: Employer may charge copying fee for each page that is equivalent to a commercial copying service fee.

Maine
Me. Rev. Stat. Ann. tit. 26, § 631

Employers affected: All

Employee access to records: Within 10 days of submitting request, employee, former employee, or authorized representative may view and copy personnel files.

Written request required: Yes

Conditions for viewing records: Employee may view records during normal business hours at the location where the files are kept, unless employer, at own discretion, arranges a time and place more convenient for employee. If files are in electronic or any other nonprint format, employer must provide equipment for viewing and copying.

Copying records: Employee entitled to one free copy of personnel file during each calendar year, including any material added to file during that year. Employee must pay for any additional copies.

Massachusetts
Mass. Gen. Laws ch. 149, § 52C

Employers affected: All

Employee access to records: Employee or former employee must have opportunity to review personnel files within 5 business days of submitting request, but not more than twice a calendar year. (Law does not apply to tenured or tenure-track employees in private colleges and universities.) Employer must notify an employee within 10 days of placing in the employee's personnel record any information to the extent that the information is, has been, or may be used, to negatively affect the employee's qualification for employment, promotion, transfer, additional compensation, or the possibility that the employee will be subject to disciplinary action. (This notification does not count toward employee's two allotted opportunities to view personnel file.)

Written request required: Yes

Conditions for viewing records: Employee may view records at workplace during normal business hours.

Copying records: Employee must be given a copy of record within 5 business days of submitting a written request.

Employee's right to insert rebuttal: If employee disagrees with any information in personnel record and cannot reach an agreement with employer to remove or correct it, employee may submit an explanatory written statement (a "rebuttal"). Rebuttal becomes a part of the personnel file.

State Laws on Access to Personnel Records (continued)

Michigan

Mich. Comp. Laws §§ 423.501 to 423.505

Employers affected: Employers with 4 or more employees

Employee access to records: Current or former employee is entitled to review personnel records at reasonable intervals, generally not more than twice a year, unless a collective bargaining agreement provides otherwise.

Written request required: Yes. Request must describe the record employee wants to review.

Conditions for viewing records: Employee may view records during normal office hours either at or reasonably near the worksite. If these hours would require employee to take time off work, employer must provide another time and place that is more convenient for the employee.

Copying records: After reviewing files, employee may get a copy; employer may charge only actual cost of duplication. If employee is unable to view files at the worksite, employer, upon receipt of a written request, must mail employee a copy.

Employee's right to insert rebuttal: If employee disagrees with any information in personnel record and cannot reach an agreement with employer to remove or correct it, employee may submit a written statement explaining his or her position. Statement may be no longer than five 8½" by 11" pages.

Minnesota

Minn. Stat. Ann. §§ 181.960 to 181.966

Employers affected: 20 or more employees

Employee access to records: Current employee may review files once per 6-month period; former employee may have access to records once only during the first year after termination. Employer must comply with written request within 7 working days (14 working days if personnel records kept

out of state). Employer may not retaliate against an employee who asserts rights under these laws.

Written request required: Yes

Conditions for viewing records: Current employee may view records during employer's normal business hours at worksite or a nearby location; does not have to take place during employee's working hours. Employer or employer's representative may be present.

Copying records: Employer must provide copy free of charge. Current employee must first review record and then submit written request for copies. Former employee must submit written request; providing former employee with a copy fulfills employer's obligation to allow access to records.

Employee's right to insert rebuttal: If employee disputes specific information in the personnel record, and cannot reach an agreement with employer to remove or revise it, employee may submit a written statement identifying the disputed information and explaining his or her position. Statement may be no longer than 5 pages and must be kept with personnel record as long as it is maintained.

Nevada

Nev. Rev. Stat. Ann. § 613.075

Employers affected: All

Employee access to records: An employee who has worked at least 60 days and a former employee, within 60 days of termination, must be given a reasonable opportunity to inspect personnel records.

Conditions for viewing records: Employee may view records during employer's normal business hours.

Copying records: Employer may charge only actual cost of providing access and copies.

Employee's right to insert rebuttal: Employee may submit a reasonable written explanation in

State Laws on Access to Personnel Records (continued)

direct response to any entry in personnel record. Statement must be of reasonable length; employer may specify the format; employer must maintain statement in personnel records.

New Hampshire
N.H. Rev. Stat. Ann. § 275:56

Employers affected: All

Employee access to records: Employer must provide employees with a reasonable opportunity to inspect records.

Copying records: Employer may charge a fee reasonably related to cost of supplying copies.

Employee's right to insert rebuttal: If employee disagrees with any of the information in personnel record and cannot reach an agreement with the employer to remove or correct it, employee may submit an explanatory written statement along with supporting evidence. Statement must be maintained as part of personnel file.

Oregon
Ore. Rev. Stat. § 652.750

Employers affected: All

Employee access to records: Within 45 days after receipt of request, employer must provide employee a reasonable opportunity to inspect personnel records used to determine qualifications for employment, promotion, or additional compensation, termination, or other disciplinary action.

Conditions for viewing records: Employee may view records at worksite or place of work assignment.

Copying records: Within 45 days after receipt of request, employer must provide a certified copy of requested record to current or former employee (if request made within 60 days of termination). If employee makes request after 60 days from termination, employer shall provide a certified copy of requested records if employer has records at

time of the request. May charge amount reasonably calculated to recover actual cost of providing copy.

Pennsylvania
43 Pa. Cons. Stat. Ann. §§ 1321 to 1324

Employers affected: All

Employee access to records: Employer must allow employee to inspect personnel record at reasonable times. (Employee's agent, or employee who is laid off with reemployment rights or on leave of absence, must also be given access.) Unless there is reasonable cause, employer may limit review to once a year by employee and once a year by employee's agent.

Written request required: At employer's discretion. Employer may require the use of a form as well as a written indication of the parts of the record employee wants to inspect or the purpose of the inspection. For employee's agent: Employee must provide signed authorization designating agent; must be for a specific date and indicate the reason for the inspection or the parts of the record the agent is authorized to inspect.

Conditions for viewing records: Employee may view records during normal business hours at the office where records are maintained, when there is enough time for employee to complete the review. Employer may require that employee or agent to view records on their own time and may also require that inspection take place on the premises and in the presence of employer's designated official.

Copying records: Employer not obligated to permit copying. Employee may take notes.

Employee's right to insert rebuttal: The Bureau of Labor Standards, after a petition and hearing, may allow employee to place a counterstatement in the personnel file, if employee claims that the file contains an error.

State Laws on Access to Personnel Records (continued)

Rhode Island

R.I. Gen. Laws § 28-6.4-1

Employers affected: All

Employee access to records: Employer must permit employee to inspect personnel file when given at least 7 days advance notice (excluding weekends and holidays). Employer may limit access to no more than 3 times a year.

Written request required: Yes

Conditions for viewing records: Employee may view records at any reasonable time other than employee's work hours. Inspection must take place in presence of employer or employer's representative.

Copying records: Employee may not make copies or remove files from place of inspection. Employer may charge a fee reasonably related to cost of supplying copies.

Washington

Wash. Rev. Code Ann. §§ 49.12.240 to 49.12.260

Employers affected: All

Employee access to records: Employee may have access to personnel records at least once a year within a reasonable time after making a request.

Employee's right to insert rebuttal: Employee may petition annually that employer review all information in employee's personnel file. If there is any irrelevant or incorrect information in the file, employer must remove it. If employee does not agree with employer's review, employee may request to have a statement of rebuttal or correction placed in file. Former employee has right of rebuttal for two years after termination.

Wisconsin

Wis. Stat. Ann. § 103.13

Employers affected: All employers who maintain personnel records

Employee access to records: Employee and former employee must be allowed to inspect personnel records within 7 working days of making request. Access is permitted twice per calendar year unless a collective bargaining agreement provides otherwise. Employee involved in a current grievance may designate a representative of the union or collective bargaining unit, or other agent, to inspect records that may be relevant to resolving the grievance.

Written request required: At employer's discretion.

Conditions for viewing records: Employee may view records during normal working hours at a location reasonably near worksite. If this would require employee to take time off work, employer may provide another reasonable time and place for review.

Copying records: Employee's right of inspection includes the right to make or receive copies. If employer provides copies, may charge only actual cost of reproduction.

Employee's right to insert rebuttal: If employee disagrees with any information in the personnel record and cannot come to an agreement with the employer to remove or correct it, employee may submit an explanatory written statement. Employer must attach the statement to the disputed portion of the personnel record.

Time Off

We all know that a little time off work is a good thing. Workers get a chance to have fun, recharge their batteries, and deal with personal and family obligations as they arise. And your company benefits, too: A company is more productive if its employees (and managers!) are healthy, rested, and focused on their jobs.

Whether your company offers a generous leave program or only the minimum required by law, this chapter will give you an overview of the rules on:

- vacation
- sick leave
- family and medical leave
- pregnancy and parental leave
- time off for jury duty
- voting leave
- leave for military service
- domestic violence leave, and
- other types of legally required leave.

If you are responsible for setting company policy, this chapter will help you create sensible leave policies that stay well within the bounds of the law. If your job is to supervise employees, this information will help you figure out how to handle requests for leave, how to enforce your company's policies, and what kinds of requests should alert you to a potential legal problem for your company.

Frequently Asked Questions About Leave

Is my company legally required to offer paid vacation and sick leave?

In most places, no. Federal law does not impose any vacation or sick leave requirements, so this area is left up to state and local laws. While no state requires vacation—paid or unpaid—a growing number of states and cities have passed paid sick leave laws in recent years. Seven states and Washington DC, along with several cities, require employers to provide at least a few days of paid sick leave to employees each year. Many other states are considering similar laws. (For more information, see "Vacation and Sick Leave," below.)

Does my company have to provide family and medical leave?

It depends on how many employees work for your company. Under the federal Family and Medical Leave Act (FMLA), employers must allow employees to take leave only if they employ 50 people or more within a 75-mile radius. To be eligible, employees must have worked for the employer for at least one year, among other things. Some states have their own leave laws in addition to the FMLA, which might apply to smaller employers. (For more on the requirements of the FMLA, see "Family and Medical Leave," below.)

Frequently Asked Questions About Leave (continued)

Can I fire a pregnant employee for poor attendance, even if the absences are pregnancy related?

It's illegal to fire an employee because she is pregnant. However, if you would fire any employee with poor attendance, you may legally fire your pregnant employee for that reason, as long as the absences for which you are firing her are not protected by the FMLA, the ADA, or similar state laws. (For more on pregnancy leave, see "Pregnancy and Parental Leave," below.)

One of the employees I supervise just got called for jury duty. If she gets seated on a jury, can I fire her?

No. Almost every state prohibits employers from firing or disciplining an employee for being called to jury duty and serving on a jury. However, most states do not require companies to pay employees for time spent on jury duty unless their own employment policies provide for such pay. (For more on employees and jury duty, see "Jury Duty and Voting," below.)

Does my company have to pay employees for time spent voting?

It depends on where your workplace is. Almost half of the states require employers to provide at least a couple of hours of paid leave so employees can vote, if the employee does not have enough time to vote outside of working hours. Even if your company does business in a state that does not require paid leave for voting, you must not discipline any employee for taking time off to cast a ballot. (For more on leave to vote, see "Jury Duty and Voting," below.)

Does my company have to give employees time off for National Guard training or other military service?

Most likely. Federal law requires employers to reinstate workers who take up to five years of leave to serve in the armed forces. And in almost every state, employers must allow their employees to take leave for certain types of military service. In some states, only employees called for active duty are entitled to leave; other states require leave for training as well. (For more on leave for military duties, see "Military Leave," below.)

Are employees entitled to take time off to handle domestic violence issues?

It depends on the situation and the laws of your state. If the employee has a serious health condition or needs to care for a family member with a serious health condition due to domestic violence, the Family and Medical Leave Act (or a similar state law) might give the employee the right to take time off. About a dozen states have separate laws that give victims of domestic violence a right to time off work to deal with medical issues, relocate, or take legal action against their abusers. (For more information, see "Domestic Violence Leave," below.)

Vacation and Sick Leave

Most employers do not currently have to provide paid sick or vacation leave, although this issue is a hot topic of debate in federal, state, and local legislatures. In recent years, a handful of states and several cities have passed laws requiring employers to provide a small number of paid sick days per year, usually in the range of three to five days. (See, "Paid Leave," below.) However, the majority of states do not require any form of paid sick leave, and no state requires paid vacation leave.

Voluntary Sick and Vacation Policies

If your company isn't required to offer paid leave, it might decide not to (although such a policy would make it tough to attract and retain high-quality employees). If your company decides to adopt a paid leave policy, keep these guidelines in mind:

- **Apply the policy consistently to all employees.** Don't make individual decisions on who can take leave and for how long. Adopt a policy that applies to all workers in a particular position or all workers at your company. If your company already has a policy, apply it evenhandedly. If some employees are offered a more attractive leave package than others in the same position, you are opening your company up to claims of unfair treatment and possible discrimination lawsuits.
- **Require employees to schedule leave in advance, if possible.** Sometimes, an employee cannot know ahead of time that he or she will need time off (for a sudden illness or family emergency, for example). In all other circumstances, however, you should ask your reports to schedule leave—especially vacations—at least a month in advance. This will help you meet your staffing needs, particularly during summers and holidays.
- **Adopt a sensible vacation accrual policy.** Many employees enjoy taking a longer vacation from time to time, and a policy that allows employees to save up a long stretch of vacation time—four weeks, for example—for this purpose is reasonable. Your company might want to cap how much vacation time an employee can accrue or specify how much vacation an employee can take at one time, however. Otherwise, you might suddenly have several employees asking for months off at a time. Employees are also less likely to suffer from burnout if they take their vacation at more regular intervals.
- **Follow your state's rules on use-it-or-lose-it policies.** A few states, including California, prohibit employers from adopting a use-it-or-lose-it vacation policy, which requires employees to use accrued vacation by a certain date or forfeit it. (California does allow a reasonable cap on vacation accrual, though.) While the majority of states allow use-it-or-lose-it policies, a handful require employers to give employees

notice and a reasonable opportunity to use the accrued vacation before it disappears. To find out what rules apply to your company, contact your state's department of labor (see appendix for contact information).

- **Don't allow abuse of sick leave time.** Some employees treat sick leave as an extra allotment of vacation days. Crack down by requiring employees to call in each day they are ill, requiring a doctor's note for serious illnesses, and monitoring patterns of sick leave use. Do you have employees who only seem to call in sick on Mondays and Fridays? Do some employees claim illness at the end of every year, in an effort to take advantage of unused sick time? Counsel these employees about the proper use of sick leave, and discipline those who abuse the system.

- **Consider what you will pay when an employee quits or is fired.** If your company allows employees to accrue vacation days, it must decide whether to pay departing employees for unused leave. Some states, including California, require employers to pay for this accrued vacation time when employment ends. (See "State Laws That Control Final Paychecks," at the end of Chapter 14, for information on your state's rules.) Although employers are generally not required to pay out unused sick days, some do anyway, perhaps believing that this encourages employees not to misuse sick leave.

State Paid Sick Leave Laws

In a growing trend over the last five years, a number of states (and cities) have passed paid sick leave laws, requiring employers to provide at least a few days off for illness and other reasons. To date, the District of Columbia and the following states have paid sick leave laws: Arizona, California, Connecticut, Massachusetts, Oregon, Vermont, and Washington. Some of these laws apply to all employers, regardless of size; other laws apply only to larger employers or have different rules for employers based on their size.

Sick leave amounts and accrual rates vary by state. However, it's common for employees to accrue one hour of sick leave for every 30 hours worked, up to a maximum of 40 hours of paid sick leave per year (the equivalent of five work days). Employees generally must be allowed to carry over accrued sick leave from year to year, but employers are not required to pay out accrued leave when the employee separates from the company.

In most states, employees may use paid sick leave for a variety of purposes, including:

- the employee's own illness, treatment, or preventative care
- a family member's illness, treatment, or preventative care, and
- to deal with the effects of domestic violence, stalking, or sexual assault.

Several other states and cities are considering similar laws. Because this area is in flux, you should check in regularly with your state and local government to find out whether any new laws apply to your company. You can also find legal updates at this book's online companion page (see the introductory chapter for the link).

Family and Medical Leave

It can be tough to balance the demands of a job with personal and family needs. In response to this much-discussed problem, Congress passed the Family and Medical Leave Act (FMLA), 29 U.S.C. §§ 2601 and following, then amended it in 2008 to cover military family leave. The FMLA requires certain employers to allow their employees up to 12 weeks of unpaid leave per year to care for a seriously ill family member, to deal with their own serious illnesses, to take care of a newborn or newly adopted child, or to handle a qualifying exigency arising out of a family member's call or deployment to active military duty. The FMLA also requires employers to allow employees to take up to 26 weeks of leave in a single leave year to care for a family member who suffered a serious injury or illness while serving on active duty.

In most cases, the employer must reinstate an employee returning from leave to either the same position or to a position that is comparable in every important respect—including pay, benefits, and status. (For detailed information on the FMLA, see *The Essential Guide to Family and Medical Leave,* by Lisa Guerin and Deborah C. England (Nolo).)

When the FMLA Applies

An employer must comply with the FMLA if it has 50 or more employees during at least 20 calendar workweeks of the current or previous year. An employee is eligible for leave if the following three requirements are met:

- The employee works at a location that has 50 or more employees within a 75-mile radius. All employees on the payroll—including those who work part time and those on leave—count toward this total.
- The employee has worked for the company for at least 12 months.
- The employee has worked at least 1,250 hours (about 25 hours a week) during the 12 months immediately preceding the leave.

Even if all three of these requirements are met, an employee is entitled to take FMLA leave only for specified reasons. Not every personal or family emergency qualifies for FMLA leave. The employee must be seeking leave for:

- **Birth, adoption, or foster care.** A new parent or foster parent may take FMLA leave within one year after a child is born or placed in the parent's home. A parent may go out on leave before the child arrives, if necessary for prenatal care or preparations for the child. If the parents are married and work for the same employer, the employer may limit them to a combined total of 12 weeks.

- **An employee's serious health condition.** The FMLA provides a specific definition of a "serious health condition." Generally, an employee who requires inpatient treatment, has a chronic health problem, or is unable to perform normal activities for three days while under the care of a doctor has a serious health condition.

- **A family member's serious health condition.** An employee who needs to care for an ill family member is also entitled to leave. Under this provision of the FMLA, only parents, spouses (including same-sex spouses), and children count as family members. Grandparents, domestic partners, in-laws, and siblings are not covered (although they may be covered under state family and medical leave laws).

- **Qualifying exigencies.** Employees may take leave to handle certain matters when a parent, spouse, or child who is a member of the reserve, National Guard, or regular armed forces is called to active duty. Qualifying exigencies include making legal and financial arrangements, changing child care, or attending military events or ceremonies, among other things.

- **Seriously injured or ill military family member.** An employee whose family member suffers or aggravates a serious injury or illness while on active military duty is eligible for FMLA leave. The law also allows time off to care for veterans who were in the military in the last five years and are undergoing treatment, therapy, or recuperation for a qualifying injury or illness. This provision is intended to cover conditions that might not manifest fully until military service has ended, such as posttraumatic stress disorder. An employee may take leave for a military member who is a spouse, parent, or child, or for whom the employee serves as "next of kin" (which could be a sibling, grandparent, or aunt or uncle, for example).

Amount of Leave Available

An employee who takes leave for a serious health condition, a family member's serious health condition, a new child, or a qualifying exigency, may take 12 weeks of leave per 12-month period. The 12-week entitlement is for all of these types of leave combined. For example, an employee who takes ten weeks off to bond with a new child has only two weeks of leave to use for any other purpose in the 12-month leave year.

Different rules apply to FMLA leave taken to care for a family member who suffers a serious illness or injury while on active military duty. Employees may take up to 26 weeks of leave for this purpose in a single 12-month leave year, beginning on the first day of leave. However, this leave entitlement doesn't renew every 12 months. Instead, it is a per-injury, per-service-member entitlement. Once an employee takes this leave, he or she cannot take it again unless the same family member suffers a different injury on active duty, or a different family member suffers an injury on active duty. Of the 26 weeks, up to 12 weeks may be used for any purpose other than military caregiver leave. For example, an eligible employee may take 12 weeks off to bond with a child and another 14 weeks for military caregiver leave.

Reinstatement and Benefits

When the employee's leave is over, the company must reinstate the employee to the same position he or she held prior to taking leave, or to a position that is comparable in every important respect, subject to the following conditions:

- Employees have no greater right to rein-statement than they would have had if they had not taken leave. For example, if an employee works in the accounting department and your company decides to cut the entire department and outsource its bookkeeping needs, the employee does not have a right to be reinstated just because he or she was on FMLA leave.
- Your company doesn't have to reinstate certain highly paid employees. The FMLA recognizes how difficult it would be for many businesses to function without their top executives. The law allows an employer to refuse reinstatement if (1) the employee is among the highest-paid 10% of the salaried workers employed within 75 miles of the

employee's workplace, and (2) taking back the employee would cause "substantial and grievous economic injury" to the company's business. (To take advantage of this exception, the employer must give the employee a written notice and an opportunity to return to the job before reinstatement is denied.)

If your company has a group health plan for employees, it must also maintain insurance coverage for employees on FMLA leave. However, if the employee chooses not to return to work when the leave ends, the company can require the employee to reimburse it for the insurance premiums it paid for the employee while on leave. This reimbursement option is not available if the employee is unable to return due to a serious health condition or other circumstances beyond the employee's control.

Employers aren't required to continue any other benefits while an employee is on leave, nor must they allow a worker to accrue seniority, vacation, sick leave. However, an employee who returns to work is entitled to benefits reinstatement as well: The company must provide the same benefits that were available to the worker previously, without any waiting periods.

You cannot discipline a worker for taking FMLA leave. This means not only that you can't fire or demote a worker for going on leave, but also that you cannot count a worker's FMLA leave as an absence under a no-fault attendance policy. For example, if

CHAPTER 5 | TIME OFF | 211

you give workers a disciplinary warning after ten absences in any year and fire workers after 15 absences, you may not count any days that a worker takes as FMLA leave as an "absence" under the policy.

Lessons From the Real World

On September 26, 1995, Chem-Tronics fired Javier Mora for violating its attendance policy. Mora had taken a number of absences to care for his teenage son, Javier Jr., who suffered from AIDS and related infections. On these occasions, Mora cared for his son at home and took his son to necessary medical appointments.

The company claimed that Mora was not entitled to FMLA leave because his wife, Javier Jr.'s stepmother, was available to care for him. However, Mora explained that his wife was not his son's biological mother, that he was closer to his son, and that his son wanted him to provide care. The court sided with Mora, holding that an eligible employee has the right to take FMLA leave, even if there is someone else available to provide care.

The company also argued that it didn't know that Javier Jr. suffered from a serious health condition covered by the FMLA. However, this argument was dramatically undercut by the company's own newsletter, in which an article appeared detailing Mora and his son's trip to the Superbowl, courtesy of the Make a Wish Foundation (a group that provides special experiences for terminally ill children).

Mora v. Chem-Tronics, Inc., 16 F.Supp.2d 1192 (S.D. Cal. 1998).

Paid Leave

FMLA leave is unpaid. However, in some circumstances, accrued paid leave can be used or "substituted" for FMLA leave at the option of the employee or the employer. Paid vacation or personal days may be used to cover any type of FMLA leave. Paid sick or family leave may be used for FMLA leave only if the employee's reason for leave is covered by your company's paid leave policy. For example, if your company's paid sick leave policy allows employees to take time off to care for sick family members, then an employee may use paid sick leave while on FMLA leave to care for a family member with a serious health condition. If your policy covers only the employee's own illness, however, the employee may not use paid sick leave in this situation.

Your company can require employees to follow its usual procedures for paid leave. For example, if your company requires employees to give two weeks' notice to use vacation time, you can require the same for substituting paid leave. However, you may not deny the employee's FMLA leave for those two weeks: Your company's policies dictate only when an employee can use paid leave, not whether the employee can take unpaid FMLA leave.

Employees might be entitled to paid leave through state-run paid family leave programs. See "State Leave Laws," below, for more information.

Scheduling and Notice Requirements

An employee's absence can disrupt the workplace. Recognizing this, the FMLA requires employees to give 30 days' notice if the need for leave is foreseeable (except for qualifying exigency leave). The most common "foreseeable" leave is leave for the birth or adoption of a child or to care for a family member recovering from scheduled surgery or other planned medical treatment.

If the employee's need for leave is not foreseeable or the employee is taking qualifying exigency leave, the employee must give whatever notice is possible and practical under the circumstances. For example, it would be impossible for an employee to give advance notice of a medical emergency such as a car accident or an appendectomy.

In some circumstances, an employee might want to take FMLA leave intermittently rather than all at once. If an employee requires physical therapy for a serious injury, for example, or needs to care for a spouse receiving periodic medical treatment, it might make more sense for the employee to take a few hours off each day or week. This arrangement could also make more sense for your company because you get to keep your employee's part-time services instead of planning for a protracted absence.

If it is medically necessary for an employee to take intermittent leave to care for a family member or for his or her own serious health condition, the employee has a right to do so. Employees may also take intermittent leave for a qualifying exigency. For time off to care for a new child, you may, but are not required to, allow the employee to take leave on an intermittent schedule.

Certifications

Your company can ask employees to provide proof that they really need leave for a qualifying FMLA purpose. If an employee is taking leave for his or her own serious health condition or to care for a family member with a serious health condition, you can require the employee to provide a medical certification from a health care provider. You may also require an employee to submit a certification for qualifying exigency leave or leave to care for a military service member. The Department of Labor has developed optional forms you can use for this purpose (available online at www.dol.gov/whd/fmla). You may not, however, require a certification for birth, adoption, or foster care placement.

There are detailed rules covering the timing of certifications, second and third opinions, and requests for recertification of a serious health condition. You can find all of the details in *The Essential Guide to Family and Medical Leave*, by Lisa Guerin and Deborah C. England (Nolo).

State Leave Laws

Some states have their own family and medical leave laws. Some state laws apply to employers with fewer than 50 employees, so your company might have to comply with the state law even if it isn't subject to the

FMLA. If your company is subject to both the FMLA and a similar state law, it will have to follow whichever law gives workers the most protection. For example, if your state has a family and medical leave law that gives workers the right to take more than 12 weeks off to bond with a new child, your company will have to follow state law. And if state and federal law offer workers different benefits, your company must follow both of them. For example, if your state law requires employers to offer family leave to allow parents to attend a child's school conference (a right that the federal law doesn't provide), your company must let parents take that time in addition to their 12 weeks of federal FMLA leave. (To find out more about your state's laws on leave, see "State Family and Medical Leave Laws," at the end of this chapter.)

Like the FMLA, most of these state laws require unpaid leave only. However, the lack of comprehensive paid family leave in this country has become a hot topic in recent years. In 2014, the International Labour Organization, part of the United Nations, published a widely reported study comparing paid maternity and paternity leave in 185 countries. The United States was one of only two countries that didn't provide any form of paid leave to new parents.

To fill this gap, more states and cities have passed paid family leave laws. These laws typically provide monetary benefits to employees who need time off to care for a new child or for a seriously ill family member. Employees are paid through a state-run program, rather than by employers directly. These programs are largely funded through employee payroll deductions. So far, the following states have paid family leave laws: California, New Jersey, New York, Rhode Island, and Washington (taking effect in 2020). The District of Columbia also has a paid family leave law (taking effect in 2020). More states and cities are considering these laws each year. For updates, visit the online companion page for this book, or contact your state or local government.

Pregnancy and Parental Leave

The birth of a new child is a special and exciting time for parents. However, it can be difficult for employees to balance the needs of work and their new family obligations. A series of federal and state laws provide some help here.

Unpaid Leave

As explained above, the Family and Medical Leave Act (FMLA) requires employers who meet certain criteria to provide up to 12 weeks of unpaid leave.

FMLA leave can be used as pregnancy or parental leave in certain situations. Here are some of the rules that apply:

- Pregnant employees are entitled to use FMLA leave if complications from pregnancy constitute a serious health condition. As a practical matter, if a woman's doctor determines that it is medically necessary for her to take time off from work, she will be able to use FMLA leave for that purpose. FMLA leave is also available for routine prenatal care, such as monthly checkups.

- New parents may use FMLA leave following the birth or adoption of a child or the placement of a foster child. This leave may be taken any time during the first year after the new child arrives. However, a worker is entitled to only 12 weeks of FMLA leave, total, in a single year (unless caring for a military family member). So, if a worker has to take two weeks off for medical reasons during her pregnancy, she will have only ten weeks of FMLA leave for parental leave (unless state law provides additional leave).

- If both parents work for your company and are married to each other, they are entitled to a combined total of 12 weeks of parental leave. The spouses may use the remainder of their leave for any other FMLA purpose. For example, suppose an employee has a difficult birth and takes six weeks of leave for her own serious health condition. She may then take another six weeks of leave to bond with the child, leaving her husband with six weeks of leave for the same purpose. The husband then has six weeks of FMLA leave for any purpose other than parental leave.

- Parental leave may be taken intermittently, but only with an employer's permission. For example, new parents might wish to work part time for a while or take some leave immediately following the birth and some leave later. As long as your company agrees, you and the employee can work out a flexible leave arrangement under the FMLA.

Some states require employers to provide more than 12 weeks of leave, particularly if the leave is for "pregnancy disability": the legal term for the period of time when women are unable to work because of pregnancy and childbirth. In a few of these states, the pregnancy disability leave provided under state law is in addition to the leave provided by the FMLA or similar state statutes. For example, in California, a pregnant employee can take up to four months of pregnancy disability leave (if deemed necessary by her doctor) and an additional 12 weeks under the FMLA. Some of these laws apply to employers with fewer than 50 employees. To find out what your state requires, see "State Family and Medical Leave Laws," at the end of this chapter.

Even if your company isn't subject to the FMLA or a similar state law, it might be required to provide time off to pregnant employees, if leave is provided to other employees with temporary disabilities. Federal law requires employers to treat pregnant employees the same as nonpregnant employees who are limited in their ability to work. For example, if your company provides time off to employees who are recovering from surgery or other injuries, you probably need to provide time off to employees who are unable to work due to pregnancy. Otherwise, your company could face claims of discrimination.

Paid Leave

In general, there is no rule that requires employers to provide paid time off for pregnancy or parental leave. However, if your company's policies provide paid time off to other workers who are unable to work (such as those recovering from surgery or broken bones), it might be required to provide the same benefits to pregnant employees.

Employees can use accrued paid vacation or sick leave during FMLA leave, as long as the reason for leave is covered by the employer's policy. For example, if your company provides vacation time or personal days, new parents must be allowed to use this accrued time off for bonding leave, provided they meet the other requirements of the policy (for example, providing adequate notice or scheduling the leave with a supervisor). If your company provides paid sick leave, a pregnant employee who takes time off for a serious health condition must be allowed to use the paid sick leave. Likewise, your company can require employees to use accrued paid leave if the policy covers the reason for the FMLA leave. Most employers choose to do this because it limits the amount of time employees are away from work. Otherwise, employees could take their full FMLA leave and then extend their time off by using paid vacation or sick time.

A handful of states (including California, Hawaii, New Jersey, New York, and Rhode Island) offer temporary disability insurance (TDI)—or require employers to provide it as a job benefit—to employees who are temporarily unable to work due to a disability, including pregnancy disability. In these states, an employee who can't work due to pregnancy or childbirth is typically entitled to some wage replacement for that time. These programs are not intended as parental leave, though. They are available only for the period of time when the employee is actually unable to work. However, a handful of states do have paid family leave programs for employees taking time off to bond with a new child. See "State Leave Laws," above, for more information.

Discrimination Claims

Federal and state laws prohibit discrimination on the basis of gender, including pregnancy. This means, of course, that you may not fire, demote, or take any other negative employment action against a worker because she is pregnant. Here are a few tips that will help you stay within the law when dealing with these issues:

- Employers cannot force a worker to take pregnancy or maternity leave. In the not-so-distant past, an employer could make a pregnant employee stop working when she reached a certain stage of her pregnancy or started "showing." This is no longer legal. As long as she can get the job done, you must allow her to work, even up to the date she gives birth.

- Treat a pregnant employee who needs time off like any other temporarily disabled worker (an employee who suffers a back injury or has a mild heart attack, for example). Employers don't have to offer special benefits to pregnant workers, but these workers should get the same treatment as other workers who are temporarily unable to do their jobs because of disability or illness. Similarly, you may fire a pregnant employee if you would fire a nonpregnant employee for the same conduct. However, be careful not to penalize a pregnant employee for taking protected leave under the FMLA or a similar state law. And check your state's laws to see if they require your company to provide pregnant employees with a reasonable accommodation (several states do). You might need to give additional time off, provide schedule modifications, or make other changes to the workplace as a reasonable accommodation. (Check with your state's fair employment agency; the appendix contains contact information.)

- Offer parental leave, not maternity leave. And don't discourage new fathers from taking parental leave or penalize them for doing so. If your company offers any time off for a parent to spend with a newborn child, make it available to both fathers and mothers. If an employer offers a benefit that can only be used by women—like maternity leave —it can be accused of gender discrimination.

Jury Duty and Voting

Under the Jury System Improvement Act, a federal law, it is illegal for employers to fire or discipline an employee for serving on a jury in federal court. (28 U.S.C. § 1875.) Almost every state has a similar law protecting employees who serve on a jury in state court.

For most employers, the most important issue is whether they must pay an employee for time spent on jury duty. Generally, unless your company has promised otherwise in your employment policies or handbook, it does not have to pay employees for leave taken to serve on a jury. However, a handful of states require at least some payment for this time off. See "State Laws on Jury Duty," at the end of this chapter, for information on your state's rules.

Special rules apply to exempt employees. Employers may not deduct an exempt employee's salary for time spent on a jury, unless the employee did no work for the entire week. Employers may, however, deduct any amount the employee receives from the state as jury fees. (For more information, see "Pay Docking and Unpaid Suspensions" in Chapter 2.)

Workers are also entitled to time off work to cast their ballots. Almost every state prohibits employers from disciplining or firing an employee who takes time off work to vote. In many states, an employer must grant at least a couple of hours of leave for employees to get to the voting booth, but only if the employee is unable to vote outside of work hours. In most of these states, an employer must pay the worker for this time off. To find out what your state requires, see "State Laws on Taking Time Off to Vote," at the end of this chapter.

Military Leave

A federal law, the Uniformed Services Employment and Reemployment Rights Act of 1994 (USERRA), 38 U.S.C. §§ 4301 and following, prohibits discrimination against members of the United States military or those who serve in the military reserves. This law also requires employers to reinstate an employee who has taken time off to serve in the armed forces, if the employee meets all of the following conditions:

- The employee must have given notice, before taking leave, that the leave was for military service.
- The employee must have spent no more than five years on leave for military service.
- The employee must have been released from military service under honorable conditions.
- The employee must report back to work or apply for reinstatement within specified time limits; these limits vary depending on the length of the employee's leave.

USERRA requires employers to reinstate workers to the "escalator position": the same positions they would have held had they been continuously employed throughout their leave, provided they are otherwise qualified for those jobs. This means that your company cannot simply return workers to their former positions; they are entitled to any promotions, raises, or additional job responsibilities that they would have received if not for taking leave, as long as they are qualified. If a worker is not qualified, your company must try to get him or her qualified. The worker is also entitled to the benefits and seniority that he or she would have earned if continuously employed. For purposes of benefits plans and leave policies, the time the worker spent on leave must be counted as time worked.

Returning members of the military receive one additional benefit: They cannot be fired without cause for up to one year after they are reinstated (the exact length of this protection depends on the length of the worker's military service). No matter what your company's employment policies say, these workers are no longer at-will employees for a limited period after they return. (For more on at-will policies and cause for firing, see "At-Will Employment" in Chapter 4.)

State Laws

Almost every state has a law prohibiting discrimination against those in the state's militia or National Guard. Most state laws also require employers to grant leave to employees for certain types of military service. Some states require leave only for employees called to active duty; other states require leave for those called for training as well. Employers typically do not have to pay employees who take military leave, although some states provide paid leave for government employees.

Lessons From the Real World

Charley Hill started working for Michelin North America in the early 1980s. In 1995, he became a member of the Naval Reserves of the United States, a position that required Hill to be absent from work for two weeks per year.

In 1998, Hill began working in the "Q-Laboratory" at Michelin. Although Hill wanted to keep working in the Q-Lab, his supervisor didn't think the lab could accommodate Hill's Navy Reserve schedule. Hill was required to transfer to another assignment, even though he wanted to stay in the Q-Lab.

Hill filed a lawsuit against Michelin, arguing that the company discriminated against him by making him transfer out of the Q-Lab. The court agreed, finding that the Q-Lab had better working conditions and a more regular work schedule, which made it superior to the job to which he was transferred. The court held that if Michelin transferred Hill because of his military service requirements, that effectively denied Hill the benefits of the Q-Lab job, in violation of the Uniformed Services Employment and Reemployment Rights Act.

Hill v. Michelin North America, Inc., 252 F.3d 307 (4th Cir. 2001).

When an employee takes military leave, your company must usually reemploy him or her without any loss of benefits or status or reduction in pay. These reemployment guarantees vary from state to state and sometimes contain additional conditions. To find out your state's rules, see "State Laws on Military Leave," at the end of this chapter.

Domestic Violence Leave

Domestic violence—mental or physical abuse at the hands of an intimate partner—often affects the victim's ability to work. According to advocacy group Legal Momentum, victims of domestic violence lose an average of 137 hours of work a year. Some need time off to seek medical attention, get a restraining order, or relocate to a safe place. Others are prevented from getting to work when an abuser disables or takes the car, sabotages child care arrangements, or leaves the victim without cash to use public transportation.

While federal law provides only limited protection to domestic violence victims under the Family Medical Leave Act, a number of states have domestic violence leave laws that provide time off to deal with the medical, legal, psychological, and practical ramifications of domestic violence. And, some states have laws that apply more broadly to employees who are victims of—or witnesses to—any crime, including domestic violence.

Family and Medical Leave Act (FMLA)

The FMLA allows eligible employees to take up to 12 weeks off every 12 months for their own serious health conditions, or to care for a family member with a serious health condition. An employee who is physically injured or develops psychological trauma as a result of domestic violence might be entitled to FMLA leave. An employee might also be able to take time off to care for a parent or child who has been a victim of domestic violence. However, FMLA leave may be used only for these health-related issues and only if they qualify as serious health conditions. See "Family and Medical Leave Act," above.

State Domestic Violence Leave Laws

Almost a dozen states—including California, Florida, Illinois, and Washington—and the District of Columbia have passed laws requiring employers to provide domestic violence leave. These laws vary significantly in the details, including:

- **Duration of leave.** Some states allow employees to take up to a set amount of days or weeks off; others allow employees to take a "reasonable" amount of leave or simply prohibit employers from disciplining or firing employees who take time off for reasons related to domestic violence.

- **Reasons for leave.** The list of covered activities varies by state, but most allow time off for medical care and psychological counseling, relocation or other safety planning, and seeking a restraining order or participating in legal proceedings relating to domestic violence.

- **Notice and paperwork requirements.** Most states require employees to give reasonable advance notice that they will need leave, although these laws also recognize that the employee might be facing an emergency and be unable to give notice. State law might also require employees to provide some written proof that they took leave for reasons related to domestic violence.

- **Use of paid leave.** State domestic violence leave laws are generally unpaid. However, some states allow employees to use their employer-provided vacation, PTO, or sick leave during this time. Other states require employees to use all of their accrued employer-provided paid leave before taking domestic violence leave. And, in states with paid sick leave laws, employees can typically use their leave for issues relating to domestic violence. (See "State Paid Sick Leave Laws," above.)

You can find information on your state's domestic violence leave laws in "State Family and Medical Leave Laws," at the end of this chapter.

State Crime Victim Laws

In addition to laws that require employers to provide domestic violence leave, most states have laws that protect employees who must take time off for legal matters relating to a criminal case in which they are a victim or witness. These laws differ in the legal matters they cover: Some states protect only employees who have been subpoenaed to appear in court and testify; others cover more activities, such as seeking a restraining order, attending court hearings, or preparing to testify.

Restraining Orders for Employers

A restraining order (often called a "stay away" order) requires a perpetrator of domestic violence to stay a certain distance away from the victim. A restraining order often also requires the abuser to stay away from certain places, such as the victim's home and the school attended by the victim's children, if applicable. The purpose of a restraining order is to allow law enforcement to step in before anyone gets hurt. A batterer who gets too close to the victim has violated the order and can be detained by the police.

Some states allow businesses to get their own restraining orders if they are threatened with violence by an employee's partner or former partner. Such a restraining order requires the batterer to stay a certain distance away from the employer's property or face

arrest. You can find detailed information about workplace restraining orders at the website of Legal Momentum, www. legalmomentum.org.

Other Types of Leave

In addition to the kinds of leave covered above, many states require employers to provide leave for specified activities. Some of these entitlements are part of the state's family and medical leave law; others are stand-alone benefits. If your company does business in a state that has any such laws and meets the other coverage requirements (most often, that it has a certain minimum number of employees), it will have to provide the mandated leave.

Details on every state law requiring employers to grant time off is beyond the scope of this book. However, here are some common state leave requirements:

- **Time off to be an organ or bone marrow donor.** A handful of states require private employers to give employees time off to donate bone marrow or be an organ donor. Sometimes, this leave counts toward the employee's entitlement to state family and medical leave.
- **Use of sick leave to care for an ill family member.** Some states give employees the right to use accrued sick leave to care for a sick family member, even if the employer's policies don't provide for it.

- **Time off for court proceedings.** Many states give employees the right to take time off to appear as a witness in a court case.
- **Time off to serve as a volunteer firefighter or other emergency worker.** Some states require private employers to give workers time off to serve as a disaster relief worker, volunteer firefighter, emergency rescue worker, or Red Cross volunteer.
- **Time off for school activities.** In some states, parents are entitled to take a certain amount of leave each year to attend school functions, parent-teacher conferences, special education meetings, and the like.

For information on some of the requirements in your state, see "State Family and Medical Leave Laws," at the end of this chapter.

CAUTION

Don't forget about the ADA. Even if an employee is not entitled to FMLA or other leave—or has already used up all of his or her leave—you might need to provide unpaid time off as a reasonable accommodation to an employee with a disability under the Americans with Disabilities Act. See Chapter 3 for more information.

Legal Dos and Don'ts: Leave

Do:

- **Help employees balance work and family.** Smart managers know that workers who can take time off occasionally to attend school conferences, care for a sick child, or take an elderly parent to the doctor will be more productive on the job. And companies that have a family-friendly reputation are better able to recruit—and retain—a high-quality workforce.

- **Be consistent.** Make sure you follow your company's policies faithfully when considering leave requests. If you play favorites, you could be setting your company up for a discrimination lawsuit.

- **Encourage employees to take accrued leave.** You don't want sick workers showing up, unable to work efficiently and infecting the rest of your team. Similarly, you don't want good employees to burn out because they never take a vacation.

Don't:

- **Allow abuse of leave.** Require sick employees to call in. Have your reports schedule vacation well in advance. And crack down on any employee who misuses leave. As long as you are evenhanded in applying these policies, they will go a long way toward keeping your workers in line.

- **Forget about fathers.** Although we've come a long way, many companies still offer only maternity leave or discourage fathers from taking leave under seemingly neutral parental leave policies. These kinds of policies and practices can lead straight to the courthouse steps in a gender discrimination lawsuit.

- **Deny a leave request without checking the law.** If an employee asks to take time off for a particular reason, check with your human resources department—or your state labor department—to find out whether your state protects that type of leave. If you leap without looking, you might be violating the law.

Test Your Knowledge

Questions

1. All companies must give their employees some paid sick leave. ☐ True ☐ False

2. Employers are not allowed to cap the amount of vacation leave employees may accrue. ☐ True ☐ False

3. Only employees who work full time are entitled to take FMLA leave. ☐ True ☐ False

4. Employers may ask employees who take FMLA leave for their own serious health conditions to provide a medical certification. ☐ True ☐ False

5. If a married couple works for the same company, each is entitled to a full 12 weeks of FMLA leave to care for their new baby. ☐ True ☐ False

6. Employees can take up to 26 weeks of FMLA leave each year to care for a family member who suffers a serious injury while serving in the military. ☐ True ☐ False

7. Some employers must pay employees for time spent on jury duty. ☐ True ☐ False

8. Employees who are reinstated after serving in the military cannot be fired without good cause for up to one year, even if they work for an at-will employer. ☐ True ☐ False

9. Employers must pay employees for time spent on military leave. ☐ True ☐ False

10. Your company might have a legal obligation to allow employees to take time off to serve as a witness in court. ☐ True ☐ False

Test Your Knowledge (continued)

Answers

1. False. Only a handful of states require employers to provide paid sick leave to their employees. However, for more serious illnesses, larger employers might have to provide unpaid leave under the FMLA, or a similar state law.

2. False. Some states prohibit employers from taking away accrued vacation time (by zeroing out an employee's balance at the end of the year, for example). But it is legal to put a reasonable limit on how much vacation time an employee may accrue in the first place.

3. False. An employee who has worked 1,250 hours for your company in the last 12 months and meets the other eligibility requirements is entitled to take FMLA leave. This works out to about 25 hours a week.

4. True. An employer may require an employee to provide a certification: proof that the employee (or the employee's family member) actually has a serious health condition.

5. False. If both parents work for one company and are married to each other, they are entitled to a combined 12 weeks of parental leave. (Unmarried parents get 12 weeks each.) However, the spouses may use the remainder of their leave for any other FMLA purposes, such as a serious health condition.

6. False. Employees may take military caregiver leave only once, unless the same family member suffers a different injury on active duty, or a different family member is injured. This right doesn't renew every 12 months, like other types of FMLA leave.

7. True. While most states do not require employers to pay for this time, some do.

8. True. Employees who are reinstated after taking military leave enjoy this special job protection for up to one year (the exact length of the protection depends on the length of the employee's military service).

9. False. Although many private employers choose to pay employees for at least some portion of their military service, this is not a legal requirement.

10. True. Some states give employees the right to take time off work to serve as a witness.

State Family and Medical Leave Laws

Arizona

A.R.S. § 23-371 and following

Employers Covered: All employers.

Eligible Employees: All employees.

Paid Sick Leave: Accrual rate depends on employer size. Employers with 15 or more employees: Employees accrue one hour paid sick time for every 30 hours worked, but cannot accrue or use more than 40 hours per year, unless the employer selects a higher limit.

Employees with fewer than 15 employees: Employees accrue one hour paid sick time for every 30 hours worked, but cannot accrue or use more than 24 hours per year, unless the employer selects a higher limit.

Employees may use sick time to deal with their own illness, to care for an ill family member, to deal with a public health emergency, to care for a child whose school or place of care has been closed due to a public health emergency, or to deal with the effects of domestic violence.

Arkansas

Ark. Code Ann. §§ 9-9-105, 11-3-205

Employers Covered: For adoption leave: employers that allow workers to take leave for the birth of a child; for leave to donate organs and bone marrow: all employers.

Eligible Employees: For adoption leave: all employees; for leave to donate organs or bone marrow: employees who are not eligible for FMLA leave.

Family Medical Leave: Employees must be given the same leave as allowed for childbirth to adopt a child no older than 18 (does not apply to stepparent or foster parent adoptions). Employees may take up to 90 days of unpaid leave to donate organs or bone marrow.

California

Cal. Govt. Code §§ 12945 and 12945.2; Cal. Lab. Code §§ 230 and following; Cal. Unemp. Ins. Code §§ 3300 and following; Cal. Lab. Code §§ 245.5, 246 and 246.5

Employers Covered: For pregnancy leave: employers with 5 or more employees; for domestic violence leave and school activity leave: employers with 25 or more employees; for family medical leave: employers with 50 or more employees; for paid family and disability leave: employers whose employees contribute to state temporary disability insurance ("SDI") fund; for paid sick leave: all employers.

Eligible Employees: For pregnancy, domestic violence, or school activity leave: all employees; for family medical leave: employee with more than 12 months of service with the employer, and who has at least 1,250 hours of service with the employer during the previous 12-month period; for paid family and disability leave benefits program: employees who contribute to SDI fund; for paid sick leave: employees who have worked at least 30 days within a year for the same employer.

Family Medical Leave: Up to 4 months for disability related to pregnancy (in addition to 12 weeks under state family leave law). Up to 12 weeks of leave per year to care for seriously ill family member, for employee's own serious illness, or to bond with new child. Employees who contribute to SDI fund may receive paid family leave benefits for up to 6 weeks of leave per year to care for a seriously ill family member (including a registered domestic partner) or bond with a new child; up to 52 weeks of leave paid by state fund for own short-term disability.

School Activities: 40 hours per year, but not more than 8 hours per calendar month, to enroll a child in a school or with a licensed child care provider or to participate in activities related to the school or licensed child care provider.

State Family and Medical Leave Laws (continued)

Domestic Violence: Reasonable time for issues dealing with domestic violence, stalking, or sexual assault, including health, counseling, and safety measures. Family member or domestic partner of a victim of a felony may take leave to attend judicial proceedings related to the crime.

Paid Sick Leave: One hour of sick leave for every 30 hours worked; however, employers may cap use of sick leave at 24 hours per year. Employees may use sick leave for their own illnesses, to care for an ill family member, or to deal with the effects of domestic violence.

Colorado
Colo. Rev. Stat. §§ 19-5-211; 24-34-402.7

Employers Covered: For adoption leave: all employers who offer leave for birth of a child; for domestic violence leave and school activities leave: employers with 50 or more employees.

Eligible Employees: For adoption leave and school activities leave: all employees; for domestic violence leave: employees with one year of service.

Family Medical Leave: Employee must be given same leave for adoption as allowed for childbirth (doesn't apply to stepparent adoption).

School Activities: 18 hours per year, no more than 6 hours per month, to attend parent teacher conferences and meetings relating to special education, truancy, attendance, discipline, drop-out prevention, or response to intervention.

Domestic Violence: Up to 3 days in any 12-month period to seek restraining order, obtain medical care or counseling, relocate, or seek legal assistance for victim of domestic violence, sexual assault, or stalking.

Connecticut
Conn. Gen. Stat. Ann. §§ 31-51kk to 31-51qq; 46a-60

Employers Covered: For pregnancy leave: employers with 3 or more employees; for family medical or serious health leave: employers with 75 or more employees; for paid sick leave: service-industry employers with at least 50 employees.

Eligible Employees: For pregnancy leave and paid sick leave: all employees; for family medical or serious health condition leave: employees with one year and at least 1,000 hours of service in last 12 months.

Family Medical Leave: Reasonable amount of leave required for a pregnancy-related disability. 16 weeks per any 24-month period for childbirth, adoption, employee's serious health condition, care for family member with serious health condition, bone marrow or organ donation, or a qualifying exigency arising out of a family member's active duty in the military. 26 weeks per 12-month period for each family member who is also a current member of the armed forces and is undergoing medical treatment.

Paid Sick Leave: One hour of paid sick leave for every 40 hours worked, up to 40 hours accrued per year, for the employee's own medical needs or to care for an ill family member.

District of Columbia
D.C. Code Ann. §§ 32-501 and following; 32-1202, 32-131.01 and following

Employers Covered: Leave other than paid sick leave: employers with 20 or more employees; paid sick leave: all employers.

Eligible Employees: Leave other than paid sick leave: employees who have worked at company for at least one year and at least 1,000 hours during the previous 12 months; paid sick leave: all employees accrue sick leave upon hire and may use sick leave after 90 days of employment.

Family Medical Leave: 16 weeks per any 24-month period for childbirth, adoption, foster care, placement of a child with the employee for whom

State Family and Medical Leave Laws (continued)

the employee permanently assumes and discharges parental responsibility, or care for family member with serious health condition. Additional 16 weeks per any 24-month period for employee's serious health condition.

School Activities: Up to 24 hours of unpaid leave per year (all employees, all employers).

Domestic Violence: Leave described under "Paid Sick Leave" may also be used for employee or family member who is a victim of stalking, domestic violence, or abuse to get medical attention, get services, seek counseling, relocate, take legal action, or take steps to enhance health and safety.

Paid Sick Leave: Paid sick leave for the employee's own illness or to care for a family member. Amount of paid leave depends on employer size: employers with 100 or more employees must provide at least one hour of paid leave for every 37 hours worked, up to seven days of leave per year; employers with 25 to 99 employees must provide at least one hour of paid leave for every 43 hours worked, up to five days of leave per year; employers with fewer than 25 employees must provide at least one hour of paid leave for every 87 hours worked, up to three days of leave per year.

Florida
Fla. Stat. § 741.313

Employers Covered: Employers with at least 50 employees.

Eligible Employees: Employees with at least 3 months of employment.

Domestic Violence: Up to 3 working days in any 12-month period if employee or family/household member is victim of domestic violence, with or without pay at discretion of employer.

Georgia
Ga. Code § 34-1-10

Employers Covered: Employers with 25 or more employees.

Eligible Employees: Employees working at least 30 hours per week.

Family Medical Leave: No requirement to provide sick leave, but if employers do, they must allow employees to use up to five days of leave each year to care for a sick immediate family member.

Hawaii
Haw. Rev. Stat. §§ 398-1 to 398-11; 378-1, 378-71 to 378-74

Employers Covered: For childbirth, adoption, and serious health condition leave: employers with 100 or more employees; for pregnancy leave, temporary disability, and domestic violence leave: all employers; for bone marrow leave: employers with 50 or more employees.

Eligible Employees: For childbirth, adoption, and serious health condition leave: employees with 6 months of service; for pregnancy, domestic violence, and temporary disability leave: all employees.

Family Medical Leave: 4 weeks per calendar year for childbirth, adoption, or care for family member with serious health condition; "reasonable period" of pregnancy/maternity leave required by discrimination statute and case law; up to 7 days' unpaid leave for bone marrow donors and up to 30 days' unpaid leave for organ donors. Up to 26 weeks of temporary disability leave paid by state insurance program.

Domestic Violence: Employer with 50 or more employees must allow up to 30 days' unpaid leave per year for employee who is a victim of domestic or sexual violence or if employee's minor child is a victim. Employer with 49 or fewer employees must allow up to 5 days' leave.

State Family and Medical Leave Laws (continued)

Illinois

820 Ill. Comp. Stat. §§ 147/1 and following; 180/1 and following

Employers Covered: For school activities leave, employers with 50 or more employees. For domestic violence leave, all employers.

Eligible Employees: For school activities leave: employees who have worked at least half time for 6 months; for domestic violence leave: all employees.

School Activities: Eight hours per year (no more than 4 hours per day); required only if employee has no paid leave available.

Domestic Violence: If employer has at least 50 employees, up to 12 weeks' unpaid leave per 12-month period for employee who is a victim of domestic violence or sexual assault or for employee with a family or household member who is a victim. If employer has at least 15 but not more than 49 employees, up to 8 weeks' unpaid leave during any 12-month period. If employer has fourteen or fewer employees, up to 4 weeks' unpaid leave during any 12-month period.

Iowa

Iowa Code § 216.6

Employers Covered: Employers with 4 or more employees.

Eligible Employees: All employees.

Family Medical Leave: Up to 8 weeks for disability due to pregnancy, childbirth, or related conditions.

Kentucky

Ky. Rev. Stat. Ann. § 337.015

Employers Covered: All employers.

Eligible Employees: All employees.

Family Medical Leave: Up to 6 weeks for adoption of a child under 7 years old.

Louisiana

La. Rev. Stat. Ann. §§ 23:341 to 23:342; 23:1015 and following; 40:1299.124

Employers Covered: For pregnancy/maternity leave: employers with 25 or more employees; for leave to donate bone marrow: employers with 20 or more employees; for school activities leave: all employers.

Eligible Employees: For pregnancy/maternity or school activities leave: all employees; for leave to donate bone marrow: employees who work 20 or more hours per week.

Family Medical Leave: "Reasonable period of time" for pregnancy disability and childbirth, not to exceed 6 weeks for normal pregnancy and 4 months for more disabling pregnancies; up to 40 hours' paid leave per year to donate bone marrow.

School Activities: 16 hours per year.

Maine

Me. Rev. Stat. Ann. tit. 26, §§ 843 and following

Employers Covered: For domestic violence leave: all employers; for family medical leave: employers with 15 or more employees at one location.

Eligible Employees: All employees for domestic violence leave; employees with at least one year of service for family medical leave.

Family Medical Leave: 10 weeks in any two-year period for childbirth, adoption (for child 16 or younger), employee's serious health condition, care for family member with serious health condition, or death or serious health condition of family member suffered while on active military duty.

Domestic Violence: "Reasonable and necessary" leave for employee who is victim of domestic violence, sexual assault, or stalking, or whose parent, spouse, or child is a victim, to prepare for and attend court, for medical treatment, and for other necessary services.

State Family and Medical Leave Laws (continued)

Maryland

Md. Code Ann., [Lab. & Empl.] §§ 3-801, 3-802, 3-803

Employers Covered: For adoption leave: employers with 15 or more employees; for military family leave: employers with at least 50 employees.

Eligible Employees: All employees for adoption leave; employees who have worked at least 12 months, and at least 1,250 hours in the last 12 months, for military family leave.

Family Medical Leave: Employee must be given same leave for adoption as allowed for childbirth. Employee must be allowed to take off the day immediate family member leaves for or returns from active military duty outside the United States.

Massachusetts

Mass. Gen. Laws ch. 149, §§ 52D, 105D, 148C; ch. 151B, § 1(5)

Employers Covered: For maternity and adoption leave: employers with 6 or more employees; for school activities leave: employers with 50 or more employees; for domestic violence leave: employers with 50 or more employees; for paid sick leave: all employers.

Eligible Employees: For maternity and adoption leave: employees who have completed the employer's probationary period, or if there is no probationary period, employees who have completed 3 months of service as full-time employees; for paid sick leave: all employees accrue sick leave upon hire and may use sick leave after 90 days of employment; for all other leave: employees who are eligible under FMLA.

Family Medical Leave: Eight weeks total for childbirth/maternity or adoption of child younger than 18 (younger than 23 if disabled); additional 24 hours total per year (combined with school activities leave) to accompany minor child or relative age 60 or older to medical and dental appointments.

School Activities: 24 hours per year total (combined with family medical leave for medical and dental appointments).

Domestic violence: 15 days of unpaid leave in 12-month period if employee, or family member of employee, is a victim of abusive behavior, to seek medical attention or counseling, obtain a protective order from a court, attend child custody proceedings, and other related purposes. Employee may also use leave described under "Paid Sick Leave" for these purposes.

Paid Sick Leave: One hour of sick leave for every 30 hours worked, although employers may cap annual accrual at 40 hours per week. Employers with 11 or more employees must provide paid time off; employers with 10 or fewer employees may provide unpaid time off. Employees may use leave for their own illnesses or to care for an ill family member.

Minnesota

Minn. Stat. Ann. §§ 181.940 and following

Employers Covered: For childbirth/maternity and adoption leave: employers with 21 or more employees at one site; for bone marrow donation: employers with 20 or more employees; for school activities: employers with 2 or more employees.

Eligible Employees: For maternity leave: employees who have worked at least half time for one year; for bone marrow donation: employees who work at least 20 hours per week; for school activities: employees who have worked at least one year.

Family Medical Leave: 12 weeks for childbirth/maternity or adoption; up to 40 hours paid leave per year to donate bone marrow; parent can use accrued sick leave to care for sick or injured child. Up to ten days if family member is killed or injured in active military service (all employers).

State Family and Medical Leave Laws (continued)

School Activities: 16 hours in 12-month period; includes activities related to child care, preschool, or special education.

Domestic violence: Employee may use sick leave for reasonable time off to receive assistance because of sexual assault, domestic violence, or stalking.

Montana

Mont. Code Ann. §§ 49-2-310, 49-2-311

Employers Covered: All employers.

Eligible Employees: All employees.

Family Medical Leave: Reasonable leave of absence for pregnancy disability and childbirth.

Nebraska

Neb. Rev. Stat. § 48-234

Employers Covered: Employers that allow workers to take leave for the birth of a child.

Eligible Employees: All employees.

Family Medical Leave: Employee must be given same leave as allowed for childbirth to adopt a child, unless child is over 8 (or over 18 for special needs child); does not apply to stepparent or foster parent adoptions.

Nevada

Nev. Rev. Stat. Ann. §§ 392.920, 613.335, 392.4577, 2017 Nevada Laws Ch. 496 (S.B. 361)

Employers Covered: All employers.

Eligible Employees: All employees. For domestic violence leave only: as of January 1, 2018, employees employed for at least 90 days and who are victims of domestic violence or whose family members are victims of domestic violence.

Family Medical Leave: Same sick or disability leave policies that apply to other medical conditions must be extended to pregnancy, miscarriage, childbirth and related medical conditions.

School Activities: Employers may not fire or threaten to fire a parent, guardian, or custodian for attending a school conference or responding to a child's emergency. Employers with 50 or more employees must provide parent with a child in public school 4 hours of leave per school year, which must be taken in increments of at least 1 hour, to attend parent-teacher conferences, attend school-related activities during regular school hours, attend school-sponsored events, or volunteer or be involved at the school.

Paid Sick Leave: Employee may take up to 160 hours of leave within one year of the incident(s) of domestic violence for the following purposes: to seek medical treatment, to obtain counseling, to participate in court proceedings, or to create a safety plan. Leave may be unpaid.

New Hampshire

N.H. Rev. Stat. Ann. § 354-A:7(VI)

Employers Covered: Employers with 6 or more employees.

Eligible Employees: All employees.

Family Medical Leave: Temporary disability leave for pregnancy/childbirth or related medical condition.

New Jersey

N.J. Stat. Ann. §§ 34:11B-1 and following; 34-11C and following; 43:21-1 and following

Employers Covered: Employers with 50 or more employees; for paid family and temporary disability leave, employers subject to the New Jersey Unemployment Compensation Law; for domestic violence leave, employers with 25 or more employees.

Eligible Employees: Employees who have worked for at least one year and at least 1,000 hours in previous 12 months; for paid family and temporary disability leave benefits program: employees who worked 20 calendar weeks in covered New Jersey employment; or earned at least 1,000 times New Jersey minimum wage during 52 weeks preceding leave.

Family Medical Leave: 12 weeks (or 24 weeks

State Family and Medical Leave Laws (continued)

reduced leave schedule) in any 24-month period for pregnancy/maternity, childbirth, adoption, or care for family member with serious health condition. Employees may receive paid family leave benefits for up to 6 weeks of leave per year to care for a seriously ill family member (including a registered domestic partner) or bond with a new child. Employee may receive temporary disability benefits while the employee is unable to work, up to 26 weeks.

Domestic violence: 20 unpaid days in one 12-month period for employee who is (or whose family member is) a victim of domestic violence or a sexually violent offense.

New Mexico

N.M. Stat. Ann. §§ 50-4A-1 and following

Employers Covered: All employers.

Eligible Employees: All employees.

Domestic Violence: Employer must provide intermittent paid or unpaid leave time for up to fourteen days in any calendar year, taken by an employee for up to eight hours in one day, to obtain or attempt to obtain an order of protection or other judicial relief from domestic abuse or to meet with law enforcement officials, to consult with attorneys or district attorneys' victim advocates or to attend court proceedings related to the domestic abuse of an employee or an employee's family member.

New York

N.Y. Lab. Law §§ 201-c, 202-a. N.Y. Workers' Compensation Law § 200 and following.

Employers Covered: Employers that allow workers to take leave for the birth of a child must allow adoption leave; employers with 20 or more employees at one site must allow leave to donate bone marrow; employers with at least one

employee for 30 days are covered by the state's temporary disability program 4 weeks later; for paid family leave, all employers.

Eligible Employees: All employees are eligible for adoption leave; employees who work at least 20 hours per week are eligible for leave to donate bone marrow; employees who have worked for a covered employer for at least 4 consecutive weeks are eligible for temporary disability benefits. For paid family leave, employees are eligible once they have worked for their employer for 26 weeks.

Family Medical Leave: Employees must be given same leave as allowed for childbirth to adopt a child of preschool age or younger, or no older than 18 if disabled; up to 24 hours' leave to donate bone marrow. Temporary disability insurance benefits available for up to 26 weeks while employee is unable to work. Beginning in January of 2018, employee may take paid leave to care for a family member with a serious health condition, to bond with a new child, or for qualifying exigency arising out of a family member's call to active duty in the military. Employee can receive 50% of average wages for up to 8 weeks in 2018, which will gradually increase to 67% of average wages for up to 12 weeks by 2021. Leave is paid by the state, not the employer.

North Carolina

N.C. Gen. Stat. §§ 95-28.3, 50B-5.5

Employers Covered: All employers.

Eligible Employees: All employees.

School Activities: Parents and guardians of school-aged children must be given up to 4 hours of leave per year.

Domestic Violence: Reasonable time off from work to obtain or attempt to obtain relief from domestic violence and sexual assault.

State Family and Medical Leave Laws (continued)

Oregon

Ore. Rev. Stat. §§ 659A.029, 659A.150 and following, 659A.312, 659A.270 and following, 653.601 and following

Employers Covered: For childbirth, adoption, and serious health condition leave: employers with 25 or more employees; for domestic violence leave: employers with 6 or more employees; for leave to donate bone marrow: all employers; for paid sick leave: all employers.

Eligible Employees: For childbirth, adoption, or serious health condition: employees who have worked 25 or more hours per week for at least 180 days (except parental leave, which only requires that the employee has worked 180 days); for leave to donate bone marrow: employees who work an average of 20 or more hours per week; for domestic violence leave: all employees; for paid sick leave: all employees accrue sick leave upon hire and may use leave after 90 days of employment.

Family Medical Leave: 12 weeks per year for pregnancy disability; additional 12 weeks per year for parental leave, serious health condition, care for family member with serious health condition, deal with the death of a family member, or care for child who has an illness, injury, or condition that requires home care; employee who takes 12 weeks of parental leave may take an additional 12 weeks to care for a sick child. Up to 40 hours or amount of accrued paid leave (whichever is less) to donate bone marrow.

Paid Sick Leave: Employees must accrue one hour of sick leave for every 30 hours worked, although employers may cap accrual and use at 40 hours per year. Up to 40 hours of accrued leave must carry over to the next year, but employers can cap total accrual to 80 hours. Employers with 10 or more employees must provide paid time off; employers with 9 or fewer employees may provide unpaid time off. Employees may use leave for their own illnesses, to care for an ill family member, to deal with domestic violence issues, or for any purpose described under the "Family Medical Leave" section. Different rules apply to Portland employers.

Domestic Violence: Reasonable leave for employee who is victim of domestic violence, harassment, sexual assault, or stalking, or whose minor child is a victim, to seek legal treatment, medical services, counseling, or to relocate/secure existing home.

Rhode Island

R.I. Gen. Laws §§ 28-48-1 and following; 28-41-34 through 28-41-42

Employers Covered: For family medical leave: employers with 50 or more employees.

Eligible Employees: For family medical leave: employees who have worked an average of 30 or more hours a week for at least 12 consecutive months; for school activities leave: all employees; for temporary disability and temporary caregiver leave: all employees who meet the earning requirements.

Family Medical Leave: 13 weeks in any two calendar years for childbirth, adoption of child up to 16 years old, employee's serious health condition, or care for family member with serious health condition. While temporarily unable to work due to disability (including pregnancy), employees can collect benefits from state insurance fund for up to 30 weeks. Four weeks of benefits are available as temporary caregiver insurance (to bond with a new child or care for a family member with a serious health condition); this time plus temporary disability time may not exceed 30 total weeks.

School Activities: Up to 10 hours a year.

South Carolina

S.C. Code Ann. § 44-43-80

Employers Covered: Employers with 20 or more workers at one site in South Carolina.

State Family and Medical Leave Laws (continued)

Eligible Employees: Employees who work an average of at least 20 hours per week.

Family Medical Leave: Employers may—but are not required to—allow employees to take up to 40 hours paid leave per year to donate bone marrow.

Tennessee

Tenn. Code Ann. § 4-21-408

Employers Covered: Employers with 100 or more employees.

Eligible Employees: Employees who have worked 12 consecutive months as full-time employees.

Family Medical Leave: Up to 4 months of unpaid leave for pregnancy, childbirth, nursing, and adoption; employee must give 3 months' notice unless a medical emergency requires the leave to begin sooner; these laws must be included in employee handbook.

Texas

Tex. Lab. Code Ann. § 21.0595

Employers Covered: Employers with 15 or more employees.

Family Medical Leave: No leave requirements, but employers that choose to provide leave to care for a sick child must allow leave to care for a foster child.

Vermont

Vt. Stat. Ann. tit. 21, §§ 471 and following

Employers Covered: For pregnancy/parental leave: employers with 10 or more employees; for family medical and school activities leave: employers with 15 or more employees; for paid sick leave: all employers.

Eligible Employees: For pregnancy/parental leave, family medical leave, and school activities leave, employees must have worked an average of 30 or more hours per week for at least one year. For paid sick leave, employees must have worked for

a covered employer for an average of 18 hours per week for at least 20 weeks.

Family Medical Leave: 12 weeks per year for pregnancy, childbirth, adoption of child age 16 or younger, employee's serious health condition, or care for family member with serious health condition; combined with school activities leave, additional 4 hours of unpaid leave in a 30-day period (up to 24 hours per year) to take a family member to a medical, dental, or professional well-care appointment or respond to a family member's medical emergency.

School Activities: Combined with leave to take family members to appointments, 4 hours' total unpaid leave in a 30-day period (up to 24 hours per year) to participate in child's school activities.

Paid Sick Leave: Employee accrues one hour of paid sick leave for every 52 hours worked. For 2017 and 2018, employer may limit accrual to 24 hours of sick leave per year. For 2019, employer may limit accrual to 40 hours per year. Employers with 5 or fewer employees do not need to comply with the law until 2018.

Washington

Wash. Rev. Code Ann. §§ 49.78.010 and following, 49.12.265 and following, 49.12.350 and following, 49.76.010 and following, 49.86.005 and following

Employers Covered: All employers must provide domestic violence leave and paid sick leave; employers with 8 or more employees must provide pregnancy disability leave; employers with 50 or more employees must provide leave to care for newborn, adopted, or foster child, or family member with serious health condition.

Eligible Employees: For parental leave and leave to care for a family member with a serious health condition, employees must have worked at least

State Family and Medical Leave Laws (continued)

1,250 hours in the previous year to be eligible.

Family Medical Leave: Up to 12 weeks during any 12-month period for the birth or placement of a child, employee's serious health condition, or care for a family member with a serious health condition. In addition to any leave available under federal FMLA and state law, employee may take leave for the period of time when she is temporarily disabled due to pregnancy or childbirth.

Domestic Violence: Reasonable leave from work, with or without pay, for employee who is victim of domestic violence, sexual assault, or stalking, or whose family member is a victim, to prepare for and attend court, for medical treatment, and for other necessary services.

Paid Sick Leave: Beginning January 1, 2018, all employees accrue at least one hour of paid sick leave for every 40 hours worked. No annual cap on accrual, but employees may only carry over 40 hours of accrued leave from year to year. Employees may use sick leave for their own illness, the illness of a family member, the closure of a child's school or day care due to a public health emergency, and to seek services relating to domestic violence.

Wisconsin

Wis. Stat. Ann. § 103.10

Employers Covered: Employers with 50 or more employees.

Eligible Employees: Employees who have worked for at least one year and have worked 1,000 hours in the preceding 12 months.

Family Medical Leave: 6 weeks per 12-month period for pregnancy/maternity, childbirth, or adoption; additional 2 weeks per 12-month period to care for family member (including domestic partner) with a serious health condition; additional 2 weeks per 12-month period to care for the employee's own serious health condition.

State Laws on Jury Duty

Alabama

Ala. Code §§ 12-16-8 to 12-16-8.1

Paid leave: Full-time employees are entitled to usual pay.

Notice employee must give: Must show supervisor jury summons the next working day; must return to work the next scheduled hour after discharge from jury duty.

Employer penalty for firing or penalizing employee: Liable for actual and punitive damages.

Note: Employers with 5 or fewer full-time employees: Court must postpone an employee's jury service if another employee is already serving as a juror.

Alaska

Alaska Stat. § 09.20.037

Unpaid leave: Yes

Additional employee protections: Employee may not be threatened, coerced, or penalized.

Employer penalty for firing or penalizing employee: Liable for lost wages and damages; may be required to reinstate the fired employee.

Arizona

Ariz. Rev. Stat. § 21-236

Unpaid leave: Yes

Additional employee protections: Employee may not lose vacation rights, seniority, or precedence. Employer may not require employee to use annual, sick, or vacation hours.

Employer penalty for firing or penalizing employee: Class 3 misdemeanor, punishable by a fine of up to $500 or up to 30 days' imprisonment.

Note: Employers with 5 or fewer full-time employees: Court must postpone an employee's jury service if another employee is already serving as a juror.

Arkansas

Ark. Code Ann. § 16-31-106

Unpaid leave: Yes

Additional employee protections: Absence may not affect sick leave and vacation rights.

Notice employee must give: Reasonable notice.

Employer penalty for firing or penalizing employee: Class A misdemeanor, punishable by a fine of up to $2,500.

California

Cal. Lab. Code §§ 230, 230.1

Unpaid leave: Employee may use vacation, personal leave, or comp time.

Notice employee must give: Reasonable notice.

Employer penalty for firing or penalizing employee: Employer must reinstate employee with back pay and lost wages and benefits. Willful violation is a misdemeanor.

Colorado

Colo. Rev. Stat. §§ 13-71-126, 13-71-133 to 13-71-134, 18-1.3-501

Paid leave: All employees (including part-time and temporary who were scheduled to work for the 3 months preceding jury service): regular wages up to $50 per day for first 3 days of jury duty. Must pay within 30 days of jury service.

Additional employee protections: Employer may not make any demands on employee which will interfere with effective performance of jury duty.

Employer penalty for firing or penalizing employee: Class 2 misdemeanor, punishable by a fine of $250 to $1,000 or 3 to 12 months imprisonment, or both. May be liable to employee for triple damages and attorneys' fees.

State Laws on Jury Duty (continued)

Connecticut

Conn. Gen. Stat. Ann. §§ 51-247 and 51-247a

Paid leave: Full-time employees: regular wages for the first 5 days of jury duty; after 5 days, state pays up to $50 per day.

Additional employee protections: Once employee serves 8 hours of jury duty, employer may not require employee to work more hours on the same day.

Employer penalty for firing or penalizing employee: Criminal contempt: punishable by a fine of up to $500 or up to 30 days' imprisonment, or both. Liable for up to 10 weeks' lost wages for discharging employee. If employer fails to pay the employee as required, may be liable for treble damages and attorneys' fees.

Delaware

Del. Code Ann. tit. 10, §§ 4514, 4515

Unpaid leave: State pays $20 per diem for travel, parking, other out-of-pocket expenses. State pays certain other expenses if jury is sequestered.

Employer penalty for firing or penalizing employee: Criminal contempt: punishable by a fine of up to $500 or up to 6 months imprisonment, or both. Liable to discharged employee for lost wages and attorneys' fees and may be required to reinstate the fired employee.

District of Columbia

D.C. Code Ann. §§ 11-1913, 15-718

Paid leave: Full-time employees: regular wages for the first 5 days of jury duty, less jury fee from state. State attendance fee: $30, if not paid full regular wages by employer. State travel allowance: $2 per day.

Employer penalty for firing or penalizing employee: Criminal contempt: punishable by a fine of up to $300 or up to 30 days' imprisonment, or both, for a first offense; up to $5,000 or up to 180 days' imprisonment, or both, for any subsequent offense. Liable to discharged

employee for lost wages and attorneys' fees and may be required to reinstate the fired employee.

Florida

Fla. Stat. Ann. §§ 40.24, 40.271

Unpaid leave: Yes. State pays $15 per day for first three days of service if juror does not receive regular wages those days. State pays $30 per day for the fourth and subsequent days.

Additional employee protections: Employee may not be threatened with dismissal.

Employer penalty for firing or penalizing employee: Threatening employee is contempt of court. May be liable to discharged employee for compensatory and punitive damages and attorneys' fees.

Georgia

Ga. Code Ann. § 34-1-3

Paid leave: According to Opinion of the Attorney General Number 89-55, issued in 1989, employers must pay an employee's wages while on jury duty, minus any funds the employee receives for jury service.

Additional employee protections: Employee may not be discharged, penalized, or threatened with discharge or penalty for responding to a subpoena or making a required court appearance.

Notice employee must give: Reasonable notice.

Employer penalty for firing or penalizing employee: Liable for actual damages and reasonable attorneys' fees.

Hawaii

Haw. Rev. Stat. § 612-25

Unpaid leave: Yes

Employer penalty for firing or penalizing employee: Petty misdemeanor: punishable by a fine of up to $1,000 or up to 30 days' imprisonment. May be liable

State Laws on Jury Duty (continued)

to discharged employee for up to 6 weeks' lost wages, reasonable attorneys' fees, and may be required to reinstate the fired employee.

Idaho

Idaho Code § 2-218

Unpaid leave: Yes

Employer penalty for firing or penalizing employee: Criminal contempt: punishable by a fine of up to $300. Liable to discharged employee for triple lost wages and reasonable attorneys' fees. May be ordered to reinstate the fired employee.

Illinois

705 Ill. Comp. Stat. § 310/10.1

Unpaid leave: Yes

Additional employee protections: A regular night shift employee may not be required to work if serving on a jury during the day. May not lose any seniority or benefits.

Notice employee must give: Must give employer a copy of the summons within 10 days of issuance.

Employer penalty for firing or penalizing employee: Employer will be charged with civil or criminal contempt, or both; liable to employee for lost wages and benefits; may be ordered to reinstate employee.

Indiana

Ind. Code Ann. §§ 34-28-4-1, 35-44.1-2-11

Unpaid leave: Yes

Additional employee protections: Employee may not be deprived of benefits or threatened with the loss of them.

Employer penalty for firing or penalizing employee: Class B misdemeanor: punishable by up to 180 days' imprisonment; may also be fined up to $1,000. Liable to discharged employee for lost wages and attorneys' fees and may be required to reinstate the fired employee.

Iowa

Iowa Code § 607A.45

Unpaid leave: Yes

Additional employee protections: Employer may not threaten or coerce employee based on jury notice or jury duty.

Employer penalty for firing or penalizing employee: Contempt of court. Liable to discharged employee for up to 6 weeks' lost wages and attorneys' fees and may be required to reinstate the fired employee.

Kansas

Kan. Stat. Ann. § 43-173

Unpaid leave: Yes

Additional employee protections: Employee may not lose seniority or benefits. (Basic and additional protections apply to permanent employees only.)

Employer penalty for firing or penalizing employee: Liable for lost wages and benefits, damages, and attorneys' fees and may be required to reinstate the fired employee.

Kentucky

Ky. Rev. Stat. Ann. §§ 29A.160, 29A.990

Unpaid leave: Yes

Additional employee protections: Employer may not threaten or coerce employee based on jury notice or jury duty.

Employer penalty for firing or penalizing employee: Class B misdemeanor: punishable by up to 89 days' imprisonment or fine of up to $250, or both. Liable to discharged employee for lost wages and attorneys' fees. Must reinstate employee with full seniority and benefits.

State Laws on Jury Duty (continued)

Louisiana

La. Rev. Stat. Ann. § 23:965

Paid leave: Regular employee entitled to one day full compensation for jury service. May not lose any sick, vacation, or personal leave or other benefit.

Additional employee protections: Employer may not create any policy or rule that would discharge employee for jury service.

Notice employee must give: Reasonable notice.

Employer penalty for firing or penalizing employee: For each discharged employee: fine of $100 to $1,000; must reinstate employee with full benefits. For not granting paid leave: fine of $100 to $500; must pay full day's lost wages.

Maine

Me. Rev. Stat. Ann. tit. 14, § 1218

Unpaid leave: Yes

Additional employee protections: Employee may not lose or be threatened with loss of employment or health insurance coverage.

Employer penalty for firing or penalizing employee: Class E crime: punishable by up to 6 months in the county jail or a fine of up to $1,000. Liable for up to 6 weeks' lost wages, benefits, and attorneys' fees. Employer may be ordered to reinstate the employee.

Maryland

Md. Code Ann., [Cts. & Jud. Proc.] §§ 8-501, 8-502

Unpaid leave: Yes

Additional employee protections: Employer cannot threaten or coerce an employee. An employee may not be required to use annual, sick, or vacation leave. An employee who spends at least 4 hours on jury service (including travel time) may not be required to work a shift that begins on or after 5 p.m. that day or before 3 a.m. the following day.

Employer penalty for firing or penalizing employee: Employer penalty for violating these provisions is a fine up to $1,000.

Massachusetts

Mass. Gen. Laws ch. 234A, §§ 48 and following

Paid leave: All employees (including part-time and temporary who were scheduled to work for the 3 months preceding jury service): regular wages for first 3 days of jury duty. If paid leave is an "extreme financial hardship" for employer, state will pay. After first 3 days, state will pay $50 per day.

Michigan

Mich. Comp. Laws § 600.1348

Unpaid leave: Yes

Additional employee protections: Employee may not be threatened or disciplined; may not be required to work in addition to jury service, if extra hours would mean working overtime or beyond normal quitting time.

Employer penalty for firing or penalizing employee: Misdemeanor, punishable by a fine of up to $500 or up to 90 days' imprisonment, or both. Employer may also be punished for contempt of court, with a fine of up to $7,500 or up to 93 days' imprisonment, or both.

Minnesota

Minn. Stat. Ann. § 593.50

Unpaid leave: Yes

Additional employee protections: Employer may not threaten or coerce employee.

Employer penalty for firing or penalizing employee: Criminal contempt: punishable by a fine of up to $700 or up to 6 months' imprisonment, or both. Also liable to employee for up to 6 weeks' lost wages and attorneys' fees and may be required to reinstate the fired employee.

State Laws on Jury Duty (continued)

Mississippi

Miss. Code Ann. §§ 13-5-23, 13-5-35

Unpaid leave: Yes

Additional employee protections: Employee may not be intimidated or threatened. Employee may not be required to use annual, sick, or vacation leave for jury service.

Notice employee must give: Reasonable notice is required.

Employer penalty for firing or penalizing employee: If found guilty of interference with the administration of justice: at least one month in the county jail or up to 2 years in the state penitentiary, or a fine of up to $500, or both. May also be found guilty of contempt of court, punishable by a fine of up to $1,000 or up to 6 months' imprisonment, or both.

Note: Employers with 5 or fewer full-time employees: Court must postpone an employee's jury service if another employee is already serving as a juror.

Missouri

Mo. Rev. Stat. § 494.460

Unpaid leave: Yes

Additional employee protections: Employer may not take or threaten to take any adverse action. Employee may not be required to use annual, sick, vacation, or personal leave.

Employer penalty for firing or penalizing employee: Employer may be liable for lost wages, damages, and attorneys' fees and may be required to reinstate the fired employee.

Montana

Mont. Admin. R. 24.16.2520

Paid leave: No paid leave laws regarding private employers.

Nebraska

Neb. Rev. Stat. § 25-1640

Paid leave: Normal wages minus any compensation (other than expenses) from the court.

Additional employee protections: Employee may not lose pay, sick leave, or vacation or be penalized in any way; may not be required to work evening or night shift.

Notice employee must give: Reasonable notice.

Employer penalty for firing or penalizing employee: Class IV misdemeanor, punishable by a fine of up to $500.

Nevada

Nev. Rev. Stat. Ann. §§ 6.190, 193.140

Unpaid leave: Yes

Additional employee protections: Employer may not recommend or threaten termination; may not dissuade or attempt to dissuade employee from serving as a juror, and cannot require the employee to work within 8 hours before jury duty or if employee's duty lasts four hours or more (including travel time to and from the court), between 5 p.m. that day and 3 a.m. the next day. Cannot be required to take paid leave.

Notice employee must give: At least three days' notice.

Employer penalty for firing or penalizing employee: Terminating or threatening to terminate is a gross misdemeanor, punishable by a fine of up to $2,000 or up to 364 days' imprisonment, or both; in addition, employer may be liable for lost wages, damages equal to lost wages, and punitive damages to $50,000 and must reinstate employee. Dissuading or attempting to dissuade is a misdemeanor, punishable by a fine of up to $1,000 or up to 6 months in the county jail, or both.

State Laws on Jury Duty (continued)

New Hampshire

N.H. Rev. Stat. Ann. § 500-A:14

Unpaid leave: Yes

Additional employee protections: Employer cannot threaten or coerce employee.

Employer penalty for firing or penalizing employee: Employer may be found guilty of contempt of court; also liable to employee for lost wages and attorneys' fees and may be required to reinstate the fired employee.

New Jersey

N.J. Stat. Ann. § 2B:20-17

Unpaid leave: Yes

Additional employee protections: Employer cannot threaten or coerce employee.

Employer penalty for firing or penalizing employee: Employer may be found guilty of a disorderly persons offense, punishable by a fine of up to $1,000 or up to 6 months' imprisonment, or both. May also be liable to employee for economic damages and attorneys' fees and may be ordered to reinstate the fired employee.

New Mexico

N.M. Stat. Ann. §§ 38-5-10.1, 38-5-18 to 38-5-19

Unpaid leave: Yes

Additional employee protections: Employer cannot threaten or coerce employee. An employee may not be required to use annual, sick, or vacation leave.

Employer penalty for firing or penalizing employee: Petty misdemeanor, punishable by a fine of up to $500 or up to 6 months in the county jail, or both.

Note: Court must postpone an employee's jury service if the employer has five or fewer full-time employees and another employee has already been summoned to appear during the same period, or if the employee is the only person performing essential services that the employer cannot function without.

New York

N.Y. Jud. Ct. Acts Law § 519

Unpaid leave: Yes

Paid leave: Employers with more than 10 employees must pay first $40 of wages for the first 3 days of jury duty.

Notice employee must give: Must notify employer prior to beginning jury duty.

Employer penalty for firing or penalizing employee: May be found guilty of criminal contempt of court, punishable by a fine of up to $1,000 or up to 30 days in the county jail, or both.

North Carolina

N.C. Gen. Stat. § 9-32

Unpaid leave: Yes

Additional employee protections: Employee may not be demoted.

Employer penalty for firing or penalizing employee: Liable to discharged employee for reasonable damages; must reinstate employee to former position.

North Dakota

N.D. Cent. Code § 27-09.1-17

Unpaid leave: Yes

Additional employee protections: Employee may not be laid off, penalized, or coerced because of jury duty, responding to a summons or subpoena, serving as a witness, or testifying in court.

Employer penalty for firing or penalizing employee: Class B misdemeanor, punishable by a fine of up to $1,500 or up to 30 days' imprisonment, or both. Liable to employee for up to 6 weeks' lost wages and attorneys' fees, and may be required to reinstate the fired employee.

State Laws on Jury Duty (continued)

Ohio

Ohio Rev. Code Ann. §§ 2313.15, 2313.19, 2313.99

Unpaid leave: Yes

Additional employee protections: An employee may not be required to use annual, sick, or vacation leave.

Notice employee must give: Reasonable notice. Absence must be for actual jury service.

Employer penalty for firing or penalizing employee: May be found guilty of contempt of court, punishable by a fine of up to $250 or 30 days' imprisonment, or both, for first offense.

Note: Employers with 25 or fewer full-time employees: Court must postpone an employee's jury service if another employee served within thirty days prior.

Oklahoma

Okla. Stat. Ann. tit. 38, §§ 34, 35

Unpaid leave: Yes

Additional employee protections: Employee can't be subject to any adverse employment action, and can't be required to use annual, sick, or vacation leave.

Notice employee must give: Reasonable notice.

Employer penalty for firing or penalizing employee: Misdemeanor, punishable by a fine of up to $5,000. Liable to discharged employee for actual and exemplary damages; actual damages include past and future lost wages, mental anguish, and costs of finding suitable employment.

Oregon

Or. Rev. Stat. § 10.090, 10.092

Unpaid leave: Yes (or according to employer's policy)

Additional employee protections: Employee may not be threatened, intimidated, or coerced, and can't be required to use annual, sick, or vacation leave. Employers with 10 or more employees that provide health, disability, life, or other insurance benefits must continue coverage during jury service at the election of the employee.

Employer penalty for firing or penalizing employee: Court may order reinstatement with or without back pay, and a $720 civil penalty.

Pennsylvania

42 Pa. Cons. Stat. Ann. § 4563; 18 Pa. Cons. Stat. Ann. § 4957

Unpaid leave: Yes (applies to retail or service industry employers with 15 or more employees and to manufacturers with 40 or more employees)

Additional employee protections: Employee may not be threatened or coerced, or lose seniority or benefits. (Any employee who would not be eligible for unpaid leave will be automatically excused from jury duty.)

Employer penalty for firing or penalizing employee: Liable to employee for lost benefits, wages, and attorney's fees; may be required to reinstate the fired employee.

Rhode Island

R.I. Gen. Laws § 9-9-28

Unpaid leave: Yes

Additional employee protections: Employee may not lose wage increases, promotions, length of service, or other benefit.

Employer penalty for firing or penalizing employee: Misdemeanor punishable by a fine of up to $1,000 or up to one year's imprisonment, or both.

South Carolina

S.C. Code Ann. § 41-1-70

Unpaid leave: Yes

Employer penalty for firing or penalizing employee: For discharging employee, liable for one year's salary; for demoting employee, liable for one year's difference between former and lower salary.

State Laws on Jury Duty (continued)

South Dakota

S.D. Codified Laws Ann. §§ 16-13-41.1, 16-13-41.2

Unpaid leave: Yes

Additional employee protections: Employee may not lose job status, pay, or seniority.

Employer penalty for firing or penalizing employee: Class 2 misdemeanor, punishable by a fine of up to $500 or up to 30 days in the county jail, or both.

Tennessee

Tenn. Code Ann. § 22-4-106

Paid leave: Regular wages minus jury fees, as long as the employer has at least 5 employees, and the employee is not a temporary worker who has been employed for less than 6 months.

Additional employee protections: Employer may not demote, suspend, or discriminate against employee. Night shift employees are excused from shift work during and for the night before the first day of jury service.

Notice employee must give: Employee must show summons to supervisor the next workday after receiving it.

Employer penalty for firing or penalizing employee: Employees are entitled to reinstatement and reimbursement for lost wages and work benefits. Violating employee rights or any provisions of this law is a Class A misdemeanor, punishable by up to 11 months, 29 days' imprisonment or a fine up to $2,500, or both. Liable to employee for lost wages and benefits and must reinstate employee.

Texas

Tex. Civ. Prac. & Rem. Code Ann. §§ 122.001, 122.002

Unpaid leave: Yes

Notice employee must give: Employee must notify employer of intent to return after completion of jury service.

Employer penalty for firing or penalizing employee: Liable to employee for not less than one year's nor more than 5 years' compensation and attorneys' fees. Must reinstate employee.

Note: Only applies to permanent employees.

Utah

Utah Code Ann. § 78B-1-116

Unpaid leave: Yes

Additional employee protections: Employer may not threaten or coerce employee or take any adverse employment action against employee. Employee may not be requested or required to use annual or sick leave or vacation.

Employer penalty for firing or penalizing employee: May be found guilty of criminal contempt, punishable by a fine of up to $500 or up to 6 months' imprisonment, or both. Liable to employee for up to 6 weeks' lost wages and attorneys' fees and may be required to reinstate the fired employee.

Vermont

Vt. Stat. Ann. tit. 21, § 499

Unpaid leave: Yes

Additional employee protections: Employee may not be penalized or lose any benefit available to other employees; may not lose seniority, vacation credit, or any fringe benefits.

Employer penalty for firing or penalizing employee: Fine of up to $200.

Virginia

Va. Code Ann. § 18.2-465.1

Unpaid leave: Yes

Additional employee protections: Employee may not be subject to any adverse personnel action and may not be forced to use sick leave or vacation.

State Law on Jury Duty (continued)

Employee who has appeared for 4 or more hours cannot be required to start a shift after 5 p.m. that day or before 3 a.m. the next morning.

Notice employee must give: Reasonable notice.

Employer penalty for firing or penalizing employee: Class 3 misdemeanor, punishable by a fine of up to $500.

Washington
Wash. Rev. Code Ann. § 2.36.165

Unpaid leave: Yes

Additional employee protections: Employee may not be threatened, coerced, harassed, or denied promotion.

Employer penalty for firing or penalizing employee: Intentional violation is a misdemeanor, punishable by a fine of up to $1,000 or up to 90 days' imprisonment, or both; also liable to employee for damages and attorneys' fees and may be required to reinstate the fired employee.

West Virginia
W.Va. Code § 52-3-1

Unpaid leave: Yes

Additional employee protections: Employee may not be threatened or discriminated against; regular pay cannot be cut.

Employer penalty for firing or penalizing employee: May be found guilty of civil contempt, punishable by a fine of $100 to $500. May be required to reinstate the fired employee. May be liable for back pay and for attorneys' fees.

Wisconsin
Wis. Stat. Ann. § 756.255

Unpaid leave: Yes

Additional employee protections: Employee may not lose seniority or pay raises; may not be disciplined.

Employer penalty for firing or penalizing employee: Fine of up to $200. May be required to reinstate the fired employee with back pay.

Wyoming
Wyo. Stat. § 1-11-401

Unpaid leave: Yes

Additional employee protections: Employee may not be threatened, intimidated, or coerced.

Employer penalty for firing or penalizing employee: Liable to employee for up to $1,000 damages for each violation, costs, and attorneys' fees. May be required to reinstate the fired employee with no loss of seniority.

State Laws on Taking Time Off to Vote

Note: States not listed in this chart do not have laws or regulations on voting leave that govern private employers. Check with your state department of labor for more information. (See appendix for contact list.)

Alabama
Ala. Code § 17-1-5

Time off work for voting: Necessary time up to one hour. The employer may decide when hours may be taken.

Time off not required if: Employee has 2 nonwork hours before polls open or one nonwork hour after polls are open.

Time off is paid: No

Employee must request leave in advance: "Reasonable notice."

Alaska
Alaska Stat. § 15.56.100

Time off work for voting: Not specified.

Time off not required if: Employee has 2 consecutive nonwork hours at beginning or end of shift when polls are open.

Time off is paid: Yes

Arizona
Ariz. Rev. Stat. § 16-402

Time off work for voting: As much time as will add up to 3 hours when combined with nonwork time. Employer may decide when hours are taken.

Time off not required if: Employee has 3 consecutive nonwork hours at beginning or end of shift when polls are open.

Time off is paid: Yes

Employee must request leave in advance: Prior to the day of the election.

Arkansas
Ark. Code Ann. § 7-1-102

Time off work for voting: Employer must schedule employees' work schedules on election days to enable employees to vote.

Time off is paid: No

California
Cal. Elec. Code § 14000

Time off work for voting: Up to 2 hours at beginning or end of shift, whichever gives employee most time to vote and takes least time off work.

Time off not required if: Employee has sufficient time to vote during nonwork time.

Time off is paid: Yes (up to 2 hours)

Employee must request leave in advance: Two working days before election.

Colorado
Colo. Rev. Stat. § 1-7-102

Time off work for voting: Up to 2 hours. Employer may decide when hours are taken, but employer must permit employee to take time at beginning or end of shift, if employee requests it.

Time off not required if: Employee has 3 nonwork hours when polls are open.

Time off is paid: Yes (up to 2 hours)

Employee must request leave in advance: Prior to election day.

Georgia
Ga. Code Ann. § 21-2-404

Time off work for voting: Up to 2 hours. Employer may decide when hours are taken.

Time off not required if: Employee has 2 nonwork hours at beginning or end of shift when polls are open.

State Laws on Taking Time Off to Vote (continued)

Time off is paid: No

Employee must request leave in advance: "Reasonable notice."

Hawaii
Haw. Rev. Stat. § 11-95

Time off work for voting: 2 consecutive hours excluding meal or rest breaks. Employer may not change employee's regular work schedule.

Time off not required if: Employee has 2 consecutive nonwork hours when polls are open.

Time off is paid: Yes

Employee required to show proof of voting: Only if employer is verifying whether employee voted when they took time off to vote. A voter's receipt is proof of voting by the employee. If employer verifies that employee did not vote, hours off may be deducted from pay.

Illinois
10 Ill. Comp. Stat. §§ 5/7-42, 5/17-15

Time off work for voting: 2 hours. Employer may decide when hours are taken except that employer must permit a 2-hour absence during working hours if employee's working hours begin less than 2 hours after opening of polls and end less than 2 hours before closing of polls.

Time off is paid: Yes

Employee must request leave in advance: Prior to the day of election. One day in advance (for general or state election). Employer must give consent (for primary).

Iowa
Iowa Code § 49.109

Time off work for voting: As much time as will add up to 3 hours when combined with nonwork time. Employer may decide when hours are taken.

Time off not required if: Employee has 3 consecutive nonwork hours when polls are open.

Time off is paid: Yes

Employee must request leave in advance: In writing "prior to the date of the election."

Kansas
Kan. Stat. Ann. § 25-418

Time off work for voting: Up to 2 hours or as much time as will add up to 2 hours when combined with nonwork time. Employer may decide when hours are taken, but it may not be during a regular meal break.

Time off not required if: Employee has 2 consecutive nonwork hours when polls are open.

Time off is paid: Yes

Kentucky
Ky. Const. § 148; Ky. Rev. Stat. Ann. § 118.035

Time off work for voting: "Reasonable time," but not less than 4 hours. Employer may decide when hours are taken.

Time off is paid: No

Employee must request leave in advance: One day before election.

Employee required to show proof of voting: No proof specified, but employee who takes time off and does not vote may be subject to disciplinary action.

Maryland
Md. Code Ann. [Elec. Law] § 10-315

Time off work for voting: Two hours

Time off not required if: Employee has 2 consecutive nonwork hours when polls are open.

Time off is paid: Yes.

Employee required to show proof of voting: Yes;

State Laws on Taking Time Off to Vote (continued)

also includes attempting to vote. Must use state board of elections form.

Massachusetts

Mass. Gen. Laws ch. 149, § 178

Time off work for voting: First 2 hours that polls are open. (Applies to workers in manufacturing, mechanical, or retail industries.)

Time off is paid: No

Employee must request leave in advance: Must apply for leave of absence (no time specified).

Minnesota

Minn. Stat. Ann. § 204C.04

Time off work for voting: May be absent for the time necessary to appear at the employee's polling place, cast a ballot, and return to work.

Time off is paid: Yes

Missouri

Mo. Rev. Stat. § 115.639

Time off work for voting: Three hours. Employer may decide when hours are taken.

Time off not required if: Employee has 3 consecutive nonwork hours when polls are open.

Time off is paid: Yes (if employee votes)

Employee must request leave in advance: "Prior to the day of election."

Employee required to show proof of voting: None specified, but pay contingent on employee actually voting.

Nebraska

Neb. Rev. Stat. § 32-922

Time off work for voting: As much time as will add up to 2 consecutive hours when combined with nonwork time. Employer may decide when hours are taken.

Time off not required if: Employee has 2 consecutive nonwork hours when polls are open.

Time off is paid: Yes

Employee must request leave in advance: Prior to or on election day.

Nevada

Nev. Rev. Stat. Ann. § 293.463

Time off work for voting: If it is impracticable to vote before or after work: Employee who works 2 miles or less from polling place may take 1 hour; 2 to 10 miles, 2 hours; more than 10 miles, 3 hours. Employer will decide when hours are taken.

Time off not required if: Employee has sufficient nonwork time when polls are open.

Time off is paid: Yes

Employee must request leave in advance: Prior to election day.

New Mexico

N.M. Stat. Ann. § 1-12-42

Time off work for voting: Two hours. (Includes Indian nation, tribal, and pueblo elections.) Employer may decide when hours are taken.

Time off not required if: Employee's workday begins more than 2 hours after polls open or ends more than 3 hours before polls close.

Time off is paid: Yes

New York

N.Y. Elec. Law § 3-110

Time off work for voting: As many hours at beginning or end of shift as will give employee enough time to vote when combined with nonwork time. Employer may decide when hours are taken.

Time off not required if: Employee has 4 consecutive nonwork hours at beginning or end of shift when polls are open.

State Laws on Taking Time Off to Vote (continued)

Time off is paid: Yes (up to 2 hours)

Employee must request leave in advance: Not more than 10 or less than 2 working days before election.

North Dakota

N.D. Cent. Code § 16.1-01-02.1

Time off work for voting: Employers are encouraged to give employees time off to vote when regular work schedule conflicts with times polls are open.

Time off is paid: No

Ohio

Ohio Rev. Code Ann. § 3599.06

Time off work for voting: "Reasonable time."

Time off is paid: Yes

Oklahoma

Okla. Stat. Ann. tit. 26, § 7-101

Time off work for voting: Two hours, unless employee lives so far from polling place that more time is needed. Employer may decide when hours are taken or may change employee's schedule to give employee nonwork time to vote.

Time off not required if: Employee's workday begins at least 3 hours after polls open or ends at least 3 hours before polls close.

Time off is paid: Yes

Employee must request leave in advance: One day before election, either orally or in writing.

Employee required to show proof of voting: Yes

South Dakota

S.D. Codified Laws Ann. § 12-3-5

Time off work for voting: Two consecutive hours. Employer may decide when hours are taken.

Time off not required if: Employee has 2 consecutive nonwork hours when polls are open.

Time off is paid: Yes

Tennessee

Tenn. Code Ann. § 2-1-106

Time off work for voting: "Reasonable time" up to 3 hours during the time polls are open. Employer may decide when hours are taken.

Time off not required if: Employee's workday begins at least 3 hours after polls open or ends at least 3 hours before polls close.

Time off is paid: Yes.

Employee must request leave in advance: Before noon on the day before the election.

Texas

Tex. Elec. Code Ann. § 276.004

Time off work for voting: Employer may not refuse to allow employee to take time off to vote, but no time limit specified.

Time off not required if: Employee has 2 consecutive nonwork hours when polls are open.

Time off is paid: Yes

Utah

Utah Code Ann. § 20A-3-103

Time off work for voting: Two hours at beginning or end of shift. Employer may decide when hours are taken.

Time off not required if: Employee has at least 3 nonwork hours when polls are open.

Time off is paid: Yes

Employee must request leave in advance: "Before election day."

State Laws on Taking Time Off to Vote (continued)

West Virginia

W.Va. Code § 3-1-42

Time off work for voting: Up to 3 hours. (Employers in health, transportation, communication, production, and processing facilities may change employee's schedule so that time off doesn't impair essential operations but must allow employee sufficient and convenient time to vote.)

Time off not required if: Employee has at least 3 nonwork hours when polls are open.

Time off is paid: Yes (if employee votes)

Employee must request leave in advance: Written request at least 3 days before election.

Employee required to show proof of voting: None specified, but time off will be deducted from pay if employee does not vote.

Wisconsin

Wis. Stat. Ann. § 6.76

Time off work for voting: Up to 3 consecutive hours. Employer may decide when hours are taken.

Time off is paid: No

Employee must request leave in advance: "Before election day."

Wyoming

Wyo. Stat. § 22-2-111

Time off work for voting: One hour, other than a meal break. Employer may decide when the hour is taken.

Time off not required if: Employee has at least 3 consecutive nonwork hours when polls are open.

Time off is paid: Yes (if employee votes).

Employee required to show proof of voting: None specified, but pay contingent on employee voting.

State Laws on Military Leave

Alabama

Ala. Code §§ 31-12-1 to 31-12-4

Members of the Alabama National Guard, or the national guard of another state, called to active duty or for federally funded duty for service other than training have the same leave and reinstatement rights and benefits guaranteed under USERRA (doesn't apply to normal annual training, weekend drills, and required schools).

Alaska

Alaska Stat. § 26.05.075

Employees called to active service in the state militia are entitled to unlimited unpaid leave and reinstatement to their former or a comparable position, with the pay, seniority, and benefits the employee would have had if not absent for service. Employee must return to work on next workday, after time required for travel. Disabled employee must request reemployment within 30 days of release; if disability leaves the employee unable to do the job, employee must be offered a position with similar pay and benefits.

Arizona

Ariz. Rev. Stat. §§ 26-167, 26-168

Members of the National Guard, Arizona National Guard, and U.S. armed forces reserves called to training or active duty have the same leave and reinstatement rights and benefits guaranteed under USERRA. Members of the National Guard called for active duty or to attend camps, formations, maneuvers, or drills are entitled to unlimited unpaid leave and reinstatement to their former or a higher position with the same seniority and vacation benefits. Employer may not dissuade employees from enlisting in state or national military forces by threatening economic reprisal.

Arkansas

Ark. Code Ann. § 12-62-413

Employees called to active state duty as a member of the armed forces (which includes the National Guard, militia, and reserves) of Arkansas or any other state have the same leave and reinstatement rights and benefits guaranteed under USERRA.

California

Cal. Mil. & Vet. Code §§ 394, 394.5, 395.06

Members of the California National Guard, or the national guard of any state, called to active duty are entitled to unlimited unpaid leave and reinstatement to their former position or to a position of similar seniority, status, and pay. Full-time employees must be reinstated (without loss of retirement or other benefits), unless the employer's circumstances have so changed as to make reinstatement impossible or unreasonable. Part-time employees must be reinstated if an open position exists. Reinstated employees cannot be terminated without cause for one year. Full-time employees must apply for reinstatement within 40 days of discharge, while part-time employees must apply for reinstatement within 5 days of discharge.

Employees in the U.S. armed forces reserves, National Guard, or Naval Militia are entitled to 17 days' unpaid leave per year for military training, drills, encampment, naval cruises, special exercises, or similar activities. Employer may not terminate employee or limit any benefits or seniority because of a temporary disability resulting from duty in the National Guard or Naval Militia (up to 52 weeks). Employer cannot discriminate against employee because of membership in the military services.

State Laws on Military Leave (continued)

Colorado

Colo. Rev. Stat. §§ 28-3-609, 28-3-610, 28-3-610.5

Members of the Colorado National Guard or U.S. armed force reserves are entitled to 15 days' unpaid leave per year for training. Employees called to active state duty in the Colorado National Guard are entitled to unlimited unpaid leave. Employees on leave for training and active duty must be reinstated to their former positions or a similar position with the same status, pay, and seniority, and they must receive the same vacation, sick leave, bonuses, benefits, and other advantages they would have had if not absent for service.

Connecticut

Conn. Gen. Stat. Ann. §§ 27-33a, 27-34a

Members of the Connecticut National Guard ordered into active state service by the governor are entitled to the same rights and benefits guaranteed under USERRA, except those pertaining to life insurance. Employees who are members of the state armed forces, any reserve component of the U.S. armed forces, or the national guard of any states, are entitled to take leave to perform ordered military duty, including meetings or drills, that take place during regular work hours, without loss or reduction of vacation or holiday benefits. Employer may not discriminate in terms of promotion or continued employment.

Delaware

Del. Code Ann. tit. 20 § 905

National Guard members who are called to state active duty shall be entitled to the same rights, privileges, and protections as they would have had if called for military training under federal law protecting reservists and National Guard members.

Florida

Fla. Stat. Ann. §§ 250.481, 250.482, 252.55, 627.6692(5)

Discrimination against members of the reserves is prohibited. Employees who are called to active duty in the Florida National Guard, or into active duty by the laws of any other state, may not be penalized for absence from work. Members of the Civil Air Patrol must be given up to 15 days of unpaid leave for training and missions. All employees must promptly notify their employers of the need for leave. Upon return from service, employees are entitled to reinstatement with full benefits unless employer's circumstances have changed to make reinstatement impossible or unreasonable or it would impose an undue hardship. Employee cannot be terminated without cause for one year after reinstatement. If a member of the National Guard or Reserves is receiving COBRA benefits and is called to active duty, the period of time when that service member is covered by TRICARE (military health benefits) won't count against his or her COBRA entitlement.

Georgia

Ga. Code Ann. § 38-2-280

Discrimination against members of the U.S. military reserves or state militia is prohibited. Employees called to active duty in the U.S. uniformed services, the Georgia National Guard, or the national guard of any other state, are entitled to unlimited unpaid leave for active service and up to 6 months' leave in any 4-year period for service school or annual training. Employee is entitled to reinstatement with full benefits unless employer's circumstances have changed to make reinstatement impossible or unreasonable. Employee must apply for reinstatement within 90 days of discharge or within 10 days of completing school or training.

State Laws on Military Leave (continued)

Hawaii

Haw. Rev. Stat. § 121-43

Members of the National Guard are entitled to unlimited unpaid leave while performing ordered National Guard service and while going to and returning from service, and reinstatement to the same or a position comparable in seniority, status, and pay. If an employee is not qualified for his or her former position because of a disability sustained during service but is qualified for another position, the employee is entitled to the position that is most similar to his or her former position, unless employer's circumstances have changed to make reinstatement impossible or unreasonable. Employee cannot be terminated without cause for one year after reinstatement. Employer cannot discriminate against employee because of any obligation as a member of the National Guard.

Idaho

Idaho Code §§ 46-224, 46-225, 46-407

Members of Idaho National Guard or national guard of another state ordered to active duty by their state's governor may take up to one year of unpaid leave and are entitled to reinstatement to former position or a comparable position with like seniority, status, and pay. If an employee is not qualified for his or her former position because of a disability sustained during service but is qualified for another position, the employee is entitled to the position that is most similar to his or her former position in seniority, status, and pay. Employee must apply for reinstatement within 30 days of release. Returning employees may not be fired without cause for one year. Members of the National Guard and U.S. armed forces reserves may take up to 15 days' leave per year for training without affecting the employee's right to receive normal vacation, sick leave, bonus, advancement, and other advantages of

employment. Employee must give 90 days' notice of training dates.

Illinois

20 Ill. Comp. Stat. §§ 1805/30.15, 1805/30.20; 330 Ill. Comp. Stat. § 60/4

Members of the National Guard called to active state duty by order of the governor are entitled to leave and reinstatement with the same increases in status, seniority, and wages that were earned during the employee's military duty by employees in like positions, or to a position of like seniority, status, and pay, unless employer's circumstances have changed so that reinstatement would be unreasonable or impossible or impose an undue hardship. If employee is no longer qualified for the position because of a disability acquired during service but is qualified for any other position, then the employee is entitled to the position that will provide like seniority, status, and pay. If reasonably possible, employee must give advance notice of military service. Members of the National Guard must submit request for reemployment the day after finishing duty if duty lasted less than 31 days, within 14 days if duty lasted longer than 30 days, or within 90 days if duty lasted longer than 180 days. Members of the U.S. uniformed services must submit request for reemployment within 90 days. Employee can't be discharged without cause for one year. Employees who quit their jobs to enter military service are entitled to restoration after receiving an honorable discharge.

Indiana

Ind. Code Ann. §§ 10-16-7-4 , 10-16-7-6, 10-16-7-23; 10-17-4-1 to 10-17-4-5

Members of the Indiana National Guard, or the national guard of any other state, who are called to state active duty have the same leave and reinstatement rights and benefits guaranteed under USERRA. Employers may not refuse to allow

State Laws on Military Leave (continued)

members of the Indiana National Guard to attend assembly for drills, training, or other duties.

Members of the U.S. armed force reserves may take up to 15 days' unpaid leave per year for training. Employees must provide evidence of dates of departure and return 90 days in advance, and proof of completion of the training upon return. Leave does not affect vacation, sick leave, bonus, or promotion rights. At the end of training, employee must be reinstated to former or a similar position with no loss of seniority or benefits.

Iowa

Iowa Code § 29A.43

Members of the Iowa National Guard, the national guard of any other state, the organized reserves of the U.S. armed forces, or the Civil Air Patrol who are called into temporary duty are entitled to reinstatement to former or a similar position. Leave does not affect vacation, sick leave, bonuses, or other benefits. Employee must provide evidence of satisfactory completion of duty and of qualifications to perform the job's duties. Employers may not discriminate against these employees or discharge them due to their military affiliations.

Kansas

Kan. Stat. Ann. §§ 48-517, 48-222

Employees called into active duty by the state of Kansas, or any other state, are entitled to unlimited leave and reinstatement to the same position or a comparable position with like seniority, status, and pay. Reemployment not required if employer's circumstances have changed so as to make reemployment impossible/unreasonable or if reemployment would impose undue hardship on employer. Reinstated employees may not be discharged without cause for one year. Members of the Kansas National Guard are entitled to 5 to 10 days' leave each year to attend annual muster

and camp of instruction. Employer's failure to allow employee to attend or punishing employee who attends is a misdemeanor.

Kentucky

Ky. Rev. Stat. Ann. §§ 38.238, 38.460

Members of National Guard are entitled to unlimited unpaid leave for active duty or training and reinstatement to former position with no loss of seniority or benefits. Employer may not in any way discriminate against employee or use threats to prevent employee from enlisting in the Kentucky National Guard or active militia.

Louisiana

La. Rev. Stat. Ann. §§ 29:38, 29:38.1

Employees called into active duty in National Guard, state militia, or any branch of the state military forces of Louisiana or any other state are entitled to reinstatement to same or comparable position with same seniority, status, benefits, and pay. If employee is not qualified for former position because of disability sustained during active duty, but is otherwise qualified to perform another position, employer or successor shall employ person in other or comparable position with like seniority, status, benefits, and pay provided the employment does not pose a direct threat or significant risk to the health and safety of the individual or others that cannot be eliminated by reasonable accommodation. Employees on leave are entitled to the benefits offered to employees who take leave for other reasons. Employee must report to work within 72 hours of release or recovery from service-related injury or illness and cannot be fired, except for cause, for one year after reinstatement. Employer cannot discriminate against employee because of any obligation as a member of the state National Guard or U.S. reserves.

State Laws on Military Leave (continued)

Maine

Me. Rev. Stat. Ann. tit. 37-B, § 342; tit. 26, §§ 811 to 813

Employer may not discriminate against employee for membership or service in National Guard or United States armed forces reserves. Employees in the National Guard or reserves are entitled to military leave in response to state or federal military orders. Upon completion of service, employees must be reinstated, at the same pay, seniority, benefits, and status, and must receive all other employment advantages as if they had been continuously employed.

For the first 30 days of an employee's military leave, the employer must continue the employee's health, dental, and life insurance at no additional cost to the employee. After 30 days, the employee may continue these benefits at his or her own expense (paying the employer's group rates).

Maryland

Md. Code Ann., [Public Safety], § 13-705

Members of the state National Guard and Maryland Defense Force ordered to military duty have the same leave and reinstatement rights and benefits guaranteed under USERRA. Maryland employers with 15 or more employees must allow employees who have been employed for at least 90 days to take at least 15 days off each year to respond to an emergency mission of the Maryland Wing of the Civil Air Patrol. Employees must give as much notice as possible of their need for this leave. After arriving at the emergency location, employees must notify their employer and estimate how long the mission will take. Employees are entitled to reinstatement upon their return from this type of leave. Employers may not penalize employees for exercising their rights under this law, nor may they retaliate against employees who complain that an employer has violated the law.

Massachusetts

Mass. Gen. Laws ch. 151B, § 4; ch 33 § 13

Employers may not discriminate against employees and applicants based on their membership in, application to perform, or obligation to perform military service, including service in the National Guard. Employees who are members of the armed forces are entitled to the same rights and protections granted under USERRA.

Michigan

Mich. Comp. Laws §§ 32.271 to 32.274

Employees who are called to active duty in the U.S. uniformed services, the National Guard, or the military or naval forces of Michigan or any other state, are entitled to take unpaid leave, and to be reinstated when their service has ended. Employees are also entitled to take time off to attend military encampment, drills, or instruction.

Employers may not discriminate against employees based on their military service, nor may an employer use threats to prevent employees from enlisting.

Minnesota

Minn. Stat. Ann. § 192.34

Employer may not discharge employee, interfere with military service, or dissuade employee from enlisting by threatening employee's job. Applies to employees who are members of the U.S., Minnesota, or any other state military or naval forces.

Mississippi

Miss. Code Ann. §§ 33-1-15, 33-1-19, 33-1-21

Employers may not discriminate against employees or applicants based on their current membership in the reserves of the U.S. armed forces or their former membership in the U.S. armed forces. Employers may not threaten employees to dissuade them from enlisting.

State Laws on Military Leave (continued)

Members of the U.S. armed forces reserves or U.S. military veterans may take time off for state or federal military training or duty, with reinstatement to their former position (or a similar position) once their leave is over. Employees must provide evidence that they have completed their training.

Missouri

Mo. Rev. Stat. §§ 40.490, 41.730

Members of the Missouri military forces, the national guard of any other state, or a reserve component of the U.S. armed forces, who are called to active duty are entitled to the same leave and reinstatement rights provided under USERRA. Employers may not discharge employees, interfere with their military service, or use threats to dissuade employee from enlisting in the state organized militia.

Montana

Mont. Code Ann. §§ 10-1-1005, 10-1-1006, 10-1-1007

Employees who are ordered to federally funded military service are entitled to all rights available under USERRA. Members of the Montana National Guard, or the national guard any other state, who are called to state military duty are entitled to leave for duration of service. Leave may not be deducted from sick leave, vacation, or other leave, although employee may voluntarily use that leave. Returning employee is entitled to reinstatement to same or similar position with the same seniority, status, pay, health insurance, pension, and other benefits, provided that the employee told the employer of membership in the military at the time of hire, or if the employee enlisted during employment, at the time of enlistment. Employer may not in any way discriminate against employee or dissuade employee from enlisting in the state organized militia.

Nebraska

Neb. Rev. Stat. § 55-161

Employees who are called into active duty in the Nebraska National Guard, or the national guard of any other state, have the same leave and reinstatement rights and benefits guaranteed under USERRA.

Nevada

Nev. Rev. Stat. Ann. §§ 412.139, 412.606

Employers may not discriminate against members of the Nevada National Guard or the national guard of another state and may not discharge any employee because he or she assembles for training, participates in field training, is called to active duty, or otherwise meets as required for ceremonies, maneuvers, and other military duties.

New Hampshire

N.H. Rev. Stat. Ann. §§ 110-B:65, 110-C:1

Members of the state National Guard or militia called to active duty by the governor have the same leave and reinstatement rights and benefits guaranteed under USERRA. Employer may not discriminate against employee because of connection or service with state National Guard or militia; may not dissuade employee from enlisting by threatening job.

New Jersey

N.J. Stat. Ann. § 38:23C-20

An employee is entitled to take unpaid leave for active service in the U.S. or state military services. Upon return, employee must be reinstated to the same or a similar position, unless employer's circumstances have changed to make reinstatement impossible or unreasonable. If same or similar position is not possible, employer shall restore such person to any available position, if requested

State Laws on Military Leave (continued)

by such person, for which the person is capable and qualified to perform the duties. Employee must apply for reinstatement within 90 days of release from service. Employee may not be fired without cause for one year after returning from service. Employee is also entitled to take up to 3 months' leave in 4-year period for annual training or assemblies relating to military service, or to attend service schools conducted by the U.S. armed forces. Employee must apply for reinstatement within 10 days.

New Mexico

N.M. Stat. Ann. §§ 28-15-1, 28-15-2, 20-4-6

Members of the U.S. armed forces, National Guard, or organized reserve may take unpaid leave for service (or for up to 1 year of hospitalization after discharge). Employee who is still qualified must be reinstated in former or similar position with like status, seniority, and pay unless employer's circumstances have changed to make reinstatement impossible or unreasonable. Employee may not be fired without cause for one year after returning from service. Employee must request reinstatement within 90 days. Employer may not discriminate against or discharge employee because of membership in the National Guard; may not prevent employee from performing military service.

New York

N.Y. Mil. Law §§ 251, 252, 317, 318

Members of the U.S. armed forces or organized militia are entitled to unpaid leave for active service; reserve drills or annual training; service school; or initial full-time or active duty training. Returning employee is entitled to reinstatement to previous position, or to one with the same seniority, status, and pay, unless the employer's

circumstances have changed and reemployment is impossible or unreasonable. Employee must apply for reinstatement within 90 days of discharge from active service, 10 days of completing school, reserve drills, or annual training, or 60 days of completing initial full-time or active duty training. Employee may not be discharged without cause for one year after reinstatement. Employers may not discriminate against persons subject to state or federal military duty.

North Carolina

N.C. Gen. Stat. §§ 127A-201, 127A-202, 127A-202.1, 127B-14

Members of the North Carolina National Guard, or the national guard of any other state, who are called to active state duty by a state governor are entitled to take unpaid leave. Unless the employer's circumstances now make it unreasonable, returning employee must be restored to previous position or one of comparable seniority, status, and salary; if no longer qualified, employee must be placed in another position with appropriate seniority, status, and salary. Employee must apply for reinstatement, in writing, within 5 days of release from duty or hospitalization continuing after release. Employer may not discriminate against or discharge an employee because of membership in the national guard of any state or discharge an employee called up for emergency military service.

North Dakota

N.D.C.C. §§ 37-29-01, 37-29-03

Employers may not terminate, demote, or otherwise discriminate against volunteer members of the North Dakota National Guard or North Dakota Air National Guard, or volunteer civilian members of the civil air patrol. The employer must allow such employees to be absent or tardy from work for

State Laws on Military Leave (continued)

up to 20 days in a calendar year because they are responding to a disaster or national emergency (20-day limit does not apply to involuntarily activated members of the North Dakota National Guard). An employee who needs this leave must make a reasonable effort to notify the employer. Upon request, the employee must also provide written verification of the dates and times of service.

Ohio

Ohio Rev. Code Ann. §§ 5903.01, 5903.02

Employees who are members of the Ohio organized militia or National Guard or in the organized militia of another state called for active duty or training; members of the commissioned public health service corps; or any other uniformed service called up in time of war or emergency have the same leave and reinstatement rights and benefits guaranteed under USERRA.

Oklahoma

Okla. Stat. Ann. tit. 44, §§ 71, 208.1

Employees in the Oklahoma National Guard who are ordered to state active duty or full-time National Guard duty have the same reinstatement rights and other benefits guaranteed by USERRA. Members of the state National Guard must be allowed to take time off to attend state National Guard drills, instruction, encampment, maneuvers, ceremonies, exercises, or other duties.

Oregon

Ore. Rev. Stat. §§ 659A.082, 659A.086

Members of Oregon or other states' organized militias called into active state service or state active duty may take unpaid leave for term of service. Returning employee is entitled to reinstatement with no loss of seniority or benefits including sick leave, vacation, or service credits under a pension

plan. Employee must return to work within 7 calendar days of release from service.

Pennsylvania

51 Pa. Cons. Stat. Ann. §§ 7301 to 7309

Employees who enlist or are drafted during a time of war or emergency called by the president or governor, along with reservists or members of Pennsylvania National Guard called into active duty, are entitled to unpaid military leave. Leave expires 90 days after enlistment/draft period, 90 days after military duty for reservists, 30 days after state duty for Pennsylvania National Guard members. Returning employee must be reinstated to same or similar position with same status, seniority, and pay. If no longer qualified due to disability sustained during military duty, employer must restore to position with like seniority, status, and pay unless employer or successor's circumstances have changed so as to make it impossible or unreasonable to do so. Employers may not discharge or discriminate against any employee because of membership or service in the military. Employees called to active duty are entitled to 30 days' health insurance continuation benefits at no cost.

Rhode Island

R.I. Gen. Laws §§ 30-11-2 to 30-11-9, 30-21-1

Members of state military forces and the National Guard of Rhode Island or any other state who are called to active duty have the same leave and reinstatement rights and benefits guaranteed under USERRA. Members of the National Guard or U.S. armed forces reserves are entitled to unpaid leave for training and are entitled to reinstatement with the same status, pay, and seniority. Employees in the U.S. armed forces are entitled to reinstatement to the same position or a position with similar seniority, status, and pay unless the employer's circumstances make reinstatement impossible or unreasonable.

State Laws on Military Leave (continued)

Employee must request reinstatement within 40 days. Employer may not discriminate against or discharge employee because of membership in the state military forces or U.S. reserves, interfere with employee's military service, or dissuade employee from enlisting by threatening employee's job.

South Carolina

S.C. Code Ann. §§ 25-1-2310 to 25-1-2340

Members of the South Carolina National Guard or State Guard, or the national or state guard of any state, who are called to active duty by a state governor are entitled to unpaid leave for service. Upon honorable discharge from service, the employee must be reinstated to the same position or a position with similar seniority, status, and pay. Employee must apply for reinstatement in writing, within 5 days of release from service or related hospitalization. Employer has no duty to reinstate if the employer's circumstances make reinstatement unreasonable.

South Dakota

S.D. Codified Laws Ann. § 33A-2-9

Members of the South Dakota National Guard ordered to active duty by governor or president have the same leave and reinstatement rights and benefits guaranteed under USERRA.

Tennessee

Tenn. Code Ann. § 58-1-604

Employer may not terminate or refuse to hire an employee because of Tennessee National Guard membership or because employee is absent for a required drill, including annual field training.

Texas

Tex. Govt. Code Ann. §§ 437.204, 437.213

Members of the state military forces are entitled to the same leave and reinstatement protections granted under USERRA. Employers may not discriminate against members of the Texas military forces, or the military forces of any other state, and have the right to be reinstated following a call to active duty or training. Employees are entitled to be reinstated to the same position they held before leaving, with no loss of time, efficiency rating, vacation time, or other benefits. An employee must give notice of his or her intent to return to work as soon as practicable after release from duty.

Utah

Utah Code Ann. § 39-1-36

Members of U.S. armed forces reserves who are called to active duty, active duty for training, inactive duty training, or state active duty may take up to 5 years of unpaid leave. Upon return, employee is entitled to reinstatement to previous employment with same seniority, status, pay, and vacation rights. Employer may not discriminate against an employee based on membership in armed forces reserves.

Vermont

Vt. Stat. Ann. tit. 21, § 491, Vt. Stat. Ann. tit. 20, § 608

Employees who are members of U.S. armed forces reserves, an organized unit of the National Guard of Vermont or any other state, or the ready reserves are entitled to 15 days per year of unpaid leave for military drills, training, or other temporary duty under military authority. Returning employee must be reinstated to former position with the same status, pay, and seniority, including any seniority that accrued during the leave of absence. Employer may not discriminate against an employee who is a member or an applicant for membership in the National Guard of Vermont or any other state. Members of the National Guard of Vermont or

State Laws on Military Leave (continued)

any other state ordered to state active duty by the governor have the right to take unpaid leave from civilian employment, and cannot be required to exhaust their vacation or other accrued leave.

Virginia

Va. Code Ann. §§ 44-93.2 to 44-93.4

Members of the Virginia National Guard, Virginia Defense Force, or the national guard of another state, called to active duty by the governor are entitled to take unpaid leave and may not be required to use vacation or any other accrued leave (unless employee wishes). Returning employee whose absence does not exceed five years must be reinstated to previous position or one with same seniority, status, and pay; if position no longer exists, then to a comparable position unless employer's circumstances would make reemployment unreasonable. Employee must apply for reinstatement, in writing, within (a) 14 days of release from service or related hospitalization if service length did not exceed 180 days, or (b) 90 days of release from service or related hospitalization if service length exceeded 180 days. Employer cannot discriminate against employees because of membership in state military service.

Washington

Wash. Rev. Code Ann. §§ 73.16.032 to 73.16.035

Employees in Washington who are members of the armed forces or the national guard of any state are entitled to take leave when called to active duty for training, inactive duty training, full-time national guard duty, or state active duty. Employees are entitled to be reinstated, following their military duty, to the position they previously held or one with like seniority, status, and pay. The time limit for requesting reinstatement depends on the length of the employee's military leave.

Employers may not discriminate against employees based on their membership in any branch of the uniformed services.

West Virginia

W.Va. Code § 15-1F-8

Employees who are members of the organized militia in active service of the state of West Virginia or any other state have the same leave and reinstatement rights and benefits guaranteed under USERRA.

Wisconsin

Wis. Stat. Ann. §§ 111.321, 321.64, 321.65, 321.66

Employees who enlist, are inducted, or are ordered to serve in the U.S. armed forces for 90 days or more, or civilian employees who are asked to perform national defense work during an officially proclaimed emergency, may take leave for military service and/or training. Employees who are called to state active duty in the Wisconsin National Guard or the national guard of any other state, or called to active service with the state laboratory of hygiene during a public health emergency, are also entitled to take military leave. Upon completion of military leave, employees are entitled to reinstatement to their prior position or to one with equivalent seniority, status, and pay. A reinstated employee may not be discharged without cause for up to one year. Employers may not discriminate against employees based on their military service.

Employers with 11 or more employees must provide up to 15 days of unpaid leave (but not more than five consecutive days at a time) to members of the Civil Air Patrol for an emergency service operation, if it wouldn't unduly disrupt the employers' operations.

State Laws on Military Leave (continued)

Wyoming

Wyo. Stat. §§ 19-11-103, 19-11-104, 19-11-107, 19-11-111

Employees of the armed forces or national guard of any state who report for active duty, training, or a qualifying physical exam may take up to 5 years' leave of absence. Employee must give advance notice of service. Employee may use vacation or any other accrued leave but is not required to do so. Returning employee is entitled to reemployment with the same seniority, rights, and benefits, plus any additional seniority and benefits that employee would have earned if there had been no absence, unless employer's circumstances have changed so that reemployment is impossible or unreasonable or would impose an undue hardship. Time limits set forth governing written application for reinstatement based on length of uniformed service. Employee is entitled to complete any training program that would have been available to employee's former position during period of absence. Employee may not be terminated without cause for one year after returning to work. Employer cannot discriminate against applicant or member of the uniformed services.

Privacy

As a manager, you might occasionally need (or want) to gather information about the employees you supervise. For example, you might want to monitor employee productivity by keeping track of Internet use, search the workspace of an employee suspected of theft, or ask applicants for promotion to take a personality test.

Before taking action, you must balance your company's need (or desire) for this information with your employees' privacy rights. You certainly don't want to go so far overboard that your workers start thinking of your company as "Big Brother." And, of course, you should be mindful of your employees' privacy in order to steer clear of potential lawsuits.

This chapter covers some employment practices that could lead your company to run afoul of privacy protections, including testing, monitoring employee communications, and looking into an employee's off-duty conduct. We explain what you can and can't do when it comes to gathering information about your employees.

Frequently Asked Questions About Workplace Privacy

Can I require a worker to take a drug test?
Generally, it's not a good idea to require every worker to submit to a drug test. However, you can require drug testing for a particular employee if you reasonably suspect drug use (if the employee has glassy or red eyes, concentration problems, or other signs of impairment at work, for example). (For more on drug testing of current employees, see "Testing Current Employees," below. For more on drug testing of job applicants, see "Testing Applicants" in Chapter 1.)

Can we prohibit personal use of the Internet by employees?
Yes, but it isn't necessarily the best policy. Consider how often most of us use the Internet and for how many purposes. Because the Internet is such a common fact of modern life, you would have to assume that your "no personal use" policy would be violated fairly often. This could lead to inconsistent enforcement of the policy and lead to claims of favoritism or worse, discrimination.

Most companies don't mind an employee's occasional check of the stock market or sports scores; what they mind is an employee who streams movies, downloads and plays games, or spends all day sending email from a personal account. The better approach is to adopt a policy that prohibits abuses like these. (For more information, see "Internet Monitoring," below.)

Can my company read employees' emails?
Probably, although it might depend on your company's policies. If you have a policy of email privacy (if you tell your employees that their email will be confidential or will not be read by the company, for example), then you should abide by it. Otherwise, you have the right to monitor employee email, as long as you have a legitimate business purpose for doing so. However, you're generally on safest legal ground if you give your employees notice beforehand that their emails aren't private. (For more information, see "Why Your Company Needs an Email Policy," below.)

Frequently Asked Questions About Workplace Privacy (continued)

Can we prohibit employees from saying anything about our company on social networking sites, like Facebook?

The National Labor Relations Board has determined that online posts and comments about the terms and conditions of employment—which includes, for example, complaining about the company's dealings with a union, taking issue with company policies, and even criticizing supervisors—qualify as protected activities, for which employees may not be disciplined or fired. This is an evolving area of law, but so far employers who prohibit employees from any online discussion of their employers or work lives have found themselves on the losing end. (For more information, see "Employee Posts and Social Networking," below.)

Can we refuse to hire smokers?

It depends on the laws of your state. Some states forbid employers from making job decisions based on an employee or applicant's legal activities outside of work, including smoking. In fact, some of these laws were passed explicitly to protect smokers from discrimination. (For more information, see "Off-Duty Conduct," below.)

Can my company randomly search employees to discourage theft?

Generally, you can perform a workplace search in order to serve important, work-related interests, as long as you don't unduly intrude on your workers' privacy rights. A search of a particular employee whom you reasonably suspect of theft is going to be more likely to pass legal muster than a random search. And, even if you have a reasonable suspicion, you must not search too invasively. (For more information, see "Workplace Searches," below.)

The Right to Privacy

Worker privacy is one of the more complex areas of law that employers have to navigate. The basic rule is fairly simple: An employer should stay out of its workers' personal lives, opinions, communications, and belongings. However, there are numerous exceptions to this basic rule. In some circumstances, an employer can intrude into these private areas, if there is a legitimate business-related reason for doing so. We explain these guidelines in detail in the sections that follow.

Privacy law is tricky, in part, because it comes from so many different legal sources. There is no single federal statute that lays out the content and limits of the right to privacy. Instead, privacy principles derive mainly from the "common law," a group of legal theories inherited from England when our nation was founded. There are additional privacy protections in the U.S. Constitution, some state constitutions, various federal and state statutes, and court decisions by federal and state judges. Here's a brief roadmap through this complicated terrain of workplace privacy law.

Common Law

The term "common law" is used by lawyers to refer to legal rules that are not codified in a statute or constitution. Many of these rules originated in England and came to this country along with the colonists. As time passes and legal issues evolve, judges apply these ancient principles to more modern situations. In the sphere of privacy, for example, judges have had to stretch the time-honored right to be left alone to cover everything from people's homes to Internet chat rooms to celebrity weddings.

Most of the privacy rules that employers must follow come from the common law. Because the common law isn't codified, however, you have to read cases—written records of court decisions—to find out precisely how judges in your state have interpreted these rules.

Generally speaking, courts recognize that employees have a right to be free from overly intrusive actions by their employers. If an employee claims that his or her right to privacy has been violated, courts generally sort it out by weighing two competing concerns. On the one hand, the court will consider the employee's legitimate expectations of privacy: whether the employee reasonably believed that the area searched or monitored (such as a locker, desk, or computer) was private, and on what basis. On the other hand, the court will look at the reason for the intrusion: whether the employer had a legitimate, job-related reason for searching or monitoring, and

whether the employer could have gathered the same information in a less intrusive way.

Constitutional Protections

The U.S. Constitution does not explicitly grant a right to privacy. Nonetheless, the U.S. Supreme Court has decided, in a series of decisions dealing primarily with sex and reproductive choice, that the Bill of Rights implies a right to privacy. However, private employers don't need to worry too much about exactly what this right entails: It applies mostly to the government. Private employers generally cannot be sued for violating the federal constitution.

However, some state constitutions also contain an explicit right to privacy, and some apply this right to private employers as well as state governments. Provisions like these can put more weight on the employee's side of the scale when a court balances the employee's right to privacy against the employer's reasons for intruding.

Federal Statutes

No single federal law lays out comprehensive rules on privacy. However, a few federal laws set down some privacy guidelines for employers. For example, the Fair Credit Reporting Act (discussed in more detail in "Background Checks" in Chapter 1) requires employers to get written consent from an employee or applicant before ordering a credit report or background check on that person. The Employee Polygraph Protection

Act generally prohibits employers from subjecting their workers to lie detector tests. (See "Testing Current Employees," below, for more information.) And the National Labor Relations Act prohibits employers from monitoring a worker's union activity, including off-the-job meetings. (See "Off-Duty Conduct," below, for more on this topic.)

State Statutes

Many states have laws banning particular privacy violations. For example, some states prohibit employers from viewing an applicant's arrest records, require employers to notify workers when they listen in to a worker's telephone conversation, or prohibit employers from using particular surveillance techniques (such as a one-way mirror or video camera) in areas like restrooms and locker rooms. To find out more about your state's privacy laws, contact your state labor department (contact information is in the appendix).

Testing Current Employees

Workplace testing has become increasingly popular as employers screen their workers in an effort to figure out who is the best candidate for promotion or who is responsible for a workplace problem. As long as a test is designed to predict a worker's actual ability to do the job and is relatively noninvasive— for example, it doesn't require a worker to reveal personal information—it is probably legal. For example, an employer can generally require typing tests for clerical jobs or agility/strength tests for positions that require certain physical skills (but make sure that the test doesn't unfairly screen out disabled workers who could do the job with a reasonable accommodation; see "Applicants With Disabilities" in Chapter 1 for more information).

Generally, an employer should have a sound, work-related reason to require a current employee to submit to a test. But that might not be enough: If the test is too intrusive or delves too deeply into personal issues, it might invade the employee's right to privacy (and result in a lawsuit).

Unfortunately for employers, there are no hard-and-fast rules about whether a particular test is legal; courts generally decide these issues on a case-by-case basis, looking at all the facts and circumstances. For the most part, employers can stay out of trouble by using common sense. An employer that inquires into an employee's sex life, religious beliefs, or political affiliations probably crosses the line, while an employer who tests only for necessary job skills is probably on safe ground.

In addition to these general consider-ations, specific rules apply to the following types of tests.

Medical Examinations

Once an employee is on the job, an employer's right to conduct a medical examination is usually limited to so-called "fitness for duty" situations. If an employee has shown objective signs that he or she is physically or mentally unfit to perform the essential functions of the job—for example, by claiming that an injury prevents him or her from working—an employer may request that the employee's fitness for the job be evaluated by a medical examiner. Although the examiner can take a full medical history and conduct any tests necessary to evaluate the employee's fitness, the employer may not be entitled to all of this information. Many states also impose strict limits on the information a doctor may disclose to an employer or an insurance company without the worker's consent.

The federal Americans with Disabilities Act (ADA) also requires certain privacy protections for the results of a medical examination. Data gathered in medical examinations must be kept in a separate file available only to those with a demonstrable need to know, such as supervisors who need information about the employee's work restrictions and first aid and safety personnel (if the employee's disability might require emergency treatment or special evacuation procedures). (Similar rules apply to records of genetic information—pursuant to the Genetic Information Nondisclosure Act, covered in Chapter 3—and medical certifications and other records gathered in connection with the Family and Medical Leave Act, covered in Chapter 5.)

Lessons From the Real World

Marya Norman-Bloodsaw worked as an accounting administrator at the Lawrence Berkeley Laboratory (a research facility jointly operated by the State of California and the federal government). When she started work, Bloodsaw and other clerical and administrative employees were given a "general physical," including a blood test.

Employees were also offered the option of further "periodic health examinations" during their employment. But the lab didn't just give workers a physical. It also tested them for syphilis, sickle cell trait, and pregnancy, without their consent or knowledge. When Bloodsaw found out, she and some of her coworkers filed a class-action complaint against the lab, arguing that the lab had violated their right to privacy.

The U.S. Court of Appeals for the Ninth Circuit agreed, saying, "[O]ne can think of few subject areas more personal and more likely to implicate privacy interests than that of one's health or genetic make-up."

The Lab agreed to settle the case, in December 1999, for $2.2 million.

Norman-Bloodsaw v. Lawrence Berkeley Laboratory, 135 F.3d 1260 (9th Cir. 1998); Dorothy Wertz, "Genetic Testing in the Workplace: The Lawrence Berkeley Labs Case," *The Gene Letter* (April 3, 2000); Matt Fleischer, "Protecting Genome Privacy Proves Hard," *The National Law Journal* (July 20, 2000).

Drug Tests

Although an employer can generally require job applicants to submit to drug testing, an employer's right to test current employees is less clear. (For more on drug testing applicants, see "Testing Applicants" in Chapter 1 and "Drugs and Alcohol" in Chapter 7.) No federal law clearly authorizes drug testing of employees, except for certain workers in the defense and transportation industries. And many state laws limit the circumstances under which an employer may test and the types of tests an employer may conduct.

Because the law of drug testing is changing rapidly, and because state laws vary widely in terms of what is allowed and prohibited, employers have to tread very carefully in this area. Before undertaking any drug testing, an employer should consult with a knowledgeable lawyer.

Employers are on safest ground if they have a strong, legitimate reason for testing workers. Your company is most likely to withstand a legal challenge if it limits testing to:

- workers whose jobs carry a high risk of injury to themselves or others (such as a pilot or a security guard who carries a gun)
- workers who have been involved in an accident that suggests the possibility of drug use (for example, a delivery person who causes a collision by driving erratically)
- workers who are currently in or have completed a drug rehabilitation program, and
- workers whom a manager or supervisor reasonably suspects of using drugs (based on obvious signs of impairment, such as slurred speech or glassy eyes).

For information on your state's current rules, see the chart entitled "State Drug and Alcohol Testing Laws," at the end of Chapter 1.

Psychological Screening

Some employers use pencil and paper (or keyboard and screen) psychological tests to attempt to predict whether an employee is a good candidate for promotion or whether the employee will engage in workplace misconduct. There are two problems with using such tests. First, mental health experts disagree about whether these tests can actually predict an employee's future conduct or work performance. Second, some of these tests include questions that are highly personal and invade the employee's privacy. For the most part, employers would be well-advised to steer clear of psychological tests absent some compelling justification and some reason to believe that the test you use will yield relevant, accurate information about the employee. (Different rules apply to applicants; for more information, see "Testing Applicants" in Chapter 1.)

Lie Detector Tests

A federal law called the Employee Polygraph Protection Act, 29 U.S.C. § 2001, prohibits all private employers from requiring workers to submit to lie detector tests, with a few exceptions. Employers that manufacture or distribute pharmaceuticals or provide certain security services might be allowed to require polygraphs. Employers might also require a worker whom they reasonably suspect of theft or embezzlement to take a polygraph test, under certain circumstances.

Aside from these limited exceptions, however, a private employer may not require a current employee to take a lie detector test, use the results of any such test in making employment decisions, or discipline or fire any employee who refuses to take one. And, even if an exception applies, the employer must meet very strict technical requirements regarding the way the test is administered and interpreted, how the test results may be used, and more.

Internet Monitoring

Remember when we had to track shipments by phone, book travel at a travel agent's office, locate information in the library, plan trips using a paper map, or go shopping in stores? The Internet sure has changed all of that! As most businesses are aware, however, the Internet's convenience comes with a dark side. As a virtual gateway in and out of the company, the Internet tempts employees to spend work time on personal pursuits like bargain hunting, watching live sports, conversing in chat rooms, posting to Facebook pages, or even looking for a new job. In addition, employees can use the Internet to access inappropriate and offensive material, such as pornography, gambling, and hate speech.

Employee access to the Web can also inadvertently damage the company's computer system and software. And, the Internet provides a backdoor way by which employees can send information out of the company, whether by transmitting company data through personal email or posting personal comments (which can be traced back to your company) to outside sites. For all these reasons and more, it's a good idea to have a company policy on use of the Internet.

Prohibited Uses of the Internet

To protect your company against abuses, your policy should explain what types of Internet activities are allowed and forbidden. In addition to banning sites with offensive material, many companies ban downloads that violate the law or could infect the company's computer system. Also, consider your company's bandwidth: Streaming audio or video can quickly overload the system, particularly during popular events like the NCAA tournament or the finale of a daytime soap opera. Your company might want to consider limits like these:

- Employees may not view websites that contain pornography, gambling, violent images, or other inappropriate content.

- Employees may not use the company's computer system to operate an outside business, online auction, or other sales site.
- Employees may not download or copy software, games, text, photos, or any other works in violation of copyright laws.
- Employees may not stream, run, or download music, video, games, widgets, or any form of multimedia.
- Employees may not use file hosting services, such as Dropbox or Rapid Share, or cloud storage services, for work-related files, unless specifically authorized by the company.

Personal Use of the Internet

Some companies ban any personal use of the Internet. This type of rule can lead to problems, however. Because most employees will probably violate the policy at some point, disciplining employees will inevitably lead to accusations of unfairness and inconsistent application of the rules. Especially if your company's employees work at computers all day long, they are likely to feel some resentment that they aren't allowed to even check the weather or take a quick look at the news headlines. A more sensible approach is to allow limited personal use of the Internet during lunch, breaks, and so on, as long as that use is not excessive and doesn't violate the company's other rules about Internet use.

Privacy Concerns

If your company doesn't already monitor employee Internet use, there might come a day when it needs to do so. To guard against potential legal problems, you should tell employees—in a written policy—that their use of the Internet on company equipment is not private and may be monitored. That way, if you have to investigate employee complaints that a manager is viewing pornography, look into online rumors about your company's products that appear to come from within the building, or find out whether declining productivity can fairly be blamed on streaming video of the World Cup, you can check up on employee Internet use without running afoul of privacy rights.

Warning employees that they may be monitored has another benefit, too: It will prevent employees from using the Internet inappropriately in the first place. All of us are less likely to break the rules if we know we can get caught. By telling employees, up front, that their Internet use is not private, you not only reserve your right to look into wrongdoing after it's taken place, but also increase the chances that employees won't commit online misconduct at all.

Why Your Company Needs an Email Policy

Does your company make computers and email available to your employees? If so, you should seriously consider adopting a policy explaining the rules for using email and reserving the company's right to monitor the messages sent and received on its equipment.

Using Work Email for Union Organizing and Other Protected Activities

Although employers are generally free to limit personal use of work email, there is an exception for union organizing and other protected activities. In 2014, the National Labor Relations Board (NLRB) ruled that employers cannot adopt a "business only" policy when it comes to work email, if it would prevent employees from using work email on their own time to engage in activities protected by the National Labor Relations Act (NLRA). This rule applies to union workers, workers trying to organize a union, and even nonunion workers who get together to discuss the terms and conditions of their employment. For example, employees who use work email to complain about pay, management, or workplace safety are typically protected.

Employees must be allowed to use work email for these purposes during nonworking time, such as meal periods, rest breaks, and the time before and after established work hours. Employers are free to prohibit such activity during work hours and can continue to monitor work emails, as long as they have a legitimate business reason and don't target their monitoring efforts to detect protected activity.

As an exception to this rule, an employer can adopt a "business only" rule if it is necessary to maintain productivity or discipline in the workplace. However, the NLRB was quick to point out that this would be a rare case.

Purple Communications, Inc., 361 NLRB No. 126 (Dec. 11, 2014).

Benefits of Having an Email Policy

There are several very good reasons to adopt an email policy. First and foremost, you need to let employees know that your company may monitor their messages. Even if you have never read employee email and don't plan to make a regular practice of it, you should protect the company's right to do so. If you don't, your company might be unable to fully investigate claims of harassment, discrimination, theft, and other misconduct. An employee might even threaten a lawsuit, claiming that your investigation violated his or her privacy.

Consider these statistics: In a survey commissioned by Elron Software, more than 60% of workers admitted to sending or receiving adult-oriented personal email at work; more than 55% admitted to sending or receiving personal emails that were racist, sexist, or otherwise offensive; one in ten employees admitted to receiving confidential information about another company in personal email; and a significant number admitted to sending messages that included confidential information about their own companies.

If your company is ever faced with an employee who uses email to transmit porno-graphic images, reveal trade secrets, or send racist or sexist messages—and these statistics demonstrate that you could very well find yourself in this position—you will have to read the messages to figure out what to do. If your company doesn't have a policy warning employees that their emails can be read at any time, an employee might sue for violation of privacy. Although these lawsuits are generally ultimately unsuccessful—that is, employees have lost most of them—your company will still have to spend time and money defending its actions in court.

In addition, some states—including Connecticut and Delaware—require employers that monitor emails to let their employees know beforehand. Every year, more states consider imposing similar requirements. Putting this information in a workplace policy helps you meet these legal obligations.

Finally, you can use an email policy to tell your employees how you expect them to use the email system and what uses are prohibited. Laying down the rules clearly, in writing, will go a long way toward preventing abuses in the first place.

What to Include in an Email Policy

Your company's email policy should address the following issues:

- **Personal use of the email system.** Explain whether employees can use email for personal messages. If your company places any restrictions on personal messages (for example, that employees can send them only during nonwork hours, must exercise discretion as to the number and type of messages sent, or may not send personal messages with large attachments), describe those rules. Also, be careful not to make your policy so broad that it would prevent employees from engaging in protected activity under the National Labor Relations Act during nonworking hours. (For more information, see "Using Work Email for Union Organizing and Other Protected Activities," above.)

- **Monitoring.** Reserve the company's right to monitor employee emails at any time. Explain that any messages employees send using company equipment are not private, even if the employee considers them to be personal. If your company will monitor regularly using a particular system—for example, a system that flags key words or copies every draft of a message—explain it briefly. This will help deter employees from sending inappropriate messages in the first place.

- **Rules.** Make clear that all of your workplace policies and rules—such as rules against harassment, discrimination, violence, solicitation, and theft of trade secrets—apply to employee use of the email system. Remind employees that all emails sent on company equipment should be professional and appropriate. Some employers also include so-called netiquette rules: style guidelines for email writing.

- **Deleting email.** Establish a regular schedule for purging emails. Otherwise, your company will eventually run into a storage problem. Let employees know how they can save important messages from the purge.

Sample Email Policy

An example of a company email policy is provided on the next two pages. This example is for illustrative purposes only; be sure any policy you adopt is appropriate for your workplace and consistent with your state's law and federal law.

Employee Posts and Social Networking

Chances are good that many of your company's employees post personal content on the Internet. Perhaps they have their own Facebook pages, tweet their observations throughout the day, keep blogs, post comments on other websites, upload photos, or chat with others online.

Many employers are understandably wary about trying to crack down on personal posts. Blogs and social media provide a creative outlet, a way for friends to keep in touch, a place to share opinions and be part of a larger community of pug owners, single parents, or recycling enthusiasts. They are, in a word, personal, and few employers really want to read employees' personal writings or be known as a company that stifles personal expression.

Unfortunately, however, not all employees like their jobs; even those who do might not successfully navigate the line between appropriate and inappropriate content. An employee blog or post that reveals company trade secrets, slams a company product, or threatens or harasses other employees can present an unmitigated disaster for a company. Even posts that have nothing to do with work can create major trouble if they express extreme or unpopular views, racist comments, or violent fantasies, for example.

A quick look through news reports shows that employees have used social networking sites and blogs to post:

- a YouTube video showing an employee of a restaurant chain stuffing cheese up his nose—before putting it on a pizza
- Facebook posts by an employee chronicling his dates with coworkers
- MySpace posts by employees of an auto club, commenting on their coworkers' weight and sexual orientation as well as their plans to slow down the company's roadside assistance to motorists
- a Facebook post by an employee threatening to punch a coworker in the face "before the end of my shift," and
- a MySpace page a teacher created to communicate with his students, which included nude photos, inappropriate conversation, and curse words.

Employers have the right to control what employees do with the time and equipment it pays for, generally speaking. However, when employees use their own computers to express their own opinions on their own time, an employer's legal rights are more limited.

Email Policy

Use of the Email System

The email system is intended for official Company business. Although you may use the email system for personal messages, you may do so during nonworking hours only. If you send personal messages through the Company's email system, you must ensure that this does not interfere in any way with your job duties or performance. Any employee who abuses this privilege may be subject to discipline.

Email Is Not Private

Email messages, including attachments, sent and received on Company equipment are the property of the Company. We reserve the right to access, monitor, read, and/or copy emails at any time, for any reason. You should not expect privacy for any email you send using Company equipment, including messages that you consider to be personal or those labeled with a designation such as "Personal" or "Private." In addition, the Company's software automatically searches the messages you send for content that violates company policy, including sexual or racial comments, threats, trade secrets, competitive information, and inappropriate language. These will be forwarded to, and read by, Company management.

All Conduct Rules Apply to Email

All of our policies and rules of conduct apply to employee use of the email system. This means, for example, that you may not use the email system to send harassing or discriminatory messages, including messages with explicit sexual content or pornographic images; to send threatening messages; or to reveal Company trade secrets or confidential information.

No Solicitation by Email

You may not use the email system to solicit others to patronize an outside business or to support an outside organization, a political candidate or cause, or a religious cause. This rule does not apply to union activities or efforts to organize a union.

Professional Tone and Content

We expect you to exercise discretion in using electronic communications equipment. When you send email using the Company's equipment, you are representing the Company. Make sure that your messages are professional and appropriate, in both tone and content. Remember, although email may seem like a private conversation, email can be printed, saved, and forwarded to unintended recipients. You should not send any email that you wouldn't want your boss, your mother, or our Company's competitors to read.

Email Security

To avoid email viruses and other threats, employees should not open email attachments from people and businesses they don't recognize, particularly if the email appears to have been forwarded multiple times or has a nonexistent or peculiar subject heading. Even if you know the sender, do not open an email attachment that has a strange name or is not referenced in the body of the email; it may have been transmitted automatically, without the sender's knowledge.

If you believe your computer has been infected by a virus, worm, or other security threat to the Company's system, you must inform the IT department immediately.

Employees also may not share their email passwords with anyone, including coworkers or family members. Revealing passwords to the Company's email system could allow an outsider to access the Company's network.

Retaining and Deleting Email Messages

Because emails are electronic records, certain messages must be retained for compliance purposes. Please refer to our record-keeping policy for guidance on which records must be kept, and for how long. If you have any questions about whether and how to retain a particular email, please ask your manager.

Because of the large volume of emails our Company sends and receives each day, we discourage employees from storing large numbers of emails that are not subject to the retention rules explained above. Please make a regular practice of deleting emails once you have read and/or responded to them. If you need to save a particular message, you may print out a paper copy, archive the email, or save it on your hard drive or disk. The Company will purge emails that have not been archived after 90 days.

The Company may have occasion to suspend our usual rules about deleting emails (for example, if the Company is involved in a lawsuit requiring it to preserve evidence). If this happens, employees will be notified of the procedures to follow to save emails. Failing to comply with such a notice could subject the Company to serious legal consequences, and will result in discipline, up to and including termination.

Legal Protections for Employees Who Post Online

A host of laws protect an employee's right to speak—at least about certain topics—online. These laws include:

- **Off-duty conduct laws.** As explained in "Off-Duty Conduct," below, a number of states have laws that prohibit employers from disciplining or firing employees for lawful activities they pursue on their own time. Although some of these laws were originally created to protect smokers from discrimination, others protect any employee conduct that doesn't break the law, which might include employee blogging or posting.

- **Protections for political views.** A handful of states protect employees from discrimination based on their political views or affiliation. In these states, disciplining an employee for a political post (for example, one that endorses a candidate or cause) could be illegal.

- **Protections for "whistle-bloggers."** An employee who raises concerns about safety hazards or illegal activity at work might be protected as a whistle-blower (called a "whistle-blogger" if the concerns are raised in a blog).

- **Prohibitions on retaliation.** Many employment laws protect employees from retaliation for complaining that their rights have been violated. If an employee complains online about workplace discrimination, harassment, violation of the Family and Medical Leave Act, wage and hour violations, or other legal transgressions, that employee might be protected from disciplinary action.

- **Concerted activity protections.** The National Labor Relations Act and similar state laws protect employees' rights to communicate with each other about the terms and conditions of employment, and to join together—in a union or otherwise—to bring concerns about these issues to their employer. Under these laws, an employee who is fired for posting about low wages, inadequate benefits, poor management, or long work hours could have a plausible legal claim. (See "Protected Concerted Activity" in Chapter 8 for more information.)

This final right has been the most likely to get employers in trouble lately. The National Labor Relations Board (NLRB), the government agency that investigates and enforces the nation's labor and union laws, has been cracking down on employers that discipline or fire employees for posting critical comments about the company on social media sites.

What do employee posts have to do with labor relations? Plenty, if employees are prohibited from, or fired or disciplined for, communicating with each other about the terms and conditions of employment and joining together to bring their concerns to their employer (called "protected concerted activity" or simply "Section 7 activity," after the provision of the National Labor Relations Act which creates them) These protections apply to union and nonunion employees alike.

In the last few years, the NLRB has become extremely active in this area, alleging unfair labor practices by employers that discipline or fire employees for what they post online. As part of these enforcement actions, the NLRB often finds that the employer's social media and posting policy is too broad, because it tends to discourage employees from exercising their rights. The board has challenged policies that prohibit disparagement or criticism of the company or management; policies that require employees not to post "confidential" or "nonpublic" information unless the policy illustrates the types of information covered (so employees aren't deterred from discussing wages or other terms of employment); policies that require employees to avoid discussing topics that are objectionable or inflammatory; and policies that require employees to check with a supervisor before posting.

Adopting a Commonsense Policy

Online posts are easy to dash off and virtually impossible to retract once published. When employees aren't at work, they probably aren't thinking of the potential consequences of making fun of a coworker's accent or revealing little-known facts about a client. Most likely, they're simply trying to be funny and attract readers.

Rules for Online Product Endorsements

If your company sells products on sites that allow users to comment or post reviews, or products that are discussed in blogs or on social networking sites or user boards, you need to make sure that employees always identify themselves—and their relationship to your company—when discussing company products online. This is required by regulations released in 2009 by the Federal Trade Commission (FTC), the federal government agency that regulates deceptive advertising.

The FTC already had rules about product endorsements, but the 2009 changes made clear that these rules also apply to statements and reviews made online. The purpose of these rules is to make sure consumers fully understand the relationship between the product and the person endorsing or discussing it, so they can make informed decisions about how much weight to give the endorser's statement. After all, a paid actor or spokesperson isn't as credible as an actual user of the product.

The upshot of these new rules is that employees must identify themselves as employees of your company when posting anything about its products online. The FTC has said that an employment relationship is the type of connection that a consumer would want to know about in evaluating product endorsements. So, your online posting policy should tell employees that they must be up front about their relationship to the company when making any statements about it or its products online.

So what can your company do to curb inappropriate employee posts without running afoul of the law or becoming known as Corporate Big Brother? Adopt a policy letting employees know that their personal pages, blogs, and posts could get them in trouble at work, and explain the types of content that could create problems.

A good social media policy should explain that, while the company appreciates that employees want to express themselves in the virtual world, problems might arise if their personal posts appear to be associated with the company or violate the rights of the company or other employees. Here are some topics you should cover:

- **Use of company resources.** Your policy should prohibit employees from using the company's equipment or network to write or publish social media posts, or from doing so on company time.

- **Company policies apply online.** It's a good idea to remind employees that company policies prohibiting harassment, protecting trade secrets, and so on apply whether an employee makes these statements online or in the bricks and mortar world.

- **Company name and marks.** Your policy should prohibit employees from using the company's trademarks, logos, or other images, and it should also prohibit employees from making false statements about the company. If employees choose to identify themselves as employees of the company in an online post, require them to clearly state that the views they

express online are their own and that they do not speak for the company.

- **Inappropriate disclosures.** Remind employees to avoid disclosing trade secrets or other confidential information. Be sure to describe what types of information are confidential, and don't make the policy so broad that it could be interpreted as prohibiting employees from discussing the terms and conditions of their employment (such as their wages). If employees have concerns about whether something they plan to post falls into this category, they should raise the issue with a manager.

- **Retaliation is prohibited.** Make it clear that employees will not be retaliated against for reporting social media activity that might be in violation of the company's policy.

For sample policy language on blogs and online posts—as well as policies on use of the Internet, email, cell phones, and much more—pick up a copy of *Smart Policies for Workplace Technologies*, by Lisa Guerin (copublished by SHRM and Nolo).

Off-Duty Conduct

Today, employers have the technological means, and occasionally the inclination, to find out what workers are doing on their own time. However, there are legal limits to a company's right to monitor its employees' conduct off the job and to make decisions based on that conduct.

Privacy Law

Employees of government and public entities have a constitutional right to privacy that protects them from most employer intrusions into their off-the-job conduct. For public employers, monitoring of off-duty activities is largely off limits.

In the private sector, a number of laws prohibit employers from intruding into their employees' private lives. As noted, some state constitutions specifically contain a right to privacy, which prevents private employers from looking into their employees' off-duty activity. Some states also have laws prohibiting employers from taking any job-related action against a worker based on that worker's lawful conduct off the job, including smoking or other use of tobacco products.

Even in states that don't provide private workers with a constitutional or statutory right to privacy, it is generally illegal for an employer to intrude unreasonably into the "seclusion" of an employee. This means that physical areas in which an employee has a reasonable expectation of privacy (personal belongings, for instance) are off-limits to employers, unless there is a very good reason to intrude. And an employer is never allowed to physically enter an employee's home without consent (even when searching for stolen company property).

The same balancing approach applies to private information. Generally speaking, employers should not inquire about or otherwise obtain facts about employees' private lives. For example, an employer may not ask employees about their sexual practices.

Courts and legislatures have created some specific rules for certain types of private, off-duty activities, as described in the sections that follow.

Union Activity

Under the National Labor Relations Act (NLRA), 29 U.S.C. §§ 151 and following, it is illegal for an employer to monitor or conduct any surveillance of employee union activities, including off-the-job meetings or gatherings. This rule applies to any concerted activity (that is, activity undertaken by workers acting together, rather than individually), even if no union is involved, as long as employees are discussing their work conditions or terms of employment. An employer who sends a supervisor to eavesdrop on such meetings or plants a spy among employees engaged in this conduct violates the NLRA. (For more on this rule, see "Representation Elections and Organizing Campaigns" in Chapter 8.)

Drug Testing

Because drug testing has the potential to reveal an employee's use of drugs outside of work hours, it has been the subject of much privacy litigation. In general, drug testing is usually allowed of job applicants, employees who perform safety or security-sensitive work, or employees who have given an employer some reason to believe that they are impaired by drugs at work. (See "Testing Current Employees," above, for more information about drug testing.)

Moonlighting

Generally speaking, working more than one job is lawful. However, an employer has the right to limit after-hours work that is in conflict with the employer's own business. For instance, going to work for the competition could provide grounds for discipline or discharge. As a general rule, the more senior the employee (and the more access to important company information), the more likely a court will take a dim view of the employee moonlighting for a competitor.

Marital Status

Many states make it illegal for employers to discriminate on the basis of marital status. Employers in these states may not keep track of whether their employees are single, married, or divorced, except as necessary for providing certain benefits such as health insurance. (To find out whether your state prohibits marital status discrimination, see "State Laws Prohibiting Discrimination in Employment" at the end of Chapter 3.)

However, tricky issues can arise when, for example, one spouse applies for a position in which he or she would supervise the other, or an applicant's spouse works for your company's major competitor. To find out how your state's law might apply to situations like these, contact your state fair employment practices agency. (You can find contact information in the appendix.)

Lawful Activities

A number of states prohibit employers from taking action against employees based on their off-the-job activities, as long as those activities are not illegal. The form of these protections varies. Some states protect an employee's right to engage in any lawful activities while off duty. These laws apply broadly to a wide range of conduct, such as volunteering for a particular political candidate or collecting signatures for a controversial ballot measure. In other states, the law is limited to the employee's right to smoke tobacco or use other lawful products off the job.

The legalization of marijuana in several states—for both medicinal and recreational purposes—has posed an interesting question under these laws: Can an employer fire an employee for smoking marijuana during nonworking hours if it's legal under state law? Most state courts to consider the issue have held that, because marijuana is still illegal under federal law, employers are free to fire employees for marijuana use. (For more on this issue, see "Drugs and Alcohol" in Chapter 7.)

Workplace Searches

It happens to even the best employers: a sudden rash of thefts, a worker threatening violence, or some other possible misconduct or illegal activity in the workplace. Your company's first step must be to investigate the situation. (See "Investigating Complaints" in Chapter 11.) As part of the investigation, you might want to search a worker's desk or locker, install some kind of monitoring device (a video camera, for example), or ask to look inside an employee's purse or backpack. The following sections explain how you can get the information you need without violating workers' right to privacy.

Reasonable Expectations of Privacy

When judges evaluate whether a particular workplace search is legal, they usually try to balance two competing concerns. First, the law considers the employer's justification for performing the search: An employer with a strong work-related reason for searching has the best chance of prevailing. For example, an employer that receives a complaint that an employee brought a gun to work and has threatened to use it has a strong justification for a locker search.

On the other hand, workers have reasonable expectations of privacy. A worker who legitimately expects, based on the employer's policies, past practice, and common sense, that the employer will not search certain areas has the strongest argument here. For example, a worker has a high expectation of privacy in an employee restroom or changing area, particularly if the employer has not warned workers that these areas might be monitored.

To decide if a workplace search is legal, a court considers the relative strengths of these two competing interests. The more steps employers take to diminish their workers' expectations of privacy and the stronger the employer's reason to search, the more likely a court is to find the search legal. Courts also have to consider whether a particular state or federal law prohibits the search.

Search Considerations

Privacy is a highly volatile area of law. Every year, workers bring lawsuits claiming that an employer invaded their privacy by conducting an improper search. The outcome of these cases depends on the judge's view of the misconduct being investigated and the employer's methods for getting to the bottom of things. Because there are no legal guarantees in this area of law, most employers should talk to a lawyer before conducting all but the most routine searches. Here are a few considerations to keep in mind:

- **Search only if necessary.** In many companies, there will rarely be a need to search. Unless your employees routinely handle large amounts of money or valuable, easily hidden items (such as prescription drugs or jewelry), you might not need to search at all. If you do want to conduct a search, make sure you have a legitimate business reason (theft, for example).

- **If you plan to search, have a policy.** If you warn your employees in advance that certain areas (like desks or lockers) might be subject to search, employees will have lower expectations of privacy in those areas, and less reason to complain about a particular search.

- **Don't conduct random searches.** Courts tend to frown on employers that conduct random searches, even if the employer's policy puts employees on notice of this possibility. These searches, particularly if conducted when the employer has no reason to suspect any wrongdoing, can get employers into trouble.

- **Never search an employee's body.** Some employers become so zealous that they want to physically search their workers for contraband or stolen items. This is always a bad idea. Workers have a very strong privacy interest in their own bodies. If your search reaches this level, consider calling the police in for help.

- **Restrooms and changing rooms are off limits.** Most workers legitimately expect that they will not be monitored while using the bathroom or changing their clothes. This expectation is highly reasonable. If you must monitor these areas, warn employees and monitor only to the extent necessary. For example, if you have received reports that some employees are selling illegal drugs in the restroom, you might install a camera or post a guard in the main part of the room, after notifying your workers. However, you would probably be going too far if you posted cameras in each stall. And some states prohibit surveillance of any kind in these private areas.

- **Consider the worker's privacy expectations.** Before you search, think about whether an average worker would consider a particular space private in your workplace. Do employees routinely lock their desk drawers? If so, they might have higher expectations of privacy. On the other hand, if no one has an assigned desk or if workers routinely use each other's desks, they shouldn't expect their desk drawers to be private.

- **Don't hold employees against their will.** Some employers detain workers in connection with a search, either to keep the worker out of the area being searched or to exert a little pressure on the worker to consent to a search ("No one is leaving this room until you show me what's in your backpack!"). This is a bad idea. Under a legal theory called "false imprisonment," an employee can sue an employer that leads the employee to believe that he or she is not free to leave. Although these claims often come up in the context of questioning (when employers refuse to let their employees leave the workplace until they have answered certain questions, for example), they also surface when searches are conducted.

Legal Dos and Don'ts: Privacy

Do:

- **Search, test, and monitor only if you really need to.** Let's face it: Most smaller businesses will never have a strong need to dig into their employees' purses, psyches, or private lives. Absent a compelling reason to pry—such as a theft problem—your best course of action is to stay out of the spy business (and, hopefully, out of the courtroom).
- **Adopt clear written policies.** The more steps your company takes to diminish employee expectations of privacy, the better its legal position will be. And, telling employees that you reserve the right to monitor and search will help deter them from engaging in misconduct in the first place.
- **Get some legal advice if you need it.** The law of workplace privacy changes all the time, and your state might have some special requirements you should know about. Before installing surveillance cameras, adopting a search policy, or tailing employees off-site, talk to a lawyer.

Don't:

- **Detain employees physically.** If you prevent workers from leaving a room or building, or you lead them to believe they are not free to go, you are buying legal trouble for your company.
- **Use lie detector tests.** In most situations, it is illegal to require a worker to take a polygraph or make any decisions based on the results of such a test. And even in the rare circumstances when polygraphs are allowed, employers must follow a number of technical rules to protect the worker's rights. The best rule of thumb for most employers: Just don't do it.
- **Become "Big Brother."** Too much monitoring will quickly lead to employee resentment. When you dig too deeply into workers' private lives, you risk alienating them. This type of resentment leads not only to lawsuits, but also to poor performance, plummeting morale, and retention problems.

Test Your Knowledge

Questions

1. Employers can require current employees to take lie detector tests as a condition of promotion. ☐ True ☐ False

2. Employers may never require employees to take a medical examination. ☐ True ☐ False

3. Employees may not post online reviews or endorsements of their own company's products. ☐ True ☐ False

4. Employers are not allowed to read employee emails if those messages are marked "private" or "confidential." ☐ True ☐ False

5. Even though it's sneaky, it isn't illegal for an employer to send a manager to eavesdrop on an off-site employee meeting to discuss forming a union. ☐ True ☐ False

6. A company can fire employees for off-duty conduct, as long as the employees work at will. ☐ True ☐ False

7. The First Amendment of the U.S. Constitution protects employees from being fired for what they write in a personal blog. ☐ True ☐ False

8. Employers are legally entitled to search the personal belongings of any one who enters or leaves company property. ☐ True ☐ False

9. If an employee won't answer legitimate questions about employee theft or other misconduct, the employer is legally entitled to detain the employee until he or she starts talking. ☐ True ☐ False

10. A company's email policy should always reserve the employer's right to read emails, even if the company has no current plans to do so. ☐ True ☐ False

Test Your Knowledge (continued)

Answers

1. False. With a few very limited exceptions, employers may not require employees to take polygraph tests.

2. False. There are circumstances in which an employer may require an employee to take a "fitness for duty" exam, to prove that the employee is able to work following an illness or injury.

3. False. Employees may post reviews, comments, and endorsements, as long as they identify themselves as company employees.

4. False, as long as the employer has warned employees that emails are not private.

5. False. Employers may not send spies or otherwise monitor employee discussions on union issues.

6. Not necessarily. It depends on the conduct and the laws of your state. Some states protect employees from being fired for lawful activity off the job, for example. And the employee's actions might be protected under other laws, such as the National Labor Relations Act (see Chapter 8).

7. False. The First Amendment protects only against actions by the government, not against the actions of private employers.

8. False. Even if an employer adopts a strict search policy, its employees might have a legitimate claim for invasion of privacy if their personal belongings are routinely searched every time they leave the worksite.

9. False. Detaining an employee against his or her will is called "false imprisonment," and it is illegal.

10. True. A company should always reserve the right to monitor, just in case it faces a situation in which it must read employee email.

Health and Safety

Most employers want to maintain a healthy and safe work environment for their employees. Not only is it the humane thing to do, but it is also good for business. Employees are happier and more productive in a safe, secure work environment. And the company will save money—with fewer workers' compensation claims and lower rates of absenteeism—by keeping employees and their work environment as healthy and safe as possible.

In addition to these practical concerns, your company also has a legal obligation to provide a safe workplace. Federal and state governments have passed laws designed to ensure healthy and safe work environments. These laws impose safety standards and posting, reporting, and record-keeping requirements on all employers. Your company will face investigations, fines, and—in serious cases—closure if it ignores these important laws.

In this chapter, we provide an overview of health and safety laws. We also look at workers' compensation statutes, drug and alcohol issues, smoking, and use of cell phones while driving.

Health and Safety Laws

All companies, regardless of size or industry, must comply with federal and state health and safety laws.

The Occupational Safety and Health Act

The major federal health and safety law is the Occupational Safety and Health Act (OSH Act), 29 U.S.C. §§ 651 to 678. The OSH Act requires employers to provide a workplace that is free of "recognized hazards" that are likely to cause serious harm or death to employees. As you can imagine, the term "recognized hazards" encompasses a wide range of things, from sharp objects to dangerous chemicals to radiation.

Employers must also conduct safety training sessions to educate employees about the materials and equipment they will be using, any workplace hazards (especially toxic chemicals), and the steps the company is taking to control those hazards.

In addition, employers must comply with some administrative requirements. For instance, companies must post a notice informing employees of health and safety regulations, report employee deaths and hospitalizations, and maintain records of employee:

- injuries and illnesses
- exposure to hazardous chemicals and substances, and
- safety training.

There are thousands of pages of federal regulations interpreting this law and defining employer duties and obligations. That's the

Frequently Asked Questions About Health and Safety

What kinds of penalties are imposed on companies that violate health and safety laws?

Penalties range from minimal to major fines. The exact penalty depends on a number of factors, including the employer's record of violations, the severity of the violation, and whether the employer acted in good faith. (See "Health and Safety Laws," below, for more information about penalties.)

Can an employee who is injured at work sue for damages?

Usually, an employee who suffers a work-related injury is limited to the benefits provided by workers' compensation; that is, the employee may not sue the employer in court. If the employer willfully or recklessly caused the injury, however (for example, if the company knew about the hazardous condition that caused the worker's accident but didn't do anything about it), then the employee might be able to bypass the workers' compensation system and sue the company for damages. (See "Workers' Compensation," below, for more information.)

Do we need any special rules for employee use of cell phones while driving?

Yes. Studies have shown that using a cell phone while driving increases the risk of accidents. Employees who dial, talk, or text while driving not only create a safety hazard for themselves, they also create a legal risk for your company, which might be liable for any harm they cause if they are having a work-related conversation or driving on company business. To minimize these dangers, every company should have cell phone rules for employees. (See "Cell Phones and Driving," below, for more information.)

Can we fire—or refuse to hire— employees who smoke?

It depends on the laws of your state. Many states prohibit employers from discriminating against workers or applicants just because they smoke; in other states, however, companies are free to make hiring and firing decisions on this basis. (See "Smoking," below, for more information.)

Can we fire an employee for being an alcoholic?

No. You cannot fire or discipline an employee merely for being an alcoholic. That would be disability discrimination. You can, however, fire an employee for drinking at work or arriving to work under the influence of alcohol. You can also fire or discipline an employee for not meeting the conduct and performance standards that apply to all workers, even if the employee's failures are caused by alcohol abuse. (For more information about this issue, see "Drugs and Alcohol," below, as well as "Disability" in Chapter 3.)

bad news. The good news is that you do not have to wade through all this paper to learn about the law. The U.S. Occupational Safety and Health Administration (OSHA), the federal agency that enforces the law, publishes lots of information designed especially for small and medium-sized businesses. You can find this information on the agency's website at www.osha.gov/dcsp/smallbusiness/index.html.

Also, each state has an OSHA-funded agency that offers free on-site consultations. If you ask for a consultation, an expert will walk through your worksite with you, pointing out risks and hazards and providing practical advice on how to correct problems and comply with the law. Because this program is separate from OSHA's inspection and enforcement division, you will not receive any citations or fines for violations found during the consult. (However, you will be required to fix serious violations within a timeframe and plan developed by you and the OSHA consultant.) To schedule a consultation, visit OSHA's website, at www.osha.gov/dcsp/smallbusiness/consult.html.

Companies that disregard their health and safety obligations run the risk of being investigated and perhaps fined by OSHA inspectors. Fines depend on a variety of factors. Generally, employers that knowingly and intentionally violate the law, fail to correct a problem that OSHA warned them about, or put their employees at risk of serious injury or death are going to face the

largest penalties. Depending on these factors, fines range from minimal all the way up to $126,749. If OSHA identifies a hazard that your company fails to eliminate, it can impose a fine of $12,675 for each day that the hazard goes uncorrected.

Lessons From the Real World

The U.S. Occupational Health and Safety Administration (OSHA) sent investigators to Party City Corporation after employees complained of unsafe conditions. When investigators looked around the workplace, they found a whole host of problems, including:

- locked fire exits
- obstructed fire exits
- no training in the use of fire extinguishers
- no handrails on stairs
- no exit signs, and
- dangerously stacked boxes.

Even though no employees had been injured or harmed by the violations, OSHA imposed a hefty $111,150 fine because the potential for harm was so high. The possibility that employees might be unable to escape a fire or another emergency was unacceptable to the agency.

If your company has ten or fewer employees and does business in an industry with a low injury rate, it is exempt from random inspections by OSHA. If not, OSHA can inspect the workplace at any time without advance notice. And it can issue citations and impose penalties based on what it finds.

In addition to fines and citations, your company could face lawsuits from an injured employee—or from the family of a deceased employee—if the employee was hurt or killed because the company intentionally violated a workplace safety law.

State Laws

In addition to the federal health and safety law, you must comply with the laws of your state. State laws regulating workplace health and safety can include occupational health and safety laws (usually similar to the federal law described above), workers' compensation laws, drug testing laws, substance abuse laws, and smoking laws, among others.

To find out about your state health and safety laws, contact your state labor department and state OSHA agency. You'll find contact information for both in the appendix.

(For more information about workers' compensation laws, see "Workers' Compensation," below. For more information about smoking laws, see "Smoking," below.)

Employee Rights

Federal and state laws give employees the right to complain about hazards in the workplace and violations of workplace safety laws. They also give employees the right to refuse to do something that endangers their safety or the safety of others.

This means that you can't discipline or take any other negative action against an employee who exercises a right under these laws. If you do, you might face additional fines or even a lawsuit.

Workers' Compensation

Through the workers' compensation system, employers purchase insurance that provides benefits to employees who suffer work-related injuries and illnesses. The system strikes a compromise between employers and employees. Employees get benefits regardless of who was at fault: themselves, their employers, a customer, or a coworker. In return, the employer gets protection from lawsuits by injured employees seeking large damages for pain and suffering or mental anguish (these damages are not available through workers' comp).

Workers' compensation systems are governed by state law, not federal law. Although each state's system differs slightly in the details, the structure and operation of the overall system is largely the same from state to state. (The main differences are the rates paid to injured employees and the procedures to be followed for making a claim, seeing a doctor, filing an appeal, and so on.) To find out the details of your state's law, contact your state department of industrial relations or division of workers' compensation.

Lessons From the Real World

The Exxon Corporation got a lesson in the limits of workers' compensation laws. Usually, these laws protect companies from lawsuits filed by employees who are injured on the job. As this case illustrates, however, the law only goes so far.

For several weeks, four workers welded sheets of steel to the inside of a huge tower at an Exxon plant in Louisiana. Exxon did not give the welders safety equipment such as masks or air-supplied respirators, provide the welders with safety instructions on the equipment they were using, or ventilate the tower with clean air. As a result, the welders inhaled carcinogenic smoke and fibers while they worked.

After just a few days of work, the welders complained of physical problems, such as nosebleeds, blurry vision, night sweats, and vomiting blood. Still, day after day, the company sent them back to work in the tower without any safety equipment or training. This went on for a period of several weeks until the welders quit.

As it turned out, the manufacturer of the equipment the welders were using had given the company a safety manual that warned of severe physical problems and that recommended safety precautions. Not only did Exxon fail to pass the warnings on to the welders, it also failed to take a single one of the safety precautions suggested by the manufacturer.

The welders sued for punitive damages. The company argued that the welders had no right to go to court, because they were limited to the benefits that they could get from the workers' compensation system.

The court disagreed, concluding that the company's actions—or inactions—amounted to intentional conduct: "When an employer repeatedly sends employees back to work without safety equipment or without remedial measures being taken, and the employees are inevitably injured each time they are sent back to work, then the employer can be considered to have committed an intentional act." And when an employer intentionally harms an employee, the employer cannot hide behind the workers' compensation laws.

Abney v. Exxon Corporation, 755 So.2d 283 (La. App. 1st Cir. 1999).

Coverage

An employee's injury or illness must be work related to be covered by workers' compensation law. It does not have to occur in the workplace, however. As long as it's job related, it's covered. For example, employees are covered if they are injured while traveling on business, running a work-related errand, or even attending a required business-related social function.

Workers' compensation covers injuries ranging from sudden accidents, such as falling off a scaffolding, to occupational illnesses, such as those resulting from exposure to workplace chemicals or radiation. Many workers receive compensation for repetitive stress injuries, including carpal tunnel syndrome and back problems. Workers may also receive compensation for illnesses and diseases that are the gradual result of work conditions, such as heart conditions, lung disease, and stress-related digestive problems.

Of course, not all problems that occur in the workplace are covered. Generally, workers' compensation will not cover injuries that are caused by an employee who is intoxicated or using illegal drugs. Coverage might also be denied in situations involving:

- self-inflicted injuries (including those caused by a person who starts a fight)
- injuries a worker suffers while committing a serious crime
- injuries an employee suffers during the commute to and from work, and
- injuries an employee suffers when engaged in conduct that violates company policy (such as horseplay).

Similarly, employers aren't protected from all employee lawsuits related to injuries. If the employee is injured because of some intentional or reckless action by the company, that employee may be able to bypass the workers' compensation system and sue the employer for a full range of damages, including punitive damages and pain and suffering.

Benefits

The workers' compensation system pays for partial wage loss, medical expenses, and sometimes vocational rehabilitation benefits, on-the-job training, education, or job placement assistance.

An employee who is temporarily unable to work often receives two-thirds of his or her average wage up to a fixed ceiling set by the state. An employee who becomes permanently unable to do the work he or she was doing prior to the injury, or unable to work at all, might be eligible for long-term or lump-sum benefits. The system also pays death benefits to surviving dependents of workers who are fatally injured in work-related incidents.

Affordable Care Act

In 2010, the Patient Protection and Affordable Care Act—commonly referred to as the "Affordable Care Act" or "Obamacare"— was passed, making significant changes to the health insurance system in this country. Using a series of incentives and penalties— some of which apply to employers—the law makes it mandatory for all Americans to have health care coverage.

Since its inception, the Affordable Care Act has undergone many legal challenges and has been the source of much political debate. As we go to press, Congress is in the midst of efforts to repeal the law. However, until then, the provisions outlined below are still in effect. (Legal updates will be posted on this book's online companion page; see the introductory chapter for the link.)

Lactation Breaks

The Affordable Care Act requires employers to allow new mothers to express breast milk. Employers must provide reasonable unpaid break time for nursing mothers to pump for up to one year after birth. State law might require additional time off or other requirements.

(For more information, see "Lactation Breaks," in Chapter 2.)

Tax Credit for Small Businesses That Offer Health Insurance

Small businesses—defined as those with fewer than 25 full-time employees (or the equivalent in part-time employees) and paying an average annual salary of less than $52,000 per employee—are eligible for a tax credit if they provide health insurance to their employees. To qualify, the business must pay at least half of the premium for covering a single person (not a family) and must purchase insurance through the Small Business Health Options Program (SHOP) (see below). Businesses can get a credit of up to 50% of the premiums they paid; nonprofit employers can get a credit of up to 35% of the premiums they paid. The exact amount of the credit depends on the size of the employer; the smallest businesses get the maximum credit.

The Small Business Health Options Program (SHOP)

As explained below, employers with at least 50 full-time employees are subject to the "play or pay" mandate (also called the "shared responsibility" payment): These employers must offer affordable health care coverage that meets certain minimum value standards or pay a penalty. However, the health care law was not intended only to require larger employers to provide adequate coverage. Another major purpose of the law was to make insurance more affordable for smaller businesses.

The tax credit explained above is one of the ways the law attempts to do this. Another is the SHOP marketplace: an online resource where employers can compare plan benefits, costs, and premiums; apply for a plan; and enroll in a plan. The SHOP marketplace is like the health care exchange available to individuals, but for businesses. It allows employers to compare plans side-by-side, to determine what will work best for them.

The SHOP marketplace has been open for business since 2014. In most states, employers with 50 or fewer full-time employees are eligible to use the marketplace. You can learn more about the marketplace, including other eligibility requirements, at www.healthcare. gov/small-business.

Requirements and Restrictions on Health Care Plans

For plan years that began on October 1, 2010 or later, new restrictions and requirements apply to health care plans. Different rules apply to new plans and grandfathered plans.

A grandfathered plan is a plan that existed in March 2010, when the health care reform law passed. Grandfathered plans don't have to comply with all of the requirements imposed on new plans. However, a plan can lose its grandfathered status by making changes that increase costs or lower benefits for employees. For example, a plan that significantly cuts coverage or significantly raises deductibles or copayments might no longer be grandfathered (and therefore, must comply with the additional rules applicable to new plans). Your benefits provider can help you determine your company's plan status.

Rules Applicable to All Plans

All health care plans, whether grandfathered or not, must meet a number of requirements, including:

- Plans must cover preexisting conditions, without charging more.
- Plans must allow children up to the age of 26 to stay on their parents' plans.
- There can be no lifetime or annual dollar limits on the care provided for essential health benefits (including emergency care, hospitalization, maternity and newborn care, prescriptions drugs, preventive care, mental health, and laboratory services).
- Plans may cancel coverage only if the insured commits fraud or intentionally misrepresents a material fact.
- Plans must spend at least 80% of premiums on health care and quality improvement, rather than overhead, administration, and marketing. Plans that don't meet this requirement must pay rebates to consumers.
- Plans must provide a plain-English summary of benefits and coverage.

Rules Applicable Only to New Plans

Although grandfathered plans provided by employers must comply with all of the rules above, they don't have to meet all of the requirements imposed on new plans. New plans only must do the following:

- offer free preventive care (including vaccines and preventive services for women)
- allow ob-gyn care without a referral
- allow patients to choose any available doctor in the plan's network
- allow emergency room visits from outside the plan's network without prior authorization, and
- provide an appeals process for denied claims and coverage decisions.

Changes to HSAs and FSAs

Over-the-counter drugs are no longer reimbursable through flexible spending accounts (FSAs) or health savings accounts (HSAs) unless a doctor prescribes them. The health care reform law also caps annual contributions to an FSA and HSA. For an individual in 2017, the maximum contribution is $2,600 for an FSA and $3,400 for an HSA (These numbers are subject to adjustments for inflation each year.) And employees under the age of 65 who make nonqualified withdrawals from their HSA (in other words, don't use the money for health care purposes) will have to pay income tax on the withdrawals and pay a 20% penalty.

Play or Pay: The Employer Mandate

The employer mandate applies to employers with 50 or more full-time employees, or the equivalent in part-time employees. A full-time employee is someone who works an average of 30 hours or more per week. For example, 20 employees working 15 hours per week each would equal 10 full-time equivalent employees.

Covered employers must provide health insurance to at least 95% of their full-time workers (and their dependents), or pay a penalty. Employers that fail to provide coverage must pay a fine of $2,260 per full-time employee in 2017. However, the first 30 employees are excluded from the fine.

Even if the employer offers health insurance coverage to 95% of its full-time workers, it must pay a separate penalty if the coverage fails to meet both of the following requirements:

- It must cover at least 60% of the total allowed cost of benefits under the plan.
- The employee's cost for coverage cannot exceed 9.69% of the employee's household income for 2017 (this percentage is adjusted each year for inflation).

If the coverage fails to meet the above requirements, a full-time employee is eligible to receive government-subsidized coverage under the Affordable Care Act. If this happens, the employer must pay the lesser of the following:

- $3,390 per full-time employee receiving government-subsidized coverage for 2017, or
- $2,260 per full-time employee working for the company, minus the first 30 full-time employees.

The IRS reviews the penalty amounts each year and adjusts for inflation. To learn more, see www.irs.gov/affordable-care-act/employers.

Reporting and Notice Requirements

The Affordable Care Act imposes several reporting and notice requirements on employers. They include:

- Employers must provide new hires with a notice about the state health insurance exchange program and coverage offered by the employer. (The U.S. Department of Labor has a model notice available at its website, www.dol.gov/agencies/ebsa.)

- Employers must report the value of the health benefits they provide to employees on each employee's W-2 form.
- Employers subject to the employer mandate must file Form 1094-C with the IRS regarding the health care plan offered to employees. Employers must also submit a 1095-C for each full-time employee enrolled in the employer-sponsored plan and send a copy to the employee.

For More Information

To learn more about the health care reform law, check out:

- www.healthcare.gov, the federal government's website on the law
- http://kff.org/health-reform, a comprehensive site maintained by the Kaiser Family Foundation, and
- www.shrm.org, the Society for Human Resource Management's site, which includes detailed articles and a timeline for health care reforms affecting employers (select "HR Topics & Strategy," then "Benefits," then "Health Care Reform").

Cell Phones and Driving

Studies show that drivers who are distracted cause more accidents and that cell phones and other forms of wireless technology are increasingly to blame for our lack of attention to the road. If your company's employees drive for work or use cell phones for work, chances are good that they occasionally do both at the same time; 81% of drivers do, according to a 2008 survey by Nationwide Insurance Company. To make sure employees are safe and don't cause harm to others (or expose the company to liability), you should have rules dictating whether and how employees may use their cell phones while driving.

State Law Restrictions

A growing number of states have passed laws that limit the use of cell phones while driving. These laws take several forms: Some prohibit only texting; some require drivers to use a hands-free device if they want to talk on the phone; some prohibit younger or less experienced drivers from using any type of cell phone; and some allow officers to cite drivers for using a hand-held cell phone if the driver is pulled over for another offense. (To learn the laws of your state, go to the website of the Governors Highway Safety Association, www.ghsa.org, and select "State Laws" and then "Distracted Driving.")

If your company does business in a state that limits the use of cell phones while driving, of course you'll want to require employees to follow the law. However, even companies in states that haven't legislated in this area need cell phone rules. Simply put, using a cell phone while driving is dangerous. And, if an employee causes an accident while doing business on a cell phone, your company could be held liable for the damages.

Employer Liability Concerns

There have been plenty of big settlements in lawsuits against companies whose employees injured or killed someone while talking on a cell phone. Why are the companies sued? Because they typically have much deeper pockets than the employee who actually caused the accident. Consider these real-life examples:

- A stockbroker from Smith Barney was making a cold call to a potential client while driving when he struck and killed a motorcyclist. Although the broker was using his own cell phone and driving to a nonbusiness event, the plaintiff argued that Smith Barney should be liable because it encouraged employees to use their cell phones for cold calling without training them on safety issues. Smith Barney eventually settled the case for $500,000.
- A lawyer was making a business call on her cell phone while driving home from work. She hit something, which she thought was a deer, and kept driving; tragically, she actually hit—and killed—a teenager. The attorney served a year in jail for hit-and-run driving and was ordered to pay the victim's family more than $2 million. Her law

firm settled its part of the case for an undisclosed amount.

- An employee of International Paper was using her company cell phone when she rear-ended another driver on the freeway, causing injuries that eventually required the other driver to have her arm amputated. The company paid $5.2 million to settle the case.

As explained in "Liability for an Employee's Actions" in Chapter 11, your company can be held liable for actions an employee takes within the scope of employment. So, if the call, the driving, or both are work-related, your company could be on the hook for damages.

Sensible Cell Phone Rules

To promote employee safety (and avoid liability), your company should adopt a policy on use of cell phones while driving. Your policy should do all of the following:

- Prohibit employees from using cell phones for work-related matters while driving.
- Tell employees what to do if they must pick up or place a call while driving: Pull over safely and stop the car before taking or making the call.
- Explain the rules on hands-free devices. If your company wants to allow employees to use hands-free equipment while driving, your policy should say so. However, it should also state that

employees must concentrate fully on the road while driving. If bad weather, traffic, or other conditions make it difficult to talk on the phone and drive safely at the same time, employees should pull over and park before having their hands-free conversation. (If you know employees use cell phones for work, it's a good idea to issue them hands-free equipment, to make sure they can comply with the policy.)

Smoking

Smoking used to be as accepted a workplace activity as drinking coffee, but not any more. Concerns about the impact of secondhand smoke and the safety of nonsmokers have prompted most states to enact laws—commonly called clean air laws—that severely restrict smoking in the workplace.

Some states prohibit smoking in all enclosed private workplaces. Other state laws prohibit smoking in private workplaces if the employer has more than a minimum number of employees, prohibit smoking except in designated areas, or prohibit smoking in certain kinds of workplaces, such as hospitals and restaurants.

In addition to these state laws, many cities and counties have enacted ordinances against smoking in the workplace.

Many employers choose to ban smoking in their workplaces, even if no state law requires them to do so. Smokers generally have higher-than-average health care costs and higher absenteeism rates than nonsmokers. In addition, nonsmokers complain about the quality of the air and about the smoking breaks that their smoking colleagues take.

However, many states prohibit employers from discriminating against smokers. This means that employers can limit an employee's on-site smoking but may not make job decisions based on an employee's or applicant's decision to smoke outside of work. (For more about this issue, see "Off-Duty Conduct" in Chapter 6.)

To learn whether your state, city, or county has a law or an ordinance that prohibits or restricts smoking in the workplace, contact your state labor department or local government offices.

Drugs and Alcohol

Employees who abuse alcohol and drugs (including illegal drugs, prescription drugs, and over-the-counter drugs)—either on their own time or at work—can pose significant and wide-ranging problems for their employers, managers, and coworkers. These problems can include diminished job performance, lowered productivity, absenteeism, tardiness, high turnover, and higher health care and workers' compensation costs. Employees who abuse drugs and alcohol can also make a workplace more volatile and dangerous, and they can expose employers to legal liability.

Alcohol Use at Work

Your company's employee handbook (or other written or verbal workplace policies) should make clear to employees that drinking on the job is not allowed. If you catch an employee actually drinking alcohol at work, you can deal with it through your company's standard disciplinary procedures. Depending on the circumstances and on your company's policies, the punishment can range from an oral reminder to immediate termination.

The consequences should depend in part on whether the employee has endangered the health and safety of others. For example, an employee who drinks a beer while operating a forklift might deserve more severe discipline than a secretary who has a beer while sitting at a desk.

Off-Hours, Off-Site Use of Alcohol

Many people drink alcohol when not at work. Most employers aren't concerned about an employee's occasional drink—or even the occasional overindulgence—as long as it doesn't affect the employee's work performance. But when off-site, off-hours drinking begins to take a toll on a worker's ability to do the job, his or her employer might have reason to take action.

Handling a worker with a drinking problem is tricky business. As discussed in Chapter 3, the federal Americans with Disabilities Act (ADA) and many state disability laws protect alcoholics from workplace discrimination. (See "Disability" in Chapter 3 for more about the ADA.) The ADA doesn't allow employers to make employment decisions based solely on the fact that an employee is an alcoholic. An employer can, however, make a decision—including a decision to discipline or terminate—based on the employee's inability to meet the same performance and productivity standards that it imposes on all employees. For example, if an employee is late or absent due to drinking, you can discipline the employee.

Legal Drug Use

Many employees properly use prescribed or over-the-counter drugs, such as sleeping aids, cold medicine, or painkillers. Most employers sensibly believe that this is none of their business, as long as the drugs don't impair the employee's job performance.

Things get trickier, however, if legitimate drug use affects an employee's ability to do the job safely and well. For example, medications that cause drowsiness might make it downright dangerous for a worker to do a job that requires driving or operating machinery. Medication might also impair judgment and abilities, which could affect a worker's ability to meet job requirements.

If an employee's performance is affected by the legal use of prescription or over-the-counter drugs, state and federal disability laws might limit an employer's options.

Depending on how the drug use affects the employee, and whether the employee suffers from a disability within the meaning of these laws, your company might have to accommodate the employee's use of the drugs. (See "Disability" in Chapter 3 for more information about disability laws and your duty to accommodate an employee's legal drug use.)

Illegal Drug Use and Possession

If an employee is under the influence of illegal drugs at work, disability laws do not limit your company's options. You may deal with that employee through your company's standard disciplinary procedures. If the drug use was relatively minor and the employee doesn't hold a highly sensitive position, a written reprimand might be appropriate for a first offense.

However, if the employee endangers the physical safety of others—for example, by driving the company van after smoking marijuana at home—something more drastic is called for. If the employee has a drug problem, one option is to suspend the worker until he or she successfully completes a treatment program. Some employers, however, opt for a zero-tolerance policy under these circumstances and immediately suspend and then terminate the employee.

Because using, selling, or possessing illegal drugs is a crime, most employers immediately terminate employees who engage in this type of behavior at work.

Off-Duty Marijuana Use

Now that marijuana is legal in many states, courts have had occasion to consider whether employers may fire employees for off-duty marijuana use. The answer depends, in part, on whether the use is for medicinal or recreational purposes. However, in most states, employers are free to fire employees even for off-duty prescription marijuana use.

Over half of the states and the District of Columbia have legalized marijuana to treat serious medical conditions, such as cancer or glaucoma. In a handful of states, such as Arizona and Massachusetts, it's illegal for employers to fire employees just because they use prescription marijuana during nonworking hours. However, the majority of states do not have such protections. In these states, several courts—including those in California and Colorado—have held that employers may fire employees who use medical marijuana while off duty. The reasoning is largely based on the fact that marijuana is still illegal under federal law.

Seven states and the District of Columbia have legalized marijuana for recreational purposes as well. None of these laws have protections for workers who smoke marijuana off-duty. In fact, these laws often explicitly state that they do not affect an employer's right to continue to enforce workplace drug policies. As a result, employers are on safer legal ground when it comes to making decisions based on an employee's recreational marijuana use.

Lessons From the Real World

Brandon Coats was working in Colorado as a customer service representative for satellite TV provider Dish Network when a random drug test revealed that he had marijuana in his system. Coats, a quadriplegic, explained to his employer that he used prescription marijuana to treat painful muscle spasms caused by his condition. Coats was legally prescribed marijuana by his doctor, and he only used it during nonworking hours. Nevertheless, Dish Network fired him for his medical marijuana use.

Coats sued Dish Network, arguing that the termination was illegal under Colorado's off-duty conduct law, which prohibits employers from firing employees for their lawful activities during nonworking hours. Dish Network, on the other hand, argued that medical marijuana was not a "lawful" activity because it was still illegal under federal law. In a holding that surprised some, the Colorado Supreme Court sided with Dish Network, stating that employers can fire employees for off-duty medical marijuana use, even though it is legal under Colorado law.

Coats v. Dish Network, LLC, 350 P.3d 849 (2015).

However, this is a rapidly evolving area of law, and public opinion on marijuana has changed significantly over the years. Depending on your workforce and geographic area, your company might find it difficult or impractical to enforce a zero tolerance marijuana policy. An alternative is to adopt a strong policy prohibiting employees from using, or being under the influence of, marijuana during work hours. Consult an employment attorney or your state labor department for information about your state's marijuana laws. (Contact information is in the appendix.)

Leave Laws

Federal and state leave laws might also come into play when an employee has substance abuse issues. As described in more detail in Chapter 5, the FMLA allows eligible employees to take time off for a serious health condition. The definition of serious health condition could include substance abuse. However, FMLA leave may be taken only for treatment by a health care provider or on the referral of a health care provider, not for the use of the substance itself. For example, an employee may take time off to enter a rehabilitation program on the advice of a doctor, but not to stay at home and recover from a drug or alcohol bender.

However, if the employer has an established policy that employees may be terminated for substance abuse in certain circumstances—and that policy has been communicated to all employees—the employer may terminate the employee regardless of whether he or she has requested or is taking FMLA leave. (But remember, the ADA might still require time off or other reasonable accommodations for alcohol or legal drug use.)

Some states also have leave laws that allow employees to take time off to enter drug or alcohol rehabilitation programs. For example, California requires employers with 25 or more employees to allow an employee to enter such a program, as long as it would not cause an undue hardship.

Because this is a complicated area of law, you should consult with an employment lawyer before taking action against an employee who has asked for time off to recover from substance abuse issues.

Drug Testing Current Employees

Drug testing is a dicey legal issue for employers, one that should be approached with extreme caution. Drug tests are highly intrusive, yet they can also be invaluable tools for preventing drug-related accidents and safety problems.

The law of drug testing is changing rapidly as more courts rule on employee lawsuits that claim that a particular drug test violated their right to privacy. Because drug testing is so intrusive, a worker who convinces a jury that a test was illegal (in violation of either your state's drug testing laws or your state's privacy laws) could cost your company a lot of money and ruin its reputation as a fair employer. Before performing any drug test or adopting a drug test policy, you should get some legal advice. If you decide to proceed with legal assistance, here are some guidelines to consider.

Whom to test. Avoid testing every employee for drugs, and avoid random drug testing. Unless all of your company's workers perform dangerous jobs, these sorts of tests cast too wide a net. A drug test is most likely to withstand legal scrutiny if you have a particular reason to suspect an employee of illegal drug use or the employee's job carries a high risk of injury.

When to test. Your company will be on the safest legal ground if your primary motive is to ensure the safety of workers, customers, and members of the general public. Employers are most likely to withstand a legal challenge if they limit testing to:

- employees whose jobs carry a high risk of injury to themselves or others (such as a forklift operator or pilot) or involve security (a security guard who carries a gun, for example)
- workers who have been involved in accidents (for instance, a delivery driver who inexplicably ran a red light and hit a pedestrian)
- employees who are currently in or have completed a drug rehabilitation program, and
- workers whom a manager or supervisor reasonably suspects of illegally using drugs.

How to test. Even if you have strong reasons for testing, your company can still get into legal trouble over the way the test is administered and interpreted. To be safe, employers should do all of the following:

- Use a test lab that is certified by the U.S. Department of Health and Human Services or an equivalent state agency.
- Consult with a lawyer in developing testing policies and procedures.
- Use a testing format that respects the privacy and dignity of each employee.
- Have a written policy in place about drug use in the workplace (including a discussion of the disciplinary steps the company will take and under what circumstances) and testing procedures (including when the test will be given, how the test will be administered, and what substances—at what levels—the test will detect).

- Require employees to read the drug and alcohol policy and testing policy and sign an acknowledgment that they have done so.
- For every drug test administered, document why it was necessary and how the test was performed.
- Keep the test results confidential.
- Be consistent in how the company deals with workers who test positive.

Employers cannot force workers to take a drug test against their will. However, an employee who refuses to take a drug test can be fired for that reason, as long as the employer had a solid basis for asking the employee to submit to the drug test in the first place.

Legal Dos and Don'ts: Health and Safety

Do:

- **Help employees stop smoking.** While many states prohibit employers from discriminating against smokers, nothing prevents your company from sponsoring programs to help employees kick the habit. It's generally easier for smokers to quit within the context of a supportive program than on their own, and your company will reap rewards like lower absenteeism and health care costs.

- **Consider rehab leave.** Workers with substance abuse problems cost a company plenty in lost productivity, higher health care costs, and missed work. Encourage these employees to clean up their acts by offering leave to enter a rehabilitation program. It will be well worth it if the worker successfully rehabilitates and returns to work more productive and more dedicated to the company.

- **Seek professional help for health and safety concerns.** Many experts offer free workplace consultations, so it makes sense to get an expert to come to your workplace and point out health and safety concerns, free of charge. This could save you a bundle in workers' compensation claims, fines, and health care costs.

Don't:

- **Disregard employee complaints.** If an employee expresses concern about a workplace hazard or another safety issue, take it seriously. If you don't, the employee might take his or her complaint to a federal or state agency. More seriously, workers might be injured or worse if the employee's fears were valid.

- **Ignore OSHA's advice.** If a federal or state inspector tells your company to make changes, do it. These agencies do not like to be ignored and won't hesitate to impose fines on employers that buck the system. Disregarding these recommendations also leaves a company more vulnerable to lawsuits from employees, customers, and vendors.

- **Go without workers' compensation coverage.** If you think your company is so safe that it doesn't need workers' compensation coverage, think again. Most states require all but the smallest employers to purchase coverage. Even smaller employers would be wise to get a policy. Otherwise, one workplace accident could wipe the company out.

Test Your Knowledge

Questions

1. Small companies don't have to worry about complying with OSHA. ☐ True ☐ False

2. Employees can be fired for complaining about a health or safety issue. ☐ True ☐ False

3. If an injury is covered by workers' compensation, the injured employee cannot sue the employer for damages. ☐ True ☐ False

4. An injury must occur at the workplace to be covered by workers' compensation. ☐ True ☐ False

5. As long as a company requires employees to use hands-free devices to use a cell phone when driving, it won't be responsible for any resulting accidents. ☐ True ☐ False

6. All employers must create a designated smoking area for employees who wish to smoke. ☐ True ☐ False

7. Employees who take breaks to smoke outside must stand at least a certain distance away from the workplace. ☐ True ☐ False

8. It is illegal to fire an employee for using alcohol at work, because that might be a sign of alcoholism, which is a disability. ☐ True ☐ False

9. Employers can fire an employee whose use of prescription or over-the-counter drugs interferes with his or her ability to do the job. ☐ True ☐ False

10. Drug testing current employees is illegal. ☐ True ☐ False

Test Your Knowledge (continued)

Answers

1. False. Although small employers (those with fewer than ten employees) and employers in industries with low injury rates are exempt from some OSHA requirements, other OSHA obligations—including the obligation to maintain a safe workplace and report serious injuries and deaths to the government—apply to all employers, regardless of size.

2. False. Retaliating against employees who complain of workplace safety or health violations is illegal.

3. True. An employee whose injury is covered by workers' compensation is entitled to the benefits that system provides but generally may not sue the employer for damages relating to the injury. (There are, however, narrow exceptions that might allow a worker to sue the employer in court.)

4. False. An injury need not take place at the worksite; it must only be work related. If an employee is injured at an off-site work event or while driving a delivery route, for example, that injury is covered by workers' compensation.

5. Not necessarily. Your policy should tell employees that they must concentrate fully on the road, no matter what technology they are using. If they can't drive safely while using a hands-free device—for example, because the conversation is heated and distracting, or because the weather makes driving difficult—they should hang up.

6. False. Employers are generally free to prohibit smoking in the workplace, if they wish to do so. Many states impose requirements on employers that choose to allow smoking (for example, that smoking areas be designated and separately ventilated).

7. It depends on local laws. Some cities prohibit smoking within a certain distance of the entrance, exit, and/or ventilation openings of certain buildings (for example, those that are open to the public).

8. False. Although the Americans with Disabilities Act prevents employers from firing an employee simply because he or she is an alcoholic, employers are free to discipline employees who are under the influence of alcohol at work.

9. It depends on whether the employee has a disability. Employers must make reasonable accommodations for employees with disabilities. One such change might involve making adjustments to an employee's job to accommodate the effects of drugs necessitated by the employee's disability.

10. It depends on state law and on how the test is administered. Most states allow some drug testing of current employees, depending on the reason for the test.

Unions

Many companies—particularly small businesses—will never have to deal with a union. In fact, union membership has steadily decreased in recent years, from 20.1% of the workforce in 1983 (the first year the government compiled statistics) to 10.7% of workers in the year 2016 (and only 6.4% of private sector employees). The type of work your company does will also dictate how much contact you have with unions, which are more common in certain industries than others. For instance, there are more union workers in government than in private industry, where union membership is concentrated heavily in the fields of transportation, utilities, manufacturing, and construction.

If there is a union in your workplace—or if workers at your company are trying to form one—a special set of rules comes into play. Federal and state labor laws dictate how management must deal with unions, as well as what rules can be imposed on workers. In this chapter, we explain the laws relating to:

- elections and organizing campaigns
- union discussions and literature in the workplace
- union dues
- union shops
- collective bargaining
- company unions, and
- strikes.

However, even if your workplace does not have a union, you're not off the hook. The National Labor Relations Act provides all employees, even nonunion employees, with certain rights to engage in protected activity designed to better their working conditions. (See "Protected Concerted Activity," below, for more information.)

The National Labor Relations Act

Several federal laws cover labor-management relations. Together, these laws make up the National Labor Relations Act (NLRA), 29 U.S.C. §§ 151 and following, which establishes the rights and obligations of employers, unions, and individual workers in the workplace.

Many states also have labor laws that apply to public employees: those who work for state or local governments and are not covered by the NLRA.

History of the NLRA

The cornerstone of the NLRA is the Wagner Act, passed in 1935. The Wagner Act guarantees covered employees the right to join a union, to bargain collectively with their employer, and to be free from discrimination or retaliation for belonging to a union. It also prohibits certain employer "union-busting" tactics and establishes the procedures for union elections. And it created the National Labor Relations Board (NLRB), the federal government agency that interprets and enforces the law. (See "The Role of the NLRB," below.)

Frequently Asked Questions About Unions

Can managers join a union?

No. Some workers are excluded from the National Labor Relations Act (NLRA, the set of federal laws that governs union issues). These workers include managers and supervisors, agricultural workers, domestic servants, those employed by a parent or spouse, and independent contractors. (For more on these laws, including how they are enforced, see "The National Labor Relations Act," above.)

If a union says it represents workers at our company, do we have to recognize it?

An employer can recognize a union as the bargaining representative of its employees only if the union has the support of a majority of workers in the "bargaining unit": a group of employees who do similar types of work and have common concerns about wages, hours, and working conditions. Even if the union can show that a majority of workers signed union authorization cards (statements indicating that the workers want a union to represent them), the employer can refuse to recognize the union. Then, the union will have to ask the NLRB for a secret election to prove its support. (For more on bargaining units, authorization cards, and elections, see "Representation Elections and Organizing Campaigns," below.)

Are there limits on what managers and other company officials can say about the union?

During an election campaign—the period of time between when the union asks for an election and when the election is actually held—management representatives have to watch their mouths.

Employers and managers may voice their opinions about the union but cannot punish or threaten union supporters, make promises to workers if they vote against the union, spy on union activities, or ask workers about the union in a coercive manner. (For more on what you can and can't do, see "Election Statements," below.)

Can the company ban workers from talking about the union on the job?

An employer may prohibit workers from talking about union matters on work time, but only if it prohibits them from talking about other nonwork issues as well. The company can also prohibit workers from holding union discussions in work areas, even during nonwork hours, but only if this rule applies across the board to all nonwork topics. But the company cannot prohibit workers from talking about the union while off the clock in nonwork areas, such as a lunchroom or locker area. (For more on union discussions and literature, see "Shop Talk," below.)

Can union workers strike whenever they want?

They can, but the strike might not be legal. There are two kinds of legal strikes: strikes to gain economic concessions from the employer and strikes to protest an employer's unfair labor practice. And even one of these two types of strikes might be illegal if it violates a no-strike provision in the collective bargaining agreement, or if the striking workers engage in serious misconduct. (For more on strikes—including when a company can replace striking workers—see "Strikes," below.)

In 1947, Congress passed the second piece of the puzzle, the Labor-Management Relations Act (LMRA), better known as the Taft-Hartley Act. The primary purpose of the LMRA was to rein in the unions' power. The act outlawed certain kinds of strikes, including the secondary boycott (a strike against a company that is not a party to a labor dispute, like a customer or client of the employer), sympathy strike (a strike by one union to show support for another), and jurisdictional strike (a strike by one of two or more unions competing to represent the same group of workers). The act also declares an individual's right not to join a union and protects this right by prohibiting unions from using violence, threats, or fraud to coerce workers to become members.

Finally, Congress passed the Labor-Management Reporting and Disclosure Act (LMRDA), also known as the Landrum-Griffin Act, in 1959. The LMRDA regulates internal union affairs: how officers are elected, what information the union must provide to its members and the government, and the rights of union members vis-à-vis the union. The LMRDA also imposes additional restrictions on union workers' rights to strike and picket.

Which Employees Are Covered

Not all workers are covered by the NLRA. The NLRA specifically excludes certain types of workers, including:

- agricultural workers

- domestic servants
- persons employed by a parent or spouse
- independent contractors
- government workers, and
- managers and supervisors.

A 2006 NLRB decision clarifies which employees qualify as supervisors or managers who aren't protected by the NLRA and cannot join a union. The NLRA says that a supervisor or manager is an employee who has the authority, in the interest of the employer, to take any of the following actions toward an employee:

- hire
- transfer
- suspend
- lay off
- recall
- promote
- discharge
- assign
- reward
- discipline
- responsibly direct
- adjust grievances, or
- effectively recommend any of the above actions.

In addition, the supervisor's actions must not be merely routine or clerical in nature, but instead must require the use of independent judgment.

This is where the 2006 decision created controversy. Previous NLRB decisions held that employees who use ordinary technical skill or judgment in directing other employees don't qualify as supervisors, because they aren't using independent judgment. These decisions meant that employees of the "assistant manager" variety, who do largely the same work as other employees but also set schedules and determine assignments, were not classified as supervisors. In the case of *Oakwood Healthcare Inc.*, 348 N.L.R.B. 37 (2006), however, the board found that employees who have the authority to make work assignments or direct the work of other employees qualify as supervisors if those tasks require some independent judgment and discretion, even if they spend only 10% to 15% of their time on these supervisory duties.

Which Employers Are Covered

The NLRA applies only to businesses that are engaged in interstate commerce. The National Labor Relations Board and the courts interpret the term "interstate commerce" very broadly, which means most employees are covered. Engaging in interstate commerce includes making phone calls to or from another state, sending mail out of state, or handling goods that have come from or will go to another state. However, the NLRB will generally step in to resolve labor disputes only if the company involved has reached a certain size, as measured by its volume of business or revenue. Thresholds vary depending on the industry. For example, the NLRB will get involved in a dispute involving a retail establishment that does $500,000 or more in annual business, while it will handle a dispute at a private university only if the school has at least $1 million in gross annual revenue.

Legal Rights and Wrongs Under the NLRA

The NLRA protects the rights of individual employees to form or join a union and to bargain collectively with their employer. An employer that interferes with these rights commits an illegal "unfair labor practice." Unfair labor practices include:

- firing, demoting, or taking other negative action (or threatening any of these actions) against employees who join or vote for a union
- threatening to close down a company if the workers unionize
- giving or promising to give benefits to workers for refusing to support a union
- asking employees about their union activities in a coercive or intimidating way
- spying on union meetings
- creating a "company union" or favoring one union over another, and
- firing, refusing to rehire, or otherwise penalizing employees for participating in legally protected union activities, such as legal strikes or proceedings before the National Labor Relations Board.

A union can also commit unfair labor practices. For example, a union may not coerce workers to join or require workers to pay excessive union fees or dues. Unions are also prohibited from taking certain actions against or making certain demands on employers, including:

- "featherbedding" (receiving payment for work that is not performed)
- striking to force the employer to bargain with a union other than the union elected by the employer's workers, and
- striking or picketing against an employer that is not a party to a labor dispute (for example, a "secondary strike" against a customer of the employer, intended to drive away business).

The Role of the NLRB

As noted above, the National Labor Relations Board (NLRB) administers and enforces the NLRA. The NLRB is run by five appointed board members who decide cases that come before the agency. The NLRB also has a general counsel (who investigates charges and issues complaints) as well as regional and field offices throughout the country.

The NLRB conducts representation elections—in which workers decide whether they want a particular union to represent them—and stops unfair labor practices. In either scenario, the NLRB gets involved only when a party to the dispute requests its help. For instance, if an employer refuses to acknowledge a union after a representation election, the NLRB will conduct a secret representation election if either party (usually, the union) requests it.

The board itself functions like a court to decide cases alleging unfair labor practices. Administrative law judges (decision makers hired by the federal government) decide these cases, which the losing party can appeal up to the five-member board. The board has the power to order unions and employers to do—or not do—certain things. At that point, the losing party must obey the board's order or ask a federal Court of Appeals to overrule the board.

Representation Elections and Organizing Campaigns

Efforts to unionize a workplace often begin with employee dissatisfaction. Workers might consider unionizing in response to an unpopular workplace rule, low wages, or a perception that the company doesn't care about their concerns.

An actual union—as opposed to a group of unhappy workers—might enter a workplace in a number of ways. A worker might contact an existing union and ask for information and help. A union might send an organizer out to the company to look into whether a union campaign is likely to succeed. Or the workers might decide to form their own union (not a typical scenario, but certainly possible). Regardless of how a union starts, its goal will be the same: to earn the right to represent workers in their dealings with the company.

Bargaining Units

A union may only represent workers who form an appropriate "bargaining unit." A bargaining unit is a group of employees who do similar types of work and have common concerns about wages, hours, and working conditions. A bargaining unit generally won't combine professional with nonprofessional employees, nor will it contain workers with significantly different job duties, skills, or working conditions. If the employer claims that a particular bargaining unit is inappropriate (a strategy often used to challenge a successful representation election), the NLRB will also consider what the workers themselves want.

A bargaining unit can include employees from several different facilities. For example, all the cashiers in a chain of retail stores might be included in a single bargaining unit. And a single workplace might contain more than one bargaining unit. In a grocery store, for example, the butchers might be represented by one union, the checkers by another, and the janitors by yet another.

Authorization and Election

In order to represent a bargaining unit in negotiations with the company, a union must have the support of a majority of the workers in the unit. The union usually demonstrates this support by asking workers to sign authorization cards: forms that workers fill in and sign to indicate that they want the union to represent them in negotiations with the employer.

If the union gets support from the majority of workers in the unit, it will probably ask the company to recognize the union voluntarily. If the company decides to do this (for example, because it has good reason to believe that the union's majority support is genuine), the company and the union can immediately begin hammering out a collective bargaining agreement. (See "Collective Bargaining," below.)

But many companies choose not to recognize a union voluntarily. Perhaps the company doubts the signatures on the authorization cards are authentic or suspects that the union coerced workers into signing. Or maybe the company just wants to do whatever it can to keep a union out of its workplace for as long as possible. For whatever reason, the company might refuse to recognize the union. In that case, the union will probably file a petition with the NLRB, asking it to hold an election.

The NLRB will then conduct a secret election in the workplace to figure out whether workers really support the union. Before the election, the union and the employer can engage in a pro- or antiunion campaign (subject to the rules discussed in "Election Statements," below). If the union receives a majority of the votes cast, the NLRB will certify it as the bargaining representative of the unit. Note that the union only has to get a majority of those workers who vote, not a majority of all the workers in a unit. This means turnout in secret elections can play a major role in the outcome.

On April 14, 2015, new NLRB regulations went into effect to speed up the election process. Among other things, the new rules permit electronic filings, shorten deadlines for employer responses, limit written briefs, and postpone most disputes until after the election is held. Prior to the revised rules, the NLRB aimed to hold an election within 42 days of a petition's being filed. While the NLRB has yet to establish a new target timeline, elections could happen as early as two or three weeks after a petition is filed under the new rules. (For more information on the revised rules, visit the NLRB's website at www.nlrb.gov and select "What We Do" and then "Conduct Elections.")

Challenging an Election

Most of the time, everyone accepts the outcome of a representation election and moves on to the negotiating table. However, either the company or the union may object to the election results. Usually, one side will claim that the other side unfairly influenced the outcome of the election. For example, if the union incites workers to violence or offers special privileges to workers who vote for the union, the NLRB might set aside a union victory. Similarly, if the company threatens to fire workers who vote for the union or promises to give benefits to workers who oppose the union, the NLRB might void the election results and could even declare the union to have won by default.

The union or the employer can also challenge how the election itself was conducted. Just as in a government election, certain NLRA rules restrict what can be posted near the voting booth. And the NLRB generally prohibits both unions and employers from making campaign speeches to groups of employees on company time within 24 hours of the election.

Decertifying a Union

Even a union once championed by employees might lose support as time goes on. This can happen for many reasons. Perhaps the union hasn't been able to negotiate successfully for the workers, has corrupt leadership, or imposes dues and fees the workers find oppressive. Employees who wish to challenge the union can file a petition for a decertification election with the NLRB. In such an election, workers will vote on whether they still want the union to represent them in negotiations with their employer. If a majority of workers voting oppose the union, the union no longer has the right to represent the workers.

Election Statements

Many employers are not eager to deal with unionized workers and want to defeat a union organizing campaign. However, there are limits to how far employers can go in discouraging the union. Employers hold the power of the purse and the pink slip, not to mention the opportunity of creating a captive audience for any opinions they might want to express. Recognizing this, the NLRA prohibits employers from using this advantage to unfairly influence the outcome of an election.

The NLRB will set aside the results of an election if the employer engages in conduct that tends to interfere with the employees' right to freely choose a union without fear of reprisal. If the employer's actions confuse or incite fear in its workers, the election won't count. However, employers—like everyone else—have free speech rights. The trick is to differentiate between free speech and coercion.

What You Cannot Do

Any of the following activities constitute unfair labor practices and might cause the NLRB to overturn a decision against union representation:

- **Punishing union supporters.** You may not retaliate or discriminate against workers who support the union.
- **Making threats.** You cannot threaten to fire, demote, impose pay cuts on, or otherwise take any negative job action against workers for supporting a union. And employers can't threaten to shut down or move the business if the union is successful.

- **Inducements.** You are not allowed to promise or give benefits to workers who oppose the union. And, once an organizing campaign has begun, the company may not increase workers' benefits—by giving pay raises or health insurance coverage, for example—to discourage them from forming or joining the union.
- **Infiltration.** Conducting surveillance of union meetings or of employees who support the union is illegal, as is planting a spy in union gatherings to report back to management.
- **Interrogation.** You may not question workers about their union membership, union meetings, or their support for the union. Similarly, you should not ask employees to report workplace union activities to you or tell you how their coworkers feel about the union.
- **Gag rules.** You may not prohibit workers from discussing the union in work areas unless you prohibit all conversations that aren't related to work. (See "Shop Talk," below.)

What You Can Do

Once you rule out the spying, threats, and strong-arming, what's left? Quite a bit, actually. Employers are free to express their opinions, present reasons why a union might not be in the workers' best interests, and give employees information about the union, as long as these actions aren't coercive and the information is accurate.

Here are some examples of employer statements and actions that courts and the NLRB have said are permissible:

- **Voicing an opinion.** Employers can tell employees that they don't want a union in the workplace and explain why.
- **Providing information.** Employers can publicize true information about the union, such as how much it charges members for dues, the rules it imposes on members, and how often it has gone on strike at other companies.
- **Explaining workplace changes.** Employers can inform workers of changes a union might bring to the workplace (for example, that workers might have to bring problems to a shop steward instead of to a supervisor).
- **Giving wage and benefit comparisons.** Employers can compare the benefits and wages they offer workers to the benefits and wages the union has been able to negotiate for employees at other companies.

Shop Talk

The one location where all of a company's workers are certain to gather is the workplace. Recognizing this, workers who are in favor of a union often spread their views or pass out union material in the workplace, whether in the lunchroom or on the assembly line.

For various reasons, some employers try to keep union organizing out of the workplace, arguing that their facilities are private company property and that management dictates what goes on within their walls. And certainly, employers want to minimize the amount of work time employees spend on nonwork activities.

The NLRB and the courts try to balance these competing concerns by creating some rules about what union-related activities are allowed in the workplace. Here are the basic rules:

- Companies may prohibit workers from talking about nonwork issues in work areas during work hours.
- Companies must allow workers to talk about union matters during nonwork hours in nonwork areas (like the company lunchroom). Union discussions may be prohibited in work areas during nonwork hours only if such a rule is necessary to maintain productivity or discipline and the rule applies to all nonwork topics.
- Companies may prohibit distribution of union literature (such as pamphlets and fact sheets) in work areas at all times, as long as the prohibition applies to all nonwork literature, not just union literature.
- Companies cannot single out union communications for special treatment. For example, an employer cannot forbid employees from distributing union materials in work areas but allow them to distribute other nonwork documents.

- Companies cannot prevent workers from wearing clothing bearing pro-union logos or symbols, such as a button or cap, unless that type of apparel creates a safety hazard.

Employers have more leeway to limit the on-site activities of nonemployees who work for the union. Employers may refuse to allow union representatives onto company property to distribute union literature, as long as the representatives have other methods of contacting the employees. And, the employer's policy must apply to all nonwork literature; in other words, it can't single out union literature for negative treatment.

Using Company Email

Email has added a modern twist to these rules. As is true of other types of communications, an employer may not single out union-related messages for harsher treatment. For example, an employer that allows employees to solicit coworkers on behalf of various organizations may not prohibit messages soliciting on behalf of a union.

Until relatively recently, the NLRB allowed employers to adopt a "business only" email policy, prohibiting employees from sending nonwork emails of any kind—including union-related emails. (*The Guard Publishing Co.*, 351 NLRB No. 70 (2007).) However, in December of 2014, the NLRB overruled this decision and held that employers cannot prohibit employees from using work email for union-related activity

on their own time. (*Purple Communications, Inc.*, 361 NLRB No. 126 (2014).)

As a result of this decision, employees must be allowed to use work emails to organize a union, participate in union activities, or engage in discussions aimed at improving the terms and conditions of their employment (see "Protected Concerted Activity," below). However, employers may limit this activity to nonworking time only, such as meal periods, rest breaks, or the time before or after established work hours.

Employers can also continue to monitor workplace emails for legitimate business reasons, according to their usual company policies. However, employers cannot change their monitoring practices to detect protected activities or discipline employees for engaging in protected activities. As long as employers follow these rules, email monitoring will not be considered illegal eavesdropping on union activities.

Protected Concerted Activity

The NLRA gives employees the right to act together to increase their pay, improve working conditions, or resolve other workplace problems (called "concerted activity"). Employees are protected whether or not they are in a union. Even in a nonunion workplace, employees who act together on workplace issues—by, for example, meeting with a manager to lobby for better benefits or having a group discussion about the company's safety record —are protected from employer retaliation.

An activity is concerted only if it involves at least two employees. For example, an employee is engaged in concerted action when he or she complains, after consulting with or on behalf of coworkers, that the company's performance evaluation system unfairly penalizes employees who speak up in safety meetings. However, an employee who simply complains about his or her own negative performance review is not engaged in concerted action. As the NLRB puts it, "personal gripes" are not protected.

Even if employees are clearly acting in a concerted way, they won't be protected if they cross the line from constructive behavior to malicious or reckless actions. Employees who reveal company trade secrets or make threats of violence, for example, won't have any recourse if they are fired for these activities.

Recently, the NLRB has shown great interest in applying these protections to online social media posts. Here are some examples:

- An employee was having a dispute with a coworker about job performance, staffing levels, and how well the employer (a nonprofit that provided services to the public) was serving its clients. In a Facebook post, the employee asked coworkers for their input on the issues, and several responded in online comments. All were fired because of the online conversation. The NLRB found that the employees were engaged in protected concerted activity, even though some of the comments were sarcastic or included profanity, because they were discussing working conditions in advance of a meeting with management.

- A supervisor denied an employee's request to have a union representative assist her in preparing a response to a customer complaint. Later that day, the employee made disparaging comments about the supervisor on Facebook, and a number of coworkers chimed in. The NLRB found that the employee's comments were protected concerted activity.

- While on a lunch break following a dispute with a supervisor, an employee updated her Facebook status to an expletive and the name of the employer's home improvement chain. Several coworkers "liked" her status. She later posted that the employer didn't appreciate its employees; no coworkers responded to this online. She was fired for the posts. The NLRB found that she was not engaged in concerted activity because she was neither acting on behalf of other employees nor seeking their input or support to turn her complaint into a group action. Instead, the NLRB found she was airing a "personal gripe," which was not protected.

- Largely in response to poor treatment by management, employees began a union organizing campaign. After a run-in with a supervisor at a catering event, an employee posted a heated message on Facebook, which included profanities toward the manager and the manager's family, and ended with a plea to "vote for the union." The NLRB held that this was protected activity, despite the vulgar nature of the post. The NLRB's decision was based, in part, on the fact that profanity was largely tolerated at the workplace and the employer had never previously fired an employee for foul language alone.

There are a number of other examples available from the NLRB's protected concerted activity page, http://nlrb.gov/concerted-activity.

As these cases show, employees are often protected if they are discussing employer policies or practices that apply broadly. Protection is also more likely if employees are having an online discussion to prepare to discuss issues with management. The more personal the post (for example, calling a supervisor names because of an isolated argument), the less likely the employee is protected. On the other hand, even if a post includes expletives and name-calling, it might still be protected if it is a complaint about working conditions and seeks, or receives, input from other employees. Because this is an evolving area of the law, you should consult with a lawyer before disciplining or firing an employee for social media posts.

Union Shops and Union Dues

A union is required to represent all workers in the bargaining unit, including employees who aren't union members. For unions, this creates the problem of so-called "free riders": workers who don't pay union dues but still reap the benefits of the union's efforts.

In general, an employee cannot be forced to become a full union member as a condition of employment. However, the employee might be required to pay at least some portion of union dues, depending on state law and the basis for his or her objection to the union.

Union Security Agreements and "Right to Work" Laws

The NLRA allows a union and an employer to enter into a contract called a "union security agreement." Although these contracts cannot require a worker to join a union, they can require workers to pay certain dues to the union as a condition of getting or keeping a job. These employees are called "dues objectors" (see below). An employer that enters into one of these agreements will be required to fire a worker who doesn't make the payments called for by the contract.

However, the NLRA also allows states to prohibit these agreements, and around half of the states have. In these states, workers who decide not to join the union cannot be required to pay any fees to the union, and they cannot be fired or otherwise penalized for failing to do so. These statutes, called "right to work" laws, basically require that every unionized workplace be an "open shop," in which workers are free to join the union or not. To find out whether your state has such a law, see "State Right to Work Laws," at the end of this chapter.

Dues Objectors

If your company is not located in a "right to work" state, employees who decide not to join the union can still be required to pay union dues. However, these employees—called "objectors"—can only be required to pay for their share of union money spent on representing the bargaining unit's workers, including the costs of collective bargaining, contract administration, and grievance processing. And, in some states, unions are required to get permission from all workers in the bargaining unit before collecting any fees for activities not related to representing the workers.

A worker who refuses to join a union or pay union dues for religious reasons can be exempt from paying dues or fees. However, these workers can be required to make a similar contribution to a nonlabor, nonreligious charity organization. And the union can require them to pay the reasonable cost of any grievances the union handles on their behalf.

Lessons From the Real World

The Washington Education Association (WEA), the state's largest teachers' union, was sued by the state of Washington and several nonunion members, claiming that it had improperly used agency fees—fees collected from teachers who did not want to join the union—to fund political causes.

Under Washington law, the union was required to get explicit authorization from nonmembers before using their fees for this purpose. Instead, the union adopted a procedure by which nonmembers had to "opt out" by objecting to this use of their fees within 30 days. When challenged, the WEA claimed that the state law requiring it to get authorization from nonmembers imposed an unconstitutional burden on the union.

The Supreme Court disagreed, however. The Court found that the voters of Washington were within their rights in passing a law that required the union to get permission before spending money it collected from state employees on political issues.

Davenport v. Washington Education Association, 551 U.S. 177 (2007).

Collective Bargaining

"Collective bargaining" refers to the negotiation process between the union (on behalf of the bargaining unit it represents) and the company to work out an agreement that will govern the terms and conditions of the workers' employment. The agreement reached through this process is called a collective bargaining agreement (CBA).

The NLRA requires a duly elected union and an employer to meet and negotiate over wages, hours, and other employment terms, as well as issues that might arise under an existing CBA. The two sides don't have to reach an agreement, but they must always bargain in good faith. Although neither side is required to make a particular concession, a party that refuses to bend on a single issue or to put any offer on the table is probably acting in bad faith.

Employers Must Supply Information

Employers have a clear bargaining advantage over the union in one important respect: Employers have access to more information. The employer is almost always better informed about a variety of issues, especially the company's financial picture.

To level the playing field a bit, the NLRB and the courts require employers to make certain types of information available to the union during the collective bargaining process. For example, if an employer claims that financial problems prohibit it from granting a requested wage increase, the union has the right to request and review documents that support the company's claims. Similarly, employers typically must supply the union with current employee salary and benefit data so the union can base its demands on accurate information.

Mandatory Bargaining Issues

An employer doesn't have to bargain over every conceivable employment issue. However, employers must bargain with the union over issues that are central to the employment relationship, such as wages, hours, and layoff procedures. Employers must give the union advance notice of any proposed workplace changes that involve these issues, but only if the union requests it. An employer that refuses to bargain or takes unilateral action in one of these mandatory bargaining areas commits an unfair labor practice. At that point, the NLRB can step in to remedy the situation. However, the union may also take certain actions against the employer, including a strike.

Given these dire consequences, you might think that there would be a clear list of mandatory bargaining topics included in the labor laws. Unfortunately, that's not the case. Although there is general agreement that mandatory bargaining is required on some issues—including wages, hours, layoff procedures, production quotas, and other substantial work rules—many other issues fall into a gray area. And this is where employers often find themselves in trouble.

Part of the problem is that some subjects may or may not qualify as mandatory bargaining topics, depending on the reasons

Lessons From the Real World

Workers at the Frontier Hotel & Casino in Las Vegas belonged to a union. When the collective bargaining agreement between the union and Frontier expired, the two sides were unable to negotiate a new agreement.

And then things got ugly. A member of Frontier's management started eavesdropping on conversations between workers and their union representative. When it didn't like what it heard, Frontier kicked the union representative out of the workplace. Then Frontier instituted 63 new work rules and stopped making contributions to the employees' pension fund.

The union filed a charge against Frontier with the NLRB. Both the NLRB and the Ninth Circuit Court of Appeals decided that Frontier's actions were illegal under the NLRA. The eavesdropping was an obvious no-no, but the court also decided that ejecting the union representative from the

premises interfered with the workers' contractual right to access their union representative.

Further, the court held that Frontier's decision to issue major changes in work rules—including a requirement that workers suspected of being intoxicated had to agree to undergo a medical exam or risk immediate termination—violated its duty to bargain with the union before implementing a major change. Even though the first collective bargaining agreement had expired, Frontier was legally required to negotiate these issues with the union, including its decision to stop paying into the pension fund. Its failure to do so—and its insistence on filing legal appeals on issues that were such clear losers—convinced the court to slap the company and its attorney with a hefty fine for wasting everyone's time.

NLRB v. Unbelievable, Inc., 71 F.3d 1434 (9th Cir. 1995).

for the employer's action. For instance, if the employer decides to close a plant in order to avoid paying union wages, that might be a mandatory bargaining topic. But if the employer bases its decision on concerns unrelated to the union—for example, if the employer's customer base in the area has dried up or the employer can reap significant tax advantages by moving to another location—the employer might not have to bargain on the issue.

What constitutes a mandatory bargaining topic is an evolving area of law. Consult

an experienced labor lawyer (a lawyer who specializes in union issues) if your company is trying to figure out whether it has to bargain on a particular issue.

Acting Unilaterally Can Get Employers in Trouble

Before changing a workplace rule or policy that clearly requires bargaining (such as adjusting pay scales or revamping a seniority system), a company must notify the union. Mandatory bargaining applies whether the changes will benefit or harm workers.

In other words, a company cannot give an across-the-board pay raise or offer more generous paid leave on its own initiative without consulting with the union.

Sounds silly? Consider that some employers make positive changes on their own to convince workers that they don't need a union. And some employers might try to disguise a controversial change as a "benefit" (for example, by tying a wage increase to higher production rates).

Yet the process of bargaining on mandatory topics isn't as onerous as it sounds. In the real world, if the proposed change is beneficial, the union is likely to agree to it without a lengthy negotiating session. And by seeking the union's approval, the employer avoids a claim that it committed an unfair labor practice.

Company Unions and Employee Committees

Under the NLRA, employers may not establish, dominate, or interfere with any labor organization. This rule exists to outlaw sham unions: company groups that appear to represent employees but are really employer controlled. The reason for this rule is simple: Fair collective bargaining requires genuine employee participation. If an employer negotiates with a union of its own creation, the employees' chair at the bargaining table is empty.

To figure out whether an employer unfairly controls a particular union, the courts and the NLRB look at all the circumstances, including whether the employer started the group, whether the employer played a role in the group's organization and function, whether management actually attends the group's meetings or otherwise tries to set its agenda, and what the group's purpose is.

Employee Committees Might Cross the Line

Many companies have established "committees": informal groups of workers and management that meet to resolve workplace problems. Common examples include committees on safety, policy review, or productivity. But even if these groups are not unions, they might still constitute employer-dominated labor organizations, which are illegal under the NLRA.

Whether these groups qualify as sham unions depends on their purpose and on the role both employees and management play in their activities. To constitute an illegal sham union, the group must deal with the employer on traditional union bargaining topics, such as wages, hours, or working conditions. The group doesn't have to bargain formally with the employer; even a group that simply comes up with proposals for management to consider could be illegal, if those proposals involve bargaining issues.

Lessons From the Real World

Crown Cork & Seal, a company that manu-factures aluminum cans, adopted an unusual decision-making structure at its Texas plant. Under the "Socio-Tech System," employees served on one of four production teams. These teams had substantial authority to make and carry out workplace decisions, including decisions on safety, discipline, training, production, and more.

One level above the production teams were three more committees, which recommended changes in policies, terms and conditions of employment, safety procedures, and pay. These committees made their recommendations to the plant manager, who always adopted them without question.

The NLRB found that these teams and committees were not illegal company unions because they did not "deal with" management; in effect, they *were* management. They had the power to make important decisions— to discipline employees, shut down the production line, or stop delivery of products— that are traditionally made by managers. Even though the plant manager had the right to disapprove some of these decisions, he never did so, instead letting the committees and teams effectively run the plant.

Crown Cork & Seal Company, Inc., 334 NLRB No. 92 (2001).

To violate the NLRA, management must also dominate or support the group. For example, if a group is established by the company, if management chooses the employee representatives of the group, if management employees sit in on the meetings, or if management sets the committee's agenda, this group is probably dominated by the company.

Strikes

Strikes are, perhaps, the most common image that comes to mind when people think of the history of unions over the last century. But strikes are much less common than they were in the past. For a number of reasons— including "no-strike" clauses in contracts, employers' rights to replace some striking workers (see below), and a decline in union membership generally—many employers will never have to face a strike.

However, if your company's employees do take to the streets, you need to know whether their actions are protected by law and what steps the company can legally take to stay open for business.

Legal Strikes

The right to strike is protected by the NLRA, but not all strikes are legal. Whether a strike is lawful depends on the purpose of the strike, when the strike takes place, and the conduct of the strikers.

To qualify for protection under the NLRA, a strike must have a legal motive. Generally, a strike has a protected purpose if the workers are striking (1) for economic reasons, or (2) to protest an unfair labor practice by the employer. In the first scenario, workers strike to try to get some economic concession from the employer, like higher wages, increased benefits, or better working conditions. In the second, workers strike because the employer has engaged in some practice that violates the NLRA, like refusing to bargain with the union or discriminating against union members.

However, even a strike that has a lawful purpose might be illegal if the workers strike in violation of a "no-strike" provision in a collective bargaining agreement (an agreement that employees won't go on strike in an attempt to resolve a dispute with the employer). With a few limited exceptions, these strikes are not protected by the act. And a strike to end or change a collective bargaining agreement might be illegal if the workers haven't complied with whatever procedures the agreement sets for such changes.

Tips for Nonunion Employers

If your workplace is not unionized, you might think that the rules in this chapter don't apply to you. However, some of these rules apply to all employers covered by the NLRA, regardless of whether their workers are represented by a union or not. The NLRA applies generally to any collective action workers take in an effort to change the terms and conditions of employment, whether or not a union is involved and whether or not workers are explicitly trying to form a union.

Here are some tips for nonunion companies:

- All of the rules described above about union discussions apply to employee discussions of wages, benefits, hours, and other working conditions as well. For example, employers cannot prohibit such discussions in nonwork areas when employees are off duty, nor can they prohibit employees from using company email to discuss such issues on their own time. And employers may not adopt a policy prohibiting workers from discussing their salaries with each other or otherwise inhibiting employees from engaging in protected concerted activities.

- All of the NLRA's prohibitions on retaliation, threats, coercion, and so on apply equally to nonunion employers. An employer may not, for example, fire employees for joining together to ask the company for a raise or a better benefit plan, plant a spy in an employee meeting where employees are discussing working conditions, threaten to demote employees who are trying to convince other workers to protest a work rule, or fire employees for social media posts that seek coworker support for improving working conditions.

- A nonunion employer may not create a company or "sham" union: an employee group that is dominated or supported by management and deals with the company on traditional bargaining issues (wages, working conditions, and so on). Even though such a group doesn't compete with an existing union, it is still illegal under the NLRA.

Finally, even a lawful strike might cross the line if the strikers engage in serious misconduct. Workers who are violent or threaten violence, who physically prevent others from entering or leaving the workplace, or who engage in a sit-down strike—a strike in which employees refuse to leave the workplace and refuse to work—are not legally protected.

Strike Replacements

Although the NLRA protects the right to strike, employers do not have to shut down their businesses for the duration of the walkout. Instead, employers are legally allowed to hire replacement workers (sometimes called "scabs" in union lingo) to take the place of strikers during the strike. Once the strike ends, employers' obligations to rehire the striking workers depends on the reasons for the strike.

Workers who strike to protest an unfair labor practice cannot be fired or permanently replaced. When the strike is over, these employees must be reinstated to their jobs, even if it means replacement workers have to be let go.

However, workers who strike for economic gain don't enjoy the same right. Although they cannot be fired, they can be replaced. And if they are replaced permanently, they aren't entitled to their jobs back. Instead, if they are unable to find similar employment, employers are required only to call them back for job openings as they occur.

Legal Dos and Don'ts: Unions

Do:

- **Keep employees happy.** If your company is intent on keeping a union out of the workplace, it should give workers what a union would get for them. This might include competitive pay, good benefits, safe working conditions, some form of job protection, and a meaningful complaint process.
- **Review your company's employee handbook.** Work rules must allow employees to exercise their rights under the NLRA. Make sure, for example, that your company's dress code doesn't prohibit workers from wearing pro-union messages, that you don't have a strict "business only" email policy, and that your social media policy doesn't prohibit critical comments about the company or management.
- **Get some help if you plan to fight the union.** The rules about what employers can and can't do to defeat a union in a representation election are very nuanced. Sometimes, a single word or act can make the difference between a sustainable victory and an unfair labor practices charge. If your company is planning to get into it, get some help from an experienced labor lawyer.

Don't:

- **Prevent employees from discussing union issues.** Although your company can prohibit workers from discussing any nonwork issue in work areas, it cannot selectively enforce this policy to prohibit only union matters, and it cannot prohibit union discussions in nonwork areas when employees are off duty. If you, as a representative of management, try to discourage workers from exercising this right, you could get the company in big trouble.
- **Bypass the union.** If your company has a union, it must bargain with the union before changing the terms and conditions of employment. This means no new policies on wages, hours, or working conditions without consulting the union.
- **Coerce workers during a union election.** As a manager, what you say and do will be attributed to the company. If you threaten to fire workers who vote for the union, promise benefits to workers who vote against the union, or otherwise put pressure on workers, the NLRB might find that you've unduly influenced the outcome of the election and declare the union to have won by default.

Test Your Knowledge

Questions

1. Managers can join a union, as long as the union is made up of managers and employees who work in the same field. ☐ True ☐ False

2. Independent contractors may not join a union. ☐ True ☐ False

3. Employers should not make any statements about the union during a union election. ☐ True ☐ False

4. If employees try to organize a union and they are unsuccessful, the employer may discipline or fire them. ☐ True ☐ False

5. Employers can prohibit employees from talking about union issues anywhere on the employer's premises. ☐ True ☐ False

6. Employers can discipline employees for their social media posts that disparage the company and hurt the company's reputation. ☐ True ☐ False

7. Although employees can be required to join a union, they cannot be forced to pay union dues. ☐ True ☐ False

8. An employer may not decide, on its own, to offer more generous benefits; it must bargain on this issue with the union. ☐ True ☐ False

9. Companies may establish safety committees, made up of employees and managers, as long as those committees don't have the power to make decisions. ☐ True ☐ False

10. Once workers go out on strike, their jobs are not protected. ☐ True ☐ False

Test Your Knowledge (continued)

Answers

1. False. Managers may not join a union, period.

2. True. Independent contractors may not join a union, even if the union is composed of employees who do similar types of work for the same company.

3. False. Although employers should not threaten, coerce, or interrogate workers during an election, they can give accurate information about the union and express their opinions about whether workers should unionize.

4. False. Employees who engage in "concerted activity" are protected from retaliation, even if they ultimately fail in their efforts.

5. False. Companies must allow workers to talk about union issues in nonwork areas—such as a lunch area, locker room, or break room—on nonwork time.

6. False. The NLRB has held that social media posts about the terms and conditions of employment—such as hours, wages, management, and workplace safety—are protected concerted activity when they seek or receive input from other coworkers. Even angry, expletive-filled posts have been protected under some circumstances.

7. False. This is exactly backwards: Employees cannot be required to join a union. However, they can be required to pay at least some portion of union dues in states that have not enacted a "right to work" law.

8. True. Even if the employer is trying to do something good for its workers, it must include the union in the decision. (If it's really a win for workers, chances are good that the union will agree to it.)

9. False. Even if the committee simply makes recommendations, it might be considered a company union if it deals with the company on traditional topics of union bargaining and is dominated by management. A committee that has the right to make important decisions might be legal if it is acting in the place of management.

10. It depends on the reason for the strike. Workers who strike over an unfair labor practice are entitled to get their jobs back when the strike is over. Workers who strike for economic gain do not have the same protections; they can be replaced.

State Right to Work Laws

Alabama.................. Ala. Code §§ 25-7-30 to 25-7-36; Ala.Const. Art. I, § 36.05

Alaska...................... No right to work law.

Arizona.................... Ariz. Const. art. 25; Ariz. Rev. Stat. §§ 23-1301 to 23-1307

Arkansas................. Ark. Const. amend. 34 § 1; Ark. Code Ann. §§ 11-3-301 to 11-3-304

California .... No right to work law.

Colorado................. No right to work law.

Connecticut .... No right to work law.

Delaware................ No right to work law.

District of
Columbia .... No right to work law.

Florida..................... Fla. Const. art. 1, § 6; Fla. Stat. Ann. § 447.17

Georgia................... Ga. Code Ann. §§ 34-6-20 to 34-6-28

Hawaii .... No right to work law.

Idaho....................... Idaho Code §§ 44-2001 to 44-2014

Illinois..................... No right to work law.

Indiana .... Ind. Code Ann. § 22-6-6-8

Iowa .... Iowa Code § 731.1 to 731.9

Kansas..................... Kan. Const. art. 15, § 12; Kan. Stat. Ann. §§ 44-808(5), 44-831

Kentucky .... Ky. Rev. Stat. Ann. §§ 336.130, 336.132, 336.135 336.180, 336.990

Louisiana .... La. Rev. Stat. Ann. §§ 23:981 to 23:987 (all workers) and 23:881 to 23:889 (agricultural workers)

Maine....................... No right to work law.

Maryland................ No right to work law.

Massachusetts.... No right to work law.

Michigan................. Mich. Comp. Laws §§ 423.1, 423.8, 423.14, 423.17

Minnesota .... No right to work law.

Mississippi............ Miss. Const. Art. 7, § 198-A; Miss. Code Ann. § 71-1-47

Missouri.................. Mo. Ann. Stat. § 290.590

Montana .... No right to work law.

Nebraska................ Neb. Const. art XV, §§ 13 to 15; Neb. Rev. Stat. § 48-217 to 48-219

Nevada .... Nev. Rev. Stat. Ann. §§ 613.230 to 613.300

New
Hampshire............. No right to work law.

New Jersey............ No right to work law.

New Mexico .... No right to work law.

New York................ No right to work law.

North Carolina.... N.C. Gen. Stat. §§ 95-78 to 95-84

North Dakota....... N.D. Cent. Code § 34-01-14

Ohio......................... No right to work law.

Oklahoma.............. Okla. Const. Art. 23, § 1A

Oregon .... No right to work law.

Pennsylvania....... No right to work law.

Rhode Island........ No right to work law.

South Carolina ... S.C. Code Ann. §§ 41-7-10 to 41-7-130

South Dakota....... S.D. Const. art. VI, § 2; S.D. Codified Laws Ann. §§ 60-8-3 to 60-8-8

Tennessee.............. Tenn. Code Ann. §§ 50-1-201 to 50-1-208

Texas....................... Tex. Lab. Code Ann. §§ 101.051 to 101.053

Utah......................... Utah Code Ann. §§ 34-34-1 to 34-34-17

Vermont.................. No right to work law.

Virginia .... Va. Code Ann. §§ 40.1-59 to 40.1-69

Washington........... No right to work law.

West Virginia .... W. Va. Code §§ 21-1A-3, 21-5G-1 through 21-5G-7

Wisconsin .... Wis. Stat. Ann. §§ 111.02, 111.04, 111.06, 947.20

Wyoming................ Wyo. Stat. §§ 27-7-108 to 27-7-115

Independent Contractors

ndependent contractors exist in virtually every type of workplace, large and small, blue collar and professional. The federal Bureau of Labor Statistics estimates that more than ten million people work as independent contractors in occupations ranging from farming to computer technology to upper-level management. Contractors go by a number of names—consultants, freelancers, the self-employed, entrepreneurs, and business owners—but they all typically have two things in common: They are in business for themselves, and they don't rely on a single employer for their livelihood.

Hiring independent contractors can be a smart, cost-effective alternative to taking on employees. They can add a lot of flexibility and expertise to a company's workforce without the financial and legal burdens of hiring employees.

Using independent contractors does have some drawbacks, however. The biggest potential problem is that numerous federal and state government agencies keep a close watch on any employer that uses independent contractors. These agencies want to make sure employers aren't taking advantage of workers (and skipping out on their tax obligations) by calling them independent contractors when they should really be classified as employees. Companies that try to get the benefits of the arrangement without following the rules can end up in legal trouble.

In this chapter, you'll find:

- an overview of the issues that arise when companies hire independent contractors
- an examination of the various government definitions of independent contractor and employee
- the benefits and drawbacks of this type of arrangement, and
- advice on creating a written independent contractor agreement.

Classifying Workers

You might think that a worker's status as an independent contractor or an employee depends on what your company and the worker decide. As long as both parties agree on the terms of the relationship, that's all that matters, right?

Wrong. The federal and state governments care a lot about how workers are classified. Not surprisingly, the root of their concern is money. Your company doesn't have to withhold or pay taxes (including expensive payroll taxes such as Social Security and Medicare) for an independent contractor, and it will have fewer legal obligations to an independent contractor than to an employee. Thus, it's often in a company's interest to call a worker an independent contractor. (For more on this, see "Benefits and Drawbacks of Using Independent Contractors," below.) By contrast, it's in the government's interest to label the worker as an employee. The more employees there are in this world, the

Frequently Asked Questions About Independent Contractors

What is an independent contractor?

Independent contractors, also sometimes referred to as freelancers or consultants, are people who are in business for themselves. In other words, they perform services for a company but are not its employees. Figuring out the difference between employees and independent contractors is not always easy, and the answer often depends on who is asking the question. (For more about this, see "Classifying Workers," above.)

What are the benefits of using independent contractors?

Because companies don't have to pay taxes or provide benefits (such as health insurance) for independent contractors, it can be less expensive to use them. Using independent contractors also gives a company more flexibility and reduces its exposure to certain kinds of lawsuits. (For more, see "Benefits and Drawbacks of Using Independent Contractors," below.)

What are the drawbacks of using independent contractors?

A company does not have the same right to control independent contractors as it does employees, nor can a company demand or expect the same type of loyalty from independent contractors. In addition, independent contractors can sue your company if they are injured while working for you, while employees cannot. (See "Benefits and Drawbacks of Using Independent Contractors," below.)

Do we need to use any special paperwork to hire independent contractors?

Your company can greatly reduce the chances of a misclassification claim by requiring the worker to fill out an independent contractor questionnaire, provide copies of business licenses, and sign a written independent contractor agreement. (For more information, see "Important Documents When Hiring Independent Contractors," below.)

Do we have to use a written agreement with independent contractors?

With a few exceptions, the law does not require companies to use a written agreement with independent contractors. Still, it's a good idea to write things down because it can avoid confusion down the road. (To learn more about this, see "Written Agreements With Independent Contractors," below.)

Who owns the rights to the intellectual property we hire an independent contractor to create for us?

Unless the work falls into one of nine categories defined by law, the intellectual property rights to any works created by an independent contractor belong to the independent contractor, not to your company. This is true even if you hired and paid the independent contractor specifically to create the product for your company. But you can use a written contract to have the independent contractor assign these rights to your company. (For more information, see "Copyright Ownership," below.)

more money flows straight into government coffers through payroll withholding (and the fewer opportunities workers have to hide or underreport their income).

Unfortunately, there are as many tests to determine whether a worker qualifies as an independent contractor as there are government agencies that deal with workers, from your state unemployment office to the federal Internal Revenue Service. Figuring out how to treat a worker so that agencies classify the worker as an independent contractor can be a complicated undertaking.

Employers that don't learn the rules before they hire an independent contractor can get into trouble with multiple agencies. To avoid problems such as audits, fines, and back taxes, you should learn the rules of all of the following agencies before you hire an independent contractor. (For more about fines and taxes, see "Benefits and Drawbacks of Using Independent Contractors," below.)

The Internal Revenue Service

The Internal Revenue Service (IRS) is probably the most important agency to satisfy when it comes to classifying a worker as an independent contractor. Under the IRS's test (sometimes called the "right to control" test), workers are considered employees if the company they work for has the right to direct and control the way they work, including the details of when, where, and how the job is accomplished. In contrast, the IRS will consider workers to be independent

contractors if the company they work for does not manage how they work, other than to accept or reject the final product.

The IRS looks at a number of factors when determining whether a worker is an employee or an independent contractor. The agency is more likely to classify a worker as an independent contractor if the worker:

- can earn a profit or suffer a loss from the activity
- furnishes the tools and materials needed to do the work
- is paid by the job
- works for more than one company at a time
- invests in his or her own equipment and facilities
- pays his or her own business and traveling expenses
- hires and pays assistants, and
- sets his or her own working hours.

On the other hand, the IRS is more likely to classify a worker as an employee if the worker:

- can be fired at any time
- is paid by the hour
- receives instructions from the company
- receives training from the company
- works full time for the company
- receives employee benefits
- has the right to quit without incurring liability, and
- provides services that are an integral part of the company's day-to-day operations.

If the IRS considers the worker to be an independent contractor, your company does not have to withhold federal payroll taxes as you would for an employee, including Social Security taxes, federal disability taxes, and federal income taxes. The independent contractor is responsible for reporting his or her income to the IRS.

If you're not sure how to classify a worker, you can ask the IRS to determine the worker's status, but we don't recommend it. Not surprisingly, the IRS will usually decide that the worker is an employee (and your company will be stuck with that decision). It's better to consult with an experienced employment lawyer if you have classification questions.

To find out more about the IRS independent contractor test, visit the agency's website at www.irs.gov/Businesses and select "Small Business and Self-Employment Tax Center."

The U.S. Department of Labor

The U.S. Department of Labor also cares about how your company classifies workers: If a worker is an independent contractor, then the worker is not covered by the Fair Labor Standards Act (FLSA), the major federal law regarding wages and hours. This means, among other things, that the worker is not entitled to minimum wage or overtime.

Like the IRS, the Department of Labor has no single rule or test for determining whether someone is an independent contractor under the FLSA. However, the following factors are significant:

- whether the worker's services are an integral part of your company's business (for example, an IT technician working for a company that provides IT services is more likely an employee)
- the permanency of the relationship (someone who is working for your company indefinitely is more likely an employee)
- whether the worker has invested in facilities and equipment (if so, this points to independent contractor status)
- how much control your company has over the worker (workers who set their own hours and have the freedom to decide how the work gets done are more likely independent contractors)
- whether the worker has opportunities to make a profit or suffer a loss (someone who always earns a set amount of money no matter what happens is more likely an employee)
- whether the worker competes in the open market for business (if so, this points to independent contractor status), and
- the extent to which the worker operates a truly independent business (workers who are in business for themselves and perform the same services for multiple clients are more likely independent contractors).

According to the Department of Labor, the following things have no bearing on whether a worker is an independent contractor or an employee:

- the time or mode of payment
- whether the parties signed an independent contractor agreement (the true working relationship is what matters, not a label used by the parties)
- whether the worker has filed papers to create a corporation or another entity, and
- whether the worker is licensed by a state or local agency.

The DOL has made employee misclassification an enforcement priority in recent years. To learn more about this issue, go to www. dol.gov/whd/workers/misclassification. For more about wages and hours, see Chapter 2.

Your State Unemployment Compensation Board

If the worker meets your state unemployment compensation board's definition of independent contractor, your company doesn't need to pay unemployment insurance taxes for the worker. If the worker does not meet this test, your company must pay unemployment insurance taxes for the worker, even if the worker qualifies as an independent contractor under other tests (such as the IRS test).

To learn more about your state unemployment department's test, contact your state unemployment compensation board or your state department of labor. You can also try your local office of the Small Business Administration (SBA). (For a list of local SBA offices, refer to the SBA's website, at www.sba.gov.)

As a manager, it's a good idea to learn about your state's unemployment department test for independent contractor status *before* you hire an independent contractor. That way, you can create an independent contractor relationship from the beginning that satisfies the test and averts possible problems later.

Your company could get into trouble if a worker who you thought was an independent contractor decides to apply for unemployment compensation, a benefit that is reserved for employees. Should this happen, it will be your company's word against the worker's: You say the worker was an independent contractor, but the worker—eager for that unemployment check—claims to have been an employee. In such a situation, you'll have to be prepared to back up your assertion.

Your State Workers' Compensation Insurance Agency

As with unemployment insurance, only employees are entitled to receive workers' compensation. If a worker meets your state workers' compensation agency's definition of independent contractor, your company does not have to provide workers' compensation coverage for that worker. Otherwise, your company must provide workers' compensation coverage, even if the worker qualifies as an independent contractor under other tests.

To find out more about the workers' compensation test in your state, contact your state workers' compensation agency or your state

Lessons From the Real World

Bennett Harrington, who worked as a hunting guide for Gueydan Duck Club in Louisiana, was injured one day when his dog stepped on a client's loaded gun, causing it to go off. The shell ripped into Harrington's leg, seriously injuring him.

When Harrington applied for workers' compensation benefits, he was surprised to learn that the club owner had classified him as an independent contractor. This meant that Harrington could not get the benefits, which were for employees only.

The Louisiana Court of Appeal looked at the relationship between Harrington and the club and decided that Harrington was entitled to benefits because he should have been classified as an employee. The court based its opinion on the amount of control the club had over Harrington. The court decided that the following facts, taken together, made Harrington an employee:

- The club had recruited Harrington to work as a guide.

- The club, not Harrington, set the price that the clients paid for the guided hunt. The clients paid the club, not Harrington.

- There was no formalized agreement between Harrington and the club, which meant that the club could choose not to use Harrington at any time, for any reason.

- The club assigned clients to Harrington.

- The club told Harrington which hunting blind to use.

- The club told Harrington how to act around the clients—to entertain them, to make them happy, and to ensure their safety.

- The club maintained facilities and land for its guides, including Harrington, to use.

- The club provided blinds and decoys for the hunts.

- The club provided cell phones and transportation to the guides.

- Harrington thought he was an employee.

Harrington v. Hebert, 789 So.2d 649 (La. App. 3d Cir. 2001).

---

labor department. Your local office of the Small Business Administration (SBA) might also have information on the subject. (For a list of SBA offices, refer to the SBA's website, at www.sba.gov.)

Again, you should find out what test your state's workers' compensation board uses before you hire an independent contractor. If an independent contractor is injured on the job and applies for workers' compensation—a benefit reserved for employees—your company might face an audit.

Your State Tax Department

If your state collects income tax, then you need to know your state tax department's rules regarding independent contractors. If the worker qualifies as an independent contractor under your state tax department's test, your company does not need to withhold state income taxes from the worker's paycheck. Otherwise, you must withhold state income taxes (if your state imposes them), even if the worker qualifies as an independent contractor under other tests. Contact your state tax board for details. This is an especially important test to learn because many independent contractor audits begin with a state tax agency: State tax agencies are often more aggressive about independent contractor audits than other state agencies.

Your State Department of Labor

If your state department of labor would consider the worker to be an independent contractor, then your company does not have to pay minimum wage or overtime according to your state wage and hour laws. (But federal wage and hour laws might apply; see above for more information.) Contact your state labor department for details on how it determines independent contractor status. (See the appendix for contact information.)

Other Agencies

The classification issue can come up in the context of several other laws, such as Title VII of the Civil Rights Act (enforced by the Equal Employment Opportunity Commission) and the National Labor Relations Act (enforced by the National Labor Relations Board). Most agencies and courts use the "right to control" test or the "economic realities" test, or some variation of these tests. For an in-depth look at the various classification methods, see *Working With Independent Contractors*, by Stephen Fishman (Nolo).

Benefits and Drawbacks of Using Independent Contractors

Using independent contractors is a double-edged sword. For every benefit, there is an equally important drawback. In the end, your company will have to weigh all of the factors and decide what is best for the business when deciding what sort of worker to hire.

Benefits

Independent contractors require a much smaller cash outlay compared to new employees. As a result, cash-strapped companies are often tempted to classify workers as independent contractors. Companies that hire independent contractors instead of employees reap the following financial benefits:

- They do not have to pay a whole host of federal taxes for independent contractors, including Social Security and Medicare taxes.
- They do not have to withhold any state or federal income taxes from an independent contractor's paycheck.
- They do not have to comply with wage and hour laws, including paying overtime.
- They do not have to pay for workers' compensation insurance for independent contractors.
- They do not have to pay for unemployment insurance for independent contractors.

- They do not have to provide employee benefits (such as health insurance, paid sick leave, and retirement benefits) to independent contractors.
- Unless the project requires otherwise, they do not have to provide facilities, equipment, or training to independent contractors.

These and other expenses associated with employees add about 20% to 30% to a company's payroll costs. Although independent contractors generally earn more per hour than employees who do the same work, the company will still pay less overall because it won't have to pay these extra employee expenses and administrative costs.

In addition to the monetary benefits, independent contractors give companies the flexibility to add expertise to their workforces as needed. A company can hire independent contractors for specific tasks and take advantage of their specialized knowledge and experience without the cost and obligations of hiring full-time employees. This allows a company to run a lean operation, using employees for integral parts of the business and independent contractors for other projects as they arise.

Companies also have less exposure to lawsuits from independent contractors than from employees. Antidiscrimination laws and wrongful termination laws are all designed to protect employees, not independent contractors. In addition, employees have the right to unionize; independent contractors do not.

Companies that hire independent contractors also have less exposure to lawsuits from third parties. Although a company is liable to third parties for most things an employee does on the job, it is not liable for what an independent contractor does unless the company had some part in causing the injury or accident (for example, it gave the independent contractor poor directions on how to complete the job or hired an independent contractor who wasn't qualified for the job).

Drawbacks

After reading about the financial and other benefits of hiring independent contractors, it might be tempting to convert your company's entire workforce to independent contractors. Not so fast: There are some definite drawbacks to using independent contractors instead of employees.

The primary drawback of classifying any worker as an independent contractor is the risk that one or more government agencies will audit your company and reclassify the worker as an employee. According to *Business Wire* magazine, the government loses about $20 billion a year in taxes due to independent contractor misclassification. The government—particularly the IRS—does not take these losses lightly, and it is happy to audit any company it suspects is misclassifying workers.

State agency audits are even more common, spurred by independent contractors who apply for unemployment

Lessons From the Real World

When Julianne Eisenberg sued the warehouse at which she worked for sexual harassment, the warehouse claimed that she was not protected by workplace discrimination laws because she was an independent contractor, not an employee. As proof of her status, the warehouse pointed to the fact that she was listed as an independent contractor in tax documents and wasn't provided with any employee benefits.

The warehouse's arguments did not convince the federal court that reviewed the case, however. Looking at the way the warehouse treated Eisenberg, the court said she was an employee, not an independent contractor. That meant the warehouse was on the hook for the sexual harassment that Eisenberg suffered.

What tipped the balance in Eisenberg's favor? The court noted the following facts:

- The warehouse gave Eisenberg, whose job was to load and unload trucks, orders on a daily basis.
- At the job site, someone from the warehouse would instruct the crew, of which Eisenberg was a member, on what objects to move and where.

- Eisenberg's job did not require any specialized skill. (Examples of jobs that require a specialized skill include computer programmers, architects, graphic artists, and photographers. A worker with specialized skills is more likely to be classified as an independent contractor than an unskilled laborer.)
- The warehouse supplied all of the necessary supplies and equipment for Eisenberg to do her job.
- Eisenberg performed her job almost exclusively in the warehouse or on its trucks.
- Eisenberg was not hired for a specific move or project. Instead, she worked on whatever move or project the warehouse had at the time.
- Eisenberg was paid on an hourly basis, not by project.
- Eisenberg's job was an integral part of the warehouse's business.

Eisenberg v. Advance Relocation & Storage, Inc., 237 F.3d 111 (2d Cir. 2000).

benefits and workers' compensation, benefits exclusively reserved for employees. If a government agency decides that your company has misclassified a worker, your company will owe all of the back taxes associated with that worker, plus interest and penalties. This could add up to quite a hefty sum. In addition, the worker might be entitled to unpaid overtime and other wages, as well as any unpaid unemployment or workers' compensation benefits.

Another drawback to classifying a worker as an independent contractor is that your company will not be able to control that worker as it could an employee (for instance, setting work hours or requiring a project to be done in a certain manner). Under all of the agency tests, control is a big factor. The more the company controls (or has the right to control) the way the worker does the job, the more likely it is that one agency or another will classify that worker as an employee instead of an independent contractor. When your company hires an independent contractor, it must allow the worker to do the job as he or she wishes, or suffer the consequences. (You can still specify standards for the final work product, though.)

Control isn't the only thing your company loses by using an independent contractor. It also loses continuity when independent contractors come and go for short-term projects. Each new independent contractor will have to become familiar with your business and the project, and you'll have to establish a working relationship with each new person you bring on. In contrast, employees know your company's inner workings and needs. They know your company's people and practices, which can improve the efficiency and consistency of your operations.

Misclassification Lawsuits on the Rise

In June of 2015, after nearly a decade of litigation, FedEx settled a class action lawsuit with 2,300 California drivers for a whopping $226 million. The drivers, who had worked for FedEx between 2000 and 2007, claimed that the company had improperly classified them as independent contractors. Among other things, the drivers brought claims for unpaid overtime, violations of the Family and Medical Leave Act, and reimbursement of business expenses.

The case made its way up to the Ninth Circuit (the federal appeals court for California), which held that the FedEx drivers were employees, not independent contractors. The court pointed out that FedEx exercised a significant degree of control over the drivers, including their appearances, their work hours, and how they performed their work. For example, FedEx required the drivers to wear FedEx uniforms, to conform their trucks to certain standards, to arrive at FedEx property at a certain time at the start and end of each day, and to deliver packages within a certain window of time. The court also noted that the drivers were not providing a specialized skill and that the drivers' work was essential to FedEx's business operations.

Instead of appealing the decision, FedEx agreed to settle the matter with the California drivers for one of the biggest employment law settlements in recent history. Less than two years later, FedEx agreed to pay another $227 million to settle misclassification lawsuits in 19 other states..

Ridesharing companies, such as Uber and Lyft, are fending off similar misclassification claims. The U.S. Department of Labor, and its state equivalents, have also made it clear that independent contractor misclassification is one of their top enforcement priorities. If you have any doubts as to whether your workers should be classified as independent contractors or employees, you should consult with an employment lawyer.

Your company also can't simply get rid of an independent contractor who isn't working out. Unlike an employee, who can usually be fired for any reason at any time (see "At-Will Employment" in Chapter 4 for more information), an independent contractor will be protected by the terms of the contract. Most contracts, for example, require that you give at least some notice to an independent contractor before terminating the agreement. (For more about contracts, see "Written Agreements With Independent Contractors," below.)

If your company hires an independent contractor to create works that can be copyrighted, the independent contractor will likely own the work unless the company secures a written agreement transferring copyright ownership in advance. This is not the case with employees; for the most part, your company automatically owns copyrightable works created by its employees. (For more about this, see "Copyright Ownership," below.)

Although independent contractors usually cannot sue your company for violating federal antidiscrimination laws, they can sue for work-related injuries, if your company was at fault. Employees, on the other hand, cannot: They are limited to the benefits provided by the workers' compensation system. (See "Workers' Compensation" in Chapter 7 for more information.)

Important Documents When Hiring Independent Contractors

If your company hires an independent contractor, there are certain key steps you can—and should—take to reduce the chances of a government agency reclassifying the contractor as an employee. You can take these steps even before the independent contractor starts work. If you gather the documents described here, you will have already gone a long way toward establishing the worker's independent contractor status.

Independent Contractor Questionnaire

Ask prospective independent contractors to complete an independent contractor questionnaire. Design the questionnaire to elicit information that will help prove that the independent contractor is a separate business entity and not merely an employee in independent contractor's clothing. The questionnaire should ask the prospective hire about the following:

- whether the independent contractor has a fictitious business name
- how the independent contractor's business is structured (for example, sole proprietorship, partnership, corporation, or limited liability company)
- the independent contractor's business address and phone number

- the number of people, if any, the independent contractor employs
- any professional licenses the independent contractor holds
- any business licenses the independent contractor holds
- contact information for other companies for whom the person has worked as an independent contractor
- how the independent contractor markets his or her business (for example, in the yellow pages or other advertising)
- whether the independent contractor has an office separate from home
- a description of the business equipment and facilities the independent contractor owns
- whether the independent contractor has business cards, professional stationery, and invoice forms, and
- a list of all types of business insurance the independent contractor carries.

The answers to these questions will help you accurately assess whether the worker is an independent contractor. However, none of them is conclusive evidence of independent contractor status. Each answer is just one factor among many you should consider when deciding how to classify the worker.

Make sure that anyone you might hire as an independent contractor fills out this questionnaire instead of your company's standard employment application. A government agency can— and probably will—try to use the fact that the independent contractor filled out an "employment" application as evidence that the worker is actually an employee.

Business Documents

Once you've received a completed questionnaire and conducted the interview, the next step is to make sure you have enough documentation to establish that the worker is a separate business entity if the government decides to audit your company. Make copies of all the following documents and file them along with the questionnaire described above:

- copies of any business or professional licenses
- certificates showing that the independent contractor has insurance, including general liability insurance and workers' compensation insurance (if the independent contractor has employees)
- copies of the independent contractor's business card and stationery
- copies of any advertising that the independent contractor has done, including advertising in the yellow pages or printouts of online ads
- a copy of the independent contractor's white pages business listing, if there is one
- if the independent contractor is operating under a fictitious or assumed business name, a copy of the fictitious or assumed business name statement or application
- a copy of the invoice form that the independent contractor uses to bill for services

- if the independent contractor rents business space, a copy of the office lease
- if the independent contractor has employees, a document containing the independent contractor's unemployment insurance number
- copies of IRS Form 1099-MISC other firms have issued to the independent contractor, and
- if the independent contractor is a sole proprietor and will agree to do so (this is a big if), copies of the independent contractor's tax returns for the previous two years showing that the independent contractor has filed a Schedule C, *Profit or Loss From a Business* (which will show that the independent contractor has been operating as an independent business).

Although the contractor may balk at showing you a few of these items—especially those that contain sensitive financial information—stress that you will keep everything confidential and that you only want these items to verify the contractor's status. The more documentation you have, the better you can defend against a claim that you misclassified the worker.

Written Agreements With Independent Contractors

For most types of projects, the law does not require companies to enter into a written contract with independent contractors. You can talk to the independent contractor, agree on the terms of the arrangement, and have a legally binding oral contract.

As your mother no doubt told you, however, just because you can do something doesn't mean you should. Oral agreements invite costly misunderstandings because there's no clear written statement of what the independent contractor is supposed to do, how much your company will pay, or what will happen if a dispute arises. These misunderstandings might be innocent—you and the independent contractor genuinely might have different memories about what was agreed to—or they might not. Either way, it'll be your word against the worker's, and there is no telling whom a judge or jury will believe. It's much safer to rely on a written document that clearly sets out the details of your relationship.

Even better, a written agreement can also help establish a worker's independent contractor status by showing the IRS and other agencies that both your company and the worker intended to create a hiring firm/independent contractor relationship, not an employer/employee relationship. But don't expect the written agreement to be a magic bullet: A written agreement won't make much difference if your company treats the worker like an employee. (For more about classification rules, see "Classifying Workers," above.)

When writing the independent contractor agreement, remember the tests for classifying workers. Don't put anything in the agreement that would tend to show the worker is an employee rather than an independent contractor. For example, don't describe in the agreement the details of how the independent contractor is to accomplish the work; remember, if the hiring company controls the details of the work, that's a sign that the worker is really an employee.

A written independent contractor agreement should contain at least the following terms:

- a general description of the services the independent contractor will perform
- a description of how much your company will pay the worker (usually either a fixed fee for a finished product or a sum based on unit of time, such as by the hour or by the week)
- a description of how and when the worker will be paid (the contractor should invoice the company)
- an explanation of who will be responsible for expenses (independent contractors are usually responsible for their own expenses, although this isn't true in every industry)
- an explanation of who will provide materials, equipment, and office space (independent contractors usually provide these things, but not always)
- a statement that your company and the worker agree to an independent contractor relationship
- a statement that the contractor is free to work for others
- a statement that the independent contractor has all of the permits and licenses that the state requires for the work
- a statement that the independent contractor will pay all state and federal income taxes
- an acknowledgment that the independent contractor is not entitled to any of the benefits your company provides employees
- a statement that the independent contractor carries liability insurance
- a description of the term of the agreement (for example, one week, one season, or until the project is completed)
- a description of the circumstances under which your company or the independent contractor can terminate the agreement, and
- an explanation of how any disputes will be resolved.

Other terms you could include range from copyright ownership (see below) to naming who will be responsible for the independent contractor's employees.

Sample Independent Contractor Agreement

Below is an example of an independent contractor agreement (the contractor is referred to as the "Consultant"). This example is for illustrative purposes only; be sure any agreement you create is appropriate for your situation and consistent with your state's and federal law. For sample contract language you can use to create your own agreements, see *Consultant & Independent Contractor Agreements*, by Stephen Fishman (Nolo).

Sometimes, You Have to Write It Down

While agreements between your company and the independent contractor can generally be oral (although we don't recommend relying on oral understandings), many states' laws require certain kinds of contracts to be in writing to be enforceable. These laws, usually called a state's "Statute of Frauds," typically require that the following types of agreements be in writing:

- any contract that will last longer than a year
- contracts for the sale of goods (tangible property, such as a work of art or a car) worth $500 or more
- a promise to pay someone else's debt
- contracts involving the sale of real estate
- real estate leases that last for more than one year, or
- any transfer of copyright ownership.

If your company's agreement with the independent contractor meets any of these definitions (for instance, your relationship will last longer than a year, or the contractor is assigning or transferring copyright ownership to the company), then the agreement will probably need to be in writing to be enforceable.

Confidentiality Agreement

Depending on what your company is hiring the independent contractor for, you might also want to have him or her sign a confidentiality agreement. A confidentiality agreement (also called a nondisclosure agreement) will prohibit the contractor from disclosing your company's trade secrets or other highly sensitive information. If your company is hiring a consultant who will have access to the company's financial records, for example, you will definitely want to protect your company's information. On the other hand, a confidentiality agreement might not be necessary if you're hiring a web designer to update your company's website.

If you do have an independent contractor sign a confidentiality agreement, make sure it is tailored specifically to consultants. In other words, don't use the same agreement you use with your employees. Not only will that agreement have multiple references to "employees" and "employment," it might also have provisions that are not appropriate for a contractor (such as a noncompete clause, restricting the contractor's ability to work with other companies). If the contractor is going to use any employees or subcontractors to do the work, make sure they sign the agreement as well. (For more on confidential information, see Chapter 10.)

Copyright Ownership

When your company hires an independent contractor to create a work for the company—such as a computer program, written work, artwork, musical work, photograph, or multimedia work—you might wonder who will own the copyright. Generally, whoever owns the copyright to a work has significant rights, including the right to use, license, or sell the work to someone else.

Although you might think that your company owns any work it pays a contractor to create, that isn't always the case. Copyright law contains a major trap for the unwary: Unless the work an independent contractor creates falls into one of nine "work for hire" categories described below, your company will *not* automatically own the copyright to the work. Rather, the independent contractor must "assign" the copyright to the company in writing. It's critical to obtain this assignment (transfer of copyright ownership) before an independent contractor starts work, so that there is no disagreement later over who owns the copyright. You can include the copyright assignment in the written independent contractor agreement (see Section 14 in the sample agreement below).

If the work was specially commissioned or ordered by the hiring company and falls into one of the nine categories described, it is considered a "work for hire" in legal parlance. The hiring company owns the copyright to such works for hire; however, your company and the independent contractor must sign a written agreement stating that the work is made for hire. You can include this statement in the independent contractor agreement described above.

Works for hire include:

- a contribution to a collective work, such as a work created by more than one author like a newspaper, magazine, anthology, or encyclopedia
- a part of an audiovisual work (for example, a motion picture screenplay).
- a translation
- supplementary works, such as forewords, afterwords, supplemental pictorial illustrations, maps, charts, editorial notes, bibliographies, appendixes, and indexes
- a compilation (for example, an electronic database)
- an instructional text
- a test
- answer material for a test, and
- an atlas.

Independent Contractor Agreement

This Agreement is made between FunWorks, Inc., ("Client"), with a principal place of business at Berkeley, California, and John Cunningham ("Consultant"), with a principal place of business at Berkeley, California.

1. Services to Be Performed
Consultant agrees to perform the following consultant services on Client's behalf: Create new design for Client's packaging and promotional materials.

2. Payment
In consideration for the services to be performed by Consultant, Client agrees to pay Consultant $10,000 according to the terms of payment set forth below.

3. Terms of Payment
Client shall pay according to the schedule of payments set forth in Exhibit A, attached to this Agreement.

4. Expenses
Consultant shall be responsible for all expenses incurred while performing services under this Agreement.

5. Materials
Consultant will furnish all materials, equipment, and supplies used to provide the services required by this Agreement.

6. Independent Contractor Status
Consultant is an independent contractor, and neither Consultant nor Consultant's employees or contract personnel are, or shall be deemed, Client's employees. In its capacity as an independent contractor, Consultant agrees and represents, and Client agrees, as follows:

- Consultant has the right to perform services for others during the term of this Agreement.
- Consultant has the sole right to control and direct the means, manner, and method by which the services required by this Agreement shall be performed.
- Consultant has the right to perform the services required by this Agreement at any place or location and at such times as Consultant may determine.
- Consultant has the right to hire assistants as subcontractors or to use employees to provide the services required by this Agreement.

- The services required by this Agreement shall be performed by Consultant, Consultant's employees, or Consultant's contract personnel, and Client shall not hire, supervise, or pay any assistants to help Consultant.
- Neither Consultant nor Consultant's employees or contract personnel shall receive any training from Client in the professional skills necessary to perform the services required by this Agreement.

7. Business Permits, Certificates, and Licenses

Consultant has complied with all federal, state, and local laws requiring business permits, certificates, and licenses required to carry out the services to be performed under this Agreement.

8. State and Federal Taxes

Client will not:

- withhold FICA (Social Security and Medicare taxes) from Consultant's payments or make FICA payments on Consultant's behalf
- make state or federal unemployment compensation contributions on Consultant's behalf, or
- withhold state or federal income tax from Consultant's payments.

9. Fringe Benefits

Consultant understands that neither Consultant nor Consultant's employees or contract personnel are eligible to participate in any employee pension, health, vacation pay, sick pay, or other fringe benefit plan of Client.

10. Workers' Compensation

Client shall not obtain workers' compensation insurance on behalf of Consultant or Consultant's employees or contract personnel. If Consultant hires employees to perform any work under this Agreement, Consultant will provide them with workers' compensation coverage and provide Client with a certificate of workers' compensation insurance before the employees begin work.

11. Term of Agreement

This agreement will become effective when signed by both parties and will terminate on the earlier of:

- the date Consultant completes the services required by this Agreement
- November 30, 20xx, or
- the date a party terminates the Agreement as provided below.

12. Terminating the Agreement

Either party may terminate this agreement at any time by giving 30 days' written notice to the other party of the intent to terminate.

13. Exclusive Agreement

This is the entire agreement between Consultant and Client.

14. Intellectual Property Ownership

Consultant assigns to Client all patent, copyright, trademark, and trade secret rights in anything created or developed by Consultant for Client under this Agreement. Consultant shall help prepare any papers that Client considers necessary to secure any patents, copyrights, trademarks, or other proprietary rights at no charge to Client. However, Client shall reimburse Consultant for reasonable out-of-pocket expenses incurred.

Consultant must obtain written assurances from Consultant's employees and contract personnel that they agree with this assignment. Consultant agrees not to use any of the intellectual property mentioned above for the benefit of any other party without Client's prior written permission.

15. Confidentiality

Consultant acknowledges that, in the course of performing services under this contract, Consultant may have access to Client's trade secrets and other confidential information. Prior to beginning any work, Consultant agrees to sign Client's confidentiality agreement and have Consultant's employees or contractors do the same. Notwithstanding such agreement, pursuant to the Defend Trade Secrets Act of 2016 (18 U.S.C. § 1833(b)), Consultant will not be held criminally or civilly liable under any federal or state trade secret law for the disclosure of a trade secret that: (a) is made (i) in confidence to a federal, state, or local government official, either directly or indirectly, or to an attorney; and (ii) solely for the purpose of reporting or investigating a suspected violation of law; or (b) is made in a complaint or other document filed in a lawsuit or other proceeding, if such filing is made under seal. If Consultant files a lawsuit for retaliation by Client for reporting a suspected violation of law, Consultant may disclose the trade secret to his or her attorney and use the trade secret information in the court proceeding, if Consultant: (a) files any document containing the trade secret under seal, and (b) does not disclose the trade secret, except pursuant to court order.

16. Resolving Disputes

If a dispute arises under this Agreement, the parties agree to first try to resolve the dispute with the help of a mutually agreed-upon mediator in Berkeley, California. Any costs and fees other than attorneys' fees associated with the mediation shall be shared equally by the parties. If the dispute is not resolved within 30 days after it is referred to the mediator, either party may take the matter to court.

17. Applicable Law

This Agreement will be governed by the laws of the state of California.

Signatures

Client: FunWorks, Inc.

By: _____   Date: _____
    Dylan Irons, President

Consultant: _____   Date: _____
        John Cunningham

Taxpayer ID#: _____

Legal Dos and Don'ts: Independent Contractors

Do:

- **Say what you mean.** Never use the words "employment" or "employee" when referring to the independent contractor. Have the worker complete an independent contractor questionnaire (*not* an employment application) and be careful when naming or referring to any written agreement you create (do *not* call it an "employment contract").

- **Spread the work around.** The more consistently someone works for your company, the more likely an agency is to view the worker as an employee who depends on your company for a living. If you can, don't use the same independent contractor every time.

- **Hire corporations.** If you have the choice, hire independent contractors who have incorporated or formed a limited liability company. While this isn't a slam dunk, it can help establish that the contractor is in business for himself or herself.

Don't:

- **Buck the trend.** When deciding whether a worker is an independent contractor, auditors will sometimes look at how others in the same industry categorize those workers. If workers who do particular types of jobs are always characterized as employees, your company is more likely to attract an audit if it tries to call them contractors.

- **Rely on labels.** When it comes to classifying workers, it's what you do that matters, not what you say. If you treat an independent contractor like an employee (especially by trying to control every aspect of how the worker does the job), you'll find yourself paying fines and taxes, no matter what you call the worker.

- **Take the worker's word for it.** Don't just accept a worker's claim that he or she operates an independent business: Get proof. You never know when the worker might decide to argue that he or she was really an employee (for instance, to receive workers' compensation or unemployment benefits).

Test Your Knowledge

Questions

1. As long as your company calls a worker an independent contractor and doesn't withhold employment taxes, it won't have to worry about government audits. ☐ True ☐ False

2. A company has essentially the same obligations to independent contractors as it does to its employees, except that it doesn't have to withhold and pay taxes for contractors. ☐ True ☐ False

3. Independent contractors are not entitled to workers' compensation benefits if they are injured on the job. ☐ True ☐ False

4. It is generally more expensive to hire employees than it is to hire independent contractors. ☐ True ☐ False

5. Someone who works for more than one company at a time cannot be classified as your company's employee. ☐ True ☐ False

6. You can use your company's regular employment application with independent contractors. ☐ True ☐ False

7. Even very basic arrangements with independent contractors should be put in writing. ☐ True ☐ False

8. Your company shouldn't hire independent contractors unless they have incorporated their own businesses. ☐ True ☐ False

9. If your company hires someone to create a work of art, the company will automatically own the copyright to the work, regardless of whether the worker is an employee or an independent contractor. ☐ True ☐ False

10. If one agency finds a worker to be an independent contractor, your company doesn't need to worry about audits from other agencies. ☐ True ☐ False

Test Your Knowledge (continued)

Answers

1. False. What matters is how your company treats the worker. Not paying taxes and calling the worker an employee are a good start, but the real issues are whether the worker is truly operating an independent business and whether the contractor has control over how the work gets done.

2. False. Employees are protected by laws that require overtime pay, prohibit discrimination, and provide benefits for on-the-job injuries. These protections generally don't extend to independent contractors.

3. True. Independent contractors are not covered by the workers' compensation system. However, if the company is at fault for the contractor's injuries, the contractor may sue in court.

4. True. Although independent contractors typically command higher pay than employees, your company won't have to pay taxes; provide benefits, workspace, and training; or otherwise lay out as much overhead for independent contractors.

5. False. If a worker has several clients at a time, that might be indicative of a contractor relationship. However, an employee can work for more than one employer and still be an employee (by working two part-time jobs, for example). What matters most is whether the worker has an independent business and whether your company controls how the worker does the job.

6. False. You shouldn't use an employment application with independent contractors. A court or agency might see that as proof that you thought the worker was really an employee.

7. True. The best course of action is to always use a written agreement, spelling out the terms of the arrangement.

8. False. Although it's safer to hire contractors who have formed corporations or LLCs, it's fine to hire an unincorporated contractor—as long as he or she is really running an independent business.

9. False. Although a company generally owns the copyright to works created by its employees, this is not the case with independent contractors. Your company must have a written agreement with the contractor either stating that the work is a work for hire (if it falls into one of the nine listed categories) or assigning the copyright to your company.

10. False. Multiple federal and state agencies are invested in how your company classifies its workers, and each agency has its own test for determining independent contractor status. While a worker might pass as a contractor under one test, he or she might be classified as an employee under another test.

Trade Secrets

Often, workers never seem more precious to their employer than they do the moment they walk out the door, taking a vast amount of knowledge and a keen understanding of the employer's business with them, perhaps to the doorstep of a competitor.

Companies do not have to sit back and just watch this happen, however. You can help protect your company's confidential business information and prevent poaching of valuable employees and independent contractors. In this chapter, we explain how the law protects company trade secrets and what steps companies can take to stop them from leaking out.

The Law of Trade Secrets

More often than not, what gives a business a competitive advantage over others is the specialized knowledge it has gained through ingenuity, innovation, or just plain old hard work. This specialized knowledge could be something as mundane as a list of customers who use or need your company's services or as glamorous as the top secret formula for its best-selling product, from a cookie recipe to an industrial chemical.

Historically, trade secret theft (or "misappropriation") was a matter left up to the states. Each state has its own trade secret law designed to protect confidential and proprietary business information. Because the vast majority of states adopted a model law called the Uniform Trade Secrets Act, there is a lot of consistency from state to state. However, court interpretations of the law have created differences among the states as well.

Until recently, there was no federal trade secret law. However, in 2016, Congress passed the Defend Trade Secrets Act (DTSA), 18 U.S.C. § 1831 and following, which creates federal trade secret protection and allows companies to pursue claims in federal court. Because the DTSA mirrors the Uniform Trade Secret Act in large part, the federal law shares many similarities with states' trade secret laws—including what qualifies as a trade secret and what constitutes illegal misappropriation. However, there are some key differences, including a company's options for enforcing its rights under the law. The DTSA does not replace state law, meaning that a company can choose to enforce its rights under federal or state law.

A trade secret generally has three main components under the law:

- **Value.** The information must have economic value to your company's business because you know it and competitors don't. Information that doesn't give your company a competitive edge is not a trade secret.
- **Secrecy.** The information cannot be generally known, nor can it be easy to find out. If a competitor could learn the same information easily

Frequently Asked Questions About Trade Secrets

What is a trade secret?

Generally speaking, a trade secret is information that gives the business a competitive advantage that is not generally known to the public, and that you take reasonable steps to keep secret. A trade secret can be anything from a formula to a marketing plan to a customer list to the recipe for Coca Cola (one of the most famous trade secrets in history). (For more information, see "The Law of Trade Secrets," above.)

Can we prevent employees from revealing the company's trade secrets?

Yes. You can take many steps to prevent current and former employees from revealing your company's trade secrets, including the most basic step of disclosing them to employees on a need-to-know basis only. (To learn how, see "Protecting Trade Secrets," below.)

What is a nondisclosure agreement?

A nondisclosure agreement is a contract that prohibits an employee or independent contractor from disclosing trade secrets and other confidential information learned while working for your company. The company must give something of value in exchange, such as a job, money, a promotion, or a raise. (For more information, see "Nondisclosure Agreements," below.)

What is a noncompete agreement?

A noncompete agreement is a contract that an employee or independent contractor signs, promising not to start a competing business or work for a direct competitor for a specified period of time after leaving your company. As it would for a nondisclosure agreement, the company must give something of value in exchange for the worker's promise. Noncompete agreements are illegal in some states. (For more information, see "Noncompete Agreements," below.)

What is a nonsolicitation agreement?

When an employee or independent contractor signs a nonsolicitation agreement, he or she promises not to solicit your company's clients and customers after leaving your company. This type of agreement can also contain a promise not to solicit other employees to leave. Again, in exchange for signing the agreement, your company must provide the worker with something of value. (For more about this, see "Nonsolicitation Agreements," below.)

Does it violate trade secret law to hire an employee from a competitor?

You can hire employees who worked for a competitor, but you should always be careful when you do so, especially if the new hire signed a nondisclosure or noncompete agreement with the previous employer. (For more information, see "Hiring From Competitors," below.)

without much work or ingenuity, it's probably not a trade secret. Similarly, if some competitors already know the information, then it is not a trade secret.

- **Effort.** Your company must take reasonable steps to keep the information as secret as possible. For example, if a company posts the information at the workplace where anyone, including employees, customers, and vendors, can see it, then it's probably not a trade secret. Similarly, it's not a trade secret if it's posted on the company's public website.

Examples of trade secrets include a formula for a sports drink, survey methods used by professional pollsters, a recipe, a new invention for which a patent application has not yet been filed, marketing strategies, manufacturing techniques, and computer algorithms.

Unlike other forms of intellectual property such as patents, copyrights, or trademarks, trade secrecy is basically a do-it-yourself form of protection. Companies don't register with the government to secure their trade secrets; it's the company's responsibility to keep the information confidential and make sure it fits the definition laid out above. Trade secret protection lasts for as long as the secret is kept confidential. Once a trade secret is made available to the public, trade secret protection ends, sometimes even if the secret was taken or disclosed without permission.

Rights of the Trade Secret Owner

A trade secret owner has the right to prevent the following groups of people from copying, using, and benefiting from its trade secrets, or disclosing them to others without permission:

- people who are automatically bound by a duty of confidentiality not to disclose or use trade secret information (for example, your company's employees)
- people who acquire a trade secret through improper means such as theft, industrial espionage, or bribery
- people who knowingly obtain trade secrets from people who have no right to disclose them (for example, a competitor who hires one of your company's employees and then intentionally tries to exploit that employee's knowledge of your company's trade secrets)
- people who learn about a trade secret by accident or mistake but have reason to know that the information is a protected trade secret (for example, a competitor who hires one of your company's employee's away and accidentally learns information from the employee that turns out to be a trade secret), and
- people who sign nondisclosure agreements (also known as "confidentiality agreements") promising not to disclose trade secrets without authorization from the owner. (For more about these, see "Nondisclosure Agreements," below.)

Lessons From the Real World

Christopher Warman devised the perfect recipe for fudge and turned it into a successful business called Christopher M's Hand Poured Fudge, Inc.

Warman hired Clyde Hennon to work as his assistant in daily operations. In the course of his employment, Hennon learned all about Warman's fudge-making operations, from the details of Warman's secret fudge recipe to Warman's unique manufacturing process.

After a year of working at Christopher M's, Hennon struck out on his own, opening his own fudge-making operation called The Fudge Works, Inc. Warman sued, arguing that Hennon was illegally using trade secret information he had learned from Warman including, among other things, Warman's secret fudge recipe.

The court agreed with Warman and ordered Hennon to stop making fudge. The court decided that the fudge recipe was a trade secret based on the following facts:

- Warman developed the recipe after several years of trial and error from a recipe that he had purchased for $140,000.
- Certain aspects of the recipe were unique and were not commonly used in the industry.
- Warman took great care to protect the secrecy of the recipe. He kept only one written copy of the recipe that he stored off the premises; he compartmentalized the manufacturing process so that employees only knew the portion of the recipe relating to their specific tasks; and he revealed the entire recipe to only a handful of people.
- The recipe had a multimillion-dollar value.

Christopher M's Hand Poured Fudge, Inc., v. Hennon and The Fudge Works, Inc., 699 A.2d 1272 (1997).

Each state imposes a duty of loyalty on current and former employees not to disclose a company's trade secrets. Because employees are automatically prohibited from disclosing trade secrets, your company does not have to ask its employees to sign a nondisclosure agreement to keep trade secrets confidential. However, it's still a good idea to do so. (See "Nondisclosure Agreements," below, for some reasons why a company might want to take this extra step.)

Unlike current and former employees, however, the only way to impose liability on independent contractors, customers, or vendors for disclosing trade secrets is to have them sign a nondisclosure agreement. (For more about this, see "Nondisclosure Agreements," below.) Unless such people sign a nondisclosure agreement, they are free to disclose any trade secrets they learn while working with or for your company.

Finally, there are some people whom your company cannot prevent from using its trade secret information: people who discover the secret independently, without using illegal means or violating agreements or state laws.

For example, it is not a violation of trade secret law to analyze (or "reverse engineer") any lawfully obtained product to determine its trade secret. Although it's highly unlikely, if someone managed to reproduce Kentucky Fried Chicken's 11-herb-and-spice recipe by experimenting in the kitchen, Kentucky Fried Chicken could not sue that person for violating trade secret laws.

Protecting Trade Secrets

Employees and independent contractors pose a thorny dilemma for businesses with valuable trade secrets. After all, your company has to let some of these people in on its trade secrets. Perhaps they need the information to do their jobs, or they helped develop the information in the first place. Yet these same people may leave your company and take that special knowledge with them, whether it's to go into business for themselves or to work for a competitor.

Fortunately, simple preventive measures can reduce the risk that departing employees or independent contractors will take your company's trade secrets with them on their way out the door. We suggest a six-step approach:

1. Identify your company's trade secrets.
2. Grant access to these trade secrets only on a need-to-know basis.
3. Tell employees and independent contractors which information the company considers confidential.
4. Use nondisclosure agreements.
5. Make sure the company keeps its own secrets.
6. Conduct exit interviews with departing employees and independent contractors.

The following sections look at each of these steps in more detail.

Identify Trade Secrets

You can't protect something if you don't know it exists. The first step in protecting your company's trade secrets is to figure out what valuable information needs to be protected.

Periodically, take an "information inventory" and ask yourself and other managers and supervisors the following questions:

- What information does my company have that gives us an advantage?
- Do our competitors know this information?
- Is it information that they would want to know or find valuable?
- How did we gain the information? Was the process difficult? Time-consuming? Expensive? Unique?
- What kind of damage would our business suffer if competitors discovered this information?
- What do we know that we really don't want our competitors to know?

Because businesses are in an almost constant process of developing this information, you should probably conduct this sort of review once a year.

Limit Access

The fewer people who know your company's trade secrets, the better. Limiting access to trade secrets limits the number of potential loose lips. And departing employees or independent contractors can't reveal secrets that they don't know.

Of course, your company won't be able to keep all of its employees and independent contractors in the dark about everything. But always carefully consider whether an individual actually needs to know a secret you or other managers are about to reveal. Once you give it some thought, you might realize that an individual needs to know only one piece of the puzzle; other times, you might realize that the individual needs only a summary of the information, not the details.

If employees or independent contractors really need to know a trade secret to work effectively, go ahead and reveal it. But before you do, make sure they know it's a trade secret and have them sign a nondisclosure agreement (see below).

Tell Workers That the Information Is Secret

Once you've identified your company's trade secrets and the employees or contractors who need to know them, the next step is to inform them that they must keep the secrets confidential. After all, you can't expect them to keep information a secret if they don't know that they are supposed to.

Often, your company's internal security procedures will be enough to put people on notice about trade secrets. (See "Keep the Secret," below.) But you should review these security procedures periodically to make sure that they're still appropriate. For example, once a formula that's been in research and development hits the production line, your company will need to change its security procedures to include the production floor and any workers involved in the manufacturing process.

Use Nondisclosure Agreements

Because employees have an automatic duty to keep trade secrets confidential, telling them that something is confidential is technically sufficient: You do not have to ask them to sign a nondisclosure agreement to impose this legal duty on them. Still, nondisclosure agreements underscore the importance of confidentiality and clear up any ambiguity about what information your company considers a trade secret. Nondisclosure agreements can also cover more than just trade secrets; they can protect a broader range of confidential information that you don't want others to know about (but that doesn't necessarily fall under the protection of trade secret law). They can also be helpful if your company ever has to haul that employee into court for revealing the trade secret, whether the employee is still working for your company or not.

Independent contractors do not have an automatic duty to protect your company's

Checklist: Trade Secret Protection Program

Once you identify your company's trade secrets, how can you keep them confidential? Here are some tips:

- ☐ Require anyone who will have access to your company's trade secrets to sign a nondisclosure agreement ahead of time.

- ☐ Maintain the physical security of your company's trade secrets by, for example, keeping them in a locked room, file cabinet, or desk drawer.

- ☐ Increase computer security to prevent unauthorized access to the system. For example, you should use secret passwords, firewalls, and access procedures; keep trade secrets in coded or encrypted form; and/or consider using a separate computer system, without Internet or network access, for your company's most sensitive information.

- ☐ Stamp or label your company's trade secrets "Confidential."

- ☐ Don't write down trade secrets; tell others what they need to know orally.

- ☐ Limit employee access to trade secrets by, for example, having them sign confidential materials in and out and creating project logs to keep track of which employees have access to which confidential information.

- ☐ Restrict photocopying. Many trade secrets are lost through unauthorized photocopying. A good way to limit this is by requiring employees to use key cards and passwords every time they use a company copy machine.

- ☐ Shred documents. Whenever anyone at your company disposes of a document that includes confidential information, it should be shredded, not left in a dumpster or garbage can for the world to see.

- ☐ Screen employee presentations. Companies can inadvertently lose trade secret protection if an employee reveals or refers to them in a speech or presentation at a trade show, convention, or professional conference.

- ☐ Restrict camera phones. Cell phones with a camera feature make it all too easy for employees to photograph confidential documents, products, or processes.

trade secrets, so you should make a practice of presenting a nondisclosure agreement to every independent contractor who will learn any trade secrets before you share them. When you disclose trade secrets or other confidential information to independent contractors, tell them that the information is confidential and remind them of their obligations under any nondisclosure agreement. (For more about this type of contract, see "Nondisclosure Agreements," below.)

Keep the Secret

As explained above, proprietary information can lose its trade secret status if you fail to take reasonable steps to protect it. Security measures might include the following:

- labeling all documents that contain trade secret information "Confidential"
- keeping a log of all confidential documents and the people who have access to them
- keeping a list of all trade secrets and the people who know them
- keeping all documents and evidence of trade secrets in a locked cabinet, locked room, or password-protected online database
- requiring employees to sign out confidential documents and materials and return them when they're done
- using a paper shredder to destroy any discarded documents that contain trade secret information

- password-protecting any computer files that contain proprietary information
- requiring all visitors to sign in, wear badges, and be accompanied by an employee at all times
- locking all exterior doors
- using nondisclosure agreements with employees, independent contractors, vendors, and customers
- using noncompete and nonsolicitation agreements with key employees (unless prohibited by your state)
- using nonsolicitation agreements with independent contractors, and
- periodically providing employees with access to confidential information with a list identifying which pieces of information your company views as confidential.

Although it's rare that a business will want to use all of these security measures, using at least some of them will go a long way toward maintaining the confidentiality of its trade secrets. Moreover, if someone does pilfer your company's trade secrets, implementing these procedures will show a judge that the company has taken reasonable steps to keep the information a secret.

Conduct Exit Interviews

When an employee or independent contractor stops working for your company—for whatever reason—you must take extra care to ensure that the individual does not turn around and disclose the company's trade secrets to competitors.

An effective way to do this is to conduct an exit interview. Identify all of the trade secrets that the employee has learned and remind him or her of the obligation to keep the information confidential. If the person leaving has any documents that are confidential, retrieve them at the interview.

If the individual has already signed a nondisclosure or nonsolicitation agreement, review it at the interview and reiterate that your company will enforce it if necessary. If not, consider asking the individual to sign such an agreement in exchange for something of value.

Finally, once employees or independent contractors are gone, make sure they no longer have access to the company's computer files and physical premises, by retrieving keys and changing passwords.

Nondisclosure Agreements

A nondisclosure agreement—also called an NDA or a confidentiality agreement—is a contract which prohibits the disclosure of confidential information learned during employment or another type of business transaction. In addition to protecting trade secrets, a nondisclosure agreement can protect a larger category of sensitive business information that your company does not want revealed to the public. For example, a nondisclosure agreement can prohibit someone from disclosing a secret invention design, an

idea for a new website, or confidential financial information about your company.

If your company has entered into a nondisclosure agreement with someone who then uses or discloses its proprietary information without permission, your company can sue for damages and ask a court to stop the violator from making any further disclosures.

These are the important elements of a nondisclosure agreement:

- definition of confidential information
- exclusions from confidential information
- obligations of receiving party
- duration
- notice of immunity, and
- miscellaneous provisions.

This section looks at each of these elements in more detail.

Definition of confidential information. Every nondisclosure agreement provides a general description of the types or categories of information that may not be disclosed. The purpose is to establish the boundaries or subject matter of the disclosure, without actually disclosing the secrets.

Exclusions from confidential information. Every nondisclosure agreement excludes some information from protection. The party signing the agreement has no obligation to protect the excluded information. Typical areas of excluded information include:

- information that is already generally known outside of the business at the time the nondisclosure agreement is signed

- information that becomes known outside of the business through no fault of the employee or independent contractor
- information the employee or independent contractor knew prior to working for your company, and
- information the employee or independent contractor learns independently (that is, outside of the working relationship).

Obligations of the receiving party. The employee or independent contractor generally must keep the information in confidence and limit its use. In general, he or she can neither reveal the information nor assist others in acquiring it improperly or revealing it.

Duration. Most nondisclosure agreements provide that the employee or independent contractor cannot disclose confidential information either during or after employment with your company. When it comes to trade secrets, nondisclosure agreements often don't impose a time limit. Because trade secrets are protected as long as they remain secret, your company could be cutting its rights short by limiting nondisclosure to a certain number of years. On the other hand, some states impose time limits on the protection of confidential information that doesn't qualify as a trade secret. In these states, failing to include a reasonable time limit for this type of information could result in the whole agreement being invalidated. Because this is a tricky area, you should run any

nondisclosure agreement you plan to use past an employment lawyer.

Notice of immunity. In order for employers to take advantage of certain remedies under the federal Defend Trade Secrets Act, they must include a notice of immunity in their nondisclosure agreements or other contracts dealing with trade secrets and confidential information (including an independent contractor agreement with a confidentiality clause; see Chapter 9). The notice must inform the party signing the agreement of the types of disclosures that do not violate the law, namely:

- disclosures made to a government agency or attorney solely for the purpose of reporting a suspected violation of the law, or
- disclosures in a legal complaint or another document in a lawsuit, filed under seal.

Employers that fail to include this notice may still sue under the DTSA, but they may not recover punitive damages or attorneys' fees. For sample language of the notice of immunity, see the sample independent contractor agreement in Chapter 9.

Miscellaneous provisions. Miscellaneous standard terms are usually included at the end of the agreement. They include such matters as which state's law will apply if the agreement is breached, whether the parties will use arbitration (a private proceeding in lieu of going to court) to settle disagreements over the contract, and whether attorneys' fees will be awarded to the party who wins.

As noted above, even if an employee already has a legal duty to keep your company's trade secrets confidential under your state's laws, it's still a good idea to ask an employee to sign a nondisclosure agreement. A nondisclosure agreement:

- shows a judge that your company takes its responsibility to protect its trade secrets seriously
- defines exactly what information the employee must keep secret
- can protect a broader range of sensitive business information, and
- can specify the state or county in which disputes will be resolved, the state's law that will apply, and any dispute resolution method the parties agree on.

Nondisclosure agreements are even more important for independent contractors, customers, and vendors, because none of these people have a duty to keep your company's trade secrets confidential without an agreement.

Noncompete Agreements

Sometimes, a worker is so integral to your company's business or so thoroughly immersed in its trade secrets that his or her departure—particularly to work for a competitor—would cause your company a great deal of harm. In such a situation, a nondisclosure agreement probably will not be sufficient to protect your company. Instead, you should ask, or require, the worker to sign a noncompete agreement. A noncompete agreement goes one step further by prohibiting the worker from performing services for a direct competitor—or from starting a competing business—for a specified period of time after leaving the company.

You do not need to ask every employee to sign a noncompete agreement. Indeed, you should reserve this type of contract for the most valuable and key members of the workforce. So how do you determine which employees fall into this category? Consider the following questions:

- Is the employee so valuable that losing him or her to a competitor would damage your company's business?
- Has the company spent a significant amount of time or money training the employee?
- Does the employee have access to a great deal of important information that you don't want revealed to a competitor?
- If the employee were to work for a competitor, is it practically inevitable that he or she would use your company's trade secrets in the new job?

Noncompete agreements are illegal in a handful of states, including California. If your company does business in one of these states, it won't be able to use noncompete agreements to protect its business. However, you might be able to use nondisclosure agreements and nonsolicitation agreements to protect trade secrets and prevent customer and employee poaching when a worker leaves.

(For more about these types of contracts, see "Nondisclosure Agreements," above, and "Nonsolicitation Agreements," below.)

While nondisclosure agreements may be used freely with both employees and independent contractors, an employer could risk a worker's status as an independent contractor by asking him or her to sign a noncompete agreement. Under most legal definitions, independent contractors are people who are in business for themselves and compete in the open market. Limiting a contractor's ability to work for other companies could lead a government agency or court to find that the worker should really be classified as an employee. (For more information on independent contractor classification, see Chapter 9.)

Make the Agreement Legal

While noncompete agreements can be an effective way to protect your company's business, the legal system also puts a high value on a person's right to earn a living. This means that a court will balance your company's interest in protecting itself against an individual's interest in being able to work where he or she wants to work. If the agreement isn't reasonable and necessary, your company will have a hard time convincing a court to enforce it.

If your company follows the guidelines set out in this section, its agreements should pass legal muster (in states that allow noncompetes).

Lessons From the Real World

Anita Walia worked as an Account Manager in the San Francisco office of Aetna U.S. Healthcare. Aetna decided, in 1997, to start requiring its employees to sign noncompete agreements. When Walia was asked to sign the agreement, which would have prohibited her from working for any health care organization in the state of California for six months after leaving Aetna, she did some research on the Internet and learned that noncompete agreements are generally illegal in California.

Walia spoke to four Aetna managers, starting with her supervisor, about her concerns. She offered to sign the nondisclosure and confidentiality provisions of the agreement if the noncompete were removed. She had a lawyer write to Aetna's president, explaining that the noncompete portion was illegal in California. Her efforts were unsuccessful, however, and Aetna eventually fired her for refusing to sign the agreement.

Walia sued, claiming that she was illegally terminated. A jury agreed, and awarded her more than $1.2 million, most of it for punitive damages. Aetna's failure to take a closer look at California law, even after Walia and her attorney told the company that its agreement was illegal, led the jury to believe that the company needed a wake-up call.

Walia v. Aetna, Inc., 93 Cal.App.4th 1213 (2001).

Have a good business reason. First and foremost, your company must have a good business reason for asking an employee to sign a noncompete agreement. In other words, you can't simply use the agreement to punish someone for leaving the company. The typical business reason is to protect trade secrets or a customer base that a company has worked long and hard to develop. By being selective about which workers are asked to sign noncompete agreements, your company can increase its chances of success; judges are much more likely to enforce noncompete agreements against workers who truly possess inside information.

Provide a benefit. Next, your company must provide a benefit to the worker in exchange for the promise not to compete. Making a job offer contingent on signing a noncompete agreement probably satisfies this requirement, because the applicant is receiving a benefit (a job) in exchange for the promise. When it comes to current employees, some states allow employers to offer continued employment in exchange for signing a noncompete. The rationale is that employers can fire at-will employees at any time, so allowing the employee to continue working is a benefit. However, other states require employers to provide something else of value for the agreement to be effective, such as a raise or promotion.

Be reasonable. A noncompete agreement must also be "reasonable." This means that the agreement can't:

- last too long
- cover too wide a geographic area, or
- prohibit a former worker from engaging in too many types of businesses.

Generally, the biggest issue with noncompete agreements is how long the noncompete agreement lasts. In most states, there's no set rule on timing, and noncompete agreements ranging from six months to two years are generally considered "reasonable," while anything longer than that will receive closer scrutiny. However, some states place statutory limits on how long a noncompete agreement can last. Check with an employment lawyer to make sure any agreement you create complies with your state's legal restrictions.

Nonsolicitation Agreements

It's inevitable: If your company is a service or sales business, workers will develop relationships with the company's best clients and customers. Similarly, employees often develop close working relationships with each other. But when an employee or independent contractor leaves, your company will probably want to stop him or her from using those relationships to solicit its clients' business and steal away other valuable workers. With a little advance planning, you can accomplish this by using a nonsolicitation agreement.

A nonsolicitation agreement is exactly what it sounds like: an agreement in which the worker promises not to solicit your company's clients and customers, for his or her own benefit or for the benefit of a competitor, after leaving your company. A nonsolicitation agreement can also contain a promise by the worker not to solicit other employees to leave when he or she quits or moves on.

Often, a nonsolicitation agreement is part of a broader employment agreement, noncompete agreement, or nondisclosure agreement. But it doesn't need to be. For example, if your company isn't concerned about a former employee starting a competing business but just wants to prevent him or her from stealing its customers and clients, a nonsolicitation agreement alone will do the trick.

Nonsolicitation agreements are effective tools for protecting your company's clients and customers. And if your company is located in a state that doesn't enforce noncompete agreements, nonsolicitation agreements might be one of your only ways to discourage employees from going to work for a competitor or opening a competing business. (However, a minority of states—including California—also prohibit nonsolicitation agreements that prevent a former employee from having contact with the employer's customers and clients.)

Of course, there are some limits on nonsolicitation agreements. If a nonsolicitation agreement makes it too difficult for an employee to earn a living or unfairly limits a competitor's ability to hire workers or solicit customers through legitimate means, a court might not enforce it. Generally, courts will weigh your company's and the employee's circumstances to judge whether a nonsolicitation agreement is fair.

As with noncompete agreements, the key to drafting an effective nonsolicitation agreement is to be reasonable. A judge who thinks the agreement is overreaching might refuse to enforce it at all. For instance, if your company is worried about an employee stealing only a specific client or group of clients, it's best to limit the nonsolicitation agreement to those clients instead of creating a blanket prohibition against all solicitation. Similarly, if there are a few specific types of employees you're afraid the departing employee will try to take, list them, too. Remember, the more limited the agreement, the easier it will be to enforce.

Nonsolicitation agreements must also comply with some other basic legal requirements before a judge will agree to enforce them.

Your company must have a valid business reason. A judge who reviews a nonsolicitation agreement will want to see a valid business reason for putting restraints on a former employee. (As tempting as it might be, a company can't keep all former employees from soliciting its customers and employees just because it wants to.) Valid business reasons include:

- protecting a valuable customer list
- protecting trade secrets and other confidential information, or
- protecting the business from the mass departure of valuable employees with specialized skills, knowledge, and access to trade secrets.

Your company's customer list must be worth protecting. If the average person could figure out who your company's customers or clients are just by looking at your website, a judge probably won't enforce a nonsolicitation agreement against a former employee who tries to get the company's business. Unless your company has spent a lot of time, energy, and money establishing its client database (and it contains information that isn't readily available to the general public), the list might not merit protection.

Employees and customers can leave voluntarily. Nonsolicitation agreements generally can't prevent a client, customer, or employee from moving to a competitor voluntarily. There isn't much a company can do to stop its other employees from leaving to join the former employee at a new company, as long as the departing employee hasn't improperly solicited them (and as long as the departing employees aren't subject to noncompete agreements). And if customers want to take their business to a competitor, a nonsolicitation agreement probably isn't going to be much help, unless the departing employee has improperly solicited them using your company's trade secrets. In other words, if customers or employees reach out to the departing employee, the employee doesn't have to turn them away.

Hiring From Competitors

Although your company is probably most concerned about protecting its own business, trade secret laws are a two-way street: Competitors are just as intent on preventing your company from taking what belongs to them. If your company oversteps the bounds of trade secret laws—even unwittingly—it might end up in a heap of trouble.

Sometimes, what makes a prospective employee most desirable is also what makes him or her a risky hire. Although no law could require a person to erase his or her memory, a new employee who uses a former employer's trade secrets while working for your company poses a serious lawsuit risk.

Some potential trade secret violations are obvious, such as explicitly asking a new employee to reveal trade secrets, violate a confidentiality agreement, or violate a nonsolicitation agreement. Always tread very carefully if you want to hire someone who is bound by a noncompete agreement; you might want some help from a good employment law attorney. Even if your company wins, fights between competitors over employees bound by noncompete agreements can be expensive and downright nasty.

Although it's less obvious, it's just as important not to create a situation in which the employee will be likely to, or even tempted to, reveal trade secrets. Even if no one at your company specifically asks for the information, the company could be liable for a trade secret law violation if an employee reveals a former employer's trade secrets and your company created a fertile environment for the deed. For example, if you hire someone who you know has knowledge of a competitor's trade secrets, and you put that employee in a job where it's likely he or she will use that trade secret information to your advantage, your company could be held liable in a trade secret misappropriation or unfair trade practices lawsuit.

To avoid winding up on the losing end of a trade secret lawsuit, consider the following:

- **Honor noncompete agreements.** If you really want to hire someone who's bound by a noncompete agreement, be honest about it. Talk to the former employer and negotiate some sort of arrangement. Sometimes, companies will allow a new employer to buy out an employee's noncompete, or they will agree to release an employee from a noncompete if your company promises to impose certain security measures.

- **Get promises from the new hire.** Before hiring new employees, verify that they will not be disclosing a former employer's trade secrets and will not need to use those trade secrets in order to do their jobs.

- **Do your own research.** Don't trust the employee's opinion about who owns what. Many employees don't understand intellectual property laws and think that anything they create belongs to them. This isn't always so. Many people also don't take agreements they signed seriously, but your company should. Ask to review any agreement the new hire signed with a former employer, even if the employee assures you it's "nothing serious" or it doesn't apply to the new job.

- **Manage the situation.** Don't put an employee in a job where use of a former employer's trade secrets is inevitable.

Legal Dos and Don'ts: Trade Secrets

Do:

- **Keep your own secrets.** Treat your company's trade secrets like the valuable commodities they are by keeping them in a secure location (such as a locked file cabinet) and revealing them only if and when necessary. If your company doesn't treat its trade secrets in a confidential way, it will be tough to convince a court to help you stop others from revealing them.

- **Keep track of who knows what.** Carefully label everything your company considers a trade secret, and implement procedures to track which employees have access to them. For example, you might require employees to use a sign-in sheet to access confidential information or keep a roster of all employees who have access to customer lists.

- **Use nondisclosure agreements.** From employees and independent contractors to customers and vendors, using confidentiality agreements gives your company a triple dose of protection. The agreements let these people know what information you consider secret, bind people to keep those secrets, and provide proof that your company actively safeguarded its trade secrets.

Don't:

- **Dip into your competitor's pool.** No matter how tempting it is, your company shouldn't hire a competitor's employee in order to get at the competitor's trade secrets. Company executives who engage in this type of sneaky behavior risk a lawsuit, fines, and possible jail time.

- **Cry "wolf."** If you classify every company document as a trade secret, employees won't know what's really worthy of protection. Courts won't know, either, and your company might actually get less protection for its real trade secrets as a result.

- **Overreach in trying to restrict your employees.** Do some research (and talk to a lawyer) before implementing a noncompete, nondisclosure, or nonsolicitation agreement. Companies that go too far in their efforts to prohibit employees from taking away customers, other employees, or information can find themselves in court.

Test Your Knowledge

Questions

1. Your company must file paper-work with the government to make sure its trade secrets are protected from unauthorized use by others. ☐ True ☐ False

2. Independent contractors have a duty not to reveal their clients' trade secrets, even if they never sign a nondisclosure agreement. ☐ True ☐ False

3. All of a company's internal documents should be marked "Confidential," just to be safe. ☐ True ☐ False

4. A company can lose its trade secret protection if it reveals the secret information on its website or in publicly available documents. ☐ True ☐ False

5. Companies can use nondisclosure agreements to prohibit nonemployees with whom it works—such as vendors or customers—from revealing trade secrets. ☐ True ☐ False

6. All companies should ask every employee to sign a noncompete agreement. ☐ True ☐ False

7. Companies should give employees something in exchange for signing a noncompete or non-solicitation agreement. ☐ True ☐ False

8. A company can use a nonsolicitation agreement to prevent customers from taking their business to a competitor. ☐ True ☐ False

9. As long as no one at your company asks a new hire to reveal a former employer's trade secrets, your company cannot be sued for trade secret theft. ☐ True ☐ False

10. It's best not to ask an applicant whether he or she is subject to a noncompete agreement, because that protects your company from legal problems. ☐ True ☐ False

Test Your Knowledge (continued)

Answers

1. False. Trade secret protection is do-it-yourself; you don't have to file anything with the government.

2. False. Although employees have an automatic duty not to reveal their employer's trade secrets, independent contractors do not. This is why they should be required to sign a nondisclosure agreement if they will learn the company's trade secrets.

3. False. You should designate only truly secret information as "Confidential," so employees will know what they are obligated to protect and courts will know that your company didn't unreasonably restrict employees.

4. True. If your company reveals its own trade secrets, it cannot expect a court to prevent others from revealing them.

5. True. Your company can enter into nondisclosure agreements with customers, vendors, businesses with which it's considering joint ventures, and others who are not employees.

6. False. Noncompete agreements are illegal in some states, and others prohibit employers from using them unless they are necessary. If you ask every employee to sign a noncompete agreement, your company will have a tough time convincing a court that it really had to go to such lengths to protect its business.

7. True. Your company should give something of value to employees whom it asks to sign a noncompete or nonsolicitation agreement, to make sure that a court treats it as a legally binding contract. While it's enough to offer continued employment in some states, it's generally safest to offer some other benefit, such as a raise or promotion.

8. False. Your customers are free to take their business wherever they wish. A nonsolicitation agreement prohibits a former employee from actively going after your customers' business but doesn't limit your customers in any way.

9. False. Your company can also get in trouble if it puts an employee in a work situation where disclosure of the former employer's trade secrets is virtually inevitable.

10. False. If your company hires an employee who is bound by a noncompete agreement with a previous employer, the previous employer might ask you to fire the employee or otherwise honor the agreement. If your company fails to comply, it could face a lawsuit.

Handling Workplace Problems

No manager likes dealing with workplace problems. Misconduct, harassment, interpersonal problems, and violent outbursts are all issues most of us would rather avoid if at all possible. But, as a manager, it's your job to get involved. If you ignore such issues, you risk even more serious problems for you and your company, ranging from poor performance and bad morale to workplace injuries, violence, and lawsuits.

In this chapter, we provide some techniques for handling common workplace problems. We cover:

- creating and enforcing disciplinary policies
- tips on handling a workplace investigation
- avoiding retaliation
- preventing violence in the workplace, and
- the company's responsibility for employees' actions.

Disciplining Workers

Most managers don't like to discipline employees. It's unpleasant to give criticism, even when an employee desperately needs it. But an effective, carefully administered disciplinary policy is an invaluable workplace tool.

Advantages of a Good Disciplinary Policy

A clear and effective disciplinary policy offers many benefits, including:

- **Clear guidelines for employee behavior.** A straightforward, easy-to-understand disciplinary policy will tell employees what the company expects of them and what conduct will not be tolerated. Enforcing the policy uniformly will show employees that you take these rules seriously and administer them fairly.
- **Improved performance.** Employees who don't know what you expect—or don't know that they aren't measuring up—are not going to improve. A disciplinary meeting allows you to let the employee know what's going on, listen to the employee's explanation, and collaborate together to come up with a solution.
- **Employee morale.** The employee you discipline is not likely to enjoy a morale boost, but the rest of your employees will. Other employees do not like to see a coworker "getting away with it." And if a problem employee is allowed to misbehave without suffering any consequences, others in the workforce will assume that they can get away with slacking off or misbehaving, creating an even larger problem.

Frequently Asked Questions About Handling Workplace Problems

How can I safely discipline employees?

Make sure your company has a clear, written disciplinary policy that sets out the consequences of failing to meet its performance and behavioral standards. Avoid claims of discrimination or favoritism by applying the policy fairly and consistently and imposing similar discipline for similar offenses. (To learn more, see "Disciplining Workers," above.)

What should I do if an employee complains of harassment or other misconduct?

The most important thing to do is to take the complaint seriously. Make sure to avoid taking any negative action against an employee who complains; this could be considered illegal retaliation. Report the complaint immediately, in accordance with company policy. If you are responsible for handling the complaint, investigate thoroughly. Once you get to the bottom of things, take action to remedy the situation, if necessary. (For more on handling workplace complaints, see "Investigating Complaints," below.)

How can my company prevent violence in the workplace?

There's no way to guarantee that violence will never occur in your company, but there are steps you can take to minimize the risk. Make sure your company has both a zero-tolerance policy for threats or violence and a strict no-weapons policy. You can also learn and train other managers about the warning signs of violence. Most importantly, treat workers— even those you must discipline or fire—with dignity and respect. (For more, see "Workplace Violence," below.)

Can I fire or discipline an employee for complaining about discrimination or another workplace problem?

No. Most antidiscrimination laws forbid retaliation against employees who assert certain rights, such as complaining about discrimination, reporting unsafe working conditions, or filing a workers' compensation claim. Any negative action constitutes retaliation, including discipline and termination. (To learn more about what retaliation is and how to avoid it, see "Retaliation," below.)

Is the company responsible if one of our workers injures a customer?

Yes and no. If the worker is doing his or her job when the injury happens, your company is probably legally responsible. The company will also be liable for criminal acts a worker commits against a customer, client, or coworker if the company knew, or should have known, that the worker was dangerous and failed to take action. (For more, see "Liability for an Employee's Actions," below.)

- **Protection against employee lawsuits.** If your company informs employees of the consequences of poor behavior and enforces its policy fairly, it can buy itself some insurance against future disputes. It will be more difficult for an employee to claim wrongful termination if the company can show that employees knew what types of conduct would result in discipline and that this particular employee violated a clearly defined workplace rule.

Writing a Disciplinary Policy

The trick to writing an effective disciplinary policy is to give employees clear notice of the consequences of poor behavior without locking the company into following one course of action in every situation. For example, even though your company might generally follow a policy of progressive discipline (for instance, a first offense is met with a verbal warning, a second offense with a written warning, and so on), you want to reserve the right to immediately fire an employee who crosses the line.

More importantly, you should avoid even a hint of a promise that employees will not be fired unless they engage in specified misconduct. This can create a binding contract, which your company will be obliged to follow before firing an employee. You might find that employees dream up bad acts you never considered or that your company

needs to fire employees for reasons entirely unrelated to their performance or behavior (an economic downturn or a plant closing, for example).

Breaking the Bad News

If an employee violates a company rule or fails to live up to performance standards, you will have to dispense the discipline outlined in your company's disciplinary policy. Here are some guidelines for doing so:

- **Don't procrastinate.** Set up a meeting with the employee right away. The sooner you give notice that there's a problem, the sooner the employee will have an opportunity to improve.
- **Keep it private.** Meet one on one with the employee to discuss the problem. Make sure to meet in a private place, out of the earshot of coworkers or others to avoid embarrassing the employee.
- **Be honest.** The purpose of this meeting is to notify the employee of his or her poor behavior or performance so that the employee can improve. You must tell the employee precisely what the problem is, so you can figure out, together, how to correct it.
- **Collaborate.** Employees are most likely to improve when they participate in coming up with an action plan for improvement. When you meet with the employee, explain why the employee's performance or conduct is creating

problems for the company and ask for the employee's help in coming up with a solution.

- **Be respectful.** Even bad news should be delivered with respect. Let the employee know that you want to see improvement and that you will help if you can. Set aside enough time for the meeting so that the employee will have an opportunity to respond. Make sure to listen to the employee's concerns; it could be that a performance problem is the result of a misunderstanding.

- **Write it down.** Document every disciplinary meeting, action, or discussion you have with an employee and place that record in the employee's personnel file. In the case of a written warning, give the employee a copy of the warning and ask him or her to sign it to acknowledge receipt. These records help the company show that you informed the employee of the problem if the employee decides to file a lawsuit down the road.

- **Follow up.** If you tell an employee that you must see improvement by a certain date, make sure to follow up. Check with the employee periodically to make sure that things are going smoothly and improving. If the problem persists, get ready to take the next step in your disciplinary policy.

Investigating Complaints

Most managers are anxious when faced with complaints of workplace misconduct, such as violence or harassment. And with good reason: Such complaints can lead to workplace tension, government investigations, and even costly legal battles. If the company mishandles the complaint, even unintentionally, it could unwittingly put itself out of business.

However, a company that takes complaints seriously and follows a careful strategy for dealing with them can reduce the likelihood of a lawsuit and even improve employee relations in the process.

This section provides some basic rules to follow if you receive a complaint of workplace misconduct. (For an in-depth discussion of how to conduct an investigation of harassment or other misconduct at work, see *The Essential Guide to Workplace Investigations*, by Lisa Guerin (Nolo).)

- **Promptly report any complaints you receive.** If your company has established procedures for making or reporting complaints, follow them to the letter. As a manager, you are considered a representative of the company. Once you know about a complaint, the company is considered to be on notice, and it will be responsible for taking swift action to resolve the issue. This means that you must report complaints to the appropriate person or department right away.

Lessons From the Real World

Rena Weeks walked into the lion's den in July of 1991, when she started working as a secretary to Martin Greenstein, a partner in the law firm of Baker & McKenzie. Greenstein treated Weeks boorishly right from the start, reaching into her breast pocket, grabbing her rear end, asking her about "the wildest thing she'd ever done," and pulling her shoulders back so he could see "which breast is bigger."

Weeks complained almost immediately. The firm transferred her to another position, but she still felt uncomfortable. Shortly thereafter, Weeks's performance was questioned, and she left the firm. Weeks's complaint was not investigated.

Sound like the wrong way to handle a complaint? The jury sure didn't like it, especially when they heard that Greenstein had been accused by at least seven other women of sexual harassment and that the firm had never done a thing about it. There was no documentation in Greenstein's file, he was never disciplined, and no investigation was ever conducted. What's worse, many of the women who complained were transferred or fired.

Perhaps the final blow to the law firm's defense was the fact that Greenstein himself was finally fired—in the midst of the lawsuit—but not for sexual harassment. He was fired immediately when the firm learned that he had been improperly dating documents. Apparently that was an offense that merited firing, but propositioning and fondling a long line of female subordinates was not. The law firm was ordered to pay Weeks almost $4 million, not including attorneys' fees.

Weeks v. Baker & McKenzie, 63 Cal.App.4th 1128 (1998).

- **Keep an open mind.** Many managers have a hard time believing that harassment, violent behavior, or other misconduct could be happening right under their noses. As a result, they often fail to take complaints seriously, assuming that the complaint could not possibly be true. Unfortunately, ignoring a complaint is a surefire way to land your company in court.

- **Treat the employee with respect.** Employees often find it extremely difficult to come forward, particularly if the complaint involves harassment. They feel vulnerable and afraid, which can have an impact on the quality of their work. It can also lead them to seek outside assistance from a lawyer. When an employee comes to you with concerns, be understanding. An employee who feels that you are taking the complaint seriously is less likely to take the complaint to a government agency or to court.

- **Don't retaliate against the complainer.** It is against the law to punish someone for complaining about discrimination, harassment, illegal conduct, or unsafe working conditions. The most obvious forms of retaliation are termination, discipline, demotion, pay cuts, or threats to do any of these things. More subtle forms of retaliation include changing the shift hours or work area of the accuser, changing the accuser's job responsibilities, or isolating the accuser by leaving him or her out of meetings and other office functions. (To learn more, see "Retaliation," below.)

- **Follow established procedures.** If your company has an employee handbook or other documented policies relating to discrimination, harassment, or other workplace misconduct, follow those policies. Don't open the company up to claims of unfair treatment by bending the rules for a favorite employee.

- **Interview the people involved.** If you are responsible for investigating the complaint, start by talking to the person who complained. Find out exactly what the employee's concerns are. Get the details: who said or did what, when, where, and who else was there. Take notes of your interviews. Then talk to the employee being accused of misconduct. Finally, be sure to interview any witnesses who might have seen or heard problematic conduct.

- **Look for corroboration or contradiction.** Many workplace complaints, especially those of harassment, come down to one person's word against another's. Often, the accuser and the accused offer conflicting versions of the incident, leaving you with no way of knowing who's telling the truth. If you conduct

the investigation, you might need to turn to other sources for clues. For example, schedules, time cards, and other attendance records (for trainings, meetings, and so on) can help you determine whether everyone was where they claimed to be. Witnesses—including coworkers, vendors, customers, or friends—might have seen all or part of an incident. And in some cases, documents will prove one side right. After all, it's hard to argue with a sexually provocative email or a written threat to harm a coworker.

- **Keep it confidential.** Complaints can polarize a workplace. Workers will likely side with either the complaining employee or the accused employee, and the rumor mill will start working overtime. Worse, if too many details about the complaint are leaked, you could be accused of damaging the reputation of the alleged victim or alleged wrongdoer, and get yourself (and the company) slapped with a defamation lawsuit. Avoid these problems by maintaining confidentiality in your investigation.

- **Write it all down.** If you conduct the investigation, take notes during your interviews. Before the interview is over, review your notes with the interviewee to make sure you got it right. Keep a log of your investigation, documenting all the steps you took to get at the truth. Include the dates and places of interviews you conduct, and keep track of any documents you review. Document any action taken against the accused or the reasons for deciding not to take action. This written record will protect the company later if the employee claims that you ignored the complaint or conducted a one-sided investigation.

- **Cooperate with government agencies.** If the employee makes a complaint with a government agency—such as the federal Equal Employment Opportunity Commission (EEOC) or Occupational Safety and Health Administration (OSHA)—the agency will investigate. It will probably ask your company to provide certain documents, give its side of the story, and explain any efforts it made to deal with the complaint. Be cautious but cooperative. Try to provide the agency with the materials it requests, but remember that the agency is gathering evidence that could be used against the company later. This is a good time to consider hiring a lawyer.

- **Consider hiring an experienced investigator.** Many law firms and private consulting agencies will investigate workplace complaints for a fee. You might consider bringing in outside help if more than one employee complains; the accused is a high-ranking official in your business (like the president or CEO); the accuser has publicized the complaint, either in the workplace or in the media; the accusations are extreme (allegations of rape or assault, for example); or you feel too personally involved to make a fair, objective decision.

- **Take appropriate action against the wrongdoer(s).** At the end of the investigation, your company will need to decide what action to take, if any. If you are responsible for making the decision, review your notes and decide what you think really happened. If you conclude that some form of misconduct occurred, figure out how to discipline the wrongdoer(s) appropriately. Termination is likely warranted for violence, extreme misconduct, or egregious harassment, such as threats, stalking, or repeated and unwanted physical contact. Lesser discipline, such as a warning or counseling, might be in order if the misconduct arises out of a misunderstanding (a blundered attempt to ask a coworker on a date, for example). Once you have decided on an appropriate action, take it quickly, document it, and notify the accuser.

Retaliation

When an employee exercises a legal right—such as complaining about discrimination, harassment, or unsafe working conditions—you must treat that employee with care. Don't take any action that the employee might see as punishment or retaliation for complaining. It is illegal to retaliate against an employee for complaining about these

Checklist: Ten Steps to an Effective Workplace Investigation

If you are tapped to conduct a workplace investigation, follow these steps to get the job done right. (For more detailed information on investigating workplace issues, including harassment, discrimination, violence, and theft, see *The Essential Guide to Workplace Investigations*, by Lisa Guerin (Nolo).)

1. **Decide whether to investigate.** Before you put on your detective's hat, take some time to decide whether you really need to investigate. In a few situations—for example, if all employees agree on what happened or the problem appears to be minor—you might reasonably decide that a full-blown investigation is unnecessary. Usually, however, it's best to err on the side of conducting an investigation. If the problem is more serious than it seemed, failing to investigate can lead to legal trouble and continuing problems. And sometimes, you just can't tell how widespread or substantial a problem is until you do a little digging.

2. **Take immediate action, if necessary.** You might have to act right away—even before you begin your investigation—if a situation is volatile or could otherwise cause immediate harm to your company or its employees. If an employee is accused of sexually assaulting a coworker, stealing valuable trade secrets, or bringing a weapon to work, you'll probably want to suspend the accused employee temporarily, with pay, while you look into the matter. But be careful not to prejudge the situation or lead the accused employee to believe that you've already made up your mind.

3. **Choose an investigator.** You'll want an investigator who is experienced in investigation techniques, is impartial and perceived as impartial by the employees involved, and is capable of acting professionally about the situation. If your company has someone who meets this job description on the payroll (perhaps you!), you're in luck. If not, you can look into hiring an outside investigator.

4. **Plan the investigation.** Take some time up front to organize your thoughts. Gather any information you already have about the problem, including an employee complaint, a supervisor's report, written warnings, or materials that are part of the problem (such as X-rated emails or threatening letters). Using this information as your guide, think about what you'll need to find out to decide what happened. Whom will you interview and what will you ask? Are there additional documents that employees or supervisors might have? Is there anyone who witnessed important events?

5. **Conduct interviews.** The goal of every investigation is to gather information, and the most basic way to do that is by asking people questions. Most investigations involve at least two interviews: one

Checklist: Ten Steps to an Effective Workplace Investigation (continued)

of the employee who complained or was the victim and another of the employee accused of wrongdoing. Sometimes, you will also want to interview witnesses who might have seen or heard something important. When you interview people, try to elicit as much information as possible by asking open-ended questions.

6. **Gather documents and other evidence.** Almost every investigation will rely to some extent on documents: personnel files, emails, company policies, correspondence, and so on. And some investigations will require you to gather other types of evidence, such as drugs, weapons, photographs, or stolen items.

7. **Evaluate the evidence.** The most challenging part of many investigations—especially if witnesses disagree or contradict each other—is figuring out what actually happened. There are some proven methods of deciding where the truth lies, which all of us use in our everyday lives. You'll want to consider, for example, whose story makes the most sense, whose demeanor was more convincing, and who (if anyone) has a motive to deceive you. And in some situations, you might just have to acknowledge that you don't have enough information to decide what happened.

8. **Take action.** If you conclude that serious wrongdoing occurred, you will have to take disciplinary action quickly to make sure your company isn't held liable for that employee's behavior and to protect your

other workers from harm. In deciding how to handle these situations, you should consider a number of factors, including how serious the misconduct was and how your company has handled similar problems in the past.

9. **Document the investigation.** Once your investigation is complete, you should write an investigation report that explains what you did and why. This will not only give the company some protection from lawsuits relating to the investigation, but it will also provide a written record in case of future misconduct by the same employee(s). Among other things, your report should explain how and when the problem came to the company's attention, what interviews you conducted, what evidence you considered, what conclusions you reached, and what you did about the problem.

10. **Follow up.** The last step is to follow up with the employees to make sure that you've solved the problem that led to the investigation. Has the misconduct stopped? Has the wrongdoer met any requirements imposed as a result of the investigation, such as a training course on sexual harassment? If the investigation revealed any systemic workplace problems (such as widespread confusion about company policy or lack of training on issues like workplace diversity or proper techniques for dealing with customers), some training might be in order.

issues, and retaliation is often in the eye of the beholder.

All employers, managers, supervisors, and human resources professionals should become familiar with the law of retaliation. Retaliation claims are becoming more and more common, especially with respect to complaints about discrimination and harassment. They are also becoming more costly: Juries seem especially offended by retaliation and tend to slam retaliating employers with high damage awards. Even if the original complaint turns out to be unfounded, employees can still win a retaliation claim by showing that something negative happened to them because of the complaint.

Retaliation Defined

An employer retaliates when it punishes a worker for reporting or complaining of discrimination, harassment, or unsafe working conditions, or for exercising other rights under federal or state law. Any negative job action, such as demotion, discipline, firing, salary reduction, negative evaluation, change in job assignment, or change in shift assignment, can constitute retaliation.

The Supreme Court has held that any materially adverse action against an employee qualifies as retaliation under Title VII, if the action taken might deter a reasonable employee from making a complaint. (*Burlington Northern & Santa Fe Railway v. White*, 548 U.S. 53 (2006).)

Because enforcement of Title VII depends on employees' willingness to come forward with complaints, the Court held that the statute must be interpreted to provide broad protection from retaliation.

Employees are also protected from retaliation for participating in an investigation of discrimination or harassment. In other words, the employee need not be the source of the complaint: If the employee acts as a witness or answers an investigator's questions about another employee's complaint, the employee is protected. (*Crawford v. Metropolitan Government of Nashville and Davidson County, Tennessee*, 555 U.S. 271 (2009).)

Once an employee makes a complaint, you must be careful in how you treat not only that employee, but his or her close associates as well. In 2011, the Supreme Court held that an employee could sue for retaliation after he was fired because of a discrimination complaint that his fiancée had filed with the EEOC three weeks earlier (the couple worked for the same employer). Even though the employer did not take action directly against the employee who filed the charge, the Court found that firing someone's fiancé would likely dissuade a reasonable employee from making a complaint in the first place. And, the Court didn't limit its holding to spouses or engaged couples: If employees have a close relationship, disciplinary action against one may count as retaliation against the other. (*Thompson v. North American Stainless*, 562 U.S. 170 (2011).)

Lessons From the Real World

Jayson Lewis and Michael Gonzales, two employees at Video Only, went to an attorney after they felt they were subjected to harassment on the basis of race, national origin, and religion. The attorney sent a letter to the store's owner, detailing a number of harassing incidents by managers and coworkers. The owner called in the store manager and the company's area manager and asked them to look into the matter and report back to him. He also asked the company's general manager to hire an investigator to investigate the complaint.

The general manager hired Lynn McKinney, a private investigator who had previously done some theft investigations for the company, to "check out" Lewis and Gonzales. He didn't tell McKinney about the harassment complaints. McKinney ran criminal background checks on Lewis and Gonzales, asked the mother of Lewis's fiancée whether Lewis had ever beaten her daughter, and asked Lewis's former coworkers if Lewis had ever sued anyone for

race discrimination. Gonzales was also told by his former manager and family members that a private investigator was asking disturbing questions about him. Gonzales and Lewis filed charges of harassment and retaliation with the EEOC.

An Oregon court found that Video Only had retaliated against Lewis and Gonzales by investigating them. The court found that the investigation was an adverse employment action that most employees would find aggravating and that might dissuade employees from complaining about harassment. The court also found that the investigation was conducted precisely because the employees complained of harassment. Although the company argued that it had intended to investigate the harassment claims rather than the employees, and its investigator had simply misunderstood what the company wanted, the court rejected that argument.

Equal Employment Opportunity Commission v. Video Only, Civil Case No. 06-1362 (D. Oregon 2008).

Good Intentions Can Still Be Retaliatory

Retaliation obviously includes any action intended to punish the employee for complaining. However, it can also include actions that managers take with the best of intentions, if those actions have a negative impact on the employee.

For example:

- A female employee complains that her supervisor is sexually harassing her. In response, you change the employee from the day shift to the night shift so that she doesn't have to work with the supervisor anymore. Even though you didn't intend to hurt the employee, this action could be retaliatory if the employee preferred the day shift.

- An African American employee complains that his coworkers tell racial jokes and refer to him by racially derogatory names. In response, you transfer the employee to another store. This action could be retaliatory if the new store is farther from the employee's home or is less desirable in some other way.

In both of the above examples, the manager made the mistake of focusing on the complaining employee rather than focusing on the problem. When someone complains or exercises a legal right, the employer's job is to fix the problem, not to avoid it by removing the complaining employee from the situation.

With discrimination and harassment, you won't need to separate workers every time someone makes a complaint. Unless the complaining worker and the accused worker share an office, work closely together, or have a reporting relationship, you can simply tell each to stay away from the other until you get to the bottom of things. However, if the complaint is serious and the employees work together, your best bet is to separate them by moving the accused worker. Even if the investigation later shows that the complaint was unfounded, the accused worker will have a hard time showing that your action was unreasonable, given the circumstances.

Strategies to Prevent Retaliation

As soon as an employee complains about discrimination, harassment, or unsafe working conditions, retaliation becomes a possibility. You can reduce your chances of facing a retaliation claim by taking the following precautionary steps:

- **Establish a policy against retaliation.** Your company should have in place a clear policy against retaliation. It should spell out exactly what retaliation is and make perfectly clear that retaliation will not be tolerated. It should also tell employees what steps to take if they feel they are being retaliated against.

- **Communicate with the complaining employee.** Explain that the company is taking the complaint seriously. Tell the employee that you want to hear about anything that the employee considers hostile or negative. Refer the employee to your company's antiretaliation policy and explain what retaliation is.

- **Keep complaints confidential.** The fewer people who know about a complaint, the smaller the chances are that someone will retaliate against the complaining employee. Of course, if you investigate the employee's complaint, you will have to tell some people about it. Make sure that you only tell the people who absolutely need to know. And when you tell them, explain what retaliation is and tell them that it is prohibited. Take immediate disciplinary action against any employee who retaliates against a complaining employee.

- **Document, document, document.** Take notes of everything you do to prevent retaliation. Send the complaining employee a letter confirming the company's policy on retaliation.

Actions That Are Not Retaliatory

An adverse action is retaliatory only if it is done *because* the employee complained. The company is free to take adverse actions against an employee for other reasons, even if that employee has complained or participated in an investigation. For example, the following actions would not qualify as retaliation:

- If the employee performs poorly, you can give the employee a negative evaluation.
- If the employee is habitually late for work, you can discipline the employee for tardiness.
- If the employee brings a gun to work, you can fire the employee.

The problem is that some employees may claim that an adverse action is retaliation even if your decision had nothing to do with the employee's complaint or participation in an investigation.

If you must take an adverse action against an employee who has complained, be prepared to show that you had valid reasons, unrelated to the complaint, for taking the action. Your reasons will be most persuasive if they are supported by documentation—like performance evaluations and disciplinary warnings—showing that the employee's performance problems predated the complaint.

(For more information on employees who report workplace safety concerns, see Chapter 7. For more information on illegal reasons to fire employees, see Chapter 12.)

Workplace Violence

Unless you've been living under a rock, you've heard horror stories in the news about violence in the workplace. A disgruntled worker, an employee's former lover, or an enraged customer or client bursts through the door, shooting first and asking questions later.

Workplace violence is a major problem in the United States: Government studies estimate that there are about two million assaults and violent threats made against workers each year. The Bureau of Labor Statistics reports that there were 417 workplace homicides in 2015 alone; nearly 85% of deaths were caused by workplace shootings. Such violence costs businesses more than $36 billion each year, according to the Workplace Violence Research Institute.

So what can you do to prevent violence in the workplace? More than you might think. While you can't guarantee your company will never face a violent incident, you can take steps to reduce the risk. And your company can adopt a policy and a safety plan to improve its chances of avoiding trouble.

Workplace Violence Defined

Workplace violence can take many forms. Perhaps the most familiar source of violence is the infamous "disgruntled employee": the former or current worker who returns to the workplace to avenge a perceived injustice or settle a score. But violence might also be committed by an angry customer or client or by a stranger intent on robbing a business or assaulting its workers. Domestic violence can also spill into the workplace.

Here are just a few of the recent tragic events caused by workplace violence in 2017 alone:

- A personal trainer who worked at a Florida gym was reportedly fired for a workplace violence incident and escorted off the premises. He returned the same day to shoot and kill two gym managers before turning the gun on himself.
- A doctor returned to a Bronx Hospital more than a year after he was forced to resign after sexual harassment complaints were made against him. After he was unable to locate a particular doctor, he opened fire at random, killing one doctor and injuring several others.
- A UPS driver in San Francisco went on a shooting rampage at the warehouse where he worked, shooting and killing several of his coworkers. Police believe that he was targeting certain coworkers whom he felt disrespected by.

You should treat any conduct that is menacing or assaulting as violence under your company's policies. This includes threats, actual assaults, unwelcome physical contact, destruction of property, stalking, and intimidation.

Warning Signs

There is no "profile" of a perpetrator of workplace violence; like any other crime, just about anyone can commit workplace violence. But experts agree that an employee who commits a violent act often exhibits certain signs of trouble. All managers should keep an eye out for clues that intervention might be necessary. They include:

- an unexplained rise in absences
- angry outbursts at coworkers and customers
- verbal abuse or threats toward coworkers
- strained workplace relationships
- overreaction or resistance to even minor changes in the workplace
- lack of attention to one's own appearance, including hygiene
- comments about firearms or weapons

- signs of paranoia ("everyone's out to get me") or withdrawal, and
- substance abuse problems.

Clearly, not every worker who displays some of these traits poses a threat. There are numerous reasonable explanations for absences (a sick child, for example) or a decline in personal appearance (perhaps the end of a personal relationship that has nothing to do with the workplace). But a worker who demonstrates a number of these indicators—especially if the behavior appears to be intensifying—might need some help.

Preventing and Addressing Violence

In addition to watching for warning signs, there are a few other things you can do to reduce the incidence of violence in the workplace:

- **Screen applicants before hiring.** Check for past criminal convictions (if your state allows it), restraining orders, or a history of difficulties with coworkers. (See "Background Checks" in Chapter 1 for more information.) This is important not only to protect other workers, but also to protect the company's bottom line. An employer that doesn't properly investigate a potentially violent employee could face a lawsuit from a coworker or customer who is injured or harmed when the employee becomes violent.
- **Conduct performance evaluations and use your company's progressive discipline policy.** Experts say that employees are more

likely to become violent if they believe they have been treated unfairly, taken by surprise, or sandbagged. Prevent these reactions by giving employees fair warning and a chance to improve on performance or conduct problems.

- **Treat workers with respect.** Always treat workers decently, especially when you have to discipline or fire them. Depriving a worker of dignity—by disparaging the person in front of coworkers or calling the employee names—can trigger violent behavior.
- **Adopt a zero-tolerance policy toward workplace violence.** Create a company policy that states that violence of any kind will not be tolerated. Violence or threats of violence should be grounds for immediate termination.
- **Never allow weapons in the workplace.** Unless employees have a compelling need to be armed (for example, they work as security guards), don't allow weapons in the workplace. Ban weapons on company property, including the parking lot (if your state allows it; some states don't allow employers to ban licensed weapons in employee vehicles). Immediately discipline any employee who violates the no weapons rule.
- **Consider an employee assistance program.** Workplace violence often begins off site, with a failing marriage, a substance abuse problem, or money troubles. Help employees manage these problems with

an employee assistance program (EAP) before they result in workplace violence. An EAP might include counseling, rehabilitation services, or anger management classes. For information on offering an EAP to employees, contact your company's insurance carrier; many offer EAP services as part of an overall mental health benefit.

- **Take threats seriously.** Investigate every incident of violence. Don't assume a worker "didn't mean it" or was just "blowing off steam." While you might think an incident was misperceived or exaggerated, you should make that decision only after looking into all the facts. If a threat seems serious, increase security and tell the police.

- **Develop a safety plan.** Instruct employees on what to do if violence happens. Plan escape routes and know where first aid supplies are. And have the telephone numbers of local police or building security handy, preferably on speed dial.

- **Require reporting.** Your company should require all employees to report any incidents of violence that they witness. Stress that employees who report incidents of violence will be assured confidentiality as much as possible.

- **Train managers.** If you are responsible for company training, make sure other managers know the warning signs for violence, the safety plan, and the requirements of your company's reporting policy.

- **Revoke access to the workplace.** Whenever an employee leaves the company, make sure to collect key cards, change keypad passwords, and otherwise revoke the employee's access to the workplace. If you have concerns about a specific departing employee, alert security or front desk personnel to be on the lookout for the employee and what to do if he or she returns to the workplace.

For more tips on how to prevent and address workplace violence, visit the website of the Occupational Safety and Health Administration (OHSA) at www.osha.gov/SLTC/workplaceviolence/index.html.

Domestic Violence in the Workplace

An employee's domestic violence issues can seep into the workplace. Because the perpetrator is usually not a company employee, this presents unique prevention concerns. Among the strategies a company can adopt to address this problem are:

- increasing security whenever you become aware that an employee is a victim of domestic violence

- encouraging employees who are victims of domestic violence to report any potential problems or developments (if the employee's violent partner made a threat or is getting out of jail, for example)

- making sure that the security staff in the office or building are aware of any outstanding restraining orders or threats against an employee and know what the abuser looks like

- getting a restraining order (or helping the employee get one) that prohibits the abuser from entering the workplace; a handful of states allow employers to apply for such orders directly, and

- moving a victim of violence so that the abuser cannot easily locate him or her (for example, to a different floor or wing), which will protect the employee and buy your company some time to defuse a potentially violent encounter.

Liability for an Employee's Actions

Under a handful of legal theories, courts have held employers responsible for injuries their employees have inflicted on others, whether the injured person is a coworker, a customer, or a complete stranger. Here, we explain those theories, along with a few steps you can take to keep your company out of this kind of trouble.

Employer Liability for Actions Within the Scope of Employment

Under a legal doctrine called "respondeat superior," an employer is legally responsible

---

Lessons From the Real World

Minimed Inc. hired a pest control company to rid its facility of fleas. The company sprayed pesticide overnight. Some employees who reported to work the next day felt nauseated and ill from the fumes. One was Irma Hernandez, who felt sick and left work at noon. Her supervisor asked whether she felt well enough to drive home, and she said she did.

On her way home, Hernandez rear-ended a car stopped at a red light. She told officers that she felt dizzy and light-headed immediately before the crash. The person Hernandez hit, Barbara Bussard, sued Minimed for her injuries, claiming

that Hernandez was acting within the scope of her employment when she drove home.

The court agreed and held Minimed responsible for the accident. Although an employer is ordinarily not legally liable for an employee's actions during his or her commute to and from work, the court found that Hernandez was acting within the scope of her employment because she was exposed to the pesticides at work. The court decided that it was fair to attribute the injuries to Minimed because they were the foreseeable result of Hernandez's work activities.

Bussard v. Minimed, Inc., 105 Cal.App.4th 798 (Ct.App., 2d District, 2003).

for the actions committed by its employees in the course and scope of their employment. In other words, if the employee was doing his or her job, carrying out company business, or acting on the employer's behalf, the employer will generally be liable.

The purpose of this rule is fairly simple: to hold employers responsible for the costs of doing business, including the cost of employee carelessness and misconduct. If the injury the employee caused is simply one of the risks of the business, the employer will be liable. But if the employee acted independently or purely out of personal motives, the employer might not be liable. Here are a couple of examples to illustrate the difference:

- A restaurant promises delivery in 30 minutes "or your next order is free." If a delivery person hits a pedestrian while trying frantically to beat the deadline, the company will likely be liable to the pedestrian.
- A technology services company gives its sales staff company cars to make sales calls. After work hours, a salesperson hits a pedestrian while using the car to run personal errands. Most likely, the company cannot be sued for the incident.

If your company is sued under this legal theory, the employee's victim generally won't have to prove that the company should have known the employee might cause harm, or even that the company did anything

Lessons From the Real World

Charles Smith was the superintendent of Amtrak's Rail Weld and Cropping Plant in New Haven, Connecticut. On March 20, 1981, Smith reprimanded one of the employees he supervised, Joseph Leonetti, for sitting in a restaurant eating breakfast when he should have been at work.

A few hours later, Leonetti came into Smith's office and shot Smith twice with a shotgun. Smith's kneecap was shattered, he was hospitalized for months, and he suffered a heart attack and a stroke related to the shooting.

Smith sued Amtrak, arguing that the company put him in harm's way by ignoring previous incidents involving Leonetti, who was never reported or disciplined for prior violent behavior. Smith argued that Amtrak's failure to take these earlier incidents seriously led to his injury.

Amtrak contended that Smith would have been injured regardless of what it did. Amtrak pointed out that Smith was the person responsible for imposing discipline. Therefore, the company argued, if Smith had disciplined Leonetti for his earlier misconduct, those disciplinary measures would have resulted in violence as well.

But the jury didn't buy it. They found that Amtrak's failure to take action after the earlier incidents led to the shooting and awarded Smith $3.5 million in damages.

Smith v. National Railroad Passenger Corporation, 856 F.2d 467 (2d Cir. 1988).

demonstrably wrong. If the employee caused the harm while acting within the scope of employment, your company can be held automatically liable.

Employer Carelessness in Hiring and Retaining Employees

Under two different legal theories, known as "negligent hiring" and "negligent retention," someone who is injured by an employee can sue the employer for failing to take reasonable care in selecting or retaining its workers. These legal theories apply even to actions workers take that fall outside the scope of employment. In fact, they often are used to hold an employer responsible for a worker's violent criminal acts on the job, such as rape, murder, or robbery. An employer is responsible under these theories only if it acted carelessly—in other words, if it knew or should have known that an applicant or employee was unfit for the job, yet did nothing about it.

Here are a few situations in which employers have had to pay up:

- A pizza company hired a delivery driver without looking into his criminal past, which included a sexual assault conviction and an arrest for stalking a woman he met while delivering pizza for another company. After he raped a customer, he was sent to jail for 25 years, and the pizza franchise was liable to his victim for negligent hiring.

- A car rental company hired a man who later raped a coworker. Had the company verified his résumé claims, it would have discovered that he was in prison for robbery during the years he claimed to be in high school and college. The company was liable to the coworker for negligent hiring.

- A furniture company hired a delivery man without requiring him to fill out an application or performing a background check. The employee assaulted a female customer in her home with a knife. The company was liable to the customer for negligent hiring.

- A corporate company was sued after it continued to employ a male employee with an escalating pattern of abusive behavior, including sexually harassing coworkers, fighting with coworkers, and making death threats. After a female employee declined his romantic advances, the male employee continued to harass her at work, scratched a death threat into her locker door, and eventually shot and killed her at her home. The court allowed the female employee's family to sue for negligent retention.

Many states have allowed claims for negligent hiring and retention. Although these lawsuits have not yet appeared in every state, the clear legal trend is to allow injured third parties to sue employers for hiring or keeping on a dangerous worker. So what can you do to keep your company out of trouble? Here are a few tips:

- **Perform background checks.** Run a routine background check before you hire an applicant. Verify information on résumés, look for criminal convictions (but only to the extent legally allowed in your state; see "Background Checks" in Chapter 1 for more information), and check driving records. These simple steps will weed out many dangerous workers and help show that your company was not careless in its hiring practices.

- **Use special care in hiring workers who will have a lot of public contact.** A company is more likely to be found responsible for a worker's actions if the job involves working with the public. Workers who go to a customer's home (those who make deliveries, perform home repairs, or manage apartment buildings, for example), workers who interact with children or the elderly, and workers whose jobs give them access to weapons (like security guards) all require more careful screening.

- **Root out problem employees immediately.** Under the theory of negligent retention, your company can be responsible for keeping a worker on after it learns (or should have been aware) that the worker posed a potential danger. If an employee has made violent threats against customers, brought an unauthorized weapon to work, or racked up a few moving violations, for example, take immediate action.

Legal Dos and Don'ts: Handling Workplace Problems

Do:

- **Consider immediate termination.** Some workplace misconduct is so serious that firing is warranted. If, after an investigation, you conclude that a worker has made serious threats of violence, committed egregious harassment, or brandished a weapon, show that worker the door.

- **Make the punishment fit the crime.** Just as some types of misconduct are clearly firing offenses, others just as clearly are not. A progressive discipline policy that differentiates between serious and minor problems will help employees know what is expected of them, and it will help you weed out the real troublemakers while getting minor offenders to shape up.

- **Get help on the tough issues.** If you are faced with a potentially violent employee and you don't know what to do, a workplace violence consultant can help. A professional investigator can help you get to the bottom of a workplace dispute, if you feel like you are in over your head. You can find these professionals in the phone book or on the Internet.

Don't:

- **Drag your feet.** Once you discover or learn about an employment problem—whether it's a performance issue, harassing conduct, or threats of violence—take action right away. It's human to want to put off unpleasant confrontations, but procrastinating will only make the problem worse.

- **Minimize threats and outbursts.** None of us wants to believe that someone we know could become violent. But if you assume that a worker who threatens or rages is only "blowing off steam," you could be putting others in danger. Take all threats and violent acts seriously.

- **Blame the messenger.** Though it might not seem like it, a worker who complains of a workplace problem is doing you a favor. You then have a chance to investigate and act quickly to nip the problem in the bud. Take action against the problem, not against the worker who brought it to your attention.

Test Your Knowledge

Questions

1. Your company's progressive discipline policy should try to anticipate every conceivable type of employee misconduct, so employees will know what discipline will be imposed. ☐ True ☐ False

2. Employees can use a poorly written progressive discipline policy as grounds for a lawsuit against your company. ☐ True ☐ False

3. If an employee complains that she was sexually harassed, but the alleged harasser denies it, there's nothing the company can do. ☐ True ☐ False

4. You don't have to investigate every workplace incident or complaint. ☐ True ☐ False

5. If an employee complains that another employee is harassing him or her, it's best to move the complaining employee to another work area until you figure out what really happened. ☐ True ☐ False

6. Keeping complaints confidential can help you avoid claims of retaliation. ☐ True ☐ False

7. There's very little a company can do to reduce its risk of a violent workplace incident. ☐ True ☐ False

8. Employers in some states can get a restraining order that prohibits an employee's domestic abuser from coming to the worksite. ☐ True ☐ False

9. A company can be sued for damage caused by an employee only for incidents that take place at the worksite, during work hours. ☐ True ☐ False

10. A company can be legally liable for an employee's criminal behavior. ☐ True ☐ False

Test Your Knowledge (continued)

Answers

1. False. You couldn't possibly list every conceivable employee offense, and you shouldn't try to. The best progressive discipline policies reserve the company's right to decide how to handle incidents on a case-by-case basis.

2. True. If the policy appears to lock the company into a particular course of action, and the company departs from it, then the worker might have a legal claim for breach of contract.

3. False. The investigator can talk to witnesses, examine relevant documents (such as emails between the workers), and consider each employee's demeanor, motives, and consistency in deciding what actually happened.

4. True. Although it's best to err on the side of investigating, there might be situations in which the alleged wrongdoing is extremely minor or the employees involved agree about what happened. In these cases, you can skip the investigation and go straight to taking action.

5. False. If you move the employee who complained, the company could be accused of retaliation. If you must separate workers temporarily, it's a better idea to move the accused employee.

6. True. A negative employment action qualifies as retaliation only if it is done because an employee complained. Only people who know about a complaint are in a position to commit illegal retaliation.

7. False. Although there are no guarantees, treating employees with respect and giving them fair warning of misconduct and performance problems through evaluations and progressive discipline, can help avert trouble.

8. True. Traditionally, only a victim of abuse could get this type of order, but the laws of some states allow employers to get them to protect an employee, as well.

9. False. A company can be held liable for any harm an employee causes within the course and scope of the employment, whether on site or off, during work hours or not. But if the employee acted independently or purely out of personal motives, the employer probably won't be liable—unless the employer failed to exercise reasonable care in hiring or continuing to employ the employee.

10. True. A company can be held liable for criminal acts a worker commits against a customer, client, or coworker if the company knew, or should have known, that the worker was dangerous and failed to prevent potential crimes (for example, by conducting a background check before hiring a delivery or repairperson who will enter customers' homes).

Firing Employees

Firing an employee is one of the toughest tasks you'll face as a manager. And because of the emotional stakes involved, it's also the task most likely to land your company in legal trouble. When you fire a worker, some amount of his or her dignity, self-esteem, and livelihood is on the line; it's understandable that a poorly handled termination might lead a disgruntled employee to the courthouse door.

Because firing an employee poses considerable risks to your company, it pays to consider the decision carefully. In this chapter, we will explain some of the legal rules that govern employment terminations, discuss some factors to consider in deciding whether to fire, and give you advice on how to break the news. We cover:

- legal and illegal reasons for firing
- special rules for employees with contracts
- how to decide whether to fire workers, and
- how to conduct the termination meeting.

(Layoffs are covered in Chapter 13. For information on your company's obligations to departing workers—whether they quit, are fired, or are laid off—see Chapter 14.)

Illegal Reasons for Firing Employees

If your company employs workers at will, you don't need good cause to fire them. You can generally let them go at any time for any reason. (See "At-Will Employment" in Chapter 4.) However, you can't fire them for illegal reasons. Here, we list some of the most common illegal reasons for firing an employee. (If you want to end your company's relationship with an independent contractor, see Chapter 9.)

Discrimination

Federal law makes it illegal for most employers to fire an employee because of the employee's race, color, gender, national origin, disability, religion, genetic information, age (if the person is at least 40 years old), or pregnancy (including birth or a pregnancy-related medical condition).

Most states also have antidiscrimination laws that protect the same characteristics listed in the federal law. Many state laws also protect additional characteristics, such as sexual orientation or marital status. Some laws apply to a wider range of employers; for example, they might cover employers with fewer employees than those covered by federal law. (For more information on antidiscrimination laws, see Chapter 3.)

Retaliation

It is illegal for employers to fire employees for asserting their rights under the state and federal antidiscrimination laws described above. You cannot fire an employee for complaining of discrimination or harassment, for filing a lawsuit or a charge with a government agency alleging discrimination or harassment, or for testifying on behalf of a coworker who was discriminated against or harassed. (For more, see "Retaliation" in Chapter 11.)

Frequently Asked Questions About Firing Employees	

Can at-will employees be fired for any reason?

In general, an employer may fire an at-will employee at any time, for any reason (or for no reason at all). But there's one big exception to this rule: An employer may not fire an at-will employee for an illegal reason. Federal and state laws establish a number of illegal reasons, including discrimination based on a protected characteristic and retaliation for an employee exercising a legal right. (See "Illegal Reasons for Firing Employees," above, for more information.)

Does a written employment contract limit our right to fire?

Typically, yes. If an employee has a written contract, the terms of the contract will dictate the circumstances under which the worker can be fired. (See "Firing Employees With Employment Contracts," below, for more on written agreements.)

How can I protect our company from lawsuits when firing workers?

Make sure you always have a legitimate, business-related reason—known in the legal world as "good cause"—to fire. (While this is not required to fire an at-will employee, it is always a good idea.) And make sure you have documented evidence that the worker didn't meet company standards, in the form of performance reviews, disciplinary warnings, and so on. (For more tips, see "Making the Decision to Fire," below.)

Does it really matter how we fire workers?

In a word, yes. Surveys have shown that the manner in which an employee is fired plays a very important role in determining whether that employee decides to file a wrongful termination lawsuit. (For more information on how to break the bad news, see "How to Fire," below.)

Refusal to Submit to a Lie Detector Test

A federal law called the Employee Polygraph Protection Act prohibits most employers from firing employees for refusing to take a lie detector test. Many state laws contain a similar prohibition. (See "Testing Current Employees" in Chapter 6 for more.)

Citizenship Status

Under the federal Immigration Reform and Control Act (IRCA), an employer cannot fire an employee based on lack of citizenship. As long as the employee is legally authorized to work in the United States, the employer cannot discriminate against the worker based on his or her status as a noncitizen.

Whistleblowing

Generally, you may not fire an employee for complaining about illegal or unethical conduct in the workplace. A number of laws protect an employee's right to complain to a government agency or to company management about potential

Lessons From the Real World

Kaaren Yarborough worked as a manager in the recruiting department of PeopleSoft, Inc., a software maker in California. Because PeopleSoft has significant contracts with the Department of Defense and other federal agencies, it was required to comply with federal guidelines relating to the recruiting and hiring of women and minority workers.

In 1995, Yarborough saw reports that management sent to the Office of Federal Contract Compliance, a government agency that monitors companies with government contracts. According to Yarborough's lawyer, these reports falsely claimed that the company had a significantly higher percentage of female and minority workers than it actually did. Although the company claimed that 60% of its workforce was female and 21.7% were racial minorities, the true figures were 45% and 13%, respectively.

Yarborough reported these problems but was fired two days before she was scheduled to meet with auditors from the federal agency. Although PeopleSoft claimed it fired Yarborough for poor performance, the Alameda County jury that heard the case thought otherwise. The jury awarded Yarborough $5.45 million in damages on August 16, 2001.

John Roemer, "Wrongful Termination Suit Brings $5.45M," *The Daily Journal*, August 17, 2001; "PeopleSoft Whistleblower Awarded $5.4 Million," Reuters, August 16, 2001.

workplace illegalities. Some of these types of whistleblowing are covered by the laws that prohibit retaliation. For example, an employee who files an OSHA complaint or a charge of discrimination with the EEOC cannot be fired for doing so.

However, protections for whistleblowers go quite a bit further. For example, an employee who complains about financial irregularities or improprieties relating to a government contract cannot be fired for doing so. A number of laws protect the right to blow the whistle on improper employer conduct, including the Sarbanes-Oxley Act of 2002, which protects employees who complain of accounting irregularities and potential shareholder fraud.

Because so many types of whistleblowing are protected, the safest course of action is to never fire an employee for complaining of illegal or unethical behavior. Before you take any disciplinary action against an employee who has made this type of complaint, talk to an experienced employment lawyer.

Violations of Public Policy

Most states prohibit employers from firing an employee in violation of public policy (that is, for reasons that most people would find morally or ethically wrong). Of course, morals and ethics are relative things, so the range of prohibited reasons for firing varies from state to state. Some state and federal laws explicitly prohibit employers from firing workers for taking advantage of certain rights, like taking family and medical leave or supporting a union. In some states, a worker can also successfully argue that he or she was fired in violation of public policy even if no statute spells out exactly what the employer can and cannot do.

Although the laws and rules vary from state to state, most states agree that firing an employee for any of the following reasons would violate public policy:

- refusing to commit an illegal act (like falsifying insurance claims or submitting false tax returns)
- complaining about illegal workplace conduct (see "Whistleblowing," above), and
- exercising a legal right (such as voting or filing a workers' compensation claim).

To find out more about the law regarding public policy in your state, contact your state labor department or your state fair employment office. (You'll find contact information in the appendix.)

Firing Employees With Employment Contracts

If an employee has an employment contract—whether written or oral, express or implied—that contract might limit your ability to fire the employee. Usually, if an employment contract exists (which is not always easy to figure out), the company must treat the employee fairly and fire him or her only for "good cause."

Is There a Contract?

Before you fire someone, you have to determine whether your company has an employment contract with that worker. This might be as simple as looking in the employee's personnel file for a document labeled "employment contract," but it's often not.

Employment contracts can be created orally—for example, if you and an employee come to an agreement in person or over the phone—even if you never commit the terms to writing. Employers can even create employment contracts without meaning to or even knowing they are doing so. These types of contracts are called implied contracts because they are not written down, but instead are inferred from your actions and statements. Oral and implied contracts are every bit as binding as signed, written contracts.

Employers create implied contracts when they promise an employee something, usually job security. You might inadvertently make these promises in all sorts of circumstances, such as during a casual conversation with an employee or as part of a discussion in an employee handbook. No matter how the promise is made, if the promise has enough weight and the employee has relied on that promise (usually by taking the job or staying there), a court might decide that the promise is a contract that your company must honor.

Figuring out whether the company has unintentionally created an implied contract can be a tricky business. However, past court decisions provide some guidance. Courts have found implied contracts in the following circumstances:

- While trying to convince a prospective employee to take a job, an employer promises the employee that he or she will be fired only if he or she does not do the job well.

- An employee handbook states that once new workers successfully complete a 90-day probation period, they become "permanent" employees.

- A progressive discipline policy in an employee handbook states that employees will not be fired until the company has gone through all steps of its disciplinary process (for example, a verbal warning, a written warning, suspension, and so on).

- During an evaluation, a supervisor gives an employee a glowing review and tells the employee he or she has a long future at the company unless he or she really messes up. (See "At-Will Employment" in Chapter 4 for more on creating implied contracts.)

Don't let the specter of implied contracts worry you too much, however. The vast majority of employees in this country are working without a contract—written, oral, or implied. If you are dealing with an employee who has only been with your company for a short time (say, a year or two) and you are sure no one ever promised the employee job security, chances are good that the employee does not have an implied contract. This means that the employee works at will and that you can fire the employee for any reason that isn't illegal. (See "Illegal Reasons for Firing Employees," above).

Remember, too, that a contract doesn't mean you can never fire a worker. It just limits the circumstances under which the worker can be terminated. For workers with implied contracts, this generally means that you must have good cause—such as poor performance or violation of important workplace rules—to fire the employee.

Firing Employees With Written Contracts

If your company has a formal written contract with an employee, it will usually list the reasons for which the employee can be fired. If you want to terminate that employee, you must follow what the contract says. Often, contracts simply state that an employee can only be terminated for good cause. Sometimes, however, the contract will be more detailed. For example, some contracts say that a worker can be fired only for gross misconduct, for committing a crime, or in connection with a sale of the company. Either way, you must follow the contract terms or risk a lawsuit.

Good Cause

As explained above, many employment contracts allow employers to terminate the employee only for good cause. What exactly constitutes good cause varies from state to state, but generally it means what it says: You must have a legitimate, business-related reason for firing the employee. Firing an employee because you want to hire your niece or nephew, for example, isn't good cause. Firing an employee because of excessive absenteeism is.

Examples of good cause include the following:

- poor job performance
- low productivity
- refusal to follow instructions
- habitual tardiness
- excessive absences from work
- possession of a weapon at work
- threats of violence
- violating reasonable company rules
- stealing or other criminal activity
- dishonesty
- endangering the health and safety of others
- revealing company trade secrets
- harassing coworkers
- disrupting the work environment
- conviction of a felony or a crime involving "moral turpitude"
- preventing coworkers from doing their jobs, and
- insubordination.

Lessons From the Real World

If an employee has a contract, you must abide by the terms of the agreement or face a breach of contract lawsuit. That's the very expensive lesson learned by Metris Companies, a credit card issuer that fired its CEO, Ronald Zebeck.

Zebeck claimed that he was fired in anticipation of a sale of the company, which triggered the generous severance provisions of his employment contract; Zebeck also argued that he was fired because he was planning to report financial improprieties to government regulators. Metris claimed that Zebeck was fired for cause, so he forfeited the right to receive severance. Ultimately, the jury sided with Zebeck and ordered Metris to pay him more than $30 million in damages.

Good Faith and Fair Dealing

If your company has a contract with an employee, then it has an obligation to be fair and honest in its dealings with that employee. Although this rule might seem to override your company's ability to terminate employees under contract, it really doesn't. To breach this obligation, employers have to engage in very egregious conduct, such as:

- firing employees to prevent them from collecting sales commissions
- firing employees just before their retirement benefits vest, or

- fabricating evidence of poor performance to fire workers when the real motivation is to replace them with employees who will work for lower pay.

Making the Decision to Fire

Most employers start thinking about firing a worker in one of two situations. In the first, a worker commits a single act of serious misconduct that's dangerous or potentially harmful to the business, such as threatening or committing violence, stealing from the company, violating major safety rules, or revealing important company information to a competitor. These problems require a quick and careful response.

More commonly, though, an employer is facing a "problem" employee who has persistent (but less severe) performance or conduct problems. An employee who is repeatedly absent or tardy, is insubordinate, or simply can't seem to meet reasonable performance and productivity goals falls into this category. Though not as urgent, these problems can also threaten your company's well-being. Left unchecked, they will eventually erode productivity and employee morale.

No matter what your reasons are, consider all the angles before you take action. Remember, firing is the one decision you will make as a manager that is most likely to land your company in court. Stay out of legal trouble by making sure you give the worker a fair shake before showing him or her the door. We provide some suggestions below.

Questions to Ask Yourself Before Firing

If you're contemplating firing an employee, ask yourself these important questions:

- **Do we have a legitimate reason?** Make sure you have good cause—that is, a solid, business-related reason—to fire the worker. (While this is not required for at-will employees, it is always a good idea. See "Practical Limitations on At-Will Employment" in Chapter 4.) If the employee has had multiple performance or misconduct issues, or has committed a serious act of misconduct, you probably have good cause. However, you should also consider the timing of the firing and whether there could be an appearance of an illegitimate reason for the firing. For example, if the employee recently disclosed a disability, it might look like the firing is discriminatory, even if you have other legitimate reasons for the firing.
- **Should we investigate first?** If the incident has already been investigated or if the accused worker admits to the misconduct in question, you can skip this step. But if the situation is not so clear-cut, you have to figure out what happened. Take the time to investigate, even when the employee is caught "in the act." There is always the possibility, no matter how slim, that things are not what they appear to be. And the worker might have an explanation or reason for the misconduct

that is not immediately apparent. (See "Investigating Complaints" in Chapter 11 for more information on performing an investigation.)

- **Does the worker's personnel file support the reasons for firing?** Always review the employee's personnel file before firing. If you are considering firing for persistent problems (poor performance or attendance, for example), make sure these problems are documented in evaluations and disciplinary warnings. And make sure the file does not contradict your reason for firing: An employee fired for poor performance should not be able to point to merit increases and glowing performance reviews, for example. If you are firing for a single serious offense, the worker's file might not mention any problems. That's fine as long as there haven't been any.

- **Have we followed company policy?** If your company has written work rules or disciplinary policies, make sure they have been followed to the letter. Was the worker notified that the conduct could result in termination? Did the worker receive any warnings or opportunities to improve, if promised? Be sure to follow any unwritten policies that were communicated to employees orally or that workers have come to expect because of the company's past behavior.

- **Does the worker have a contract?** If the worker has a written employment contract, you can fire only for the reasons stated in the contract. If the worker doesn't have a written contract, consider whether a company representative made any promises or statements that the worker would be fired only for certain reasons. Also, check to see if your company's employee handbook or other written policies include promises of job security—for example, that employees will be fined only for serious misconduct or that they will receive a certain disciplinary process before being fired. If promises like these have been made, make sure you have honored them. (See "Firing Employees With Employment Contracts," above, for more information.)

- **Would firing this worker be consistent with the way the company has handled similar problems?** Think about how your company has dealt with other employees who have committed similar offenses. Have they always been fired? Or have some of them been given a second chance? If your company isn't consistent with discipline, it could be at risk for a claim of discrimination or unfair treatment.

- **Is this worker likely to sue?** Although it's always hard to predict what another person will do, you should take some time to consider whether this worker seems likely to sue. Has he or she threatened to sue, thrown legal terms around with ease, or talked about hiring a lawyer? Does the employee have a history of butting heads with people—such as neighbors or previous employers—and running to the courthouse? Will the employee have difficulty finding another job? Does the employee consistently see himself or herself as a victim? Has your company treated the employee unfairly? If your answer to any of these questions is "yes," your company might be at higher risk for a lawsuit, so handle the termination very carefully.

- **Is there an alternative to firing?** Would less extreme discipline be effective? Do you think it's likely that the employee will be able and willing to improve? If so, you might want to give the employee some time to fix things instead of firing him or her immediately. Just make sure you don't play favorites or bend the rules without a good reason. In particular, you might want to consider an alternative to termination if the worker's problems are due to difficulties outside of work, increased work responsibilities that the employee can't handle, or trouble working with a particular supervisor, or if your company has made some managerial missteps with the worker.

- **Is the firing decision impartial and fair?** Make sure your decision makes sense, is well supported, and can be defended if necessary. Ask a colleague to review your decision to make sure it is based on objective, work-related concerns and

has not been influenced by favoritism, discrimination, or other subjective factors.

- **Should we talk to a lawyer?** If it's a close call, or if the company has made some management mistakes, consider talking to a lawyer before firing the employee. For example, getting legal help is probably a good idea if the firing would dramatically change workplace demographics, if the worker recently complained of discrimination or harassment, if the worker has an employment contract that strictly limits your company's right to fire, if the worker is due to vest pension or other benefits soon, if the worker has recently revealed a disability or taken family and medical leave, or if the worker denies the acts for which you are firing him or her.

Once you have run through these questions and are satisfied with the answers, the only thing left to do is to document your decision. Write an internal memo to the worker's personnel file explaining why you have decided to fire the worker. It doesn't have to be a novel; a concise statement of your reasons for firing is enough. Describe any misconduct the worker has committed and, if the worker has had ongoing performance or other problems, the dates and details of any prior evaluations or warnings and any efforts the company has made to try to help the worker improve.

How to Fire

The 15 minutes or so you spend telling an employee that you are terminating his or her employment might be the most important in your company's relationship with that worker. And they will certainly be the most unpleasant: Surveys have shown that managers dread this aspect of their jobs more than any other.

Although you might be tempted to rush the process—a hurried review of the employee's personnel file, a quick check-in with other managers to make sure they're on board with the decision—this isn't the best approach. While you might want to get the task off your plate as soon as possible, the time you spend planning this meeting (such as where it will be held, who will break the news, and what will be said) will pay off in the long run. Prior planning helps ensure that you treat the employee with respect, provide all necessary information, and avoid doing or saying anything unnecessarily cruel or provocative, all of which will make the meeting a bit easier and help you avoid future legal trouble.

Who Should Break the News

The person who actually fires the employee should be someone with whom the worker has a positive, or at least a neutral, relationship. Don't assign someone who has clashed frequently with the worker or who is emotionally involved in the decision to fire the employee. This means the employee's supervisor may not always be the right person for the job. If you have a human resources manager, that person might be another good option.

Where and When to Hold the Meeting

There are many different theories about when an employee should be fired. Some say it's best to fire a worker early in the week, to give him or her the chance to immediately begin the job search and hook up with outplacement services. Others advise waiting until Friday, reasoning that this will give the worker a chance to exit quietly and use the weekend to let the news sink in. Unless you fear violence from a fired worker, you should do whatever feels right. (If you think an employee might get violent, it's best to break the news at the end of the day on a Friday, when fewer people are around. You should also have security present.)

Whichever day you choose, it's usually best to tell the worker earlier in the day. This will give him or her the chance to pack, tie up loose ends, and say goodbye to coworkers. However, holding the meeting first thing on Monday morning might not be the best option, especially if the worker has a long commute to work. (The employee might feel resentful for the waste of his or her time.)

Above all, respect the worker's privacy. Hold the meeting in a private, quiet place away from prying eyes. An open cubicle is a lousy spot for a termination meeting, as is a glass conference room, a lunchroom, or any other area where coworkers can see or hear what's going on. If possible, avoid holding the meeting in a location that will require the worker to make a long, embarrassing march past coworkers after the meeting is over. The best place to break the news is probably the worker's own office, if it is private. This will allow you to end the meeting when you wish (by getting up and leaving), and it will give the fired worker a chance to process the news privately before having to face coworkers.

What to Say

At the meeting, be firm but kind. Don't joke around or make pleasant small talk with the employee to put off the inevitable. It will ring hollow or, worse, seem cruel once the real purpose of the meeting becomes apparent.

Start the meeting by telling the employee that his or her employment is being terminated and why. Long explanations or justifications will only draw the worker into an argument or a plea to change your mind, so keep it brief. It can be tough to strike the right tone in giving this information: If you're too direct, you risk seeming cold. But if you sugarcoat it, the worker won't understand why he or she is being fired

and might use your sympathetic words in a lawsuit claiming that the termination wasn't justified. It's a difficult line to walk; the best you can do is to try for an honest, professional tone.

Once the deed is done, explain what will happen next and tie up loose ends. Give the worker his or her final paycheck and any accrued vacation pay (if your state or company policies require it). Although not all states require you to hand over the final paycheck at the time of termination, it's usually best to take care of this right away. (To find out your state's requirements for final paychecks, see "State Laws That Control Final Paychecks," at the end of Chapter 14.) Explain the worker's severance package, if you will offer one. (See "Severance " in Chapter 14.) Let the worker know whether you will continue to pay for benefits for any period of time, or of his or her right to continued health insurance coverage under COBRA. Explain your company's reference policy. (See "References" in Chapter 14.) This is also a good time to review any confidentiality or noncompete agreements the worker has signed, to make sure those obligations are clear. (See Chapter 10 for more information on these agreements.)

Finally, try to end the meeting on a positive note. Shake hands, wish the worker good luck, and give him or her the name of someone at the company to contact with any questions.

Company Property

Figuring out when and how to collect company property and block the employee's access to the building and computer system is a matter of judgment and tact. If you trust the employee and don't fear violence or sabotage, don't treat the employee like a criminal, especially at a time when he or she is apt to be feeling pretty low. Unless you have a good reason, you shouldn't march the worker off the premises. Give the worker time to digest the termination before you start cancelling passwords and collecting company property.

If you do fear violence, theft, or sabotage—or if the employee held a highly sensitive position in your company (such as managing your computer system)—act quickly to block the employee's access to the computer system, confidential files, trade secrets, and the building. If you can arrange it, the best time to have access blocked is while you are in the termination meeting with the employee. If you choose this route, explain it to the employee during the meeting. Offer to help the employee retrieve any personal information that might be located on your computer network or in his or her email account. After the meeting, forward the employee's incoming emails and voicemails to someone else in the company and remove the employee's name from the company's website and contact lists.

Documenting the Meeting

As soon as possible after the meeting, write down what happened. Note what you said and how the employee responded. Also keep a record of any issues left up in the air (for example, if the employee wants to negotiate a different severance package or to have the termination messaged in a certain way to others).

Checklist: Things to Do Before the Termination Meeting

- ☐ Cut a final paycheck for the employee that includes all unused accrued vacation time (if required by company policy or your state's law). Also include earned commissions.

- ☐ Issue any outstanding expense reimbursements.

- ☐ Have the employee dropped from payroll.

- ☐ Determine who else needs to know about the termination and inform them.

- ☐ Choose someone (if not you) to conduct the termination meeting.

- ☐ Choose someone to be the employee's contact after the meeting.

- ☐ Make sure that the person who conducts the meeting is familiar with the employee's work history, personnel file, and benefits status.

- ☐ Plan an exit interview, if you choose to conduct one.

- ☐ Decide whether the employee will be offered a severance package.

- ☐ Create an action plan for handing off the employee's current projects.

- ☐ Decide how the company will handle calls from prospective employers seeking a reference for the employee.

- ☐ Decide what you will tell the employee's coworkers about the termination.

- ☐ If you think the employee might turn violent, arrange for security personnel and an escort for the employee.

- ☐ Make arrangements to have the employee's computer privileges turned off.

- ☐ If the employee has an assigned parking space, remove the employee's name from the list and reassign the space.

- ☐ Cancel the employee's company credit card.

- ☐ Identify someone to handle any mail that comes in for the employee after his or her departure.

- ☐ Remove the employee's name from the company's website, email lists, and telephone rosters. Also remove the employee's name from the company's letterhead, if applicable.

Legal Dos and Don'ts: Firing Employees

Do:

- **Document everything.** We can't say it enough: You should always have a written record to back up your reasons for firing an employee. If you are firing someone for ongoing problems, the employee's personnel file should reflect that the employee has had notice of those problems and an opportunity to correct them. Nothing in the file should contradict your reasons for firing.

- **Consider your decision carefully.** It's important to think through your decision to fire. Are your reasons legitimate and documented? Are you sure you know the facts? Have you followed company policy and past practice? Is there any reason why it might make sense to talk to a lawyer? Taking the time to troubleshoot your decision now will save your company a lot of time (and money) down the road.

- **Fire only for good cause.** Although your company has the right to fire an at-will worker for any reason that is not illegal, you shouldn't exercise that right very often. If you fire only for legitimate business reasons, you give workers an incentive to perform well and follow workplace rules. And your company will gain a reputation for being fair and reasonable, which will help in recruiting new workers, retaining employees, and fending off wrongful termination lawsuits.

Don't:

- **Treat fired employees like criminals.** The way you fire someone has a big impact on whether your company will face a lawsuit over that termination. Unless you have legitimate concerns about violence, sabotage, or other extreme behavior, let workers gather their thoughts and belongings, say goodbye to coworkers, and exit your company for the last time on their own accord.

- **Take workers by surprise.** A firing should never come as a complete surprise to the employee who gets the bad news. A worker fired for cause should have been on notice that his or her actions or performance were unsatisfactory and might lead to termination.

- **Postpone the inevitable.** We know that it's difficult to fire an employee. But it's often the best thing for your company. Once an employee has proven that he or she can't meet the company's expectations or has committed serious misconduct, it's time to terminate. The longer you put it off, the more intractable the employee's problems will become.

Test Your Knowledge

Questions

1. An at-will employee can be fired for any reason. ☐ True ☐ False

2. If an employee has an employment contract, he or she can be fired only for good cause. ☐ True ☐ False

3. As long as an employee works at will, you don't need to bother reviewing the personnel file before you fire him or her. ☐ True ☐ False

4. It's a good idea to give an employee an in-depth explanation as to why he or she is being fired. ☐ True ☐ False

5. An employee's direct supervisor should always be the one to do the firing. ☐ True ☐ False

6. You should always ask security to escort someone you've fired off the premises, just in case. ☐ True ☐ False

7. You might have to pay a fired employee on the spot, rather than issuing a final paycheck on your usual payroll schedule. ☐ True ☐ False

8. As long as you have a good reason to fire an employee, it doesn't really matter how other managers handle similar problems. ☐ True ☐ False

9. An employee can have a valid legal claim for breach of contract even without a written employment agreement. ☐ True ☐ False

10. To avoid sabotage, you should always turn off an employee's access to the company's network and computer system before the termination meeting. ☐ True ☐ False

Test Your Knowledge (continued)

Answers

1. False. At-will employees cannot be fired for reasons that are illegal, such as discrimination or retaliation.

2. It depends on the contract. Many written and oral contracts (and virtually all implied contracts) require good cause for termination, but some contracts might impose different requirements. For example, a contract might say the employee can be fired only for committing a crime or for serious financial mismanagement.

3. False. A terminated employee's personnel file should support the reasons for firing. An employee who is fired for persistent performance problems or misconduct should have been on notice that the problems could lead to termination.

4. False. Although you should tell an employee why his or her employment is being terminated, you should keep it brief. Getting into the details will only encourage arguments.

5. It depends on the relationship between the employee and the supervisor. If the relationship is generally good, the supervisor should handle the firing. If there is friction, however, another manager might be better suited to the task.

6. False. Unless you have a legitimate concern about violence or sabotage, don't have the worker escorted off the premises. This only leads to bad feelings, for the employee you fired and the employees who see how you treated him or her.

7. True. This issue is governed by state law, and some states require you to give a fired employee a final paycheck right away. See "State Laws That Control Final Paychecks," at the end of Chapter 14, for information on your state's rules.

8. False. Inconsistent treatment can lead to claims of unfairness and discrimination. You should make sure that all managers at your company are handling employee problems according to the same set of rules.

9. True. The employee could have an oral contract or an implied contract (based on the company's actions or statements) that limits the company's right to fire, even if nothing was ever put in writing.

10. False. If you turn off access before the termination meeting, the employee will already know that there's a problem before you have a chance to fire him or her. If you fear sabotage, you can arrange to have access turned off while you are meeting with the employee.

Layoffs

During economic downturns, many companies have had to lay off employees to stay in business. Many more have tried to be creative in coming up with other ways to cut payroll, either in addition to or instead of layoffs. Furloughs, cuts in pay and/or hours, and trimming benefits have all become common strategies to save jobs.

Even if your company absolutely must trim its staff, that doesn't make the job of deciding whom to lay off—and actually delivering the bad news—any easier. Layoffs are very delicate, for legal and practical reasons. First and foremost, layoffs are painful, most especially for the employees who lose their jobs, but also for those who remain (and for the managers who have to carry out the decision). If your decisions don't rest on sound business reasons, your company could face lawsuits arising out of layoffs, which is exactly what you don't need when money is tight. And, layoffs that aren't handled in a professional, reassuring manner can lead to anxiety, poor morale, and high turnover among your remaining employees.

This chapter explains some of the legal rules that govern layoffs and other cost-cutting measures, as well as some practical strategies to help you keep employees on track. We cover:

- how to figure out whether layoffs are necessary
- how to handle alternatives to layoffs, such as hour or pay cuts, without violating the law

- how to decide whom to lay off
- how to conduct a layoff, and
- how to make sure your company meets its notice requirements.

Before Conducting a Layoff

When you're considering layoffs, it pays to understand the most common mistakes companies make when letting workers go and how to avoid them. Here, we cover some of the issues to think about before deciding to lay workers off. (If you aren't responsible for making layoff decisions, you can skip to the sections on how to conduct a layoff.)

If your company is faced with the tough decision of whether to lay off workers—many of whom you may like and wish you could keep—you have a lot to consider. Your company's first priority is probably turning the business around, by cutting costs to make the company more profitable. However, surveys have shown that downsizing doesn't always pay off in this way. According to the American Management Association, only a minority of companies that downsize report any increase in productivity or long-term gains in shareholder value.

Layoffs can be costly in other ways as well. Your company might have to pay for an increase in unemployment claims, for severance packages, and for outplacement services. And it will certainly risk declines in productivity and morale in the workers

Frequently Asked Questions About Layoffs

What should we consider before laying workers off?

Think carefully about whether the company really needs to lay workers off. If other, less drastic alternatives would help, start there. Make sure your company has valid, business-related reasons for the layoffs. Also consider possible constraints on your company's right to lay off workers, such as a collective bargaining agreement or employment contracts. (For more information on deciding whether to lay workers off, see "Before Conducting a Layoff," above.)

We're cutting employee hours and pay in order to save as many jobs as possible; are there any potential legal pitfalls we should be aware of?

Yes. Wage and hour laws might limit your ability to cut hours or pay, or they might restrict the ways you can implement these measures. Even though employees generally support cuts like these if they're necessary to avoid layoffs, you could still face legal problems if you aren't careful. (See "Alternatives to Layoffs," below, for more information.)

How should we choose the workers who will be laid off?

From a legal perspective, it's safest to use objective criteria: factors that can be measured and compared, such as seniority, productivity, or sales figures. If you want to use some subjective measures—like quality of work, skills, or teamwork—you must apply them consistently in evaluating workers. And, make sure your list doesn't include a disproportionately large number of workers in a protected class. (For more on deciding whom to lay off, see "Making the Cut," below.)

How should we tell our workforce about the layoffs?

Resist the temptation to just get it over with by laying workers off in a group meeting, in an email, or in a rush. Meet with each targeted employee, explain the decision, and take the time to answer questions about what will happen next. And, don't forget about the employees who haven't been laid off: You should also meet with them, once the layoffs have been carried out, to explain why cuts were made and how your company plans to move forward. (See "Conducting a Layoff," below, for more information.)

Can we wait until the last minute to tell employees about a layoff, to avoid unnecessary gossip and wasted work time?

Legally, it depends on the size of your company, how many people are losing their jobs, and why. If the layoff is subject to the Worker Adjustment Retraining and Notification (WARN) Act, you must give employees who will be laid off at least 60 days' advance notice of the layoff, with a few exceptions. Even if you aren't legally required to give this much notice, however, your plan to avoid gossip might not be furthered by laying people off suddenly. Whatever work time you save up front will probably be lost after the layoffs become public anyway. (For more information about the WARN Act and layoff notice, see "Notice Requirements for Layoffs," below.)

who remain. It might even face lawsuits, depending on how the layoffs are conducted. Given the risks, companies should carefully consider whether they really need to conduct layoffs and whether they can do so legally. Consider the following questions:

- **Are there good business reasons for the layoffs?** Before handing out pink slips, consider why a layoff is necessary. Make sure there's a legitimate business reason for the layoff, such as a decrease in sales, overstaffing, changes in the company's direction, or technological changes that render some employees obsolete. If your company has a sound justification for the layoff, workers will have a more difficult time challenging the decision in court. However, if your company has illegal motives for laying off workers—such as a desire to get rid of older workers or retaliate against union supporters—it could find itself on the receiving end of a lawsuit.

- **Will layoffs solve your company's problem?** It's worth remembering an obvious point: When you lay employees off, there are fewer employees left to do the work. Although cutting payroll costs will save you some money, that won't help much if your company can't turn a profit with the employees it has left. A company that really is supporting too many employees to do the available work can realize significant benefits from layoffs. A company

whose employees all have plenty to do might be better served by looking at ways to make more money rather than to cut costs. For example, the company might want to focus its energy and resources on the most profitable areas of the business for now, leaving more speculative or long-term growth possibilities for better days.

- **Are there alternatives to layoffs?** Think about whether your company can achieve its cost-cutting goals with less drastic measures. Some alternatives might include a freeze on hiring, promotions, or pay raises; cutting back on budgets for things like continuing education, travel, or entertainment; or a freeze on filling positions left vacant when employees leave voluntarily. You might also consider cutting pay, asking employees to take time off, or reducing authorized overtime. (For more information on all of these options, see "Alternatives to Layoffs," below.) Finally, some employers provide voluntary termination incentives to allow employees to decide whether to quit in exchange for a package of benefits. If your company considers or implements some of these alternatives before laying workers off, fewer workers will question whether the layoff was truly necessary.

- **Do the company's written personnel policies address layoffs?** Gather together your company's employee handbook, employee manual, or other written personnel policies. Do they discuss layoffs? If so, you will have to follow the company's guidelines or risk a lawsuit for breach of contract. Some company policies lay down specific rules about when and how layoffs will be conducted, give workers bumping rights (the right to take the job of a worker with less seniority rather than be laid off), or promise severance pay to laid-off workers. You'll need to factor in these limits—and the additional costs they often entail—when determining whether layoffs make economic sense.

- **Do the company's oral policies or past practices limit its ability to lay workers off?** Even if your company's written policies don't deal with layoffs, your company might have restricted its ability to lay workers off by its actions or statements. For example, if the company president has announced that no one who is performing well will be fired, the company could face legal trouble if it lays off good performers. Or, if your company has previously given severance pay to every worker fired for economic reasons, it might have to provide severance to workers who are laid off this time around.

- **Are layoff decisions limited by employment contracts?** If a worker has an employment contract, that contract might limit the company's right to fire the worker. (See "Firing Employees With Employment Contracts," in Chapter 12.) For example, a worker whose contract says that he or she can be fired only for serious misconduct cannot be laid off for economic reasons. Similarly, if a contract gives the worker bumping rights or promises severance pay if the worker is laid off, you will have to abide by that agreement.

- **Is the workplace unionized?** If so, check the collective bargaining agreement for any limitations on the company's right to lay workers off. Workers may be entitled to bumping rights, to be retained according to seniority, or to be paid severance. Also consider whether the company will have to negotiate with the union over how layoffs are conducted. (See "Collective Bargaining" in Chapter 8.)

- **Will the company offer severance or other termination benefits?** Even if severance is not legally required (see "Severance" in Chapter 14), providing it can be very beneficial. By giving laid-off workers something to tide them over until they find another job, you show them that the company values their contributions and is concerned for their welfare. This will only improve the company's standing in the eyes of the laid-off workers, the remaining workforce, and the public.

Alternatives to Layoffs

Layoffs generally come from a need to cut payroll costs. After all, payroll is often the largest single line item in a company's budget, and it's often the first place companies look when they need to save some money. However, before your company lets any workers go, it's a good idea to consider other ways to cut costs. You might be able to save enough money to avoid layoffs altogether. And, even if you still need to cut some staff, at least employees will know that layoffs were a last resort. Here are some alternatives to consider, as well as some legal restrictions on your company's ability to cut wages and hours.

Attrition and Freezes

Before you cut anything, it makes sense to consider a freeze on hiring, promotions, and raises. A freeze is one of the least cruel means of saving payroll dollars, because it doesn't take anything away from employees. Employees continue on in their same positions, at their same salaries; it's status quo for everyone.

There are a couple of drawbacks to counting on a freeze to save money. For one, it takes a while to pay off. Because your company isn't taking anything away from anyone, it won't realize any savings right away. However, if your company's budget allowed for several new hires, raises, and so on, that money will be freed up for other things (or, if your company is doing poorly, you won't have to figure out a way to come up with that money in the first place).

Also, a freeze might not be the best way to plan for your company's future. You may really need to expand in some areas of the company and contract in others, rather than simply limiting the company's overall size. Especially if you combine a freeze with an attrition program (by which employees who leave the company aren't replaced), you might not have enough people—or enough of the right people with the right skills—to keep the company moving forward.

Despite these drawbacks, however, a freeze is often a good first cost-cutting step. It should free up at least some money, and it will also lay the groundwork for further cuts, if necessary. After all, your employees won't be pleased to learn that, while they have seen their pay cut or watched colleagues lose their jobs, the company has been bringing on new workers. By putting a freeze on new hires, your company can demonstrate that it's trying to put its existing employees first.

Overtime

If employees at your company routinely work overtime, cutting back on authorized overtime hours is another good way to cut costs. But remember: Even though overtime looks like extra pay to you, it probably doesn't look that way to employees. An employee who routinely works overtime likely does so because he or she needs the money, and cutting that employee's paycheck is going to hurt, no matter how you classify the cut.

Furloughs and Hour Cuts

Many companies have resorted to reducing the number of hours employees work each week as a way to save money. Some employers (including some state and local governments) have introduced furloughs, by which employees take, for example, every other Friday off, or take off one week per month, in order to cut payroll cuts. Some companies have simply cut employee hours across the board by 10% or 20%.

If your company must actually reduce employee pay, this is the fairest way to do it. At least employees get some time off to compensate for their lost pay. But therein lies the legal rub: If you institute a cut in hours, you must make sure that you don't violate the law.

Before you cut an employee's pay or hours, be sure to check for any employment contracts that limit your ability to do so. If the employee has an agreement promising a certain rate of pay, your company will need to stick to its promise. Likewise, if your company has created policies or made statements that imply a promise not to reduce pay, you won't be able to institute salary cuts without risking a lawsuit.

You must also be careful not to violate wage and hour laws. The rules are different for nonexempt and exempt employees.

Nonexempt Employees

Nonexempt employees (those entitled to overtime) must be paid for all of the time they spend working. So, if your company institutes a furlough or hours cut, you must make sure that nonexempt employees are not actually working during this time. If they are, you will have to pay them for those hours. And, if they are working enough extra hours to merit overtime, you must pay them at the overtime rate.

To avoid this liability, your company must make very clear that it does not expect employees to work during the cut hours. This can be tricky, especially because your company probably cut hours in the first place because times are tough. But you must make sure that you don't send the message, inadvertently or otherwise, that employees who don't work the cut hours aren't "team players." Your company will probably need to adjust employee workloads to account for the reduced hours. If you expect your workers to do the same amount of work in a shorter period of time, employees might end up working "off the clock" in order to get the job done. Your company will be responsible for paying for this time (and can face penalties in a wage claim or lawsuit).

Some lawyers advise companies to take steps to make it harder for employees to work remotely during cut hours, such as requiring employees to leave laptops or smartphones at work when they leave for a furlough, or disabling outside access to the company's network during the cut hours. As long as this won't hamper employees from getting their work done during the hours they are expected to work, these measures could be a sensible way to make sure that employees aren't putting in unauthorized time.

Exempt Employees

For exempt employees, the issues are a bit different. As explained in Chapter 2, exempt employees must be paid on a salary basis. This means they must be paid a set salary of at least $455 every week, no matter how much work they do. An employer may reduce an employee's salary only in limited circumstances. Improper deductions in a salaried employee's compensation can result in that employee—and all other employees in the same job classification—losing exempt status and therefore becoming eligible to earn overtime.

A furlough or hours cut—with an accompanying cut in salary—might be considered illegal pay docking, depending on how it's handled. One sure way to avoid this problem is to furlough employees for an entire week. Exempt employees are entitled to their full salary in any week in which they do any work. So, as long as you furlough them for a solid week, you may pay nothing for that week without worrying about the pay docking rule. Of course, you'll have to make sure that exempt employees do absolutely no work during that week. And, you'll have to weigh whether you can really get along without your exempt employees (who are probably your most senior staff) for an entire week.

There's more risk involved in a shorter furlough (for example, every other Friday off) or hours cut (such as half a day off each week). However, the DOL has said that a reduced workweek and accompanying pay cut does not violate the salary basis test as long as all the following are true:

- The exempt employee still receives at least $455 per week.
- The pay cut is prospective (meaning applied to the future only).
- The employer has a bona fide reason for the cuts (that is, the employer isn't just trying to get around the salary basis requirement).

The cuts must also reflect the long-term needs of the business. This typically means that the cuts must be consistent and not adjusted on a day-to-day or week-to-week basis. For example, an employer may cut an exempt employee's salary from $1,000 to $900 per week, if that cut is intended to continue as long as necessary, in response to the economic downturn. But it may not cut the employee's salary to $900 one week, $800 the next, and bump it back up to $1,000 the following week, based on its day-to-day levels of business. If your company doesn't follow these rules, it can lose the exemption for these salaried employees (and all employees in the same job position). This means that your company will have to start paying these employees overtime when they work more than 40 hours per week, which could be quite often.

Pay Cuts

Some employers cut employee pay without reducing hours. There are a number of ways to do this. Some companies give everyone the same percentage wage reduction across the board; others reduce the wages of highly paid employees by a greater percentage. Sometimes, a company's top executives will also cut their own pay publicly and drastically (for example, by reducing their annual salary to one dollar), as a way both to cut costs and to demonstrate to employees that they are not suffering alone.

For exempt employees, pay cuts raise some of the same issues discussed above. For example, your company must make sure that the exempt employee's salary meets the minimum required by the exemption. The cut must also be prospective and reflect long-term business needs. In other words, there can't be daily, weekly, or monthly "adjustments" based on cash flow or available work.

For nonexempt employees, you don't need to worry about the salary basis test. However, you must make sure that employees are still receiving at least the minimum wage after the cut. (See Chapter 2 for more on the minimum wage.)

Making the Cut

If your company decides that layoffs are necessary, you'll have to figure out who gets the axe. If the company is getting rid of an entire department or outsourcing particular work tasks, the answer will be obvious. However, if you need to make cuts across the board or simply reduce staff in some areas, there will be some tough decisions to make.

Ultimately, whom you lay off should depend on your company's needs and projected future: What is your strategic plan,

and what kinds of employees will you need to get there? It's also a very good idea to have a lawyer review your layoff plan before you actually start breaking the news, to make sure the layoffs are fair and legally defensible. Here are some tips that will help you come up with your initial plan:

- **Decide what the company will need going forward.** Before deciding whom to cut, the company will need to think about its future direction. Is the company shrinking in some areas? Expanding in others? Is the corporate focus shifting? What are the essential positions that must be filled for this plan to succeed? The decision makers should meet to hash out these issues.

- **Figure out which departments or positions will be cut.** Now that you know your company's goals, you will be able to figure out which areas need to be scaled back. For example, if the company is cutting back on direct sales to focus more attention on research and development, the sales department can be safely targeted for cuts. At this point, you should be focusing on jobs and positions, not on individual workers. At the end of this step, you should have a sense of which departments will face cuts and how many workers will have to be laid off.

- **Establish the criteria for layoff decisions.** Once you have a sense of what skills the company will need going forward,

The Reasonable Factor Other Than Age (RFOA) Defense

As explained in Chapter 3, an employer whose facially neutral policies or practices have a disproportionately negative effect on a protected class could face a disparate impact discrimination lawsuit. In age discrimination cases, these claims often involve layoffs. An employer can defend itself by proving that its decision was based on a "reasonable factor other than age" (RFOA).

To prove an RFOA, the employer must show both that the employment practice it used was reasonably designed to achieve a legitimate business purpose, and it was applied in a way that reasonably achieves that purpose. In other words, an employer won't succeed in arguing that it made layoff decisions based on performance evaluations if some younger employees with poor evaluations were kept, while some older employees with stellar records were laid off. Similarly, an employer that claims it is trying to save money by laying off its most senior workers (with the largest salaries) will lose if employees can show that some older workers who were recent hires were let go.

When evaluating an RFOA defense, a court will consider all of the relevant facts and circumstances, including:

- **The factor's relationship to the employer's stated business purpose.** An employer that claims it laid off older workers in order to save money won't fare well in court if the employer is now paying more to outsource that work.
- **The extent to which the employer defined the factor accurately and applied it fairly,** including whether managers received training in how to apply the factor in making layoff decisions and how to avoid discrimination.

For example, if an employer's stated criterion for layoffs was technical expertise, it would need to define this term. It might also need to explain to managers that they shouldn't use age as a proxy for technological savvy.

- **Whether (and how much) the employer limited supervisors' discretion to evaluate employees subjectively,** particularly if the factor is known to be subject to negative stereotypes based on age. For instance, suppose that a company decides to save money by laying off some manufacturing employees and cross-training the rest tells managers to retain employees who are "flexible" and "willing to learn new things." The problem is that these qualities are often used as euphemisms for youth. The company should instead explain what managers should look for, such as "willingness to complete a two-month training," or "demonstrated facility with BuildIt software."
- **Whether the employer assessed the adverse impact of its practice on older employees.** An employer should at least consider how the criteria will affect older workers.
- **How much the practice harmed older workers (in severity and number) and whether the employer took steps to reduce that harm,** given the burden involved in taking such steps. If the employer's criteria result in laying off a group of employees who are all over 60 years old, for example, that indicates a serious problem, particularly if remaining workers are significantly younger.

you can decide how to select workers for layoff. The safest course, legally, is to use objective criteria, like seniority, productivity, sales numbers, client base, and so on. After all, it's hard to argue with numbers that can be double-checked and agreed upon. However, many companies also prefer to consider subjective criteria, such as quality of work, skills, ability to supervise, willingness to learn new tasks, communication, leadership skills, or team spirit. If you decide to consider subjective qualities, make sure everyone applies these criteria consistently.

- **Make a list.** After the criteria are set, apply them to the workers in the targeted departments to come up with an initial layoff list. Some companies choose to rank or rate their workers according to how well they meet the criteria and then weed out those with the lowest scores.
- **Check it twice.** Once the initial list is finished, look it over for potential problems. Consider the demographics of the workforce before the layoff and after. If you lay off the workers on your list, will the company be getting rid of a disproportionate number of women or older workers? If so, the company could face a discrimination lawsuit. (See Chapter 3 for more information about discrimination claims.)
- **Keep enough people to do the work.** Make sure the workers who are left will be able to do the work that remains, and don't get rid of anyone who is essential to the business. Even after the layoffs, the company still has to function. Workers who remain will quickly begin searching for new jobs if they are asked to do twice as much work to make up the shortfall. If the company makes drastic reductions in its workforce, you will also have to adjust the workload you expect the remaining workers to handle.

Conducting a Layoff

Layoffs are stressful for everyone. The workers whose jobs are cut will face unemployment, job searches, money worries, and possibly worse. The workers who remain will feel uncertain about their future with the company. And the managers who have to break the news will have to be the bad guys.

There is nothing you can do to make layoffs pleasant for everyone; it's an undeniably bad situation for the entire company. But you can take a few steps to make sure that layoffs are handled respectfully, with full recognition of workers' concerns and contributions to the company.

Before Announcing the Layoffs

Realistically, by the time the pink slips get passed around, most of the workforce will know that layoffs are coming. Why? Because layoffs are an open secret. Workers will likely have some inkling of the reasons

Lessons From the Real World

Schott North America made a decision to change its business operations in the United States. Previously, the company had produced optical glass (typically used in military, medical, aerospace, and other highly technical fields) and ophthalmic glass (used in ordinary eyeglasses). It decided to move all of its ophthalmic glass production to a plant in Germany and to reorganize its U.S. plant to produce only optical glass.

At the time, the company's production process required two types of workers: workers on the "hot end," who were mostly male, and workers on the "cold end," who were mostly female. Instead of laying off all of the employees in the ophthalmic glass production line, the company decided to create a new position for the optical glass line that monitored both the "hot" and "cold" ends. The company chose the employees for the position by coming up with a list of required job skills, asking managers to assign those skills a relative weight in terms of their importance to the job, and then grading each employee for each skill. The top 40 employees were offered a position; the rest lost their jobs either through layoff or voluntary resignation.

A group of women sued the company, claiming that the layoff was discriminatory because many more men than women were offered positions. The company tried to have the lawsuit thrown out, arguing that it made its layoff decisions based on legitimate criteria.

The former employees argued that the plant had been highly segregated by gender before the reorganization, and that sex discrimination against women had been rampant. They also argued that the rating system for determining who would get the new jobs unfairly gave more weight to the skills associated with positions largely held by men, and it didn't accurately measure the skills necessary for the new position. They also claimed that managers ranked individual employees unfairly, based on gender. Because the former employees presented evidence supporting each of these arguments, the court allowed the case to continue to trial.

EEOC v. Schott North America, Inc., No. 06CV1246, 2009 WL 310897 (M.D. Pa. Feb, 5, 2009).

for the layoff, whether job cuts are required by declining profits, changes in the marketplace, or the elimination of a product line. Savvy employees might have noticed the closed-door management meetings, the human resources department working overtime, or the stress on the faces of their supervisors.

Because news of layoffs often leaks out, some experts advise employers to take the initiative by announcing that reductions might be necessary, even before layoff plans are finalized. If your company chooses to go this route, a company officer or manager should gather employees together and let them know that the company is considering job cuts. Explain why the cuts are necessary, when decisions will be made, and how the layoffs will be handled (for example, whether severance will be offered, whether employees will be given incentives to quit, and so on). And be sure to address any actions the company is taking to try to tighten its belt; workers are more likely to cooperate in cost-cutting efforts if they know that layoffs could be next.

Of course, other experts advise employers to keep their lips sealed until all of the layoff plans have been hammered out. The aim of this approach is to keep things confidential for as long as possible and prevent good workers from leaving like rats fleeing a sinking ship.

If you're in on this decision, you'll have to consider what makes sense for your company. Consider how many people will be involved in the layoff planning, how likely it is that others will find out about the layoffs, and how the company has handled communications with employees in the past. Also, consider your company's philosophy on worker involvement. If it places a high value on open communication and group decision making, keeping layoffs a secret might do serious damage to the company's credibility with its workers.

Breaking the News to Laid-Off Workers

We have all heard layoff horror stories: groups of employees herded into conference rooms to be canned en masse, workers fired by email, staff marched out of the office by armed security guards, and so on. Each of these actions illustrates a callous disrespect for employees and their contributions to the company. And employers reap the negative consequences, by creating legions of disgruntled ex-employees whose righteous anger at the way they were treated fuels their march to a lawyer's office.

The lesson to be learned from these fiascoes is clear: Be respectful when you lay workers off. Remember that they have made valuable contributions to the company, often for many years, and are suffering a significant loss. Here are a few tips to help you keep things positive:

- **Involve the top brass.** Layoffs are a major event and should be handled by top company executives. Employees might not expect every layoff to be conducted personally by the CEO, but higher-ups should show their faces at meetings and make sure laid-off employees don't feel unimportant or ignored.

- **Give advance notice.** A federal law called the Workers Adjustment and Retraining Notification Act (WARN) requires employers with 100 or more employees to give workers 60 days' notice before a plant closing or mass layoff. (To learn more, see "Notice Requirements for Layoffs," below.) Many states have similar laws; see "State Layoff and Plant-Closing Laws," at the end of this chapter.

- **Don't lay off workers in a group.** Whenever possible, take the time to inform workers individually that they will be laid off. Hold the meeting confidentially and allow enough time to answer the worker's questions and give any necessary information. Don't rush through the meeting or make the worker feel like one stop on the layoff express.

- **Timing is everything.** Don't let laid off workers be the last to know that they're losing their jobs. They deserve to learn the news from their managers, before the rest of the workforce. At the same time, don't wait too long to tell the rest of the company: It isn't a good idea for everyone else to learn of a layoff from a former coworker's "keep in touch" email or from a hallway parade of departing employees carrying cardboard boxes. Experts advise breaking the news to the company while employees are being laid off, or very shortly thereafter.

- **Explain the decision.** Tell the worker why layoffs are necessary and why he or she was chosen to be laid off. Also discuss whether the worker will be eligible for recall or will have any bumping rights to take the position of less senior workers.

- **Be gracious.** A layoff hits workers who have done a good job for the company. Be sure to express your gratitude for the worker's contributions and your sympathy about the termination.

- **Discuss what will happen next.** If the company will offer severance, explain the package. Tell the worker when his or her last day will be and what will happen in the meantime. And give the worker the name of someone in the company to contact with questions.

Handling Security Concerns

One reason why some companies treat laid-off workers disrespectfully is that they fear violence or sabotage. And these are legitimate concerns: In 2014, the FBI announced that computer sabotage by disgruntled former employees was on the rise, costing businesses between $5,000 and $3 million in damages.

So how can you protect your company without treating workers like criminals? First, bring in security personnel only if you legitimately fear violence. If workers are resentful or have made threats, or if the situation seems particularly volatile, consider having extra security on hand for the layoffs. But don't ask them to guard the doors, escort workers out, or use any strong-arm tactics unless things really get out of hand.

Protect your company's computer system by turning off employee email and disabling passwords. The best time to do this is during the layoff meeting itself. Do it too early and the employee will be left wondering what's going on; do it too late and you leave yourself open to sabotage. Also, make sure to collect company property—keys, credit cards, cell phones, laptop computers, and so on—on the worker's last day. And once the layoffs are through, most companies take the extra step of changing locks and security codes.

Lessons From the Real World

According to *The New York Times*, one company's layoff practices might have cost it millions of dollars in damage to its computer system.

The employer, a chemical company in New Jersey, laid off 50 people in February 2001. One of the unfortunate pink slip recipients was the company's manager of information management systems, who had the inside scoop on the company's computer network. After he was fired, he used another executive's password to tap into the computer system and delete important inventory and personnel files, costing the company $20 million in damages and postponing a public stock offering indefinitely.

Why did he resort to sabotage? In a not-so-anonymous letter he wrote to the company president, he gave some clues about the source of his anger: "I have been loyal to the company in good and bad times for over 30 years. ... I was expecting a member of top management to come down from his ivory tower to face us with the layoff announcement, rather than sending the kitchen supervisor with guards to escort us off the premises like criminals. You will pay for your senseless behavior."

Eve Tahmincioglu, "Electronic Workplace Vulnerable to Revenge," *The New York Times*, Aug. 6, 2001.

Dealing With the Rest of the Workforce

No one would dispute that the workers hit hardest by a layoff are those who lose their jobs. But a layoff is no picnic for the workers who avoid the axe either. They are likely to feel wary about their employment prospects and quite possibly resentful of the company for firing their coworkers. At the same time, they will likely be expected to work harder, take on new responsibilities, and pick up the work done by their former coworkers. It's no wonder that studies have shown employee turnover rises significantly after a layoff.

To ease the burden and reassure the employees who remain, you can:

- **Provide training.** Unless your company is eliminating an entire product line or company service, the work that used to be done by the laid-off workers still has to get done. This means that remaining employees might have to take on new jobs or added responsibilities. Consider providing some job training to these employees, so they will have an opportunity to learn their new roles. Training can reduce the frustration and anxiety employees feel after a layoff. It can also keep the business running more smoothly.

- **Be communicative.** After a layoff, employees are going to be worried about the future of the company and the security of their jobs. Especially if your company had to lay workers off because it isn't doing well financially, make an effort to let employees know how the company plans to turn things around. Check in frequently to tell employees about the company's progress toward its goals. The more you can keep employees in the loop, the more likely you will be able to hold on to your most valued workers.

- **Prevent burnout.** Employees burn out when they are asked to do more work than they can handle. Remember, if the company is getting rid of a significant number of employees, it is not enough simply to cut those jobs. You must also adjust the workload required of the new, streamlined workforce. If you expect remaining employees to simply pick up the slack and do all the work that used to be done by a much larger group, those employees will quickly move on to greener pastures.

- **Retain the employees you keep.** One unfortunate consequence of a layoff is that your company might lose the employees it chooses not to lay off. After all, the best of these employees are likely to be able to find work elsewhere and might not want to stick around to see how things shake out after the layoffs. To keep these employees, reward good performance. Recognize employees who do well with positive performance evaluations and promotions, even if you can't afford any raises right now.

- **Boost morale.** After a layoff, workers will likely have questions and concerns. You and other managers should be available to provide answers, including the reasons for the layoff. While you should not make promises that the company

can't keep, you can tell workers about the company's future plans and expectations. Assure workers that you value their contributions and appreciate them staying on in this difficult time.

- **Share the pain.** If your company laid off workers to save money and increase profitability, the yearly management team retreat to Aspen isn't going to go over well with the remaining workforce. Employees want the company to turn around financially, but they also want to know that management- and executive-level employees are in the same boat and feel their pain. Now is not the time to order fancy new office furniture or throw a big expensive party.

Notice Requirements for Layoffs

The Worker Adjustment and Retraining Notification (WARN) Act requires larger employers to give some advance notice of an impending plant closing or mass layoff that will result in job losses for a large number of employees. The law was passed to help ease the transition for workers who lose their jobs in these circumstances. The WARN Act requires employers to give notice not only to the employees and unions that will be affected by the job cuts, but also to state government agencies that provide assistance to dislocated workers.

Many states have similar laws. See the "State Layoff and Plant-Closing Laws" chart at the end of this chapter for more information.

WARN Act Coverage

The WARN Act doesn't apply to every employer, every employee, or even every layoff. Only large private employers must comply with the WARN Act, and only then if they engage in a plant closing or mass layoff.

Which Employers Are Covered

Federal, state, and local governments are not covered by the WARN Act. Private employers are covered if they have either:

- 100 or more full-time employees, not counting employees who work less than 20 hours per week or who have been employed for less than six months before the date when notice would be required under the WARN Act, or
- 100 or more employees (including part-time employees and employees who have been employed for less than six months) who work a combined total of at least 4,000 hours per week.

Independent contractors don't count toward the total. However, employees who are on temporary layoff or leave must be counted, if they have a reasonable expectation of being recalled or otherwise returning to work. For example, an employee who is on FMLA leave should be counted because he or she is entitled to reinstatement after the leave is over. (See Chapter 5 for more on the FMLA).

Lessons From the Real World

After the attacks of September 11, 2001, Congress transferred responsibility for airport security to the federal government. This change meant that many passenger screeners and other security employees who worked for private employers lost their jobs (although some were rehired by the federal agency in charge of airport security).

A group of security employees who were laid off by a company that provided security at San Jose International Airport sued their employers, claiming that they should have received 60 days' notice under the WARN Act. The Ninth Circuit Court of Appeals disagreed, however. The Court found that the WARN Act applies only when an employer orders a layoff or plant closing. Because the layoffs at the airport were due to government action rather than an employer order, the WARN Act didn't apply and the employees were not entitled to notice.

Deveraturda v. Globe Aviation Security Services, 454 F.3d 1043 (9th Cir. 2006).

Which Employees Are Covered

All employees who may reasonably be expected to lose their jobs, or to have their hours cut by more than 50%, for six consecutive months due to a covered layoff are entitled to notice under the WARN Act. Part-time employees are entitled to notice, even though they are not necessarily counted in determining whether the WARN Act applies.

Independent contractors are not covered by WARN and are not entitled to notice.

Which Layoffs Are Covered

Not every reduction in force by a covered employer triggers the WARN Act's notice requirements. An employer must comply with the WARN Act only if it plans to conduct a:

- **Plant closing:** the permanent or temporary shutdown of a single employment site or one or more facilities or operating units within a single employment site, which results in job loss for 50 or more employees (not including part-time employees) during a 30-day period

- **Mass layoff:** a reduction in force that results in job loss at a single employment site, during a 30-day period, for (1) 500 or more employees (excluding part-time employees), or (2) 50 to 499 employees (excluding part-time employees) if the laid off employees make up at least 1/3 of the employer's active workforce, or

- **Staged plant closing or mass layoff:** a plant closing or mass layoff, as defined above, that occurs in stages over a 90-day period. This rule is intended to prevent employers from getting around the WARN Act's requirements by conducting a series of smaller layoffs.

Under the act, a reduction in hours of more than 50% qualifies as a job loss.

Required Notice

If a layoff is covered by the WARN Act, the employer must give written notice of the layoff at least 60 days in advance. The notice must be provided to:

- each employee who will be affected (except those in a union)
- the bargaining representative(s) of all union members who will be affected
- the state's dislocated worker unit (sometimes called the rapid response coordinator), and
- the local government in the area where the layoff will occur (for example, the mayor).

The contents of the notice depend on the recipient. For example, employees who are not in a union must be told whether the planned action is expected to be temporary or permanent; whether an entire plant will be closed; the date when the layoff or closure is expected to begin; the date when the employee will be terminated; whether the employee will have bumping rights; and the name and phone number of a company official the employee can call for more information. (For detailed information on the WARN Act, including the contents of the notice required to each recipient, check out the resources at the Department of Labor's WARN Act page, www.doleta.gov/layoff/warn.cfm.)

The notice must be based on the best available information when it is given. If that information later proves to be wrong because of subsequent changes in events or inadvertent errors, the employer will not be liable.

Employers that don't provide the required notice can be required to pay each employee up to 60 days of compensation and benefits, pay a fine of up to $500 for each day of violation, and pay attorneys' fees and court costs of workers who sue the employer successfully for violating the law.

Exceptions

In some circumstances, an employer does not have to give notice, or may give notice less than 60 days before a covered layoff.

No Notice Required

The WARN Act doesn't apply—and therefore, an employer need not give any advance notice of a layoff—in the following circumstances:

- **Temporary facilities or projects.** If an employer closes a facility that was intended to be open only temporarily or lays off workers who were hired only for a specific project, no notice is required. However, this exception applies only if the laid-off workers understood when they were hired that their employment was limited to the duration of the facility or project.

- **Strikes and lockouts.** If a layoff results from a union strike or an employer lockout, no notice is required.

Notice of Less Than 60 Days Allowed

If one of the following exceptions applies, the employer must give as much notice as possible and must explain in the written notice why it couldn't give the 60 days' notice that would otherwise be required:

- **Natural disasters.** If an earthquake, flood, or other natural disaster forces a layoff, an employer may give less than 60 days' notice.

- **Unforeseeable business circumstances.** If the layoff is caused by business circumstances that were not reasonably foreseeable 60 days in advance (for example, a major client suddenly cancelling its business), a shorter notice period is allowed.

- **Faltering company.** If a company is struggling financially and trying to avoid a plant closing, it can give a shorter period of notice. However, the company must show that it was actively seeking business or money that would have allowed it to avoid or postpone the closing, and that it reasonably believed, in good faith, that providing the 60 days' notice would have precluded it from obtaining the necessary business or money. This exception does not apply to mass layoffs.

Lessons From the Real World

A group of laid-off employees sued Hale-Halsell Co. ("HHC"), a grocery distribution and warehouse center, for failing to give 60 days' notice as required by the WARN Act. HHC argued that it couldn't give notice because the layoffs occurred unexpectedly, after it lost a key account on top of other economic problems, and it was therefore covered by the unforeseeable business circumstances exception to the WARN Act.

The employees argued that they should have received notice because it was foreseeable that the company would lose the account. There had been problems brewing with the account for more than a year, which had resulted in declining orders from the customer and numerous discussions about the problem.

However, the court found in favor of HHC. Although the problems in the relationship were evident, the loss of the account was not a reasonably foreseeable event "Free enterprise always involves risk ... [b]usiness downturns in a cyclical economy are not unusual, and we should not burden employers with the task of notifying employees of possible contract cancellation and concomitant layoffs every time there is a cost overrun or similar difficulty" (internal quotations omitted).

Gros v. Hale-Halsell Co., 554 F.3d 870 (10th Cir. 2009).

Legal Dos and Don'ts: Layoffs

Do:

- **Plan layoffs carefully.** Surveys have shown that layoffs often cost more than they are worth. Companies might cut too deep, lose critical performers to post-layoff attrition, or have to hire contract workers to pick up the slack. And layoffs are fraught with potential danger, including lawsuits. Savvy managers should think long and hard before undertaking layoffs and make sure the layoff plan is legally and practically sound.

- **Research notice requirements.** Companies that are struggling and laying off workers piecemeal must be especially careful: A series of smaller layoffs can turn into a "staged" layoff that's covered by the WARN Act. And don't forget to research state law, which might impose additional requirements.

- **Overcommunicate with workers who remain.** If you want to hang on to your best employees, you must give them reasons to stay. Attrition is often high after a layoff because employees are worried about the company's future. Keeping workers in the loop is a good way to quell this anxiety. Tell workers how the company plans to turn things around, mention deadlines by which you expect to see progress, and discuss milestones that will indicate better prospects for the future. Even if your company already holds regular quarterly or annual meetings, it's a good idea to meet more frequently and explain how things are going.

Don't:

- **Disrespect workers on the way out the door.** The way in which you lay off workers is hugely important for many reasons. Remaining workers will judge you and the company by these actions. And your actions will play a major role in determining whether the worker decides to sue over the layoff.

- **Start with layoffs.** Before anyone loses a job, your company should already have tried some less drastic measures, such as a hiring or promotion freeze, cutting back on overtime, or even pay or hours cuts. Workers should see that the company is tightening its belt. If layoffs become necessary, employees will know that they were a last resort.

- **Go it alone.** Pay and hour cuts can lead to potential wage and hour problems, and layoffs can lead straight to the courthouse. If you have any concerns or questions about your plans to cut costs, consult with an employment attorney.

Test Your Knowledge

Questions

1. A company is free to cut hours, cut pay, or furlough employees, as long as employees agree to it as a way to save jobs. ☐ True ☐ False

2. You should keep your layoff plans secret for as long as possible, to make sure you don't lose employees you wanted to keep. ☐ True ☐ False

3. Layoffs provide a good cover for getting rid of employees with performance, attendance, or conduct problems. ☐ True ☐ False

4. As long as you tell employees that their hours have been cut, it's okay for some employees to keep putting in a full week; after all, the company needs all the help it can get. ☐ True ☐ False

5. Employees should be laid off in a group meeting, to make sure everyone gets the same information. ☐ True ☐ False

6. Layoffs are a great way to increase profit. ☐ True ☐ False

7. Companies should decide which departments or positions will be cut before deciding which particular employees will be laid off. ☐ True ☐ False

8. Companies should try to use objective criteria when deciding who will be laid off. ☐ True ☐ False

9. Workers are generally entitled to at least 60 days' advance notice of a layoff. ☐ True ☐ False

10. Before laying workers off, a company should try to cut costs in other ways. ☐ True ☐ False

Test Your Knowledge (continued)

Answers

1. Not necessarily. Cutting pay, hours, or both, can lead to wage and hour violations, even if employees are fully on board. Before resorting to these cost-cutting measures, companies should consult with a lawyer.

2. It depends. Your company might have an obligation to tell employees of an impending layoff under the WARN Act. Even if it doesn't, employees may learn that layoffs are brewing. Rather than keeping it a secret, some companies choose to be more open about the possibility of layoffs, so that employees know how serious the situation is and are more willing to cut costs in other ways.

3. False. Your company's business needs and future goals should shape your layoff criteria (which departments will have to be cut and by how many people). Although you can consider performance and other issues in deciding who is laid off, you shouldn't try to shoehorn problem employees on to the layoff list if they wouldn't be there otherwise. This could cause them to doubt the reasons you give for firing them, which can lead to a lawsuit. It could also lead other employees to question whether layoffs are really necessary, or if your company is just using them to "clean house."

4. False. Your company must pay nonexempt employees for every hour they work, even if you have told them not to work that time.

5. False. Although you might hold a group follow-up meeting to explain severance, continuing benefits, and so on, the initial layoff should be conducted individually and in person.

6. False. Studies show that most companies that downsize don't realize any increases in productivity or long-term gains in shareholder value. Also, the company will be losing workers in a layoff, so to realize a net gain, the savings will have to make up for the lost productivity, sales, and/or other contributions of those workers.

7. True. A layoff should target the company's problem areas, not its problem employees. If the company is using layoffs as a way to get rid of certain workers, it might face a lawsuit claiming that the layoff was just an excuse for an illegal firing.

8. True. Although companies are allowed to consider subjective factors when deciding whom to lay off, the safest plan is to use objective criteria. This will make it harder for workers to argue that they were improperly targeted for layoffs.

9. False. Workers are not entitled to advance notice of a layoff unless the WARN Act applies. The act applies only to plant closings and mass layoffs by large employers.

10. True. Workers are more likely to accept layoffs if they believe that the company is really trying to reduce expenses and that layoffs were a last resort.

State Layoff and Plant-Closing Laws

California
Cal. Labor Code §§ 1400 to 1408

Covered employers: Industrial or commercial facility that employs at least 75 employees.

When law applies: Mass layoff (of at least 50 employees); relocation 100 or more miles away; or closing of industrial or commercial facility with at least 75 employees.

Notification requirements: Employer must give at least 60 days' advance notice, in writing, before mass layoff, relocation, or closing of facility. Notice must include the elements required by the federal WARN Act and must be provided to affected employees, Employment Development Department, local workforce investment board, and chief elected official of each city or county where job losses occur. Employer that fails to give notice to employees is liable for back pay and benefits for the period of the violation, up to 60 days or one-half the length of the employee's tenure with the company, whichever is shorter.

Exceptions: Notice not required if job loss due to physical calamity or act of war; or if employer was actively seeking capital that would have avoided or postponed job losses when notice should have been given.

Connecticut
Conn. Gen. Stat. Ann. §§ 31-51n, 31-51o

Covered employers: Industrial, commercial, or business facility with 100 or more employees at any time during the last 12 months.

When law applies: Permanent shutdown of facility or relocation of facility out of state.

Severance requirements: Employer must pay for existing group health insurance coverage for terminated employee and dependents for 120 days or until employee is eligible for other group coverage, whichever comes first.

Exceptions: Notice not required if facility closure is due to bankruptcy or natural disaster.

District of Columbia
D.C. Code Ann. §§ 21-101 to 32-103

Covered employers: Contractors and subcontractors who employ 25 or more nonprofessionals as food service, health service, security, janitorial, or building maintenance workers.

When law applies: When a new contractor takes over a service contract.

Severance requirements: Within 10 days after new contract is awarded, previous contractor must give new contractor names of all employees. New contractor must retain all employees who have worked for the past 8 months for a 90-day transition period. If fewer employees are needed, the new contractor must retain by seniority within job classifications; otherwise, employees may not be fired without cause during the transition period. After transition period ends, new contractor must give written performance evaluations and retain all employees with satisfactory performance. Contractor whose contract is not renewed and is awarded a similar contract within 30 days must hire at least half of the employees from the former site(s).

Hawaii
Haw. Rev. Stat. §§ 394B-1 to 394B-13

Covered employers: Industrial, commercial, or other business entity with at least 50 employees at any time during the last 12 months.

When law applies: Permanent or partial closing of business; relocation of all or substantial portion of business operations out of state.

Severance requirements: Employer must pay dislocated worker allowance for 4 weeks to supplement unemployment compensation; amount is the difference between the employee's former weekly wage

State Layoff and Plant-Closing Laws (continued)

and the employee's weekly unemployment benefit. Employer who does not pay severance is liable to each employee for 3 months of compensation.

Notification requirements: Employer must give notice to employees 60 days in advance of closing or relocation. Employer who fails to provide notice is liable to each employee for back pay and benefits for the period of the violation, up to 60 days.

Illinois
820 Ill. Comp. Stat 65/1 to 65/55

Covered employers: Any business enterprise that employs at least 75 full-time employees or at least 75 employees who work an aggregate of 4,000 hours a week (not including overtime).

When law applies: Mass layoff (of at least 250 employees or at least 25 employees who make up 33% or more of the workforce); relocation; or plant closing (shutdown of a site or operating unit resulting in job loss for at least 50 full-time employees).

Notification requirements: Employer must give at least 60 days' written notice to affected employees, their representatives, the Department of Commerce & Economic Opportunity, and the chief elected official of each municipal and county government where job losses occur. Employer that doesn't give notice is liable for back pay and benefits for the period of the violation, up to 60 days or one-half the length of the employee's tenure with the company, whichever is shorter.

Exceptions: Notice not required if job loss due to completion of temporary project or closure of temporary facility; unforeseen circumstances; strike or lockout; physical calamity or war; or if employer was seeking capital in good faith that would have avoided or postponed job losses when notice should have been given.

Iowa
Iowa Code §§ 84C.1 to 84C.4

Covered employers: Employers with at least 25 full-time employees.

When law applies: Business closing (permanent or temporary shutdown) or mass layoff that will affect 25 or more full-time employees.

Notification requirements: Employer must give 30 days' notice or amount of notice required by collective bargaining agreement. Employer may pay wages in lieu of notice.

Exceptions: Notice not required if job loss due to strike or lockout; unforeseeable business circumstances; or natural disaster; or if employer was seeking capital in good faith that would have avoided or postponed job loss when notice should have been given.

Maine
Me. Rev. Stat. Ann. tit. 26, § 625-B

Covered employers: Employers with at least 100 employees at any time during the last 12 months.

When law applies: Closing, discontinuation or relocation of business operations at least 100 miles distant; mass layoff (job loss for at least 500 employees or at least 50 employees, if they represent at least 33% of the workforce).

Severance requirements: Employer must give one week of severance pay for each year of employment and partial pay for any partial year of employment to all employees who have worked for at least 3 years.

Notification requirements: Employer must give employees at least 60 days' notice, in writing, before relocating or closing. Employer must also notify the director of the Bureau of Labor Standards and municipal officials where plant is located. Employers initiating mass layoffs must report to the director,

State Layoff and Plant-Closing Laws (continued)

within 7 days, the expected duration of the layoff, and whether the layoff is definite or indefinite.

Exceptions: No fine for failure to give notice if closing is due to physical calamity or final order by the government, or if unforeseen circumstances prevent giving notice.

Maryland
Md. Code Ann. [Lab. & Empl.] §§ 11-301 to 11-304; Md. Code Regs. tit. 9 § 09.33.02.04

Covered employers: Employers with at least 50 employees that have been in business for at least one year.

When law applies: Shutdown of workplace or portion of operations resulting in layoffs of at least 25% of the workforce or 15 employees, whichever is greater, over any 3-month period.

Severance requirements: Employers are encouraged to follow Department of Labor voluntary guidelines for severance pay, continuation of benefits, and notification.

Notification requirements: Employers should provide 90 days' notice whenever possible.

Exceptions: Notice not required if job loss is due to bankruptcy; seasonal factors common to industry; labor disputes; or the closure of a construction site or temporary workplace.

New Hampshire
N.H. Rev. Stat. Ann. §§ 275-F:1 to 275-F:12

Covered employers: Employers with at least 100 full-time employees or at least 100 employees who work a total of at least 3,000 hours per week.

When law applies: Plant closing (shutdown of a single employment site, facility, or operating unit resulting in job loss for at least 50 full-time employees); mass layoff (job loss for at least 250

full-time employees or at least 25 employees, if they represent at least 33% of the workforce).

Notification requirements: Employer must give 60 days' notice of plant closing or mass layoff to affected employees, their representatives, the state labor commissioner and attorney general, and the chief elected official of each municipality where job losses occur.

Exceptions: Notice is not required if job loss due to shutdown of a temporary facility; physical calamity; natural disaster; act of war; or strike or lockout. Notice is also not required if need for notice was not reasonably foreseeable or if the company was actively seeking capital, in good faith, that would have postponed or avoided job loss when notice should have been given.

New Jersey
N.J. Stat. Ann. 34:21-1 to 34:21-7

Covered employers: Employers that have operated a business establishment for at least 3 years.

When law applies: Mass layoff (at least 500 full-time employees or at least 50 full-time employees that represent at least one-third of the full-time employees at that establishment); termination or relocation of operations resulting in job loss for at least 50 full-time employees.

Severance requirements: Employer that does not provide at least 60 days' notice must pay laid-off full-time employees one week of severance for each year of employment.

Notification requirements: Employers with 100 or more employees must provide 60 days' notice or such notice as is required by the federal WARN Act. Notice must be given to affected employees, their collective bargaining units, the commissioner of Labor and Workforce Development, and the chief elected official of each municipality where job losses occur.

State Layoff and Plant-Closing Laws (continued)

New York

N.Y. Lab. Law 860 to 860-i

Covered employers: Employers with at least 50 employees.

When law applies:

- Plant closing: permanent or temporary shutdown of single site, facility, or operating unit that results in job loss for at least 25 full-time employees in a 30-day period.
- Mass layoff: reduction in force at a single site that results in job loss for at least 25 full-time employees representing at least 33% of the employer's workforce or at least 250 full-time employees in a 30-day period.
- Relocation: moving employer's entire operation at least 50 miles away.

Notification requirements: Employer must give notice at least 90 days before a mass layoff, plant closing, or relocation to affected employees, their representatives, the department of labor, and local workforce investment boards where job losses occur. Employer that fails to give required notice to employees is liable for back pay and lost benefits for up to 60 days.

Exceptions: Notice not required if job loss due to physical calamity or act of terrorism or war; closure of a temporary facility; natural disaster; or strike or lockout. Notice is also not required if job losses were not reasonably foreseeable or if employer was actively seeking capital that would avoid or postpone job losses when notice should have been given.

Tennessee

Tenn. Code Ann. 50-1-601 to 50-1-604

Covered employers: Employers with 50 to 99 full-time employees within the state.

When law applies: Closing, modernization, relocation, or new management policy of a workplace or portion of operations that permanently or indefinitely lays off 50 or more employees during any 3-month period.

Notification requirements: Employer must notify employees who will lose their jobs, then the commissioner of Labor and Workforce Development.

Exceptions: Notice not required if job loss due to closure of construction site; labor disputes; or seasonal factors common to industry.

Vermont

Vt. Stat. Ann Tit. 21 §§ 411 to 418

Covered employers: Employers with 50 or more full-time employees; employers with 50 or more part-time employees each working at least 1,040 hours per year; or employers with a combination of 50 or more full-time employees and part-time employees each working at least 1,040 hours per year.

When law applies: "Business closing" permanent shutdown of a facility, or cessation of operations at one or more worksites that results in the layoff of 50 or more employees over a 90-day period; or cessation of operations not scheduled to resume within 90 days that affects 50 or more employees.

Mass layoff (permanent layoff of 50 or more employees at one or more worksites in a 90-day period); Business closing (permanent shutdown of a facility, permanent cessation of operations at one or more worksites that results in layoff of 50 or more employees in a 90-day period, or the cessation of operations not scheduled to resume within 90 days that affects 50 or more employees).

Severance requirements: If employer fails to give notice, it must pay each employee up to ten days' severance pay and up to one month of continuing medical and dental coverage.

State Layoff and Plant-Closing Laws (continued)

Notification requirements: Employer must give at least 30 days' notice to affected employees, municipal government, and employees collective bargaining representatives. Employer must provide 45 days notice to the Agency of Commerce and Community Development and the Vermont Department of Labor.

Exceptions: Compliance not required: when closing or mass layoff is caused by strike or lockout, by business circumstances that were not reasonably foreseeable, by disaster beyond the control of the employer, or due to the conclusion of seasonal employment or a particular project; when affected employees were hired with the understanding that their employment was limited to the duration of the season or project; or when the employer is actively trying to secure funds to avoid a closing or mass layoff and it reasonably believes that giving notice would have precluded securing such funds.

Wisconsin

Wis. Stat. Ann. 106.15; 109.07

Covered employers: Employers with at least 50 employees in the state.

When law applies:
- Business closing: permanent or temporary shutdown of an employment site, facility, or operating unit(s) at one site or within one town that affects 25 or more full-time employees.
- Mass layoff: reduction in force that affects at least 25% or at least 25 full-time employees, whichever is greater, or at least 500 employees.

Employees include only those who have worked at least 6 of the last 12 months and work at least 20 hours a week.

Notification requirements: Employer must give at least 60 days' written notice to affected employees, their collective bargaining representatives, the Dislocated Worker Committee in the Department of Workforce Development, and the highest official in the municipality where job losses occur. Employer who fails to give required notice to employees is liable for up to 60 days of back pay and lost benefits.

Exceptions: Notice not required if job loss due to sale of company, if buyer agrees to hire affected employees with no more than 6-month break in employment; end of seasonal or temporary work; unforeseeable business circumstances; or disaster.

Departing Workers

Whether an employment relationship is good or bad, odds are it will end one day, and perhaps sooner than you think. Employment statistics show that the days of an employee staying with a company until retirement are long gone: According to a 2014 study by the U.S. Bureau of Labor Statistics, workers spend a median of 4.5 years with a company before moving on.

Observing legal rules is especially important at the end of the employment relationship. Departing workers (especially those who are leaving involuntarily) may be unhappy, angry, or dissatisfied with the way they've been treated by your company. If you show respect to departing employees, and observe all of their legal rights, you have a much better chance of averting lawsuits and other problems.

In this chapter, we look at some common issues you'll face when workers leave, paying special attention to trouble spots. Regardless of why a worker leaves—whether he or she was fired, was laid off, or quit—you'll face many of the same issues as the employment relationship wraps up. These issues include how to give references, how to extend health benefits, whether to dispute unemployment benefits, and whether to provide severance.

References

Whenever an employee leaves, your company will have to decide what to say to prospective employers that call for a reference. The decision is pretty straightforward if the employee left on good terms: You and the former employee can come up with a mutually agreeable statement to explain the departure. Or, you can simply tell the whole glowing truth to any prospective employer who calls for a reference. But if the employee was fired, or left on bad terms, you face a more difficult task.

Defamation

If you're not careful in your statements about former employees, your company might find itself facing a defamation lawsuit. And, because defamation is a personal injury claim that can be brought against individuals as well as organizations, you could even be sued personally for your comments.

To prove defamation, a former employee typically must show that company representatives intentionally damaged his or her reputation by making harmful statements about the employee that they knew or should have known to be false.

Frequently Asked Questions About Departing Workers

Do we have to give references for every worker who leaves?

No law requires employers to give a reference for a former employee, just as no law prohibits employers from telling the truth about a former employee. However, there are some steps you should take to make sure you don't create unnecessary legal problems when you provide a reference. (For more about this issue, see "References," above.)

What should we say to our remaining workers when an employee leaves?

It depends on why the employee is leaving. If the employee is separating on good terms, you can let other workers know where and when the employee is going. For employees who are fired, however, you should probably be less forthcoming. (See "What to Tell Coworkers When an Employee Leaves," below, for more information.)

Do we have to continue to pay a former employee's health insurance premiums?

No. Under federal and state health insurance continuation laws, employees have the option of continuing coverage at their own expense. Employers are not required to pay for any portion of the premium. However, some employers choose to continue paying for health insurance premiums for a period of time as part of a severance package.

Are we legally required to pay severance?

Probably not. Unless your company has promised severance, or has led employees to believe that they are entitled to severance, there is no obligation to provide it. (For more information, see "Severance," below.)

Is there anything we can do to protect the company from lawsuits by former employees?

Yes. In exchange for something of value, you can ask employees to sign a release in which they agree not to sue the company. Some companies routinely ask employees to sign a release as a condition of receiving a severance package. (For more about this, see "Releases," below.)

Are all departing workers entitled to unemployment compensation?

No. Unemployment laws vary from state to state, but in general, workers who quit voluntarily or who lose their jobs because of misconduct are not entitled to receive benefits. (For more information, see "Unemployment Benefits," below.)

At first glance, it might seem like only the most spiteful manager would get caught in this trap. But, if you make an unflattering statement that you don't absolutely know to be true, it could happen to you. Let's face it: Most reasons for firing make the employee look bad. And managers often cannot prove what they strongly believe to be true: that an employee is stealing from the company, is incompetent, or lied about job qualifications, for example. A manager who makes such statements about a former employee could get into trouble. Your best policy is to say as little as possible and stick to facts you can prove.

Rules for Giving References

When a potential employer calls for a reference, you may feel trapped between wanting to tell the truth and fearing a lawsuit if you say anything unflattering. Unfortunately, this fear is not unfounded. Plenty of defamation lawsuits have been filed over negative references. And, even if a former employee can't successfully prove that you defamed him or her, your company (and possibly you) will have to spend precious time and money fighting the allegation.

Here are some tips to help you avoid problems:

- **Warn a difficult employee that your reference won't be good.** Yes, the employee should know this already. But you can avoid problems at the outset by stating the obvious: "I cannot provide a positive reference for you." Smart employees will leave your company off their reference lists.

- **Keep it brief.** Some companies adopt a policy of only giving out dates of employment, job title, and final salary to prospective employers. If your company chooses to tell more, keep it to a minimum.

- **Stick to the facts.** Now is not the time to speculate about a former employee's bad qualities or to opine on the reasons for his or her failures. Limit your comments to accurate, verifiable facts.

- **Don't be spiteful.** Many states offer some protection for former employers that are called upon to provide a reference. These laws generally shield employers from defamation lawsuits as long as they provide information in good faith. This is a fairly nebulous legal standard, but it clearly does not cover nasty or mean-spirited gripes.

- **Don't give false flattery.** If you had to fire a real bad egg (for example, a worker who was violent in the workplace or threatened coworkers), don't lie about it. You may choose to give only name, rank, and serial number, but, if you give a more expansive reference, don't hide the bad news. If you fail to warn the new employer about serious problems, and the employee ends up harming coworkers or the public, you and your company could be held responsible.

Lessons From the Real World

Randi was a female student at a California middle school when she was called into the vice principal's office one day in 1992. Later, she claimed that the vice principal, Robert Gadams, sexually molested her while she was in his office.

As it turned out, the school hired Gadams after receiving positive recommendations from another school district where Gadams had worked. Even though supervisors in his former school district knew that Gadams had been accused of sexual misconduct and impropriety with students, it failed to mention these claims when the new middle school asked for a reference. In fact, the former district gave letters of recommendation for Gadams that contained unconditional praise. One letter recommended Gadams "for an assistant principalship or equivalent position without reservation."

When Randi sued Gadams's previous school district, the district claimed that she had no legal grounds for suit. After all, it argued, it didn't have any sort of obligation to her, a student in a different district. The California Supreme Court disagreed. It said that Randi could sue because the school district had a duty to not misrepresent the facts when describing the character and qualifications of an employee to a prospective employer (in this case, the middle school that Randi attended).

Randi W. v. Muroc Joint Unified School District, et al., 14 Cal.4th 1066 (1997).

- **Designate one person to give references.** Choose one trusted person in the company to be responsible for all references, and tell employees to direct inquiries to that person. Make sure that your company keeps a record of every request for a reference and every response, in case of trouble down the road. Some companies provide only written references, to make sure they have proof of exactly what was said.

- **Insist on a written release.** To make absolutely sure your company is protected against lawsuits, require former employees to sign a release: an agreement that gives you permission to provide information to prospective employers and that promises the former employee not sue over the information you provide.

What to Tell Coworkers When an Employee Leaves

Before a departing employee walks out the door, sit down and discuss what you will tell coworkers about the situation. If the employee is leaving on good terms, this decision shouldn't be difficult. You'll probably want to thank the worker for his or her service, tell coworkers where the worker is going, and express high hopes for the worker's future.

You'll need to take extra steps if a worker is fired, however. Imagine how other employees will feel when they learn that a coworker—perhaps even a friend—has been fired. Not only will they want to know why that person was fired, but they might also start to fear for their own jobs. Rumors will circulate. Morale might drop. This is especially true if you're terminating a popular employee or someone who's been with the company for a number of years.

You might be tempted to say nothing to other workers about the termination. Although this instinct is understandable, it's not a good one. Employees are not going to ignore or forget about the termination, no matter how much they may have wanted the employee gone. Every employee secretly fears being fired, so it is unsettling at best when it happens to a coworker.

So what should you do? You can keep other workers informed, boost morale, and avoid any legal missteps by following these tips:

- **Call a meeting.** Consider calling a meeting with employees to announce the termination, so you can acknowledge the event on behalf of the company and encourage workers to move past it.
- **Relay the facts.** At the meeting, tell employees who has been terminated and as of what date. Do not explain why the employee was fired.
- **Keep it neutral.** Do not express anger or relief. Be professional and calm. Tell

workers that you can't go into details because you must respect the fired employee's privacy.

Of course, this doesn't mean managers can never discuss the reasons for termination with anyone. If there is a compelling business need to tell an employee why a coworker was terminated (for example, an employee is taking on the terminated worker's projects and needs to know how to fix the worker's mistakes), then do it one on one, in a private and confidential setting. Instruct the employee not to reveal anything you say to anyone else in the organization.

Health Insurance

With the astronomical increases in the costs of medical care, health insurance has become a coveted—if not essential—employee benefit. The importance of health care coverage means that this will be one of the first issues a terminated employee will ask about.

Many companies offer to foot the bill for continued insurance coverage—at least for a while—as part of an employee's severance package. Often, this benefit helps give former workers peace of mind and makes them feel more kindly disposed toward a former employer. (See "Severance," below, for more about this issue.)

Federal and state laws often require employers to make continued coverage available to former employees, although it is generally at the employees' own cost.

Federal Law

A federal workplace law, called the Consolidated Omnibus Budget Reconciliation Act (COBRA), 29 U.S.C. § 1162, applies to companies with 20 or more employees that offer a group health care plan. Among other things, it requires companies to offer departing employees the option of continuing their health care coverage for up to 18 months, if they quit or are fired for any reason other than gross misconduct. Companies must also make this opportunity available to the employee's spouse and dependents.

Former employees are responsible for paying the full cost of continuing coverage under COBRA, including both the employee's and the company's share of the premiums. To learn more about COBRA, go to www.dol.gov/dol/topic/health-plans/cobra.htm.

State Laws

Most states have laws similar to COBRA that give former employees the right to continue group health insurance after they leave a job. Your company must comply with both state and federal law. In other words, you must follow whichever law is more generous to employees. State laws are generally more detailed and more generous to workers than COBRA. In addition, even small businesses (those with fewer than 20 employees) that escape COBRA may have to comply with state laws.

To learn more about your state's law, see "State Health Insurance Continuation Laws," at the end of this chapter.

Severance

Some employers assume they have to offer a severance package—some combination of money and continuing benefits—to fired employees. In most cases, however, a company is not legally required to pay employees severance. (A few states require some employers to pay a small amount of severance when they lay off a significant number of workers at one time; see "State Layoff and Plant-Closing Laws," at the end of Chapter 13, for more information.)

The law requires a company to provide severance to former employees only if it led them to believe they would receive it by:

- signing a written contract agreeing to pay severance
- promising employees severance pay in an employee handbook or personnel policy
- having a history of paying severance to other employees in the same position, or
- verbally promising severance to the employee.

Even if not required to by law, many employers routinely give severance packages to long-term employees, unless they were terminated for serious misconduct. Many employers do this to soften the blow of being fired or laid off and to buy a little insurance against lawsuits. A severance package may help sweeten the sour grapes workers feel about losing their jobs. And, a happier former employee is a less litigious former employee.

If your company decides to pay severance, the most important rule is to be consistent. The amount of severance can vary depending on how long the employee has worked for the company and on the employee's job category. But be sure to treat similarly situated employees equally. A company that is evenhanded and uniform in paying severance is less likely to face claims of discrimination (for example, that men received higher severance pay than women).

What to Include in a Severance Package

There are no hard-and-fast rules about what should be included in a severance package. The idea is to ease the burden on the soon-to-be-jobless employee. You might consider including any or all of the following benefits:

- **Pay.** Realistically, this is what is most important to employees. Many employers pay a set amount—a week or two of salary, for example—for every year of employment.
- **Insurance benefits.** Some employers offer to continue to pay for insurance coverage for a period of time after an employee leaves the company. Although COBRA requires most employers to allow their employees to continue their health insurance, it does not require employers to foot the bill. (For more about COBRA, see "Health Insurance," above.) An employer may also want to continue other benefits, such as life or disability insurance.
- **Uncontested unemployment compensation.** Employees can apply for unemployment benefits if they were fired for reasons other than misconduct. After an employee applies for benefits, the employer has the opportunity to contest the employee's claim. By agreeing not to contest an employee's claim, a company makes it more likely that the employee will receive benefits. (For more information about how unemployment works, see "Unemployment Benefits," below.)
- **Outplacement services.** Outplacement programs help employees find new jobs. They may offer counseling on career goals and job skills, tips on résumé writing, leads for potential jobs, practice interview sessions, and help in negotiating with potential employers.
- **References.** You might agree to come up with a mutually agreeable letter of reference for an employee to use in job hunting. But proceed with caution here: Giving references carries with it some possible risks. (For more about this issue, see "References," above.)
- **Other benefits.** Certain benefits or items may be particularly important to a

departing employee. If possible, have an honest discussion to find out what the worker would like in a severance package. You might want to consider allowing the employee to keep advances or money paid for moving expenses, giving the employee equipment such as a cell phone or computer, or releasing an employee from contractual obligations, like a covenant not to compete.

As you can see, severance means more than just money. If you think creatively and communicate with the employee, you should be able to come up with some valuable benefits that won't break the bank.

Releases

Firing or laying off a worker is never pleasant. But sometimes, it's actually risky. Perhaps the employee complains a lot or stirs up trouble in the workplace. Or maybe you've made some mistakes in your management of the employee and are concerned how a judge or jury might view your decisions.

Either way, if your company is worried about a lawsuit, you might want to ask the employee to sign a release: an agreement not to sue the company in exchange for receiving something of value. Some employers routinely ask employees to sign a release as a condition of receiving a severance package. After all, if they are voluntarily providing a benefit, they might as well get some security out of it. The downside to this approach, however, is that it

Checklist: Collecting Company Property

Before a departing worker walks out the door for the last time, you'll need to disable the employee's passwords and security codes to the company's computers, telephone system, and workplace. You'll also need to get back any company property in the employee's possession; it's much easier to do this before the employee leaves rather than to try to track the employee (and the property) down later. Here are some of the things you may need to collect:

- [ ] company car
- [ ] keys and security cards that allow access to the workplace
- [ ] company credit card (you should also call the credit card issuer to cancel the account)
- [ ] computer password
- [ ] confidential files, client lists, manuals, and other company documents
- [ ] laptop computer, and
- [ ] cell phone.

may get an employee thinking about a lawsuit when that was the furthest thing from his or her mind. For that reason, other employers ask for releases only from employees who might have legitimate legal claims against the company or who seem especially motivated to sue.

The employee might even have legal claims unrelated to the firing that could cause trouble for your company. This often happens with wage and hour claims. For example, suppose you improperly classified an employee as exempt when he or she should have been a nonexempt employee who earns overtime. Even if you had more than enough reason to fire the employee, the employee can file an overtime claim worth several thousands of dollars. In this case, you might want to offer some severance in exchange for a release, even if the employee's behavior was egregious and clearly grounds for termination. An employee's on-the-job conduct generally doesn't matter when it comes to wage and hour violations.

Because some states have specific requirements about what language must go into a release, you should consult an attorney for help in crafting a legal agreement that will hold up in court. Here are some general considerations to keep in mind:

- **Give the employee something in exchange for the release.** You are asking the employee to waive the right to sue the company, and that right is worth something. A signed release will be worthless if you don't give the employee something in exchange for the promise not to sue. This means that if your company is already obligated to provide severance (for example, by a written employment contract), or your company is offering severance packages to employees who don't sign releases, it will have to give something extra on top of the severance (for example, more money or other benefits).

- **Be clear about the rights the employee is waiving.** The release might state that the employee is waiving the right to sue for any claims arising out of the employment relationship, including the termination of that relationship. Make sure the agreement is specific enough to prevent employees from later claiming that they didn't know what rights they were giving up.

- **Give the employee plenty of time to decide whether to sign.** It's reasonable for an employee to take a week or two to decide whether to give up the right to sue. You might even suggest that the employee consult with a lawyer to review the agreement.

- **Avoid any hint of coercion.** An employee must sign the release voluntarily or courts will not enforce it. Don't threaten or talk tough with employees to convince them to sign; a release that gets thrown out of court won't do your company any good.

- **Special rules apply to older workers.** If the employee is 40 years of age or older, a federal law—the Older Workers' Benefit Protection Act (OWBPA)—dictates what language must be included in a release. Among other things, these employees must have a longer period of time to review the release, be able to revoke the agreement (change their minds) for a limited time after they sign, and be advised in writing to consult with an attorney. (For more information, see Chapter 3 under "Age" discrimination.)

Unemployment Benefits

Not everyone who's out of work is entitled to unemployment benefits. A couple of factors dictate whether a former employee will receive unemployment: the circumstances of the employee's departure and whether the former employer decides to contest the employee's claim. This means your company has a lot of power over whether the worker will receive unemployment benefits.

Employee Eligibility

Employees are eligible for unemployment benefits only if they are out of work through no fault of their own. Whether an employee is "at fault" depends on whether the employee quit, was laid off, or was fired.

If an employee quits. An employee who quits or resigns from a job will be eligible for benefits only if he or she did so for "good cause." Good cause means that the reason for quitting was "compelling": that is, the worker would have suffered some sort of harm or injury by staying. Put another way, the reason must be of the sort that would have made any reasonable person leave.

A good reason for quitting a job isn't necessarily good cause. For example, leaving a job because it doesn't offer opportunities for career advancement might be a good reason, but it won't make a worker eligible for unemployment benefits. Similarly, regular job dissatisfaction does not amount to good cause.

In many states, the compelling reason must be job related. If an employee leaves the job because of intolerable working conditions (such as being sexually harassed) or because he or she was offered the opportunity to quit in lieu of being fired, most states would allow the worker to collect unemployment. Similarly, leaving a job because it poses a serious threat to the worker's health or safety is usually good cause. In some states, compelling personal reasons will also qualify as good cause (for example, quitting to relocate with a spouse or to care for an ill family member).

If an employee is laid off. An employee who loses a job through a layoff or reduction in workforce is eligible for benefits.

If an employee is fired. Fired employees can generally claim unemployment benefits if they were terminated because they lacked the necessary skills to do the job or because they were not a good fit. They can also receive benefits if the employer had a good reason to fire but the infractions were relatively minor, unintentional, or isolated.

In most states, however, an employee who is fired for misconduct will not be able to receive unemployment benefits. Although you might think that any action that leads to termination should constitute misconduct, the unemployment laws don't look at it that way. Not all actions that result in termination are serious enough to qualify as misconduct.

So, what qualifies as misconduct? Generally speaking, an employee engages in misconduct by willfully doing something that injures the company's interests. Revealing trade secrets or sexually harassing coworkers is misconduct; simple inefficiency or an unpleasant personality is not. Other common types of misconduct include extreme insubordination, chronic tardiness, numerous unexcused absences, intoxication on the job, and dishonesty.

Common actions that often result in firing —but do not constitute misconduct—are poor performance because of lack of skills, good-faith errors in judgment, off-duty conduct that does not have an impact on the employer's interests, and poor relations with coworkers.

It is important to remember that what qualifies as misconduct is a matter of interpretation and degree. Annoying one coworker might not be misconduct, but intentionally bothering an entire department even after repeated warnings might be.

Should Your Company Contest the Claim?

Your state's unemployment office—not your company—will ultimately decide whether the former employee can receive unemployment benefits. You do, however, have the option of contesting the employee's application—which gives your company a great deal of power. In California, for example, the unemployment board presumes that a terminated employee did not engage

in misconduct unless the employer contests the claim. Thus, in California, terminated employees who claim unemployment benefits receive them unless the former employer intervenes.

Remember, there are no grounds to contest an unemployment claim if the employee was laid off. There are also typically no grounds to contest the claim for run-of-the-mill performance or conduct issues.

Even if an employee does engage in misconduct, your company might want to give up its right to contest an unemployment claim as part of a severance package. This is especially true if the fired employee seems likely to sue. (See "Severance," above, for more about severance packages and unemployment claims.)

Your company should contest a claim only if it has grounds to do so (because the employee engaged in misconduct or quit without a compelling reason). And even then, your company should also have a good, practical reason to contest it. Employers typically fight unemployment claims for one of two reasons:

- **Increase in unemployment insurance rates.** The employer—not the employee— pays for unemployment insurance. The amount the employer pays is often based in part on the number of claims made against the employer by former employees.

- **Anticipating a wrongful termination lawsuit.** The unemployment application process can be a valuable time to discover the employee's side of the story, and it can also provide an excellent opportunity for gathering evidence, both from the employee and from witnesses. (It's a good idea to get a lawyer involved at this stage.)

If your company plans to contest an unemployment claim, proceed with caution. These battles not only cost time and money, but they also ensure that the former employee will become an enemy. The employee might even file a wrongful termination lawsuit that otherwise could have been avoided. If the fired worker has friends who remain on the job, they too may doubt and distrust your company's tactics.

Before making any decisions, you might want to do some research by contacting your state's unemployment office for specific information about the law in your state. This office can tell you what effect a successful claim will have on your company's rates. If it's relatively small, backing off might be a good idea.

Anatomy of an Unemployment Compensation Claim

Although the unemployment compensation system is different in each state, some general principles apply in most cases. An unemployment claim will typically proceed through the steps described below.

Step 1: Claim filing. The process starts when the former employee files a claim with the state unemployment office. Your company will receive written notice of the claim and an opportunity to file a written objection.

Step 2: Eligibility determination. The state agency makes an initial determination of whether the former employee is eligible for unemployment benefits. Usually there's no hearing at this stage.

Step 3: Hearing. Your company or the former employee can appeal the initial eligibility decision, which results in a hearing before a referee: a hearing officer who is on the staff of the state agency. Normally conducted in a private room at the unemployment office, this is the most important step in the process. At the hearing, the company and the former employee will each have an opportunity to speak. In addition, you are entitled to have a lawyer there and to present witnesses and any relevant documents, such as employee evaluations or disciplinary warnings.

Step 4: Administrative appeal. Either your company or the former employee can appeal the referee's decision to an administrative agency, such as a board of review.

Step 5: Judicial appeal. Either side can appeal through the state court system, but this is rare.

Legal Dos and Don'ts: Departing Workers

Do:

- **Fight fair.** As a practical matter, it makes sense to contest an unemployment claim only in limited circumstances, such as when you know the employee plans to file a lawsuit (your company can use the information you gather at the unemployment hearing to help build a defense). Otherwise, let it go: Pursuing a vendetta against a former employee will only take up time and money. It might even convince the employee to sue.

- **Negotiate creatively.** If you can offer a fired or laid-off worker something—anything—to ease the pain of losing a job, you will reduce the risk of a lawsuit. You don't have to break the bank to offer a meaningful severance package; the employee might want something that you hadn't considered, such as keeping a company laptop.

- **Show respect for departing employees.** Even if an employee leaves on bad terms, you shouldn't trash the employee to other workers or prospective employers. Bad-mouthing a former employee can lead to defamation lawsuits, and it will give remaining workers a sour taste of what they can expect should they ever leave the company.

Don't:

- **Ask every employee who leaves to sign a release.** There's a big downside to using releases: Some employees who otherwise wouldn't consider a lawsuit might start thinking about it when faced with a document that asks them to give up their legal rights. Reserve releases for employees who you suspect might sue or for situations in which your company's conduct has been questionable.

- **Play favorites.** You might be tempted to treat some departing workers better than others. However, treating workers differently can lead to resentment and discrimination claims. Make sure you have legitimate, business-related reasons for your actions.

- **Make life difficult for terminated employees.** If you treat former employees fairly, they are much less likely to sue your company. Remember this simple rule when deciding whether to contest an unemployment claim, give an angry reference, or deny a fired employee a simple benefit or two, such as paying for a couple of months of continued health insurance.

Test Your Knowledge

Questions

1. Your company can be sued for giving an honest but negative reference about a former employee, if the reference prevents the employee from getting another job. ☐ True ☐ False

2. The best reference policy is to say only positive things, even if a former employee was truly dreadful. ☐ True ☐ False

3. Managers should not go into detail when telling workers that an employee has been terminated. ☐ True ☐ False

4. Companies must continue to pay for health insurance for former employees for up to 18 months. ☐ True ☐ False

5. Employers are legally required to pay one week of severance for every year an employee has worked for the company. ☐ True ☐ False

6. A company might have to pay severance to a fired employee if it has always paid severance to employees who held that position in the past. ☐ True ☐ False

7. A company can refuse to pay an employee severance unless he or she signs a release agreeing not to sue the company. ☐ True ☐ False

8. A release is valid only if the employee has talked to a lawyer before signing it. ☐ True ☐ False

9. Employees who are fired cannot collect unemployment benefits. ☐ True ☐ False

10. Companies should always contest unemployment claims. ☐ True ☐ False

Test Your Knowledge (continued)

Answers

1. False. To sue for defamation, an employee must be able to prove that your statements were false. As long as you are honest, stick to facts, and aren't motivated by malice or ill will toward the employee, a defamation lawsuit will fail.

2. False. If you give a detailed reference (that is, you go beyond name, salary, and position) for an employee who was dangerous, violent, or otherwise posed a risk to others but you omit that information, the prospective employer (or its employees or customers) may have a legal claim against you if that employee goes on to cause harm. If you choose to be expansive, you must give the bad news as well as the good.

3. True. The safest course is simply to say that the employee has been terminated and explain who will be responsible for that employee's projects going forward.

4. False. Although most companies are required to allow departing employees to continue their health insurance benefits, the company is not required to foot the bill.

5. False. Except for the few states that require employers that conduct mass layoffs to pay a small amount of severance, employers are not legally required to pay severance unless they led employees to believe that they would receive it (for example, through a written contract or company policies).

6. True. If your company has always paid severance to employees who are fired from certain positions, an employee could argue that this is company policy, and that your failure to adhere to it constitutes a breach of contract or discrimination.

7. It depends on your company's severance policies. If employees at your company are already entitled to receive severance, you cannot require them to sign a release to get it. If, however, an employee is not entitled to receive severance, you can condition a severance package on the employee's agreement not to sue.

8. False. In some circumstances—for example, if your company is firing an older worker or your state's law requires it—you might have to advise workers of their right to talk to a lawyer before signing a release. However, if the worker decides not to heed this advice, the release will still be valid.

9. False. A worker who is fired for misconduct is probably not entitled to benefits, but a worker who is fired for poor performance or being a poor fit generally is.

10. False. In fact, there are very few situations when it makes sense to contest an unemployment claim. Fighting an employee's effort to collect unemployment will take time and money. It could also convince the employee to try to get money out of your company through a lawsuit.

State Laws That Control Final Paychecks

Note: Some states are not included in this chart because they do not have laws specifically controlling final paychecks. Contact your state department of labor for more information. (See appendix for contact list.)

Alaska

Alaska Stat. § 23.05.140(b)

Paycheck due when employee is fired: Within 3 working days after termination.

Paycheck due when employee quits: Next regular payday that's at least 3 days after employee gives notice.

Unused vacation pay due: Only if agreed to by employer or required by company policy or practice.

Arizona

Ariz. Rev. Stat. §§ 23-350, 23-353

Paycheck due when employee is fired: Next payday or within 7 working days, whichever is sooner.

Paycheck due when employee quits: Next regular payday or by mail at employee's request.

Unused vacation pay due: No provision.

Arkansas

Ark. Code Ann. § 11-4-405

Paycheck due when employee is fired: Upon request, within 7 days of discharge; otherwise, next regular payday.

Paycheck due when employee quits: No provision.

Unused vacation pay due: No provision.

Special employment situations: Railroad or railroad construction: day of discharge.

California

Cal. Lab. Code §§ 201 to 202, 227.3

Paycheck due when employee is fired: Immediately.

Paycheck due when employee quits: Immediately if employee has given 72 hours' notice; otherwise, within 72 hours.

Unused vacation pay due: Yes.

Special employment situations: Motion picture business: next payday.

Oil drilling industry: within 24 hours (excluding weekends and holidays) of termination.

Seasonal agricultural workers: within 72 hours of termination.

Colorado

Colo. Rev. Stat. § 8-4-109

Paycheck due when employee is fired: Immediately. (Within 6 hours of start of next workday, if payroll unit is closed; 24 hours if unit is off-site.) When paycheck is not due immediately, employer may make the check available at the worksite, the employer's local office, or the employee's last-known mailing address.

Paycheck due when employee quits: Next payday.

Unused vacation pay due: Yes.

Connecticut

Conn. Gen. Stat. Ann. §§ 31-71c, 31-76k

Paycheck due when employee is fired: Next business day after discharge.

Paycheck due when employee quits: Next payday.

Unused vacation pay due: Only if policy or collective bargaining agreement requires payment on termination.

Delaware

Del. Code Ann. tit. 19, § 1103

Paycheck due when employee is fired: Next payday.

Paycheck due when employee quits: Next payday.

State Laws That Control Final Paychecks (continued)

Unused vacation pay due: Only if required by employer policy or agreement, in which case vacation must be paid within 30 days after it becomes due.

District of Columbia

D.C. Code Ann. §§ 32-1301, 32-1303

Paycheck due when employee is fired: Next business day unless employee handles money, in which case employer has 4 days.

Paycheck due when employee quits: Next payday or 7 days after quitting, whichever is sooner.

Unused vacation pay due: Yes, unless there is an agreement to the contrary.

Hawaii

Haw. Rev. Stat. § 388-3

Paycheck due when employee is fired: Immediately or next business day, if timing or conditions prevent immediate payment.

Paycheck due when employee quits: Next payday or immediately, if employee gives one pay period's notice.

Unused vacation pay due: No.

Idaho

Idaho Code §§ 45-606, 45-617

Paycheck due when employee is fired: Next payday or within 10 days (excluding weekends and holidays), whichever is sooner. If employee makes written request for earlier payment, within 48 hours of receipt of request (excluding weekends and holidays).

Paycheck due when employee quits: Next payday or within 10 days (excluding weekends and holidays), whichever is sooner. If employee makes written request for earlier payment, within 48 hours of receipt of request (excluding weekends and holidays).

Unused vacation pay due: No provision.

Illinois

820 Ill. Comp. Stat. § 115/5

Paycheck due when employee is fired: At time of separation if possible, but no later than next payday. Employer must comply with employee's written request to mail final paycheck.

Paycheck due when employee quits: At time of separation if possible, but no later than next payday. Employer must comply with employee's written request to mail final paycheck.

Unused vacation pay due: Yes.

Indiana

Ind. Code Ann. §§ 22-2-5-1, 22-2-9-1, 22-2-9-2

Paycheck due when employee is fired: Next payday.

Paycheck due when employee quits: Next payday. (If employee has not left address, (1) 10 business days after employee demands wages or (2) when employee provides address where check may be mailed.)

Unused vacation pay due: If employer agrees to vacation pay, absent an agreement to the contrary, employer must pay out accrued unused vacation upon termination.

Special employment situations: Does not apply to railroad employees.

Iowa

Iowa Code §§ 91A.4, 91A.2(7)(b)

Paycheck due when employee is fired: Next payday.

Paycheck due when employee quits: Next payday.

Unused vacation pay due: Yes.

Special employment situations: If employee is owed commission, employer has 30 days to pay.

State Laws That Control Final Paychecks (continued)

Kansas

Kan. Stat. Ann. § 44-315

Paycheck due when employee is fired: Next payday.

Paycheck due when employee quits: Next payday.

Unused vacation pay due: Only if required by employer's policies or practice.

Kentucky

Ky. Rev. Stat. Ann. §§ 337.010, 337.055

Paycheck due when employee is fired: Next payday or within 14 days, whichever is later.

Paycheck due when employee quits: Next payday or within 14 days, whichever is later.

Unused vacation pay due: Yes.

Louisiana

La. Rev. Stat. Ann. § 23:631

Paycheck due when employee is fired: Next payday or within 15 days, whichever is earlier.

Paycheck due when employee quits: Next payday or within 15 days, whichever is earlier.

Unused vacation pay due: Yes.

Maine

Me. Rev. Stat. Ann. tit. 26, § 626

Paycheck due when employee is fired: Next payday.

Paycheck due when employee quits: Next payday.

Unused vacation pay due: Yes, accrued vacation is considered wages and must be paid out upon termination.

Special employment situations: Employer must pay employees all wages due within two weeks of the sale of a business.

Maryland

Md. Code Ann., [Lab. & Empl.] § 3-505

Paycheck due when employee is fired: Next scheduled payday.

Paycheck due when employee quits: Next scheduled payday.

Unused vacation pay due: Yes.

Massachusetts

Mass. Gen. Laws ch. 149, § 148

Paycheck due when employee is fired: Day of discharge.

Paycheck due when employee quits: Next payday. If no scheduled payday, then following Saturday.

Unused vacation pay due: Yes.

Michigan

Mich. Comp. Laws §§ 408.471 to 408.475; Mich. Admin. Code § 408.9007

Paycheck due when employee is fired: Next payday.

Paycheck due when employee quits: Next payday.

Unused vacation pay due: Only if required by written policy or contract.

Special employment situations: Hand-harvesters of crops: within one working day of termination.

Minnesota

Minn. Stat. Ann. §§ 181.13, 181.14, 181.74

Paycheck due when employee is fired: Within 24 hours.

Paycheck due when employee quits: Next regular payday. If next payday is less than 5 days after employee's last day, employer may delay payment until payday after that. But in no event may payment exceed 20 days from employee's last day.

Unused vacation pay due: Only if required by written policy or contract.

Special employment situations: If employee was responsible for collecting or handling money or property, employer has 10 days after termination or resignation to audit and adjust employee accounts before making payment.

State Laws That Control Final Paychecks (continued)

Commissions must be paid to sales employees within 3 days if employee is fired or quits with at least 5 days' notice. Otherwise, commissions must be paid within 6 days.

Migrant agricultural workers who resign: within 5 days.

Missouri

Mo. Rev. Stat. § 290.110

Paycheck due when employee is fired: Day of discharge.

Paycheck due when employee quits: No provision.

Unused vacation pay due: No.

Special employment situations: Requirements do not apply if employee is paid primarily based on commission and an audit is necessary or customary to determine the amount due.

Montana

Mont. Code Ann. § 39-3-205; Mont. Admin. Code § 24.16.7521

Paycheck due when employee is fired: Immediately if fired for cause or laid off (unless there is a written policy extending time to earlier of next payday or 15 days).

Paycheck due when employee quits: Next payday or within 15 days, whichever comes first.

Unused vacation pay due: Yes.

Nebraska

Neb. Rev. Stat. §§ 48-1229 to 48-1230

Paycheck due when employee is fired: Next payday or within 2 weeks, whichever is earlier.

Paycheck due when employee quits: Next payday or within 2 weeks, whichever is earlier.

Unused vacation pay due: Only if required by agreement.

Special employment situations: Commissions due on next payday following receipt.

Nevada

Nev. Rev. Stat. Ann. §§ 608.020, 608.030

Paycheck due when employee is fired: Immediately.

Paycheck due when employee quits: Next payday or within 7 days, whichever is earlier.

Unused vacation pay due: No.

New Hampshire

N.H. Rev. Stat. Ann. §§ 275:43(v), 275:44

Paycheck due when employee is fired: Within 72 hours. If laid off, next payday.

Paycheck due when employee quits: Next payday, or within 72 hours if employee gives one pay period's notice.

Unused vacation pay due: Yes.

New Jersey

N.J. Stat. Ann. § 34:11-4.3

Paycheck due when employee is fired: Next payday.

Paycheck due when employee quits: Next payday.

Unused vacation pay due: Only if required by policy.

New Mexico

N.M. Stat. Ann. §§ 50-4-4, 50-4-5

Paycheck due when employee is fired: Within 5 days. 10 days for commission or piece-based workers. § 50-4-4(A).

Paycheck due when employee quits: Next payday.

Unused vacation pay due: No provision.

Special employment situations: If paid by task or commission, 10 days after discharge.

New York

N.Y. Lab. Law §§ 191(3), 198-c(2)

Paycheck due when employee is fired: Next payday.

Paycheck due when employee quits: Next payday.

Unused vacation pay due: Yes, unless employer has a contrary policy.

State Laws That Control Final Paychecks (continued)

North Carolina
N.C. Gen. Stat. §§ 95-25.7, 95-25.12

Paycheck due when employee is fired: Next payday.

Paycheck due when employee quits: Next payday.

Unused vacation pay due: Yes, unless employer has a contrary policy.

Special employment situations: If paid by commission or bonus, on next payday after amount calculated.

North Dakota
N.D. Cent. Code § 34-14-03; N.D. Admin. Code § 46-02-07-02(12)

Paycheck due when employee is fired: Next payday.

Paycheck due when employee quits: Next payday.

Unused vacation pay due: Yes. However, if an employer provides written notice at the time of hire, employer need not pay out vacation that has been awarded, but not yet earned. And, if an employee quits with less than 5 days' notice, employer may withhold accrued vacation, as long as the employer gave written notice of the limitation at the time of hire and the employee was employed for less than one year.

Ohio
Ohio Rev. Code Ann. § 4113.15

Paycheck due when employee is fired: First of month for wages earned in first half of prior month; 15th of month for wages earned in second half of prior month.

Paycheck due when employee quits: First of month for wages earned in first half of prior month; 15th of month for wages earned in second half of prior month.

Unused vacation pay due: Yes, if company has policy or practice of making such payments.

Oklahoma
Okla. Stat. Ann. tit. 40, §§ 165.1(4), 165.3

Paycheck due when employee is fired: Next payday.

Paycheck due when employee quits: Next payday.

Unused vacation pay due: Yes.

Oregon
Ore. Rev. Stat. §§ 652.140, 652.145

Paycheck due when employee is fired: End of first business day after termination.

Paycheck due when employee quits: Immediately, with 48 hours' notice (excluding weekends & holidays); without notice, within 5 business days or next payday, whichever comes first (must be within 5 days if employee submits time records to determine wages due).

Unused vacation pay due: Only if required by policy.

Special employment situations: Seasonal farmworkers: fired or quitting with 48 hours' notice, immediately; quitting without notice, within 48 hours or next payday, whichever comes first. If the termination occurs at the end of harvest season, the employer is a farmworker camp operator, and the farmworker is provided housing at no cost until wages are paid, employer must pay by noon on the day after termination.

Pennsylvania
43 P.S. §§ 260.2a, 260.5

Paycheck due when employee is fired: Next payday.

Paycheck due when employee quits: Next payday.

Unused vacation pay due: Only if required by policy or contract.

State Laws That Control Final Paychecks (continued)

Rhode Island

R.I. Gen. Laws § 28-14-4

Paycheck due when employee is fired: Next payday. Paycheck is due within 24 hours if employer liquidates, merges, or disposes of the business, or moves it out of state.

Paycheck due when employee quits: Next payday.

Unused vacation pay due: Yes, if employee has worked for one full year and the company has verbally or in writing awarded vacation.

South Carolina

S.C. Code Ann. §§ 41-10-10(2), 41-10-50

Paycheck due when employee is fired: Within 48 hours or next payday, but not more than 30 days.

Paycheck due when employee quits: No provision.

Unused vacation pay due: Only if required by policy or contract.

South Dakota

S.D. Codified Laws Ann. §§ 60-11-10, 60-11-11, 60-11-14

Paycheck due when employee is fired: Next payday (or until employee returns employer's property).

Paycheck due when employee quits: Next payday (or until employee returns employer's property).

Unused vacation pay due: No.

Tennessee

Tenn. Code Ann. § 50-2-103

Paycheck due when employee is fired: Next payday or within 21 days, whichever is later.

Paycheck due when employee quits: Next payday or within 21 days, whichever is later.

Unused vacation pay due: Only if required by policy or contract.

Special employment situations: Applies to employers with 5 or more employees.

Texas

Tex. Lab. Code Ann. §§ 61.001, 61.014

Paycheck due when employee is fired: Within 6 days.

Paycheck due when employee quits: Next payday.

Unused vacation pay due: Only if required by policy or contract.

Utah

Utah Code Ann. §§ 34-28-5; Utah Admin. Code § 610-3

Paycheck due when employee is fired: Within 24 hours.

Paycheck due when employee quits: Next payday.

Unused vacation pay due: Only if required by policy or contract.

Special employment situations: Requirements do not apply to commissioned sales employees if audit is necessary to determine the amount due.

Vermont

Vt. Stat. Ann. tit. 21, § 342(c)

Paycheck due when employee is fired: Within 72 hours.

Paycheck due when employee quits: Next regular payday or next Friday, if there is no regular payday.

Unused vacation pay due: No provision.

Virginia

Va. Code Ann. § 40.1-29(A.1)

Paycheck due when employee is fired: Next payday.

Paycheck due when employee quits: Next payday.

Unused vacation pay due: Only if agreed to in a written statement.

Washington

Wash. Rev. Code Ann. § 49.48.010

Paycheck due when employee is fired: End of pay period.

State Laws That Control Final Paychecks (continued)

Paycheck due when employee quits: End of pay period.

Unused vacation pay due: No provision.

West Virginia
W.Va. Code §§ 21-5-1, 21-5-4

Paycheck due when employee is fired: Next regular payday.

Paycheck due when employee quits: Next regular payday.

Unused vacation pay due: Only if required by policy or contract.

Wisconsin
Wis. Stat. Ann. §§ 109.01(3), 109.03

Paycheck due when employee is fired: Next payday or within 1 month, whichever is earlier. If termination is due to merger, relocation, or liquidation of business, within 24 hours.

Paycheck due when employee quits: Next payday.

Unused vacation pay due: Yes.

Special employment situations: Does not apply to managers, executives, or sales agents working on commission basis.

Wyoming
Wyo. Stat. Ann. §§ 27-4-104, 27-4-501, 27-4-507(c)

Paycheck due when employee is fired: Next regular payday.

Paycheck due when employee quits: Next regular payday.

Unused vacation pay due: No, if employer's policies state that vacation is forfeited upon termination of employment and the employee acknowledged the policy in writing.

Special employment situations: Requirements do not apply to commissioned sales employees if audit is necessary to determine the amount due.

State Health Insurance Continuation Laws

Alabama

Ala. Code § 27-55-3(a)(4)

Special Situations: 18 months for subjects of domestic abuse who have lost coverage they had under abuser's insurance and who do not qualify for COBRA.

Arizona

Ariz. Rev. Stat. §§ 20-1377, 20-1408

Employers affected: All employers that offer group disability insurance.

Length of coverage for dependents: Insurer must either continue coverage for dependents or convert to individual policy upon death of covered employee or divorce. Coverage must be the same unless the insured chooses a lesser plan.

Qualifying event: Death of an employee; change in marital status; any other reason stated in policy (other than failure to pay premium).

Time employer has to notify employee: No provisions for employer. Insurance policy must include notice of conversion privilege. Clerk of court must provide notice to anyone filing for divorce that dependent spouse entitled to convert health insurance coverage.

Time employee has to apply: 31 days after termination of existing coverage.

Arkansas

Ark. Code Ann. §§ 23-86-114 to 23-86-116

Employers affected: All employers that offer group health insurance.

Eligible employees: Employees continuously insured for previous 3 months.

Length of coverage for employee: 120 days.

Length of coverage for dependents: 120 days.

Qualifying event: Termination of employment; change in insured's marital status. Employer may—

but is not required to—continue benefits on death of employee.

Time employee has to apply: 10 days.

California

Cal. Health & Safety Code §§ 1373.6, 1373.621; Cal. Ins. Code §§ 10128.50 to 10128.59

Employers affected: Employers that offer group health insurance and have 2 to 19 employees.

Eligible employees: All covered employees are eligible.

Length of coverage for employee: 36 months.

Length of coverage for dependents: 36 months.

Qualifying event: Termination of employment; reduction in hours; death of employee; change in marital status; loss of dependent status; covered employee's eligibility for Medicare (for dependents only).

Time employer has to notify employee: 15 days.

Time employee has to apply: 60 days.

Special situations: Employee who is at least 60 years old and has worked for employer for previous 5 years may continue benefits for self and spouse beyond COBRA or Cal-COBRA limits (also applies to COBRA employers). Employee who began receiving COBRA coverage on or after 1/1/03 and whose COBRA coverage is for less than 36 months may use Cal-COBRA to bring total coverage up to 36 months.

Colorado

Colo. Rev. Stat. § 10-16-108

Employers affected: All employers that offer group health insurance.

Eligible employees: Employees continuously insured for previous 6 months.

Length of coverage for employee: 18 months.

Length of coverage for dependents: 18 months.

State Health Insurance Continuation Laws (continued)

Qualifying event: Termination of employment; reduction in hours; death of employee; change in marital status.

Time employer has to notify employee: 60 days.

Time employee has to apply: 30 days after termination; 60 days if employer fails to give notice.

Connecticut

Conn. Gen. Stat. Ann. §§ 38a-512a, 31-51n, 31-51o

Employers affected: All employers that offer group health insurance.

Eligible employees: All covered employees are eligible.

Length of coverage for employee: 30 months, or until eligible for Medicare benefits.

Length of coverage for dependents: 30 months, or until eligible for Medicare benefits; 36 months in case of employee's death, divorce, or loss of dependent status.

Qualifying event: Layoff; reduction in hours; termination of employment; death of employee; change in marital status; loss of dependent status.

Special situations: When facility closes or relocates, employers with 100 or more employees must pay for insurance for employee and dependents for 120 days or until employee is eligible for other group coverage, whichever comes first. (Does not affect employee's right to conventional continuation coverage, which begins when 120-day period ends.)

Delaware

18 Del. Code Ann. § 3571F

Employers affected: Employers that offer group health insurance and have 1 to 19 employees.

Eligible employees: Employees continuously insured for previous three months.

Length of coverage for employee: 9 months.

Length of coverage for dependents: 9 months.

Qualifying event: Employee's death; termination of employment; divorce or legal separation; employee's eligibility for Medicare; loss of dependent status.

Time employer has to notify employee: Within 30 days of the qualifying event.

Time employee has to apply: 30 days.

District of Columbia

D.C. Code Ann. §§ 32-731 to 32-732

Employers affected: Employers with fewer than 20 employees.

Eligible employees: All covered employees are eligible.

Length of coverage for employee: Three months

Length of coverage for dependents: Three months

Qualifying event: Any reason employee or dependent becomes ineligible for coverage, except employee's termination for gross misconduct.

Time employer has to notify employee: Within 15 days of termination of coverage.

Time employee has to apply: 45 days after termination of coverage.

Florida

Fla. Stat. Ann. § 627.6692

Employers affected: Employers with fewer than 20 employees.

Eligible employees: Full-time (25 or more hours per week) employees covered by employer's health insurance plan.

Length of coverage for employee: 18 months.

Length of coverage for dependents: 18 months.

Qualifying event: Layoff; reduction in hours; termination of employment; death of employee; change in marital status.

State Health Insurance Continuation Laws (continued)

Time employer has to notify employee: Carrier notifies within 14 days of learning of qualifying event (beneficiary has 63 days to notify carrier of qualifying event).

Time employee has to apply: 30 days from receipt of carrier's notice.

Georgia
Ga. Code Ann. §§ 33-24-21.1 to 33-24-21.2

Employers affected: All employers that offer group health insurance.

Eligible employees: Employees continuously insured for previous 6 months.

Length of coverage for employee: 3 months plus any part of the month remaining at termination.

Length of coverage for dependents: 3 months plus any part of the month remaining at termination.

Qualifying event: Termination of employment (except for cause).

Special situations: Employee, spouse, or former spouse, who is 60 years old and who has been covered for previous 6 months may continue coverage until eligible for Medicare. (Applies to companies with more than 20 employees; does not apply when employee quits for reasons other than health.)

Hawaii
Haw. Rev. Stat. §§ 393-11, 393-15

Employers affected: All employers required to offer health insurance (those paying a regular employee a monthly wage at least 86.67 times state hourly minimum—about $542).

Length of coverage for employee: If employee is hospitalized or prevented from working by sickness, employer must pay insurance premiums for 3 months or for as long employer continues to pay wages, whichever is longer.

Qualifying event: Employee is hospitalized or prevented by sickness from working.

Idaho
Idaho Code § 41-2213

Employers affected: All employers that offer group disability insurance

Eligible employees: Employees or dependents who are totally disabled at the time the policy ends. (Applies to policies that provide benefits for loss of time during periods of hospitalization, benefits for hospital or medical expenses, or benefits for dismemberment.)

Length of coverage for employee: Must provide a reasonable extension of coverage (in the case of medical and hospital expenses, a reasonable extension is at least 12 months).

Length of coverage for dependents: Must provide a reasonable extension of coverage (in the case of medical and hospital expenses, a reasonable extension is at least 12 months).

Illinois
215 Ill. Comp. Stat. §§ 5/367e, 5/367.2, 5/367.2-5

Employers affected: All employers that offer group health insurance.

Eligible employees: Employees continuously insured for previous 3 months.

Length of coverage for employee: 12 months.

Length of coverage for dependents: Upon death or divorce, 2 years' coverage for spouse under 55 and eligible dependents who were on employee's plan; until eligible for Medicare or other group coverage for spouse over 55 and eligible dependents who were on employee's plan. A dependent child who has reached plan age limit or who was not already covered by plan, is also entitled to 2 years' continuation coverage.

State Health Insurance Continuation Laws (continued)

Qualifying event: Termination of employment; reduction in hours; death of employee; divorce.

Time employer has to notify employee: 10 days.

Time employee has to apply: 30 days after termination or reduction in hours or receiving notice from employer, whichever is later, but not more than 60 days from termination or reduction in hours.

Iowa
Iowa Code §§ 509B.3, 509B.5

Employers affected: All employers that offer group health insurance.

Eligible employees: Employees continuously insured for previous 3 months.

Length of coverage for employee: Nine months.

Length of coverage for dependents: Nine months.

Qualifying event: Any reason employee or dependent becomes ineligible for coverage.

Time employer has to notify employee: 10 days after termination of coverage.

Time employee has to apply: 10 days after termination of coverage or receiving notice from employer, whichever is later, but not more than 31 days from termination of coverage.

Kansas
Kan. Stat. Ann. § 40-2209(i)

Employers affected: All employers that offer group health insurance.

Eligible employees: Employees continuously insured for previous 3 months.

Length of coverage for employee: 18 months.

Length of coverage for dependents: 18 months.

Qualifying event: Any reason employee or dependent becomes ineligible for coverage.

Time employer has to notify employee: Reasonable notice.

Kentucky
Ky. Rev. Stat. Ann. § 304.18-110

Employers affected: All employers that offer group health insurance.

Eligible employees: Employees continuously insured for previous 3 months.

Length of coverage for employee: 18 months.

Length of coverage for dependents: 18 months.

Qualifying event: Any reason employee or dependent becomes ineligible for coverage.

Time employer has to notify employee: Employer must notify insurer as soon as employee's coverage ends; insurer then notifies employee.

Time employee has to apply: 31 days from receipt of insurer's notice, but not more than 90 days after termination of group coverage.

Louisiana
La. Rev. Stat. Ann. §§ 22:1045, 22:1046

Employers affected: All employers that offer group health insurance and have fewer than 20 employees.

Eligible employees: Employees continuously insured for previous 3 months.

Length of coverage for employee: 12 months.

Length of coverage for dependents: 12 months.

Qualifying event: Termination of employment; death of insured; divorce.

Time employee has to apply: By the end of the month following the month in which the qualifying event occurred.

Special situations: Surviving spouse who is 50 or older may have coverage until remarriage or eligibility for Medicare or other insurance.

State Health Insurance Continuation Laws (continued)

Maine

Me. Rev. Stat. Ann. tit. 24-A, § 2809-A

Employers affected: All employers that offer group health insurance and are not subject to COBRA.

Eligible employees: Employees employed for at least 6 months.

Length of coverage for employee: One year.

Length of coverage for dependents: One year.

Qualifying event: Temporary layoff; permanent layoff if employee is eligible for federal premium assistance for laid-off employees who continue coverage; loss of employment because of a work-related injury or disease.

Time employee has to apply: 31 days from termination of coverage.

Maryland

Md. Code Ann., [Ins.] §§ 15-407 to 15-409

Employers affected: All employers that offer group health insurance.

Eligible employees: Employees continuously insured for previous 3 months.

Length of coverage for employee: 18 months.

Length of coverage for dependents: 18 months upon death of employee; upon change in marital status, 18 months or until spouse remarries or becomes eligible for other coverage.

Qualifying event: Termination of employment; death of employee; change in marital status.

Time employer has to notify employee: Must notify insurer within 14 days of receiving employee's continuation request.

Time employee has to apply: 45 days from termination of coverage. Employee begins application process by requesting an election of continuation notification form from employer.

Massachusetts

Mass. Gen. Laws ch. 175, §§ 110G, 110I; ch. 176J, § 9

Employers affected: All employers that offer group health insurance and have fewer than 20 employees.

Eligible employees: All covered employees are eligible.

Length of coverage for employee: 18 months; 29 months if disabled.

Length of coverage for dependents: 18 months upon termination or reduction in hours; 29 months if disabled; 36 months upon divorce, death of employee, employee's eligibility for Medicare, or employer's bankruptcy.

Qualifying event: Involuntary layoff; death of insured employee; change in marital status.

Time employer has to notify employee: Carrier must notify beneficiary within 14 days of learning of qualifying event.

Time employee has to apply: 60 days.

Special situations: Termination due to plant closing: 90 days' coverage for employee and dependents, at the same payment terms as before closing.

Minnesota

Minn. Stat. Ann. §§ 62A.17; 62A.20; 62A.21

Employers affected: All employers that offer group health insurance and have 2 or more employees.

Eligible employees: All covered employees are eligible.

Length of coverage for employee: 18 months; indefinitely if employee becomes totally disabled while employed.

Length of coverage for dependents: 18 months for current spouse or child after termination of employment; divorced or widowed spouse can continue until eligible for Medicare or other group health insurance. Upon divorce or death of

State Health Insurance Continuation Laws (continued)

employee, dependent children can continue until they no longer qualify as dependents under plan.

Qualifying event: Termination of employment; reduction in hours.

Time employer has to notify employee: Within 14 days of termination of coverage.

Time employee has to apply: 60 days from termination of coverage or receipt of employer's notice, whichever is later.

Mississippi
Miss. Code Ann. § 83-9-51

Employers affected: All employers that offer group health insurance and have fewer than 20 employees.

Eligible employees: Employees continuously insured for previous 3 months.

Length of coverage for employee: 12 months.

Length of coverage for dependents: 12 months.

Qualifying event: Termination of employment; divorce; employee's death; employee's eligibility for Medicare; loss of dependent status.

Time employer has to notify employee: Insurer must notify former or deceased employee's dependent child or divorced spouse of option to continue insurance within 14 days of their becoming ineligible for coverage on employee's policy.

Time employee has to apply: Employee must apply and submit payment before group coverage ends; dependents or former spouse must elect continuation coverage within 30 days of receiving insurer's notice.

Missouri
Mo. Rev. Stat. § 376.428

Employers affected: All employers that offer group health insurance and are not subject to COBRA.

Eligible employees: All employees.

Length of coverage for employee: 18 months.

Length of coverage for dependents: 18 months if eligible due to termination or reduction in hours; 36 months if eligible due to death or divorce.

Qualifying event: Termination of employment; death of employee; divorce; reduction in hours; employee's eligibility for Medicare; loss of dependent status.

Time employer has to notify employee: Same rules as COBRA.

Time employee has to apply: Same rules as COBRA.

Montana
Mont. Code Ann. §§ 33-22-506 to 33-22-507

Employers affected: All employers that offer group disability insurance.

Eligible employees: All employees.

Length of coverage for employee: One year (with employer's consent).

Qualifying event: Reduction in hours.

Special situations: Insurer may not discontinue benefits to child with a disability after child exceeds age limit for dependent status.

Nebraska
Neb. Rev. Stat. §§ 44-1640 and following, 44-7406

Employers affected: Employers not subject to federal COBRA laws.

Eligible employees: All covered employees.

Length of coverage for employee: Six months.

Length of coverage for dependents: One year upon death of insured employee. Subjects of domestic abuse who have lost coverage under abuser's plan and who do not qualify for COBRA may have 18 months' coverage (applies to all employers).

Qualifying event: Involuntary termination of employment (layoff due to labor dispute not considered involuntary).

State Health Insurance Continuation Laws (continued)

Time employer has to notify employee: Within 10 days of termination of employment must send notice by certified mail.

Time employee has to apply: 10 days from receipt of employer's notice.

Nevada

Nev. Rev. Stat. Ann. § 689B.0345

Employers affected: All employers that offer group health insurance.

Eligible employees: Employees who are on unpaid leave due to total disability.

Length of coverage for employee: Coverage must continue for 12 months, unless one of the following events occurs sooner: the employee is terminated, the employee obtains another health insurance policy, or the group health insurance policy is terminated.

Length of coverage for dependents: Coverage must continue for 12 months, unless one of the following events occurs sooner: the employee is terminated, the employee obtains another health insurance policy, or the group health insurance policy is terminated.

New Hampshire

N.H. Rev. Stat. Ann. § 415:18

Employers affected: All employers that offer group health insurance.

Eligible employees: All insured employees are eligible.

Length of coverage for employee: 18 months; 29 months if disabled at termination or during first 60 days of continuation coverage.

Length of coverage for dependents: 18 months; 29 months if disabled at termination or during first 60 days of continuation coverage; 36 months upon death of employee, divorce or legal separation, loss

of dependent status, or employee's eligibility for Medicare.

Qualifying event: Any reason employee or dependent becomes ineligible for coverage.

Time employer has to notify employee: Carrier must notify beneficiary within 30 days of receiving notice of loss of coverage.

Time employee has to apply: Within 45 days of receipt of notice

Special situations: Layoff or termination due to strike: 6 months' coverage with option to extend for an additional 12 months. Surviving, divorced, or legally separated spouse who is 55 or older may continue benefits available until eligible for Medicare or another employer-based group insurance.

New Jersey

N.J. Stat. Ann. §§ 17B:27-51.12, 17B:27A-27

Employers affected: Employers with 2 to 50 employees.

Eligible employees: Employed full time (25 or more hours).

Length of coverage for employee: 18 months; 29 months if disabled at termination or during first 60 days of continuation coverage.

Length of coverage for dependents: 18 months; 36 months upon death of employee, divorce or legal separation, loss of dependent status, or employee's eligibility for Medicare.

Qualifying event: Termination of employment; reduction in hours; change in marital status; death.

Time employer has to notify employee: At time of qualifying event.

Time employee has to apply: Within 30 days of qualifying event.

State Health Insurance Continuation Laws (continued)

Special benefits: Coverage must be identical to that offered to current employees.

Special situations: Total disability: Employee who has been insured for previous 3 months and employee's dependents entitled to continuation coverage that includes all benefits offered by group policy (applies to all employers).

New Mexico
N.M. Stat. Ann. § 59A-18-16

Employers affected: All employers that offer group health insurance.

Eligible employees: All insured employees are eligible.

Length of coverage for employee: Six months.

Length of coverage for dependents: Six months for termination of employment. May continue group coverage or convert to individual policies upon death of covered employee or divorce or legal separation.

Qualifying event: Termination of employment.

Time employer has to notify employee: Insurer or employer must give written notice at time of termination.

Time employee has to apply: 30 days after receiving notice.

New York
N.Y. Ins. Law § 3221(m)

Employers affected: All employers that offer group health insurance.

Eligible employees: All covered employees are eligible.

Length of coverage for employee: 36 months.

Length of coverage for dependents: 36 months.

Qualifying event: Termination of employment; death of employee; divorce or legal separation; loss of dependent status; employee's eligibility for Medicare.

Time employee has to apply: 60 days after termination or receipt of notice, whichever is later.

North Carolina
N.C. Gen. Stat. §§ 58-53-5 to 58-53-40

Employers affected: All employers that offer group health insurance.

Eligible employees: Employees continuously insured for previous 3 months.

Length of coverage for employee: 18 months.

Length of coverage for dependents: 18 months.

Qualifying event: Termination of employment.

Time employer has to notify employee: Employer has option of notifying employee as part of the exit process.

Time employee has to apply: 60 days.

North Dakota
N.D. Cent. Code §§ 26.1-36-23, 26.1-36-23.1

Employers affected: All employers that offer group health insurance.

Eligible employees: Employees continuously insured for previous 3 months.

Length of coverage for employee: 39 weeks.

Length of coverage for dependents: 39 weeks; 36 months if required by divorce or annulment decree.

Qualifying event: Termination of employment; change in marital status, if divorce or annulment decree requires employee to continue coverage.

Time employee has to apply: Within 10 days of termination or of receiving notice of continuation rights, whichever is later, but not more than 31 days from termination.

Ohio
Ohio Rev. Code Ann. §§ 3923.38, 1751.53

Employers affected: All employers that offer group health insurance.

State Health Insurance Continuation Laws (continued)

Eligible employees: Employees continuously insured for previous 3 months who were involuntarily terminated for reasons other than gross misconduct on the part of the employee.

Length of coverage for employee: 12 months.

Length of coverage for dependents: 12 months.

Qualifying event: Involuntary termination of employment.

Time employer has to notify employee: At termination of employment.

Time employee has to apply: Whichever is earlier: 31 days after coverage terminates; 10 days after coverage terminates if employer notified employee of continuation rights prior to termination; 10 days after employer notified employee of continuation rights, if notice was given after coverage terminated.

Oklahoma
Okla. Stat. Ann. tit. 36, § 4509

Employers affected: All employers that offer group health insurance.

Eligible employees: Employees insured for at least 6 months; (all other employees and their dependents entitled to 30 days' continuation coverage).

Length of coverage for employee: 63 days for basic coverage; 6 months for major medical at the same premium rate prior to termination of coverage (only for losses or conditions that began while group policy in effect).

Length of coverage for dependents: 63 days for basic coverage; 6 months for major medical at the same premium rate prior to termination of coverage (only for losses or conditions that began while group policy in effect).

Qualifying event: Any reason coverage terminates (except employment termination for gross misconduct).

Time employer has to notify employee: Carrier must notify employee in writing within 30 days of receiving notice of termination of employee's coverage.

Time employee has to apply: 31 days after receipt of notice.

Special benefits: Includes maternity care for pregnancy begun while group policy was in effect.

Oregon
Ore. Rev. Stat. §§ 743B.343 to 743B.347

Employers affected: Employers not subject to federal COBRA laws.

Eligible employees: Employees continuously insured for previous 3 months.

Length of coverage for employee: 9 months.

Length of coverage for dependents: 9 months.

Qualifying event: Termination of employment; reduction in hours; employee's eligibility for Medicare; loss of dependent status; termination of membership in group covered by policy; death of employee.

Time employer has to notify employee: 10 days after qualifying event.

Time employee has to apply: Within the time limit determined by the insurer, which must be at least 10 days after the qualifying event or employee's receipt of notice, whichever is later.

Special situations: Surviving, divorced, or legally separated spouse who is 55 or older and dependent children entitled to continuation coverage until spouse remarries or is eligible for other coverage; must include dental, vision, or prescription drug benefits, if they were offered in original plan (applies to employers with 20 or more employees).

State Health Insurance Continuation Laws (continued)

Pennsylvania

Pa. Stat. 40 P.S. § 764j

Employers affected: Employers that offer group health insurance and have 2 to 19 employees.

Eligible employees: Employees continuously insured for at least 3 months.

Length of coverage for employee: 9 months.

Length of coverage for dependents: 9 months.

Qualifying event: Termination of employment; reduction in hours; death of employee; change in marital status; employer's bankruptcy.

Time employer has to notify employee: 30 days after qualifying event.

Time employee has to apply: 30 days after receiving notice.

Rhode Island

R.I. Gen. Laws §§ 27-19.1-1, 27-20.4-1 to 27-20-4-2

Employers affected: All employers that offer group health insurance.

Eligible employees: All insured employees are eligible.

Length of coverage for employee: 18 months (but not longer than continuous employment); cannot be required to pay more than one month premium at a time.

Length of coverage for dependents: 18 months (but not longer than continuous employment); cannot be required to pay more than one month premium at a time.

Qualifying event: Involuntary termination of employment; death of employee; change in marital status; permanent reduction in workforce; employer's going out of business.

Time employer has to notify employee: Employers must post a conspicuous notice of employee continuation rights.

Time employee has to apply: 30 days from termination of coverage.

Special situations: If right to receiving continuing health insurance is stated in the divorce judgment, divorced spouse has right to continue coverage as long as employee remains covered or until divorced spouse remarries or becomes eligible for other group insurance.

South Carolina

S.C. Code Ann. § 38-71-770

Employers affected: All employers that offer group health insurance.

Eligible employees: Employees continuously insured for previous 6 months.

Length of coverage for employee: 6 months (in addition to part of month remaining at termination).

Length of coverage for dependents: 6 months (in addition to part of month remaining at termination).

Qualifying event: Any reason employee or dependent becomes ineligible for coverage.

Time employer has to notify employee: At time of termination, employer must clearly and meaningfully advise employee of continuation rights.

South Dakota

S.D. Codified Laws Ann. §§ 58-18-7.5, 58-18-7.12; 58-18C-1

Employers affected: All employers that offer group health insurance.

Eligible employees: All covered employees.

Length of coverage for employee: 18 months; 29 months if disabled at termination or during first 60 days of continuation coverage.

State Health Insurance Continuation Laws (continued)

Length of coverage for dependents: 18 months; 29 months if disabled at termination or during first 60 days of continuation coverage; 36 months upon death of employee, divorce or legal separation, loss of dependent status, employee's eligibility for Medicare.

Qualifying event: Termination of employment; death of employee; divorce or legal separation; loss of dependent status; employee's eligibility for Medicare.

Special situations: When employer goes out of business: 12 months' continuation coverage available to all employees. Employer must notify employees within 10 days of termination of benefits; employees must apply within 60 days of receipt of employer's notice or within 90 days of termination of benefits if no notice given.

Tennessee
Tenn. Code Ann. § 56-7-2312

Employers affected: All employers that offer group health insurance.

Eligible employees: Employees continuously insured for previous 3 months.

Length of coverage for employee: Three months (in addition to part of month remaining at termination).

Length of coverage for dependents: 3 months (in addition to part of month remaining at termination); 15 months upon death of employee or divorce (in addition to part of month remaining at termination).

Qualifying event: Termination of employment; death of employee; change in marital status.

Special situations: Employee or dependent who is pregnant at time of termination entitled to continuation benefits for 6 months following the end of pregnancy.

Texas
Tex. Ins. Code Ann. §§ 1251.252 to 1251.255; 1251.301 to 1251.310

Employers affected: All employers that offer group health insurance.

Eligible employees: Employees continuously insured for previous 3 months.

Length of coverage for employee: Nine months; for employees eligible for COBRA, 6 months after COBRA coverage ends.

Length of coverage for dependents: 9 months; for employees eligible for COBRA, 6 months after COBRA coverage ends. Three years for dependents with coverage due to the death or retirement of employee or severance of the family relationship.

Qualifying event: Termination of employment (except for cause); employee leaves for health reasons; severance of family relationship; retirement or death of employee.

Time employee has to apply: 60 days from termination of coverage or receiving notice of continuation rights from employer or insurer, whichever is later. Must give notice within 15 days of severance of family relationship. Within 60 days of death or retirement of family member or severance of family relationship, dependent must give notice of intent to continue coverage.

Utah
Utah Code Ann. § 31A-22-722

Employers affected: All employers that offer group health insurance.

Eligible employees: Employees continuously insured for previous 3 months.

Length of coverage for employee: 12 months.

Length of coverage for dependents: 12 months.

State Health Insurance Continuation Laws (continued)

Qualifying event: Termination of employment; retirement; death; divorce; reduction in hours; sabbatical; disability; loss of dependent status.

Time employer has to notify employee: In writing within 30 days of termination of coverage.

Time employee has to apply: Within 60 days of qualifying event.

Vermont

Vt. Stat. Ann. tit. 8, §§ 4090a to 4090c

Employers affected: All employers that offer group health insurance.

Eligible employees: All covered employees are eligible.

Length of coverage for employee: 18 months.

Length of coverage for dependents: 18 months.

Qualifying event: Termination of employment; reduction in hours; death of employee; change of marital status; loss of dependent status.

Time employer has to notify employee: Within 30 days of qualifying event.

Time employee has to apply: Within 60 days of receiving notice following the occurrence of a qualifying event.

Virginia

Va. Code Ann. §§ 38.2-3541 to 38.2-3452

Employers affected: All employers that offer group health insurance.

Eligible employees: Employees continuously insured for previous 3 months.

Length of coverage for employee: 12 months.

Length of coverage for dependents: 12 months.

Qualifying event: Any reason employee or dependent becomes ineligible for coverage.

Time employer has to notify employee: 14 days from termination of coverage.

Time employee has to apply: Within 31 days of receiving notice of eligibility, but no more than 60 days following termination.

Special situations: Employee may convert to an individual policy instead of applying for continuation coverage (must apply within 31 days of termination of coverage).

Washington

Wash. Rev. Code Ann. § 48.21.075

Employers affected: All employers that offer disability insurance.

Eligible employees: Insured employees on strike.

Length of coverage for employee: Six months if employee goes on strike.

Length of coverage for dependents: Six months if employee goes on strike.

Qualifying event: If employee goes on strike.

Special situations: All employers have option of offering continued group health benefits.

West Virginia

W.Va. Code §§ 33-16-2, 33-16-3(e); W. Va. Code St. R. 114-93-3

Employers affected: Employers providing insurance for between 2 and 20 employees.

Eligible employees: All employees are eligible.

Length of coverage for employee: 18 months in case of involuntary layoff.

Qualifying event: Involuntary layoff.

Time employer has to notify employee: Carrier must notify beneficiaries within 15 days of receiving notice from beneficiary of intent to apply.

Time employee has to apply: 20 days to send notice of intention to apply; 30 days to apply after receiving election and premium notice.

State Health Insurance Continuation Laws (continued)

Wisconsin

Wis. Stat. Ann. § 632.897

Employers affected: All employers that offer group health insurance.

Eligible employees: Employees continuously insured for previous 3 months.

Length of coverage for employee: 18 months (or longer at insurer's option).

Length of coverage for dependents: 18 months (or longer at insurer's option).

Qualifying event: Any reason employee or dependent becomes ineligible for coverage (except employment termination due to misconduct).

Time employer has to notify employee: 5 days from termination of coverage.

Time employee has to apply: 30 days after receiving employer's notice.

Wyoming

Wyo. Stat. § 26-19-113

Employers affected: Employers not subject to federal COBRA laws.

Eligible employees: Employees continuously insured for previous 3 months.

Length of coverage for employee: 12 months.

Length of coverage for dependents: 12 months.

Time employee has to apply: 31 days from termination of coverage.

Resources

Federal Agencies

This section includes contact information for the federal agencies that enforce the laws covered in this book. You can find more information on each agency's authority, enforcement powers, and resources for employers in the chapter that covers the law the agency administers.

Department of Health and Human Services

Administration for Children & Families (ACF)
Office of Child Support Enforcement
330 C Street, SW
Washington, D.C. 20201
Phone: 202-401-9373
www.acf.hhs.gov
The ACF enforces PRWORA.

Department of Justice

Civil Rights Division
Office of the Special Counsel for Immigration-Related Unfair Employment Practices (OSC)
950 Pennsylvania Avenue, NW
Washington, D.C. 20530
Phone: 202-616-5594
Employer Hotline: 800-255-8155
TTY: 800-237-2515
www.justice.gov/crt/about/osc
The OSC enforces the antidiscrimination provisions of IRCA.

Department of Labor

Employee Benefits Security Administration (EBSA)

Frances Perkins Building
200 Constitution Avenue, NW
Washington, D.C. 20210
Phone: 866-444-EBSA (3272)
www.dol.gov/ebsa
The EBSA shares enforcement responsibility for COBRA with the IRS.

Employment and Training Administration (DOLETA)

Office of National Response
200 Constitution Avenue, NW
Room N-5422
Washington, D.C. 20210
Phone: 877-872-5627
www.doleta.gov/layoff
DOLETA issued the regulations interpreting WARN and has some explanatory resources available.

Occupational Safety and Health Administration (OSHA)

200 Constitution Avenue, NW
Washington, D.C. 20210
Phone: 800-321-OSHA (6742)
TTY: 877-889-5627
www.osha.gov
OSHA enforces the OSH Act and the whistleblower provisions of Sarbanes-Oxley (SOX).

Veterans Employment and Training Service (VETS)

200 Constitution Avenue, Room S-1325
Washington, D.C. 20210
Phone: 866-237-0275
www.dol.gov/vets
The VETS enforces USERRA.

Wage and Hour Division (WHD)

Employment Standards Administration
200 Constitution Avenue, NE
Washington, D.C. 20210
Phone: 866-487-9243
TTY: 877-889-5627
www.dol.gov/whd
The WHD enforces the EPPA, FLSA, and FMLA.

Equal Employment Opportunity Commission (EEOC)

131 M Street, NE
Washington, D.C. 20507
Phone: 202-663-4900 or 800-669-4000
TTY: 202-663-4494 or 800-669-6820
www.eeoc.gov
The EEOC enforces the ADA, ADEA, EPA, OWBPA, PDA, and Title VII.

Federal Trade Commission (FTC)

600 Pennsylvania Avenue
Washington, D.C. 20580
Phone: 202-326-2222
www.ftc.gov
The FTC enforces the FCRA.

Internal Revenue Service (IRS)

U.S. Treasury Department
1500 Pennsylvania Avenue, NW
Washington, D.C. 20220
Phone: 800-829-4933 (for businesses)
TTY: 800-829-4059
www.irs.gov
The IRS shares enforcement responsibility for COBRA with the EBSA.

National Labor Relations Board (NLRB)

1099 14th Street, NW
Washington, D.C. 20570
Phone: 844-762-NLRB (6572)
www.nlrb.gov
The NLRB enforces the NLRA.

Securities and Exchange Commission (SEC)

100 F Street, NE
Washington, D.C. 20549
Phone: 800-732-0330
TTY: 800-877-8339
www.sec.gov
The SEC enforces the complaint procedures provision of Sarbanes-Oxley (SOX).

U.S. Citizenship and Immigration Services (USCIS)

111 Massachusetts Avenue, NW
Washington, D.C. 20539
Phone: 800-357-5283
TTY: 800-767-1833
www.uscis.gov
The USCIS enforces the employment verification provisions of IRCA.

State Labor Departments

Note: Phone numbers listed are for each department's headquarters. Check the website for regional office locations and numbers.

Alabama
Department of Labor
Montgomery, AL
334-242-8055
www.labor.alabama.gov

Alaska
Department of Labor and Workforce
    Development
Juneau, AK
907-465-2700
www.labor.state.ak.us

Arizona
Industrial Commission
Phoenix, AZ
602-542-4411
www.azica.gov

Arkansas
Department of Labor
Little Rock, AR
501-682-4500
www.labor.arkansas.gov

California
Labor Commissioner's Office
Department of Industrial Relations
Oakland, CA
510-285-2118
www.dir.ca.gov/DLSE/dlse.html

Colorado
Department of Labor and Employment
Denver, CO
303-318-9000
www.colorado.gov/CDLE

Connecticut
Department of Labor
Wethersfield, CT
860-263-6000
www.ctdol.state.ct.us

Delaware
Department of Labor
Wilmington, DE
302-761-8000
http://dol.delaware.gov

District of Columbia
Department of Employment Services
Washington, D.C.
202-724-7000
www.does.dc.gov

Florida
Department of Economic Opportunity
Tallahassee, FL
850-245-7105
www.floridajobs.org

Georgia
Department of Labor
Atlanta, GA
404-232-7300
http://dol.georgia.gov

Hawaii
Department of Labor and Industrial Relations
Honolulu, HI
808-586-8844
http://labor.hawaii.gov

State Labor Departments (continued)

Idaho
Department of Labor
Boise, ID
208-332-3575
http://labor.idaho.gov

Illinois
Department of Labor
Chicago, IL
312-793-2800
www.state.il.us/agency/idol

Indiana
Department of Labor
Indianapolis, IN
317-232-2655
www.in.gov/dol

Iowa
Division of Labor
Des Moines, IA
515-281-3606
www.iowadivisionoflabor.gov

Kansas
Department of Labor
Topeka, KS
785-296-5000
www.dol.ks.gov

Kentucky
Labor Cabinet
Frankfort, KY
502-564-0684
www.labor.ky.gov

Louisiana
Louisiana Workforce Commission
Baton Rouge, LA
225-342-3111
www.ldol.state.la.us

Maine
Department of Labor
Augusta, ME
207-623-7900
www.state.me.us/labor

Maryland
Department of Labor, Licensing, and Regulation
Baltimore, MD
410-767-2241
www.dllr.state.md.us/labor

Massachusetts
Labor and Workforce Development
Boston, MA
617-626-7122
www.mass.gov/lwd

Michigan
Department of Licensing and Regulatory Affairs
Lansing, MI
517-373-1820
www.michigan.gov/lara

Minnesota
Department of Labor and Industry
St. Paul, MN
800-342-5354
651-284-5005
www.dli.mn.gov

Mississippi
Department of Employment Security
Jackson, MS
601-321-6000
www.mdes.ms.gov

Missouri
Department of Labor and Industrial Relations
Jefferson City, MO
573-751-3215
www.labor.mo.gov

State Labor Departments (continued)

Montana
Department of Labor and Industry
Helena, MT
406-444-2840
www.dli.mt.gov

Nebraska
Department of Labor
Lincoln, NE
402-471-9000
www.dol.nebraska.gov

Nevada
Office of the Labor Commissioner
Las Vegas, NV
702-486-2650
http://labor.nv.gov

New Hampshire
Department of Labor
Concord, NH
603-271-3176
800-272-4353
www.nh.gov/labor

New Jersey
Department of Labor and Workforce Development
Trenton, NJ
609-659-9045
http://lwd.state.nj.us/labor

New Mexico
Department of Workforce Solutions
Albuquerque, NM
505-841-8405
www.dws.state.nm.us

New York
Department of Labor
Albany, NY
518-457-9000
888-469-7365
www.labor.ny.gov/home

North Carolina
Department of Labor
Raleigh, NC
919-807-2796
800-625-2267
www.nclabor.com

North Dakota
Department of Labor and Human Rights
Bismarck, ND
701-328-2660
800-582-8032
www.nd.gov/labor

Ohio
Division of Industrial Compliance
Reynoldsburg, OH
614-644-2223
www.com.ohio.gov/dico

Oklahoma
Department of Labor
Oklahoma City, OK
405-521-6100
www.ok.gov/odol

Oregon
Bureau of Labor and Industries
Portland, OR
971-673-0761
www.oregon.gov/boli

Pennsylvania
Department of Labor and Industry
Harrisburg, PA
800-932-0665
www.dli.pa.gov

Rhode Island
Department of Labor and Training
Cranston, RI
401-462-8000
www.dlt.state.ri.us

State Labor Departments (continued)

South Carolina
Department of Labor, Licensing, and Regulation
Columbia, SC
803-896-4300
www.llr.state.sc.us/labor

South Dakota
Department of Labor and Regulation
Pierre, SD
605-773-3101
www.dlr.sd.gov

Tennessee
Department of Labor and Workforce
   Development
Nashville, TN
844-224-5818
www.tn.gov/workforce

Texas
Texas Workforce Commission
Austin, TX
512-463-2222
www.twc.state.tx.us

Utah
Labor Commission
Salt Lake City, UT
801-530-6800
801-530-5090
www.laborcommission.utah.gov

Vermont
Department of Labor
Montpelier, VT
802-828-4000
www.labor.vermont.gov

Virginia
Department of Labor and Industry
Richmond, VA
804-371-2327
www.doli.virginia.gov

Washington
Department of Labor and Industries
Tumwater, WA
360-902-5800
www.lni.wa.gov

West Virginia
Division of Labor
Charleston, WV
304-558-7890
www.wvlabor.com

Wisconsin
Department of Workforce Development
Madison, WI
608-266-3131
http://dwd.wisconsin.gov

Wyoming
Department of Workforce Services
Cheyenne, WY
307-777-7261
www.wyomingworkforce.org

State Agencies That Enforce Laws Prohibiting Discrimination in Employment

Note: Phone numbers listed are for each department's headquarters. Check the website for regional office locations and numbers.

United States
Equal Employment
Opportunity Commission
131 M Street, NW
Washington, DC 20507
800-669-4000
TTY: 800-669-6820
www.eeoc.gov

Alabama
Birmingham District Office
Equal Employment Opportunity Commission
Birmingham, AL
800-669-4000
www.eeoc.gov/field/birmingham/index.cfm

Alaska
Commission for Human Rights
Anchorage, AK
907-274-4692
800-478-4692
http://humanrights.alaska.gov

Arizona
Civil Rights Division
Arizona Attorney General
Phoenix, AZ
602-542-5263
877-491-5742
www.azag.gov/civil-rights

Arkansas
Little Rock Area Office
Equal Employment Opportunity Commission
Little Rock, AR
800-669-4000
www.eeoc.gov/field/littlerock/index.cfm

California
Department of Fair Employment and Housing
Elk Grove, CA
800-884-1684
www.dfeh.ca.gov

Colorado
Colorado Civil Rights Division
Department of Regulatory Agencies
Denver, CO
303-894-2997
www.colorado.gov/dora/civil-rights

Connecticut
Commission on Human Rights and Opportunities
Hartford, CT
860-541-3400
www.ct.gov/chro/site

Delaware
Division of Industrial Affairs
Department of Labor
Wilmington, DE
302-761-8200
http://dia.delawareworks.com/discrimination

District of Columbia
Office of Human Rights
Washington, D.C.
202-727-4559
http://ohr.dc.gov

Florida
Commission on Human Relations
Tallahassee, FL
850-488-7082
800-342-8170
http://fchr.state.fl.us

State Agencies That Enforce Laws Prohibiting Discrimination in Employment (continued)

Georgia
Atlanta District Office
Equal Employment Opportunity Commission
Atlanta, GA
800-669-4000
http://www.eeoc.gov/field/atlanta

Hawaii
Hawaii Civil Rights Commission
Honolulu, HI
808-586-8636
http://labor.hawaii.gov/hcrc

Idaho
Idaho Commission on Human Rights
Boise, ID
208-334-2873
888-249-7025
http://humanrights.idaho.gov

Illinois
Department of Human Rights
Chicago, IL
312-814-6200
www2.illinois.gov/dhr

Indiana
Civil Rights Commission
Indianapolis, IN
317-232-2600
800-628-2909
www.in.gov/icrc

Iowa
Civil Rights Commission
Des Moines, IA
515-281-4121
800-457-4416
https://icrc.iowa.gov

Kansas
Human Rights Commission
Topeka, KS
785-296-3206
www.khrc.net

Kentucky
Commission on Human Rights
Louisville, KY
502-595-4024
800-292-5566
www.kchr.ky.gov

Louisiana
Commission on Human Rights
Baton Rouge, LA
225-342-6969
http://gov.louisiana.gov/page/lchr

Maine
Human Rights Commission
Augusta, ME
207-624-6290
www.maine.gov/mhrc

Maryland
Commission on Civl Rights
Baltimore, MD
410-767-8600
800-637-6247 (in state only)
http://mccr.maryland.gov

Massachusetts
Commission Against Discrimination
Boston, MA
617-994-6000
www.mass.gov/mcad

State Agencies That Enforce Laws Prohibiting Discrimination in Employment (continued)

Michigan
Department of Civil Rights
Detroit, MI
313-456-3700
800-482-3604
www.michigan.gov/mdcr

Minnesota
Department of Human Rights
St. Paul, MN
651-539-1100
800-657-3704
http://mn.gov/mdhr

Mississippi
Jackson Area Office
Equal Employment Opportunity Commission
Jackson, MS
800-699-4000
www.eeoc.gov/field/jackson

Missouri
Commission on Human Rights
Jefferson City, MO
573-751-3325
877-781-4236
www.labor.mo.gov/mohumanrights

Montana
Human Rights Bureau
Employment Relations Division
Department of Labor and Industry
Helena, MT
800-542-0807
http://erd.dli.mt.gov/human-rights/human-rights

Nebraska
Nebraska Equal Opportunity Commission
Lincoln, NE
402-471-2024
800-642-6112
www.neoc.ne.gov

Nevada
Equal Rights Commission
Las Vegas, NV
702-486-7161
http://detr.state.nv.us/nerc.htm

New Hampshire
Commission for Human Rights
Concord, NH
603-271-2767
www.nh.gov/hrc

New Jersey
Division on Civil Rights
Office of the Attorney General
Trenton, NJ
609-292-4605
www.nj.gov/oag/dcr/index.html

New Mexico
Human Rights Bureau
Santa Fe, NM
505-827-6838
800-566-9471
www.dws.state.nm.us/Human-Rights-
  Information

New York
Division of Human Rights
Bronx, NY
888-392-3644
www.dhr.ny.gov

North Carolina
Employment Discrimination Bureau
Department of Labor
Raleigh, NC
919-807-2796
800-NC-LABOR
www.nclabor.com/edb/edb.htm

State Agencies That Enforce Laws Prohibiting Discrimination in Employment (continued)

North Dakota
Human Rights Division
Department of Labor and Human Rights
Bismarck, ND
701-328-2660
800-582-8032
www.nd.gov/labor/human-rights/index.html

Ohio
Civil Rights Commission
Columbus, OH
614-466-2785
888-278-7101
www.crc.ohio.gov

Oklahoma
Office of Civil Rights Enforcement
Office of the Attorney General
Tulsa, OK
918-581-2910
www.ok.gov/oag/About_the_Office/OCRE.html

Oregon
Civil Rights Division
Bureau of Labor and Industries
Portland, OR
971-673-0764
www.oregon.gov/BOLI/CRD

Pennsylvania
Human Relations Commission
Harrisburg, PA
717-787-4410
www.phrc.state.pa.us

Rhode Island
Commission for Human Rights
Providence, RI
401-222-2661
www.richr.ri.gov

South Carolina
Human Affairs Commission
Columbia, SC
803-737-7800
800-521-0725
www.schac.sc.gov

South Dakota
Division of Human Rights
Department of Labor and Regulation
Pierre, SD
605-773-3681
www.dlr.sd.gov/default.aspx

Tennessee
Human Rights Commission
Nashville, TN
800-251-3589
www.tennessee.gov/humanrights

Texas
Civil Rights Division
Texas Workforce Commission
Austin, TX
512-463-2642
888-452-4778
www.twc.state.tx.us/customers/jsemp/
jsempsubcrd.html

Utah
Antidiscrimination and Labor Division
Labor Commission
Salt Lake City, UT
801-530-6801
800-222-1238
www.laborcommission.utah.gov/divisions/
AntidiscriminationAndLabor/index.html

State Agencies That Enforce Laws Prohibiting Discrimination in Employment (continued)

Vermont
Attorney General's Office
Civil Rights Unit
Montpelier, VT
802-828-3657
888-745-9195
http://ago.vermont.gov/divisions/civil-rights.php

Virginia
Office of the Attorney General
Division of Human Rights
Richmond, VA
804-225-2292
www.oag.state.va.us/index.php/programs-
  initiatives/human-rights

Washington
Human Rights Commission
Olympia, WA
800-233-3247
www.hum.wa.gov

West Virginia
Human Rights Commission
Charleston, WV
304-558-2616
888-676-5546
www.hrc.wv.gov

Wisconsin
Division of Equal Rights
Department of Workforce Development
Madison, WI
608-266-6860
http://dwd.wisconsin.gov/er

Wyoming
Labor Standards Office
Department of Workforce Services
Cheyenne, WY
307-777-7261
www.wyomingworkforce.org/workers/labor

Index

A

Ability to perform the job
  as valid interviewing question, 14
  and workers' compensation record
    information, 20
Absences and absenteeism
  and decision to terminate, 406
  discipline for, not allowed for family and
    medical leave taken, 210–211, 216
  family-friendly workplace policies and, 191
  as good cause for termination, 405
  as violence warning sign, 389–390
Accent rules, 130–131
Accommodation of persons with disabilities
  flexible interactive process to determine needs,
    146
  flextime and other family-friendly workplace
    policies as, 89, 193
  interviewing applicants and questions about
    need for, 14
  legal drug use, 147, 299
  medical records of employee and, 266
  pregnancy and, 136
  request by employee, as requirement, 146
  testing of applicants and, 15–16
  undue hardship and, 146–147
  unpaid leave as, 221
Accommodation of religious belief, 143–145
ADA. *See* Americans with Disabilities Act (ADA)
Address, as preemployment inquiry, 32
ADEA (Age Discrimination in Employment
  Act), 127, 133, 134–135
Administrative employees. *See* Exempt employees
Adoption, family and medical leave and, 208

Adverse action notice, for consumer report, 22
Affordable Care Act. *See* Health care reform
  (ACA)
Age
  as preemployment inquiry, 32
  and special rules for language of release not to
    sue, 454
Age discrimination
  and advertisements for jobs, 9
  and benefits, 134
  defined, 132
  federal law, 127, 133, 134–135
  harassment and, 133
  as illegal reason for firing, 400
  layoffs and, 426
  and neutral practices with disparate impacts,
    133, 426
  reasonable factor other than age (RFOA), 133,
    426
  state laws, 134
  waiver of ADEA rights, 134–135
Age Discrimination in Employment Act
  (ADEA), 127, 133, 134–135
Agricultural work and workers
  child labor laws, 24–25
  as ineligible for overtime pay or minimum
    wage, 66
Alcohol testing. *See* Drug and alcohol testing
Alcohol use
  alcoholism as disability, 147, 298
  injuries in workplace while under influence,
    291
  off-hours, off-site use of, 298
  problems in workplace caused by, 297
  at work, 298

⚖ NOLO *Online Legal Forms*

Nolo offers a large library of legal solutions and forms, created by Nolo's in-house legal staff. These reliable documents can be prepared in minutes.

Create a Document

- **Incorporation.** Incorporate your business in any state.
- **LLC Formations.** Gain asset protection and pass-through tax status in any state.
- **Wills.** Nolo has helped people make over 2 million wills. Is it time to make or revise yours?
- **Living Trust (avoid probate).** Plan now to save your family the cost, delays, and hassle of probate.
- **Trademark.** Protect the name of your business or product.
- **Provisional Patent.** Preserve your rights under patent law and claim "patent pending" status.

Download a Legal Form

Nolo.com has hundreds of top quality legal forms available for download—bills of sale, promissory notes, nondisclosure agreements, LLC operating agreements, corporate minutes, commercial lease and sublease, motor vehicle bill of sale, consignment agreements and many, many more.

Review Your Documents

Many lawyers in Nolo's consumer-friendly lawyer directory will review Nolo documents for a very reasonable fee. Check their detailed profiles at **Nolo.com/lawyers**.